PETERSON'S
#1 IN COLLEGE PREP

GED

SUCCESS

Marion B. Castellucci • Bernadette Manzo
Valerie Crossling • Linda Mazumdar • Westmore Holmes
Charlie Perkins • Marjorie Jacobs • Vera Polak

P Peterson's
Thomson Learning™

Reviewer Team

Marion B. Castellucci
Cranston, RI

Valerie Crossling
GED Instructor
Fayetteville Technical College
Fayetteville, NC

Westmore Holmes
GED Coordinator
Milwaukee Area Technical College
Milwaukee, WI

Marjorie Jacobs
GED Program Coordinator
Community Learning Center
Cambridge, MA

Bernadette Manzo
Science & Health Teacher
Cleveland Extension High School
Cleveland, OH

Linda Mazumdar
Goldsboro, NC

Charlie Perkins
GED Instructor
La Guardia Community College
New York, NY

Vera Polak
Assistant Coordinator
GED Institute
Community College of Denver
Denver, CO

Visit Peterson's Education Center on the Internet (World Wide Web) at
www.petersons.com

GED Success is adapted from GED Comprehensive published by South-Western Educational publishing.

Copyright © 1997 by Peterson's

Library of Congress Cataloging-in-Publication Data
GED success / Marion B. Castellucci . . . [et al.].
    p. cm.
  "Adapted from GED comprehensive published by South-Western Educational Publishing"—T.p. verso.
   ISBN 0-7689-0408-0
   1. General educational development tests—Study guides. I. Castellucci, Marion. II. South-Western GED comprehensive.
  LB3060.33.G45G44   1997
  373.12'62—dc21
                                                          97-29631
                                                             CIP

Printed in the United States of America

10 9 8 7 6 5 4 3 2 1

CONTENTS

CONTENTS

Part 5: Mathematics

Posttests

Practice Tests

Index

ACKNOWLEDGMENTS

Literary Credits

page 19   HENRY PAYNE. Reprinted with permission of UFS, Inc.

page 24   Drawing by Alan Dunn. © 1968 *The New Yorker Magazine*, Inc.

page 38   OLIPHANT copyright 1992. Reprinted with permission of UNIVERSAL PRESS SYNDICATE. All rights reserved.

page 42   Excerpts from NIGHT by Elie Wiesel. Copyright © 1960 and copyright renewed © 1988 by the Collins Publishing Group. Reprinted by permission of Hill and Wang, a division of Farrar, Straus & Giroux, Inc.

page 42   From the review of Donald Brown's "Cause and Effect" by Zan Stewart in DOWN BEAT, May 1993. Copyright © 1993 Mather Publications. Reprinted with permission from DOWN BEAT.

page 43   From CHINA MEN by Maxine Hong Kingston. Copyright © 1980 by Maxine Hong Kingston. Reprinted by permission of Alfred A. Knopf, Inc.

page 44   LAST NIGHT I HAD THE STRANGEST DREAM. Words and Music by Ed McCurdy. TRO-© Copyright 1950 (Renewed) and 1955 (Renewed). Almanac Music, Inc., New York, NY. Used by permission.

page 45   "The Truth" by Clyde Fitch. From BEST PLAYS OF THE EARLY AMERICAN THEATRE: FROM THE BEGINNING TO 1916 by John Glassner, ed. Copyright © 1967 by Crown Publishers, Inc. Reprinted by permission from Crown Publishers, Inc.

page 46   From "Hazards Aloft" by Philip Elmer-Dewitt in TIME, February 22, 1993. Copyright © Time Inc. Reprinted by permission.

page 48   From "Making Bricks Soar" by Calcb Bach in AMERICAS, Volume 45, No. 2, 1993. © 1993 Americas. Reprinted from AMERICAS bimonthly magazine published by the General Secretariat of the Organization of American States in Spanish and English.

page 142   Don Hesse, reprinted with permission of LA Times Syndicate.

page 168   Don Hesse, reprinted with permission of LA Times Syndicate.

page 169   © Mark Shelton. Reprinted with special permission of King Features Syndicate.

page 239   From "Home Bodies" by Pamela Stone. As appeared in CHICAGO TRIBUNE, January 24, 1993. Reprinted by permission of the author.

page 246   John Kennedy Toole, A CONFEDERACY OF DUNCES. Baton Rouge: Louisiana State University Press, 1980.

page 251   "Do Not Boast of Your Speed" by Hwang Chin-i from ANTHOLOGY OF KOREAN LITERATURE: FROM EARLY TIMES TO THE NINETEENTH CENTURY, edited by Peter H. Lee. Reprinted by permission of University of Hawaii Press.

page 252   Reprinted by permission of the publishers and the Trustees of Amherst College from THE POEMS OF EMILY DICKINSON, Thomas H. Johnson, ed., Cambridge, Mass: The Belknap Press of Harvard University Press, Copyright © 1951, 1955, 1979, 1983 by the President and Fellows of Harvard College.

page 256   From THE GUITARRON by Lynne Alvarez. Copyright © 1983 by Lynne Alvarez. CAUTION NOTE: All inquiries concerning production or other rights to THE GUITARRON should be addressed in writing to the author's agent, Helen Merrill, Ltd., 435 West 23rd Street, Suite 1A, New York, NY 10011, USA. No amateur performance or reading of the play may be given without obtaining, in advance, the written permission of Helen Merrill, Ltd.

page 256   From FENCES by August Wilson. Copyright © 1986 by August Wilson. Used by permission of Dutton Signet, a division of Penguin Books USA Inc.

ACKNOWLEDGMENTS

page 257   From COME BACK, LITTLE SHEBA by William Inge. Copyright © 1949 by William Inge. CAUTION: Professionals and amateurs are hereby warned that COME BACK, LITTLE SHEBA is subject to a royalty. It is fully protected under the copyright laws of the United States of America, the British Commonwealth, including Canada, and all other countries of the Copyright Union. All rights, including professional, amateur, motion pictures, recitation, lecturing, public reading, radio broadcasting, television, and the rights of translation into foreign languages are strictly reserved. In its present form the play is dedicated to the reading public only. For all other rights than those stipulated above, apply to International Creative Management, Inc., 40 West 57th Street, New York, NY 10019.

page 260   "Wanderers and References" by Barbara Mujica in AMERICAS, Vol. 45, No. 2, 1993. © 1993 Americas. Reprinted from AMERICAS bimonthly magazine published by the General Secretariat of the Organization of American States in Spanish and English.

page 261   From "The Color Between Earth and Sky" by Ron Butler in AMERICAS, Vol. 45, No. 2, 1993. © 1993 Americas. Reprinted from AMERICAS bimonthly magazine published by the General Secretariat of the Organization of American States in Spanish and English.

page 263   From "Remembering Dizzy" by John McDonough in DOWN BEAT, April 1993. Copyright © 1993 Maher Publications. Reprinted with permission from DOWN BEAT.

page 263   From "A Blast from the Past, Muffled" by Gary Graff in the DETROIT FREE PRESS, June 5, 1993. Reprinted by permission of the DETROIT FREE PRESS.

page 265   From "Life after fashion" by Hugh Hart in CHICAGO TRIBUNE, May 26, 1993. Reprinted by permission of Hugh Hart, special to the CHICAGO TRIBUNE.

page 265   From "Johnny's Song" by Douglas Lathrop in MAINSTREAM, May 1993. Reprinted with permission from MAINSTREAM Magazine, 2973 Beech St., San Diego, CA 92102.

page 319   Reprinted courtesy of *The Boston Globe.*

page 320   Reprinted courtesy of *The Boston Globe.*

page 408   Le Pelley in *The Christian Science Monitor*, © 1984

page 414   Garner© 1977, The Commercial Appeal, Memphis, Tennessee. Used with permission.

page 430   From THE GLASS MENAGERIE by Tennessee Williams. Copyright © 1945 by Tennessee Williams and Edwina D. Williams and renewed 1973 by Tennessee Williams. Reprinted by permission of Random House, Inc.

page 431   Selected excerpt from "Montiel's Widow" from NO ONE WRITES TO THE COLONEL AND OTHER STORIES by Gabriel Garcia Marquez. Copyright © 1968 in the English translation by Harper & Row, Publishers, Inc. Reprinted by permission of Random House, Inc.

page 432   BOOKSHELF: "Female Suspicions" by Erica Abeel, NEW WOMAN (July 1993): 22. Reprinted by permission.

page 433   Denise Levertov: LIFE IN THE FOREST. Copyright © 1978 by Denise Levertov. Reprinted by permission of New Directions Publishing Corp.

page 433   From "Perspective of Literature" by Ralph Ellison. Originally published in AMERICAN LAW: THE THIRD CENTURY, The Law Bicentennial Volume. New York: Fred B. Rothman & Co., 1967.

page 434   From A RAISIN IN THE SUN by Lorraine Hansberry. Copyright © 1958 by Robert Nemiroff, as an unpublished work. Copyright © 1959, 1966, 1984 by Robert Nemiroff. Reprinted by permission of Random House, Inc.

page 435   Excerpted with permission from the Winter 1992 issue of *Media & Values* magazine, published by the Center for Media and Values in Los Angeles, CA.

page 435   From the book KITCHEN by Banana Yoshimoto, Copyright © 1993 GROVE ATLANTIC MONTHLY PRESS. Used with the permission of Grove/Atlantic Monthly Press.

page 436   From MACHINAL by Sophie Treadwell. Copyright 1928.

page 437   From "The Kind of Light That Shines on Texas" by Reginald McKnight in THE KENYON REVIEW, Vol. XI, No. 3, Summer 1989. Copyright © 1989 by Reginald McKnight. Reprinted by permission of the author.

page 437   Reprinted by permission of Louisiana State University Press from *Mama's Promises,* by Marilyn Nelson Waniek. Copyright © 1985 by Marilyn Nelson Waniek.

page 439   From "More closed captions open communications" by Donna Gable in USA TODAY, June 29, 1993. Copyright 1993, USA TODAY. Reprinted with permission.

page 485   Dick Locher/Tribune Media Services.

page 487   John Danziger in *The Christian Science Monitor*. © 1994.

page 488   Dick Locher/Tribune Media Services.

page 489   Dick Locher/Tribune Media Services.

page 509   From ABLAZE: THE STORY OF CHERNOBYL by Piers Paul Read. Copyright © 1993 by Piers Paul Read. Reprinted by permission of Random House, Inc., and the author.

page 510   From MAN AND SUPERMAN by George Bernard Shaw. Reprinted by permission of the Society of Authors on behalf of the Estate of Bernard Shaw.

page 510   From "The Boy with Yellow Eyes" by Gloria Gonzalez. Copyright © 1987 Gloria Gonzalez. Reprinted by permission of Brandt & Brandt.

page 511   Anne Tyler, THE ACCIDENTAL TOURIST. New York: Alfred A. Knopf, Inc., 1985.

page 512   From "At Home on the Range" by Nancy F. Smith in AUDUBON MAGAZINE, January/February 1993. Copyright © by Nancy F. Smith. Reprinted by permission.

page 515   From COLLECTED POEMS by Langston Hughes. Copyright © 1994 by the Estate of Langston Hughes. Reprinted by permission of Alfred A. Knopf, Inc.

page 516   From NEWSWEEK, April 5, 1993. Copyright © 1993, Newsweek, Inc. All rights reserved. Reprinted by permission.

page 517   © Jo Whitehorse Cochran, 1985.

pages 464, 475, 476, 492, 507, 518   Reprinted with permission of the American Council on Education.

How have adults who have prepared for and passed the GED Tests described their experience? As a major life achievement. A milestone. A turning point.

This introduction will give you general information about the GED Tests and answer some basic questions you may have, such as:

- What are the GED Tests?
- What do the GED Tests look like?
- What does it take to pass the GED Tests?
- How can this book help you to pass the GED Tests?

WHAT ARE THE GED TESTS?

The Tests of General Educational Development (GED) are developed and administered by the GED Testing Service of the American Council on Education. Each year they provide close to one million adults with the chance to earn a certificate or diploma that is widely recognized as the equivalent of a high school diploma. Since 1942, when the GED program began, more than 12 million adults have earned GED credentials. Among their names are some you may recognize, such as Bill Cosby, Waylon Jennings, Mary Lou Retton, and Dave Thomas.

Because the GED credential is recognized and accepted by over 95 percent of businesses, industries, schools, and colleges, it is often a step to further achievements. Perhaps most importantly, the GED credential proves to those who have earned it that they are indeed achievers with potential for further success.

The GED Tests are five separate tests: Writing Skills, Social Studies, Science, Interpreting Literature and the Arts, and Mathematics. A GED certificate or diploma is earned by obtaining a passing score based on the results of all five tests.

WHAT DO THE GED TESTS LOOK LIKE?

The GED Tests are made up entirely of multiple-choice questions, except for the Writing Skills Test, which includes an essay section.

Test Number	Test Name	Number of Test Items	Time	Content Areas
Test 1	Writing Skills:			Sentence Structure 35%
	Part I	55 items	75 min.	Usage: 35%
	Part II	1 topic	45 min.	Mechanics: 30%
				Essay Writing
Test 2	Social Studies	64 items	85 min.	History: 25%
				Geography: 15%
				Political Science: 20%
				Economics: 20%
				Behavioral Science: 20%
Test 3	Science	66 items	95 min.	Life Sciences: 50%
				Physical Sciences: 50%

Test Number	Test Name	Number of Test Items	Time	Content Areas
Test 4	Interpreting Literature and the Arts	45 items	65 min.	Popular Literature: 50% Classical Literature: 25% Commentary: 25%
Test 5	Mathematics	56 items	90 min.	Arithmetic: 50% Algebra: 30% Geometry: 20%

Note: In Canada, 20 percent of the items on the GED Social Studies Test are based on geography and 15 percent of the items are based on behavioral science.

WHAT DOES IT TAKE TO PASS THE GED TESTS?

To earn a GED credential, you need to earn a minimum passing score on each of the five tests as well as a passing average score overall. If you do not achieve a passing score on any one test or an overall passing score on all five tests, it is possible to retake one or more of the individual tests. By retaking a test, you can improve individual test scores, and that will increase your overall average score.

Note: You will want to find out more about the requirements of the GED Tests where you live. Each state, U.S. territory, and Canadian province sets its own specific requirements for taking and passing the GED Tests. This region-specific information is available by contacting a local adult education center, community college, or library, or simply by calling the toll-free number 1-800-62-MY GED.

In general, you will need to show that you have the skills of an average graduating high school senior to pass the GED Tests. You will be tested on your knowledge of broad concepts and generalizations—not on how well you can remember exact details or facts. Your ability to use knowledge, information, and skills to solve problems is the key to passing the tests. A good test-preparation tip is to read as much as you can of everything that interests you—general and specific. Studies show that GED candidates who read more tend to do better on the tests. Read books, newspapers, and magazines—whatever you enjoy reading. Just read!

You probably already have many of the skills you need and know much of what you need to know. Getting ready for the tests means finding out what you already know and what you need to work on, choosing a study plan for self-improvement, and spending the necessary time to follow through on your plan.

HOW TO USE THIS BOOK

This book has been written to help you prepare for the five subject areas of the GED Test. There is a logical approach to each section of study. Take a minute now to become familiar with the features and format of this book.

Pretest: This book begins with a full-length sample GED test. This pretest is similar in content to the test you will eventually take. The purpose of the pretest is to help you diagnose your strengths and weaknesses. With this information, you can plan how to best use your time to prepare for the actual test. If you score less well than you would like in a particular subject area, you can allot more time to studying for that subject. Likewise, if you do very well in a subject area, you may choose to spend less time on that subject.

Following the pretest are detailed answers and explanations for each item. Carefully review the explanation for any items you may have answered incorrectly. Once you have completed the pretest, you are ready to go on to the subject area reviews.

Review Section: Each of the five subject review sections begins with a three-page introduction to the question types you will be asked to answer in that subject area test. You will also find information about what content areas will be covered. In this introduction, you will see an example of each question type and how best to approach it.

Next, you will be given a review for each content area. After every one or two pages of information, you will have a chance to practice answering sample GED test questions about the material. As you answer the multiple-choice questions, read all the choices carefully. You are asked to choose the one best answer to each item. Although an answer choice may contain facts from the material you have read, only choose it if it is the best answer for that particular item.

Posttest: After you review the five subject areas, you are ready to take the posttest. The posttest is a full-length sample GED test. As you take the test, approximate the testing conditions. Choose a quiet place to work. Set a timer. If you do not finish in the allotted time, mark your place and then continue to answer the questions. If you finish early, go back and review your work. Working under timed conditions will help you adjust to the pacing of the actual test.

Next, check your answers to the posttest. Carefully study the explanations for the items you missed. If you had trouble with a particular subject area, review that section of the book. Then proceed to the Practice Tests.

Practice Tests: The five full-length Practice Tests contain the same questions types and cover the same content areas that you will find on the GED Test. Read the instructions for each test carefully. These are the same instructions you will see on the actual test. By reading and understanding the instructions now, you will save time when you take the GED Test. Again, approximate the testing conditions. Choose a quiet place to work. Time your work. If possible, complete all five Practice Tests in the same day, allowing short breaks between tests as needed. Use the answer sheets printed in the book and fill in the ovals with a No. 2 pencil.

When you have completed all five tests, check your answers. Carefully study the explanations for any items you may have missed. At the end of each set of explanations, use the chart to find out which areas of content and question types you may still need to review. Review pages as indicated on the chart. Your performance on the Practice Tests will help you determine whether you are ready for the GED Tests.

Now, it's time to get to work! Begin with the Pretest and go on to review each subject area. The material in this book will help you develop the test-taking skills you need to do well on the GED Test. Make sure you carefully read and answer each exercise in the book. The exercises and sample tests will give you all the practice you need to take the GED Tests with confidence.

GED PRETESTS

WRITING SKILLS

75 Minutes ❖ 55 Questions

Part I

> **Directions**
> Choose the <u>one best answer</u> to each item.

> Items 1 to 7 refer to the following paragraph.

(1) Advances in miniaturization and computer technology have revolutionized our world, they have also saved our lives. (2) Machines play an important roll in medical treatment. (3) Computers monitor the pulse, heartbeat and respiration of patients during surgery and recovery. (4) Nurse's stations stay in constant contact with patients via computer hookups. (5) Surgery has benefitted a great deal from new technology. (6) Pacemakers, organ transplants, and artificial hearts have literally give people life. (7) After they make a small incision surgeons can insert tiny cameras and surgical instruments into people's bodies. (8) Then they can perform operations by looking at the surgical area on a television monitor. (9) Less trauma to the patient speeds recovery from this type of surgery. (10) Clearly, the use of high-tech tools have resulted in marvelous advances in medicine today.

1. Sentence 1: **Advances in miniaturization and computer technology have <u>revolutionized our world, they have also</u> saved our lives.**

   Which of the following is the best way to write the underlined portion of this sentence? If you think the original is the best way, select choice (1).

   (1) revolutionized our world, they have also
   (2) revolutionized our world, they have, also
   (3) revolutianized our world. They have also
   (4) revolutionized our world. They have also
   (5) revolutionized our World, they have also

2. Sentence 2: **Machines play an important roll in medical treatment.**

   What correction should be made to this sentence?

   (1) change the spelling of <u>Machines</u> to <u>Mashines</u>
   (2) change <u>play</u> to <u>plays</u>
   (3) change the spelling of <u>roll</u> to <u>role</u>
   (4) insert a comma after <u>roll</u>
   (5) change <u>medical treatment</u> to <u>Medical Treatment</u>

3. Sentence 3: **Computers monitor the <u>pulse, heartbeat and respiration of patients during surgery</u> and recovery.**

   Which of the following is the best way to write the underlined portion of this sentence? If you think the original is the best way, select choice (1).

   (1) pulse, heartbeat and respiration of patients during surgery
   (2) pulse, heartbeat, and respiration of patients during surgery
   (3) pulse heartbeat and respiration of patients during surgery
   (4) pulse, heartbeat and respiration of patients, during surgery
   (5) pulse, heartbeat and respiration, of patients during surgery

4. Sentence 4: **Nurse's stations stay in constant contact with patients via computer hookups.**

What correction should be made to this sentence?

(1) change Nurse's to Nurses
(2) change Nurse's to Nurses'
(3) change stations to station's
(4) change patients to patient's
(5) change patients to patients'

5. Sentence 6: **Pacemakers, organ transplants, and artificial hearts have literally give people life.**

What correction should be made to this sentence?

(1) insert a comma after organ
(2) remove the comma after transplants
(3) change give to gave
(4) change give to given
(5) no correction is necessary

6. Sentence 7: **After they make a small incision surgeons can insert tiny cameras and surgical instruments into people's bodies.**

Which of the following is the best way to write the underlined portion of this sentence? If you think the original is the best way, select choice (1).

(1) After they make a small incision surgeons can insert
(2) After they make a small incision, surgeons can insert
(3) After they make a small incision surgeons, can insert
(4) After they makes a small incision surgeons can insert
(5) After they make a small incision Surgeons can insert

7. Sentence 10: **Clearly, the use of high-tech tools have resulted in marvelous advances in medicine today.**

Which of the following is the best way to write the underlined portion of this sentence? If you think the original is the best way, select choice (1).

(1) use of high-tech tools have resulted
(2) use of high-tech tools have result
(3) use of high-tech tools, have resulted
(4) use of high-tech tools, have result
(5) use of high-tech tools has resulted

Items 8 to 14 refer to the following paragraphs.

(1) Many social critics worrying about a decline in reading among Americans. (2) They cite surveys that show that 72 percent of eighth graders watch 3 or more hours of television a day. (3) Only 27 percent of eighth graders say they spend time. (4) Reading for pleasure. (5) Television is not the only factor contributing to a population that doesnt read. (6) Computers also plays a role. (7) People are becoming used to flashing, noisy, and instantaneous electronic information. (8) Reading, on the other hand, is private and quiet. (9) Electronic communication lacks the subtlety of the written word, but reading demands more effort than watching television.

(10) Nevertheless, the number of bookstores increases 76 percent in the 1980s. (11) Independent bookstores, especially, try to entice customers with a wide selection of titles and a homelike atmosphere. (12) Many install wooden shelves for their books and provide comfortable chairs so consumers can read while they browse through books.

8. Sentence 1: **Many social critics worrying about a decline in reading among Americans.**

What correction should be made to this sentence?

(1) change worrying to worried
(2) change worrying to are worrying
(3) insert a comma after reading
(4) change the period to a semicolon
(5) no correction is necessary

9. Sentences 3 and 4: **Only 27 percent of eighth graders say they spend time. Reading for pleasure.**

Which of the following is the best way to write the underlined portion of these sentences? If you think the original is the best way, select choice (1).

(1) they spend time. Reading for pleasure.
(2) they spend time reading. For pleasure.
(3) they spend time, reading for pleasure.
(4) they spend time reading for pleasure.
(5) he or she spends time. Reading for pleasure.

10. Sentence 5: **Television is not the only factor contributing to a population that doesnt read.**

What correction should be made to this sentence?

(1) insert a comma after factor
(2) change the spelling of contributing to contributeing
(3) change contributing to contributed
(4) change doesnt to does'nt
(5) change doesnt to doesn't

11. Sentence 6: **Computers also plays a role.**

What correction should be made to this sentence?

(1) insert a comma after Computers
(2) change plays to play
(3) change plays to will play
(4) insert a comma after plays
(5) no correction is necessary

12. Sentence 9: **Electronic communication lacks the subtlety of the written word, but reading demands more effort than watching television.**

Which of the following is the best way to write the underlined portion of this sentence? If you think the original is the best way, select choice (1).

(1) word, but reading demands
(2) word, if reading demands
(3) word, or reading demands
(4) word; therefore, reading demands
(5) word, even though reading demands

13. Sentence 10: **Nevertheless, the number of bookstores increases 76 percent in the 1980s.**

What correction should be made to this sentence?

(1) remove the comma after Nevertheless
(2) change increases to increase
(3) change increases to increased
(4) change increases to will increase
(5) insert a comma after increases

14. Sentence 12: **Many install wooden shelves for their books and provide comfortable chairs so consumers can read while they browse through the books.**

If you rewrote sentence 12 beginning with

Wooden shelves and comfortable chairs the next word should be

(1) encourage
(2) repel
(3) browse
(4) read
(5) install

Items 15 to 21 refer to the following paragraph.

(1) Checking accounts offer convenience to many people. (2) When you pay bills by mail, it's much safer to mail a check than mailing cash. (3) Checking accounts do, however, require some care. (4) Balancing a checkbook is the most important way of keeping your account in good shape. (5) Being confusing and frustrating, many people simply don't bother to reconcile their accounts. (6) Don't despair, however; bank statements include forms to guide you through the process of balancing your account. (7) You do have to solve some addition and subtraction problems, but it usually isn't complicated. (8) The main reason to reconcile your account with the bank's monthly statement is to be sure you have the funds you think you have. (9) Errors carry over from month to month, so you might end up with a Bounced Check even though you thought you had enough money in your account to cover it. (10) Bouncing a check makes things difficult for the person you wrote the check for, and it can be expensive for you because most places charge a penalty for bounced checks. (11) It's important to use the account wisely and carefully. (12) That way, you had all the benefits of a checking account and none of its perils.

15. Sentence 2: **When you pay bills by mail, it's much safer to mail a check than mailing cash.**

Which of the following is the best way to write the underlined portion of the sentence? If you think the original is the best way, select choice (1).

(1) to mail a check than mailing cash
(2) to mail a check than by mailing cash
(3) to mail a check than mailing some cash
(4) to mail a check, then mailing cash
(5) to mail a check than to mail cash

16. Sentence 3: **Checking accounts do, however, require some care.**

What correction should be made to this sentence?

(1) remove the comma after do
(2) remove the comma after however
(3) remove however
(4) change require to required
(5) no correction is necessary

17. Sentence 5: <u>**Being confusing and frustrating, many people**</u> **simply don't bother to reconcile their accounts.**

Which of the following is the best way to write the underlined portion of this sentence? If you think the original is the best way, select choice (1).

(1) Being confusing and frustrating, many people
(2) Being confused and frustrating, checking accounts
(3) Because people are confusing and frustrating, many
(4) Because balancing a checking account is often confusing and frustrating, many people
(5) Because they confuse and frustrate them, many people

18. Sentence 7: **You do have to solve some addition and subtraction problems, <u>but it usually isn't complicated.</u>**

Which of the following is the best way to write the underlined portion of this sentence? If you think the original is the best way, select choice (1).

(1) but it usually isn't complicated
(2) but it usually wasn't complicated
(3) and it usually isn't complicated
(4) but they usually aren't complicated
(5) it usually isn't complicated

19. Sentence 9: **Errors carry over from month to month, so you might end up with a Bounced Check even though you thought you had enough money in your account to cover it.**

What correction should be made to this sentence?

(1) remove the comma after <u>month</u>
(2) change <u>Bounced Check</u> to <u>bounced check</u>
(3) insert a comma after <u>Check</u>
(4) replace <u>it</u> with <u>them</u>
(5) no correction is necessary

20. Sentence 10: **Bouncing a check makes things difficult for the person you wrote the check for, and it can be expensive for you because most places charge a penalty for bounced checks.**

If you rewrote sentence 10 beginning with <u>Bouncing a check creates many problems and costs</u> the next word should be

(1) little
(2) nothing
(3) them
(4) me
(5) you

21. Sentence 12: **That way, you had all the benefits of a checking account and none of its perils.**

What correction should be made to this sentence?

(1) remove the comma after <u>way</u>
(2) change <u>had</u> to <u>have</u>
(3) insert a comma after <u>account</u>
(4) change <u>its</u> to <u>it's</u>
(5) change <u>perils</u> to <u>peril's</u>

Items 22 to 28 refer to the following paragraphs.

(1) Tuberculosis once thought eradicated from the civilized world is returning. (2) The disease is spreading in American slums and poor cities throughout the world. (3) TB is not the only returning disease doctors thought they had conquered. (4) New strains of cholera that doesn't respond to vaccines have been seen in Africa and Asia. (5) The World Health Organization, an agency of the United Nations, says malaria is another one. (6) Typhoid and diphtheria has resurfaced in Russia. (7) Although these diseases appear mostly in underdeveloped countries, they threaten developed nations too. (8) There, tuberculosis already worries health officials.

(9) Health professionals blame the threatening epidemics on poverty and poor health care in over-populated third world countries, new strains of bacteria that resist drugs, and growth in world travel, which spreads diseases across continents and oceans. (10) The world must improve sanitation, step up vaccination programs, and practice better hygiene. (11) To prevent epidemics.

22. Sentence 1: **Tuberculosis once thought eradicated from the civilized world is returning.**

    What correction should be made to this sentence?

    (1) insert commas after tuberculosis and world
    (2) insert a comma after once
    (3) change tuberculosis to tuberculoses
    (4) change is to are
    (5) no correction is necessary

23. Sentence 3: **TB is not the only returning disease doctors thought they had conquered.**

    If you rewrote sentence 3 beginning with Doctors thought they had conquered TB and many other diseases, the next word should be

    (1) so
    (2) or
    (3) and
    (4) but
    (5) if

24. Sentence 4: **New strains of cholera that doesn't respond to vaccines have been seen in Africa and Asia.**

    What correction should be made to this sentence?

    (1) replace that with who
    (2) replace doesn't with don't
    (3) insert a comma after vaccines
    (4) change seen to saw
    (5) no correction is necessary

25. Sentence 5: **The World Health Organization, an agency of the United Nations, says malaria is another one.**

    Which of the following is the best way to write the underlined portion of this sentence? If you think the original is the best way, select choice (1).

    (1) says malaria is another one.
    (2) say malaria is another one.
    (3) says malaria was another growing health problem.
    (4) say malaria is another growing health problem.
    (5) says malaria is another growing health problem.

26. Sentence 6: **Typhoid and diphtheria has resurfaced in Russia.**

    Which of the following is the best way to write the underlined portion of this sentence? If you think the original is the best way, select choice (1).

    (1) has resurfaced in Russia.
    (2) have resurfaced in Russia.
    (3) has resurface in Russia.
    (4) has resurfaced in russia.
    (5) will resurface in Russia.

27. Sentences 7 and 8: **Although these diseases appear mostly in underdeveloped countries, they threaten developed nations too. There, tuberculosis already worries health officials.**

    The most effective combination of sentences 7 and 8 would include which of the following groups of words?

    (1) Underdeveloped countries don't worry about disease
    (2) mostly tuberculosis
    (3) Underdeveloped diseases worry health officials
    (4) where health officials already worry about tuberculosis
    (5) because developed nations are free of these diseases

28. Sentences 10 and 11: **The world must improve sanitation, step up vaccination programs, and practice better hygiene. To prevent epidemics.**

    What correction should be made to these sentences?

    (1) remove the comma after sanitation
    (2) remove the comma after programs
    (3) insert a comma after and
    (4) change hygiene. To to hygiene to
    (5) change hygiene. To to hygiene, to

Items 29 to 37 refer to the following paragraphs.

(1) The Great Depression of the 1930s. (2) One of the most devastating periods in American history. (3) It was a time many people still remember filled with pain. (4) Not everyone was devastated by the Depression, but most people were at least touched by it. (5) Whether it was unemployment, food shortages, or the landlord kicked them out, people remember the anguish of those years. (6) This period of economic crisis began with the Stock Market Crash of 1929 and continued until World War II created a demand for new goods and services. (7) Which put people back to work.

(8) During the Depression, more than five thousand banks closed. (9) Causing people to lose all their savings. (10) Wealthy people who had made fortunes in the stock market lost everything, even though many of them committed suicide. (11) Unemployment reached 25 percent, with 15 million people out of jobs. (12) Many young people who were ready to go to work for the first time had no hope of employment so they wandered around the country. (13) Aimlessly riding freight trains, many of these hoboes were injured or killed. (14) The railroads added empty cars to help them. (15) Years of drought in the part of the country known as the Great Plains drove people west. (16) Families abandoned their unproductive farms, loaded their possessions into their beat-up cars, and California seemed to promise a better life. (17) They found little relief when they got there unless things were bad all over. (18) A famous book by John Steinbeck, called *The Grapes of Wrath*, tells the story of some of these people.

29. Sentences 1 and 2: **The Great Depression of the 1930s. One of the most devastating periods in American history.**

What correction should be made to these sentences?

(1) change 1930s. One to 1930s, one
(2) change 1930s. One to 1930s was one
(3) change 1930s. One to 1930s, being one
(4) replace one of the with a
(5) change periods in to periods. In

30. Sentence 3: **It was a time many people still remember filled with pain.**

Which of the following is the best way to write the underlined portion of this sentence? If you think the original is the best way, select choice (1).

(1) time many people still remember filled with pain.
(2) time filled with pain many people still remember.
(3) painful time many people still remember.
(4) time many people fill with pain.
(5) painful memory to many people most of the time.

31. Sentence 5: **Whether it was unemployment, food shortages, or the landlord kicked them out, people remember the anguish of those years.**

What correction should be made to this sentence?

(1) remove Whether
(2) replace it was with people faced
(3) replace the landlord kicked them out with eviction from their homes
(4) replace the landlord kicked them out with they had no place to live
(5) change anguish of to anguish. Of

32. Sentence 7: **Which put people back to work.**

What correction should be made to this sentence?

(1) replace Which with The war
(2) insert finally before put
(3) replace put people with saw people go
(4) insert again after work
(5) no correction is necessary

33. Sentences 8 and 9: **During the Depression, more than five thousand banks closed. Causing people to lose all their savings.**

If you rewrote sentences 8 and 9 beginning with

The closing of the banks the next word should be

(1) people
(2) lost
(3) savings
(4) Depression
(5) caused

34. Sentence 10: **Wealthy people who had made fortunes in the stock market lost <u>everything, even though many</u> of them committed suicide.**

Which of the following is the best way to write the underlined portion of this sentence? If you think the original is the best way, select choice (1).

(1) everything, even though many
(2) everything even though many
(3) everything. Even though many
(4) everything, and many
(5) everything because many

35. Sentence 12: **Many young people who were ready to go to work for the first time had no hope of employment so they wandered around the country.**

What correction should be made to this sentence?

(1) change <u>work for</u> to <u>work. For</u>
(2) change <u>time had</u> to <u>time. Had</u>
(3) insert a comma after <u>employment</u>
(4) replace <u>so</u> with <u>or</u>
(5) change <u>wandered around</u> to <u>wandered. Around</u>

36. Sentence 16: **Families abandoned their unproductive farms, loaded their possessions into their beat-up cars, and <u>California seemed to promise a better life.</u>**

Which of the following is the best way to write the underlined portion of this sentence? If you think the original is the best way, select choice (1).

(1) California seemed to promise a better life
(2) headed to California for a better life
(3) California looked better to them
(4) better things awaited them in California
(5) life would improve in California

37. Sentence 17: **They found little relief when they got there unless things were bad all over.**

What correction should be made to this sentence?

(1) change <u>relief when</u> to <u>relief. When</u>
(2) insert a comma after <u>there</u>
(3) change <u>there unless</u> with <u>there. Unless</u>
(4) replace <u>unless</u> with <u>although</u>
(5) replace <u>unless</u> with <u>since</u>

Items 38 to 44 refer to the following paragraph.

(1) Nutritionists and doctors tell us that breakfast may be the most important meal of the day, yet many people skips this meal. (2) They say breakfast is too time-consuming or food is unappealing early in the morning. (3) They find many reasons for skipping breakfast. (4) Nevertheless, studies show that people perform better at work and at school if they have eaten a nutritious breakfast. (5) Breakfast didn't have to take a lot of time. (6) In fact, we're now told not to eat the huge bacon-and-egg breakfasts of the past. (7) Those meals, who do take time to prepare, contain too much fat and cholesterol. (8) Lighter breakfasts is better. (9) A bowl of cereal with milk, a piece of toast, fruit, juice, and perhaps a cup of coffee provide a wholesome breakfast in very little time. (10) People who skip breakfast often experience a sudden attack of hunger midmorning. (11) He or she may satisfy this hunger quickly with something like doughnuts, potato chips, and canned soda. (12) It's high in calories and fat but low in nutritional value. (13) Even if it seems hard at first, it's important to try to eat a good breakfast.

38. Sentence 1: **Nutritionists and doctors tell us that breakfast may be the most important meal of the day, yet many people skips this meal.**

What correction should be made to this sentence?

(1) replace <u>us</u> with <u>you</u>
(2) replace <u>meal</u> with <u>one</u>
(3) change <u>skips</u> to <u>skip</u>
(4) change <u>skips</u> to <u>skipping</u>
(5) change <u>skips</u> to <u>skipped</u>

39. Sentence 4: **Nevertheless, studies show that people perform better at work and at school if they have eaten a nutritious breakfast.**

If you rewrote sentence 4 beginning with

<u>Nevertheless, studies show better performance</u> at <u>work and school by people</u> the next word should be

(1) which
(2) whom
(3) who
(4) that
(5) skipping

40. Sentence 5: **Breakfast didn't have to take a lot of time.**

What correction should be made to this sentence?

(1) change <u>didn't</u> to <u>don't</u>
(2) change <u>didn't</u> to <u>doesn't</u>
(3) replace <u>didn't</u> with <u>won't</u>
(4) replace <u>didn't</u> with <u>does</u>
(5) replace <u>didn't</u> with <u>will</u>

41. Sentence 7: **Those meals, <u>who do take time to prepare,</u> contain too much fat and cholesterol.**

Which of the following is the best way to write the underlined portion of this sentence? If you think the original is the best way, select choice (1).

(1) who do take time to prepare,
(2) which do take time to prepare,
(3) who spend a lot of time preparing,
(4) who prepare for a long time,
(5) which are quick,

42. Sentence 8: **Lighter breakfasts is better.**

What correction should be made to this sentence?

(1) insert <u>A</u> before <u>lighter</u>
(2) change <u>Lighter</u> to <u>Light</u>
(3) change <u>is</u> to <u>were</u>
(4) change <u>is</u> to <u>are</u>
(5) no correction is necessary

43. Sentence 11: **He or she may satisfy this hunger quickly with something like doughnuts, potato chips, and canned soda.**

What correction should be made to this sentence?

(1) replace <u>He or she</u> with <u>It</u>
(2) replace <u>He or she</u> with <u>One</u>
(3) replace <u>He or She</u> with <u>They</u>
(4) replace <u>He or She</u> with <u>We</u>
(5) replace <u>He or She</u> with <u>You</u>

44. Sentence 12: **It's high in calories and fat but low in nutritional value.**

What correction should be made to this sentence?

(1) replace <u>It's</u> with <u>This is</u>
(2) replace <u>It's</u> with <u>These foods are</u>
(3) replace <u>It's</u> with <u>Doughnuts, potato chips, and canned soda are</u>
(4) replace <u>It's</u> with <u>Which are</u>
(5) no correction is necessary

Items 45 to 51 refer to the following paragraph.

(1) There is considerable debate among politicians and voters as to weather English should be noted as the official language of the United States. (2) Supporters of an official language policy argue that it costs to much to provide education, voter ballots, and other services in several different languages. (3) Opponents argue that its important to serve the millions of non-English speakers in their native languages so that they can learn more quickly to function productively in American society. (4) Teaching school in languages other than English, they argue, helps children learn the basic skills everyone needs. (5) An opposing view, on the other hand, says immigrants should not be able to avoid English so easily. (6) Without English language skills, the argument goes, people are stuck in jobs with low pay. (7) Such jobs also offer little opportunity for advancment. (8) America's earlier waves of immigrants had less available in their native languages, so they were forced to learn english. (9) Which approach is better? (10) The experts, who hold widely different opinions may not come to agreement on this issue for a long time.

45. Sentence 1: **There is considerable debate among politicians and voters as to weather English should be noted as the official language of the United States.**

What correction should be made to this sentence?

(1) replace <u>There</u> with <u>Their</u>
(2) change the spelling of <u>considerable</u> to <u>considerible</u>
(3) replace <u>weather</u> with <u>whether</u>
(4) change <u>English</u> to <u>english</u>
(5) change the spelling of <u>language</u> to <u>langauge</u>

46. Sentence 2: **Supporters of an official language policy argue that <u>it costs to much to provide</u> education, voter ballots, and other services in several different languages.**

Which of the following is the best way to write the underlined portion of this sentence? If you think the original is the best way, select choice (1).

(1) it costs to much to provide education
(2) it cost to much to provide education
(3) it costs to much too provide education
(4) it costs too much to provide education
(5) it costs to much to provide, education

47. Sentence 3: **Opponents argue that its important to serve the millions of non-English speakers in their native languages so that they can learn more quickly to function productively in American society.**

What correction should be made to this sentence?

(1) change the spelling of argue to argu
(2) change its to it's
(3) change the spelling of millions to milions
(4) insert a comma after languages
(5) no correction is necessary

48. Sentence 5: **An opposing view, on the other hand, says immigrants should not be able to avoid English so easily.**

If you rewrote sentence 5 beginning with

On the other hand, opponents believe it's too easy for the next word should be

(1) everyone
(2) teachers
(3) Americans
(4) politicians
(5) immigrants

49. Sentence 7: **Such jobs also offer little opportunity for advancment.**

Which of the following is the best way to write the underlined portion of this sentence? If you think the original is the best way, select choice (1).

(1) little opportunity for advancment.
(2) little oppertunity for advancment.
(3) little opportunity, for advancment.
(4) little opportunity to advancment.
(5) little opportunity for advancement.

50. Sentence 8: **America's earlier waves of immigrants had less available in their native languages, so they were forced to learn english.**

What correction should be made to this sentence?

(1) change America's to Americas
(2) change the spelling of available to avalable
(3) change native languages to Native Languages
(4) remove the comma after languages
(5) change english to English

51. Sentence 10: **The experts, who hold widely different opinions may not come to agreement on this issue for a long time.**

What correction should be made to this sentence?

(1) change experts to expert's
(2) change experts to experts'
(3) remove the comma after experts
(4) insert a comma after opinions
(5) no correction is necessary

Items 52 to 55 refer to the following paragraph.

(1) Among nature's animals are many that can harm human beings. (2) Most people know insects and snake's can be poisonous. (3) Not everyone realizes, however, that the oceon is also home to poisonous creatures. (4) One such animal is a deadly jellyfish. (5) It's sting affects the victim's circulatory system. (6) The impact of the vicious sting is felt immediatelly. (7) A disasterous encounter with such a creature could amount to a tragedy that ends in death. (8) Because of their dramatic reputation, we usually think of sharks when we think of the dangers of the sea. (9) Clearly, sharks are not the only fish to avoid.

52. Sentence 2: **Most people know insects and snake's can be poisonous.**

What correction should be made to this sentence?

(1) replace know with no
(2) change insects to insect's
(3) change snake's to snakes'
(4) change snake's to snakes
(5) no correction is necessary

53. Sentence 3: **Not everyone realizes, however, that the oceon is also home to poisonous creatures.**

What correction should be made to this sentence?

(1) change realizes to realize's
(2) remove the comma before however
(3) change the spelling of oceon to ocean
(4) replace to with too
(5) change the spelling of poisonous to poisinous

14

54. Sentence 5: **It's sting affects the victim's circulatory system.**

What correction should be made to this sentence?

(1) change It's to Its
(2) change affects to effects
(3) change victim's to victims
(4) change the spelling of circulatory to sirculatory
(5) no correction necessary

55. Sentence 6: **The impact of the vicious sting is felt immediatelly.**

What correction should be made to this sentence?

(1) change impact to Impact
(2) change the spelling of vicious to visious
(3) change is to was
(4) change the spelling of immediatelly to imediatelly
(5) change the spelling of immediatelly to immediately

Part II

In Part II of the Writing Skills Test, you are asked to write an essay. Read the entire essay topic carefully before you begin writing. After you are sure you understand the topic, take some time to plan what you want to say. Be sure to check your essay after you write it to correct any errors in structure, content, or mechanics.

TOPIC

Political campaigns can cost candidates hundreds of thousands or even millions of dollars. To reach voters, politicians spend huge amounts of money to hire professional advertising firms and to buy television time. Through the technology of television, the American people can see, hear, and evaluate candidates without having to leave home. Sometimes, however, we get more image than substance through televised politics.

In an essay of about 200 words, discuss the value of television as a source of information during political campaigns.

SOCIAL STUDIES

85 Minutes ❖ 64 Questions

Items 1 and 2 refer to the following passage.

Operant conditioning occurs when you learn from the consequences of your behavior. For example, if you park your car in a handicapped-designated parking space and receive a parking ticket, you probably will not park your car in a handicapped space again.

1. According to the passage, which of the following statements is true?

   (1) Your behavior "operates" on the outside world to produce a consequence.
   (2) Operant conditioning is only a theory.
   (3) Your behavior has no effect on operant conditioning.
   (4) Only handicapped persons are to use handicapped parking spaces.
   (5) People change their actions depending on the consequences of their previous actions.

2. In the example given in the passage, the stimulus, or the factor that influences your change in behavior, is

   (1) the handicapped parking space
   (2) the car that you parked
   (3) the parking ticket
   (4) the fact that you got caught
   (5) your reaction to the ticket

Items 3 and 4 refer to the following information.

Economist: one who studies production, distribution, and consumption of wealth and ways of supplying the material wants of people.

Psychologist: one who studies behavior and the human mind in their many aspects, operations, powers, and functions.

Sociologist: one who studies human society and social phenomena, the progress of civilization, and the laws controlling human institutions and functions.

Historian: one who studies and explains the record of past events.

Geographer: one who studies the planet Earth, including its climate, products, natural features, and inhabitants.

3. John Maynard Keynes, who wrote *The General Theory of Employment, Interest, and Money* was a(n):

   (1) economist
   (2) psychologist
   (3) sociologist
   (4) historian
   (5) geographer

4. Someone who examines the effects of poverty on preschool children living in urban areas of the American Southwest is a(n):

   (1) economist
   (2) psychologist
   (3) sociologist
   (4) historian
   (5) geographer

Items 5 and 6 refer to the following information.

The Eastern Woodland peoples of North America lived in what is now the northeastern part of the United States. The Mohawk, Oneida, Seneca, and other groups lived by hunting, farming corn and squash, fishing, and gathering berries. By contrast, peoples of the Northwest, including Nootka, Tillamook, and Coos, survived by fishing for salmon, cod, herring, and halibut in the crowded streams and coastal waters and by using the trees of the huge forests of the area for many of their needs.

5. Salmon was a staple in the diet of the

   (1) Tillamook
   (2) Seneca
   (3) Mohawk
   (4) Oneida
   (5) peoples of the Northeast

6. The passage indicates that a native people's way of living depended on

   (1) the fish available in the region
   (2) the proximity of streams and coastal waters
   (3) the crops and berries that grew in the region
   (4) the geography and resources of the region
   (5) the proximity of large forests

7. When you enter a grocery store, you may find that the produce section is located near the entrance. Store owners believe the smells of fresh fruits and vegetables will make you hungry, which in turn will cause you to

   (1) sample the fresh produce as you shop
   (2) leave the store and return after you have eaten
   (3) purchase more food items
   (4) search the shelves for your favorite brands
   (5) rush through your shopping so you can go home to eat

8. Forty-nine of the fifty states have bicameral, or two-house, legislatures. Nebraska is the only state with a unicameral, or one-house, legislature. What is one possible disadvantage of Nebraska's unicameral legislative system?

   (1) Bills might pass too quickly, without adequate consideration.
   (2) Voters would have fewer choices in elections.
   (3) Fewer people would have the opportunity to run for office.
   (4) One interest group could dominate the entire legislature.
   (5) The efficiency of state government could be obstructed.

Items 9 and 10 refer to the following information.

Unemployment of qualified workers has three basic causes:

1. Cyclical unemployment is caused by slowdowns in the economy. Businesses sell fewer goods and thus need fewer workers. These same workers often are rehired when business picks up again.
2. Seasonal unemployment occurs in industries such as farming that need many workers during some seasons but not during others.
3. Structural unemployment takes place when businesses move from one location to another or when skills of certain workers become obsolete or are no longer needed for some reason.

Occasionally, unemployment can be caused by more than one of these situations at a time.

9. Peter is a ski instructor in Colorado. When the economy is slow, fewer people ski, but Peter is still hired by the ski resort. Every year, though, he has trouble finding someone who will hire him for about five months when there is no skiing.

   Peter's unemployment is

   (1) cyclical
   (2) seasonal
   (3) structural
   (4) cyclical and seasonal
   (5) seasonal and structural

Squash=
herring=
halibut=
cod =

10. Critics of the North American Free Trade Agreement (NAFTA) argue that many Americans' jobs will be lost as companies take advantage of opportunities to move their operations to Mexico. The fear is that workers will experience which type of unemployment?

    (1) cyclical
    (2) seasonal
    (3) structural
    (4) cyclical and seasonal
    (5) cyclical and structural

Items 11 and 12 refer to the time zone map below.

TIME ZONES IN THE 48 CONTIGUOUS STATES

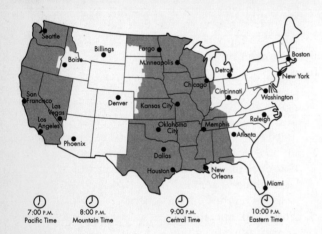

11. When it is 1 a.m. in Atlanta, what time is it in Los Angeles?

    (1) midnight
    (2) 2 a.m.
    (3) 1 p.m.
    (4) 11 p.m.
    (5) 10 p.m.

12. When it is 2 p.m. in Seattle, what time is it in San Francisco?

    (1) noon
    (2) 1 p.m.
    (3) 2 a.m.
    (4) 2 p.m.
    (5) 11 a.m.

Items 13 to 15 refer to the following graph.

COST OF AN AVERAGE TRADITIONAL WEDDING

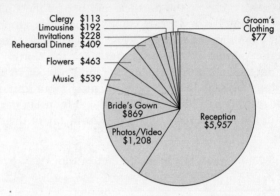

13. According to the graph, which two categories cost less than the limousine?

    (1) invitations and clergy
    (2) music and the flowers
    (3) clergy and groom's clothing
    (4) rehearsal dinner and invitations
    (5) groom's and bride's clothing

14. A couple on a limited budget would save the most money by cutting back on which category?

    (1) the rehearsal dinner
    (2) the reception
    (3) the invitations
    (4) the photographs and video
    (5) the music

15. The average traditional wedding shown in the graph costs slightly more than $10,000. About what portion of that amount is the cost of the reception?

    (1) less than 10 percent
    (2) about 90 percent
    (3) about 30 percent
    (4) a little less than half
    (5) about 60 percent

Items 16 and 17 refer to the cartoon.

16. Which statement best summarizes the point of this 1990 cartoon?

(1) Farmers in the Soviet Union were sometimes able to raise bumper crops.

(2) Despite huge resources, the Soviet system managed to produce practically nothing.

(3) The Soviet Union used a highly centralized distribution system.

(4) People in the Soviet Union had to endure a low standard of living.

(5) By the 1990s, machinery in the Soviet Union was quite antiquated by Western standards.

17. With which statement would the cartoonist be most likely to agree?

(1) Communism provided a decent living to its citizens.

(2) Few people believed that communism would fail so completely in the Soviet Union.

(3) People who lived in the Soviet Union got what they deserved.

(4) Communism was a system that took advantage of the people forced to endure it.

(5) The Soviet Union had many lazy workers.

18. In the first years of the existence of the United States, the right to vote was limited to white male landowners aged 21 or over. Since then there has been a gradual extension of this right to include women, minorities, and people aged 18 and over, regardless of economic status. Which statement best describes why this extension of rights has taken place?

(1) The great growth in overall population has been the major cause of the extension of voting rights.

(2) The idea has grown that all people are equal and should be treated as such.

(3) The westward movement of white settlers in the 1800s led to the need for more voters west of the Mississippi River.

(4) The elimination of slavery in 1865 was the main reason for this extension of rights.

(5) More people today feel qualified to elect responsible leaders.

19. Which of the following men is best known as the leader of the American civil rights movement of the 1960s?

(1) W. E. B. Du Bois

(2) Jesse Jackson

(3) Martin Luther King Jr.

(4) Booker T. Washington

(5) Marcus Garvey

20. In his January 1961 inaugural address, a new American president said, "Ask not what your country can do for you—ask what you can do for your country." Which president was this?

(1) George Washington

(2) Abraham Lincoln

(3) Theodore Roosevelt

(4) John F. Kennedy

(5) Bill Clinton

Regardless =
overrall =

Items 21 to 23 refer to the globe.

Items 24 to 26 refer to the following information.

LATITUDE AND LONGITUDE

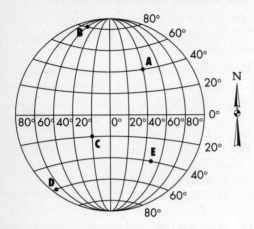

21. Which point on the globe can be found at 80 degrees north, 60 degrees west?

   (1) point A
   (2) point B
   (3) point C
   (4) point D
   (5) point E

22. Which point probably has the warmest year-round weather?

   (1) point A
   (2) point B
   (3) point C
   (4) point D
   (5) point E

23. A traveler going from point B to point E would travel in which direction?

   (1) north
   (2) west
   (3) southeast
   (4) southwest
   (5) northwest

To help America recover from the Great Depression, President Franklin Delano Roosevelt's administration got Congress to enact laws that created the following programs:

Rural Electrification Administration, which provided low-cost electricity to isolated rural areas.

Civilian Conservation Corps, which provided jobs for young, single men on conservation projects for the federal government.

Works Progress Administration, which created as many jobs as possible as quickly as possible, from electrician to violinist, and paid wages with government funds.

Banking Act of 1935, which created a seven-member board of public officials to regulate the nation's money supply and interest rates on loans.

Tennessee Valley Authority, which developed natural resources of the Tennessee Valley.

24. Today's powerful Federal Reserve Board, which sets interest rates charged by the Federal Reserve Bank, is an outgrowth of which legislative initiative of the 1930s?

   (1) the Rural Electrification Administration
   (2) the Civilian Conservation Corps
   (3) the Works Progress Administration
   (4) the Banking Act of 1935
   (5) the Tennessee Valley Authority

25. A farmer in rural Oregon was probably most interested in which of the five government initiatives?

   (1) the Rural Electrification Administration
   (2) the Civilian Conservation Corps
   (3) the Works Progress Administration
   (4) the Banking Act of 1935
   (5) the Tennessee Valley Authority

enact=

26. The social legislation of the 1930s had a profound and lasting effect on American society. Today some people believe that this effect was not an entirely positive one. Which statement probably best describes those people's beliefs today?

   (1) The federal government spends too much money on foreign aid.

   (2) The federal government should take more control of public education and agencies that deal with child abuse.

   (3) The Tennessee Valley Authority was an overly ambitious project that destroyed the natural beauty of the Tennessee Valley.

   (4) Too many social programs of today are not as well administered as were those of the 1930s.

   (5) Social programs have created a nation of people who depend on the government too much for the everyday things of life.

27. From 1919 to 1933, Americans lived with a constitutional amendment that forbade the making, selling, or transporting of intoxicating liquors for drinking purposes. During that time, now often referred to as the Roaring 20s, a great deal of liquor was illegally manufactured, transported, sold, and consumed. Large, well-organized groups of violent criminals made huge profits on this illegal activity. Which of the following people may cite that national experience to support his or her point of view today?

   (1) someone who favors the decriminalization of drugs

   (2) someone who wants to increase the number of government drug inspectors at major seaports and airline terminals

   (3) someone who works for a liquor manufacturer today

   (4) someone who believes there is too much violence on TV

   (5) someone who wants much higher "sin taxes" on items such as liquor and tobacco products

---

Items 28 to 30 refer to the following information.

The collapse of the Soviet Union in the early 1990s led to a drastic fall in the birth rate across Russia. The birth rate fell from 2.1 children per woman in 1988 to 1.4 children per woman in 1993. At the same time, the death rate soared. In 1993, there were 800,000 more deaths than births.

28. If this trend continues, you can safely predict that Russia's population will

   (1) decrease by half by the year 2010

   (2) increase when the country achieves economic stability

   (3) decrease sharply in the coming years

   (4) decrease sharply, then increase after the year 2000

   (5) follow the same patterns as other countries in the former Soviet Union

29. What is the most likely reason for the falling birth rate?

   (1) the large number of women compared to men after World War II

   (2) a national problem of alcoholism

   (3) the large percentage of the population that is already over age 65

   (4) uncertainty about the future as a result of economic and political chaos

   (5) an increase in the suicide rate

30. In the far northern villages of Russia, the average life expectancy for men is now below 50 years of age. Which of these choices would not be a factor contributing to this declining life expectancy?

   (1) the increasing rate of alcoholism

   (2) the growing number of suicides

   (3) the increasingly difficult economic conditions in the country

   (4) the generally cold climate in the region

   (5) the increasing number of industrial accidents resulting in death due to lack of medical supplies

forbade =
trend =

31. George Washington was chosen president of the Constitutional Convention in 1787 and was then overwhelmingly elected to serve as the first president of the new republic in 1789 and 1792. Washington is associated with which of the following wars?

(1) the French and Indian War
(2) the Revolutionary War
(3) the War of 1812
(4) the Civil War
(5) the Spanish-American War

32. With which act of government is President Abraham Lincoln most closely associated?

(1) the Monroe Doctrine
(2) the Louisiana Purchase
(3) the Emancipation Proclamation
(4) the Roosevelt Corollary
(5) the Truman Doctrine

Item 33 refers to the following passage.

In the early 1800s, the decision to send a child to school was a private one. By the middle of the century, a change was brought about by reformers such as Horace Mann of Massachusetts, who believed that education promoted inventiveness and economic growth and allowed workers to increase their incomes. More and more states began to use tax money to pay for public schools. By 1870, about 57 percent of the nation's children were enrolled in public school and by 1920, 75 percent of American children were in school.

33. During the 1800s, education became not a privilege for the few but

(1) an obligation for everyone
(2) a tax burden on society
(3) a right for everyone
(4) an economic decision
(5) a business decision

Overwhelmingly=
Rift=
burden

34. The southern colonies were favored with fertile land and a warm climate—perfect conditions for growing tobacco, cotton, rice, and other cash crops, or crops grown for profit. To grow these cash crops, large farms, or plantations, were developed. Plantations, with their need for tremendous numbers of workers, gave rise to a "peculiar institution" in the colonies and then in the United States. This institution was

(1) democracy
(2) colonialism
(3) land development
(4) cash crop economy
(5) slavery

35. In his first campaign speech, Abraham Lincoln referred to the rift that was dividing the nation: "A house divided against itself cannot stand. I believe this government cannot endure permanently half slave and half free. I do not expect the Union to be dissolved; I do not expect the house to fall; but I do expect it will cease to be divided. It will become all one thing, or all the other." This statement reflects Lincoln's main purpose in fighting the Civil War. That purpose was

(1) to preserve the Union
(2) to preserve slavery in the South
(3) to abolish slavery
(4) to divide the country
(5) to extend slavery to the territories

Items 36 and 37 refer to the following passage.

The removal of Native Americans from land desired by white settlers began long before Americans crossed the Mississippi River. The Indian Removal Act of 1830 gave the U.S. government authority to relocate the native peoples of the South and Northwest to Indian Territory, an area set aside west of the Mississippi. There they would "cast off their savage habits and become an interesting, civilized, and Christian community," said President Jackson. During the forced migration, disease, severe weather, and hardships on the trail took their toll; thousands of Native Americans died. The Cherokee had a particularly hard time. Of about 20,000 removed from their homes, 4,000 died on the journey, which came to be known as the "Trail of Tears."

36. The Indian Removal Act was a justification of the American policy of

    (1) Manifest Destiny
    (2) expansion
    (3) "civilizing" Native Americans
    (4) Native American relocation
    (5) settlement west of the Mississippi River

37. The Cherokees' name for their journey, "Trail of Tears," suggests that they

    (1) were forced to migrate against their will
    (2) were not as civilized as other tribes
    (3) planned to hurt the people responsible for their move
    (4) wept constantly on the trail
    (5) viewed the journey with bitterness and sorrow

Items 38 and 39 refer to the following passage.

The railroad changed the way Americans viewed time. Before, most people used the sun to set their clocks. Because the sun appears to move across the sky from east to west, a city a little to the east of a neighboring town marked noon a few minutes earlier. In the early days of the railroad, each city and each railroad had its own time. The main terminal in Buffalo, New York, had four clocks, one for each railroad using the train station and one on "Buffalo time." In 1883, an association of railroad managers ended the confusion with Standard Railway Time. They divided the nation into time zones, and every community within a time zone was on the same time. An Indianapolis newspaper noted, "The sun is no longer [the boss]. People—55,000,000 people—must now eat, sleep, and work, as well as travel by railroad time." In 1918, Standard Railway Time became federal law.

38. Standard Railway Time most likely had the effect of

    (1) placing all cities in the same time zone
    (2) confusing the public
    (3) establishing two main time zones
    (4) improving railroad efficiency
    (5) making trains run faster

39. The Indianapolis newspaper viewed railroad time as

    (1) a great innovation
    (2) a dangerous move
    (3) an example of the power of the railroad
    (4) unnecessary
    (5) unnatural

40. Mapmakers use parallels of latitude and meridians of longitude to determine the exact locations of places on earth. The exact location of any place is where

    (1) the prime meridian crosses the equator
    (2) two meridians intersect
    (3) two parallels intersect
    (4) a particular parallel intersects a particular meridian
    (5) 60° north latitude intersects 30° west longitude

Items 41 and 42 refer to the following information.

Other factors besides latitude may affect the climate of a region.

Ocean currents can warm or cool shorelines as they pass.

Oceans and large lakes, which do not lose or gain heat as quickly as land does, may cause milder temperatures nearby.

Mountains affect rainfall by forcing clouds to rise up and over them. As air rises, it cools. Since cold air cannot hold as much moisture as warm air, the clouds drop their moisture as they rise.

41. Inland areas, away from the coast, are likely to be

    (1) colder in winter than places near a coast
    (2) warmer in winter than places near a coast
    (3) rainier than places near a coast
    (4) drier than places near a coast
    (5) similar in temperature and rainfall to places near a coast

42. Although Valdez, a port in Alaska, lies near the Arctic Circle, it is free of ice all year long. The most likely explanation is that

    (1) winds that blow over water are warmer than winds that blow over land
    (2) mountains block the cold winds
    (3) Valdez is warmed by an ocean current
    (4) the ocean does not gain or lose heat as quickly as land
    (5) Valdez is affected by prevailing winds

43. For which of the following activities would knowledge of relative location be more helpful than information about longitude and latitude?

    (1) piloting a plane
    (2) driving a car
    (3) sailing on the ocean
    (4) surveying a state's borders
    (5) laying out a new city

Item 44 refers to the circle graph below.

WATER SUPPLY

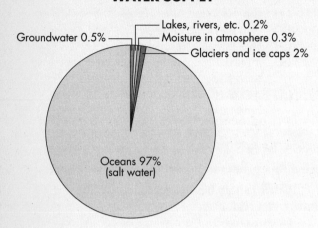

Lakes, rivers, etc. 0.2%
Moisture in atmosphere 0.3%
Groundwater 0.5%
Glaciers and ice caps 2%

Oceans 97%
(salt water)

44. The graph suggests that people could increase their fresh water supply significantly if they could find an inexpensive way to

(1) melt the glaciers
(2) reach aquifers and other sources of ground-water
(3) turn salt water into fresh water
(4) channel water from places that have too much water to those that have too little
(5) clean polluted rivers and lakes

45. In the United States, power is divided among several branches of government so that no one branch has too much power. This division is called

(1) separate-but-equal policy
(2) the system of checks and balances
(3) the process of amendment
(4) judicial review
(5) representative democracy

Items 46 and 47 refer to the cartoon.

"Isn't it about time we issued some new guidelines about something?"

46. To what federal government group or segment does the cartoon refer?

(1) the judicial system
(2) lobbyists
(3) the bureaucracy
(4) special districts
(5) state government

47. With which of the following statements would the cartoonist most likely agree?

(1) Government is needlessly complex and confusing because there are too many local special districts.
(2) The bureaucracy creates too many rules that aren't really necessary.
(3) The bureaucracy is an efficient system when properly controlled by the executive and legislative branches of government.
(4) The judicial system meddles in citizens' lives too much and should step back from trying to set policy for the government.
(5) Lobbyists have too much influence at all levels of government.

48. The New Deal programs of the 1930s changed the role of government in citizens' lives. Social Security and other programs had some success in helping Americans recover from the Great Depression. As a result, many Americans now believe the government

   (1) has an obligation to help individual citizens
   (2) should stay out of people's private lives
   (3) does not care about individual citizens
   (4) caused the Great Depression
   (5) has become too big

49. President Thomas Jefferson encouraged westward movement when he sponsored the Lewis and Clark expedition in the early 1800s. His farsighted action is just one of many examples of how presidents

   (1) seek publicity for themselves
   (2) see that bills become laws
   (3) let others influence them
   (4) influence American policy and history
   (5) control the executive branch

50. The Supreme Court's reversals of some of its earlier rulings demonstrate that

   (1) the Court changes the meaning of laws when it wants to
   (2) the Court is flexible and recognizes the need to interpret a 200-year-old document in terms of modern life
   (3) the Court doesn't take its decision-making role seriously
   (4) the justices don't think carefully enough about the possible results of their decisions
   (5) Supreme Court justices should be forced to retire at age seventy

Items 51 and 52 refer to the following information.

The Constitution provides for changing times with a process for amendment, or change. Today, the Constitution includes 26 amendments. The first 10 amendments, called the Bill of Rights, are outlined below.

BILL OF RIGHTS

First Amendment: religious and political freedom

Second Amendment: the right to bear arms

Third Amendment: the right to refuse to house soldiers in peacetime

Fourth Amendment: protection against unreasonable search and seizure

Fifth Amendment: the right of accused persons to due process of the law

Sixth Amendment: the right to a speedy and public trial

Seventh Amendment: the right to a jury trial in civil cases

Eighth Amendment: protection against cruel and unusual punishment

Ninth Amendment: the rights of the people to powers that may not be spelled out in the Constitution

Tenth Amendment: the rights of the people and the states to powers not otherwise given to the federal government, states, or people

51. Which two amendments provide for changes over time in the circumstances and realities of American life?

   (1) the First and Second Amendments
   (2) the Fifth and Sixth Amendments
   (3) the Third and Fourth Amendments
   (4) the Ninth and Tenth Amendments
   (5) the Seventh and Eighth Amendments

52. A family that was forced by the U.S. Army to provide housing and food for a group of soldiers could appeal to the courts based on which amendment to the Constitution?

   (1) the Sixth Amendment
   (2) the Third Amendment
   (3) the Second Amendment
   (4) the Ninth Amendment
   (5) the Tenth Amendment

Trial =
bear =
Otherwise =

53. Which choice best describes the meaning of the word "democracy"?

(1) multiple branches of government
(2) rule by the few
(3) freedom for all
(4) rule by the people
(5) balance of power

54. Economics is concerned with the distribution of goods and services. It deals with all of the following except

(1) the best ways to make money
(2) the allocation of limited resources
(3) scarcity, the condition in which wants exceed resources
(4) the demand for goods and services
(5) the production of goods and services

Items 55 and 56 refer to the following passage.

When people make economic decisions, they must often give up something; for example, they give up taking a vacation in order to save for a car. The value of the thing given up is called opportunity cost. In another example, Maria is trying to decide whether to take a part-time night job that pays $200 per week or take courses for credit at the local community college. Her uncle will pay for her tuition and books if she decides to go to college. In addition, he will give her $100 per week.

55. What is Maria's opportunity cost of going to college?

(1) $100 per week
(2) college credits
(3) the $200-per-week job
(4) payment for tuition and books
(5) working too slowly toward her degree

56. Why does Maria's decision involve opportunity cost?

(1) She doesn't want her uncle to pay her college costs.
(2) She wants both to work and to go to school.
(3) Her resources (her uncle's money) are endless, so she can choose to take classes.
(4) Her resources (time and money) are limited, so she must make a choice.
(5) She would rather go to college than work at night.

57. In recent years, mail-order catalog sales have increased substantially over previous years. What is the best explanation for this increase?

(1) People are too lazy to shop in stores.
(2) People respond favorably to lower prices in catalogs and the convenience of ordering by mail.
(3) People respond favorably to lower catalog prices.
(4) People like the convenience of ordering by mail.
(5) People are effectively persuaded to buy from catalogs.

Items 58 and 59 refer to the following graph.

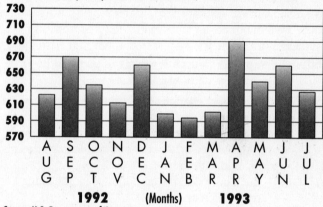

NEW HOME SALES
Seasonally Adjusted Annual Rate, Thousands of Units

1992 (Months) **1993**
Source: U.S. Department of Commerce

58. Which is the best description of the market for new homes shown in the graph?

(1) The market is on a decreasing trend.
(2) The market is on an increasing trend.
(3) Compared to 1991, the market is good.
(4) There doesn't seem to be an overall <u>trend in</u> the market for the time period shown.
(5) Sales of between 600,000 and 700,000 houses are pretty good for the time period shown.

59. For the period April through July 1993, the home sales trend is

(1) flat
(2) increasing
(3) neither increasing nor decreasing
(4) decreasing
(5) lower than it should be

Overall Trend =

60. Which of the following does not describe a cultural change that has occurred in America over the past twenty to thirty years?

- **(1)** Men in America earn more pay than women in the same jobs.
- **(2)** Many men in America share the responsibilities of housework and child-rearing with their wives.
- **(3)** African Americans and Hispanic Americans are being elected to political office.
- **(4)** Many women in America have both families and careers.
- **(5)** Divorce and remarriage are increasingly accepted in America.

Items 61 and 62 refer to the following passage.

In 1993, Michael Jordan's father was shot to death as he slept in his car on the side of a North Carolina road. Two eighteen-year-olds were charged with the murder. Both boys, who grew up in very poor families in the area, had lengthy police records that included violent crimes.

61. Many people believe that we can prevent such crimes only by teaching youngsters our values and by showing them that these values work. These people think that crime can be prevented through

- **(1)** diffusion, or the spread of values from one culture to another through contact between societies
- **(2)** cultural transmission, or the sharing of information about what works in a certain situation
- **(3)** enculturation, or the transmission of knowledge and values from one generation to another
- **(4)** trial-and-error learning, or the type of learning that occurs when a person tries out a behavior without first knowing whether or not it will work
- **(5)** internal conflict, or the struggle within society resulting from opposing ideas, needs, wishes, or drives

62. Youngsters who commit violent crimes probably do so mostly as a result of

- **(1)** technological advances made by their society
- **(2)** material things that their society has made from resources in the environment
- **(3)** the beliefs and values that their society thinks are important
- **(4)** the educational institutions they have attended
- **(5)** their social environments, or contact with other groups of people who have influenced their behavior patterns

63. Many parents are angry about the amount of violence that children see on television. These parents are afraid that their children will

- **(1)** give in to what they think most people on TV want them to do (conformity)
- **(2)** shape their behavior to match the behaviors they see on TV (modeling)
- **(3)** do what they are told to do by people on TV (obedience)
- **(4)** form attitudes and opinions due to the arguments of people on TV (persuasion)
- **(5)** form inaccurate generalizations about a group of people they see on TV (prejudice)

64. Salaries of women executives at the highest levels have more than doubled in the past ten years. These American businesswomen of the 1990s are raising families as well as pursuing careers. American society seems to be undergoing

- **(1)** an internal conflict resulting from opposing ideas, needs, wishes, and drives
- **(2)** the spread of ideas and technology from one culture to another
- **(3)** the enculturation of special knowledge passed from one generation to the next
- **(4)** a cultural change resulting from beliefs and ways of doing things that are different from those of our parents
- **(5)** an evolutionary change resulting from a change in the biological makeup of the human race

Undergoing =

SCIENCE

95 Minutes ❖ 66 Questions

Directions
Choose the one best answer to each item.

Items 1 to 5 refer to the following passage.

Charles Darwin, a famous naturalist, believed that animals' colors and patterns were necessary to their survival. Camouflage is nature's defense—an adaptation that confuses an animal's enemies or prey. Camouflage can be classified according to the following types.

Cryptic coloration: Body colors match or blend with an animal's environment. As a result, the animal is difficult to see.

Warning coloration: Vivid colors or patterns on an animal warn others of danger because some of these animals bite, sting, or emit foul odors.

Disruptive coloration: Irregular patches or bold patterns on an animal break up, or disrupt, the visible shape of the animal. As a result, the animal is hard to recognize.

Mimicry: One animal's behavior or physical appearance resembles that of another animal, plant, or object. This similarity in appearance deceives its enemies.

Masking: An animal collects materials from its surroundings and arranges them around its body to create a disguise.

Disrupt=
Warn=
deceives=
disguise=
skunk =
beneath=
Seaweed=

1. Two campers are hiking through the woods. From a distance, they spot a black furry animal with a bold white stripe down its back. Immediately identifying this animal as a skunk, the campers avoid it and head in another direction. The skunk is an example of

   (1) cryptic coloration
   (2) warning coloration
   (3) disruptive coloration
   (4) mimicry
   (5) masking

2. The orchid mantis lives in southern Asia. This pink insect could easily be mistaken for the petals of a flower. The insect is an example of

   (1) cryptic coloration
   (2) warning coloration
   (3) disruptive coloration
   (4) mimicry
   (5) masking

3. A white snowshoe rabbit is barely noticeable as it hops across a winter landscape. At night, a black bat flies unseen across the dark sky. The rabbit and bat are examples of

   (1) cryptic coloration
   (2) warning coloration
   (3) disruptive coloration
   (4) mimicry
   (5) masking

4. The kelp crab's true identity is concealed beneath a disguise that it cleverly creates from seaweed. The kelp crab gathers strips of green seaweed and rubs them on its body until its outer shell is covered. The kelp crab is an example of

   (1) cryptic coloration
   (2) warning coloration
   (3) disruptive coloration
   (4) mimicry
   (5) masking

5. The military has borrowed camouflage tricks from animals such as leopards and giraffes. For combat in the jungle, soldiers' uniforms are often marked with spots or <u>blotches</u> of different shades of green and brown. These patterns distract the enemy from seeing the actual outlines of the soldiers' bodies. The soldiers' uniforms are an example of

(1) cryptic coloration
(2) warning coloration
(3) disruptive coloration
(4) mimicry
(5) masking

Items 6 and 7 refer to the following information.

As shown in the graph below, alcoholic drinks contain various percentages of a chemical called ethyl alcohol or ethanol. Its chemical formula is $C_x^2H^6O$. As a pure chemical, ethyl alcohol has a powerful odor and a burning taste. Drinking pure ethyl alcohol is both dangerous and unpleasant.

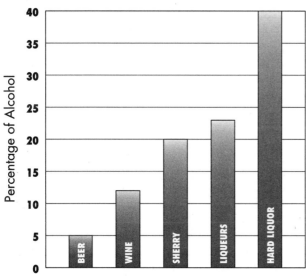

AVERAGE PERCENTAGE OF ALCOHOL IN DRINKS

6. Based on the data in the bar graph, which two drinks are most similar in their alcohol content?

(1) beer and wine
(2) wine and sherry
(3) sherry and liqueurs
(4) liqueurs and hard liquor
(5) hard liquor and sherry

7. The alcohol content of hard liquor is expressed as proof. Proof equals twice the percentage of alcohol. Therefore, based on data in the bar graph, you can conclude that hard liquor is about

(1) 20 proof
(2) 40 proof
(3) 60 proof
(4) 80 proof
(5) 100 proof

Items 8 to 10 refer to the following definitions.

Mixture: A combination of substances that are not chemically united. Each substance retains its unique chemical properties.

Element: A substance that cannot be broken down into a simpler chemical.

Atom: The smallest possible piece of an element that can be part of a chemical reaction.

Compound: Two or more substances joined together chemically. A compound can be broken down into simpler parts by chemical means.

Colloid: A finely divided substance spread evenly throughout a second, chemically separate, substance. A colloid separates out very slowly, if at all.

8. Iron (Fe) is an example of a(n)

(1) mixture
(2) element
(3) atom
(4) compound
(5) colloid

9. Carbon dioxide (CO^2) is an example of a(n)

(1) mixture
(2) element
(3) atom
(4) compound
(5) colloid

10. Hot cocoa is an example of a(n)

(1) mixture
(2) element
(3) atom
(4) compound
(5) colloid

blotches

Items 11 and 12 refer to the following passage.

Experiments on mice have led to important medical breakthroughs, especially cures for diseases. In a typical research experiment, a scientist injects the germs that cause a certain disease into several healthy mice. After the mice become ill, some are tested with a new drug, and the scientist observes the results. Other mice receive no medication; they are called the control group. The only difference between the control group and the other group is the medication provided or not provided. The scientist then closely compares the medicated mice with the control group. The findings are carefully recorded. Drawing conclusions based on the results of experiments conducted in this way helps scientists evaluate the effectiveness of newly developed drugs.

11. Which of the following data recorded in the experiment with mice would be the least useful in determining the value of a new drug?

   (1) the number of mice that died
   (2) the number of mice that remained ill
   (3) the kinds of food eaten by the mice
   (4) the number of mice that were cured
   (5) the length of time it took for mice to recover

12. Which of the following would cause the greatest error in the results of drug tests using laboratory mice?

   (1) using mice with the identical genetic makeup
   (2) recording the symptoms developed by the infected mice
   (3) repeating the same experiment several times
   (4) injecting all the infected mice with the experimental drug
   (5) measuring the dosage of the drug given to the mice

Item 13 refers to the following graph.

The U.S. Department of Agriculture conducted a study of the pain that research animals feel during scientific experiments. The circle graph below summarizes the department's findings.

BREAKDOWN OF EXPERIMENTS
(by percentage)

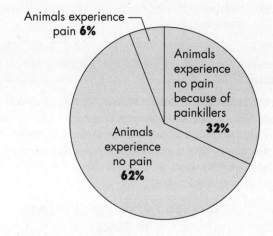

Animals experience pain **6%**

Animals experience no pain because of painkillers **32%**

Animals experience no pain **62%**

13. Which of the following states an opinion, rather than a fact, about the data in the graph?

   (1) The majority of research animals feel no pain.
   (2) About one third of research animals are given doses of painkillers.
   (3) Animals used in scientific experiments are treated cruelly.
   (4) Less than 10 percent of research animals feel pain.
   (5) A government agency analyzed the pain felt by research animals.

Items 14 and 15 refer to the following passage.

People once thought that gases exploding in the air caused lightning. Benjamin Franklin, however, believed that lightning was a form of electricity. In 1752, Benjamin Franklin proved his belief by conducting a risky experiment. He attached a metal key to the string of a kite and flew the kite during a rainstorm. He predicted that the electricity from a thundercloud would flow along the wet string to the key. His prediction was accurate. Immediately after a flash of lightning and a boom of thunder, an electrical spark jumped from the key to his finger.

14. Which of the following is the best conclusion based on the data provided?

   (1) The explosion of gases in the atmosphere produces lightning.
   (2) Electrical energy from lightning can be used to run machines.
   (3) Many different types of electricity exist in the universe.
   (4) The energy from lightning raises the temperature of air.
   (5) Lightning results from electricity discharged from a cloud.

15. Which of the following examples would be most similar to electricity flowing along a wet kite string?

   (1) a bucket of water being lifted from a well
   (2) water moving through a pipe
   (3) a spark plug igniting fuel in a car engine
   (4) a fan circulating air throughout a room
   (5) a dam controlling the flow of water

Items 16 and 17 refer to the following map.

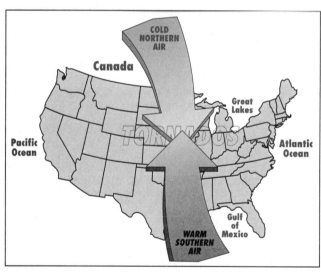

In the United States, warm, moist air colliding with cold, dry air often causes winds to rotate at high speeds. These destructive whirling winds, accompanied by funnel-shaped clouds, are called tornadoes.

16. Where do currents of warm air come from?

   (1) Canada
   (2) the Gulf of Mexico
   (3) the Great Lakes
   (4) the Pacific Ocean
   (5) the Atlantic Ocean

17. In which part of the United States would scientists most likely observe weather conditions that create tornadoes?

   (1) the Northeast
   (2) the Southeast
   (3) the Midwest
   (4) the Northwest
   (5) the Southwest

18. Vibrations traveling through the air or other substances cause sounds to be produced. Based on this information, which of the following conditions explains why the moon is completely silent?

   (1) There is no air on the moon.
   (2) Dangerous radiation is emitted on the moon.
   (3) The temperatures on the moon are extremely hot or cold.
   (4) The pull of gravity is weak on the moon.
   (5) The moon is uninhabited by people.

Items 19 and 20 refer to the following passage and illustration.

According to Sir Isaac Newton's Third Law of Motion, for every action there is an equal and opposite reaction. Two objects are always involved in the reaction. When you exert a force on an object, the object, in turn, exerts a similar but opposite force on you. This law can be illustrated in many different sports activities, including swimming, as shown below.

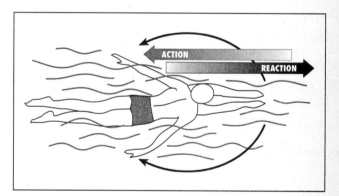

As the swimmer uses his arms to push the water backward, the water propels him forward.

19. Which of the following statements summarizes the main idea of the paragraph?

    (1) Sir Isaac Newton established laws about movement.
    (2) For every action there is an equal and opposite reaction.
    (3) Many sports activities can be explained scientifically.
    (4) Two objects are always involved in a reaction.
    (5) Water exerts a force on swimmers.

20. Which of the following examples illustrates Newton's Third Law of Motion?

    (1) A baseball travels in a curved path as the pitcher hurls it to the catcher.
    (2) The faster a football player runs, the more difficult it becomes for him to suddenly slow down.
    (3) When a basketball strikes the backboard, the backboard pushes the ball back with the same force exerted on it by the ball.
    (4) As an ice skater twirls quickly on one foot, she pulls in her arms in order to maintain her balance.
    (5) The steeper the slope, the faster a skier races down a snow-covered mountainside.

Items 21 to 24 refer to the following passage.

In 1910, Dr. Alice Hamilton served as director of the Occupational Disease Commission in Illinois. She specialized in investigating the causes and effects of lead poisoning in the state. She inspected the lead industries and examined the hospital records of workers suffering from lead poisoning. Dr. Hamilton also interviewed druggists and doctors living in working-class neighborhoods. Her research led her to discover the cause of lead poisoning—breathing in lead dust and lead fumes. The solution to the problem was obvious. The air in factories must be cleansed of lead dust and lead fumes. However, many factory owners opposed her solution because of the expense.

Dr. Hamilton wrote articles and made speeches to make the public aware of this important health issue. She discussed the typical symptoms of lead poisoning: drooping head; bowed shoulders; limp, dangling arms; trembling muscular movements; and excessive weight loss. Later she conducted surveys of lead and other poisonous industries for the United States government.

Throughout her long career, from the 1890s to the 1930s, Dr. Hamilton sought to protect the health and safety of millions of workers in the United States. She devoted herself to studying work-related diseases. In 1936, Eleanor Roosevelt, the nation's First Lady, expressed her admiration of Dr. Hamilton "because she had the courage to pioneer in research in industrial medicine."

21. Which of the following questions best summarizes the main purpose of Dr. Hamilton's investigation of lead industries in Illinois?

    (1) How will clean air in factories reduce the cases of lead poisoning?
    (2) What are the causes and effects of lead poisoning?
    (3) What do druggists and doctors know about treating lead poisoning?
    (4) What do workers' hospital records reveal about lead poisoning?
    (5) Why won't factory owners help solve the problem of lead poisoning?

22. All of the following are symptoms of lead poisoning except

    (1) hanging head
    (2) trembling muscles
    (3) weight loss
    (4) limp arms
    (5) difficulty in breathing

23. Which of the following best explains how Dr. Hamilton supported her conclusion about why workers develop lead poisoning?

    (1) gathering data
    (2) testing a hypothesis
    (3) conducting scientific experiments
    (4) delivering speeches
    (5) writing scientific articles

24. Which of the following assumptions about lead poisoning is supported by information given?

    (1) Chemical analysis of blood samples is a current method for diagnosing lead poisoning.
    (2) Factory workers in lead industries were exposed to a form of indoor air pollution.
    (3) Today most states have laws that protect workers from industrial diseases.
    (4) Lead poisoning is currently a very rare disease in the United States.
    (5) In the early 1900s, Illinois had the highest number of lead-poisoning victims.

Limp-

Items 25 to 28 refer to the following passage.

Soil contains nutrients that are essential to the growth of plants. When farmers repeatedly plant the same crop every growing season, the crop can rob the soil of nutrients that are not replenished. After a while, the crop does not grow as well and the soil becomes worn out. As a result, the soil is more easily eroded by wind or water.

Soil erosion occurs when soil is transported from one place to another. For example, powerful winds can lift soil and carry it for long distances. Wind erosion is most prevalent in areas where there is a drought—a long period of hot weather and little rainfall.

In the 1930s, a drought, coupled with poor farming practices, created the conditions for soil erosion in the midwestern United States. People living in this region, known as the Dust Bowl, witnessed one of the worst farming disasters in American history. Strong winds blew dry soil into mounds of worthless dirt. When rain finally did fall, further soil erosion resulted. The rain could not soak into the surface of the bare, hard ground. Instead, the water carved gullies, washing the soil away.

25. Which of the following farming practices would help conserve nutrients in the soil?

   A.   rotating crops on different fields
   B.   stripping the land of all plants
   C.   grazing many animals on the same plot of land

   (1) A only
   (2) B only
   (3) C only
   (4) A and B only
   (5) B and C only

26. Which of the following best explains the cause of droughts?

   (1) water erosion
   (2) unwise farming methods
   (3) high temperatures and little rainfall
   (4) dried, hardened soil
   (5) wind erosion

27. Which of the following would be most similar to the mounds of dirt formed during a windstorm?

   (1) mountain peaks covered with snow
   (2) hillsides eroded by running water
   (3) glaciers of ice
   (4) earthquakes under the sea
   (5) sand dunes on a desert

28. In nature, soil erosion is a slow, long-term process. Which of the following statements best explains this phenomenon?

   (1) Soil is a grainy material made up of rocks, minerals, water, and air.
   (2) Many microscopic organisms, such as bacteria and fungi, live in the soil.
   (3) Extreme weather conditions, such as powerful winds and rainstorms, rarely occur.
   (4) Grasses, trees, and other vegetation tend to hold the soil in place.
   (5) Since the Dust Bowl, scientists have been investigating ways to prevent erosion.

Items 29 and 30 refer to the following chart.

Biome*	Avg. Rainfall per Year (centimeters)
Tundra	12
Desert	25
Taiga	35–40
Grassland	25–75
Temperate Forest	100
Tropical Rain Forest	200

* A biome is composed of several communities with the same major life forms.

29. Which of the following biomes has the lowest annual rainfall?

   (1) tundra
   (2) desert
   (3) taiga
   (4) grassland
   (5) temperate forest

30. Which of the following biomes is most likely to have an abundant growth of plants?

   (1) tundra
   (2) taiga
   (3) grassland
   (4) temperate forest
   (5) tropical rain forest

31. Tides occur approximately twice a day. About how long are the intervals for each tide?

   (1) 3 hours
   (2) 6 hours
   (3) 12 hours
   (4) 18 hours
   (5) 24 hours

Tides→

32. At the University of Limburg in the Netherlands, researchers investigated the link between emotion and heart disease. About 3,500 men participated in the study. According to the findings, the men who reported feeling tired or depressed had a 400 percent greater chance of developing heart disease than the men who did not experience such feelings. Which of the following statements best explains the main goal of the study?

(1) to discover the relationship between feelings and heart disease

(2) to learn why the rate of heart disease is high in the Netherlands

(3) to investigate the causes of exhaustion and depression

(4) to analyze the emotional reactions of 3,500 men

(5) to determine ways of reducing stress

33. The four major blood types are A, B, AB, and O. People with the same type of blood can safely give and receive transfusions to and from one another. People with type O blood are called universal donors because they can donate blood to anyone. Which of the following statements is incorrect according to the information given?

(1) A person with type A blood can receive transfusions from another person with type A blood.

(2) A person with type O blood can receive transfusions from people of all blood types.

(3) Injecting people with the wrong blood type is an unsafe medical procedure.

(4) People with type A, B, AB, and O can all receive transfusions of type O blood.

(5) A person with type B blood can be a donor for another person with type B blood.

Items 34 and 35 refer to the following paragraph.

A virus is a tiny organism, much smaller than a cell. A virus by itself is not really alive; it becomes active only after it has entered a living cell. Once inside the cell, the virus takes over the parts of the cell that direct the cell's activities, so that instead of producing the proteins it normally produces, the cell produces more viruses. Eventually, the host cell is destroyed. The new viruses invade other cells.

34. Which part of a cell would be the primary target of an invading virus?

(1) cytoplasm

(2) endoplasmic reticulum

(3) mitochondria

(4) nucleus

(5) vacuole

35. In order to make the cell produce copies of a virus, the virus must contain something like one of the following cell components. Which one?

(1) chromosome

(2) Golgi apparatus

(3) nucleolus

(4) organelle

(5) ribosome

36. In complex organisms, cells combine to form tissues, and tissues combine to form organs. Each organ performs a specific function. For example, the heart pumps blood throughout the body. Which of the following is another example of a vital organ?

(1) pupil

(2) chloroplast

(3) brain

(4) hair

(5) pollen

37. The male spider makes a package of sperm enveloped in silk and inserts it into the female spider's body with one of his feelers. What should be the immediate outcome of this process?

(1) germination

(2) fertilization

(3) incubation

(4) mating ritual

(5) maturation

38. The placenta is a protective sac around the fetus. Scientists have found that alcohol passes directly through the placenta to the fetus soon after being consumed by the mother. For the fetus, alcohol acts as a toxic substance. Which of the following conclusions is supported by this evidence?

(1) Alcohol interferes with or damages the development of the fetus.
(2) The placenta protects the fetus from dangerous substances such as alcohol.
(3) The fetus is immune to the effects of alcohol because it is not a completely developed human being.
(4) Pregnant women are a high-risk group for developing alcoholism.
(5) Women can consume moderate amounts of alcohol during their pregnancies without injuring their fetuses.

39. Normal red blood cells are disc-shaped. However, in sickle-cell anemia, a hereditary disease, some of the red blood cells are distorted into the shape of a crescent or <u>sickle</u>. Sickle-cell anemia is common among African Americans. Which of the following statements presents evidence that supports this fact?

(1) Many ancestors of African Americans originally came from West Africa.
(2) Among African Americans, sickle-cell anemia occurs in one out of 500 births.
(3) Sickle-cell anemia occurs in people whose ancestors came from the Mediterranean area.
(4) In 1978, sickle-cell anemia was diagnosed in an infant before birth by DNA analysis.
(5) The rate of occurrence for the majority of single-gene disorders is one out of 2,000 humans.

Items 40 and 41 refer to the following passage.

An ancient Chinese manuscript described a freak incident that occurred among a group of black crucian carp in a fish pond. One of the fish born there looked distinctly different from other offspring of the same species: the fish was red instead of black. Did the birth of this one red fish have far-reaching implications?

In 1914, Dr. Yoshiichi Matsui, a famous Japanese geneticist, searched for the answer to this question. He conducted thousands of experiments to prove his hypothesis—that every present-day goldfish descended from that first red carp. For twenty years, he <u>crossbred</u> about two million goldfish. The results of these experiments confirmed his hypothesis. All species of modern

goldfish are mutations that descended from the black crucian carp in one pond in ancient China.

40. What was the purpose of Dr. Matsui's scientific investigations?

(1) to find the origin of all goldfish species
(2) to prove Darwin's theory of evolution
(3) to decipher the meaning of an ancient Chinese manuscript
(4) to crossbreed various species of fish
(5) to conduct a twenty-year experiment

41. Which of the following triggered an evolutionary change in the black crucian carp?

(1) migration
(2) isolation
(3) sexual selection
(4) mutation
(5) environmental change

Item 42 refers to the following bar graph.

DOCUMENTED EXTINCTION OF BIRDS

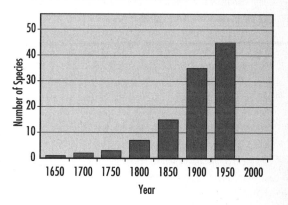

42. During which years did the sharpest increase occur in the number of birds known to have become extinct?

(1) 1650–1700
(2) 1700–1750
(3) 1800–1850
(4) 1850–1900
(5) 1900–1950

Sickle =
Crossbred =
triggered -

43. In 1985, *Business Week* magazine sponsored a poll on the topic of genetic engineering. Two thirds of the participants questioned agreed that medical treatments in which genes are altered to cure people with fatal diseases should continue. The participants' viewpoint can best be classified as

(1) an assumption
(2) a hypothesis
(3) a fact
(4) an opinion
(5) irrelevant information

Items 44 to 48 refer to the following information.

Animals and plants frequently share the same environment, in which they form various kinds of relationships. These relationships are based on nourishment, habitat, and other interactions. Here are five classifications of relationships that typically exist within a community of different organisms.

Mutualism: two types of organisms live in a mutually beneficial association. The two species help one another in a certain way.

Commensalism: one organism benefits, whereas the other organism is neither benefited nor harmed.

Parasitism: one organism, called the parasite, benefits, whereas the other organism, called the host, is usually injured or harmed. The host is useful only while alive.

Predation: one organism kills another organism and eats it, usually right away.

Saprophytic relationship: one organism feeds on dead or decaying organic matter from another organism.

44. Pilot fish frequently swim along with a school of sharks searching for food in the ocean. After the sharks kill their prey, the pilot fish reap the rewards of this association by feeding on the sharks' leftovers. The relationship of pilot fish to sharks can best be classified as

(1) mutualism
(2) commensalism
(3) parasitism
(4) predation
(5) a saprophytic relationship

45. In a tropical rain forest, some acacia trees provide homes and food for ants. In turn, the ants help the acacia trees survive by stinging other insects that might feed on the trees' leaves. The association between the acacia trees and the ants can best be classified as

(1) mutualism
(2) commensalism
(3) parasitism
(4) predation
(5) a saprophytic relationship

46. For centuries, Eskimos in northwestern Alaska have hunted bowhead whales, which they kill for food. The relationship of the Eskimos to the bowhead whales can best be classified as

(1) mutualism
(2) commensalism
(3) parasitism
(4) predation
(5) a saprophytic relationship

47. People can get tapeworms by eating improperly cooked beef. Tapeworms attach themselves to the walls of the intestines, where they live on food digested by the human host. The relationship of tapeworms to humans can best be classified as

(1) mutualism
(2) commensalism
(3) parasitism
(4) predation
(5) a saprophytic relationship

48. The people who create exhibits of animal skeletons at natural history museums sometimes use carrion beetles to clean the bones of dead animals. The relationship of the carrion beetles to the dead remains of other animals can best be classified as

(1) mutualism
(2) commensalism
(3) parasitism
(4) predation
(5) a saprophytic relationship

Nourishment
whereas

Items 49 and 50 refer to the following diagram.

THE MOVEMENT OF THE DIAPHRAGM DURING RESPIRATION

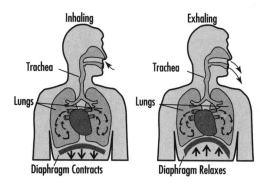

49. Which of the following statements best summarizes the main idea illustrated in the diagram?

    (1) The diaphragm is a sheet of muscle located underneath the lungs.
    (2) The diaphragm contracts and relaxes as a person inhales and exhales.
    (3) Every person has a pair of lungs that are shaped like footballs.
    (4) Each lung branches out from a tubelike structure called the trachea.
    (5) The organs located in the chest control the respiratory system.

50. In which of the following situations would a person intentionally relax the diaphragm for several seconds during respiration?

    (1) swimming underwater
    (2) sucking on a straw
    (3) blowing a horn
    (4) hiccupping
    (5) smelling flowers

Hiccupping =
whirlpool =
Streams =
Valley =

51. Although the Earth is not the center of the universe, it seems as if distant galaxies are moving away from the Earth in all directions. In fact, the entire universe is expanding. Which of the following is most similar to the expansion of the universe?

    (1) the bubbles rising to the surface in a glass of soda
    (2) the revolution of the planets and comets around the sun
    (3) the expansion of a car tire when it is filled with air
    (4) the whirlpool formed by water going down a bathtub drain
    (5) the increasing distance between raisins in a rising cake

Items 52 and 53 refer to the following information.

Streams and rivers erode rocks and soil from their banks as they flow. As a river grows older, it widens its valley. The shape of a river valley tells how much erosion has taken place.

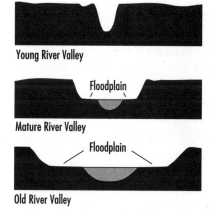

Young River Valley

Mature River Valley

Old River Valley

52. Which of the following is characteristic of a young river valley?

    (1) The river deepens the valley.
    (2) The river broadens the valley.
    (3) The valley has many cities and towns.
    (4) The river overflows into its floodplain.
    (5) The floodplain is very wide.

53. The Mississippi River is an old river. Many cities along the river have elaborate levee systems designed to prevent flooding when the river waters rise. If levees prevent flooding upstream, then in unprotected areas downstream the river would

  (1) rise more than normal, but flooding would be less likely

  (2) rise more than normal, and flooding would be more likely

  (3) rise less than normal, without flooding

  (4) rise less than normal, with flooding

  (5) not rise, and flooding would be less likely

54. Physical weathering breaks rocks into smaller pieces without changing the substances of which they are made. Chemical weathering breaks down rocks by changing their substances. Weathering can be caused by natural processes or by human activities. Which of the following is an example of chemical <u>weathering</u>?

  (1) cracking of rock by freezing and thawing

  (2) lifting and cracking of a sidewalk by a tree root

  (3) cutting of limestone in a quarry

  (4) formation of a cave by acid dissolution of limestone

  (5) cutting of a highway by dynamite blasting

Items 55 to 57 refer to the following information.

Coral reefs are built primarily of the skeletal remains and secretions of coral and certain algae. They form in shallow, warm ocean water where the sun is bright. A barrier reef is a coral reef that surrounds an island. An atoll is a barrier reef whose island has sunk beneath the ocean's surface.

55. What is a lagoon?

  (1) the buildup of coral around an extinct volcanic island

  (2) an underwater atoll in the Pacific Ocean or the Caribbean Sea

  (3) a shallow body of water that is near or linked with the ocean

  (4) a deep trench off the shore of an active volcanic island

  (5) a type of barrier reef in which coral reaches above the ocean's surface

56. Which of the following facts supports the hypothesis that an <u>atoll</u> once had an island in its center?

  (1) Atolls are made of the skeletal remains of coral and the secretions of algae.

  (2) An atoll provides food and shelter for many species of fish.

  (3) There is no land above the ocean surface in the middle of an atoll.

  (4) Coral reefs form only in warm ocean waters.

  (5) Coral reefs form only in shallow, sunlit water where there is a foundation for their growth.

57. Which of the following statements is supported by the information provided?

  (1) All barrier reefs were once atolls.

  (2) All atolls eventually sink beneath the surface of the ocean.

  (3) All atolls were once barrier reefs.

  (4) Active reef building takes place only during the barrier reef stage.

  (5) Coral reefs can form in deep tropical waters.

levees=
atoll=
weathering=

Items 58 and 59 refer to the following information.

Chemical Change	Physical Change
	no change in
substances used up	chemical composition
energy absorbed or released	new substances formed

58. Which of the following involves a physical change?

(1) an ozone molecule breaking down into oxygen atoms
(2) ice melting
(3) iron rusting
(4) calcium oxide breaking down into calcium and oxygen
(5) hydrogen and oxygen combining to form water

59. In an experiment, a scientist analyzes the chemical content of a substance, then exposes the substance to heat. After a certain period of time, the substance changes. At this point, which of the following methods would be most valuable in determining whether the change is physical or chemical?

(1) measuring the area of the substance
(2) weighing the substance
(3) analyzing the chemical content of the substance
(4) smelling the substance
(5) studying the color of the substance

60. A scientist performed an experiment to analyze the results of mixing two substances. When substance A was added to substance B, the crystals of A dissolved. The molecules of A spread out evenly among the molecules of B. Which of the following terms best describes substance A?

(1) solvent
(2) solute
(3) solution
(4) concentration
(5) equilibrium

61. The following equation shows a change in electrical charge.

$$HF + H_2O \rightarrow H_3O^+ + F^-$$

Which of the following terms best describes both H_3O^+ and F^- in this equation?

(1) atoms
(2) elements
(3) compounds
(4) ions
(5) catalysts

62. The following chart lists the atomic numbers of certain elements that exist in nature as gases.

Element	Atomic Number
Argon	18
Chlorine	17
Hydrogen	1
Krypton	36
Nitrogen	7
Oxygen	8
Radon	86

Air consists mainly of oxygen and nitrogen gases. Which of the following gases is lighter than air?

(1) chlorine
(2) argon
(3) krypton
(4) hydrogen
(5) radon

Items 63 and 64 refer to the following illustration.

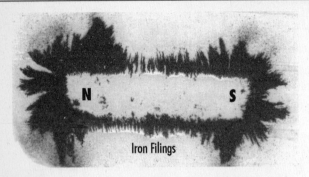

Iron Filings

63. Which of the following statements about magnetism is best illustrated by this diagram?

(1) Opposite poles attract and like poles repel.
(2) One end of a magnet held from a string will always point north.
(3) The magnetic field is strongest around the poles.
(4) Sometimes magnetism is only temporary.
(5) The north magnetic pole is located in Canada, 1,500 miles from the geographic North Pole.

64. Which of the following statements best describes what happens if a magnet is placed near iron filings?

(1) The arrangement of the iron filings will be random.
(2) The iron filings will repel each other and the magnet.
(3) The iron filings will be evenly distributed around the magnet.
(4) There will be no change in the arrangement of the iron filings.
(5) Most of the iron filings will be attracted to the ends of the magnet.

65. Static electricity can be produced by rubbing two objects against each other, which transfers electrons from one object to another. Materials charged with static electricity attract each other if they have opposite electrical charges (positive and negative) and repel each other if they have like electrical charges (negative and negative). Stroking a piece of hard rubber with fur gives the rubber a negative charge and the fur a positive charge. Which of the following statements best explains how this happens?

(1) The rubber gives up some electrons to the fur.
(2) The fur gives up some electrons to the rubber.
(3) The rubber gives up some protons to the fur.
(4) The fur gives up some protons to the rubber.
(5) The fur gives up some neutrons to the rubber.

66. Electricity ordinarily travels the shortest path between two points. A short circuit occurs when electricity takes the shortest path through an appliance and cuts out part of its intended route through a planned electrical circuit. Which of the following statements best explains why insulation can prevent a short circuit?

(1) Insulation prevents electricity from leaving its intended path.
(2) Insulation directs electricity in two directions at one time.
(3) Most appliances do not have insulation on their power cords.
(4) Insulation can cause static electricity to rest on the surface of an appliance.
(5) Insulation is a good conductor of electricity.

INTERPRETING LITERATURE AND THE ARTS

65 Minutes ❖ 45 Questions

Directions
Read each passage; then answer the questions that follow. Choose the one best answer to each question.

Items 1 to 3 refer to the following poem.

Line   What Is the Poet's Advice?
     The saddest day will have an <u>eve</u>,
     The darkest night, a <u>morn</u>;
     Think not, when clouds are thick
5   and dark,
     Thy way is too forlorn.
     For, ev'ry cloud that e'er did rise,
     To shade thy life's bright way,
     And ev'ry restless night of pain,
10   And ev'ry weary day,
     Will bring thee gifts, thou'lt value
      more,
     Because they cost so dear;
     The soul that faints not in the storm,
15   Emerges bright and clear.

          —From "Hope"
          by Clara Ann Thompson

eve =
morn =
forlorn =
betrothals =

1. The poet includes all of the following to symbolize life's problems except

  (1) dark nights
  (2) dark clouds
  (3) rough waters
  (4) weary days
  (5) thick clouds

2. The tone of this poem could best be described as

  (1) depressed
  (2) hopeful
  (3) carefree
  (4) uncertain
  (5) troubled

3. If confronted with the death of a friend, this poet probably would

  (1) be unable to carry on with everyday life
  (2) try not to react at all to the sad event
  (3) check to see if the clouds outside were dark and stormy
  (4) act bravely and believe in a brighter tomorrow
  (5) bring food and gifts to the grieving family

Items 4 to 7 refer to the following excerpt from an autobiography.

WHAT ARE POSSIBLE CONSEQUENCES OF THE GERMANS' ADVANCE?

Line Spring 1944. Good news from the Russian front. No doubt could remain now of Germany's defeat. It was only a question of time—of months or weeks perhaps.
5   The trees were in blossom. This was a year like any other, with its springtime, its <u>betrothals</u>, its weddings and births.
     People said: "The Russian army's making gigantic strides forward . . . Hitler won't be able
10 to do us any harm, even if he wants to."
     Yes, we even doubted that he wanted to exterminate us.

Was he going to wipe out a whole people? Could he exterminate a population scattered
15 throughout so many countries? So many millions! What methods could he use? And in the middle of the twentieth century! . . .

The following day, there was more disturbing news: with government permission, German
20 troops had entered Hungarian territory.

Here and there, anxiety was aroused. One of our friends, Berkovitz, who had just returned from the capital, told us: "The Jews in Budapest are living in an atmosphere of fear and terror. There
25 are anti-Semitic incidents every day, in the streets, in the trains. The Fascists are attacking Jewish shops and synagogues. The situation is getting very serious."

This news spread like wildfire through
30 Sighet. Soon it was on everyone's lips. But not for long. Optimism soon revived.

"The Germans won't get as far as this. They'll stay in Budapest. There are strategic and political reasons . . ."
35 Before three days had passed, German army cars had appeared on our streets.

—From *Night* by Elie Wiesel

4. Which of the following events occurs last in the passage?

(1) Berkovitz returns from the capital with frightening news.
(2) German troops enter Hungarian territory.
(3) German troops arrive in Sighet.
(4) Berkovitz's news spreads through Sighet.
(5) Good news arrives from the Russian front.

5. Which of the following can you assume from the last line in the passage?

(1) A great number of army cars will soon be arriving.
(2) The German army cars will not stay long in Sighet.
(3) The townspeople will soon feel calm and relieved.
(4) The atmosphere of fear and anxiety is warranted.
(5) The Germans will cause no harm to the townspeople.

6. What was one cause of anxious feelings in Sighet?

(1) the unusually long winter
(2) news from the front that Germany would surrender
(3) the number of betrothals that spring
(4) the Russian army's steady advance
(5) Berkovitz's account of events in the capital

7. Which of the following contrasted pairs adds irony to this passage?

(1) the number of weddings and the beautiful spring
(2) the cruelty of the Germans and the kindness of the Russians
(3) fire in Sighet and the warm spring weather
(4) Berkovitz's fear and the news from the front
(5) the quiet beauty of spring and the disturbing rumors

Items 8 to 11 refer to the following excerpt from an audio review.

WHAT KIND OF ALBUM HAS DONALD BROWN MADE?

Line Memphis-native [Donald] Brown, continuing to stretch as a composer, has come up with a series of provocative pieces that, except for the standard "I Should Care," express various aspects of the
5 black life experience. These selections often have a dynamic rhythmic underpinning—"Theme For Mandela" is old-fashioned, back-beat funk, "The Power of the Drums" is driven by a foot-tapping groove. To drive home his message further, Brown
10 on four tracks has included texts by Marshall Stephens, Nancy Tobin, and Dorothy Jean Brown that discuss such topics as "How free can a person be who has witnessed, or been held, in slavery?" The words are potent, are read with
15 authority and passion by narrator Saunders, and are deftly bolstered by complementary instrumental statements.

Despite the thematic aspect, the album is musically moving, and abounds with prime
20 moments. . . . Brown remains a more individualistic writer than pianist, and here his strong ties to Herbie Hancock and McCoy Tyner are readily apparent. He embraces the latter's richness of tone and approach on "Drums," while a Hancock
25 funkiness prevails on "Theme For Mandela."

—From "Donald Brown" by Zan Stewart

8. Which of the following words best describes the music on Donald Brown's new album?

(1) instrumental
(2) funky
(3) revolutionary
(4) moving
(5) old-fashioned

Despite

9. Which of the following statements best expresses the main idea of this passage?

    (1) On this album, Brown covers familiar musical ground.
    (2) The song "I Should Care" has been recorded too many times.
    (3) Brown's album is an artistic and thematic success.
    (4) This new album will be controversial.
    (5) Brown's album does not have a thematic focus.

10. Based on the information in lines 5-6, which of the following works of art would be most similar to Brown's new album?

    (1) a movie sound track that tells the story of two best friends
    (2) a sculpture that depicts the richness of Native American culture
    (3) a painting that shows key events in the life of Nelson Mandela
    (4) a biography of jazz greats such as Herbie Hancock and McCoy Tyner
    (5) a blues album that is dedicated to the career of Ray Charles

11. How does the structure of this passage support the reviewer's message?

    (1) by offering suggestions on how to compose music
    (2) by arguing that everyone should buy Brown's album
    (3) by referring to the texts by Marshall Stephens and Nancy Tobin
    (4) by providing detailed descriptions of songs on the album
    (5) by implying that jazz greats admire the work of Donald Brown

Items 12 to 16 refer to the following excerpt from a book.

WHAT DOES THE SPEAKER SEE?

Line I swam out to Chinaman's Hat. We walked partway in low tide, then put on face masks. Once you open your eyes in the water, you become a flying creature. Schools of fish—zebra fish,
5 rainbow fish, red fish—curve with the currents, swim alongside and away; balloon fish puff out their porcupine quills. How unlike a dead fish a live fish is. We swam through spangles of silver-white fish, their scales like sequins. Sometimes we
10 entered cold spots, deserts, darkness under clouds,

where the sand churned like gray fog, and sometimes we entered golden chambers. There are summer forests and winter forests down there. Sea cucumbers . . . rocked side to side. A sea
15 turtle glided by and that big shell is no encumbrance in the water. We saw no sharks, though they spawn in that area, and pilot fish swam ahead in front of our faces. The shores behind and ahead kept me unafraid.
20   Approaching Chinaman's Hat, we flew around and between a group of tall black stones like Stonehenge underwater, and through there, came up onto the land, where we rested with arms out holding on to the island. We walked
25 among the palm trees and bushes that we had seen from the other shore. Large white birds were nesting on the ground under these bushes. We hurried to the unseen part of the island.

—From *China Men*
by Maxine Hong Kingston

12. In the passage, the speaker mentions all of the following except

    (1) zebra fish
    (2) rainbow fish
    (3) sharks
    (4) flying fish
    (5) sea cucumbers

13. "How unlike a dead fish a live fish is." (lines 7-8)

    Which of the following best restates the meaning of this statement?

    (1) Whether alive or dead, all fish are beautiful.
    (2) There is no way to understand the difficulties of fishing.
    (3) Even dead, fish retain much of their natural beauty.
    (4) To truly understand the beauty of fish, a person must go scuba diving.
    (5) Seeing a fish in its natural environment is an enlightening experience.

14. From the descriptions in this passage, you can conclude that the speaker

    (1) wants to become a professional deep-sea diver
    (2) enjoys observing fish more than she enjoys birdwatching
    (3) has never had a more successful diving expedition
    (4) feels as if she has entered another world
    (5) is afraid of the potential danger around her

43

15. The speaker's comparison between fish scales and sequins in lines 8-9 emphasizes

(1) the deep, dark colors of the fish
(2) the speaker's attraction to colorful things
(3) the bright underwater sparkle of the fish
(4) the sunlight that enters the ocean waters
(5) the pale color of most of the fish's scales

16. Which of the following series of events is most similar to events in the passage?

(1) a trip across the country, followed by a long vacation
(2) a visit to a famous art museum, followed by the writing of an essay
(3) an afternoon of swimming in a pool, followed by more exercise in the gym
(4) a flight into space, followed by a return to Earth
(5) a relaxing vacation in Jamaica, followed by a bumpy plane flight home

Items 17 to 19 refer to the following song lyrics.

WHAT IS THE SPEAKER'S DREAM?

Line Last night I had the strangest dream,
I'd ever dreamed before,
I dreamed the world had all agreed
To put an end to war.
5 I dreamed I saw a mighty room
Filled with women and men,
And the paper they were signing said
They'd never fight again.
And when the paper was all signed,
10 And a million copies made,
They all joined hands and bowed their heads
And grateful prayers were prayed.
And the people in the streets below
Were dancing 'round and 'round.
15 While swords and guns and uniforms
Were scattered on the ground.
        —From "Last Night I Had the
        Strangest Dream" by Ed McCurdy

17. Which of the following best restates the main dream event in this poem?

(1) People joined hands and prayed.
(2) People signed a paper.
(3) People danced in the street.
(4) The world put an end to war.
(5) People scattered their guns and uniforms.

18. Based on this poem, you can assume that the speaker

(1) secretly wants to fight in a war
(2) would like war to cease
(3) is not a spiritual person
(4) once served his country in war
(5) frequently dreams about unusual events

19. Based on lines 1-4, with which of the following statements would this speaker agree?

(1) A world without war could exist only in a dream.
(2) The world would never agree to put an end to war.
(3) Most people occasionally have strange dreams.
(4) A world without war is an unfamiliar concept.
(5) The world will soon agree to put an end to war.

Items 20 to 23 refer to the following excerpt from a play.

WHY IS BECKY SURPRISED?

Line Becky: Tom, you frighten me! Eve has made you jealous again. (Goes to him and puts both arms about his neck) Now, my darling, I give you my word of honor I
5   love only you and never have loved Fred Lindon and never could! Say you believe me!

    Warder: Haven't I always believed you?

    Becky: Ye—s.

10 Warder: But if I find your word of honor is broken in one thing, how can I ever trust it in another?

    Becky: Of course you can't—but you needn't worry, because it won't be broken.

15 Warder: Then, now we're alone, tell me the truth, which you didn't tell me when you said you'd not seen Lindon often.

    Becky: (turns away) It was the truth. I haven't—so very often.

20 Warder: Not every day?

    Becky: (sits in the chair by the writing table.) How could I?

    Warder: Nor telephoned him Thursday, breaking off an engagement after you told me
25   absolutely you'd parted with him for good—and had no appointment?

    Becky: Of course not! The idea! (But she shows she is a little worried.) Even Lindon never could tell the truth!

44

30 Warder: The telephone girl must have lied too or
else the statement was made out of
whole cloth. *(Throwing the envelope on
the desk.)*
    Becky: What statement?
35 Warder: *(sitting on sofa)* From these detectives.
(He begins to look through the papers.)
    Becky: Detectives! *(Stunned)* What detectives?
*(Picks up envelope and looks at it, puts
it back on the desk.)*
                    —From *The Truth* by Clyde Fitch

20. Based on lines 10–12, you can conclude that
Warder

(1) is a well-respected man
(2) always tells the truth
(3) relies on a person's word of honor
(4) doesn't believe what people say
(5) has hired detectives to discover the truth

21. Which of the following statements best summarizes the events in this passage?

(1) Becky confronts Warder about his adulterous
behavior.
(2) Warder confronts Becky and then apologizes
to her.
(3) Becky becomes angry at Warder for using
detectives.
(4) Warder confronts Becky and discovers that
she has lied.
(5) Becky admits to Warder that she is seeing
Lindon.

22. The purpose of the stage directions in this passage
(in *italics*) is to

(1) hide the fact that Becky has lied
(2) show that Becky loves Warder
(3) reveal Becky's increasing discomfort
(4) describe the sofa, writing table, and desk
(5) emphasize Warder's growing anger

23. If Becky came to Warder two weeks after this
discussion and promised never to see Lindon
again, Warder probably would

(1) assume that she is lying
(2) believe in her promise
(3) be sorry he had doubted her
(4) feel grateful to Becky and Lindon
(5) leave Becky for good

dwell = to live.

Items 24 to 28 refer to the following poem.

WHAT IS THIS SPEAKER SAYING TO DEATH?
Line Death, be not proud, though some have called
        thee
      Mighty and dreadful, for thou art not so;
      For those whom thou think'st thou dost over-
5   throw
      Die not, poor Death, nor yet canst thou kill me.
      From rest and sleep, which but thy pictures be
      Much pleasure; then from thee much more must
        flow,
10   And soonest our best men with thee do go,
      Rest of their bones, and soul's delivery.
      Thou art slave to fate, chance, kings, and desper-
        ate men,
      And dost with poison, war, and sickness dwell,
15   And poppy or charms can make us sleep as well
      And better than thy stroke; why swell'st thou
        then?
      One short sleep past, we wake eternally
      And death shall be no more; Death, thou shalt die.
                    —"Sonnet 10" by John Donne

24. Which of the following best summarizes the
speaker's message to Death?

(1) "I fear that you will vanquish me."
(2) "You are a monstrous devil."
(3) "Nothing can ever stop you."
(4) "You have no real power over me."
(5) "You have every reason to be arrogant."

25. "Thou art slave to fate, chance, kings, and
desperate men,/And dost with poison, war, and
sickness dwell. . . ." (lines 12–14)

In these lines, the speaker portrays Death as

(1) unyieldingly strong
(2) peaceful and attractive
(3) weak and unappealing
(4) exaggerated and laughable
(5) threatening but unbelievable

26. To "wake eternally" (line 18) means to

(1) survive illness
(2) enter Heaven
(3) embrace Death
(4) understand life
(5) regain one's faith

thee = you
thou = pron. (old) you.
thy = your.

45

27. In line 7, the speaker personifies Death as

   (1) an evil leader who chases people
   (2) a teacher who instructs learned men
   (3) a guide who takes people away
   (4) a sea captain
   (5) a kind and gentle savior

28. Who would be most likely to appreciate the main idea of this poem?

   (1) a doctor
   (2) a pastor or rabbi
   (3) new parents
   (4) a woman who is about to be married
   (5) a person with AIDS

Items 29 to 34 refer to the following excerpt from a magazine article.

WHAT PROBLEM IS THE AIRLINE INDUSTRY FACING?

Line Unless you are born with feathers, flying requires a leap of faith. Passengers have to assume, when they strap themselves in, that a 500,000-lb. machine hurtling through the air is firmly in the
5 pilot's control. That faith was shaken last week by a report that a DC-10 coming into New York's Kennedy Airport recently almost crashed when a passenger in first class turned on his portable compact disc player.
10   The story . . . set off what one airline called "a tidal wave" of concern. Can jets really be diverted from their flight paths by something as small as a battery-powered CD player? Or a video-game machine? Or any of a dozen electronic
15 gadgets and computers that passengers regularly carry on board?
      Farfetched as it may sound, it can't be ruled out. Every electrical device creates a certain amount of radiation. Portable phones, remote-
20 control toys, and other radio transmitters emit signals that can carry for miles, and their use on planes has long been <u>banned</u>.

               —From "Hazards Aloft"
                by Philip Elmer-Dewitt

Banned-

29. According to this passage, flying "requires a leap of faith" (lines 1–2) because

   (1) airplanes make leaping motions when they take off
   (2) people must give up control and trust their pilot
   (3) like birds, people enjoy being airborne
   (4) airplane technology is not very complex
   (5) airplanes weigh 500,000 pounds

30. Which of the following best states the topic of this passage?

   (1) the effect of strong winds on airline passengers' safety
   (2) people's fear of flying
   (3) the cause of a series of recent airplane crashes
   (4) recent developments in electronics
   (5) the possible danger of electronic devices on airplanes

31. According to the article, what may happen when airplane passengers use electronic gadgets?

   (1) radiation from the devices may cause planes to go off course
   (2) passengers may annoy each other by making noise
   (3) pilots may be distracted by the noise
   (4) flights may be delayed because of signal interruptions
   (5) people enjoy the travel time more

32. "The story . . . set off what one airline called 'a tidal wave' of concern." (lines 10–11)

The image of a tidal wave shows that the concern was

   (1) weak, isolated, and never resolved
   (2) temporary
   (3) strong and widespread
   (4) ignored by officials
   (5) unimportant

33. Which is most similar to an airplane "hurtling through the air" (lines 3–4)?

   (1) a car at a stop sign
   (2) a bus full of people
   (3) an auto graveyard
   (4) a bicycle on a country road
   (5) a train at full speed

34. Based on the information in this passage, what else could emit small amounts of radiation?

   (1) a book
   (2) a handheld TV
   (3) a motorcycle
   (4) a travel bag
   (5) another airplane

> Items 35 to 40 refer to the following excerpt from a novel.

HOW IS THIS WOMAN SPENDING HER LIFE?

Line   "Nearly twenty years since I set out to seek my
fortune. It has been a long search, but I think I
have found it at last. I only asked to be a useful,
happy woman, and my wish is granted: for I
5   believe I am useful; I know I am happy."

     Christie looked so as she sat alone in the
flower parlor one September afternoon, thinking
over her life with a grateful, cheerful spirit. Forty
today, and pausing at that halfway house between
10   youth and age, she looked back into the past
without bitter regret or unsubmissive grief, and
forward into the future with courageous patience;
for three good angels attended her, and with faith,
hope, and charity to brighten life, no woman need
15   lament lost youth or fear approaching age. Christie
did not, and though her eyes filled with quiet tears
as they were raised to the faded cap and sheathed
sword hanging on the wall, none fell. . . .

     A few evenings before she had gone to one
20   of the many meetings of working women, which
had made some stir of late. . . .

     The workers poured out their wrongs and
hardships passionately or plaintively, demanding
or imploring justice, sympathy, and help; display-
25   ing the ignorance, incapacity, and prejudice,
which make their need all the more pitiful, their
relief all the more imperative.

          —From *Work: A Story of Experience*
               by Louisa May Alcott

35. Christie's mood in this passage is one of

   (1) contentment *- being contented.*
   (2) unhappiness
   (3) laziness
   (4) ambition
   (5) sympathy

36. Based on this passage, you can assume that Christie

   (1) is a wealthy woman
   (2) frequently argues with her husband
   (3) is a working woman
   (4) does not approve of working women
   (5) is happily married

37. In lines 15–18, Christie's sadness most likely results from

   (1) remembering a sad first marriage
   (2) remembering a loved one who has died
   (3) her failure to find her fortune
   (4) the realization that she is forty years old
   (5) sympathizing with the working women

38. Which of the following statements best captures the theme of this passage?

   (1) A middle-aged woman has good reason to fear the approach of old age.
   (2) Caring for a family is harder work than most people believe it to be.
   (3) All workers deserve justice, sympathy, and hope.
   (4) Middle age is a time to reflect upon past events and to look forward with hope.
   (5) At the age of forty, this woman is happy.

39. Based on this passage, which of the following events is most likely to happen later?

   (1) Christie's husband will divorce her.
   (2) The working women will arrive at Christie's house.
   (3) Christie will lose hope regarding the future.
   (4) Christie will regret being a mother.
   (5) Christie will attend another meeting.

40. The statement that Christie is " . . . pausing at that halfway house between youth and age" (lines 9–10) suggests that she

   (1) believes halfway houses can help people
   (2) is afraid that time will pass quickly
   (3) has been longing for her youth
   (4) is at a reflective point in her life
   (5) has decided to move

Items 41 to 45 refer to the following excerpt.

WHAT MAKES THIS ARCHITECT'S WORK SPECIAL?

Line   In this age of high technology when construction projects seem invariably to carry multimillion-dollar price tags, it is refreshing to encounter the work of Eladio Dieste. Working quietly for nearly a
5   half century, often in remote corners of his native Uruguay, this structural engineer has designed large buildings for communities and industries that are at once inexpensive and of high aesthetic quality. Avoiding costly steel or reinforced
10   concrete structural systems characteristic of so many twentieth-century buildings, Dieste has favored fired brick, a material both attractive and easily produced locally. . . .
    Rooted in tradition yet futuristic in feeling,
15   Dieste's buildings are sturdy, easily maintained, and possessed of genuinely beautiful lines. His humane structures are so light and airy they almost seem to flap in the wind.
    It is no accident that two of Dieste's best
20   known buildings are churches. He brings to all of his work (even industrial projects) a serious kind of devotion that borders on the spiritual. As he has said, "Besides its obvious functions, architecture has in common with other arts the ability to help
25   us contemplate the universe. All the spiritual activity of man is a conscious or unconscious search for such contemplation. A building cannot be as profound as art without serious and subtle fidelity to the laws of the materials; only reverence
30   to this fidelity can make our works serious, lasting, worthy companions for our daily contemplative discourse."
    —From "Making Bricks Soar" by Caleb Bach

41. Which of the following best summarizes Dieste's opinions on architecture as expressed in lines 23–25?

(1)   Architecture is not a true art form.
(2)   The most important element of a building is its materials.
(3)   Architecture and spirituality are not related.
(4)   Good architecture helps us contemplate the universe.
(5)   The universe is unfathomable to humans.

42. Which of the following best describes why the reviewer admires Dieste's buildings?

(1)   They are beautiful and inexpensive.
(2)   Dieste has built beautiful churches.
(3)   Dieste often uses steel and concrete.
(4)   They seem a part of the natural environment.
(5)   They have many windows.

43. Comparing Dieste's buildings to flags being lifted by the wind (lines 17–18)

(1)   shows how flimsy and thin the walls are
(2)   reveals Dieste's love of nature
(3)   suggests the buildings' open, inspirational feel
(4)   emphasizes that they seem full of motion
(5)   illustrates how costly Dieste's work is

44. If Dieste were a jewelry maker, which material would he most likely use?

(1)   diamonds
(2)   emeralds
(3)   copper
(4)   gold
(5)   rubies

45. In lines 1–3, why does this reviewer emphasize the high cost of architecture today?

(1)   to highlight the low-cost simplicity of ancient buildings
(2)   to provide a contrast with Dieste's elegant, low-cost works
(3)   to praise Dieste's policy of working free of charge
(4)   to criticize the high cost of home insurance
(5)   to prove that, decades ago, materials were less expensive

MATHEMATICS

90 Minutes ❖ 56 Questions

Directions

Choose the <u>one best answer</u> to each item.

Items 1 and 2 refer to the following information.

State Football Championship

Admission	$8.00
Hot Dog	$1.50
Bucket of Popcorn	$2.00
Soda	$1.00

1. Vickie and Bill went to the game together. While Bill bought their tickets, Vickie got one bucket of popcorn to share and a soda for each of them. How much money did they spend altogether?

    (1) $4
    (2) $16
    (3) $19
    (4) $20
    (5) Not enough information is given.

2. If 2,500 people attended the game, what were the total proceeds from admission fees?

    (1) $2,500
    (2) $3,750
    (3) $16,000
    (4) $20,000
    (5) $200,000

3. Joan must consume at least 12 grams of dietary fiber daily. For breakfast she eats bran cereal containing 4.3 grams of fiber. During the day, Joan drinks two high-fiber milkshakes, each containing 3.8 grams of fiber. Which of the following expressions could she use to figure out how many grams of fiber she still needs?

    (1) $2(3.8) + 4.3 - 12$
    (2) $12 - 4.3 - 3.8$
    (3) $12 - 2(4.3 + 3.8)$
    (4) $12 - (4.3 + 3.8)$
    (5) $12 - 4.3 - 2(3.8)$

Items 4 to 6 refer to the following information.

The following table shows the GED test scores of three students. A total of 225 points is required in order to earn the GED certificate.

Subject	Joanne	Fidelia	Mike
Writing Skills	51	48	49
Social Studies	49		52
Science	52	50	50
Literature and the Arts	53	52	45
Math	50	40	49
TOTAL POINTS	225		
Average	51		

4. What is Mike's mean (average) score?

    (1) 45
    (2) 49
    (3) 50
    (4) 51
    (5) 52

5. When values are arranged from smallest to largest, the median value is the middle value. Rearrange Joanne's scores from smallest to largest. What is her median score?

    (1) 49
    (2) 50
    (3) 51
    (4) 52
    (5) 53

6. Which of the following expressions can be used to find the social studies score that Fidelia needs in order to get a total of 225 points on the GED tests?

   (1) 225 − (48 + 50 + 52 + 40)
   (2) (48 + 50 + 52 + 40) − 225
   (3) 225 − 48 + 50 + 52 + 40
   (4) 225 − 48 + (50 + 52 + 40)
   (5) Not enough information is given.

Items 7 to 9 refer to the following information.

7. If Yolanda buys 2 bottles of Delicious Apple Juice at the advertised price and uses the coupon shown above, what is her final cost per bottle of apple juice?

   (1) $1.39
   (2) $1.69
   (3) $1.89
   (4) $3.38
   (5) $3.78

8. To the nearest penny, how much would 2.2 pounds of ground beef cost?

   (1) $2.69
   (2) $5.38
   (3) $5.92
   (4) $6.58
   (5) $6.78

9. What is the price per ounce of the advertised peanut butter?

   (1) $0.27
   (2) $0.39
   (3) $0.46
   (4) $0.52
   (5) Not enough information is given.

Item 10 refers to the following graph.

**PERCENT OF CHANGE IN
U.S. MEDIAN FAMILY INCOME**
(from 1981 to 1990)

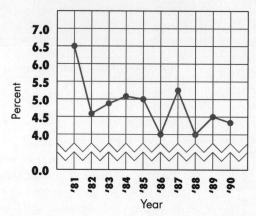

10. In which years did the percent of change in median family income decrease 0.5 percent or more?

   (1) 1981, 1985, and 1987
   (2) 1982, 1985, and 1990
   (3) 1983, 1985, and 1990
   (4) 1982, 1986, and 1988
   (5) 1981, 1982, and 1986

11. The record high temperature for the state of Maine is 105° F. The record low temperature for the state is 48° below zero. Which of the following expressions could be used to find the difference between the record high and low temperatures?

   (1) 105° − 48°
   (2) −105° + (−48°)
   (3) 105° + (−48°)
   (4) 105° − (−48°)
   (5) −105° − 48°

12. An elementary school ordered 14 packs of color ribbons for its computer printers. Each pack contains 6 ribbons. If the school uses about 8 ribbons per month, approximately how long will the ribbons last?

  (1) Between 7 and 8 months
  (2) Between 8 and 9 months
  (3) Between 9 and 10 months
  (4) Between 10 and 11 months
  (5) Between 11 and 12 months

Items 13 and 14 refer to the following information.

SPENDING CALORIES
Approximate Calories Burned per 15 Minutes

Activity	Calories
AEROBIC DANCING	105
BASKETBALL	141
CLIMBING HILLS	123
CYCLING*	66
DOWNHILL SKIING	101
GOLF**	87
JUDO	199
RUNNING***	174
SQUASH	216
SWIMMING****	143
WALKING*****	99

      * level ground 5.5 mph
    ** walking the course
  *** 10-minute miles
 **** moderate pace
***** level ground 4 mph

13. How many calories are burned by playing basketball for 15 minutes?

  (1) 105
  (2) 141
  (3) 143
  (4) 199
  (5) 282

14. How many calories are burned by walking for an hour at the pace of 4 miles per hour?

  (1) 99
  (2) 198
  (3) 297
  (4) 396
  (5) 495

15. Eric plans to drive 275 miles. If he leaves at 8:30 a.m. and averages 55 miles per hour, at what time will he arrive at his destination?

  (1) 12:30 p.m.
  (2) 1:30 p.m.
  (3) 2:30 p.m.
  (4) 5:00 p.m.
  (5) Not enough information is given.

Items 16 and 17 refer to the following packages and formulas.

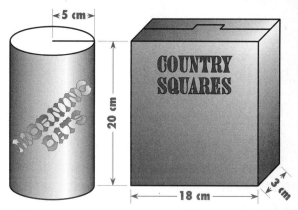

Volume (*V*) of a:

Rectangular Container:
    $V = lwh$; where l = length, w = width, h = height

Cylinder:
    $V = \pi r^2 h$; where π = 3.14, r = radius, h = height

16. Which of the following expressions represents the volume of the package of Morning Oats in cubic centimeters?

  (1) 3.14(5)(20)
  (2) $3.14(5)^2(20)$
  (3) 3.14(10)(20)
  (4) $3.14(10)^2(20)$
  (5) Not enough information is given.

17. How many cubic centimeters are contained in the package of Country Squares?

  (1) 480
  (2) 960
  (3) 1,080
  (4) 1,880
  (5) 2,880

Items 18 to 20 refer to the following information.

MARISOL SANCHEZ'S PAY STUB

HOURS	TOTAL EARNED	DEDUCTIONS	
40	$420.00	Fed. Tax	$37.80
		State Tax	21.00
		Soc. Sec.	18.90
		Health Plan	9.25
		NET PAY	

18. Using the information given on the pay stub, how much does Marisol earn per hour?

   (1) $9.25
   (2) $10.50
   (3) $37.80
   (4) $42.00
   (5) Not enough information is given.

19. What is her net pay (after deductions)?

   (1) $86.95
   (2) $279.04
   (3) $333.05
   (4) $420.00
   (5) $506.95

20. What percent of her total pay is taken out for state tax?

   (1) 5%
   (2) 9%
   (3) 10%
   (4) 14%
   (5) 25%

21. Marisol's friend, Gabe, earns $11 an hour. When he works overtime, he is paid "time and a half" or 1½ times his regular hourly wage. How much is Gabe paid per hour for overtime?

   (1) $5.50
   (2) $11.00
   (3) $13.25
   (4) $16.50
   (5) $22.00

Items 22 and 23 refer to the following information.

MICKIE'S WEEKLY EXPENDITURES

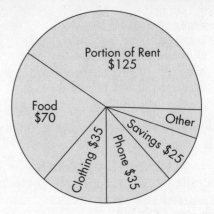

22. What is the ratio of money Mickie spent for clothing to the money she spent for food?

   (1) $\frac{3}{25}$
   (2) $\frac{3}{14}$
   (3) $\frac{3}{7}$
   (4) $\frac{7}{25}$
   (5) $\frac{1}{2}$

23. The amount that Mickie spent on food this week is 25% of her monthly food budget. How much does Mickie budget for food each month?

   (1) $25
   (2) $70
   (3) $140
   (4) $280
   (5) $350

24. An amusement park received a shipment of 5,000 necklaces to use as prizes. Of the necklaces, $\frac{3}{10}$ were found to be defective. Of the defective necklaces, $\frac{3}{4}$ could be repaired. How many necklaces could be repaired?

   (1) 200
   (2) 375
   (3) 660
   (4) 1,125
   (5) 1,500

Items 25 and 26 refer to the following information.

Dan is saving money to redecorate his living room and dining room. Dan made this sketch of the rooms with the measurements in feet shown.

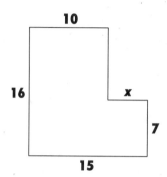

25. What is the length of the side labeled *x*?

(1) 5
(2) 7
(3) 9
(4) 10
(5) 16

26. If 1 gallon of paint covers 500 square feet, what additional information does Dan need to determine how many gallons to buy to paint the walls in both rooms?

(1) The price per gallon
(2) The perimeter of the ceiling
(3) The height of the walls
(4) The width of the ceiling
(5) The area of the floor

27. In the 1992 Summer Olympic Games, the United States won ten more than twice the number of medals won by China. The total number of medals won by China and the United States was 262. Which of the following equations could be used to find how many medals the athletes from the United States won?

(1) $2x + 10 = 262$
(2) $x(2x + 10) = 262$
(3) $x + (2x + 10) = 262$
(4) $x + 2x = 262 + 10$
(5) $(2x + 10) - x = 262$

Item 28 refers to the following diagram.

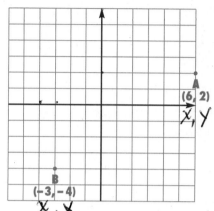

28. Points *A* and *B* lie on the same plane and are drawn on a graph at the coordinates shown. What is the approximate distance between the two points?

(1) Between 9 and 10
(2) Between 10 and 11
(3) Between 11 and 12
(4) Between 12 and 13
(5) Between 13 and 14

29. In a suburban area covering 18.6 square miles, homeowners occupy the predominantly 3- and 4-bedroom houses by a ratio of 5 owners to 1 renter. What number of these homes are occupied by renters?

(1) 60
(2) 774
(3) 930
(4) 1,080
(5) Not enough information is given.

30. The Acme Novelty Company plans to increase its workforce by ⅓ to meet seasonal demand for its products. The company currently employs 828 workers. How many workers will be on the payroll once the additional employees are hired?

(1) 276
(2) 552
(3) 828
(4) 1,104
(5) 2,484

31. The Orange Grove Municipal Library recently received an endowment of $19,200, an amount that represented 8% of the library's annual budget. What is the annual budget of the library?

(1) $17,664
(2) $20,870
(3) $153,600
(4) $184,000
(5) $240,000

Item 32 refers to the following graph.

COPIER PAPER INVENTORY
Monday, October 18

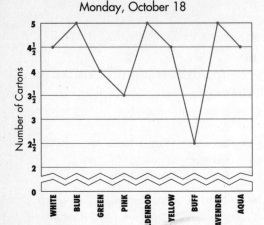

32. The Quick Copy Center takes inventory of its paper stock at the end of each day. If there are 12 reams of paper in each carton, how many reams of pink paper were in stock at the end of Monday, October 18?

(1) 12
(2) 30
(3) 33
(4) 42
(5) Not enough information is given.

33. Christina jogs 1¾ miles five days per week and 2½ miles on Saturday. How many miles does she run weekly?

(1) $4\frac{1}{4}$
(2) $9\frac{1}{4}$
(3) $11\frac{1}{4}$
(4) $14\frac{1}{4}$
(5) $21\frac{7}{8}$

34. Kesha earns $7.20 per hour. Her boss has promised her a 10% raise next month. If she works 40 hours per week, how much will she earn per week after she gets her raise?

(1) $259.20
(2) $288.00
(3) $292.00
(4) $298.60
(5) $316.80

Item 35 refers to the following chart.

JOB OUTLOOK FOR THE FUTURE

Occupation	Estimated Employment in 1990	New Jobs by 2005
Salespersons (retail)	4,754,000	1,381,000
Truck Drivers	2,701,000	659,000
Elementary School Teachers	1,521,000	350,000
Cashiers	2,633,000	685,000
Registered Nurses	1,727,000	767,000
Medical Assistants	165,000	122,000

35. Which of the following occupations will show the greatest percent of increase in numbers of jobs from 1990 to 2005?

(1) truck drivers
(2) elementary school teachers
(3) cashiers
(4) registered nurses
(5) medical assistants

Items 36 and 37 refer to the following information.

A customer service representative logs the following times for the first 8 calls of the morning.

Call 1	5.0 minutes	Call 5	12.5 minutes
Call 2	8.0 minutes	Call 6	8.5 minutes
Call 3	2.5 minutes	Call 7	10.0 minutes
Call 4	3.0 minutes	Call 8	4.5 minutes

36. To the nearest minute, what is the average time spent per call by the customer service representative?

(1) 5 minutes
(2) 6 minutes
(3) 7 minutes
(4) 8 minutes
(5) 9 minutes

37. What is the median time of the calls listed?

    (1) 5.0 minutes
    (2) 6.5 minutes
    (3) 7.5 minutes
    (4) 8.0 minutes
    (5) Not enough information is given.

> **Item 38 refers to the following information.**

Kina has 12 black marbles, 10 white marbles, and 8 red marbles in a bag.

38. If Kina pulls out one marble without looking, what is the probability that the marble will not be black?

    (1) $\dfrac{1}{18}$

    (2) $\dfrac{1}{12}$

    (3) $\dfrac{2}{5}$

    (4) $\dfrac{3}{5}$

    (5) Not enough information is given.

> **Items 39 and 40 refer to the following information.**

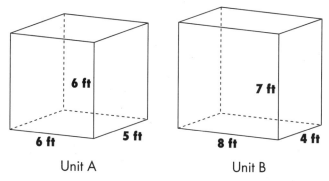

Unit A   Unit B

The Jacksons have decided to rent a storage unit in their apartment building. The two units now available are shown in the diagram above.

39. Ms. Jackson is most concerned about the surface area of the storage unit's floor. Which of the following expressions could be used to find the difference in the floor area of the two units?

    (1) $2(6) + 2(5)$
    (2) $2(8) + 2(4)$
    (3) $8(7)(4) - 6(6)(5)$
    (4) $\dfrac{8(4)}{6(5)}$
    (5) $8(4) - 6(5)$

40. Mr. Jackson wants to rent both units. What is the total volume of the two units in cubic feet?

    (1) 40,320
    (2) 960
    (3) 404
    (4) 323
    (5) 092

41. Bob and Rick set up new computers for the school computer lab. In 2½ hours they were able to set up 15 computers. Bob connected twice as many computers as Rick. How many computers did Bob connect?

    (1) 5
    (2) 6
    (3) 10
    (4) 12
    (5) 15

42. Marie, an art teacher, budgets $15 per week to spend on glue sticks. The glue sticks cost $0.65 each including sales tax. Which of the following inequalities could be used to find the greatest number (n) of glue sticks Marie could buy in a week?

    (1) $\$15 - \$0.65 \geq n$
    (2) $\dfrac{n}{\$0.65} \leq \$15n$
    (3) $\$0.65 + \$15 \leq n$
    (4) $\$0.65n \geq \$15$
    (5) $\$0.65n \leq \$15$

43. A coeducational sports program requires that each basketball team of five starting players include two women. At the same ratio, how many women must be included on a ten-player coed softball team?

    (1) 2
    (2) 3
    (3) 4
    (4) 5
    (5) Not enough information is given.

44. What is the sum of 8, −12, 5, and −3?

(1) 28
(2) 22
(3) −2
(4) −12
(5) −28

45. Which of the following inequalities is true when x is replaced by 2?

A. $6x + 2(5 − 3) \geq 16$
B. $5x − (8x + 4) \geq 20$
C. $3x + 9 \leq 16$

(1) A and B
(2) B only
(3) A and C
(4) A, B, and C
(5) Not enough information is given.

46. Which of the following statements is true?

(1) 6.3×10^5 is greater than 6,000,000
(2) 6.3×10^5 is equal to 630,000
(3) 6.3×10^5 is equal to 63,000
(4) 6.3×10^5 is less than 60,000
(5) 6.3×10^5 is equal to 6,300

47. Paul has three baseball rookie cards worth a total of $40.50. The first card is worth three times the value of the second card. The third card is worth one-half the value of the second card. What is the value of the first card?

(1) $27.00
(2) $18.00
(3) $13.50
(4) $09.00
(5) $04.50

48. Which of the following is equal to the expression $3n^2 + 2n + n^2 + 5 − 6n − 8$?

(1) $8n − 3$
(2) $4n^2 − 4n − 3$
(3) $3n^2 − 2n + 3$
(4) $n^2 − 13$
(5) $4n^2 + 4n − 3$

Items 49 and 50 refer to the following diagram.

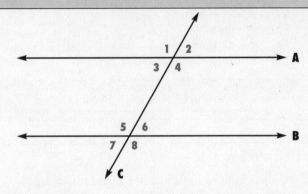

49. Lines A and B are parallel. If $\angle 2$ measures 60°, what is the measure of $\angle 8$?

(1) 30°
(2) 60°
(3) 90°
(4) 120°
(5) Not enough information is given.

50. Which of the following do not have equal measures?

(1) $\angle 1$ and $\angle 4$
(2) $\angle 2$ and $\angle 7$
(3) $\angle 4$ and $\angle 5$
(4) $\angle 3$ and $\angle 6$
(5) $\angle 1$ and $\angle 7$

51. An apartment complex uses a boiler to provide hot water for 10 apartments. The cylindrical boiler is 7 feet high with an 8-foot diameter. What is the volume of the boiler to the nearest cubic foot?

(1) 176
(2) 352
(3) 615
(4) 1,407
(5) Not enough information is given.

Items 52 to 54 refer to the following graph.

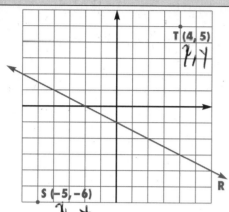

Item 55 refers to the following figure.

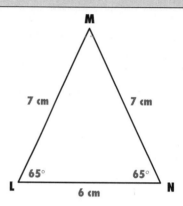

52. What is the distance between points S and T on the graph to the nearest whole number?

(1) 5
(2) 11
(3) 14
(4) 21
(5) Not enough information is given.

53. Which of the following points is not found on line R?

(1) $(-6, 2)$
(2) $(-4, 1)$
(3) $(-2, 0)$
(4) $(1, -1)$
(5) $(4, -3)$

54. What would be the slope of a line that passes through points S and T?

(1) $\dfrac{5}{12}$

(2) $\dfrac{11}{20}$

(3) $\dfrac{11}{9}$

(4) $\dfrac{3}{4}$

(5) Not enough information is given.

55. What is the measure of $\angle M$?

(1) 50°
(2) 65°
(3) 130°
(4) 230°
(5) Not enough information is given.

56. The legs of a right triangle measure 6 inches and 12 inches. Which of the following expressions could be used to find the measure in inches of the hypotenuse of the triangle?

(1) $\sqrt{12^2 + 6^2}$

(2) $12^2 + 6^2$

(3) $\sqrt{12 + 6}$

(4) $\sqrt{(12 + 6)^2}$

(5) $\dfrac{12^2 + 6^2}{2}$

Slope = slating surface (Flat)

ANSWERS TO PRETESTS 1–5

WRITING SKILLS		SOCIAL STUDIES		SCIENCE		LITERATURE AND THE ARTS		MATHEMATIACS	
Part I		1. 5	33. 3	1. 2	34. 4	1. 3	24. 4	1. 4	29. 5
1. 4	40. 2	2. 3	34. 5	2. 4	35. 1	2. 2	25. 3	2. 4	30. 4
2. 3	41. 2	3. 1	35. 1	3. 1	36. 3	3. 4	26. 2	3. 5	31. 5
3. 2	42. 4	4. 3	36. 2	4. 5	37. 2	4. 3	27. 3	4. 2	32. 4
4. 2	43. 3	5. 1	37. 5	5. 3	38. 1	5. 4	28. 5	5. 3	33. 3
5. 4	44. 2	6. 4	38. 4	6. 3	39. 2	6. 5	29. 2	6. 1	34. 5
6. 2	45. 3	7. 3	39. 3	7. 4	40. 1	7. 5	30. 5	7. 2	35. 5
7. 5	46. 4	8. 4	40. 4	8. 2	41. 4	8. 4	31. 1	8. 3	36. 3
8. 2	47. 2	9. 2	41. 1	9. 4	42. 4	9. 3	32. 3	9. 5	37. 2
9. 4	48. 5	10. 3	42. 3	10. 1	43. 4	10. 2	33. 5	10. 4	38. 4
10. 5	49. 5	11. 5	43. 2	11. 3	44. 2	11. 4	34. 2	11. 4	39. 5
11. 2	50. 5	12. 4	44. 3	12. 4	45. 1	12. 4	35. 1	12. 4	40. 3
12. 4	51. 4	13. 3	45. 2	13. 3	46. 4	13. 5	36. 3	13. 2	41. 3
13. 3	52. 4	14. 2	46. 3	14. 5	47. 3	14. 4	37. 2	14. 4	42. 5
14. 1	53. 3	15. 5	47. 2	15. 2	48. 5	15. 3	38. 4	15. 2	43. 3
15. 5	54. 1	16. 2	48. 1	16. 2	49. 2	16. 4	39. 5	16. 2	44. 3
16. 5	55. 5	17. 4	49. 4	17. 3	50. 3	17. 4	40. 4	17. 3	45. 3
17. 4		18. 2	50. 2	18. 1	51. 5	18. 2	41. 4	18. 2	46. 2
18. 4	**Part II**	19. 3	51. 4	19. 2	52. 1	19. 4	42. 1	19. 3	47. 1
19. 2	Turn to	20. 4	52. 2	20. 3	53. 2	20. 3	43. 4	20. 1	48. 2
20. 5	page 15.	21. 2	53. 4	21. 2	54. 4	21. 4	44. 3	21. 4	49. 4
21. 2		22. 3	54. 1	22. 5	55. 3	22. 3	45. 2	22. 5	50. 5
22. 1		23. 3	55. 3	23. 1	56. 5	23. 1		23. 4	51. 2
23. 4		24. 4	56. 4	24. 2	57. 3			24. 4	52. 3
24. 2		25. 1	57. 2	25. 1	58. 2			25. 1	53. 4
25. 5		26. 5	58. 4	26. 3	59. 3			26. 3	54. 3
26. 2		27. 1	59. 4	27. 5	60. 2			27. 3	55. 1
27. 4		28. 3	60. 1	28. 4	61. 4			28. 2	56. 1
28. 4		29. 4	61. 3	29. 1	62. 4				
29. 2		30. 4	62. 5	30. 5	63. 3				
30. 3		31. 2	63. 2	31. 3	64. 5				
31. 3		32. 3	64. 4	32. 1	65. 2				
32. 1				33. 2	66. 1				
33. 5									
34. 4									
35. 3									
36. 2									
37. 5									
38. 3									
39. 3									

Answers and Explanations
PRETESTS

Writing Skills
Part I

1. **The correct answer is (4): revolutionized our world. They have also** Choice (4) corrects this run-on sentence by making each of its complete thoughts a separate sentence. Choice (2) inserts still another unnecessary comma. There is a spelling error in choice (3), and in choice (5) a word is capitalized for no reason.

2. **The correct answer is (3): change the spelling of roll to role** Choice (3) uses the correct sound-alike word. Choice (1) introduces a spelling error. Choice (2) lacks subject-verb agreement. There is no reason for the comma in choice (4), and there is no reason to capitalize the words in choice (5).

3. **The correct answer is (2): pulse, heartbeat, and respiration of patients during surgery** Choice (2) includes a comma before the last item in a series of three. Choice (1) omits that comma. Choice (3) omits all series commas. Choice (4) inserts a comma before a prepositional phrase that follows the main clause. There is no reason for the comma in choice (5).

4. **The correct answer is (2): change Nurse's to Nurses'** Choice (2) places the apostrophe in the correct place to show a plural possessive. Choice (1) changes the possessive to a plural, and the other choices change plurals to possessives.

5. **The correct answer is (4): change give to given** Choice (4) uses the correct past participle. Choice (1) changes the meaning of the sentence, choice (2) removes the comma before the last item in a series, and choice (3) shifts to the past tense.

6. **The correct answer is (2): After they make a small incision, surgeons can insert** Choice (2) places a comma after the introductory dependent clause. Choice (1) omits this comma. Choice (3) wrongly uses a comma to separate the subject (*surgeons*) from its verb (*can insert*), choice (4) uses the singular verb makes with the plural subject they, and there is no reason to capitalize the general term in choice (5).

7. **The correct answer is (5): use of high-tech tools has resulted** Choice (5) matches the singular subject (*use*) with a singular verb (*has*). Choice (2) uses an incorrect verb form for the past participle, choice (3) incorrectly inserts a comma between the subject and the verb, and there is no reason for the comma in choice (4).

8. **The correct answer is (2): change worrying to are worrying** Choice (2) completes the sentence by supplying the missing verb part. Choice (1) incorrectly puts the sentence into the past tense. There is no reason to insert a comma as in choice (3) or a semicolon as in choice (4), and neither option completes the verb.

9. **The correct answer is (4): they spend time reading for pleasure** Choice (4) corrects two sentence fragments by eliminating the period at the end of sentence 3 and the capital letter at the beginning of sentence 4. Choices (2) and (5) do not correct the fragments, and choice (5) uses pronouns incorrectly. Choice (3) uses a comma inappropriately to join the fragment to the preceding sentence.

10. **The correct answer is (5): change doesnt to doesn't** Choice (5) indicates a contraction by replacing the missing letter with an apostrophe. There is no reason for the comma in choice (1), choice (2) does not drop the *e* before adding *ing*, choice (3) uses a past participle instead of a present participle, and choice (4) puts the apostrophe in the wrong place.

11. **The correct answer is (2): change plays to play** Choice (2) uses a verb that agrees with the subject. Choice (1) separates the subject and verb with a comma, choice (3) shifts to the future tense, and there is no reason for the comma in choice (4).

12. **The correct answer is (4): word; therefore, reading demands** Choice (4) uses a connecting word that shows the correct relationship between the two ideas stated in this compound sentence. The other choices use inappropriate connecting words.

13. **The correct answer is (3): change increases to increased** Choice (3) uses the past tense, which is appropriate because the action being described took place in the 1980s. Choice (1) removes a comma after an introductory word, choice (2) lacks subject-verb agreement, choice (4) shifts to the future tense, and there is no reason for the comma in choice (5).

14. **The correct answer is (1): encourage** Choice (1) is the only word that maintains the meaning of the original sentence.

15. **The correct answer is (5): to mail a check than to mail cash** In choice (5), repeating the verb *to mail* makes the sentence's structure parallel. Simply adding a word, as in choices (2) and (3), does not improve the structure. Choice (4) changes the meaning of the sentence and makes no sense.

16. **The correct answer is (5): no correction is necessary**

17. **The correct answer is (4): Because balancing a checking account is often confusing and frustrating, many people** Choice (4) corrects the misplaced modifier by making it clear that balancing checking accounts is often confusing and frustrating. The misplaced modifier in choice (1) makes it seem as if people, not the task of balancing checking accounts, are confusing and frustrating. Choice (2) incorrectly puts checking accounts near the modifier. Choice (3) incorrectly states that people are confusing. Choice (5) uses unclear pronoun references.

18. **The correct answer is (4): but they usually aren't complicated** Choice (4) uses a pronoun that agrees in number with its antecedent. Choice (1) lacks pronoun-antecedent agreement, choice (2) shifts to the past tense, choice (3) uses an inappropriate connecting word between the clauses, and choice (5) creates a run-on sentence because it deletes a connecting word and a comma.

19. **The correct answer is (2): change Bounced Check to bounced check** Choice (2) is correct because there is no reason to capitalize *bounced check*. Choice (1) removes a comma that is required with the connecting word *so that* separates two independent clauses. Choice (3) incorrectly inserts a comma before a dependent clause, and choice (4) uses the plural pronoun *them* with the singular antecedent *bounced check*.

20. **The correct answer is (5): you** Choice (5) is the only choice that maintains the meaning of the original sentence: bouncing a check costs *you* money.

21. **The correct answer is (2): change had to have** Choice (2) continues the paragraph's use of the present tense. Choice (1) removes a comma that is required after an introductory phrase, there is no reason for the comma in choice (3), choice (4) changes the possessive to a contraction, and choice (5) changes a plural to a possessive.

22. **The correct answer is (1): insert commas after tuberculosis and world** Choice (1) uses commas to set off an interrupting phrase from the rest of the sentence, which would make sense even without that information. In choice (2) an unnecessary comma is added. Choice (3) introduces a spelling error, while choice (4) lacks subject-verb agreement.

23. **The correct answer is (4): but** Choice (4) is the only choice that shows the contrast between what doctors thought (diseases had been eradicated) and what is really happening (diseases are returning).

24. **The correct answer is (2): replace doesn't with don't** Choice (2) uses the plural form of the verb to agree with the plural subject (*strains*). Choice (1) uses the wrong pronoun (*who* instead of *that*) to refer to a thing, there is no reason for the comma in choice (3), and choice (4) changes the past participle (*seen*) of the verb *to see* to the past tense (*saw*).

25. **The correct answer is (5): says malaria is another growing health problem** Choice (5) replaces the pronoun *one*, which had no clear antecedent, with a noun. None of the other choices corrects *one's* vague reference.

26. **The correct answer is (2): have resurfaced in Russia** Choice (2) uses the plural verb *have* to agree with the plural subject *Typhoid and diphtheria*. Choices (1), (3), and (4) do not correct this subject-verb agreement error, and choice (5) shifts to the future tense.

27. **The correct answer is (4): where health officials already worry about tuberculosis** Choice (4) is the only choice that maintains the meaning of the original sentences.

28. **The correct answer is (4): change hygiene. To to hygiene to** Choice (4) eliminates the sentence fragment by joining it to the complete sentence. Choice (5) eliminates the fragment but joins the words to the complete sentence with incorrect punctuation. Choices (1) and (2) omit commas between items in a series of three, and choice (3) inserts a comma after the *and* at the end of the series.

29. **The correct answer is (2): change 1930s. One to 1930s was one** Choice (2) connects the two fragments with a verb and creates a complete sentence. The other choices do not correct the fragments.

30. **The correct answer is (3): painful time many people still remember** Choice (3) places the modifier *painful* next to the word it modifies. Choices (1) and (2) misplace the modifier. Choices (4) and (5) change the meaning of the sentence.

31. **The correct answer is (3): replace the landlord kicked them out with eviction from their homes** Choice (3) is the only choice that corrects the faulty parallel structure. Choice (5) creates a fragment.

32. **The correct answer is (1): replace Which with The war** Choice (1) gives the fragment a subject to make a complete sentence. The other choices don't correct the fragment.

33. **The correct answer is (5): caused** Choice (5) provides a verb to follow the subject. *Lost*, in choice (2), changes the meaning of the sentence. The other choices are nouns.

34. **The correct answer is (4): everything, and many** Choice (4) uses the appropriate connecting word to link the two clauses. The other choices use incorrect connecting words, and choice (3) creates a fragment as well.

35. **The correct answer is (3): insert a comma after employment** Choice (3) uses a comma and a connecting word together to separate the two clauses in a compound sentence. Choices (1), (2), and (5) create fragments. Choice (4) uses an inappropriate connecting word.

36. **The correct answer is (2): headed to California for a better life** Choice (2) is the only choice that corrects for parallel structure.

37. **The correct answer is (5): replace unless with since** Choice (5) supplies the appropriate connecting word for the two clauses in this sentence. Choice (4) is not an appropriate connector. Choices (1) and (3) create fragments, and choice (2) inserts an unneeded comma.

38. **The correct answer is (3): change skips to skip** Choice (3) uses a plural verb (*skip*) to match a plural subject (*people*). The other choices do not correct for subject-verb agreement.

39. **The correct answer is (3): who** Choice (3) is the required relative pronoun to connect the two parts of the sentence. Choices (1) and (4) assume a nonhuman antecedent. Choice (2) uses the object form of the pronoun, and choice (5) changes the meaning of the sentence.

40. **The correct answer is (2): change didn't to doesn't** Choice (2) uses the present tense, which is consistent throughout the paragraph. Choice (1) uses a verb that doesn't agree with the subject in number. Choices (3) and (5) switch to future tense, and choice (4) changes the meaning of the sentence.

41. **The correct answer is (2): which do take time to prepare** Choice (2) uses a pronoun that agrees with a nonhuman antecedent. Choices (1), (3), and (4) assume human antecedents; choice (5) changes the meaning of the sentence.

42. **The correct answer is (4): change is to are** Choice (4) uses a plural verb to agree with a plural subject. Choices (1) and (2) don't correct for subject-verb agreement, and choice (3) shifts to past tense.

43. **The correct answer is (3): replace He or she with They** Choice (3) uses a plural pronoun to agree with a plural antecedent (people). Choices (1) and (2) use singular pronouns, choice (4) shifts to first person, and choice (5) shifts to second person.

44. **The correct answer is (2): replace It's with These foods are** Choice (2) provides a clear subject for the sentence instead of a pronoun without a clear antecedent. Choice (1) doesn't correct for an unclear antecedent, choice (3) awkwardly repeats all the nouns, and choice (4) uses a relative pronoun incorrectly as a subject.

45. **The correct answer is (3): replace weather with whether** Choice (3) uses the correct word. Choice (1) uses the wrong sound-alike word, choices (2) and (5) each misspell a word, and choice (4) fails to capitalize the name of a language.

46. **The correct answer is (4): it costs too much to provide** Choice (4) uses the correct sound-alike words. Choices (1), (3), and (5) use the wrong sound-alike words, choice (5) uses a comma for no reason, and choice (2) lacks subject-verb agreement.

47. **The correct answer is (2): change its to it's** Choice (2) uses an apostrophe for a contraction. Choices (1) and (3) misspell words, and there is no reason for the comma in choice (4).

48. **The correct answer is (5): immigrants** Choice (5) is correct because the sentence speaks of immigrants having it too easy. The other choices change the meaning of the sentence.

49. **The correct answer is (5): little opportunity for advancement** Choice (5) spells *advancement* correctly. Choices (1) and (2) misspell words, and choice (3) inserts a comma for no reason. Choice (4) is incorrect because the infinitive is *to advance*.

50. **The correct answer is (5): change english to English** Choice (5) capitalizes the name of a language. Choice (1) omits the apostrophe in a possessive, choice (2) misspells the word, choice (3) capitalizes a general word, and choice (4) removes the comma required before a connecting word in a compound sentence.

51. **The correct answer is (4): insert a comma after opinions** Choice (4) places a comma after the interrupter. Choices (1) and (2) change plurals to possessives, and choice (3) removes the comma at the beginning of an interrupter.

52. **The correct answer is (4): change snake's to snakes** Choice (4) uses the plural, not the possessive. Choice (2) changes a plural to a possessive, and choice (3) uses a possessive.

53. **The correct answer is (3): change the spelling of oceon to ocean** There's no reason for the apostrophe in choice (1). Choice (2) is incorrect because an interrupting word must be set apart by commas, choice (4) uses the wrong sound-alike word, and choice (5) spells *poisonous* incorrectly.

54. **The correct answer is (1): change It's to Its** Choice (1) uses the possessive rather than the contraction. Choice (2) uses the wrong sound-alike word, choice (3) changes a possessive to a plural, and choice (4) uses the wrong initial letter.

55. **The correct answer is (5): change the spelling of immediatly to immediately** Choice (5) adds *ly* to a word without changing the main word's spelling. There's no reason to capitalize the word in choice (1), choice (2) misspells *vicious*, and choice (3) uses the incorrect verb tense. Choice (4) misspells the main word.

PART II

Although it is difficult to evaluate your own essay, the scoring information on page 453 will help you estimate a score for your essay. For your use, make a list of your essay's strengths and weaknesses based on the self-evaluation questions that follow. If you can, ask an instructor, friend, or family member to read and comment on your essay.

- Did you write about the assigned topic? Did you stick to the point?

- Does your essay have a clear controlling idea that is developed throughout?

- Does your essay have a clear structure (introduction, body, and conclusion)?

  - Does the introduction tell the reader what the topic is and what you are going to say about it?

  - Does the body contain details and examples to support each point?

  - Does the conclusion sum up what you have written?

- Did you revise your essay to correct errors?

SOCIAL STUDIES

1. **The correct answer is (5): (Analysis)** The consequence of receiving a ticket will probably decrease or completely eliminate the behavior that caused you to get the ticket.

2. **The correct answer is (3): (Application)** The parking ticket will probably influence your decision not to park in handicapped spaces in the future.

3. **The correct answer is (1): (Application)** Keynes was an economist, as indicated by the title of his most famous book.

4. **The correct answer is (3): (Application)** Someone who studies the social effects of circumstances on a group is a sociologist.

5. **The correct answer is (1): (Comprehension)** The Tillamook group lived in the Northwest, where the tribes fished for salmon.

6. **The correct answer is (4): (Comprehension)** The passage shows that the native peoples in both areas of the country relied on locally available game and plants (such as fish and berries) for food and on geographic characteristics, such as forests, for their other needs.

7. **The correct answer is (3): (Analysis)** Store owners hope that your hunger will cause you to buy more food.

8. **The correct answer is (4): (Analysis)** The system of checks and balances, which prevents one group from gaining too much power, might not operate as well in Nebraska's one-house legislature as it does in two-house legislatures. There is no evidence that bills pass too quickly in Nebraska as suggested in choice (1). Government efficiency (5) might be improved with only one house, and voters might welcome fewer choices (2). In a state with a small population, fewer candidates (3) would be an advantage.

9. **The correct answer is (2): (Application)** Peter's temporary unemployment is seasonal. According to the passage, he always has a job during ski season, even when the economy is slow. He has difficulty finding employment only during the months when the ski slopes are not open.

10. **The correct answer is (3): (Application)** When companies change locations, their employees are subject to structural unemployment.

11. **The correct answer is (5): (Application)** As the map shows, the later times are in the east, and the time difference is three hours from east coast to west coast.

12. **The correct answer is (4): (Application)** A time zone covers all of one north-to-south area (a vertical strip on the map). Seattle and San Francisco both lie on the Pacific Ocean and therefore are in the same time zone.

13. **The correct answer is (3): (Comprehension)** According to the circle graph, the clergy costs $113 and the groom's clothing costs $77, which are both less than $192, the cost of the limousine.

14. **The correct answer is (2): (Application)** Since the reception is by far the greatest single expense, the greatest saving probably could be made there.

15. **The correct answer is (5): (Analysis)** If the wedding cost about $10,000 and the cost of the reception was just under $6,000, then a little more than half, or about 60 percent, of the total cost was for the reception.

16. **The correct answer is (2): (Analysis)** The cartoon shows huge resources being turned into tiny results.

17. **The correct answer is (4): (Evaluation)** Nothing in the cartoon supplies evidence for support of choices (2), (3), or (5). Choice (1) is completely denied by the image of the cartoon. Choice (4) is correct because the tiny image of the citizen in relation to the huge state apparatus can be seen as evidence of victimization of the people.

18. **The correct answer is (2): (Evaluation)** A growing belief in the essential equality of all people is the core factor that has led to an extension of voting rights.

19. **The correct answer is (3): (Application)** Martin Luther King Jr. was the great leader of the 1960s American civil rights movement. Choices (1), (4), and (5) are African-American leaders of the early 1900s, and choice (2) is a leader of today.

20. **The correct answer is (4): (Application)** The sentence is probably the most famous utterance of John F. Kennedy throughout his entire presidency. A clue to the correct answer is the part of the question that tells in what year the statement was made.

21. **The correct answer is (2): (Comprehension)** Point B is at about 80 degrees north latitude and 60 degrees west longitude.

22. **The correct answer is (3): (Application)** Places near the equator generally have warmer climates than places near either the North Pole or South Pole.

23. **The correct answer is (3): (Application)** A traveler would move in a south-easterly direction when going from point B to point E.

24. **The correct answer is (4): (Analysis)** The 1935 Banking Act created a group to regulate the money supply and interest rates, very much as the Federal Reserve Board does today.

25. **The correct answer is (1): (Analysis)** The nationwide spread of cheap electricity to rural areas probably would have held the most interest for an Oregon farmer, so choice (1) is correct. Choice (2) might have been involved in conservation projects nearby, but there is nothing to indicate an even national spread. Choices (3) and (4) would have had no more effect on a rural farmer than on any other person in the nation, and choice (5) was for a specific geographic region of which Oregon was not a part.

26. **The correct answer is (5): (Evaluation)** Since the programs of the 1930s created many jobs with the government and brought new services to citizens, the dependence on the government grew. Many efforts of government since the 1930s have also meant a larger role in peoples' lives for official agencies. Some people believe this growing role has led to a dependence that is not a positive factor of American life today.

27. **The correct answer is (1): (Evaluation)** The similarity of crime today because of illegal drug sales to the crime caused in the 1920s by illegal liquor sales could be cited as a possible reason to change drug laws by someone who favors such a decriminalization.

28. **The correct answer is (3): (Evaluation)** The passage provides enough information to predict that the population will decline, but not enough information to predict either choice (1) or choice (2). Nothing in the passage suggests that (4) is true, and while (5) may be true, there is no information in the passage to support it.

29. **The correct answer is (4): (Analysis)** The tremendous problems now facing Russia have caused many couples to wonder how well they could provide for a family in such circumstances. Therefore, some have decided against having children.

30. **The correct answer is (4): (Analysis)** Only choice (4) would not be related to the falling life expectancy. The cold climate has always been a factor in Russia and would not become more or less important now.

31. **The correct answer is (2): (Application)** George Washington was a general and commander-in-chief of the colonial armies in the American Revolution. The dates of his presidency are clues you can use to arrive at the correct answer (the Revolution was fought between 1775 and 1783). The French and Indian War was earlier in the 18th century (1754-1763), while the remaining three wars were fought in the 19th century.

32. **The correct answer is (3): (Application)** Abraham Lincoln issued the Emancipation Proclamation in 1865. Choices (1), (4), and (5) all include the names of other presidents, which should tell you that these choices are incorrect, even if the specific action or stance is not well known. The Louisiana Purchase (2), made by President Thomas Jefferson in 1803, more than doubled the size of the United States at that time.

33. **The correct answer is (3): (Analysis)** The growth of publicly funded education suggests that an education became a citizen's right regardless of status or ability to pay. The other choices are not incorrect, but choice (3) is the best answer.

34. **The correct answer is (5): (Application)** Plantations could not have existed without slavery. Democracy (1) and colonialism (2) were discussed in the text, but they were not associated with plantations. Land development (3) and a cash crop economy (4) were associated with the plantation system, but they were not caused by it, as slavery was.

35. **The correct answer is (1): (Analysis)** Lincoln's speech gives several clues to his view on the matter of preserving the Union. He makes no reference to abolishing slavery (3) or extending it (5), and choices (2) and (4) are contradicted by the speech.

36. **The correct answer is (2): (Analysis)** The information in Lesson 2 and in the passage indicates that white settlers wanted more land. This passage shows that the U.S. government pursued a policy of helping the settlers take the land from the native peoples. Manifest Destiny (1) was a feeling, not a policy. The government was interested in land, not Native American civilization (3), and Native American relocation (4) was an effect of the policy of expansion. Settlement west of the Mississippi (5) was not an issue in 1830.

37. **The correct answer is (5): (Comprehension)** The Cherokees viewed their forced migration (1) with great bitterness. There is no evidence in the passage that they actually wept (4) or planned to hurt people (3). Their level of civilization (2) was not related to their hardships.

38. **The correct answer is (4): (Analysis)** The passage strongly implies that different times caused confusion and standard time lessened the confusion. The fact that the entire country adopted Standard Railway Time indicates that the new standard time had improved efficiency.

39. **The correct answer is (3): (Comprehension)** The writer complained that railroad time controlled 55 million people—an example of the railroad's power.

40. **The correct answer is (4): (Comprehension)** The grid system of intersecting parallels and meridians allows the identification of specific locations. Choices (1) and (5) each identify a specific place. Choices (2) and (3) are not possible.

41. **The correct answer is (1): (Application)** The passage refers to the effect of large bodies of water on temperature. It suggests that such bodies of water have a moderating effect on temperatures. Therefore, places inland are likely to be colder in winter and warmer in summer than places near a coast.

42. **The correct answer is (3): (Analysis)** As a port, Valdez lies along an ocean, so choice (2) is incorrect. Choices (1) and (4) are incorrect because they explain only why Valdez might have more moderate temperatures than places inland. They do not explain why those temperatures are above freezing. Choice (5) is incorrect because prevailing winds can bring warm or cold temperatures to a place.

43. **The correct answer is (2): (Analysis)** Drivers rely on landmarks to find their way. The other activities require a knowledge of absolute location.

44. **The correct answer is (3): (Evaluation)** The graph shows that most of the world's water is salt water.

45. **The correct answer is (2): (Comprehension)** Any one branch of government is prevented from growing too powerful by the system of checks and balances.

46. **The correct answer is (3): (Application)** The bureaucracy, which is mostly responsible for creating policies and guidelines to implement new laws, is the target of this cartoon.

47. **The correct answer is (2): (Evaluation)** The devil-may-care attitude of the two government workers in the cartoon implies that they don't think the job they do is entirely worthwhile or necessary.

48. **The correct answer is (1): (Application)** Most people now believe that the government has some obligation to help citizens in need.

49. **The correct answer is (4): (Application)** Starting with George Washington, presidents have promoted policies that have shaped American policy and history.

50. **The correct answer is (2): (Analysis)** The ability to be flexible is vital to the role of the Supreme Court. Without this ability, the justices would not be able to play a positive role in a nation that has changed greatly since the Constitution was written more than two centuries ago.

51. **The correct answer is (4): (Analysis)** The Ninth and Tenth Amendments give powers not otherwise described to the people and to the states.

52. **The correct answer is (2): (Application)** The Third Amendment protects citizens from having to house and feed troops during peacetime.

53. **The correct answer is (4): (Comprehension)** The best way to describe "democracy" is with the phrase "rule by the people."

54. **The correct answer is (1): (Comprehension)** Although economic reasoning can help a person make money, the study of economics is not about how to do so.

55. **The correct answer is (3): (Application)** By choosing to attend college, Maria gives up the opportunity of earning $200 per week.

56. **The correct answer is (4): (Analysis)** Maria's decision involves a choice between the part-time job and college classes. Because she can't be in two places at once or pay her college costs, choosing one means giving up the other.

57. **The correct answer is (2): (Analysis)** While people may like lower prices (3) and convenience (4), a combination of these reasons is a better explanation.

58. **The correct answer is (4): (Analysis)** Home sales are up one month and down the next, meaning that there is no discernible trend in this market.

59. **The correct answer is (4): (Analysis)** With the exception of the month of June 1993, there is a decreasing trend over the four-month period.

60. **The correct answer is (1): (Evaluation)** Choice (1) does not constitute a cultural change, because men have always made more money than women who do the same work. Choices (2) to (5) describe cultural changes that have occurred in America recently.

61. **The correct answer is (3): (Application)** People who believe that we can prevent violent crimes by teaching young people our values and showing them that these values work are espousing enculturation.

62. **The correct answer is (5): (Analysis)** The physical environments in which many young people are raised probably have negative effects on their behavior.

63. **The correct answer is (2): (Evaluation)** By seeing violent behaviors modeled, or portrayed, rather consistently in the media, children may think of these behaviors as normal and may tend to imitate them.

64. **The correct answer is (4): (Analysis)** Ten years ago, few women held high executive positions in companies. Those who did usually did not have growing families. Our culture is moving toward increasing acceptance of career women who are mothers as well.

SCIENCE

1. **The correct answer is (2): (Application)** The skunk's bold white stripe is its warning coloration, signaling danger because of the foul odor skunks emit.

2. **The correct answer is (4): (Application)** The physical appearance of the orchid mantis resembles the petals of a flower. This similarity confuses its predators.

3. **The correct answer is (1): (Application)** The colors of the white snowshoe rabbit and the black bat match the background colors of their environment.

4. **The correct answer is (5): (Application)** The kelp crab collects materials from its surroundings and arranges them around its body to create a disguise.

5. **The correct answer is (3): (Application)** The irregular patches of green and brown on the soldiers' uniforms disrupt the visible shapes of the soldiers' bodies, making them difficult to see in the jungle.

6. **The correct answer is (3): (Comprehension)** The difference between sherry and liqueurs is 3 percent, which is the smallest difference between any two categories in the graph.

7. **The correct answer is (4): (Analysis)** Because the bar graph shows that hard liquor is 40 percent alcohol, you can conclude that it is 80 proof (2×40).

8. **The correct answer is (2): (Application)** Iron is an element. The symbol Fe is a clue.

9. **The correct answer is (4): (Application)** Carbon dioxide is a compound. The formula CO_2 contains symbols for two chemical elements—carbon (C) and oxygen (O). This is a clue that carbon dioxide is a chemical compound.

10. **The correct answer is (1): (Application)** Hot cocoa is a mixture. The substances could be separated back into their original forms. The cocoa settles out too quickly to be a colloid.

11. **The correct answer is (3): (Evaluation)** Choices (1), (2), (4), and (5) are all essential in evaluating a new drug. These choices are related to the possible effects of a drug administered to diseased mice. What the mice eat is not as important as observed reactions to the drug; in such an experiment, all the mice would be fed the same diet.

12. **The correct answer is (4): (Evaluation)** If all the mice were given the drug and then recovered from the disease, the scientist would not be able to prove that the drug was the reason for the cure. The possibility would exist that some mice might have recovered without any treatment.

13. **The correct answer is (3): (Analysis)** A general statement about the cruel treatment of animals cannot be proved or disproved based on data in the graph. The other choices are all factual statements of information in the graph.

14. **The correct answer is (5): (Evaluation)** The passage states that Benjamin Franklin predicted that electricity from a thundercloud would flow along the wet string to the key. The electrical spark that jumped from the key to his finger after the lightning flash supports this choice. Choices (1), (2), and (3) are untrue. Choice (4) is a true statement but is not supported by information in the passage.

15. **The correct answer is (2): (Application)** The word *flowing* in the question is a clue that electricity moves like a fluid—in this case, water. The other choices do not describe movement along a path.

16. **The correct answer is (2): (Comprehension)** The arrow pointing north on the map shows that warm air comes from the Gulf of Mexico. The other choices do not correctly indicate the source of this air.

17. **The correct answer is (3): (Analysis)** The two arrows on the map representing the collision of cold, dry air with warm, moist air are positioned in the middle section of the United States. This is where the necessary conditions exist for tornadoes. You can conclude that tornadoes are not likely to occur in the places stated in the other choices.

18. **The correct answer is (1): (Analysis)** Because air is required in order for sounds to be produced, you can conclude that the moon's silence is due to the absence of air. Although the other choices also accurately describe conditions on the moon, they do not explain why the moon is completely silent.

19. **The correct answer is (2): (Comprehension)** The main idea of the passage is Newton's Third Law of Motion, defined in choice (2). Choices (1) and (3) are too general to be the main idea. Choices (4) and (5) are supporting details and are too specific to be the main idea.

20. **The correct answer is (3): (Application)** The basketball exerts a force when it strikes the backboard. In turn, the backboard exerts a similar but opposite force when it pushes the basketball back. Although the other choices can be explained scientifically, they are not examples of Newton's Third Law of Motion.

21. **The correct answer is (2): (Analysis)** The purpose of a scientific investigation is often stated as a question. The passage states that Dr. Hamilton specialized in investigating the causes and effects of lead poisoning. Choice (1) states a solution to the problem of lead poisoning. Choices (3) and (4) are specific questions Dr. Hamilton probably asked during the course of her investigation. Choice (5) is related to factory owners' reaction to Dr. Hamilton's findings.

22. **The correct answer is (5): (Comprehension)** Choices (1), (2), (3), and (4) restate symptoms of lead poisoning listed in the passage. Difficulty in breathing is not a symptom.

23. **The correct answer is (1): (Evaluation)** Dr. Hamilton's research consisted of gathering data based on firsthand observation of lead industries, examination of hospital records, and interviews with doctors and druggists. Her conclusion was based on the information she collected. Choices (2) and (3) are inaccurate because she did not form a hypothesis and test it in scientific experiments. Choices (4) and (5) are approaches Dr. Hamilton used to publicize her conclusion about lead poisoning.

24. **The correct answer is (2): (Analysis)** An assumption is information that the author of a passage takes for granted is already known by the reader. Since polluted air contains dust and fumes, you can assume that workers in lead industries were exposed to indoor air pollution because they were breathing in lead dust and lead fumes. Although choices (1) and (3) are true, they are not supported by information in the passage. Choice (4) is inaccurate. Although you can assume that many workers in Illinois suffered from lead poisoning, choice (5) is not supported by information in the passage.

25. **The correct answer is (1): (Application)** When crops are rotated, planting is planned so that nutrients depleted by one year's crop are replaced in the soil by the plants raised the following year. This is the only choice that describes a method of restoring nutrients to the soil. The other choices describe methods that would cause the loss of nutrients in the soil and contribute to further soil erosion.

26. **The correct answer is (3): (Analysis)** The cause of a drought is stated in the passage. Choices (1), (4), and (5) are typical effects of drought. Choice (2) can worsen the effects of a drought.

27. **The correct answer is (5): (Application)** Previous knowledge about sand dunes should lead you to this answer. Strong winds blowing across a desert cause sand dunes to form, just as strong winds blowing across dry soil cause mounds of dirt to form. None of the other choices involves wind blowing a grainy material.

28. **The correct answer is (4): (Evaluation)** You have learned in the passage that the action of wind and water removes soil. Because vegetation holds the soil in place, soil erosion therefore occurs slowly over a long period. Choices (1), (2), and (5) state factual information about soil, but they do not explain why soil erosion is a slow, long-term process. Choice (3) is inaccurate.

29. **The correct answer is (1): (Comprehension)** The chart shows that the tundra receives 12 cm of rain per year, which is the lowest number listed on the chart.

30. **The correct answer is (5): (Analysis)** Many kinds of plants thrive in a warm, moist environment with a long growing season. Because the tropical rain forest receives the highest amount of rainfall, you can conclude that plants would more than likely grow best there. The word *tropical* also provides you with a clue that this biome has warm temperatures, which also contribute to the growth of many species of plants.

31. **The correct answer is (3): (Analysis)** Because there are 24 hours in a day, you can conclude that tides occur about every 12 hours (twice daily).

32. **The correct answer is (1): (Comprehension)** This choice restates the goal of the study—to investigate the relationship between emotions and heart disease. None of the other choices accurately states what the study was intended to accomplish.

33. **The correct answer is (2): (Analysis)** People with type O blood can donate blood to people with type A, B, or AB blood. However, the information does not state that people with type O blood can receive other types of blood. The other choices logically follow from the information given.

34. **The correct answer is (4): (Analysis)** Because the goal of the virus is to take over the cell, its primary target would be the cell's activity center—the nucleus.

35. **The correct answer is (1): (Analysis)** The key words here are *produce copies*. Chromosomes contain the instructions a cell uses to make copies of itself; a virus must have something similar in order to make its own copies.

36. **The correct answer is (3): (Application)** The brain is the only example of an organ listed among the choices. Choice (1) refers to part of an organ (the eye). Choice (2) refers to a plant cell organelle. Choice (4) refers to a protein outgrowth from the skin. Choice (5) refers to the sperm cell of a flowering plant.

37. **The correct answer is (2): (Analysis)** You have learned that the union of male and female sex cells results in fertilization. Careful analysis should lead you to rule out the other choices because none describes the cause-and-effect relationship presented in the question.

38. **The correct answer is (1): (Evaluation)** This conclusion is supported by the fact that alcohol passing through the placenta is toxic to the fetus. The scientists' findings do not support the other choices.

39. **The correct answer is (2): (Evaluation)** Although all the choices present factual information, only choice (2) offers evidence that sickle-cell anemia is common among African Americans.

40. **The correct answer is (1): (Comprehension)** This choice is suggested by Dr. Matsui's hypothesis as stated in the passage. The other choices do not precisely state the focus of his scientific investigations.

41. **The correct answer is (4): (Analysis)** The word *mutations*, mentioned in the final sentence of the passage, is a clue that mutation was the trigger for the evolutionary change in the black crucian carp. Although the other choices are triggers of evolutionary change according to Darwin, none of them correctly explains the incident of the red crucian carp.

42. **The correct answer is (4): (Comprehension)** By correctly reading the vertical and horizontal scales on the bar graph, you can figure out that from 1850 to 1900 the number of known extinct species increased from about 15 to about 35. This is the sharpest increase among the choices.

43. **The correct answer is (4): (Analysis)** Opinions are beliefs that can be neither proved nor disproved. The words *agreed* and *viewpoint* in the question are clues that the participants' response can best be classified as an opinion.

44. **The correct answer is (2): (Application)** The pilot fish and the sharks have a one-sided relationship. The pilot fish benefit, whereas the sharks are neither helped nor harmed.

45. **The correct answer is (1): (Application)** The acacia trees and the ants are engaged in a two-sided relationship in which each organism benefits.

46. **The correct answer is (4): (Application)** The Eskimos play the role of predators, killing the bowhead whales because these animals provide an immediate source of food.

47. **The correct answer is (3): (Application)** Tapeworms are parasites that benefit from their presence in the human host. This relationship, however, harms the human.

48. **The correct answer is (5): (Application)** The carrion beatles clean the bones by feeding on the dead remains left on the bones.

49. **The correct answer is (2): (Comprehension)** The title of the illustration is the main clue that should lead you to choice (2). The labels "Inhaling," "Exhaling," "Diaphragm contracts," and "Diaphragm relaxes" should also be helpful. Choices (1), (3), and (4) describe structures in the illustration, rather than the process. Choice (5) presents an inaccurate interpretation of the illustration.

50. **The correct answer is (3): (Application)** The diaphragm relaxes when a person exhales. When a person blows a horn, he or she is exhaling air. Choice (1) involves holding one's breath, whereas choices (2) and (5) involve inhaling. Hiccupping, choice (4), is caused by muscle spasms in the diaphragm.

51. **The correct answer is (5): (Application)** As the cake rises, all the raisins move away from each other, just as all the galaxies are moving away from earth and from each other. Choice (1) is incorrect because all the bubbles are going in one direction. Choice (2) is incorrect because the planets and comets are not moving away from the sun. Choice (3) is incorrect because a tire has a boundary; at some point it can no longer expand. Choice (4) is incorrect because a whirlpool is a circular movement.

52. **The correct answer is (1): (Analysis)** A young river cuts downward, deepening its valley, rather than sideways, as shown by the lack of a floodplain. Choices (2) and (4) are characteristic of both mature and old river valleys. Choice (3) is incorrect because the shape of the young river valley, with its steep slopes, is not suitable for much urban development. Choice (5) is characteristic of an old river valley.

53. **The correct answer is (2): (Analysis)** Because levees near the cities would prevent the river from overflowing, much more water than normal would continue to flow downstream, where it would be more likely to cause flooding. Choice (1) is partially correct, but the river would be more, not less, prone to flooding. Choices (3), (4), and (5) are all incorrect because downstream the river would rise more than normal.

54. **The correct answer is (4): (Evaluation)** Dissolution of limestone by acid is a chemical action because it changes the limestone into other substances. All the other choices are examples of physical weathering because the rock is broken but not otherwise changed.

55. **The correct answer is (3): (Comprehension)** The second and third sections of the diagram both show lagoons as shallow bodies of water near or connected with the deeper ocean beyond the reef.

56. **The correct answer is (5): (Analysis)** The key word here is *shallow*. Formation of a coral reef requires bright sunlight in shallow water. Thus, at some time in the past, an atoll must have had land upon which to build—an island surrounded by shallow water. The other choices, although true, do not provide an explanation for the hypothesis.

57. **The correct answer is (3): (Evaluation)** The sequence shown in the diagram indicates that atolls were once barrier reefs. Choices (1), (4), and (5) are untrue. Choice (2) may or may not be true, but you cannot tell from the information provided.

58. **The correct answer is (2): (Application)** Melting of ice, a change of state, is a physical change. All of the other choices describe chemical reactions.

59. **The correct answer is (3): (Evaluation)** By comparing the chemical content of the substance before and after the experiment, the scientist could determine whether the change was physical or chemical.

60. **The correct answer is (2): (Analysis)** Substance A is a solute, or dissolved substance. The other choices all have to do with solutions, but none of them is consistent with the fact that substance A dissolved and spread evenly throughout substance B.

61. **The correct answer is (4): (Application)** The + and − signs in H_3O+ and F− indicate that they are charged particles, or ions. None of the other choices describes charged particles.

62. **The correct answer is (4): (Analysis)** The atomic number represents the weight of an element. Hydrogen's atomic number shows it to be lighter than both oxygen and nitrogen. All of the other elements in the chart are too heavy.

63. **The correct answer is (3): (Analysis)** The fact that the iron filings are most dense around the poles suggests that the magnetic field is strongest around the poles. The other statements provide accurate information about magnetism, but they do not explain the diagram.

64. **The correct answer is (5): (Comprehension)** Most of the iron filings will be attracted to the ends of the magnet. None of the other statements is true.

65. **The correct answer is (2): (Analysis)** The addition of electrons gives the rubber a negative electrical charge. If choice (1) were true, the rubber would become positively charged. None of the other choices describes a transfer of electrons.

66. **The correct answer is (1): (Analysis)** Insulation can prevent electricity from taking unwanted paths. Choices (2), (3), and (5) are all untrue. Choice (4) is true, but it does not explain why insulation can prevent a short circuit.

INTERPRETING LITERATURE AND THE ARTS

What Is the Poet's Advice? *(page 41)*

1. **The correct answer is (3): (Literal comprehension)** The poet mentions dark nights (line 3), dark clouds (lines 4-5), thick clouds (line 4), and weary days (line 10). The poet does not refer to rough waters.

2. **The correct answer is (2): (Inferential comprehension)** The poet is saying that hard times are always followed by happier moments: "The soul that faints not in the storm,/emerges bright and clear" (lines 14-15). Her tone is hopeful. Choices (1), (4), and (5) are incorrect because they are negative. Though the poet is optimistic, her description of sadness and pain shows that she is not carefree, as choice (3) suggests.

3. **The correct answer is (4): (Application)** The poet indicates that even during hard times, it is important to remember that brighter days will follow. Therefore, if a friend passed away, she would probably try to be brave and believe that things would get better. Choice (1) does not suggest the poet's optimism and hope. Choice (2) can be eliminated since the poet does seem to recognize and respond to sadness. The images of clouds in this poem are figurative, so choice (3) is incorrect. Though choice (5) is possible, it does not refer to the poet's personal philosophy.

What Are Possible Consequences of the Germans' Advance? *(page 41)*

4. **The correct answer is (3): (Literal comprehension)** The last event that occurs is the arrival of German troops in Sighet (lines 29-30). Choices (1), (2), (4), and (5) precede this event.

5. **The correct answer is (4): (Inferential comprehension)** Throughout the passage, the speaker describes anxiety over the thought that the German army may arrive. In lines 35-36, the fear and worry become reality. There is no evidence that more army cars are coming, as choice (1) suggests, or that they will stay only a brief time, as choice (2) suggests. The townspeople are afraid of what the Germans may do, so choices (3) and (5) are unlikely.

6. **The correct answer is (5): (Inferential comprehension)** Berkovitz's report in lines 21–28 causes anxiety among the townspeople. Choices (1), (2), (3), and (4) are all positive events or normal events that would not cause fear.

7. **The correct answer is (5): (Analysis)** The warm weather, weddings, and news of the Russian army's success (lines 1–7) are contrasted with the frightening rumors about the Germans' advance (lines 13–17). The events in choices (1) and (4) are not contrasted, but are paired together as evidence of positive events and negative events, respectively. The Russians' behavior is not described, so choice (2) is incorrect. Choice (3) can be eliminated because the "wildfire" in line 29 refers figuratively to the spread of the rumors.

What Kind of Album Has Donald Brown Made?
(page 42)

8. **The correct answer is (4): (Literal comprehension)** Brown's album is "musically moving" (line 19). The text of four tracks is "bolstered by complementary instrumental statements" (lines 16–17); the album is not entirely instrumental, so choice (1) can be eliminated. Only "Theme For Mandela" is described as "old-fashioned . . . funk" (lines 6–7), so choices (2) and (5) can be eliminated. There is no evidence to support choice (3).

9. **The correct answer is (3): (Inferential comprehension)** The reviewer describes the album as "provocative" and its theme as expressing "various aspects of the black life experience" (lines 4–5). Only the song "I Should Care" is "standard," so choice (1) is incorrect. The reviewer does not state that "I Should Care" has been recorded too often, so choice (2) is incorrect. The term "provocative" means the album might inspire discussion and interest, but not necessarily controversy, so choice (4) can be eliminated. The reviewer states the album's theme, so choice (5) is incorrect.

10. **The correct answer is (2): (Application)** Like an album that describes one group of people's experiences, a sculpture depicting Native American culture would depict experiences common to a certain group. Choices (1), (3), (4), and (5) can be eliminated since they describe experiences particular to one or two people only.

11. **The correct answer is (4): (Analysis)** The reviewer supports his positive comments about the album by offering specific descriptions of the sounds and lyrics of songs on the album. There are no hints on how to compose music, and the reviewer does not directly suggest the reader should buy Brown's album, so choices (1) and (2) can be eliminated. The reviewer refers to Stephens and Tobin, but this is just one of the reviewer's supporting details, so choice (3) can be eliminated. There is no evidence to support choice (5).

What Does the Speaker See? *(page 43)*

12. **The correct answer is (4): (Literal comprehension)** The speaker states, "Once you open your eyes in the water, you become a flying creature" (lines 2–3). She does not mention "flying fish." She refers to "zebra fish" (line 4), "rainbow fish" (line 5), "sharks" (line 16), and "sea cucumbers" (line 14), so choices (1), (2), (3), and (5) are incorrect.

13. **The correct answer is (5): (Literal comprehension)** Seeing the color and movement of the swimming fish shows the speaker how different a live fish is from one that is dead—and how much more beautiful. The speaker is contrasting live and dead fish, so choices (1) and (3) are incorrect. Observing fish while diving isn't fishing, so choice (2) is incorrect. There are other ways besides diving to observe live fish, so choice (4) is incorrect.

14. **The correct answer is (4): (Inferential comprehension)** The speaker describes a different world underwater of "cold spots, deserts, darkness under clouds . . . and golden chambers" (lines 10–12) and "summer forests and winter forests" (line 13). She does not mention becoming a professional diver or enjoying birdwatching, so choices (1) and (2) can be eliminated. There is no evidence that the speaker has gone diving before, so choice (3) is incorrect. The speaker mentions being "unafraid," so choice (5) is incorrect.

15. **The correct answer is (3): (Analysis)** Sequins are sparkly objects, so comparing the fish's scales to sequins means that the fish look bright and sparkling underwater. The fish are "silver-white" (lines 8–9), so choice (1) is incorrect. The primary characteristic of sequins is their sparkle, so the speaker is not describing her love of colorful objects, sunlight, or pale colors as choices (2), (4), and (5) suggest.

16. **The correct answer is (4): (Application)** The speaker journeys underwater and then returns to land, much like an astronaut flying into space and then returning to Earth. Choices (1), (2), (3), and (5) are not correct because they do not contrast two dramatically different places and experiences.

What Is the Speaker's Dream? *(page 44)*

17. **The correct answer is (4): (Literal comprehension)** The main dream event, stated in lines 3–4, is that the world put an end to war. Choices (1), (2), (3), and (5) can be eliminated because they are only details of the main event.

18. **The correct answer is (2): (Inferential comprehension)** In lines 9–17, the speaker describes people celebrating and praying, so the reader can conclude that ending war is a positive event that the speaker would like to see. Since the speaker wants war to cease, choice (1) is unlikely. The speaker makes references to praying, so choice (3) is not supported. There is no evidence to support choices (4) and (5).

19. **The correct answer is (4): (Inferential comprehension)** The speaker describes his dream as "strange," and says he has never dreamed this before, so the concept of a world without war is probably unfamiliar to the speaker. The speaker does not state whether he believes this dream could come true or not, so choices (1), (2), and (5) can be eliminated. Choice (3) is incorrect because the speaker does not comment on other people's dreams.

Why Is Becky Surprised? *(page 44)*

20. **The correct answer is (3): (Inferential comprehension)** Warder's questioning whether he can trust Becky's word of honor if she breaks it (lines 10–12) suggests that he relies on a person's word of honor. There is no evidence for choices (1) and (2). Although Warder may not believe Becky, there is no evidence that he doesn't believe what people say in general, so choice (4) can be eliminated. Choice (5) is supported by lines 25–29, but not by lines 10–12.

21. **The correct answer is (4): (Literal comprehension)** Throughout the passage, Warder asks Becky questions about her actions. In lines 30–33, Warder has divulged that he knows Becky is lying to him. Choice (1) states the opposite. The passage does not end with an apology from Warder, so choice (2) is incorrect. The fact that Warder has hired detectives worries Becky (line 37), so choice (3) is incorrect. Becky denies seeing Lindon, so choice (5) can be eliminated.

22. **The correct answer is (3): (Analysis)** The stage directions first show Becky comfortably hugging Warder (lines 2–3) and then describe her as "worried" (line 28). They help reveal that she is lying, so choice (1) is incorrect. Becky says that she loves Warder but, since the stage directions do not reveal this, choice (2) can be eliminated. The stage directions refer to the furniture, but do not describe it, as choice (4) suggests. Choice (5) is incorrect since Warder's emotions are not made clear.

23. **The correct answer is (1): (Application)** In lines 10-12, Warder asks, ". . . if I find your word of honor is broken in one thing, how can I ever trust it in another?" so, after discovering that Becky is lying, he probably would assume she is lying again. Choice (2) states the opposite. He would be angry, so choices (3) and (4) are incorrect. Choice (5) is a possibility, but Warder might leave Becky after this first lie. Also, choice (1) applies more directly to his statement in lines 7-8.

What Is This Speaker Saying to Death? *(page 45)*

24. **The correct answer is (4): (Inferential comprehension)** In line 1, the speaker states, "Death, be not proud . . ." The rest of the poem describes why Death can be conquered and is not as mighty as many believe. Choices (1), (3), and (5) contradict this message. Though the speaker might agree with choice (2), this is not the point of his message to Death.

25. **The correct answer is (3): (Analysis)** Describing Death as a "slave to fate" (line 12) and a friend of poison and sickness creates a weak and unattractive image of Death. Choices (1) and (2) can be eliminated because they are positive characterizations. Since the speaker's tone is sincere, he does not exaggerate or distort his description of Death; thus, choice (4) is incorrect. Choice (5) can be eliminated, for while Donne is not afraid, he does believe that Death is real.

26. **The correct answer is (2): (Literal comprehension)** The speaker describes entering a place where Death cannot reach people any longer; only an afterlife could be described in that way. Of the other choices, only choice (5) comes close to that meaning; it can be eliminated, however, because the expression is meant literally rather than figuratively.

27. **The correct answer is (3): (Analysis)** This description, of people going somewhere with Death, creates an image of Death as a guide who leads people away. Choice (1) can be eliminated because the people do not seem to be running from Death. Choices (2), (4), and (5) are incorrect because there is no reference to teaching, the sea, or being saved in this personification.

28. **The correct answer is (5): (Application)** The message of this poem—that one need not fear Death—probably would be most appreciated by someone who is facing death. Choices (3) and (4) can be eliminated because they refer to people who could generally be described as looking to a bright future, in a time of new beginnings. The people named in choices (1) and (2) might have more reason to appreciate Donne's message, but that message would be more immediate to a person with a deadly illness.

What Problem Is the Airline Industry Facing? *(page 46)*

29. **The correct answer is (2): (Literal comprehension)** The author says that, unless you are a bird, flying requires a "leap of faith"—people must simply have faith in the plane and the pilot. The speaker is not referring literally to the motion of a plane taking off, so choice (1) is incorrect. Choices (3) and (5) are not relevant to this figurative expression, and choice (4) is not true.

30. **The correct answer is (5): (Inferential comprehension)** The article discusses the possibility that electronic gadgets such as CDs, video games, and computers can cause problems on a plane. Choices (1), (2), and (4) are incorrect because the author does not address strong winds, fear of flying, or advances in electronics. The author mentions one plane that nearly crashed, so choice (3) is inaccurate.

31. **The correct answer is (1): (Literal comprehension)** Line 12 states the possibility that jets may be "diverted from their flight paths" by the radiation from small electronic devices. Choices (2), (3), and (4) can be eliminated because the author does not address the noise made by electronic gadgets or any flight delays that such noise causes. Choice (5) can be assumed as a supporting detail, but it is not the main focus of the passage.

32. **The correct answer is (3): (Analysis)** A tidal wave of concern would be strong and widespread, much like the force and size of a real tidal wave. The other choices all downplay the strength of concern that this figurative expression suggests.

33. **The correct answer is (5): (Application)** Of these choices, only a train at full speed nearly resembles the strength of an airplane hurtling through the air.

34. **The correct answer is (2): (Application)** The passage suggests that all small electronic devices emit radiation. Of the choices provided, only a hand-held TV would be both small and electronic.

How Is This Woman Spending Her Life? *(page 47)*

35. **The correct answer is (1): (Literal comprehension)** In line 8, Christie is described as "grateful" and "cheerful." Choice (2) implies a negative mood. Choices (3) and (4) are incorrect since she describes herself as already feeling useful (line 3). Though Christie shows sympathy to other working women, this trait does not describe her general mood in this passage, so choice (5) is incorrect.

36. **The correct answer is (3): (Inferential comprehension)** Since Christie "set out to seek [her] fortune" (lines 1-2) and "found it" (line 2), considers herself "useful" (line 3), and went to a meeting for working women, she is most likely a worker too, though happier than many. Christie may be wealthy and happily married, but there is not enough information in these lines to draw these conclusions; thus, choices (1), (2), and (5) can be eliminated. There is no evidence for choice (4).

37. **The correct answer is (2): (Inferential comprehension)** Christie's sadness results from looking at a "faded cap and sheathed sword" (lines 17-18), which probably belonged to a loved one who died. Choices (1) and (5) are incorrect, respectively, because there is no mention of a first marriage, and she is not thinking of the workers. Although Christie has suffered losses and is now forty years old, she is at peace with both facts and states that she has found her fortune; thus, choices (3) and (4) can be eliminated.

38. **The correct answer is (4): (Literal comprehension)** The theme of middle age as a turning point is described in lines 8-15. Choice (1) is contradicted in line 13; choice (5) is too narrow a statement to be called a theme. The passage mentions only certain workers not all workers as choice (3) suggests. There is no reference to Christie's hard work on behalf of her family, so choice (2) is incorrect.

39. **The correct answer is (5): (Inferential comprehension)** There is no foreshadowing of a bad turn of events in Christie's life, so choices (1), (3), and (4) are unlikely. Choice (2) is possible, but choice (5) is even more likely.

40. **The correct answer is (4): (Inferential comprehension)** The phrase "half-way house" figuratively suggests a stopping point, or resting spot. Since the statement is figurative, choice (1) can be eliminated. Choices (2) and (3) are incorrect because Christie is content with her age and her life. There is no evidence to support choice (5).

What Makes This Architect's Work Special? *(page 48)*

41. **The correct answer is (4): (Literal comprehension)** In lines 23-25, Dieste states that "architecture has in common with other arts the ability to help us contemplate the universe." Dieste considers architecture both an art and something spiritual; thus, choices (1) and (3) can be eliminated. Although Dieste might agree with choices (2) and (5), the ideas in those choices are not related to this quotation.

42. The correct answer is (1): (Literal comprehension) In lines 8-9, the reviewer states that Dieste's buildings "are at once inexpensive and of high aesthetic quality." Though choices (2) and (4) are true, they are not the main reason the reviewer admires Dieste. Choice (3) is incorrect because Dieste avoids "costly steel" (line 9). There is no mention of windows, so choice (5) can be eliminated.

43. The correct answer is (4): (Analysis) The correct response is reinforced by the author's frequent reminders of the spiritual quality of Dieste's buildings. Dieste's buildings are "sturdy" (line 15), so choice (1) is incorrect. There is no mention of nature or openness, as choices (2) and (3) suggest. Dieste's buildings are "inexpensive" (line 8), so choice (5) is incorrect.

44. The correct answer is (3): (Application) Since Dieste favors inexpensive materials, he would probably use copper, the least expensive of the choices.

45. The correct answer is (2): (Analysis) The reviewer contrasts the "multimillion-dollar price tags" of most architects with Dieste's work. Choices (1) and (3) are incorrect because Dieste's work is modern and low in cost, not free. The reviewer does not discuss home insurance or prices decades ago, so choices (4) and (5) can be eliminated.

MATHEMATICS

1. The correct answer is (4): $20

2. The correct answer is (4): $20,000

3. The correct answer is (5): 12 − 4.3 − 2(3.8) From 12, subtract 4.3 grams for the cereal and 3.8 grams for each of the two milkshakes.

4. The correct answer is (2): 49

5. The correct answer is (3): 51 Arrange the scores from smallest to largest.

49
50
51   Middle Value
52
53

6. The correct answer is (1): 225 − (48 + 50 + 52 + 40) Add her scores, and subtract the total from 225.

7. The correct answer is (2): $1.69 Divide the value of the coupon by 2, and subtract that amount from the price of each bottle.

8. The correct answer is (3): $5.92

Multiply: $2.69
             × 2.2
            ─────
             538
            538
            ─────
           $5.918

Round $5.918 to the nearest penny, or estimate 2($3) = $6.

9. The correct answer is (5): Not enough information is given. The ad does not say how many ounces are in the jar.

10. The correct answer is (4): 1982, 1986, and 1988 Read the graph carefully. The scale is marked in increments of 0.5 percent. Look for any decrease on the graph for a one-year period that is equal to or greater than one increment, or 0.5 percent.

11. The correct answer is (4): 105 − (−48) Let 105 represent 105° above zero, and let −48 represent 48° below zero. Then subtract −48 from 105 to find the difference.

12. The correct answer is (4): Between 10 and 11 months Multiply the number of packs by the number of ribbons in each pack. Then divide the total number of ribbons by 8 per month.

$84 \div 8 = 10.5$

13. The correct answer is (2): 141 The graph shows the number of calories burned per 15 minutes.

14. The correct answer is (4): 396

Use a proportion.

1 hour = 60 minutes

$$\frac{calories}{minutes} \quad \frac{99}{15} = \frac{x}{60} \quad \frac{calories}{minutes}$$

$$\frac{60(99)}{15} = 396$$

15. The correct answer is (2): 1:30 p.m. Use the formula $d = rt$; where d = distance, r = rate, and t = time. Divide 275 miles (the distance) by 55 (the rate) to find the number of hours (5). Add 5 hours to 8:30 a.m. Eric will arrive at 1:30 p.m.

16. The correct answer is (2): 3.14(5)^2(20) Substitute the values for π, radius, and height into the formula.

17. The correct answer is (3): 1,080   3(18)(20)

18. The correct answer is (2): $10.50 Divide her total earned by the number of hours she worked.

19. The correct answer is (3): $333.05

Add the deductions; then subtract from $420.

    $37.80
     21.00
     18.90 $420.00
   + 9.25   −86.95
    ──────   ───────
    $86.95 $333.05

20. The correct answer is (1): 5%

Use a proportion.

$$\frac{\%}{100} \quad \frac{x}{100} = \frac{\$21}{\$420} \quad \frac{state\ tax}{earnings}$$

$$\frac{100(\$21)}{\$420} = 5\%$$

21. The correct answer is (4): $16.50

Multiply 1½ or 1.5 times $11.

$$1\frac{1}{2} \times \$11 = 3 \times \$11 = \frac{\$33}{2} = \$16.50$$

    $ 11
    ×1.5
    ────
     55
     11
    ────
   $16.50

22. The correct answer is (5): ½ $\frac{35}{70} = \frac{1}{2}$

23. The correct answer is (4): $280

Use a proportion.

$$\frac{\%}{100} \quad \frac{25}{100} = \frac{\$70}{x} \quad \frac{food\ this\ week}{food\ budget} \quad \frac{100(\$70)}{25} = \$280$$

24. The correct answer is (4): 1,125 Find the number of defective necklaces, then find the number repaired.

5,000 × ³⁄₁₀ = 1,500
1,500 × ¾ = 1,125

25. **The correct answer is (1): 5** Subtract 10 from 15.

26. **The correct answer is (3): The height of the walls** To determine the area of the walls, he needs to know their length and width. The diagram shows only the width of each wall.

27. **The correct answer is (3):** $x + (2x + 10) = 262$ Let x = the number of medals won by China. Let $2x + 10$ equal the number won by the United States. The sum is equal to 262.

28. **The correct answer is (2): Between 10 and 11** Use the formula for finding the distance between two points in a plane.

$$d = \sqrt{(x_2 - x_1)^2 + (y_2 - y_1)^2}$$
$$d = \sqrt{(-3 - 6)^2 + (-4 - 2)^2}$$
$$d = \sqrt{(-9)^2 + (-6)^2}$$
$$d = \sqrt{81 + 36}$$
$$d = \sqrt{117}$$
$$d = 10.82$$

To find the square root of 117, estimate using the numbers in the problem. You know the square of 10 is 100 and the square of 11 is 121, so the correct answer must be choice (2).

29. **The correct answer is (5): Not enough information is given.** You need to know the total number of homes in the area.

30. **The correct answer is (4): 1,104** First find ⅓ of 828 to find out the number of employees that will be hired. Then add that number (276) to 828 to find the total number of employees after the hiring.

31. **The correct answer is (5): $240,000**

Set up a proportion, and solve.

$$\frac{8}{100} = \frac{\$19,200}{x}$$
$$\frac{100(\$19,200)}{8} = \$240,000$$

32. **The correct answer is (4): 42** Multiply 3½ (the number of cartons from the graph) by 12 (the number of reams in each carton).

33. **The correct answer is (3): 11¼** Multiply 1¾ by 5; then add 2½. You may want to use decimals to calculate the answer.

34. **The correct answer is (5): $316.80** Find Kesha's new hourly wage.
10% of $7.20 is $0.72. Her new hourly wage is $7.92.
Multiply the new wage by 40 hours. $7.92(40) = $316.80

35. **The correct answer is (5): Medical assistants** You can calculate the percent of change for each job among the choices. You can also set up ratios for the jobs in the list and compare them. Use rounding to make the work easier. Another way to think about the problem is to ask yourself, "Which job comes closest to doubling its numbers by the year 2005?" Only the number of new jobs for medical assistants comes close to approaching the number of jobs in 1990. The medical assistant profession shows the greatest percent of change.

36. **The correct answer is (3): 7 minutes** Add the time of the calls, and divide by 8. Round the result to the nearest whole minute.

37. **The correct answer is (2): 6.5 minutes** Because the list has an even number of times, you must find the two middle times and average them. After arranging the times in order, you find that 5 minutes and 8 minutes are the middle times.
Add: $5 + 8 = 13$.
Then **divide** by 2: $\frac{13}{2} = 6.5$ minutes.

38. **The correct answer is (4): ⅗** There are 18 chances out of 30 that the marble will not be black. The fraction $\frac{18}{30}$ is equal to ⅗.

39. **The correct answer is (5): 8(4) − 6(5)** To find the area of a rectangle, multiply the length by the width. To find the difference in square feet of the floors of the storage units, subtract the smaller area from the larger.

40. **The correct answer is (3): 404** Use the formula. $V = lwh$
Find the volume of each storage unit and add.
$6(5)(6) + 8(4)(7) = 404$ cubic feet

41. **The correct answer is (3): 10** Write an equation. Let x = the number of computers set up by Rick. Let $2x$ = the number set up by Bob.
$$2x + x = 15$$
$$x + 3x = 15$$
$$x = 5$$
Remember, the problem asks for the number set up by Bob.
If $x = 5$, then $2x = 10$.

42. **The correct answer is (5)** $0.65n ≤ $15 The number of glue sticks multiplied by $0.65 must be less than or equal to $15.

43. **The correct answer is (3): 4** Set up a proportion and solve.
$$\frac{2 \text{ women}}{5 \text{ players}} = \frac{x \text{ women}}{10 \text{ players}}$$
$$20 = 5x$$
$$4 = x$$

44. **The correct answer is (3): −2**
$8 + (-12) + 5 + (-3)$

45. **The correct answer is (3): A and C** Replace the variable x with the value 2 in each inequality to evaluate each statement.

46. **The correct answer is (2):** 6.3×10^5 is equal to 630,000 To expand the notation, move the decimal point 5 places to the right, adding zeros as needed.
6.30000

47. **The correct answer is (1): $27.00** Write an equation.
x = value of the second card
$3x$ = value of the first card
$\frac{1}{2}x$ or $0.5x$ = value of the third card
$$x + 3x + 0.5x = \$40.50$$
$$4.5x = \$40.50$$
$$x = \$9$$
The value of the first card is $3x$, or $27.

48. **The correct answer is (2):** $4n^2 - 4n - 3$ Combine like terms.
$$3n^2 + n^2 = 4n^2$$
$$2n - 6n = -4n$$
$$5 - 8 = -3$$

49. **The correct answer is (4): 120°** Angles 2 and 6 are corresponding angles so $\angle 6$ must measure 60° as well. Angle 8 is a supplementary angle to $\angle 6$, which means that the sum of angles 6 and 8 must equal 180°.

Subtract to find the measure of $\angle 8$. $180 - 60 = 120$

50. **The correct answer is (5): $\angle 1$ and $\angle 7$** Angles 1, 4, 5, and 8 are congruent. Angles 2, 3, 6, and 7 are congruent. Only choice (5) pairs two angles that are not equal.

51. **The correct answer is (2): 352** Use the formula:

$V = \pi r^2 h$; where $\pi = 3.14$, r = radius, and h = height. Remember that the radius is ½ of the diameter.

$V = \pi r^2 h$

$V = 3.14(4)^2(7)$

$V = 3.14(16)(7)$

$V = 351.68$ cu ft

52. **The correct answer is (3): 14** You can use the formula for finding distance between two points.

$d = \sqrt{(x_2 - x_1)^2 + (y_2 - y_1)^2}$

$d = \sqrt{(4 - (-5))^2 + (5 - (-6))^2}$

$d = \sqrt{(9)^2 + (11)^2}$

$d = \sqrt{81 + 121}$

$d = \sqrt{202}$

$14^2 = 196$

$15^2 = 225$

The square root of 202 is between 14 and 15. Since 202 is closer to 196 than to 225, you know the distance is closer to 14 units.

53. **The correct answer is (4): (1, −1)** Find the coordinates listed in the answer choices on the graph. All lie on line R but the coordinates in choice (4).

54. **The correct answer is (3): $\dfrac{11}{9}$** Use the formula for finding the slope of a line. Choose two points on the line; you can use the coordinates for S and T: $(-5, -6)$ and $(4, 5)$.

55. **The correct answer is (1): 50°** The sum of the angles of a triangle equals 180°. Find the sum of the given angles.

$65 + 65 = 130$

Subtract to find the missing angle. $180 - 130 = 50$

56. **The correct answer is (1): $\sqrt{12^2 + 6^2}$** Use the formula for the Pythagorean relationship:

$c^2 = a^2 + b^2$

$c^2 = 12^2 + 6^2$

$c = \sqrt{12^2 + 6^2}$

Part 1
WRITING SKILLS

RED ALERT

The GED Writing Skills Test is Test One of the GED Tests. It measures your knowledge of written English and your ability to write. The GED Writing Skills Test is an opportunity for you to demonstrate how well you read and that you can think logically and express yourself clearly. It is *not* a measure of how many grammar rules you know.

PART I

Part I of the GED Writing Skills Test measures your ability to use the conventions of standard written English. These conventions include sentence structure, usage, and mechanics.

All items in Part I are multiple-choice questions. Each question has five answer choices. You are first asked to read a paragraph or two. Then, you respond to a series of questions that focus on certain sentences within those paragraphs.

Three types of multiple-choice questions appear on the test: sentence correction questions (50 percent of all items), sentence revision questions (35 percent), and construction shift questions (15 percent).

SENTENCE CORRECTION QUESTIONS

These questions ask you to find what is wrong with a sentence and to determine how it can be corrected. Here is a sample:

1. Sentence 2: **Dorothy and her assistant evaluates 20 applications every day.**

   What correction should be made to this sentence?
   - **(1)** insert a comma after Dorothy
   - **(2)** insert a comma after assistant
   - **(3)** change the spelling of assistant to assistent
   - **(4)** change evaluates to evaluate
   - **(5)** no correction is necessary

To find the correct answer to this sample, you need to know something about commas, spelling, and verbs because those are the kinds of changes covered by the choices. If you know when and why to use commas, you will know that choices (1) and (2) are not correct. Choice (3) has a misspelled word. Looking back at the sample sentence, you can see that the verb doesn't agree in number with the subject. Choice (4), therefore, is the correct answer. The plural verb *evaluate* agrees with the plural subject *Dorothy and her assistant.*

Note: *If you are offered an answer choice that says* no correction is necessary, *do not assume that it is the correct choice. Occasionally it will be, but not always. You must consider all answer choices as possibilities.*

SENTENCE REVISION QUESTIONS

These questions have a specific portion of a sentence underlined. Your task is to choose the answer that best improves the underlined portion:

2. Sentence 4: **After they attended the technology workshop the accounting clerks felt more confident about using computers.**

   Which of the following is the best way to write the underlined portion of the sentence? If you think the original is the best way, choose option (1).
   - **(1)** workshop the accounting clerks felt
   - **(2)** workshop, the accounting clerks felt

- **(3)** workshop the Accounting Clerks felt
- **(4)** workshop the accounting clerks will feel
- **(5)** workshop. The accounting clerks felt

To find the correct answer to this sample, you need to know something about punctuation, capitalization, and verb tense because those are the kinds of changes offered by the choices. The correct answer is choice (2). It inserts a comma after the dependent clause that introduces the sentence.

CONSTRUCTION SHIFT SENTENCES

These questions ask you to choose a better way to write a sentence that contains no mechanical errors, but may be awkwardly written. The same idea must be expressed in a clearer, smoother way, or you may be asked to combine two sentences more effectively. Either way, to find the correct answer, you must understand the meaning of the original sentence (or sentences). Here is a sample:

3. Sentence 5: **Schools all across America are seeking ways to address the needs of children who have a wide range of ethnic backgrounds, which is a major problem that educators struggle to solve.**

   If you rewrote sentence 5 beginning with <u>American educators seek ways to</u> the next word should be

   - **(1)** struggle
   - **(2)** need
   - **(3)** help
   - **(4)** separate
   - **(5)** employ

Here, the original sentence tells you that *educators want to find ways to meet the needs of students with varying ethnic backgrounds.* The answer that most closely expresses this idea is choice (3): *help.*

Note: *It is in your best interest to answer every question on the test whether or not you know the answer. There is no penalty for guessing. When you are stuck, relax and then make your best guess.*

PART II

Part II of the GED Writing Skills Test measures your ability to state an opinion on a given topic or to explain something. You will need to write an essay that clearly states ideas and supports them effectively with detailed reasons and examples. Your essay will be evaluated on how clear, well organized, and free of mechanical errors it is. It will need to be about 200 words in length.

You will not have a choice of topics. You will make decisions, however, on how to respond to the topic that is given to you. Notice in the example that follows that the GED essay topic has two parts. The first part introduces the topic by giving you some background information about it. The second part tells what the topic is; that is, it tells you what you must write about.

SAMPLE ESSAY TOPIC

As electronic devices become easier to use, more and more homes will have things like telephone answering machines, compact disc players, computerized games, and personal computers. One of the most popular electronic inventions is the videocassette recorder (VCR).

In an essay of 200 words, discuss the advantages, disadvantages, or both of owning a VCR. Be sure to support your ideas with details and examples.

For this sample topic, you might choose to discuss as advantages the convenience of recording television shows to watch later and the wide choice of movies a VCR owner can watch comfortably at home. As disadvantages, you could mention that a VCR is expensive and that it may encourage people to watch too much television.

SENTENCE STRUCTURE

Avoiding Sentence Fragments

When we speak to each other, we don't worry about complete sentences. Even if we hear only pieces or fragments of sentences, the situation in which we hear the words fills in for the sentence's missing words.

When we write, complete sentences help our readers understand us.

A **complete sentence** must meet three requirements:

1. It must *have a subject.*
2. It must *have a complete verb.*
3. It must *express a complete thought.*

A **fragment** is a word group that may *look like* a sentence because it begins with a capital letter and ends with a period. However, a fragment is not a sentence because it lacks either a subject, a verb, or a verb part or because it does not express a complete thought.

Usually, if you read a word group out loud, you can tell if it's not a complete sentence because it won't sound finished. Something will be missing, and you will have questions like Who? or What? or What about it?

Being late to work.

What about being late to work? To complete the sentence, we have to answer the question: *Being late to work can cost you your job.*

It's true that we often can figure out what a fragment means because of the preceding sentence or sentences. But a complete sentence must have meaning on its own, regardless of what the sentences before and after it say.

A fragment may lack a subject. The following words look like a sentence:

Fell off the horse.

However, the words make no sense because we can't tell who or what fell off the horse. There's no subject. The **subject** of a sentence tells us who or what the sentence is about. To correct this fragment, add a subject:

The *jockey* fell off the horse.

---

complete sentence: a sentence that contains a subject and a complete verb that expresses a complete thought

---

fragment: a word group that may look like a sentence but lacks a subject, a verb, or part of a verb, or is not a complete thought

---

subject: the person or thing that performs the action in a sentence and tells who or what the sentence is about

When you're looking for the subject of a sentence, look for the doer or the actor. Ask yourself who or what is doing something in the sentence. If you can't find an answer, there probably is no subject, and you're probably looking at a sentence fragment.

Here is another word group that looks like a sentence but isn't:

Five dogs in our neighborhood.

These words don't make sense because you don't know anything about the five dogs. You don't know who they are or what they are doing because there is no **verb.** The verb in a sentence tells what the subject *does* or what it *is*.

Action verbs show that the subject is *doing* something. To correct this fragment, add a verb.

Five dogs in our neighborhood <u>growled</u>. *(sound made in the troat expresing anger.)*

Linking verbs show no action, but tell what the subject *seems like,* what it *is,* or how it *feels.*

The five dogs in our neighborhood *seem* ferocious. Actually, they *are* harmless unless they *feel* threatened.

✳ Sometimes fragments occur because the verb is not complete.

Music blaring outside my window.

Because *blaring* expresses an action, you may see it as a verb. But it really is only part of a verb, and without the other part, the word group doesn't make sense. To correct this fragment, complete the verb by adding *is*.

Music <u>is</u> blaring outside my window.
+ loud noise.

---

verb: the word in a sentence that shows what the subject is or what it does

---

action verb: a verb that shows the subject doing something

---

linking verb: a verb that shows what the subject is, seems, or feels

Exercise 1

Items 1 to 3 refer to the following paragraph.

(1) AIDS is a devastating disease that the medical profession has trouble. (2) Understanding or treating. (3) The name is an abbreviation for *acquired immunodeficiency syndrome*. (4) People with AIDS suffer a breakdown. (5) In their bodies' immune systems. (6) In a healthy body, a certain type of white blood cell attacks foreign substances that enter it. (7) That type of cell protects us from disease. (8) Scientists believe that AIDS is caused by a virus that kills this particular type of blood cell. (9) Leaving the AIDS victim defenseless against infection and tumors. (10) Researchers hope to produce a vaccine against AIDS.

1. Sentences 1 and 2: **AIDS is a devastating disease that the medical profession has trouble. Understanding or treating.**

   Which of the following is the best way to write the underlined portion of these sentences? If you think the original is the best way, select choice (1).

   (1) trouble. Understanding or
   (2) trouble. To understand or
   (3) trouble understanding or
   (4) trouble understanding. Or
   (5) trouble. With understanding or

2. Sentences 4 and 5: **People with AIDS suffer a breakdown. In their bodies' immune systems.**

   Which of the following is the best way to write the underlined portion of these sentences? If you think the original is the best way, select choice (1).

   (1) breakdown. In their
   (2) breakdown in their
   (3) breakdown in. Their
   (4) breakdown. That's in
   (5) breakdown that's also in

3. Sentence 9: **Leaving the AIDS victim defenseless against infection and tumors.**

   What correction should be made to this sentence?

   (1) change Leaving to Leaves
   (2) replace Leaving with This leaves
   (3) replace victim defenseless with victim. Defenseless
   (4) insert is after victim
   (5) replace defenseless against with defenseless. Against

Items 4 and 5 refer to the following paragraph.

(1) After becoming concerned about the environment, many people have decided to try recycling. (2) Most commonly, newspapers, glass, and aluminum cans. (3) However, automotive oil, cardboard, and plastic can be recycled too. (4) In most communities, several recycling centers taking these materials. (5) Some are private operations, and others are public.

4. Sentence 2: **Most commonly, newspapers, glass, and aluminum cans.**

   What correction should be made to this sentence?

   (1) insert they before newspapers
   (2) insert collect before newspapers
   (3) insert they collect before newspapers
   (4) insert collecting before newspapers
   (5) insert collected before newspapers

5. Sentence 4: **In most communities, several recycling centers taking these materials.**

What correction should be made to this sentence?

(1) replace <u>communities, several</u> with <u>communities. Several</u>

(2) replace <u>centers taking</u> with <u>centers. Taking</u>

(3) remove <u>taking</u>

(4) change <u>taking</u> to <u>take</u>

(5) no correction is necessary

To check your answers, turn to page 131.

CLAUSES

A **clause** is a group of words containing a subject and a verb.

Independent clauses

Independent clauses can stand alone. They can also be combined with other clauses to make longer sentences.

Example: I have a headache.

Some clauses have no meaning by themselves.

Example: <u>Whenever I drink milk.</u>

any time

They *depend* on another word group for their meaning and, therefore, are called **dependent clauses.**

por eso

Example: When the lions entered the circus ring.

Dependent Clauses

A dependent clause is a sentence fragment. One way to correct this kind of fragment is to attach the dependent clause to an independent clause:

The crowd roared with excitement when the lions entered the circus ring.

Another way is to eliminate the word that makes the clause dependent:

The lions entered the circus ring.

The following words often begin a dependent clause:

after	even though	until
although	if	when
as	since	whenever
because	though	where
before	unless	wherever

Exercise 2

> **Directions**
> Choose the <u>one best answer</u> to each item.

> Items 1 to 3 refer to the following paragraph.

(1) While she prepares to become an American citizen. (2) Kimiko attends a class once a week. (3) In the class, students from all over the world. (4) Studying U.S. government. (5) Kimiko will be ready to pass the naturalization examination after completing the class. (6) It will be a proud day for her and the others when they receive their U.S. citizenship.

1. Sentences 1 and 2: **While she prepares to become an <u>American citizen. Kimiko</u> attends a class once a week.**

   Which of the following is the best way to rewrite the underlined portion of these sentences? If you think the original is the best way, select choice (1).

   (1) American citizen. Kimiko

   (2) American citizen, Kimiko

   (3) American citizen: Kimiko

   (4) American citizen Kimiko

   (5) American citizen; Kimiko

---

clause: a word group that contains a subject and a verb but is not necessarily a complete thought

---

independent clause: a clause that includes a subject and a verb and has meaning on its own (a complete sentence)

---

dependent clause: a clause that depends on the rest of the sentence for its meaning

2. Sentences 3 and 4: **In the class, students from all over the <u>world. Studying</u> U.S. government.**

Which of the following is the best way to write the underlined portion of these sentences? If you think the original is the best way, select choice (1).

(1) world. Studying
(2) world studying
(3) world that studying
(4) world are studying
(5) world have studying

3. Sentence 5: **Kimiko will be ready to pass the naturalization examination after completing the class.**

If you rewrote sentence 5 beginning with <u>After she completes the class</u>, the next word should be

(1) they
(2) everyone
(3) Kimiko
(4) students
(5) citizens

To check your answers, turn to page 131.

AVOIDING RUN-ON SENTENCES AND COMMA SPLICES

A **run-on sentence** is simply a string of two or more sentences written as a single sentence.

Incorrect: Charles worked late last night he didn't get enough sleep he fell asleep in class today.

Correct: Charles worked late last night and he didn't get enough sleep. He fell asleep in class today.

When you write, if you have more than one thought to express, you must take care to separate the thoughts with proper punctuation and connecting words. Sometimes writers try to avoid run-ons by inserting commas after each complete thought. Then it becomes a list of ideas rather than a sentence:

A series of thoughts separated by commas is called a **comma splice**.

Incorrect: The lawn mower made too much noise in the early morning, it annoyed Dorothy, she asked the neighbor to mow the lawn later in the day, the neighbor agreed, Dorothy felt better, it was quiet for a while.

Correct: The lawn mower made too much noise in the early morning and it annoyed Dorothy. She asked the neighbor to mow the lawn later in the day. The neighbor agreed. Dorothy felt better. It was quiet for a while.

To correct a run-on or comma splice:

- Write the thoughts as separate sentences.

- Separate closely related thoughts using a semicolon.

- Connect the thoughts using a comma and a conjunction. Some common conjunctions are <u>and</u>, <u>or</u>, <u>but</u>, <u>for</u>, <u>yet</u>, and <u>so</u>.

- Connect the thoughts using a semicolon and a transitional word or phrase followed by a comma.

Incorrect: The movie was sold out, we didn't get in.

Corrections: The movie was sold out. We didn't get in.

The movie was sold out; we didn't get in.

The movie was sold out, so we didn't get in.

The movie was sold out; as a result, we didn't get in.

If either of the independent clauses in a run-on already contains commas, you should always use a semicolon to separate the independent clauses.

Akemi, Maria, Lucas, and Tom enjoyed the movie; but Sumio, Mario, and Irene didn't like it.

---

run-on sentence: two or more complete sentences not separated by punctuation

---

comma splice: two or more complete sentences separated only by commas

Exercise 3

Items 1 to 3 refer to the following paragraph.

(1) Although the reunification of Germany and the breakdown of the Soviet Union held out hope for a more peaceful world, the ending of the Cold War has had a serious economic impact on Americans. (2) As the defense industry cut back, many people found themselves unemployed highly skilled workers suddenly faced an uncertain future. (3) Military personnel no longer felt secure about their career choice. (4) The government closed bases at home and abroad this affected service people and also hurt the civilians who worked on these bases. (5) We must find ways to turn defense industries to peaceful endeavors it's tragic to waste the skills of former defense workers.

1. Sentence 2: **As the defense industry cut back, many people found themselves unemployed highly skilled workers suddenly faced an uncertain future.**

   What correction should be made to this sentence?

   (1) replace back, many with back. Many
   (2) replace people found with people. Found
   (3) remove many
   (4) insert a semicolon after unemployed
   (5) insert a semicolon after workers

2. Sentence 4: **The government closed bases at home and abroad this affected service people and also hurt the civilians who worked on these bases.**

   Which of the following is the best way to write the underlined portion of this sentence? If you think the original is the best way, select choice (1).

   (1) home and abroad this affected
   (2) home and abroad. This affected
   (3) home. And abroad this affected
   (4) home and abroad this affecting
   (5) home and abroad affected

3. Sentence 5: **We must find ways to turn defense industries to peaceful endeavors it's tragic to waste the skills of former defense workers.**

   If you rewrote sentence 5 beginning with Because it's tragic to waste the skills of former defense workers, the next word would be

   (1) skills
   (2) peaceful
   (3) endeavors
   (4) we
   (5) there

Items 4 to 6 refer to the following paragraph.

(1) "Doves" and "hawks" are terms that came into use during the Vietnam War. (2) Doves are birds that symbolize peace, but that became the name applied to people who opposed the war. (3) They wanted the United States to negotiate peace. (4) Hawks are more aggressive birds their name was applied to those who wanted to step up the fighting. (5) The terms continue to be used to identify people according to their attitudes toward global conflict. (6) For example, the media refer to those who advocate negotiated settlements as doves those who believe military force is the answer are called hawks.

4. Sentence 2: **Doves are birds that symbolize peace, but that became the name applied to people who opposed the war.**

   What correction should be made to this sentence?

   (1) remove the comma
   (2) replace peace, but with peace. But
   (3) replace the comma with a semicolon
   (4) replace but with yet
   (5) replace but with so

5. Sentence 4: **Hawks are more aggressive birds their name was applied to those who wanted to step up the fighting.**

   Which of the following is the best way to write the underlined portion of this sentence? If you think the original is the best way, select choice (1).

   (1) birds their
   (2) birds, but their
   (3) birds, so their
   (4) birds; and their
   (5) birds, their

6. Sentence 6: **For example, the media refer to those who advocate negotiated settlements as doves those who believe military force is the answer are called hawks.**

Which of the following is the best way to write the underlined portion of this sentence? If you think the original is the best way, select choice (1).

(1) doves those
(2) doves, because those
(3) doves, or those
(4) doves, those
(5) doves; those

To check your answers, turn to page 131.

LINKING IDEAS OF EQUAL IMPORTANCE

A **simple sentence** contains one subject and one verb and expresses a complete thought, but a string of simple sentences is not very interesting to read. To make your writing more appealing, you should occasionally combine two or more ideas into one sentence.

Charles was thirsty. He poured a glass of juice.

Charles was thirsty, so he poured a glass of juice.

Both examples express the same ideas, but the second flows more smoothly.

When you combine independent clauses into single sentences, you're writing compound sentences. A **compound sentence** links ideas of equal importance. That is, each idea could stand by itself and make sense.

However, not all independent clauses can be combined effectively into compound sentences. Be sure to link only those ideas that are closely related.

The following two ideas, for example, would not make an effective compound sentence, since they have little to do with each other:

Armando borrowed three books from the library. Leah has always enjoyed browsing in libraries.

But the following two ideas are so closely related that it does make sense to link them into one sentence:

Armando borrowed three books from the library, but Leah was unable to find the books she wanted.

To clarify the relationship between two ideas, you must use connecting words.

To choose the proper connecting words, you must understand the relationship between the ideas in the two independent clauses. For example, it would be senseless to say

Milton was ill; however, he had to stay home from work.

The writer really means

Milton was ill; consequently, he had to stay home from work.

In this case, *however* is an inappropriate connector because it shows contrast between ideas. *Consequently* makes more sense because it shows that the second idea is the result of the first.

Some common connectors are *however, therefore, for example, furthermore,* and *then.*
also, in addition.

Exercise 4

Directions
Choose the one best answer to each item.

Items 1 to 3 refer to the following paragraphs.

(1) Some states charge a sales tax on food. (2) It seems like a fair tax because everyone has to buy food everyone pays the tax. (3) There are those, however, who think this kind of tax is unfair. (4) They point out that people with little money have to buy just as much food as people with lots of money. (5) These people spend a larger portion of their income on food, so they also pay a larger portion of their income on the taxes.

(6) Taxes that cost some people a higher proportion of their income than others are called regressive taxes. (7) Income taxes are called progressive taxes they increase proportionately as the taxpayer's income goes up. (8) Thus, a person earning $60,000 a year pays a higher tax than someone earning $18,000. (9) Because sales tax is regressive, many states do not apply it to

simple sentence: a sentence containing one complete thought

compound sentence: a sentence that contains two or more independent clauses

food. (10) On the other hand, some states collect no state income tax they rely instead on other taxes, including sales tax on food.

1. Sentence 2: **It seems like a fair tax because everyone has to buy <u>food everyone</u> pays the tax.**

Which of the following is the best way to write the underlined portion of this sentence? If you think the original is the best way, select choice (1).

(1) food everyone
(2) food, everyone
(3) food but everyone
(4) food and everyone
(5) food. Everyone

2. Sentence 7: **Income taxes are called progressive taxes they increase proportionately as the taxpayer's income goes up.**

What correction should be made to this sentence?

(1) replace <u>progressive taxes</u> with <u>progressive. Taxes</u>
(2) insert a comma after the second <u>taxes</u>
(3) insert a semicolon after the second <u>taxes</u>
(4) replace <u>proportionately as</u> with <u>proportionately. As</u>
(5) remove <u>as</u>

3. Sentence 10: **On the other hand, some states collect no state income tax they rely instead on other taxes, including sales tax on food.**

What correction should be made to this sentence?

(1) replace <u>hand, some</u> with <u>hand. Some</u>
(2) replace <u>income tax they</u> with <u>income tax. They</u>
(3) insert a comma after <u>income tax</u>
(4) remove <u>they</u>
(5) replace <u>taxes, including</u> with <u>taxes. Including</u>

Items 4 to 6 refer to the following paragraph.

(1) Advertising is an essential feature of our economy. (2) Clever ads can entertain the public as they introduce them to goods and services. (3) Advertising gives consumers useful information on new products, so it also makes consumers want things they don't need. (4) Ads are everywhere; however, they appear on television, on the radio, in magazines, and in newspapers. (5) Some ads are misleading, so they cause people to spend money unwisely. (6) The wise consumer approaches advertising claims carefully.

4. Sentence 3: **Advertising gives consumers useful information on new products, so it also makes consumers want things they don't need.**

What correction should be made to this sentence?

(1) remove the comma after <u>products</u>
(2) replace <u>so</u> with <u>but</u>
(3) change <u>products, so</u> to <u>products. So</u>
(4) replace <u>so</u> with <u>then</u>
(5) no correction is necessary

5. Sentence 4: **Ads are everywhere; however, they appear on television, on the radio, in magazines, and in newspapers.**

What correction should be made to this sentence?

(1) replace <u>however</u> with <u>for example</u>
(2) replace <u>however</u> with <u>nevertheless</u>
(3) replace the comma after <u>however</u> with a semicolon
(4) remove the comma after <u>however</u>
(5) no correction is necessary

6. Sentence 5: **Some ads are misleading, so they cause people to spend money unwisely.**

If you rewrote sentence 5 beginning with <u>Misleading ads</u> The next word should be

(1) and
(2) people
(3) cause
(4) prevent
(5) help

To check your answers, turn to page 131.

81

LINKING IDEAS OF UNEQUAL IMPORTANCE

Besides combining two equally important ideas into one sentence, you can vary your sentence structure and make your writing more interesting with complex sentences.

Like a compound sentence, a **complex sentence** links two ideas into one sentence. However, in a complex sentence, one of the ideas is less important than the other and depends on the main idea for its meaning. The main idea appears in the independent clause.

> Because he was late, Jeff decided not to stop at the cleaners on the way to work.

You see that, by itself, *Because he was late* doesn't make sense. When it's added to the independent clause *Jeff decided not to stop at the cleaners on the way to work* you understand it.

Dependent clauses may precede the main clause or they may follow it. If the dependent clause comes first, it is followed by a comma. If the dependent clause appears at the end of the sentence, a comma is not needed.

> Because it was 102 degrees in the shade, they stayed in the house all day.

> They stayed in the house all day because it was 102 degrees in the shade.

The connectors in complex sentences must accurately express the relationship between the ideas in the two clauses. Complex sentences relate ideas in several different ways.

- cause and effect
  Since the house was dark, they didn't ring the doorbell.
- contrast
  Leona turned down the invitation *despite the fact that* she loved parties.

- time
  They screamed *until* their throats hurt.

- place
  They put the key *where* no one would see it.

- condition
  If you work hard, you'll get good grades.

- similarity between the ideas in the two clauses
  Terry felt *as if* he could eat a horse.

Exercise 5

Directions

Choose the one best answer to each item.

Items 1 to 3 refer to the following paragraph.

(1) The history of ice cream, perhaps America's favorite dessert, goes back to colonial times. (2) It was enjoyed by people like George Washington and Dolly Madison. (3) Although ice cream is delicious by itself. (4) It also forms the basis for other wonderful treats. (5) According to legend, in 1874 a businessman in Philadelphia combined ice cream with a carbonated beverage to create the ice-cream soda. (6) Laws were passed prohibiting the sale of ice-cream sodas on Sundays. (7) Because the drink was so sinfully delicious. (8) This led to a new creation. (9) A druggist in Illinois put noncarbonated syrup over ice cream and called it a Sunday. (10) The spelling changed over the years, and the ice-cream sundae became a favorite dessert.

1. Sentences 3 and 4: **Although ice cream is delicious by itself. It also forms the basis for other wonderful treats.**

   Which of the following is the best way to write the underlined portion of these sentences? If you think the original is the best way, select choice (1).

   (1) itself. It
   (2) itself, it
   (3) itself, and it
   (4) itself, so it
   (5) itself because it

2. Sentence 5: **According to legend, in 1874 a businessman in Philadelphia combined ice cream with a carbonated beverage to create the ice-cream soda.**

   What correction should be made to this sentence?

   (1) insert a period after legend
   (2) insert a comma after Philadelphia
   (3) insert a period after beverage
   (4) insert a comma after create
   (5) no correction is necessary

complex sentence: a sentence containing a closely related independent clause and a dependent clause

3. Sentences 6 and 7: **Laws were passed prohibiting the sale of ice-cream sodas on Sundays. Because the drink was so sinfully delicious.**

What correction should be made to these sentences?

(1) insert a semicolon after <u>passed</u>
(2) replace <u>sodas on Sundays</u> with <u>sodas. On Sundays</u>
(3) replace <u>Sundays. Because</u> with <u>Sundays, but</u>
(4) replace <u>Sundays. Because</u> with <u>Sundays because</u>
(5) insert a comma after <u>drink</u>

Items 4 and 5 refer to the following paragraph.

---

(1) We can remember things more easily if we write them down. (2) Some people use calendars or appointment books, although others just use a piece of paper. (3) Then we have to remember to look at the reminder we wrote. (4) Jean forgot to look at her calendar. (5) She missed her dental appointment.

4. Sentence 2: **Some people use calendars or appointment books, although others just use a piece of paper.**

What correction should be made to this sentence?

(1) replace <u>books, although</u> with <u>books. Although</u>
(2) replace the comma with a semicolon
(3) remove the comma after <u>books</u>
(4) replace <u>although</u> with <u>in order that</u>
(5) replace <u>although</u> with <u>whenever</u>

5. Sentences 4 and 5: **Jean forgot to look at her calendar. She missed her dental appointment.**

The most effective combination of sentences 4 and 5 would begin with which of the following words?

(1) Unless
(2) As soon as
(3) Until
(4) Because
(5) Although

To check your answers, turn to page 132.

USING MODIFIERS

A **modifier** is a word or word group that describes another word or word group in a sentence. Single-word modifiers (adjectives and adverbs) don't usually cause many problems with sentence structure, but it's important to be able to recognize them. **Adjectives** describe **nouns,** which are words that often represent persons, places, or things (*angry* citizens). **Adverbs** describe verbs (meet *regularly*), adjectives (*very* angry), and other adverbs (*quite* regularly).

Prepositional phrases and verb phrases are the modifiers most likely to cause problems in writing.

When writers are careless about where they put modifiers, they confuse readers with unclear sentences.

The police officer spoke about heroic crime stoppers at the local high school.

The sentence suggests that the crime stoppers were from the local high school. The modifier *at the local high school* seems to be modifying *crime stoppers* because it appears next to it.

The police officer spoke at the local high school about heroic crime stoppers.

This time the modifier is next to *spoke,* the word it modifies.

---

modifier: a word or group of words that describes another word or group of words in a sentence

---

adjective: a word that modifies a noun

---

noun: a word that names a person, place, or thing

---

adverb: a word that modifies a verb, adjective, or another adverb

---

Some sentences are unclear because of *dangling modifiers*. These phrases are confusing because there is nothing in the sentence they could logically modify.

Diving into the pool, the tension was extreme.

Who was diving into the pool? Who was feeling the tension?

To correct dangling modifiers, you must change the main part of the sentence so that it includes something for the modifier to describe:

Diving into the pool, *the athlete* felt extreme tension.

You may turn the modifier into a prepositional phrase:

Before diving into the pool, the athlete felt extreme tension.

You may also turn the modifier into a dependent clause:

The athlete felt extreme tension *before she dove into the pool.*

Exercise 6

Directions

Choose the <u>one best answer</u> to each item.

Items 1 to 3 refer to the following paragraph.

(1) Counting on public transportation, schedules are very important. (2) People who ride buses count on them to be on time. (3) Most buses and commuter trains do stick closely to the advertised schedule. (4) Missing a bus is often the fault of the rider. (5) Carmela often gets last-minute phone calls at work that force her to miss her bus. (6) Tired from working late, missing the bus can be extremely annoying. (7) Carmela wonders whether it's any worse to be stuck in a traffic jam in her car. (8) Out of patience, another bus is seen coming down the street. (9) Once she boards the bus, she settles down and reads or naps.

1. Sentence 1: **Counting on public transportation, schedules are very important.**

   If you rewrote sentence 1 beginning with <u>For people who count on</u> the next word(s) should be

   (1) schedules
   (2) public transportation
   (3) work
   (4) importance
   (5) advertised

2. Sentence 6: **Tired from working late, missing the bus can be extremely annoying.**

   If you rewrote sentence 6 beginning with <u>Because Carmela is tired from working late,</u> the next word should be

   (1) missing
   (2) annoying
   (3) working
   (4) the
   (5) while

3. Sentence 8: **Out of patience, <u>another bus is seen coming</u> down the street.**

   Which of the following is the best way to write the underlined portion of this sentence? If you think the original is the best way, select choice (1).

   (1) another bus is seen coming
   (2) the bus is coming
   (3) the bus sees
   (4) Carmela sees another bus coming
   (5) Carmela is seen coming

To check your answers, turn to page 132.

PARALLEL STRUCTURE

You've already learned about compound sentences, which contain two or more complete thoughts. Many sentences also contain compound elements. This means parts within the sentence are linked with connecting words, such as *and, but,* and *or.* To maintain clarity in your writing, it's important to put elements that play similar roles within a sentence into the same form. Consider the following sentences:

> Incorrect: JoAnn does billing for a dentist, a law firm, and one doctor's office also employs her.

> Correct: JoAnn does billing for a dental group, a law firm, and a doctor's office.

The sentence names three businesses JoAnn does billing for, so all three play the same role in the sentence. They should be written in the same form, which we call **parallel structure**. As you can see, a sentence that lacks parallel structure does not flow smoothly.

Sometimes sentences lack parallel structure because the writer adds an entire clause when a single word is better. For example:

> Dogs require food, shelter, and you have to bathe them.

The sentence above tells us three things about dogs. Two of those things are expressed as nouns (*food* and *shelter*), but the third is expressed as a clause, with a subject (*you*) and a verb (*have*).

Parallel structure expresses each requirement as a noun and changes the sentence:

> Dogs require food, shelter, and baths.

Sometimes sentences lack parallel structure because the writer switches subjects in midsentence. Think about this example:

> At parks, people play baseball, toss Frisbees, and parks are good places to talk to friends.

This sentence has three word groups, but the third one changes subjects from *people* to *parks,* which spoils the parallel structure. A better sentence would be:

> At parks, people play baseball, toss Frisbees, and talk to friends.

Exercise 7

Directions

Choose the one best answer to each item.

Items 1 to 3 refer to the following paragraphs.

(1) The Peace Corps was established in 1961, during President John F. Kennedy's administration. (2) That year, about three thousand volunteers worked in Asia, in Africa, and countries in Latin America to help the natives improve their standard of living. (3) Peace Corps workers live among the natives, learn their language, and their standard of living is just like that of the natives. (4) Their pay, about $75 a month, is deposited for them in the United States, and they receive travel and living expenses. (5) Although most Peace Corps volunteers are young men and women, the age range is from eighteen to sixty.

(6) Not only has this program developed good will between the United States and underdeveloped countries, it has taught people in hundreds of communities to help themselves improve their lives. (7) Some people believe all Americans, when they reach the age of eighteen, should be required to serve for two years either at home or go to foreign countries.

1. Sentence 2: **That year, about three thousand volunteers worked in Asia, in Africa, and countries in Latin America to help the natives improve their standard of living.**

   Which of the following is the best way to write the underlined portion of this sentence? If you think the original is the best way, select choice (1).

   (1) and countries in Latin America
   (2) and other countries in Latin America
   (3) and in Latin America
   (4) and the many countries of Latin America
   (5) and countries that are in Latin America

parallel structure: putting similar elements in a sentence into the same form

2. Sentence 3: **Peace Corps workers live among the natives, learn their language, and their standard of living is just like that of the natives.**

Which of the following is the best way to write the underlined portion of this sentence? If you think the original is the best, select choice (1).

(1) their standard of living is just like that of the natives

(2) share their standard of living

(3) their standard of living is the same

(4) their standard of living matches that of the natives

(5) standard of living goes down

3. Sentence 7: **Some people believe all Americans, when they reach the age of eighteen, should be required to serve for two years either at home or go to foreign countries.**

What correction should be made to this sentence?

(1) replace of eighteen, should with of eighteen. Should

(2) replace years either with years. Either

(3) remove at

(4) replace go to with in

(5) no correction is necessary

Items 4 to 9 refer to the following paragraph.

---

(1) One way to give children a sense of family history is to share memories with them. (2) Through memories, children can learn about relatives they may not see often, such as aunts, uncles, cousins, or even grandparents. (3) It can be fun for parents to share family memories with their children. (4) They can do this through photographs, scrapbooks, and the children ask questions. (5) Modern technology makes it easier than ever to capture the past. (6) Many types of cameras help people record family events, capture vacation highlights, and remembering all kinds of things. (7) Cameras come in a wide range of prices and sophistication, from video cameras that record sound to disposable cameras that are used once and turned in with the film. (8) With the help of cameras, tape recorders, and by keeping diaries, parents can easily look back on their children's growing up. (9) Adults are often amused by their own childhood photos, drawings, report cards, and to remember special times from years back. (10) To record your children's growing up is giving them a precious gift for their later years.

4. Sentence 2: **Through memories, children can learn about relatives they may not see often, such as aunts, uncles, cousins, or even grandparents.**

What correction should be made to this sentence?

(1) replace relatives they with relatives. They

(2) replace often, such as with often. Such as

(3) insert including before cousins

(4) insert their before grandparents

(5) no correction is necessary

5. Sentence 4: **They can do this through photographs, scrapbooks, and the children ask questions.**

Which of the following is the best way to write the underlined portion of this sentence? If you think the original is the best way, select choice (1).

(1) the children ask questions

(2) when the children ask questions

(3) children's questions

(4) whenever the children ask questions

(5) the parents answer questions

6. Sentence 6: **Many types of cameras help people record family events, capture vacation highlights, and remembering all kinds of things.**

What correction should be made to this sentence?

(1) change record to recording

(2) insert to before capture

(3) change remembering to to remember

(4) change remembering to remember

(5) no correction is necessary

7. Sentence 8: **With the help of cameras, tape recorders, and by keeping diaries, parents can easily look back on their children's growing up.**

What correction should be made to this sentence?

(1) replace by keeping diaries with diaries

(2) replace With the help of with By

(3) remove can easily

(4) replace can easily look with by looking

(5) no correction is necessary

8. Sentence 9: **Adults are often amused by their own childhood photos, drawings, report cards, and to remember special times from years back.**

What correction should be made to this sentence?

(1) replace <u>photos</u> with <u>pictures</u>
(2) replace <u>drawings</u> with <u>they drew pictures</u>
(3) replace <u>to remember</u> with <u>memories of</u>
(4) remove <u>report cards</u>
(5) remove <u>from years back</u>

9. Sentence 10: **To record your children's growing up is giving them a precious gift for their later years.**

What correction should be made to this sentence?

(1) replace <u>To</u> with <u>Parents who</u>
(2) replace <u>To record</u> with <u>When you record</u>
(3) insert <u>like</u> before <u>giving</u>
(4) change <u>giving</u> to <u>to give</u>
(5) remove <u>their</u>

To check your answers, turn to page 132.

amused = To give

USAGE AND GRAMMAR

Subject-Verb Agreement

You already know that subjects and verbs are the basic components of a complete sentence. To do well on the GED Writing Skills Test, you must also understand how to write those subjects and verbs in their correct forms.

Can you tell that something is wrong with the following sentence?

Lee and Melva <u>lives</u> in a mountain community 65 miles from the nearest city.

The problem is that the verb *lives* doesn't match the subject *Lee and Melva. And* is the key word here. In discussing language, when we talk about one thing, we call it **singular.**

A tree grows in the park.

This sentence contains two singular nouns: *tree* and *park.* One of those nouns, *tree,* is the subject of the sentence. We can say this sentence has a singular subject. But if there is more than one tree in the park, the subject would be **plural:**

Several trees grow in the park.

Subject-verb agreement means that singular subjects take singular verbs and plural subjects take plural verbs. In English, we usually make a noun plural by adding *s* or *es* to it: *tree* becomes *trees.* A plural verb, however, never ends in *s.*

Here is a sentence with a *singular* subject and verb:

He goes to night school.

This sentence has a *plural* subject and verb:

Mark and Hakeem go to night school.

Remember that *compound* subjects are two words linked by *and.* They always take plural verbs:

Naomi and Judson sell hot dogs from a corner stand.

If the sentence has one subject and two verbs, be sure both verbs agree with the subject:

Every month, a *firefighter speaks* to our club and *shows* slides.

---

singular: one

---

plural: more than one

---

subject-verb agreement: singular subjects take singular verbs; plural subjects take plural verbs

Exercise 1

> **Directions**
>
> Choose the correct verb from the pair in each of the following sentences.

1. Bruce Lee (was/were) a good actor.

2. They (cheer/cheers) for different teams.

3. Flashing yellow lights (warn/warns) drivers of road hazards.

4. Four-way stops (confuse/confuses) some drivers.

5. Elsa (take/takes) the bus everywhere.

> **Directions**
>
> Correct the following sentences for subject-verb agreement. Some sentences may not contain errors.

6. Charles play card games with his friends and sometimes he win.

7. Michelle seem to win every time she play.

8. Carla enjoys her job at the hardware store.

9. Computers scare my mother.

10. Mr. Chan hate long lines and becomes impatient in them.

> **Directions**
>
> Choose the one best answer to each item.

> Items 11 to 13 refer to the following paragraph.

(1) Strikes is the most powerful weapon workers have against unfair treatment by employers. (2) Strikes usually occur over wages, but working conditions can also be a source of dissatisfaction for laborers. (3) When all negotiation attempts fails, labor union members may vote to strike. (4) This means they stop work so that the employer will lose money. (5) The hope are that this tactic will force the employer to meet their demands. (6) They gamble that the employer would rather give in to them than risk the financial ruin of the company. (7) Strikes can last for weeks or even months and can be a severe hardship to the striking workers as well as to the company they work for. (8) The economic impact of these battles of will between labor and management can be felt in communities or across the nation for a long time.

11. Sentence 1: **Strikes is the most powerful weapon workers have against unfair treatment by employers.**

    What correction should be made to this sentence?

    (1) change is to are
    (2) change weapon to weapons
    (3) change have to has
    (4) replace have against with have. Against
    (5) replace treatment by with treatment. By

12. Sentence 3: **When all negotiation attempts fails, labor union members may vote to strike.**

    Which of the following is the best way to write the underlined portion of this sentence? If you think the original is the best way, select choice (1).

    (1) negotiation attempts fails
    (2) negotiation attempts fail
    (3) negotiation attempt fail
    (4) negotiations attempt to fail
    (5) negotiation fails to attempt

13. Sentence 5: **The hope are that this tactic will force the employer to meet their demands.**

    What correction should be made to this sentence?

    (1) replace The with They
    (2) replace The with Their
    (3) change hope are to hopes is
    (4) change are to is
    (5) no correction is necessary

To check your answers, turn to page 132.

attempt = to try
fail = failure

Recognizing Singular and Plural Subjects

There are some nouns that seem to be plural because they refer to groups of individuals. However, these words usually take a singular verb:

The *team practices* daily.

Here are some other nouns that take a singular verb:

group   congress   choir   audience

There are also nouns that appear to be plural because they end in *s*, but they are actually singular and require a singular verb:

No *news is* good news.

Here are some other nouns that appear to be plural but take a singular verb:

physics   measles   athletics   economics   series

When a sentence has two subjects that are connected by *either/or* or *neither/nor*, the verb must agree with the subject closest to it. Compare the following two sentences:

Either the doctor or the *nurses answer* questions.

Either the nurses or the *doctor answers* questions.

Personal pronouns (*I, we, you, he, she, they,* and *it*) have their own set of subject-verb agreement rules. *He, she,* and *it* take a singular verb, while all the others (including the singular *I* and the singular *you*) take a plural verb:

- He/she/it (singular) goes.
- They (plural) go.
- I (singular) go.
- We (plural) go.
- You (singular or plural) go.

Sometimes beginning writers have trouble with subject-verb agreement when they work with the verb *to be.* You must learn the correct forms of that verb to avoid problems.

Incorrect: They be late again.

Correct: They are late again.

Here are the personal pronouns with correct forms for the verb *to be*:

I am   you are   he/she/it is   we/they are
I was   you were   he/she/it was   we/they were

To learn other tricky singular and plural subjects, study the lists below. These words always take *singular* verbs:

another	either	one	nothing
anyone	everybody	other	somebody
anybody	everyone	either	someone
anything	everything	nobody	something
each	much	no one	

Example: *Everything costs* too much these days.

These words always take *plural* verbs:

both   few   many   several

Example: *Few put* forth their best effort.

Exercise 2

Directions

Determine whether the subjects in the following sentences are singular or plural and choose the correct verb from each pair.

1. Congress (vote/votes) on every tax law.
2. You (go/goes) first.
3. Today's news (look/looks) good.
4. The city council (choose/chooses) the site for games.
5. They (ask/asks) too many questions.

Directions

Choose the correct verb form for the following sentences.

6. She (say/says) to hurry back from the store.
7. No one (know/knows) the park rules.
8. I (am/be) too tired for a movie tonight.
9. Most (run/runs) on regular gasoline.

Directions

Choose the one best answer to each item.

Items 10 and 11 refer to the following paragraph.

(1) A three-day weekend is coming up. (2) No one wants to waste a weekend, but Holly and Kent has no particular plans. (3) Kent thinks about going to the beach for at least one day. (4) Holly fears bad weather, so she suggest staying home instead. (5) Kent doesn't mind, as long as they find something relaxing to do.

10. Sentence 2: **No one wants to waste a weekend, but Holly and Kent has no particular plans.**

What correction should be made to this sentence?

   (1) change <u>wants</u> to <u>want</u>
   (2) remove the comma
   (3) replace <u>has</u> with <u>be without</u>
   (4) change <u>has</u> to <u>have</u>
   (5) change <u>Kent has</u> to <u>Kent. Has</u>

11. Sentence 4: **Holly fears bad weather, so she suggest staying home instead.**

What correction should be made to this sentence?

   (1) change <u>fears</u> to <u>fear</u>
   (2) remove the comma
   (3) change <u>weather, so</u> to <u>weather. She</u>
   (4) change <u>suggest</u> to <u>suggests</u>
   (5) replace <u>staying</u> with <u>they stays</u>

To check your answers, turn to page 132.

When Subjects Are Separated from Their Verbs

Matching a verb to a plural or a singular subject isn't difficult if you know what the subject is. Occasionally, however, you may be confused by phrases that appear between the subject and the verb. For example, can you select the correct verb in the following sentence?

Millie, like her sisters and her mother, (has/have) small feet.

To choose the correct verb, you must first determine who or what the subject is. Is *Millie* the subject in this sentence? Or is it *Millie and her mother and sisters*?

Remember: Two or more words *must* be joined by *and* to be a plural subject. In the sentence above, only *Millie* is the subject. The verb form must be the singular, *has.* To take a plural verb, the subjects would have to be linked by *and:*

Millie, her sisters, *and* her mother have small feet.

Notice that in the original sentence, the interrupting words *like her sisters and her mother* are set off by commas. Sometimes, however, words that separate the subject and verb are not set apart by commas, so it's easier to mistake them for the subject. These interrupters are the prepositional phrases. One way to be certain of the subject is to identify the prepositional phrase and see how the sentence sounds without it. Try this sentence:

One of the dancers (is/are) especially graceful.

If you set aside the prepositional phrase *of the dancers*, you can see the subject next to the verb:

One . . . is.

Verb phrases can sometimes be subjects of sentences.

Studying for three straight hours (make/makes) me tired.

To identify the subject of this sentence, you might look at the verb and ask *who* or *what makes* me tired. You'll see that *studying*, not *hours*, is the subject of the sentence.

Exercise 3

Directions

Choose the one best answer to each item.

Items 1 to 3 refer to the following paragraphs.

(1) Mr. Brewer wants his adult education students to learn math in the context of real life. (2) He feels it's not enough for them just to work problems from a book. (3) To show his class how math can really help them, he holds or has them enter several contests during the year. (4) The contests allow his students to have fun while they practice math and raises money.

(5) Once they filled a fishbowl with marbles, asked people to guess how many marbles there was, and awarded a free lunch to the winner. (6) Another time they entered and won a contest to guess how many soda cans the back of a pickup truck held. (7) To win, they had to practice their skills at estimating,

multiplying, dividing, and measuring. (8) They used most of the prize money for an end-of-the-year field trip. (9) The class thinks the best thing about entering contests are winning.

1. Sentence 4: **The contests allow his students to have fun while they practice math and raises money.**

   What correction should be made to this sentence?

   (1) change <u>allow</u> to <u>allows</u>
   (2) change <u>fun while</u> to <u>fun. While</u>
   (3) change <u>fun while</u> to <u>fun, while</u>
   (4) change <u>practice</u> to <u>practices</u>
   (5) change <u>raises</u> to <u>raise</u>

2. Sentence 5: **Once they filled a fishbowl with marbles, asked people to guess how many marbles there was, and awarded a free lunch to the winner.**

   Which of the following is the best way to write the underlined portion of this sentence? If you think the original is the best way, select choice (1).

   (1) asked people to guess how many marbles there was
   (2) asked people to guess how many marbles was there
   (3) asked how many could guess the right number
   (4) asked people to guess how many marbles there were
   (5) asked people how many marbles there was

3. Sentence 9: **The class thinks the best thing about entering contests are winning.**

   What correction should be made to this sentence?

   (1) change <u>thinks</u> to <u>think</u>
   (2) remove <u>entering</u>
   (3) change <u>are</u> to <u>is</u>
   (4) change <u>contests are</u> to <u>contests. Are</u>
   (5) no correction is necessary

To check your answers, turn to page 133.

When the Verb Comes Before the Subject

As you have seen in this lesson, sometimes the structure of the sentence can make it difficult to spot errors in subject-verb agreement. This is especially true when the verb comes before the subject.

In sentences that begin with *There* or *Here*, the verb comes before the subject: *Here come the clowns.* The verb in the preceding sentence is *come,* but when we ask who or what comes, we see the subject is *the clowns,* which appears after the verb. As always, the subject must agree with the verb. It would be incorrect to write *Here comes the clowns* because that would put a singular verb with a plural subject.

Questions pose an additional problem for subject-verb agreement because they often split the verb into two parts with the subject in between: *Does Judith have her shoes?* The singular verb, *does,* must agree with the singular subject, *Judith.* It would be incorrect to write: *Do Judith have her shoes?*

Both the subject and the verb sometimes appear at the ends of sentences, which can cause some confusion:

In the back yard are two peach trees.

The subject of the sentence above, *peach trees,* is plural, so it must take a plural verb: *are.* If you think *back yard* is the subject, you will use a singular verb, which would be incorrect. *Back yard* is part of the prepositional phrase.

Follow these tips to ensure subject-verb agreement:

- Find the verb.

- Ask *who* or *what* is performing the action.

- Make the verb agree in number (*singular* or *plural*) with the subject.

Exercise 4

> **Directions**
> Choose the correct verb from the pairs in the sentences below.

1. There (is/are) too many leaves to rake in one afternoon.

2. (Does/Do) both of them want to go to the game?

3. In the cupboard (is/are) all the things you need to bake a cake.

4. Upstairs (is/are) two more bedrooms.

5. Here (is/are) the information you asked for.

Directions

Choose the <u>one best answer</u> to each item.

Items 6 to 11 refer to the following paragraph.

(1) Many people hate to cook, but others find cooking is a good way to relax. (2) There is many ways to learn to cook. (3) One of the best ways are watching other people do it. (4) This can be done in an actual kitchen, in a cooking class, or by watching cooking programs on television. (5) There are all kinds of cooks. (6) Some people follow recipes carefully, measuring and counting with precision. (7) Others prefers to create as they go, tasting and testing along the way. (8) Cooks, especially when modifying recipes, has to use some basic math skills, such as estimating amounts. (9) In a well-stocked kitchen is many kinds of ingredients. (10) A creative cook must also be familiar with them all. (11) Otherwise, it would be difficult to know which herbs and spices goes best with different foods. (12) The kitchen is a place where creative people can experiment and expand their talents.

6. Sentence 2: **There is many ways to learn to cook.**

What correction should be made to this sentence?

(1) replace <u>There</u> with <u>Here</u>
(2) change <u>is</u> to <u>are</u>
(3) replace <u>to learn</u> with <u>for learn</u>
(4) change <u>learn</u> to <u>learning</u>
(5) change <u>cook</u> to <u>cooking</u>

7. Sentence 3: **One of the best ways are watching other people do it.**

What correction should be made to this sentence?

(1) change <u>are</u> to <u>is</u>
(2) change <u>are</u> to <u>be</u>
(3) insert <u>to</u> before <u>watching</u>
(4) change <u>watching</u> to <u>to watch</u>
(5) change <u>do</u> to <u>did</u>

8. Sentence 7: **Others prefers to create as they go, tasting and testing along the way.**

What correction should be made to this sentence?

(1) replace <u>Others</u> with <u>Other people</u>
(2) change <u>prefers</u> to <u>prefer</u>
(3) replace <u>to create</u> with <u>creating</u>
(4) insert <u>they are</u> before <u>tasting</u>
(5) insert <u>everything</u> before <u>along</u>

9. Sentence 8: **Cooks, especially when modifying recipes, has to use some basic math skills, such as estimating amounts.**

If you rewrote sentence 8 beginning with <u>When modifying recipes, cooks</u> the next word should be

(1) has
(2) uses
(3) use
(4) estimates
(5) modify

10. Sentence 9: <u>**In a well-stocked kitchen is many kinds**</u> of ingredients.

Which of the following is the best way to write the underlined portion of this sentence? If you think the original is the best way, select choice (1).

(1) In a well-stocked kitchen is many kinds
(2) In a well-stocked kitchen many kinds
(3) A well-stocked kitchen have many kinds
(4) A well-stocked kitchen has many kinds
(5) Many kinds of well-stocked kitchens

11. Sentence 11: **Otherwise, it would be difficult to know which herbs and spices goes best with different foods.**

What correction should be made to this sentence?

(1) remove <u>would</u>
(2) change <u>to know</u> to <u>knowing</u>
(3) replace <u>know which</u> with <u>know. Which</u>
(4) change <u>goes</u> to <u>go</u>
(5) insert <u>kinds of</u> after <u>different</u>

To check your answers, turn to page 133.

Using Verb Phrases

Understanding subject-verb agreement is important for clear writing. Verbs tell us not only *what* the subject does or is, but also *when*—past, present, or future. The form of the verb changes to show an action's place in time. Those forms indicate **verb tense**.

Notice that some tenses require more than one word in the verb form:

The relatives *have arrived* for the wedding.

A verb form with more than one word is called a **verb phrase,** containing a helping verb *(have)* and some form of the main verb *(arrive).*

To see how verb phrases affect meaning, look at the two sentences below:

Jake and Brigitte have gone to the store.

Jake and Brigitte went to the store.

From the first sentence we learn that the action (going to the store) happened at some unclear time in the past, but not too long ago. They are probably still at the store. That is, the action began in the past and continues into the present. Notice that the verb form includes two words, or a *verb phrase.*

The second sentence tells us something slightly different. We learn from that sentence that Jake and Brigitte went to the store at a particular time in the past, perhaps *this morning,* and the action is complete. (Presumably, they are back.) This verb form is in the simple past tense and uses only one word *(went).*

In the first sentence, the word *gone* is a **participle**. Because the action started in the past, it is a past participle. Participles may not be used alone as verbs. They must appear with a helping verb, such as *have.*

Participles can also be used to show action taking place in the present:

Ruth *is mowing* the lawn.

When we add *ing* to a verb to show action that is occurring in the present, we form a present participle. This form of the verb also requires a helping verb, like *is.*

Gerunds are present participles that are used in sentences as nouns rather than as parts of verb phrases.

Her *dancing* on the table shocked everyone.

Compare the following sentences:

Their *working* extra hours impressed the boss.

Because of the new project, they are *working* extra hours this month.

In the first sentence, *working* is a gerund that is the subject of the sentence. The verb is *impressed.* In the second sentence *working* is part of a verb phrase. *They* is the subject of the sentence; *are working* is the verb.

Exercise 5

> **Directions**
> Identify the participles in the following sentences, paying attention to the meaning of the sentence, and determine whether the participle is past or present.

1. Jill and Evan are planning a party for next week.
2. Maurice had helped with the presentation.
3. The boss is sitting at Eva's table.

> **Directions**
> Choose the one best answer to each item.

> Items 4 to 6 refer to the following paragraph.

(1) Although much of the country suffers from crippling snowstorms, Californians usually have to drive to the mountains to see snow. (2) The California Highway Patrol knows that many people will be plan trips to the snow during wet winters. (3) The authori-

---

verb tense: form of the verb that indicates the time of the action

---

verb phrase: a verb form with more than one word: a helping verb and some form of the main verb

---

participle: a form of the main verb that follows a helping verb in a verb phrase

---

gerund: present participle used in a sentence as a noun

ties warn people to prepare well for trips to the mountains. (4) A sudden storm could close roads and tie up traffic for hours. (5) Traveling without tire chains, good windshield wipers, plenty of gasoline, and antifreeze in your radiator is foolish. (6) Start out on a mountain drive without blankets and extra food and water could also be regrettable. (7) If you get stuck in the snow, you'll know you should have pay attention to the highway patrol's advice.

4. Sentence 2: **The California Highway Patrol knows that many people will be plan trips to the snow during wet winters.**

    What correction should be made to this sentence?

    (1)   change knows that to knows. That
    (2)   change plan to planning
    (3)   change plan to planned
    (4)   change snow during to snow. During
    (5)   no correction is necessary

5. Sentence 6: **Start out on a mountain drive without blankets and extra food and water could also be regrettable.**

    What correction should be made to this sentence?

    (1)   change Start to Starting
    (2)   change drive to driven
    (3)   insert take before blankets
    (4)   change be to been
    (5)   change regrettable to regretting

6. Sentence 7: **If you get stuck in the snow, you'll know you should have pay attention to the highway patrol's advice.**

    Which of the following is the best way to write the underlined portion of this sentence? If you think the original is the best way, select choice (1).

    (1)   you should have pay attention
    (2)   you should have paying attention
    (3)   you should have been pay attention
    (4)   you should have attention
    (5)   you should have paid attention

To check your answers, turn to page 133.

Using the Correct Verb Form

For most verbs in English, the past participle looks exactly like the simple past tense form of the verb. We merely place a helper in front of it:

> The ponies *trotted* around the track.

> The ponies *have trotted* around the track many times before.

The chart below shows some frequently used regular verbs.

Present Tense (Today I . . .)	Past Tense (Yesterday I . . .)	Past Participle (Many times I have . . .)
sit	sat	sat
walk	walked	walked
play	played	played

Unfortunately, English contains numerous *irregular verbs* that have past participles that differ from their past-tense forms. There is, for example, the *I, A, U* group of verbs:

> sing, sang, sung

> ring, rang, rung

But watch out for these exceptions:

> bring, brought, brought

> swing, swung, swung

Because there are so many irregular verbs in English, you must listen and read carefully to become alert to them. The chart below shows you the forms of some frequently used irregular verbs.

Present Tense (Today I . . .)	Past Tense (Yesterday I . . .)	Past Participle (Many times I have . . .)
am	was	been
bring	brought	brought
choose	chose	chosen
come	came	come
do	did	done
eat	ate	eaten
forget	forgot	forgotten
go	went	gone
know	knew	known
see	saw	seen
take	took	taken
throw	threw	thrown
write	wrote	written

Be careful not to use participles alone, as if they were complete verbs. *"I seen you at the restaurant"* is incorrect. The writer means either *"I saw you at the restaurant"* (past tense) or *"I have seen you at the restaurant"* (verb phrase).

One other verb form to consider is the **infinitive**—a verb form with *to* in front of it: *to go, to stare, to study.* Infinitives function as nouns in sentences. It is important not to *split* an infinitive (separate its parts) in a sentence.

Incorrect: She didn't mean *to rudely stare* at the woman's unusual hat.

Correct: She didn't mean *to stare rudely* at the woman's unusual hat.

Exercise 6

Directions

Choose the one best answer to each item.

Items 1 to 3 refer to the following paragraph.

(1) Not long ago, people thought the way to lose weight was to cutting out starchy foods like potatoes, pasta, and bread. (2) Believing that protein was better for them than carbohydrates, weight-conscious individuals ate extra meat. (3) High-protein diets made the dieters feel hungry and frustrated with their failed efforts to lose weight. (4) They would give up counting calories and go on eating binges, which caused them to gain back whatever pounds they had lose. (5) Nutritionists now understand the best way to reach and maintain a healthful weight is to cut fat rather than carbohydrates out of the diet. (6) It had not been the bread, potatoes, and pasta that caused weight problems. (7) Actually, it had been the butter, sour cream, and rich sauces that people were put on them. (8) Pasta and fresh vegetables has become one of the most popular meals among health-conscious people.

1. Sentence 1: **Not long ago, people thought the way to lose weight was to cutting out starchy foods like potatoes, pasta, and bread.**

   What correction should be made to this sentence?

   (1) change <u>thought</u> to <u>thinked</u>
   (2) change <u>thought</u> to <u>thinking</u>
   (3) change <u>lose</u> to <u>losing</u>
   (4) change <u>lose</u> to <u>lost</u>
   (5) change <u>cutting</u> to <u>cut</u>

2. Sentence 4: **They would give up counting calories and go on eating binges, which caused them to gain back whatever pounds they had lose.**

   If you rewrote sentence 4 beginning with <u>Any weight they had</u> the next word should be

   (1) lose
   (2) losing
   (3) lost
   (4) gained
   (5) eaten

3. Sentence 7: **Actually, it had been the butter, sour cream, and rich sauces that people were put on them.**

   What correction should be made to this sentence?

   (1) change <u>been</u> to <u>being</u>
   (2) replace <u>had been</u> with <u>be</u>
   (3) remove <u>had</u>
   (4) change <u>put</u> to <u>putting</u>
   (5) change <u>put</u> to <u>putten</u>

To check your answers, turn to page 133.

---

infinitive: form of the verb that consists of the word *to* followed by the present tense form of the verb

Using Verb Tenses

When you use verbs, their tense tells your reader when the action in a sentence or paragraph takes place. It is important to know whether an event happened in the past, is happening right now, happens all the time, or will happen later. Verb tense affects a reader's reaction to information.

When you write, you must be careful not to change tenses in midsentence or midparagraph. The following sentence is confusing because it changes from past to future tense:

> The crowd *went* wild when the team *will enter* the stadium.

Does the writer mean the crowd *will go* wild or that the team *entered* the stadium?

The verb tense that uses a present tense helping verb with a past participle *(has gone)* is called present perfect. It may mean the action occurred over a period of time in the past, or that it occurred in the past but continues into the present.

A past tense helping verb with a past participle *(had gone)* is called past perfect, and it indicates that an action was completed in the past after another past action occurred:

> By the time the sun came up, the street cleaners had finished their work.

Sometimes verbs use a past participle with the verb *to be* rather than *to have.* We call these verbs *passive.* They occur in sentences where the subject doesn't perform the action:

> The ladder was placed against the fence.

In the sentence above, we don't see the actor—whoever placed the ladder against the fence. We see only the ladder that someone has placed against the fence. In passive sentences, the subject doesn't perform action; it receives it. Compare the following two sentences.

> The telephone pole was hit hard.

> The truck hit the telephone pole hard.

In the first sentence, no actor is apparent. Instead, the subject *(the telephone pole)* receives action. In the second sentence, the subject *(the truck)* appears and performs an action *(hits the telephone pole).* Good writing tends most often to use active, rather than passive, verb structure.

Exercise 7

> ### Directions
> Circle the time clues in the following sentences and then choose the correct verb tense.

1. When she heard thunder, the kitten (will crawl/ crawled) under the chair.

2. Whenever it rains, I (feel/felt) cold all over.

3. By the time his roommate arrived, Guy (walks/had walked) home.

4. Now Jonathan loves cross-country skiing, but last year he (refuses/refused) to try it.

5. Currently, we (receive/received) only one newspaper, but next fall we will subscribe to two.

6. Now that school has started, I (am/was) ready to study.

7. Last year, Ken and Lucille (will have/had) a long vacation.

> ### Directions
> Choose the one best answer to each item.

> Items 8 to 10 refer to the following passage.

(1) Schools are frequently under attack for not teaching basic reading, writing, and math skills. (2) But even those children who do acquire basic skills in school may be poorly prepared for the world of work. (3) Included among workplace skills are being able to listen, speak, and work well with others. (4) A successful worker needs critical thinking skills, too. (5) Knowing how to handle information and modern technology also will help in the workplace. (6) Equally important were a sense of personal responsibility. (7) Business and labor are working with educators to close the skills gap between the classroom and the job.

Crawl = creeping on hands & knees. (gatea)
acquire = to get

8. Sentence 3: **Included among workplace skills are being able to listen, speak, and work well with others.**

   If you rewrote sentence 3 beginning with <u>Workplace skills</u> the next word should be

   (1) will
   (2) had
   (3) meant
   (4) include
   (5) were

9. Sentence 5: **Knowing how to handle information and modern technology also will help in the workplace.**

   What correction should be made to this sentence?

   (1) change <u>Knowing</u> to <u>Know</u>
   (2) change <u>handle</u> to <u>handling</u>
   (3) change <u>will help</u> to <u>helps</u>
   (4) change <u>will help</u> to <u>helped</u>
   (5) change <u>help in</u> to <u>help. In</u>

10. Sentence 6: **Equally important were a sense of personal responsibility.**

    What correction should be made to this sentence?

    (1) change <u>important were</u> to <u>important. Were</u>
    (2) change <u>were</u> to <u>is</u>
    (3) change <u>were</u> to <u>are</u>
    (4) change <u>were</u> to <u>was</u>
    (5) no correction is necessary

To check your answers, turn to page 133.

Keeping Verb Tense Consistent Throughout a Paragraph

Within paragraphs, the clue for tense in one sentence often comes from the other sentences. This is an important concept to know for the multiple-choice section of the GED Writing Skills Test. For example, if the first three sentences in a paragraph are written in the present tense, the fourth sentence should also be in the present tense. In the paragraph below, you can see what happens when tense changes unnecessarily:

> Kim's parents watch the news every evening. They like to keep up with current events. Kim watches with them, but she preferred game shows.

The sudden shift to past tense in the last sentence is incorrect and confusing. The writer probably meant that Kim *prefers* game shows.

There are times, however, when one sentence in a paragraph could require a different tense from the others. When this is the case, there will be a clue, as in the following example:

Last year the school parking lot *was* a disaster. Cars *parked* in no-parking zones, *blocked* driveways, and *hemmed* in other cars. No one *paid* attention to signs or directions. People *came* in and *went* out the same driveways, and there *were* several accidents. Finally, the police *were called* in to direct traffic and give tickets to illegally parked cars. *This year,* our parking lot *is* easy to use.

All the italicized clues call for past-tense verbs except for the last one, which calls for a present-tense verb.

Exercise 8

Directions: Write the word *present, past,* or *future* to indicate which verb tense would follow each of the clues below.

1. yesterday
2. when I get old
3. the other day
4. next summer
5. right now
6. when I was at my brother's house
7. whenever I hear loud noises
8. at this time tomorrow
9. for the next three months
10. last time

Directions
Correct the following paragraph for appropriate verb tense. All the verbs appear in *italics.* Not all the verbs are incorrect.

11. Last summer, the Orangerie Produce Co. *had* an employee picnic. The picnic *is* a great success, thanks to the Planning Committee. The committee members *will work* for weeks by the time picnic day *arrived.* The employees *had played* games, *danced, swam,* and *ate* hot dogs and apple pie by the end of the day. Everyone *will hope* there *was* another picnic next year.

Directions

Choose the one best answer to each item.

Items 12 to 15 refer to the following paragraphs.

(1) For generations, the United States has been a haven for people from vastly different cultures. (2) The first wave of immigrants, who came primarily from Europe, poured into the country, learned American ways, and become part of the huge American "melting pot." (3) The idea of a melting pot suggests that everyone became the same, adopting the same attitudes, language, and customs.

(4) A new wave of immigration in the 1970s and 1980s has change this view of America. (5) While people continue to seek freedom and opportunity in the United States, they clung with pride to the culture of their homelands. (6) No longer wanting to be like everyone else, American citizens are taking renewed pride in their heritage. (7) It's common to hear a variety of languages in American schools. (8) Restaurants and food stores offer many kinds of ethnic foods. (9) Cultural fairs and festivals gave Americans an opportunity to learn about the music, stories, and costumes of each other's native countries.

12. Sentence 2: **The first wave of immigrants, who came primarily from Europe, poured into the country, learned American ways, and become part of the huge American "melting pot."**

Which of the following is the best way to write the underlined portion of this sentence? If you think the original is the best way, select choice (1).

(1) poured into the country, learned American ways, and become part of
(2) pour into the country, learn American ways, and become part of
(3) poured into the country, learned American ways, and became part of
(4) poured into the country, learn American ways, and become part of
(5) pour into the country, learn American ways, and became part of

13. Sentence 4: **A new wave of immigration in the 1970s and 1980s has change this view of America.**

What correction should be made to this sentence?

(1) replace has change with is changing
(2) replace has change with has changed
(3) change has to had
(4) remove has
(5) no correction is necessary

14. Sentence 5: **While people continue to seek freedom and opportunity in the United States, they clung with pride to the culture of their homelands.**

Which of the following is the best way to write the underlined portion of this sentence? If you think the original is the best way, select choice (1).

(1) they clung with pride to
(2) they clinged with pride to
(3) they clang with pride to
(4) they cling with pride to
(5) they were proud of

15. Sentence 9: **Cultural fairs and festivals gave Americans an opportunity to learn about the music, stories, and costumes of each other's native countries.**

What correction should be made to this sentence?

(1) change gave to give
(2) change gave to had given
(3) replace to with for
(4) remove to
(5) replace to with and

To check your answers, turn to page 134.

Using Pronouns

Writing stays both interesting and clear when we use pronouns. **Pronouns** are words used to refer to nouns, where otherwise we would have to repeat the noun. Without them, both speech and writing would not only sound ridiculous but would be difficult to understand.

This is what would happen if we eliminated pronouns from our writing:

Jason and Peter were longtime friends, Jason and Peter worked together in construction, and Jason and Peter shared Jason's and Peter's tools.

Three repetitions of the subjects' names would confuse the reader and sound very strange. Here's how pronouns improve writing:

Jason and Peter were longtime friends who worked together in construction and shared their tools.

English has a variety of pronouns for several different purposes. The most common group of pronouns refers to specific people or things:

I	you	he	she
it	me	him	her
we	they	us	them

Example: The lifeguard said *we* can swim today.

Another group of pronouns refers to nonspecific people or things; that is, nouns that are not specified elsewhere in the sentence:

anyone	everybody	no one	anything
each	one	both	nothing
many	others	one	

Example: *Many* disagreed.

Some pronouns suggest ownership:

yours	his	hers	its
mine	theirs	ours	

Example: Joel said to keep *your* hands off *his* car.

Others are used for emphasis or to reflect back on the noun:

myself	ourselves	yourself	itself
himself	herself	themselves	

Examples: The children can tie their shoes by *themselves.* I, *myself,* wouldn't do that.

Exercise 9

Directions
Choose the one best answer to each item.

Items 1 to 4 refer to the following paragraph.

(1) About 35 million Americans suffer from an illness called Seasonal Affective Disorder. (2) These 35 million Americans lack energy and feel sad and hopeless during the long nights and dreary days of winter. (3) Victims of SAD, as the disorder is called by psychiatrists, often overeat, gain weight, lose interest in his jobs, and have trouble with their relationships. (4) Children and adolescents, who suffer from SAD just like adults, exhibit disruptive behavior in school, have short attention spans, and lack interest in learning. (5) The illness affects more women than men. (6) Researchers think the dim light of winter causes a reduction in certain brain chemicals and that people who are sensitive to this deprivation feel the symptoms of SAD. (7) It's possible to buy special lights that are twenty times brighter than ordinary indoor lights. (8) To control the symptoms for many people. (9) Anyone who suffers from SAD should consult a physician for advice and treatment.

1. Sentence 2: **These 35 million Americans lack energy and feel sad and hopeless during the long nights and dreary days of winter.**

    Which of the following is the best way to write the underlined portion of this sentence? If you think the original is the best way, select choice 1.

    (1) These 35 million Americans
    (2) Everyone
    (3) Because they
    (4) Sometimes
    (5) They

pronoun: a word that replaces or refers to a noun

2. Sentence 3: **Victims of SAD, as the disorder is called by psychiatrists, often overeat, gain weight, lose interest in his jobs, and have trouble with their relationships.**

   What correction should be made to this sentence?

   (1) change <u>called</u> to <u>call</u>
   (2) change <u>psychiatrists, often</u> to <u>psychiatrists. Often</u>
   (3) change <u>overeat</u> to <u>overeats</u>
   (4) change <u>gains</u> to <u>gained</u>
   (5) change <u>his</u> to <u>their</u>

3. Sentence 8: **To control the symptoms for many people.**

   Which of the following is the best way to write the underlined portion of this sentence? If you think the original is the best way, select choice (1).

   (1) To control the symptoms
   (2) They control the symptoms
   (3) Their control the symptoms
   (4) Its control of the symptoms
   (5) They themselves control the symptoms

4. Sentence 9: **Anyone who suffers from SAD should consult a physician for advice and treatment.**

   What correction should be made to this sentence?

   (1) replace <u>Anyone</u> with <u>They</u>
   (2) change <u>suffers</u> to <u>suffer</u>
   (3) change <u>consult</u> to <u>consulted</u>
   (4) change <u>physician for</u> to <u>physician. For</u>
   (5) no correction is necessary

To check your answers, turn to page 134.

Choosing the Correct Pronoun

The form of personal pronouns, those that substitute for specific people, is determined by the role the pronoun plays in the clause it appears in. That means if the pronoun is the actor in the clause, it must be in the subject form *(we, he, she, they)*. If it's the receiver of the action, it must be in the object form *(us, him, her, them)*.

Just as verbs must agree with the nouns they go with in a sentence, pronouns must agree with the nouns they replace. The noun that is replaced by a pronoun is called an **antecedent,** and pronouns must agree with their antecedents in two ways.

First, the pronoun and antecedent must agree in number. That is, if the noun is plural, the pronoun must be plural, and if the noun is singular, the pronoun must be singular. The most common mistake with pronoun agreement in number is to confuse *their* with *his* or *her* and *them* with *him* or *her*.

Incorrect: Each applicant must turn in their cards.

This sentence is incorrect because the antecedent, *applicant*, is singular, but the pronoun, *their*, is plural. The sentence should read:

Correct: Each applicant must turn in his or her card.

You can make the pronoun and antecedent agree in number in the above sentence by rewriting it and by changing the antecedent:

Correct: All applicants must turn in their cards.

This construction actually is preferable because it avoids the awkwardness of using *his or her*.

The following table shows that pronouns and antecedents must also agree by person.

Type of Pronoun	Pronoun
First-person pronouns (refer to *me*)	I, we, me, us, my, mine, our, ours, myself, and ourselves
Second-person pronouns (refer to *you*)	you, your, yourself, and yourselves
Third-person pronouns (refer to everyone and everything other than *me* or *you*)	he, she, it, they, him, her, them, his, hers, its, theirs, himself, herself, and themselves

antecedent: the noun that a pronoun substitutes for or replaces

If you write one part of a sentence or a paragraph in the third person, it would be incorrect to shift suddenly to first- or second-person pronouns. For example, if you're talking about *Marjorie* (third person), do not shift to *you* for the pronoun:

Incorrect: Marjorie knows that if she wants to win, *you* must practice every day.

Correct: Marjorie knows that if she wants to win, *she* must practice every day.

Exercise 10

Directions
Correct the pronouns in the following sentences, making sure they agree with the nouns and are in the proper form.

1. Manuel and Umeki agreed to share one's study notes with each other.

2. A baby seal can swim by themselves right away.

3. The basketball team lost their third game in a row.

Directions
Choose the one best answer to each item.

Items 4 to 6 refer to the following paragraph.

(1) If you're looking for a bargain, many people love to shop in consignment stores. (2) For low prices, these stores sell used clothing and other items that are in good condition. (3) It's possible to find wonderful bargains and hidden treasures. (4) One might find great clothing for yourself and gifts for your friends. (5) Consignment items might come from people who need new clothes because they have gained or lost weight. (6) Some people just get tired of their perfectly good clothes and want to sell them. (7) After selling an item, the owner of the store gives a portion of the money to the original owner and keeps the rest. (8) They make money, and you get our bargain.

4. Sentence 1: **If you're looking for a bargain, many people love to shop in consignment stores.**

Which of the following is the best way to write the underlined portion of this sentence? If you think the original is the best way, select choice (1).

(1) many people love to shop
(2) they love to shop
(3) you might like to shop
(4) everyone loves to shop
(5) I would prefer to shop

5. Sentence 4: **One might find great clothing for yourself and gifts for your friends.**

What correction should be made to this sentence?

(1) replace One with I
(2) replace One with We
(3) replace One with They
(4) replace One with You
(5) replace One with It

6. Sentence 8: **They make money, and you get our bargain.**

What correction should be made to this sentence?

(1) replace They with We
(2) replace They with You
(3) replace you with we
(4) replace you with they
(5) replace our with your

To check your answers, turn to page 134.

Does the Pronoun Fit the Rest of the Sentence?

In some GED Writing Skills Test items, you will need to correct the use of pronouns and their antecedents. You've seen how confusing it can be when pronouns do not agree with their antecedents in number and person. Sometimes, antecedents are so unclear that readers can't tell whether or not the pronouns agree with them. Can you tell what all the pronouns refer to in the following passage?

> A group of us had hoped to go fishing over the weekend. We had gathered several times at one person's house to plan the trip. We agreed that some of us would have to go to the store to purchase supplies, while the others would get the boat and fishing gear ready. The day before the trip, when it was time to buy the food, they were so tired that we decided to forget it.

The last sentence raises a few questions: Who are *they?* Are they the people who were going on the trip? Are they the people who sold supplies? What is *it* they decided to forget? Is it shopping for supplies or it is the entire fishing trip?

When you use pronouns, you must make sure the antecedents are clear. Otherwise, the reader can't tell what the pronoun refers to and probably won't be able to understand what you mean.

Unclear pronoun references usually occur for one of three reasons:

1. There are two possible antecedents for a single pronoun.

   Mario told Albert *he* was wrong.

Because either *Mario* or *Albert* could be the antecedent for the pronoun *he*, the reader can't tell who was wrong.

2. The antecedent is placed too far away from the pronoun.

   At the bottom of the hill was a huge forest. Hundreds of trees crowded together to hide the sky. Pine needles covered up the paths, and overgrown shrubs and vines blocked the view. Hiking to the other side was difficult. The campers were frightened by *it*.

The pronoun *it* is so far from its antecedent *forest* that a reader might wonder what *it* is.

3. There is no antecedent.

   Patricia always loved school, which made her want to become a teacher.

The pronoun *which* doesn't refer to any particular noun. You might rewrite the sentence to read: *The fact that Patricia always loved school made her want to become a teacher.*

Exercise 11

Directions
Choose the one best answer for each item.

Items 1 to 3 refer to the following paragraph.

(1) Historians and sociologists study periods of time and attach labels to them. (2) Some decades, for example, carry names that suggest their main characteristics. (3) We refer to the last decade of the 1800s as the Gay Nineties because of its general prosperity. (4) These were years when people had jobs. (5) They were industrially productive. (6) The Roaring Twenties suggests a time of wild behavior, when women cut her hair short and smoked cigarettes. (7) Wild dances like the Charleston were popular, and young people drove fast cars and partied a great deal. (8) Student protest, the sexual revolution, and feminism characterize the radical '60s and '70s. (9) The 1980s are seen as a time of greed, when selfish pursuit of money is what drove them.

1. Sentences 4 and 5: **These were years when people had jobs. They were industrially productive.**

   The most effective combination of sentences 4 and 5 would include which of the following groups of words?

   (1) Although people had jobs
   (2) Although they were industrially productive
   (3) During these industrially productive years
   (4) Despite their productivity
   (5) Even though most people had jobs

2. Sentence 6: **The Roaring Twenties suggests a time of wild behavior, when women cut her hair short and smoked cigarettes.**

   What correction should be made to this sentence?

   (1) replace her with our
   (2) replace her with their
   (3) replace her with its
   (4) replace her with hers
   (5) no correction is necessary

3. Sentence 9: **The 1980s are seen as a time of greed, when <u>selfish pursuit of money is what drove them.</u>**

Which of the following is the best way to write the underlined portion of this sentence? If you think the original is the best way, select choice (1).

(1) selfish pursuit of money is what drove them
(2) they were driven by selfish pursuit of money
(3) selfish pursuit of money motivated them
(4) people selfishly pursued money
(5) they were selfish and drove big cars

To check your answers, turn to page 134.

Using Relative Pronouns

Relative pronouns are a special kind of pronoun; they don't actually replace a noun but refer to it.

| who | whom | which |
| whoever | whomever | that |

Relative pronouns give you another way to combine ideas into a single sentence.

Simple sentence with a relative pronoun clause: People *who want muscular bodies* work out regularly.

When we refer to <u>animals</u> or <u>things</u>, we use *that* or *which*, but when we refer to <u>people</u>, we use *who* or *whom*.

❂ The birds *that* sing all morning have built a nest in our tree.

❂ The people *who* sing in the choir have nice voices.

Many people are troubled by *who* and *whom* because they can't figure out which one to use. You can solve this problem by remembering that *who* is used in the subject or actor position in a sentence or clause, and *whom* is used in the object or receiver position.

In the sentence below, the relative pronoun *who* is used as the subject of a clause. *Is going* is the verb.

Give a ticket to everyone *who* is going.

In the following sentence, the relative pronoun *whom* is used as an object:

The man *whom* the police suspected was proved innocent.

When you're not sure whether to use *who* or *whom*, look only at the words in the clause. Mentally substitute *he* or *him* for the pronoun, and if *he* fits, use who; if *him* fits, use whom.

The officer told the jury *(who/whom)* was at the scene of the crime.

Make the *he/him* substitution, and you find that only *he* makes sense:

The officer told the jury *(he/who)* was at the scene of the crime.

Exercise 12

1. All the dogs (who/that) went to obedience school can perform tricks.

2. Everyone (who/that) asked received an announcement.

3. Mrs. Doak, (who/which) lives next door, travels every summer.

4. (Who/Whom) shall I ask to help?

5. They finally fixed the car (who/that) had broken down four times.

6. (Whoever/Whomever) wants to come is welcome.

Items 7 to 11 refer to the following paragraph.

(1) Because of their convenience, more and more people are running businesses out of their homes. (2) A home-based business is good for anyone who can discipline themselves. (3) Some companies allow employees to work at home, so they can have a home office without owning their own business. (4) People that work at home might miss the company of other workers and become lonely. (5) However, some people do very well on your own. (6) Working at home means one must be careful not to get caught up in the distractions of family, housework, or watching television instead of working; it can be a problem. (7) Some

relative pronoun: does not replace a noun but refers to it people who work at home find they snack all day long and gain weight. (8) Some home-based workers work late into the night and fail to get enough sleep, but others find the quiet of night hours the most appealing part of working in a home office.

7. Sentence 1: **Because of their convenience, more and more people are running businesses out of their homes.**

   Which of the following is the best way to write the underlined portion of this sentence? If you think the original is the best way, select choice (1).

   (1) Because of their convenience,
   (2) Because they find it convenient,
   (3) Being convenient,
   (4) For your convenience,
   (5) Because of your convenience,

8. Sentence 2: **A home-based business is good for anyone who can discipline themselves.**

   What correction should be made to this sentence?

   (1) replace anyone with someone
   (2) replace anyone with people
   (3) replace anyone with a person
   (4) change themselves to themself
   (5) no correction is necessary

9. Sentence 4: **People that work at home might miss the company of other workers and become lonely.**

   What correction should be made to this sentence?

   (1) replace People with Someone
   (2) replace People with Anyone
   (3) replace that with whom
   (4) replace that with who
   (5) replace that with which

10. Sentence 5: **However, some people do very well on your own.**

    What correction should be made to this sentence?

    (1) replace your with his or her
    (2) replace your with our
    (3) replace your with their
    (4) replace your with one's
    (5) no correction is necessary

11. Sentence 6: **Working at home means one must be careful not to get caught up in the distractions of family, housework, or watching television instead of working; it can be a problem.**

    If you rewrote sentence 6 beginning with Home-based workers must beware of the next word should be

    (1) working
    (2) them
    (3) it
    (4) him or her
    (5) distractions

To check your answers, turn to page 134.

MECHANICS

Capitalization

When you refer to general items, like *cities*, you don't capitalize the word. But if you refer to a specific city, like *Dallas*, you must capitalize its name.

Examples of specific and general names appear in the table below.

Names of Specific People, Places, and Things	People, Places, and Things in General
Governor Pataki will speak.	The governor will speak.
We live at 2511 Oak Street.	Our street is shady.
I'm reading *War and Peace*.	There could be a war.
They went rafting on the Colorado River.	They went rafting on the river.
He lives in the West.	She lives on the west side of the street.
They enjoyed *Gone with the Wind*.	They enjoyed last night's movie.

The following paragraph, which contains no capitalization errors, shows the distinction between general and specific words:

When Jim decided to open a bank account with some money his aunt had given him, he looked for a bank that was both open on Saturdays and located close to his home. Looking in the phone book's yellow pages, he discovered First Continental Bank had a branch near his house on Olive Street. His Aunt Millie's check was large enough for him to open the account and still have some extra cash to buy *A Tale of Two Cities,* the book he needed for his class on the French Revolution. At the bank, he was assisted by Mr. Collier, an account clerk.

You see that words that name specific people or places are capitalized, while more general words are not.

We learn that Jim received money from his *aunt*, which could be any of his aunts. Later in the paragraph, we learn that the money came from *Aunt Millie*. In this instance, *Aunt* is part of someone's name. It refers to a specific person, so it must be capitalized. Jim was assisted by *an account clerk*, which could be any unnamed account clerk. But the writer could have said, "Jim was assisted by Account Clerk Collier." In this case, *Account Clerk* is capitalized because it is someone's title.

Exercise 1

Directions
Some of the specific names in the following sentences lack capitalization. Correct the sentences by capitalizing those words. Not all the sentences contain errors.

1. The notice says dr. Juanita Moreno will speak tonight.

2. We heard a deputy sheriff at the july meeting.

3. The governor answered questions for more than an hour.

4. Ryan likes old movies; his favorite is *casablanca*.

5. Chidori speaks several languages, including japanese, english, and french.

Directions
Choose the one best answer to each item.

Items 6 and 7 refer to the following paragraph.

(1) Our legislator is senator Sperling. (2) He shows a genuine interest in his constituents. (3) Every month he sends out a newsletter and a questionnaire to survey voters' opinions on several issues. (4) He occasionally holds meetings at a public library. (5) Last month he spoke about health care at the Brownsville public library. (6) This is one politician who understands the need for voters to be informed. (7) He wants to keep in touch with the people.

6. Sentence 1: **Our legislator is senator Sperling.**

What correction should be made to this sentence?

(1) change Our to our
(2) change legislator to Legislator
(3) change senator to Senator
(4) change Sperling to sperling
(5) no correction is necessary

7. Sentence 5: **Last month he spoke about health care at the Brownsville public library.**

What correction should be made to this sentence?

(1) change month to Month
(2) change health to Health
(3) change Brownsville to brownsville
(4) change public library to Public Library
(5) no correction is necessary

To check your answers, turn to page 135.

Some Words Are *Always* Capitalized

Distinguishing between the general and the specific helps you determine when to capitalize many words. Certain words, however, always need to be capitalized. The best way to recognize them is to learn the following rules of capitalization.

Always capitalize:

1. Names of people and places

   Shirley Chisholm, John F. Kennedy, Lincoln Center, Museum of Modern Art, Grand Canyon

2. Titles of works (books, movies, paintings) Note: Do not capitalize *and*, *or*, *the*, *a*, *an*, or prepositions of fewer than five letters in titles unless they are the first or last word of the title.

   For Whom the Bell Tolls, *The Witches of Eastwick*, *Jurassic Park*, Leonardo da Vinci's *The Last Supper*

3. Names of streets, cities, states, and countries

   They live in the United States, at 555 Elm Street, Montgomery, Alabama.

4. Titles of people

   Doctor (Dr.) Hobart, Mayor Wallace, Princess Diana, Aunt Ethel, the President of the United States

   A person may serve up to eight years as President of the United States.

5. Days of the week, months, and holidays (but not seasons)

   The third Saturday in August is when we begin our vacation every summer, and we return after Labor Day.

6. Historic eras or events

   the Renaissance, World War II, the Stone Age

7. Languages or nationalities

   He speaks Spanish and loves Mexican food.

8. Direction words when used as the name of a place

   They moved to the West. Our cousins live in Northern Ireland.

   Do *not* capitalize directions when they are used to describe something:

   The southern side of the house needs shade.

   Their house faces east.

Exercise 2

Directions
Choose the one best answer to each item.

Items 1 to 5 refer to the following paragraph.

(1) The United States has almost fifty National Parks ranging from the western edge of the continent to the eastern edge. (2) Some, like yellowstone, cover territory in more than one state. (3) Each park boasts something beautiful and special. (4) For example, the Great Smoky Mountains are the largest eastern Mountain Range. (5) California's Yosemite national park is famous for having the nation's highest waterfall. (6) Mammoth cave in Kentucky has 144 miles of underground passages. (7) Our national parks preserve the scenic wonders of our land.

1. Sentence 1: **The United States has almost fifty National Parks ranging from the western edge of the continent to the eastern edge.**

   What correction should be made to this sentence?

   (1) change <u>United States</u> to <u>united states</u>
   (2) change <u>National Parks</u> to <u>national parks</u>
   (3) change <u>western</u> to <u>Western</u>
   (4) change <u>continent</u> to <u>Continent</u>
   (5) change <u>eastern</u> to <u>Eastern</u>

2. Sentence 2: **Some, like yellowstone, cover territory in more than one state.**

   What correction should be made to this sentence?

   (1) change <u>Some</u> to <u>some</u>
   (2) change <u>yellowstone</u> to <u>Yellowstone</u>
   (3) change <u>territory</u> to <u>Territory</u>
   (4) change <u>state</u> to <u>State</u>
   (5) no correction is necessary

3. Sentence 4: **For example, the Great Smoky Mountains are the largest eastern Mountain Range.**

   What correction should be made to this sentence?

   (1) change <u>example</u> to <u>Example</u>
   (2) change <u>Great Smoky Mountains</u> to <u>great smoky mountains</u>
   (3) change <u>largest</u> to <u>Largest</u>
   (4) change <u>eastern</u> to <u>Eastern</u>
   (5) change <u>Mountain Range</u> to <u>mountain range</u>

4. Sentence 5: **California's Yosemite national park is famous for having the nation's highest waterfall.**

   What correction should be made to this sentence?

   (1) change <u>Yosemite</u> to <u>yosemite</u>
   (2) change <u>national park</u> to <u>National Park</u>
   (3) change <u>nation's</u> to <u>Nation's</u>
   (4) change <u>highest</u> to <u>Highest</u>
   (5) change <u>waterfall</u> to <u>Waterfall</u>

5. Sentence 6: **Mammoth cave in Kentucky has 144 miles of underground passages.**

   What correction should be made to this sentence?

   (1) change <u>Mammoth</u> to <u>mammoth</u>
   (2) change <u>cave</u> to <u>Cave</u>
   (3) change <u>Kentucky</u> to <u>kentucky</u>
   (4) change <u>underground</u> to <u>Underground</u>
   (5) change <u>passages</u> to <u>Passages</u>

To check your answers, turn to page 135.

Punctuation

In writing, punctuation is essential to make the meaning clear. Periods, question marks, and exclamation points appear at the ends of sentences and rarely present problems.

Commas, on the other hand, are used internally in sentences for a variety of reasons. They indicate pauses in thought, and they show relationships among the ideas in a sentence.

Separating Items in a Series

Occasionally, you will write a sentence that lists three or more items:

A good baseball player must be able to *bat*, *run*, *throw*, and *catch*.

The items in the list are separated by commas. Notice that the last comma appears before *and*.

It's incorrect to place a comma *after* the conjunction that links the last two items in the series:

Incorrect: Everyone loved the movie's action, romance, and, suspense.

Correct: Everyone loved the movie's action, romance, and suspense.

It's also incorrect to place a comma at the end of the series:

Incorrect: The acting, the scenery, and the music, thrilled the audience.

Correct: The acting, the scenery, and the music thrilled the audience.

If your list contains only two items, you don't need a comma:

Marilee's strengths were *running and throwing*.

Mel could neither *run nor throw*.

If you use conjunctions between items in a list, you don't need commas. Both of these sentences are correct:

They can find a chair or stand up or sit on the floor.

They can find a chair, stand up, or sit on the floor.

Exercise 3

Directions

In the following sentences, use commas to separate the items in a series. Not all the sentences require commas.

1. Mr. and Mrs. Suarez took their tent their cooking utensils and their fishing gear to the campsite in the woods.

2. They preferred camping in the summer when they could count on warm weather long days and good fishing.

3. They only had room for one extra lawn chair or a picnic basket or some extra blankets.

4. They forgot to bring the hot dogs and the mustard.

5. They did have plenty of equipment for swimming fishing and hiking.

6. Some people would rather vacation in cities than in mountains woods or the country.

7. They enjoy bustling city life with all that it offers, such as museums theater and restaurants.

8. Still others prefer to stay home to rest or work on projects around the house.

9. Winter vacations can be nice if you live in a climate that is cold or wet.

10. It can be fun to spend time exploring your own city neighborhood and community.

Directions

Choose the one best answer to each item.

Items 11 to 13 refer to the following paragraph.

(1) People plant trees for many reasons. (2) Large trees cool yards in summer because of their shade, and their green color. (3) Some trees are chosen for their beauty. (4) They may be covered with flowers in spring or change color in fall or have unusual leaves. (5) Fruit trees have beautiful blossoms in spring, tasty peaches, or cherries in summer, and good climbing branches all year round. (6) Scientists now believe trees also help counteract the greenhouse effect. (7) Some local governments are considering communitywide tree-planting campaigns to keep cities cool and attractive.

11. Sentence 2: **Large trees cool yards in summer because of their shade, and their green color.**

    What correction should be made to this sentence?

    (1) remove the comma after <u>shade</u>
    (2) remove <u>and</u>
    (3) insert a comma after <u>and</u>
    (4) insert a comma after <u>green</u>
    (5) no correction is necessary

12. Sentence 4: **They may be covered with flowers <u>in spring or change color in fall or have</u> unusual leaves.**

    Which of the following is the best way to write the underlined portion of this sentence? If you think the original is the best way, select choice (1).

    (1) in spring or change color in fall or have
    (2) in spring, or change color in fall or have
    (3) in spring or change color in fall or, have
    (4) in spring or change color in fall but have
    (5) in spring or change color in fall so have

13. Sentence 5: **Fruit trees have beautiful blossoms in spring, tasty peaches, or cherries in summer, and good climbing branches all year round.**

    What correction should be made to this sentence?

    (1) remove the comma after <u>spring</u>
    (2) remove the comma after <u>peaches</u>
    (3) remove the comma after <u>summer</u>
    (4) insert a comma after <u>and</u>
    (5) no correction is necessary

To check your answers, turn to page 135.

Linking Ideas into One Sentence

To add variety to your writing, you will sometimes join two or more ideas together into one sentence.

You must use a comma between independent clauses when you join the clauses with the connecting words (conjunctions) *and, so, but,* and *or.* The connecting word in compound sentences always appears in between the two clauses.

Late movies on television put me to *sleep, so* I don't watch them.

Certain connecting words in compound sentences take a semicolon and a comma. The semicolon precedes the connector, and the comma follows:

Movies on television put me to *sleep; however,* I never fall asleep in a movie theater.

These connectors are usually preceded by a semicolon and followed by a comma:

however	nevertheless	otherwise	on the other hand
finally	instead	likewise	moreover
besides	furthermore	in addition	consequently
thus	therefore	as a result	for example

Writing complex sentences is another way to link ideas into a single sentence. In complex sentences, one of the ideas will have a connecting word attached to it that makes it dependent upon the rest of the sentence for its meaning. That dependent clause, with the connecting word attached, can appear at the beginning or at the end of the sentence.

If the dependent clause appears at the beginning, before the independent clause, you must follow it with a comma:

Whenever I drink tea, I put lemon in it.

If the dependent clause appears at the end, after the independent clause, you do not use a comma:

I add lemon *whenever I drink tea.*

Exercise 4

Directions

Choose the one best answer to each item.

Items 1 to 4 refer to the following paragraph.

(1) Enormous parking lots near shopping malls, hospitals, business districts, supermarkets, and movie theaters attest to the vast numbers of cars in America and the amount of time people spend in them. (2) Once people buck traffic jams to get to these parking lots they face the problem of finding a convenient parking place. (3) Because physical disabilities make it truly difficult for some people to walk long distances a few spaces for the disabled are often reserved close to the buildings. (4) Parking in these spots requires a special license plate. (5) It's not uncommon to find these spaces illegally occupied. (6) Parking in these spaces illegally carries a heavy fine. (7) Law enforcement officers have little time to patrol parking lots, but some communities have solved that problem with volunteers. (8) These volunteers cite illegally parked cars, inform the driver and report the car to the authorities.

1. Sentence 2: **Once people buck traffic jams to get to these parking lots they face the prob-lem of finding a convenient parking place.**

   Which of the following is the best way to write the underlined portion of this sentence? If you think the original is the best way, select choice (1).

   (1) to get to these parking lots they face
   (2) to get to these parking lots. They face
   (3) to get to these, parking lots they face
   (4) to get to these parking lots, they face
   (5) to get, to these parking lots they face

2. Sentence 3: **Because physical disabilities make it truly difficult for some people to walk long distances a few spaces for the disabled are often reserved close to the buildings.**

   What correction should be made to this sentence?

   (1) insert a comma after difficult
   (2) insert a comma after distances
   (3) insert a comma after spaces
   (4) insert a comma after disabled
   (5) no correction is necessary

3. Sentences 4 and 5: **Parking in these spots requires a special license plate. It's not uncommon to find these spaces illegally occupied.**

   The most effective combination of sentences 4 and 5 would include which of the following groups of words?

   (1) Parking is not uncommon
   (2) Illegally parked cars occupy
   (3) Even though spaces are illegal
   (4) Special license plates require
   (5) Cars without spaces

4. Sentence 8: **These volunteers cite illegally parked cars, inform the driver and report the car to the authorities.**

   What correction should be made to this sentence?

   (1) insert a comma after volunteers
   (2) remove the comma after cars
   (3) insert a comma after driver
   (4) insert a comma after and
   (5) insert a comma after report

To check your answers, turn to page 135.

Using Commas to Set Off Parts of Sentences

Commas help readers understand your writing. Commas can indicate a pause in thought, or they may tell the reader that some information is set apart from the main part of the sentence.

Single words or word *groups* (called **phrases**) sometimes appear at the beginning of sentences to give the reader additional information. Introductory words, phrases, and clauses must be followed by a comma:

Across town, crowds watched the Fourth of July parade.

Hoping for a miracle, Louis searched the house for his lost keys.

Eagerly, Yolanda opened the letter from her brother.

Before the car started, the passengers fastened their seat belts.

When addressing someone directly in a sentence, you use a comma:

Mother, please don't tell me what to wear.

Occasionally, a sentence contains a word or a phrase that interrupts the main thought. If you remove the word or phrase, you still have a sentence that makes sense.

Roy attended night school, exhausting himself in the process, to become a car mechanic.

The main idea of the sentence is that Roy attended school at night to become a car mechanic. The fact that he was exhausting himself in the process is informative, but not necessary to make the sentence clear.

Another kind of interrupter describes a noun in the sentence:

Dmitri, *a Russian immigrant,* was eager to master English.

Common interrupters that are set off by commas include such expressions as *for example* and *I believe*, as well as people's names:

Consider, *for example,* yesterday's discussion.

Their favorite cousins, *Jeff and Lee,* were coming to visit.

You must not use commas to set apart information in the middle of a sentence if that information is *essential* to the meaning of the sentence. If you're tempted to set off some words or phrases with commas, try reading the sentence without those words to be sure it still makes sense. Remember, the commas mean you can omit the words between them without changing the meaning of the sentence.

Exercise 5

Directions

Choose the <u>one best answer</u> to each item.

Items 1 to 3 refer to the following paragraph.

(1) One of the most famous English writers of the last century was Charles Dickens, a novelist who lived from 1812 to 1870. (2) When he was alive his novels appeared in magazines in serial form. (3) People read the stories in monthly installments, and had to wait for the next issue to find out about the next plot twist. (4) Acclaimed during his lifetime, Dickens remains a popular novelist whose offbeat characters and satiric plots are well known to people around the world. (5) Among his books are the well-known titles, *David Copperfield, Oliver Twist, A Tale of Two Cities,* and *A Christmas Carol.*

1. Sentence 2: **When he was alive his novels appeared in magazines in serial form.**

   What correction should be made to this sentence?

   (1) change <u>was</u> to <u>were</u>
   (2) insert a comma after <u>alive</u>
   (3) change <u>appeared</u> to <u>will appear</u>
   (4) change the spelling of <u>magazines</u> to <u>magisines</u>
   (5) no correction is necessary

phrase: a word group that does not contain a subject and verb; a phrase often appears at the beginning of a sentence as introductory material

2. Sentence 3: **People read the stories in monthly installments, and had to wait for the next issue to find out about the next plot twist.**

Which of the following is the best way to write the underlined portion of this sentence? If you think the original is the best way, select choice (1).

(1) monthly installments, and had to wait
(2) monthly installments, and have to wait
(3) monthly installments, and will wait
(4) monthly installments and had to wait
(5) Monthly Installments, and had to wait

3. Sentence 5: **Among his books are the well-known titles, *David Copperfield, Oliver Twist, A Tale of Two Cities*, and *A Christmas Carol*.**

What correction should be made to this sentence?

(1) insert a comma after are
(2) change titles to Titles
(3) remove the comma after titles
(4) change of to Of
(5) remove the comma after *Cities*

To check your answers, turn to page 135.

Avoiding Overuse of Commas

Inserting a comma that doesn't belong in a sentence can confuse readers just as much as omitting one that does. Avoid the following common errors:

1. Separating the subject and verb in a sentence

Incorrect: Some gas *stations, let* you pay with a credit card.

Correct: Some gas stations let you pay with a credit card.

2. Separating compound subjects and verbs

Incorrect: *Ricardo, and* Cameron rented a truck to move furniture.

Correct: Ricardo and Cameron rented a truck to move furniture.

3. Separating independent clauses without a connecting word

Incorrect: Oliver H. Perry was an important naval hero in the *1800s, he* defeated the British and their Indian allies.

Correct: Oliver H. Perry was an important naval hero in the 1800s, and he defeated the British and their Indian allies.

4. Putting a comma after the connecting word

Incorrect: There are many legends about the origins of the American flag *so, historians* aren't sure who designed the original.

Correct: There are many legends about the origins of the American flag, so historians aren't sure who designed the original.

5. Putting a comma before the first item in a series

Incorrect: Most school districts *require, history, English, science, and math* for high school graduation.

Correct: Most school districts require history, English, science, and math for high school graduation.

6. Putting a comma after the conjunction in a series

Incorrect: The reasons people take the GED examination include *preparing for higher education, seeking a better job, or, feeling a sense of accomplishment.*

Correct: The reasons people take the GED examination include preparing for higher education, seeking a better job, or feeling a sense of accomplishment.

7. Putting a comma after the last item in a series

Incorrect: Americans often take things like *hot running water, telephones, and automobiles,* for granted.

Correct: Americans often take things like hot running water, telephones, and automobiles for granted.

8. Separating an adjective from the noun it describes

Incorrect: You can recognize black widow spiders by the *hourglass, markings* on their bodies.

Correct: You can recognize black widow spiders by the hourglass markings on their bodies.

Exercise 6

Directions
Choose the one best answer to each item.

Items 1 to 4 refer to the following paragraph.

(1) The designers of the U.S. government, were radical thinkers in their day. (2) But that was more than

200 years ago. (3) Our nation's founders would be amazed today to see women in the President's Cabinet, on the Supreme Court and, in Congress. (4) Although they designed a democratic government, these men did not include women even among the voters. (5) Women have made huge strides in government participation and a woman probably will become president someday.

1. Sentence 1: **The designers of the U.S. government, were radical thinkers in their day.**

   What correction should be made to this sentence?

   (1) insert a comma after designers
   (2) remove the comma after government
   (3) insert a comma after radical
   (4) insert a comma after thinkers
   (5) no correction is necessary

2. Sentence 3: **Our nation's founders would be amazed today to see women in the President's Cabinet, on the Supreme Court and, in Congress.**

   Which of the following is the best way to write the underlined portion of this sentence? If you think the original is the best way, select choice (1).

   (1) in the President's Cabinet, on the Supreme Court and, in Congress
   (2) in the President's Cabinet, on the Supreme Court, and, in Congress
   (3) in the President's Cabinet, on the Supreme, Court, and in Congress
   (4) in the President's Cabinet, on the Supreme Court, and in Congress
   (5) in the President's Cabinet, on the Supreme Court and in Congress

3. Sentence 4: **Although they designed a democratic government, these men did not include women even among the voters.**

   What correction should be made to this sentence?

   (1) insert a comma after Although
   (2) remove the comma after government
   (3) insert a comma after men
   (4) insert a comma after women
   (5) no correction is necessary

4. Sentence 5: **Women have made huge strides in government participation and a woman probably will become president someday.**

   Which of the following is the best way to write the underlined portion of this sentence? If you think the original is the best way, select choice (1).

   (1) participation and a woman
   (2) participation a woman
   (3) participation and, a woman
   (4) participation, and a woman
   (5) participation; and a woman

To check your answers, turn to page 136.

Overcoming Spelling Problems

A good essay can be marred by misspelled words. Spelling skills are also important on the multiple-choice section of the GED Writing Skills Test. You will need to know some basic rules, memorize exceptions to the rules, and practice. Study the list on page 123. A dictionary can also help you with difficult words.

It's easier to spell words if you divide them into **syllables**. A syllable is a part of a word that is pronounced as a single unit: go + ing = going; fe + ver + ish = feverish. Say the word first, to hear how many syllables there are, and spell each one as you write. Notice that each syllable contains at least one vowel.

con + cen + trate = concentrate

op + por + tu + ni + ty = opportunity

syllable: a part of a word that is pronounced as a single unit; a syllable always contains a vowel

ADDING *ING* OR *ED* TO A VERB

When you change verb tense or use verb phrases, you change the form of the verb, frequently by adding *ed* or *ing* to the main part of the verb.

1. If the verb ends in *e*, drop the *e* before adding *ing*:

   use becomes *using*
   ride becomes *riding*

2. If the verb has *one syllable and a single consonant preceded by a single vowel*, double the final consonant before adding *ed* or *ing*:

   let becomes *letting*

   hit becomes *hitting*

3. If the word does not meet these criteria, do not double the consonant:

   listen becomes *listened*

   sleep becomes *sleeping*

WORDS WITH *IE* AND *EI*

1. If the vowel sound is *ee*, put the *i* first, except after *c*:

   believe, thief, niece, receive

   Exceptions to this rule include *seize*, *either*, *neither*, *leisure*, *weird*.

2. If the vowel sound is *a* or *i*, put the *e* before the *i*:

   neighbor, freight, height

WORDS THAT END IN *CEDE, SEDE, CEED*

1. Only one word ends in *sede*:

   supersede

2. Only three words end in *ceed*:

   exceed, proceed, succeed

3. All the others end in *cede*:

   precede, recede, secede, concede

Exercise 7

Items 1 to 3 refer to the following paragraph.

(1) To encourage recycling, some service stations and oil-changing facilities are begining to accept used motor oil from people who change the oil in their own cars. (2) Stations that recieve used oil have to pass government standards to obtain certification to recycle it. (3) Oil must not be contaminated, and there must be arrangements with waste-oil haulers to take the oil to recycling plants. (4) Many people, unsure of how to dispose of their used motor oil, pour it down storm drains, into garbage cans, or directly into the ground. (5) Each gallon of oil has the potential to damage one million gallons of groundwater, but it is important that oil be disposed of properly.

1. Sentence 1: **To encourage recycling, some service stations and oil-changing facilities are begining to accept used motor oil from people who change the oil in their own cars.**

   What correction should be made to this sentence?

   (1)   change begining to beginning
   (2)   change accept to acept
   (3)   change facilities to facillities
   (4)   replace people with people's
   (5)   change people to People

2. Sentence 2: **Stations that recieve used oil have to pass government standards to obtain certification to recycle it.**

   What correction should be made to this sentence?

   (1)   change recieve to reccieve
   (2)   change recieve to receive
   (3)   replace obtain with obtains
   (4)   change certification to certafication
   (5)   no correction is necessary

3. Sentence 5: **Each gallon of oil has the potential to damage one million gallons of groundwater, but it is important that oil be disposed of properly.**

   What correction should be made to this sentence?

   (1)   change has to had
   (2)   remove to
   (3)   change damage to damaged
   (4)   replace but with or
   (5)   replace but with so

To check your answers, turn to page 136.

Changing Nouns: Singular to Plural

If you write that Lorenzo drives *a truck*, you are using a singular noun. But if Lorenzo drives *several trucks*, you change the noun to plural.

You change words from singular to plural all the time, both in speaking and in writing. In English, nouns change to their plural form in several ways, so the trick is to spell the plural correctly. The following six rules will help you.

1. Most nouns can be made plural by adding *s*. If the noun ends in *s*, *x*, *ch*, or *sh*, make it plural by adding *es*:

   loss becomes *losses*

   fox becomes *foxes*

   wrench becomes *wrenches*
   lash becomes *lashes*

2. Nouns that end in a consonant plus *y* become plural by changing the *y* to *i* and adding *es*:

   city becomes *cities*

   penny becomes *pennies*

   party becomes *parties*
   doily becomes *doilies*

3. Some nouns that end in a consonant plus *o* add *es*:

   hero becomes *heroes*

   potato becomes *potatoes*

   tomato becomes *tomatoes*
   halo becomes *haloes*

4. Some nouns that end in *f* change the *f* to *v* and add *es* for the plural:

   leaf becomes *leaves*

   wolf becomes *wolves*

   calf becomes *calves*
   half becomes *halves*

5. Some nouns that end in *fe* change the *f* to *v* and add *s*:

   knife becomes *knives*

   wife becomes *wives*

   life becomes *lives*

6. Some nouns don't change at all when they become plural:

   The *deer* were hiding among the trees.
   I saw a *deer* by the side of the road.

   On a trip to Alaska, several *moose* crossed the street in front of us.

   To see a *moose* up close is an amazing sight.

Exercise 8

Directions

Circle and correct the misspelled words in the sentences that follow.

1. They had hopped to find more clues at the scene of the crime.

2. Some adults think there are no heros for youngsters to admire.

3. Guido's directions were so good, we found both address in less than an hour.

4. There were too many boxs to fit into the back of the car.

5. Marguerita planted tomatos and carrots in her garden.

6. After three trys, Madeline got the basketball through the hoop.

Directions

Choose the <u>one best answer</u> to each item.

Items 7 to 9 refer to the following paragraph.

(1) With a weak economy and a high rate of unemployment, people seek ways to save money. (2) Several books and articles have been written to help people save money and change bad spending habits. (3) There are even classes available for helping people reduce their debts. (4) Some people have started newsletters that show how to save money. (5) Among a variety of ways to avoid exorbitent prices, they suggest cutting out coupons, buying food in bulk, making your own bread, and growing vegetables in a home garden. (6) Newspapers and magazines also publish ideas for saving money; there are plenty of tips for anyone who is serious about financiel cutbacks.

7. Sentence 3: **There are even classes available for helping people reduce their debts.**

   What correction should be made to this sentence?

   (1) change <u>classes</u> to <u>class's</u>
   (2) change the spelling of <u>helpping</u> to <u>helping</u>
   (3) change <u>their</u> to <u>thier</u>
   (4) change the spelling of <u>debts</u> to <u>debtes</u>
   (5) no correction is necessary

8. Sentence 5: **Among a variety of ways to avoid exorbitent prices, they suggest cutting out coupons, buying food in bulk, making your own bread, and growing vegetables in a home garden.**

What correction should be made to this sentence?

(1) change the spelling of <u>variety</u> to <u>vareity</u>
(2) change the spelling of <u>exorbitent</u> to <u>exorbitant</u>
(3) change the spelling of <u>making</u> to <u>makeing</u>
(4) change the spelling of <u>vegetables</u> to <u>vegetabels</u>
(5) no correction is necessary

9. Sentence 6: **Newspapers and magazines also publish ideas for saving money; there are plenty of tips for anyone who is serious about financiel cutbacks.**

What correction should be made to this sentence?

(1) change the spelling of <u>magazines</u> to <u>magezines</u>
(2) insert a comma after <u>ideas</u>
(3) replace the semicolon with a comma
(4) change <u>who</u> to <u>whom</u>
(5) change the spelling of <u>financiel</u> to <u>financial</u>

To check your answers, turn to page 136.

Adding Suffixes

A **suffix** is one or more letters or syllables added to the end of a word. You have already learned the common suffixes *ed* and *ing*.

Some words change their spelling when a suffix is added to them; others don't. A few rules will help you correctly spell words that have suffixes.

1. When a word ends in a consonant and the suffix begins with a consonant, just add the suffix:

   fear + ful = fearful; mind + less = mindless

2. When a word ends with the letter *e* and the suffix begins with a consonant, just add the suffix:

   care + ful = careful; sense + less = senseless

   Exceptions include *truly, argument, ninth, wholly,* and *judgment.*

3. When a word ends with the letter *e* and the suffix begins with a vowel, drop the final *e:*

   value + able = valuable; confuse + ion = confusion

   Words that end in *ce* or *ge* are often exceptions to this rule:

   advantageous, replaceable, courageous, noticeable

4. Add *ly* and *ness* without changing the spelling of the main word:

   final + ly = finally; eager + ly = eagerly; careless + ness = carelessness

5. If a word ends in *y* following a consonant, change the *y* to *i* before adding a suffix:

   silly + er = sillier; forty + eth = fortieth

6. Don't change the *y* before adding *ing*:

   cry + ing = crying

7. If a word ends in *y* following a vowel, do not change the *y:*

   pay + ment = payment; annoy + ed = annoyed

   Exceptions include *paid* and *said.*

Exercise 9

Directions
Choose the one best answer to each item.

Items 1 to 3 refer to the following paragraph.

(1) Medical technology is so far advanced that it's possible for a team of surgeons to operate on an unborn baby with out removing it from the mother's body. (2) If doctors see that a fetus is not developing normaly, they may be able to fix it surgically. (3) If, for example, a fetus's organs are not in the proper location, doctors can relocate the organs within the tiny body of the fetus. (4) Fetal surgery involves operating on the mother, too. (5) To reach the fetus, the surgeons have to make one incision in the mother to reach the womb, and then they have to open the womb to reach the fetus. (6) After the fetal operation, they seal the uterus with staples and a material like glue. (7) Then they stitch the mother's incision. (8) It takes couragous parents and highly skilled doctors to give babies this chance at a healthy life.

---

suffix: one or more letters added to the end of a word

1. Sentence 1: **Medical technology is so far advanced that it's possible for a team of surgeons to operate on an unborn baby with out removing it from the mother's body.**

   What correction should be made to this sentence?

   (1) change possible to posible
   (2) change the spelling of operate to oporate
   (3) change with out to without
   (4) change the spelling of removing to remove-ing
   (5) no correction is necessary

2. Sentence 2: **If doctors see that a fetus is not developing normaly, they may be able to fix it surgically.**

   What correction should be made to this sentence?

   (1) change the spelling of developing to developeing
   (2) change the spelling of normaly to normally
   (3) remove the comma after normaly
   (4) change the spelling of surgically to surgicaly
   (5) no correction is necessary

3. Sentence 8: **It takes couragous parents and highly skilled doctors to give babies this chance at a healthy life.**

   What correction should be made to this sentence?

   (1) change couragous to courageous
   (2) change couragous to courrageous
   (3) change highly to highlly
   (4) change skilled to skilld
   (5) no correction is necessary

To check your answers, turn to page 136.

Using Apostrophes

The **apostrophe** is the punctuation mark that looks like a comma but appears at the top of a word ('). Apostrophes are used in only two situations: to form contractions and to show possession.

A **contraction** combines two words into one by omitting one or more letters. The apostrophe takes the place of the missing *letter* or *letters*.

> *are* + *not* becomes *aren't*

> *it* + *is* becomes *it's*

The second reason to use an apostrophe is to show that one thing belongs to another:

> the *soldier's* weapon

> the *truck's* front wheel

Note, however, that we use apostrophes to show possession *only with nouns*. Pronouns that show possession (*yours, hers, his, theirs, ours, its, whose*) do not take apostrophes:

> *Her* house is around the corner.

> *Their* values are different from *ours*.

To show possession with a singular noun, add an *apostrophe* + *s*:

> *Marci's* coat looks warm.

> The *boss's* car was stolen yesterday.

With nouns that become plural by adding *s* or *es*, put the apostrophe after the *s*:

> The *bosses'* privileges seemed more numerous than ours.

The sentence above shows that there was more than one boss.

With nouns that become plural in other ways, add *apostrophe* + *s* to show possession:

> *Women's* fashions change more dramatically than *men's* fashions.

> The *oxen's* strength made them essential on farms before tractors were invented.

---

apostrophe: a punctuation mark used to indicate either ownership or that a letter has been omitted

---

contraction: a word formed by combining two words; one or more letters are omitted and an apostrophe is put in their place

Exercise 10

> **Directions**
> Place apostrophes in the contractions in the following sentences. Identify the missing letters.

1. Being late so often, youre going to have trouble keeping the job.

2. Itll be hard to find any place open at this hour.

3. They arent selling that item any longer.

4. He hasnt missed a single game all season.

5. Youll have to wait until the report is published.

6. Sam saw that theyd been there already.

7. Shes completely dependable.

8. Take whatever theyll give you.

9. It really isnt hard to understand.

10. By now, its too late to get tickets.

> **Directions**
> Choose the one best answer to each item.

> Items 11 to 13 refer to the following paragraph.

(1) Nutritionists agree that snacks are an important part of our food intake. (2) Snacks keep us from feeling hungry before the next meal. (3) It's also fun to eat. (4) However, most people who work all day depend on vending machines for snacks, and there more likely to buy candy bars than a more healthful snack like pretzels. (5) Apparently, its necessary to bring something from home if we want a healthful snack during the workday.

11. Sentence 3: **It's also fun to eat.**

    What correction should be made to this sentence?

    (1) change It's to Its
    (2) change It's to They're
    (3) insert a comma after fun
    (4) change fun to to fun. To
    (5) no correction is necessary

12. Sentence 4: **However, most people who work all day depend on vending machines for snacks, and there more likely to buy candy bars than a more healthful snack like pretzels.**

    What correction should be made to this sentence?

    (1) remove the comma after However
    (2) remove the comma after snacks
    (3) change there to they're
    (4) change there to theyr'e
    (5) change the spelling of healthful to healthfull

13. Sentence 5: **Apparently, its necessary to bring something from home if we want a healthful snack during the workday.**

    What correction should be made to this sentence?

    (1) remove the comma after Apparently
    (2) change its to its'
    (3) change its to it's
    (4) insert a comma after home
    (5) change snack during to snack. During

> **Directions:** Choose the one best answer to each item.

> Items 14 to 17 refer to the following paragraph.

(1) A college computer students' project led to a fascinating discovery about jump rope rhymes. (2) While watching some children jumping rope on a school playground, the student decided to research the origins of their jingles. (3) Children who jump rope and chant jingles while they jump usually think they invented the rhymes. (4) Their older brothers and sisters claim the rhymes are their's. (5) However, the project revealed that the same or similar rhymes are sung by rope-jumping children all over the world. (6) Not only do the rhymes cross national boundaries, they cross generations. (7) They're the same rhymes that have been sung by children for decade's. (8) The projects conclusions not only led to information about jump rope rhymes, but show the similarity among people, no matter where they live or when they lived.

14. Sentence 1: **A college computer students' project led to a fascinating discovery about jump rope rhymes.**

What correction should be made to this sentence?

(1) change students' to students
(2) change students' to student's
(3) change the spelling of fascinating to fasinating
(4) insert a comma after discovery
(5) no correction is necessary

15. Sentence 4: **Their older brothers and sisters claim the rhymes are their's.**

What correction should be made to this sentence?

(1) change brothers to brother's
(2) change sisters to sister's
(3) change claim to claims
(4) change their's to theirs
(5) change their's to theirs'

16. Sentence 7: **They're the same rhymes that have been sung by children for decade's.**

What correction should be made to this sentence?

(1) change They're to Theyre
(2) change sung to sang
(3) change sung to singed
(4) change children to children's
(5) change decade's to decades

17. Sentence 8: **The projects conclusions not only led to information about jump rope rhymes, but show the similarity among people, no matter where they live or when they lived.**

Which of the following is the best way to write the underlined portion of this sentence? If you think the original is the best way, select choice (1).

(1) the projects conclusions
(2) the projects' conclusions
(3) the project's conclusion
(4) the project's conclusions
(5) the projects conclusion's

To check your answers, turn to page 136.

Words to Watch Out For

Memory and practice are essential tools for mastering spelling. In this lesson you'll find a list of word pairs or groups that sound the same but have different meanings and different spellings. Study the list and use it for reference.

COMMONLY CONFUSED WORD PAIRS AND GROUPS

Word Pair	Meaning	Example
affect	verb meaning to have an impact	How did the exercise affect you?
effect	noun meaning a result	Did it have the effect you hoped for?
already	previously	He had already filled the gas tank.
all ready	entirely prepared	The class was all ready for the field trip.
altogether	entirely	She was altogether confused by the map.
all together	everyone or everything in the same place	The books were all together on the correct shelves.
capitol	the building in which government officials work	Pictures on the capitol walls show all of the governors.
capital	the city that serves as the seat of government; also wealth or money owned or used in business	The capital of the United States is Washington, D.C.
desert	a dry, arid place	The desert blooms in the spring.
dessert	the last course of a meal	Ice cream is a popular dessert.
lead	a metal; the graphite in a pencil	A lead weight is hard to move.
led	past tense of the verb *to lead*	The captain led his team to victory.
passed	past tense of the verb *to pass*	She passed the exam easily.
past	time that has gone by	In the past, dress was more formal.
principal	head of a school; most important	The principal kept the school running smoothly. It was our principal demand.
principle	basic law or rule	He liked to study the principles of chemistry.
role	a part in a play	She wanted to play the role of the detective.
roll	to turn over and over; a single-serving loaf of bread; a list of names	The car would roll down the hill if the brake slipped. A roll and butter make a good snack. After roll call, the class started.
stationary	not moving	Riding a stationary bicycle is good exercise.
stationery	paper	She found note cards at the stationery store.
there	in that place	The ball is over there.
their	belonging to them	It's their problem.
they're	contraction of *they are*	They're able to solve it.
to	indicates direction	Turn to the left.
too	also; excessive	I'll go too. Too many movies are sad.
two	a number	Two people lost their cameras.
who's	contraction of *who is* or *who has*	Who's riding in the station wagon?
whose	possessive pronoun	Whose jacket is this?

Exercise 11

> **Directions**
> Choose the one best answer to each item.

> Items 1 to 4 refer to the following paragraph.

(1) The seen of the collision was a four-way-stop intersection. (2) It was hard to tell whose fault it was. (3) Three cars were involved, but their were no other witnesses to the accident. (4) Even after questioning the three drivers, the police were not sure what had happened. (5) One driver claimed neither of the other two applied the breaks. (6) Another driver said he was already to go when the other one ran the stop sign.

1. Sentence 1: **The seen of the collision was a four-way-stop intersection.**

   What correction should be made to this sentence?

   (1) change the spelling of seen to scene
   (2) change collision to Collision
   (3) change four-way to for-way
   (4) change four-way to fore-way
   (5) change intersection to inter section

2. Sentence 3: **Three cars were involved, but their were no other witnesses to the accident.**

   What correction should be made to this sentence?

   (1) replace their with there
   (2) replace their with they're
   (3) replace no with know
   (4) replace to with too
   (5) replace to with two

3. Sentence 5: **One driver claimed neither of the other two applied the breaks.**

   What correction should be made to this sentence?

   (1) replace one with won
   (2) change the spelling of neither to niether
   (3) replace two with to
   (4) replace breaks with brakes
   (5) no correction is necessary

4. Sentence 6: **Another driver said he was already to go when the other one ran the stop sign.**

   What correction should be made to this sentence?

   (1) insert a comma after said
   (2) change already to all ready
   (3) change ran to run
   (4) change stop sign to Stop Sign
   (5) no correction is necessary

To check your answers, turn to page 137.

Frequently Misspelled Words

Below is a list of commonly misspelled words. Some of these follow the spelling rules you have already learned, but some are exceptions to the rules and must simply be memorized. To find out which words on this list you need to study, ask someone to quiz you.

MASTER SPELLING LIST FOR THE GED WRITING SKILLS TEST

MASTER LIST OF FREQUENTLY MISSPELLED WORDS

a lot	arrangement	circumstance	describe	exercise	inevitable	mischievous	personality	recommend	successful
ability	article	congratulate	description	exhausted	influence	misspelled	personnel	recuperate	sudden
absence	artificial	citizen	desert	exhaustion	influential	mistake	persuade	referred	superintendent
absent	ascend	clothes	desirable	exhilaration	initiate	momentous	persuasion	rehearsal	suppress
abundance	assistance	clothing	despair	existence	innocence	monkey	pertain	reign	surely
accept	assistant	coarse	desperate	exorbitant	inoculate	monotonous	picture	relevant	surprise
acceptable	associate	coffee	dessert	expense	inquiry	moral	piece	relieve	suspense
accident	association	collect	destruction	experience	insistent	morale	plain	remedy	sweat
accommodate	attempt	college	determine	experiment	instead	mortgage	playwright	renovate	sweet
accompanied	attendance	column	develop	explanation	instinct	mountain	pleasant	repeat	syllable
accomplish	attention	comedy	development	extreme	integrity	mournful	please	repetition	symmetrical
accumulation	audience	comfortable	device	facility	intellectual	muscle	pleasure	representative	sympathy
accuse	August	commitment	dictator	factory	intelligence	mysterious	pocket	requirements	synonym
accustomed	author	committed	died	familiar	intercede	mystery	poison	resemblance	technical
ache	automobile	committee	difference	fascinate	interest	natural	policeman	resistance	telegram
achieve	autumn	communicate	different	fascinating	interfere	narrative	political	resource	telephone
achievement	auxiliary	company	dilemma	fatigue	interference	necessary	population	respectability	temperament
acknowledge	available	comparative	dinner	February	interpreted	needle	portrayal	responsibility	temperature
acquaintance	avenue	compel	direction	financial	interrupt	negligence	positive	restaurant	tenant
acquire	awful	competent	disappear	financier	invitation	neighbor	possess	rhythm	tendency
across	awkward	competition	disappoint	flourish	irrelevant	neither	possession	rhythmical	tenement
address	bachelor	compliment	disappointment	forcibly	irresistible	newspaper	possessive	ridiculous	therefore
addressed	balance	conceal	disapproval	forehead	irritable	newsstand	possible	right	thorough
adequate	balloon	conceit	disapprove	foreign	island	niece	post office	role	through
advantage	bargain	conceivable	disastrous	formal	its	noticeable	potatoes	roll	title
advantageous	basic	conceive	discipline	former	it's	obedient	practical	roommate	together
advertise	beautiful	concentration	discover	fortunate	itself	obstacle	prairie	sandwich	tomorrow
advertisement	because	conception	discriminate	fourteen	January	occasion	precede	Saturday	tongue
advice	become	condition	disease	fourth	jealous	occasional	preceding	scarcely	toward
advisable	before	conference	dissatisfied	frequent	judgment	occur	precise	scene	tragedy
advise	beginning	confident	dissection	friend	journal	occurred	predictable	schedule	transferred
advisor	being	conquer	dissipate	frightening	kindergarten	occurrence	prefer	science	treasury
aerial	believe	conscience	distance	fundamental	kitchen	ocean	preference	scientific	tremendous
affect	benefit	conscientious	distinction	further	knew	o'clock	preferential	scissors	tries
affectionate	benefited	conscious	division	gallon	knock	offer	preferred	season	truly
again	between	consequence	doctor	garden	know	often	prejudice	secretary	twelfth
against	bicycle	consequently	dollar	gardener	knowledge	omission	preparation	seize	twelve
aggravate	board	considerable	doubt	general	labor	omit	prepare	seminar	tyranny
aggressive	bored	consistency	dozen	genius	laboratory	once	prescription	sense	undoubtedly
agree	borrow	consistent	earnest	government	laid	operate	presence	separate	United States
aisle	bottle	continual	easy	governor	language	opinion	president	service	university
all right	bottom	continuous	ecstasy	grammar	later	opportune	prevalent	several	unnecessary
almost	boundary	controlled	ecstatic	grateful	latter	opportunity	primitive	severely	unusual
already	brake	controversy	education	great	laugh	optimist	principal	shepherd	useful
although	breadth	convenience	effect	grievance	leisure	optimistic	principle	sheriff	usual
altogether	breath	convenient	efficiency	grievous	length	origin	privilege	shining	vacuum
always	breathe	conversation	efficient	grocery	lesson	original	probably	shoulder	valley
amateur	brilliant	corporal	eight	guarantee	library	oscillate	procedure	shriek	valuable
American	building	corroborate	either	guess	license	ought	proceed	siege	variety
among	bulletin	council	eligibility	guidance	light	ounce	produce	sight	vegetable
amount	bureau	counsel	eligible	half	lightning	overcoat	professional	signal	vein
analysis	burial	counselor	eliminate	hammer	likelihood	paid	professor	significance	vengeance
analyze	buried	courage	embarrass	handkerchief	likely	pamphlet	profitable	significant	versatile
angel	bury	courageous	embarrassment	happiness	literal	panicky	prominent	similar	vicinity
angle	bushes	course	emergency	healthy	literature	parallel	promise	similarity	vicious
annual	business	courteous	emphasis	heard	livelihood	parallelism	pronounce	sincerely	view
another	cafeteria	courtesy	emphasize	heavy	loaf	particular	pronunciation	site	village
answer	calculator	criticism	enclosure	height	loneliness	partner	propeller	soldier	villain
antiseptic	calendar	criticize	encouraging	heroes	loose	pastime	prophet	solemn	visitor
anxious	campaign	crystal	endeavor	heroine	lose	patience	prospect	sophomore	voice
apologize	capital	curiosity	engineer	hideous	losing	peace	psychology	soul	volume
apparatus	capitol	cylinder	English	himself	loyal	peaceable	pursue	source	waist
apparent	captain	daily	enormous	hoarse	loyalty	pear	pursuit	souvenir	weak
appear	career	daughter	enough	holiday	magazine	peculiar	quality	special	wear
appearance	careful	daybreak	entrance	hopeless	maintenance	pencil	quantity	specified	weather
appetite	careless	death	envelope	hospital	maneuver	people	quarreling	specimen	Wednesday
application	carriage	deceive	environment	humorous	marriage	perceive	quart	speech	week
apply	carrying	December	equipment	hurried	married	perception	quarter	stationary	weigh
appreciate	category	deception	equipped	hurrying	marry	perfect	quiet	stationery	weird
appreciation	ceiling	decide	especially	ignorance	match	perform	quite	statue	whether
approach	cemetery	decision	essential	imaginary	material	performance	raise	stockings	which
appropriate	cereal	decisive	evening	imbecile	mathematics	perhaps	realistic	stomach	while
approval	certain	deed	evident	imitation	measure	period	realize	straight	whole
approve	changeable	definite	exaggerate	immediately	medicine	permanence	reason	strength	wholly
approximate	characteristic	delicious	exaggeration	immigrant	million	permanent	rebellion	strenuous	whose
argue	charity	dependent	examine	incidental	miniature	perpendicular	recede	stretch	wretched
arguing	chief	deposit	exceed	increase	minimum	perseverance	receipt	striking	
argument	choose	derelict	excellent	independence	miracle	persevere	receive	studying	
arouse	chose	descend	except	independent	miscellaneous	persistent	recipe	substantial	
arrange	cigarette	descent	exceptional	indispensable	mischief	personal	recognize	succeed	

Exercise 12

Directions

Choose the one best answer to each item.

Items 1 to 3 refer to the following paragraph.

(1) Isabel and Felix attended a sychology seminar. (2) They hoped to learn some things that would help them solve problems with their families. (3) Isabel felt she had to sholder most of the responsibility in her family because her younger brothers wouldn't help around the house. (4) Felix was especially interested in learning how to deal with his demanding boss. (5) They found the seminar helpful in those areas and others as well. (6) There were talks on marriage, tragedy, and predjudice. (7) By the time they left, they had much to talk about.

1. Sentence 1: **Isabel and Felix attended a sychology seminar**.

   What correction should be made to this sentence?

   (1) change the spelling of sychology to psychology
   (2) change the spelling of sychology to phsychology
   (3) change the spelling of seminar to semanar
   (4) change the spelling of seminar to semenar
   (5) no correction is necessary

2. Sentence 3: **Isabel felt she had to sholder most of the responsibility in her family because her younger brothers wouldn't help around the house.**

   What change should be made to this sentence?

   (1) change the spelling of sholder to shuolder
   (2) change the spelling of sholder to shoulder
   (3) change the spelling of responsibility to responsability
   (4) change the spelling of responsibility to responsibleity
   (5) no correction is necessary

3. Sentence 6: **There were talks on marriage, tragedy, and predjudice.**

   What correction should be made to this sentence?

   (1) replace There with They're
   (2) change the spelling of marriage to marrage
   (3) change the spelling of marriage to marrige
   (4) change the spelling of tragedy to tradgedy
   (5) change the spelling of predjudice to prejudice

To check your answers, turn to page 137.

ESSAY WRITING

In Part II of the GED Writing Skills Test, you are given 45 minutes to write an essay approximately 200 words in length. An **essay** is a written argument or discussion. Its purpose is to say something about an issue or a topic in a clear, logical way so that the reader understands the writer's points and is convinced that they make sense.

Like the sample in Figure 1, your GED essay needs a clear beginning, middle, and end. You can achieve this by planning four or five paragraphs. The first paragraph is the **introduction**. The middle two or three paragraphs are the **body** of the essay. The last paragraph contains the **conclusion**.

Each paragraph in your essay serves only one purpose. The introduction tells the reader what your essay will do. It introduces the main idea of your essay and each of your main supporting points. Each paragraph of the body discusses one of those supporting points and gives details and examples. Finally, the concluding paragraph briefly sums up the discussion to end the essay.

Look at the sample essay in Figure 1. The introduction briefly states three ways in which animals are useful to people. Notice that no specific examples or details are given in the introduction.

The second paragraph opens with a topic sentence, or a general statement, about animals as friends. Then the entire paragraph illustrates this point. The next two paragraphs begin in a similar way, each with a topic sentence (one about animals who assist disabled people and the other about animals as workers). Each goes on to discuss only that one main idea.

The fifth paragraph is the conclusion. It ties together everything in the essay. Like the introduction, it is general. Examples and details appear only in the body of the essay.

essay: a written argument or discussion

introduction: the first paragraph of an essay

body: the middle two or three paragraphs of an essay

conclusion: the last paragraph of an essay

FIGURE 1. SAMPLE ESSAY

Introduction

Some people spend large amounts of money and time on animals. They do this because animals can bring them friendship if they're lonely and aid if they're disabled. Animals also help people with their work.

Body

People who live alone might count on a pet for company. An eager dog wagging its tail, might welcome them home from a tiring day at work. A warm kitten might snuggle up and keep them company while they read or watch television.

For the physically disabled, an animal can make life easier. Guide dogs help blind people get around. highly skilled dogs and chimpanzees can turn lights on and off and get food for people who are paralyzed.

Some people depend on animals in their work. The police rely on dogs to catch criminals. Scientists use dolphins and other animals to study behavior. People who work in the wilderness can use pack animals, such as horses and lamas, to provide transportation or carry heavy loads.

Conclusion

Animals serve as friends, as helpers, and as workers. That's why people are willing to spend time and money caring for them.

This sample meets all the criteria for a good essay.

Use Your Time Well

In order to write a good essay in 45 minutes, you will need to use your time well. The following time frame is suggested:

5 Minutes	Think about your essay.
	Understand the essay topic.
	Brainstorm ideas.
5 Minutes	Organize your ideas.
	Group your ideas.
	Create a brief outline.
30 Minutes	Write your essay.
	Introduce the subject in the first paragraph.
	Develop the body.
	Tie up your ideas in the conclusion.
5 Minutes	Revise and edit your work.
	Check your sentence structure.
	Make grammar, spelling, capitalization, and punctuation corrections.

Understanding the Topic

In Part II of the GED Writing Skills Test, a series of paragraphs, called the *prompt*, will give you a topic on which you must write your essay. GED essay prompts contain three parts:

- some *background information* to introduce you to the topic

- the *topic* itself

- some *instructions* on how to write the essay

Here's an example of the kind of prompt you'll see:

Many adults worry about the amount of violence on television. They think television is a bad influence on young people, who spend far too much time watching it. Others take a different view, believing that television has many good features for children under the age of 18.

Write an essay of about 200 words in which you discuss the positive effects television has on young people. Be sure to use examples.

At first glance, you might assume the essay topic is *violence on television* because that's the topic of the first sentence you read. But, in this prompt, violence on television is background to the topic. The topic is *the positive effects television has on young people*. If you don't read everything in the prompt, you could mistakenly write about the wrong topic, and even if your essay were otherwise perfect, you'd get no credit because you didn't write about the assigned topic.

Use these guidelines to find the topic when you read a GED essay prompt:

- Look for a statement that tells you to do something.

- Look for a question that you must answer.

Organizing Your Ideas

After you read a prompt and understand the topic, you need to decide what to say about it. Start with the topic and brainstorm some ideas that would support it. If you are asked by the topic to take a position on an issue, choose your position and brainstorm main ideas to support it. To **brainstorm** means to write down every idea about the topic that comes to your mind.

Consider the topic—the positive effects of television on young people. You might brainstorm these main ideas:

- television provides entertainment

- television stars may provide good role models

- television provides information

- television models family relationships

- television shows people at work, which helps children make career goals

Now narrow your ideas to no more than three main points. If some ideas are closely related, you can perhaps combine them. Eliminate ideas that seem short, dull, or inappropriate. Suppose you have chosen these three main points.

I. television provides entertainment

II. television provides information

III. television helps young people choose life goals

From these ideas, you can now create an **outline** for the body of your essay. An outline is a plan to get you from the beginning of your essay to the end. It helps you stick to the subject of each paragraph and keeps your essay organized and under control.

Remember, as you write the body of your essay, you will need to support each point with details and specific examples. Your details and examples should reinforce the main idea of the paragraph. An outline keeps you on track.

You can use any method you like to write your outline. You may choose to make simply a list of points and examples or you may choose to use a formal numbering system. You will not be scored on your outline. Its only purpose is to organize your writing. To see how an outline works, look at this possible outline for the second paragraph of the essay on the positive effects of television.

brainstorm: to write down *every* idea about a topic that comes to your mind

outline: a brief plan or list that guides you in writing an essay

II. Television provides information

    A. Current events

1. News

2. Elections

3. Talk shows (concerns of society)

    B.   School subjects

1. Documentaries

2. Children's programs (*Sesame Street*)

    C. Commercials

1. Consumer products (cars, toys, food)

2. Services (credit cards, telephone companies)

At the outline state, you may find that you have too much material for a 200-word essay. If that happens, you can eliminate one or two subgroups as you write. But, remember, it's always better to go into the writing stage knowing you won't be at a loss for something to say.

Writing Your Essay

Your essay's first paragraph, the introduction, tells the reader two things: (a) what the topic is and (b) what you are going to say about that topic. Stated in a single sentence, these ideas form a **thesis statement**. Your thesis statement is the central idea of your entire essay and clarifies your position as the writer of the essay.

Here is a possible thesis statement for an essay on the positive effects of television on young people: *Although adults worry that television is bad for children, television provides entertainment and information for young people and helps them set goals.*

Combined with another general sentence, you have a well-written introduction:

Although adults worry that television is bad for children, television provides entertainment and information for young people and helps them set goals. Used wisely, television is a positive influence on young people.

Notice what the introductory paragraph does *not* do:

- **It doesn't announce what it will say.** It doesn't say *"In this essay, I will show. . . ."* If you have a clearly stated thesis, you don't need to *tell* the reader what you are going to say, you *just say it.*

- **It doesn't apologize for not being a good essay.** It doesn't say *"I'll do the best I can, but this is a hard topic."*

- **It doesn't wander away from the topic.** It doesn't say *"We have two television sets in our house, but my sister and I still fight over what to watch. I wouldn't spend 5 minutes watching the stuff she likes. I don't even like the same music she listens to. And I can't stand her clothes. Even her friends are hard to take."*

- **It doesn't contain specific details or examples.** The introduction must be general; examples will come later.

---

thesis statement: the introduction of an essay that tells the reader two things: what the topic is and what you are going to say about that topic

Exercise 1

> **Directions**
> Read the following GED essay prompt.

America is facing a health-care crisis. Many politicians and health-care professionals believe we can keep medical costs down only if we take better care of ourselves and try to prevent illness.

   Write a 200-word essay in which you show how people can accept responsibility for their own health care.

Your topic: Show how people can accept responsibility for their own health to keep medical costs down.

Your main points:

- People must become informed.

- People must pay attention to diet and exercise.

- People must create a safe home environment.

   Now use this information to write an introduction. When you have written your introduction, check for the following:

- Will the opening grab the reader's attention?

- Will the reader know what the topic is?

- Will the reader know what you intend to say about the topic?

   In other words, is your thesis clear?

To check your answer, turn to page 137.

Developing the Body and Conclusion

Once you've written the introduction, you're ready to develop the body of the essay. These middle paragraphs are the most complicated paragraphs in your essay because they contain details and supporting examples. Your job now is to expand your outline into sentence and paragraph form. Supporting details and examples should offer some new level of information; they can't be just a restatement of the introduction.

   Each paragraph in the body should begin with a topic sentence. Here's a possible topic sentence:

> One reason television is a positive experience for young children is that it delivers complex information in a way that they can easily understand.

Notice that the sentence not only makes a point, but also reminds the reader that the entire essay is about the positive effects of television on children. Based on our earlier outline, the rest of the paragraph might read:

> Through the use of graphics and sound, news shows help children to understand current events. Maps and graphs help children to understand election reports. Talk shows explore human relationships and the concerns of society. Documentaries and other educational programs aim to deliver actual academic content in interesting, engaging ways. Even commercials inform as they introduce children to the products and services they may someday choose as consumers.

   You may end a paragraph, if it seems complete, before you've included everything on your outline, or you may add new ideas if they fit the topic sentence.

   As you know, the last paragraph of an essay will always be a conclusion. Regardless of what the topic is, a conclusion, like an introduction, does two things:

- It restates the thesis or the ideas contained in the thesis.

- It contains a closing thought, something the reader can think about after reading the essay.

   Here's one possible conclusion to the essay on the positive effects of television.

> Television enriches the lives of young people in many ways. Not only does it entertain, it also teaches. Through the depiction of people from every walk of life, children identify models of behavior for life in the family and on the job. No other artistic medium has a greater opportunity to affect the lives of young people in such a positive way.

Notice that the first sentence reminds the reader of the essay's topic. The paragraph also lists the main points of the thesis (that television entertains, informs, and helps children set goals). The last sentence strengthens the argument and ties the ideas together.

   Notice, too, what the concluding paragraph does not do:

- **It doesn't report what you have just said.** It doesn't say *"In this essay, I talked about the positive effects of television on young people."*

- **It doesn't apologize for not being a good essay.** It doesn't say *"This probably isn't very clear, but I hope you understand it."*

- **It doesn't change the subject at the very end.** It doesn't say *"When I was a child, I watched only cartoons, which are very violent."*

Exercise 2

Directions

Write a possible conclusion for an essay that asks you to consider why people enjoy horror movies. The essay has the following thesis statement: *Horror movies help me forget my problems, entertain me with special effects, and let me enjoy fantastic drama.*

Be sure your conclusion

- restates the thesis
- contains a closing thought
- does not change the subject

If possible, try out different conclusions on a friend or family member to see which have the most impact. Read the possibilities and ask what works and what doesn't, or why one ending seems more effective than another.

To check your answer, turn to page 137.

Revising and Editing Your Work

Before you submit your GED essay, take 5 minutes and revise and edit your work. If you find a mistake, draw a single line through the words you want to omit or change and write any correction neatly and clearly above. You may want to change some words or phrases to add variety and interest. You can improve the sophistication of your writing by choosing accurate words. For example, instead of writing *a lot*, try phrases like *several dozen*, *countless*, or *more than a thousand*.

Use these questions to help you revise and edit your work:

- Did you write about the topic?
- Did you stick to the subject?
- Does your essay have a clear structure?
- Did you use clear and interesting examples?
- Did you choose the best words?
- Are the sentences complete?
- Is the essay free of spelling, capitalization, and punctuation errors?
- Have you followed the rules of grammar?

Exercise 3

Directions

Write an essay based on the following sample GED prompt.

Topic

In our culture, it is impossible to escape the influence of advertising. Advertising is a multi-billion dollar industry that bombards consumers with information about countless products and services.

In an essay of 200 words, discuss some ways advertisers influence the buying public. Be sure to use examples to support your ideas.

To check your essay, turn to page 137.

Answers and Explanations
WRITING SKILLS

Unit 1: Sentence Structure

Exercise 1 (page 76)

1. **The correct answer is (3): trouble understanding or** Removing the period corrects the fragment by attaching it to the rest of a complete sentence. The other choices create different fragments.

2. **The correct answer is (2): breakdown in their** Removing the period corrects the fragment by attaching it to the rest of a complete sentence. Choice (3) creates different fragments. Choices (4) and (5) change the meaning of the sentence.

3. **The correct answer is (2): change Leaving to This leaves** Choice (2) creates a sentence that makes sense. The other choices create more fragments.

4. **The correct answer is (3): insert they collect before newspapers** Choice (3) gives the sentence a subject and a verb. The other choices do not correct the fragment.

5. **The correct answer is (4): change taking to take** The verb must be complete to complete the sentence. The other choices create different fragments.

Exercise 2 (page 77)

1. **The correct answer is (2): American citizen, Kimiko** When a dependent clause precedes the main clause, it takes a comma. The other choices use incorrect punctuation.

2. **The correct answer is (4): world are studying** Choice (4) completes the verb. The other choices do not complete the verb.

3. **The correct answer is (3): Kimiko** Kimiko is the subject of the sentence. The other choices don't make sense.

Exercise 3 (page 79)

1. **The correct answer is (4): insert a semicolon after unemployed** *Unemployed* marks the end of the first complete thought. A semicolon is the appropriate punctuation. Choices (1), (2), and (5) create fragments. Choice (3) doesn't correct the run-on.

2. **The correct answer is (2): home and abroad. This affected** *Abroad* marks the end of the first complete thought. A period or semicolon is the appropriate punctuation. Choice (3) forms two complete sentences but the intended meaning is changed in the second sentence. The other choices do not correct the run-on.

3. **The correct answer is (4): we** The other choices don't make sense in this sentence.

4. **The correct answer is (5): replace but with so** *So* is a more appropriate connecting word than either the original *but* or *yet*, which is given in choice (4). The other choices punctuate incorrectly.

5. **The correct answer is (3): birds, so their** Choice (3) uses the best connecting word and punctuates correctly.

6. **The correct answer is (5): doves; those** Choice (5) uses a semicolon to separate two independent clauses. Choice (1) is a run-on sentence. Choices (2) and (3) link the two independent clauses with a comma and a connecting word, but the connecting words are inappropriate. Choice (4) is punctuated incorrectly.

Exercise 4 (page 80)

1. **The correct answer is (5): food. Everyone** The first independent clause ends with *food*. The two clauses are not closely connected, so a period should be used to separate them. The other choices do not correct the run-on.

2. **The correct answer is (3): insert a semicolon after the second taxes** Because of the close connection between the clauses, a semicolon is the best way to link them into one sentence. However, making two separate sentences would also work. Choice (1) creates two complete sentences, but the second one contains an extra word. Choice (4) creates a fragment. Choices (2) and (5) don't correct the run-on.

3. **The correct answer is (2): replace income tax they with income tax. They** *Income tax* marks the end of the first complete thought. The other choices either create fragments or do not correct the run-on.

4. **The correct answer is (2): replace so with but** The connector *but* shows the correct relationship between the two ideas. Choice (1) creates a run-on. Choices (3) and (4) show the wrong relationship between the ideas.

5. **The correct answer is (1): replace however with for example** Choice (1) provides the proper connecting word. Choice (2) uses the wrong connecting word. Choices (3) and (4) incorrectly punctuate a compound sentence.

6. **The correct answer is (3): cause** Choice (3) provides an appropriate verb for the sentence. Choices (1) and (2) don't make sense, and choices (4) and (5) change the meaning of the sentence.

Exercise 5 *(page 82)*

1. **The correct answer is (2): itself, it** A dependent clause at the beginning of the sentence should be followed by a comma. Choice (1) creates a fragment. The other choices don't make sense.

2. **The correct answer is (5): no correction is necessary**

3. **The correct answer is (4): replace Sundays. Because with Sundays because** A dependent clause that follows the main clause should not be separated from the main clause by a comma. The other choices don't make sense.

4. **The correct answer is (3): remove the comma after books** When the dependent clause follows the main clause, there is no need for a comma. Choice (1) creates a fragment, choice (2) uses incorrect punctuation, and choices (4) and (5) use inappropriate connecting words.

5. **The correct answer is (4): Because** The relationship is cause and effect. The other choices use inappropriate connecting words.

Exercise 6 *(page 84)*

1. **The correct answer is (2): public transportation** Choice (2) doesn't change the sentence's meaning and it clarifies the modifier. The other choices change the meaning of the sentence.

2. **The correct answer is (1): missing** The main part of the sentence doesn't need to change. The other choices change the meaning of the sentence.

3. **The correct answer is (4): Carmela sees another bus coming** Choice (4) puts the modifier next to the word it modifies. Choice (5) changes the meaning of the sentence, and the other choices do not correct the dangling modifier.

Exercise 7 *(page 85)*

1. **The correct answer is (3): and in Latin America** Choice (3) is the only choice that maintains parallel structure.

2. **The correct answer is (2): share their standard of living** Choice (2) is the only choice that maintains parallel structure.

3. **The correct answer is (4): replace go to with in** Choice (4) is the only choice that maintains parallel structure.

4. **The correct answer is (5): no correction is necessary**

5. **The correct answer is (3): children's questions** Choice (3) is the only choice that maintains parallel structure.

6. **The correct answer is (4): change remembering to remember** Choice (4) is the only choice that maintains parallel structure.

7. **The correct answer is (1): replace by keeping diaries with diaries** Choice (1) is the only choice that maintains parallel structure.

8. **The correct answer is (3): replace to remember with memories of** Choice (3) is the only choice that maintains parallel structure.

9. **The correct answer is (4): change giving to to give** Choice (4) is the only choice that maintains parallel structure.

Unit 2: Usage and Grammar

Exercise 1 *(page 89)*

1. was
2. cheer
3. warn
4. confuse
5. takes
6. Charles *plays* card games with his friends and sometimes he *wins*. *Charles* is singular, so the verbs must be singular.
7. Michelle *seems* to win every time she *plays*. *Michelle* is a singular subject and takes singular verbs.
8. Correct
9. Correct
10. Mr. Chan *hates* long lines and becomes impatient in them. *Mr. Chan* is a singular subject and takes a singular verb.
11. **The correct answer is (1): change is to are** Choice (1) has a plural subject *(strikes)* that requires a plural verb. Choices (2) and (3) do not correct for subject-verb agreement. Choices (4) and (5) create fragments.
12. **The correct answer is (2): negotiation attempts fail** Choice (2) has a plural subject *(attempts)* that requires a plural verb. Choices (1) and (3) do not correct for subject-verb agreement; choices (4) and (5) change the meaning of the sentence.
13. **The correct answer is (4): change are to is** Choice (4) has a singular subject *(hope)* that requires a singular verb. The other choices don't correct for subject-verb agreement.

Exercise 2 *(page 90)*

1. votes
2. go
3. looks
4. chooses
5. ask
6. says
7. knows
8. am
9. run
10. **The correct answer is (4): change has to have** Choice (4) matches a plural verb *(have)* with a plural subject *(Holly and Kent)*. Choice (1) does not correct for subject-verb agreement. Choice (2) is incorrect punctuation for a compound sentence. Choice (3) is an incorrect verb form, and choice (5) creates sentence fragments.
11. **The correct answer is (4): change suggest to suggests** Choice (4) matches the singular verb *(suggests)* with a singular subject *(Holly)*. Choice (2) is incorrect punctuation for a compound sentence. Choices (1), (3), and (5) don't correct for subject-verb agreement.

Exercise 3 (page 91)

1. **The correct answer is (5): change <u>raises</u> to <u>raise</u>** Choice (5) uses a plural verb *(raise)* to agree with a plural subject *(they)*. Choices (1) and (4) lack subject-verb agreement, choice (2) creates a fragment, and choice (3) inserts a comma before a dependent clause.

2. **The correct answer is (4): asked people to guess how many marbles there were** Choice (4) uses a plural verb *(were)* to agree with a plural subject *(marbles)*. Choices (1), (2), and (5) lack subject-verb agreement, and choice (3) changes the meaning of the sentence.

3. **The correct answer is (3): change <u>are</u> to <u>is</u>** Choice (3) uses a singular verb *(is)* to agree with a singular subject *(thing)*. Choice (1) lacks subject-verb agreement, choice (2) doesn't correct for subject-verb agreement, and choice (4) creates a fragment.

Exercise 4 (page 92)

1. There *are* too many leaves to rake in one afternoon. (subject = leaves)

2. *Do* both of them want to go to the game? (subject = both)

3. In the cupboard *are* all the things you need to bake a cake. (subject = things)

4. Upstairs *are* two more bedrooms. (subject = bedrooms)

5. Here *is* the information you asked for. (subject = information)

6. **The correct answer is (2): change <u>is</u> to <u>are</u>** Choice (2) uses a plural verb to agree with the plural subject *(ways)*. Choice (1) changes the meaning of the sentence. Choices (3), (4), and (5) do not correct for subject-verb agreement.

7. **The correct answer is (1): change <u>are</u> to <u>is</u>** Choice (1) uses a singular verb to agree with a singular subject *(one)*. Choice (2) uses *be* alone as a verb, choice (3) is not a correct infinitive form, choice (4) doesn't correct for subject-verb agreement, and choice (5) shifts to past tense.

8. **The correct answer is (2): change <u>prefers</u> to <u>prefer</u>** Choice (2) matches a plural verb to a plural subject *(others)*. The other choices do not affect subject-verb agreement.

9. **The correct answer is (3): use** Choice (3) uses a plural verb form to agree with a plural subject *(cooks)*. Choices (1), (2), and (4) do not correct for subject-verb agreement, and choice (5) changes the meaning of the sentence.

10. **The correct answer is (4): A well-stocked kitchen has many kinds** Choice (4) restructures the sentence to put the subject and verb closer to the beginning. Choices (1) and (3) lack subject-verb agreement, choice (2) lacks a verb, and choice (5) changes the meaning of the sentence.

11. **The correct answer is (4): change <u>goes</u> to <u>go</u>** Choice (4) matches a plural verb with a plural subject *(herbs and spices)*. Choice (1) incorrectly uses *be* by itself, choice (3) creates a fragment, and the other choices do not affect subject-verb agreement.

Exercise 5 (page 94)

1. planning—present

2. helped—past

3. sitting—present

4. **The correct answer is (2): change <u>plan</u> to <u>planning</u>** Choice (2) uses a present participle to complete the verb and to show future action. Choices (1) and (4) create fragments, and choice (3) incorrectly uses a past participle.

5. **The correct answer is (1): change <u>Start</u> to <u>Starting</u>** Choice (1) uses a gerund as the subject of the sentence so that the sentence makes sense. Choice (2) changes the meaning of the sentence, choices (3) and (4) use incorrect verb forms, and choice (5) changes an adjective to a verb.

6. **The correct answer is (5): you should have paid attention** Choice (5) uses a past participle to complete the verb. Choices (1), (2), and (3) use incorrect verb forms, and choice (4) omits the participle.

Exercise 6 (page 96)

1. **The correct answer is (5): change <u>cutting</u> to <u>cut</u>** Choice (5) uses the correct infinitive form. Choice (1) is an incorrect verb form, choice (2) uses a participle by itself, and choices (3) and (4) are incorrect infinitive forms.

2. **The correct answer is (3): lost** Choice (3) is the correct past participle of *to lose*. Choices (1) and (2) are not past participle forms, and choices (4) and (5) change the meaning of the sentence.

3. **The correct answer is (4): change <u>put</u> to <u>putting</u>** Choice (4) uses the correct participle. Choice (1) is not the correct participle, choice (2) is an incorrect verb form, choice (3) eliminates the required helper in a verb phrase, and choice (5) does not use the correct form of the past participle of *to put*.

Exercise 7 (page 97)

1. she heard/crawled

2. Whenever it rains/feel

3. by the time/had walked

4. last year/refused

5. Currently/receive

6. Now/am

7. Last year/had

8. **The correct answer is (4): include** Choice (4) uses a present-tense verb, which is consistent with the rest of the paragraph. The other choices use incorrect tenses.

9. **The correct answer is (3): change <u>will help</u> to <u>helps</u>** Choice (3) uses a present-tense verb, which is consistent with the rest of the paragraph. Choice (1) removes the gerund that serves as the subject of the sentence, choice (2) uses an incorrect infinitive form, choice (4) uses the past tense, and choice (5) creates a fragment.

10. **The correct answer is (2): change <u>were</u> to <u>is</u>** Choice (2) uses a present-tense singular verb to agree with the singular subject *(sense)*. Choice (1) creates a fragment, choice (3) lacks subject-verb agreement, and choice (4) uses the past tense.

Exercise 8 (page 98)

1. past
2. future
3. past
4. future
5. present
6. past
7. present
8. future
9. future
10. past
11. Last summer, the Orangerie Produce Co. had an employee picnic. The picnic was a great success, thanks to the Planning Committee. The committee members had worked for weeks by the time picnic day arrived. The employees had played games, danced, swum, and eaten hot dogs and apple pie by the end of the day. Everyone hopes there will be another picnic next year.
12. **The correct answer is (3): poured into the country, learned American ways, and became part of** Choice (3) maintains past tense throughout the sentence. The tenses of the other choices are inconsistent.
13. **The correct answer is (2): replace has change with has changed** Choice (2) uses the correct past participle for to change. Choices (1) and (3) switch tense, and choice (4) lacks subject-verb agreement.
14. **The correct answer is (4): they cling with pride to** Choice (4) maintains the present tense that is used throughout the second paragraph. Choices (1) and (5) switch to past tense, and the other choices use incorrect verb forms.
15. **The correct answer is (1): change gave to give** Choice (1) maintains the present tense that is used throughout the paragraph. Choice (2) shifts tense, and choices (3), (4), and (5) are incorrect infinitive forms.

Exercise 9 (page 100)

1. **The correct answer is (5): They** Choice (5) is the appropriate pronoun to match the antecedent. Choice (1) repeats the lengthy subject. Choice (2) is not the appropriate pronoun and does not agree with the verb. Choices (3) and (4) create sentence fragments.
2. **The correct answer is (5): change his to their** Choice (5) uses a plural pronoun (their) to agree with a plural subject (victims). Choice (1) is not a participle, choice (2) creates a fragment, choice (3) lacks subject-verb agreement, and choice (4) shifts to the past tense.
3. **The correct answer is (2): They control the symptoms** Choice (2) corrects the fragment by giving the sentence a subject. Choice (1) is a fragment, choice (3) doesn't make sense, and choices (4) and (5) change the meaning of the sentence.
4. **The correct answer is (5): no correction is necessary**

Exercise 10 (page 102)

1. Manuel and Umeki agreed to share their study notes with each other.
2. A baby seal can swim by itself right away.
3. The basketball team lost its third game in a row.
4. **The correct answer is (3): you might like to shop** Choice (3) maintains the pronoun you that already has been used in the sentence. Choice (1) switches from second person to an indefinite pronoun. Choices (2) and (4) switch from second person to third person. Choice (5) shifts to first person.
5. **The correct answer is (4): replace One with You** Choice (4) maintains second-person pronoun consistency in the sentence. The other choices shift from second person.

6. **The correct answer is (5): replace our with your** Choice (5) maintains second person in the sentence. The other choices change the meaning of the sentence and do not correct the mismatched pronoun our.

Exercise 11 (page 103)

1. **The correct answer is (3): During these industrially productive years** Choice (3) corrects the pronoun (they), which lacks a clear antecedent. The other choices change the meaning of the sentence.
2. **The correct answer is (2): replace her with their** Choice (2) correctly provides a plural third-person pronoun their to fit the plural antecedent women. The other choices do not fit the antecedent.
3. **The correct answer is (4): people selfishly pursued money** Choice (4) uses a noun (people) instead of the pronoun them, which has no clear antecedent. The other choices lack clear antecedents.

Exercise 12 (page 104)

1. **The correct answer is that**—The pronoun has a nonhuman antecedent.
2. **The correct answer is who**—The pronoun has a human antecedent.
3. **The correct answer is who**—The pronoun has a human antecedent.
4. **The correct answer is Whom**—The pronoun is used in object position (substitute him).
5. **The correct answer is that**—The pronoun has a nonhuman antecedent.
6. **The correct answer is Whoever**—The pronoun is used in actor position (substitute he).
7. **The correct answer is (2): Because they find it convenient,** Choice (2) is correct because it clears up the vague pronoun reference. Choice (1) is incorrect because the reader can't tell what their refers to. Choice (3) changes the meaning of the sentence; choices (4) and (5) are incorrect because there is no antecedent for your.
8. **The correct answer is (2): replace anyone with people** Choice (2) provides a plural antecedent to go with a plural pronoun (themselves). Choices (1) and (3) do not correct the pronoun problem, and choice (4) is incorrect because themself is not an accepted English word.
9. **The correct answer is (4): replace that with who** Choice (4) is correct because who is the pronoun to use for people. Choices (1) and (2) use singular subjects (Someone and Anyone) with a plural verb (work). Choice (3) uses the object form of the pronoun, and choice (5) assumes a nonhuman antecedent.
10. **The correct answer is (3): replace your with their** Choice (3) is correct because their agrees with the antecedent people. The other choices use pronouns that do not agree with the antecedent.
11. **The correct answer is (5): distractions** Choice (5) expresses the meaning of the original sentence: workers must be aware of distractions (such as family, housework, etc.). Choice (1) changes the meaning of the sentence; choices (2), (3), and (4) use pronouns without antecedents.

Unit 3: Mechanics

Exercise 1 (page 107)

1. The correct answer is *Dr.*
2. The correct answer is *July.*
3. The correct answer is *Correct.*
4. The correct answer is *Casablanca.*
5. The correct answer is *Japanese, English, and French.*
6. **The correct answer is (3): change senator to Senator** In this sentence, *Senator* must be capitalized because it is a title used as part of someone's name. Choice (1) is incorrect because the first word in a sentence must be capitalized. Choice (2) is incorrect because *legislator* is a general term, and choice (4) is incorrect because a person's name must be capitalized.
7. **The correct answer is (4): change public library to Public Library** Choice (4) capitalizes both words because in this sentence they are part of the name of a specific public library. The other choices either capitalize general words or fail to capitalize specific names.

Exercise 2 (page 108)

1. **The correct answer is (2): change National Parks to national parks** Choice (2) is correct because the writer is speaking of national parks in general, so there is no need for capital letters. Choice (1) is incorrect because the name of a country must be capitalized. Choice (3) is incorrect because we do not capitalize directions unless they are used as the name of a place. There is no reason to capitalize the nouns in choices (4) and (5).
2. **The correct answer is (2): change yellowstone to Yellowstone** Choice (2) capitalizes the name of a specific national park. Choice (1) is incorrect because the first word of a sentence must be capitalized. There's no reason to capitalize the words in choices (3) and (4).
3. **The correct answer is (5): change Mountain Range to mountain range** Choice (5) is correct because there is no need to capitalize when speaking of mountain ranges in general. There is no reason to capitalize the words in choices (1), (3), and (4). Choice (2) is incorrect because the entire name of a specific mountain range must be capitalized.
4. **The correct answer is (2): change national park to National Park** Choice (2) capitalizes all the words that are part of a name. Choice (1) fails to capitalize all the words in a name, and there is no reason to capitalize the words in choices (3), (4), and (5).
5. **The correct answer is (2): change cave to Cave** Choice (2) capitalizes the name of a particular cave. Choice (1) is incorrect because the first word of a sentence and the name of a particular place must be capitalized. Choice (3) fails to capitalize the name of a state, and there is no reason to capitalize the words in choices (4) and (5).

Exercise 3 (page 109)

1. Mr. and Mrs. Suarez took their tent, their cooking utensils, and their fishing gear to the campsite in the woods.
2. They preferred camping in the summer when they could count on warm weather, long days, and good fishing.
3. Correct
4. Correct
5. They did have plenty of equipment for swimming, fishing, and hiking.
6. Some people would rather vacation in cities than in mountains, woods, or the country.
7. They enjoy bustling city life with all that it offers, such as museums, theater, and restaurants.
8. Correct
9. Correct

10. It can be fun to spend time exploring your own city, neighborhood, and community.
11. **The correct answer is (1): remove the comma after shade** Choice (1) omits the comma because there are only two items in the list. Choice (2) uses a comma instead of a conjunction between the two items. It's incorrect to place a comma after the *and* that precedes the last item in a series, as in choice (3), and there is no reason for the comma in choice (4).
12. **The correct answer is (1): in spring or change color in fall or have** Choice (1) uses no commas because the conjunction is repeated. Choices (2) and (3) incorrectly use commas, and choices (4) and (5) use inappropriate connecting words.
13. **The correct answer is (2): remove the comma after peaches** Choice (2) omits the comma because the second item in the list is *tasty peaches or cherries in summer.* Choices (1) and (3) remove the required comma between items in a series. Choice (4) incorrectly places a comma after the *and* that precedes the last item in a series.

Exercise 4 (page 111)

1. **The correct answer is (4): to get to these parking lots, they face** Choice (4) places a comma after the dependent clause at the beginning of the sentence. Choice (1) omits the comma, choice (2) creates a fragment, and choices (3) and (5) put the comma in the wrong places.
2. **The correct answer is (2): insert a comma after distances** Choice (2) places a comma after the dependent clause at the beginning of the sentence. The other choices put commas in the wrong places.
3. **The correct answer is (2): Illegally parked cars occupy** Choice (2) is the only choice that maintains the meaning of the original sentence.
4. **The correct answer is (3): insert a comma after driver** Choice (3) places a comma before the last item in a series. There's no reason for the comma in the other choices.

Exercise 5 (page 112)

1. **The correct answer is (2): insert a comma after alive** Choice (2) inserts a comma after a dependent clause. Choice (1) lacks subject-verb agreement, choice (3) shifts to the future tense, and choice (4) introduces a misspelling.
2. **The correct answer is (4): monthly installments and had to wait** Choice (4) removes the comma that separates the two parts of a compound verb. Choice (1) separates the parts of the compound verb with a comma, choice (2) shifts to the present tense, choice (3) shifts to the future tense, and choice (5) capitalizes general words.
3. **The correct answer is (3): remove the comma after titles** Choice (3) removes the comma before the beginning of the items in a series. There's no reason for the comma in choice (1), choice (2) capitalizes a general word, choice (4) capitalizes a two-letter preposition in a title, and choice (5) removes the comma before the last item in a series.

Exercise 6 (page 113)

1. **The correct answer is (2): remove the comma after government** Choice (2) does not separate a subject and verb with a comma. There is no reason for the commas in the other choices.

2. **The correct answer is (4): in the President's Cabinet, on the Supreme Court, and in Congress** Choice (4) places a comma after the last item in the series *before* the connecting word. Do not put a comma *after* the connecting word. The other choices punctuate the series incorrectly.

3. **The correct answer is (5): no correction is necessary**

4. **The correct answer is (4): participation, and a woman** Choice (4) places a comma before the connecting word that links two independent clauses into a compound sentence. Choices (1) and (2) create run-on sentences. Choice (3) incorrectly places a comma after the conjunction rather than before, and choice (5) uses a semicolon instead of a comma.

Exercise 7 (page 115)

1. **The correct answer is (1): change begining to beginning** Choice (1) shows the correct spelling of *beginning*. Choices (2) and (3) show incorrect spellings. Choice (4) shows an incorrect use of the posessive. Choice (5) shows an incorrect use of capitalization.

2. **The correct answer is (2): change recieve to receive** Choice (2) shows the correct spelling of *receive*. Choices (1) and (4) show incorrect spellings. Choice (3) shows an incorrect use of present tense.

3. **The correct answer is (5): replace but with so** Choice (5) uses the correct connecting word to show contrast. Choice (1) shifts to the past tense, choice (2) omits part of a verb, choice (3) uses a past participle as part of the infinitive, and choice (4) uses an inappropriate connecting word.

Exercise 8 (page 116)

1. **The correct answer is *hoped*.**

2. **The correct answer is *heroes*.**

3. **The correct answer is *addresses*.**

4. **The correct answer is *boxes*.**

5. **The correct answer is *tomatoes*.**

6. **The correct answer is *tries*.**

7. **The correct answer is (2): change the spelling of helping to helping** Choice (2) is correct because the consonant is doubled before *ing* is added to a one-syllable verb only if the consonant is preceded by a vowel. Choice (1) incorrectly changes a plural noun to a possessive. Choice (3) reverses the *ei* in *their*. Choice (4) adds *es* to a noun that becomes plural simply by adding *s*.

8. **The correct answer is (2): change the spelling of exorbitent to exorbitant** Choices (1) and (4) misspell words by reversing letters, and choice (3) fails to drop the *e* before adding *ing*.

9. **The correct answer is (5): change the spelling of financiel to financial** Choice (1) is a misspelling. There is no reason for the comma in choice (2). Choice (3) is incorrect because a comma between independent clauses requires a connecting word. Choice (4) is the incorrect form of the relative pronoun.

Exercise 9 (page 117)

1. **The correct answer is (3): change with out to without** Do not separate prefixes and suffixes from the main word even if the suffix or prefix is a complete word. Choices (1) and (2) are misspellings, and choice (4) fails to drop the final *e* before adding *ing*.

2. **The correct answer is (2): change the spelling of normaly to normally** Choice (2) adds the suffix *ly* without changing the spelling of the main word. Choice (1) fails to drop the final *e* before adding *ing*. Choice (3) removes the comma after a dependent clause in a compound sentence, and choice (4) changes the spelling of the main word before adding the suffix *ly*.

3. **The correct answer is (1): change couragous to courageous** Choice (1) correctly spells *courageous*. Choices (2), (3), and (4) misspell words.

Exercise 10 (page 119)

1. Being late so often, *you're* going to have trouble keeping the job. *a*

2. *It'll* be hard to find any place open at this hour. *wi*

3. They *aren't* selling that item any longer. *o*

4. He *hasn't* missed a single game all season. *o*

5. *You'll* have to wait until the report is published. *wi*

6. Sam saw that *they'd* been there already. *ha*

7. *She's* completely dependable. *i*

8. Take whatever *they'll* give you. *wi*

9. It really *isn't* hard to understand. *o*

10. By now, *it's* too late to get tickets. *i*

11. **The correct answer is (2): change It's to They're** Choice (2) uses a plural pronoun (*they*) to agree with a plural antecedent (*snacks*). Choice (1) removes an apostrophe from a contraction, choice (3) uses a comma for no reason, and choice (4) creates a fragment.

12. **The correct answer is (3): change there to they're** In choice (3) the wrong word *there* becomes a contraction meaning *they are*. Choices (1) and (2) remove necessary commas, choice (4) puts the apostrophe in the wrong place, and choice (5) misspells *healthful*.

13. **The correct answer is (3): change its to it's** Choice (3) makes a contraction out of *it is*. Choice (1) removes a comma after an introductory word, and choice (2) misplaces the apostrophe. Choice (4) places a comma before a dependent clause, and choice (5) creates a fragment.

14. **The correct answer is (2): change students' to student's** Choice (2) places the apostrophe to indicate that the possessive noun is singular. Choice (1) fails to use an apostrophe for a possessive noun. Choice (3) misspells *fascinating*, and there's no reason for the comma in choice (4).

15. **The correct answer is (4): change their's to theirs** Possessive pronouns do not use apostrophes. Choices (1) and (2) change plural words to singular possessives, choice (3) lacks subject-verb agreement, and choice (5) uses an apostrophe with a possessive pronoun.

16. **The correct answer is (5): change decade's to decades** Choice (5) removes the apostrophe from a word that is neither possessive nor a contraction. Choice (1) removes the apostrophe from a contraction, choices (2) and (3) use incorrect past participles, and choice (4) makes a noun possessive for no reason.

17. **The correct answer is (4): the project's conclusions** Choice (4) uses the apostrophe for the possessive and leaves it out of the plural word. Choice (1) has no possessive, choice (2) places the apostrophe after the *s* in a singular possessive, choice (3) changes a noun from plural to singular and will result in faulty subject-verb agreement (*conclusion show*), and choice (5) reverses the plural and the possessive words.

Exercise 11 (page 122)

1. **The correct answer is (1): change the spelling of seen to scene** There's no reason to capitalize *collision*, as in choice (2). Choices (3) and (4) use the wrong sound-alike words, and choice (5) is incorrect because there's no reason to separate the prefix from the main word.

2. **The correct answer is (1): replace their with there** Choice (1) uses *there* to indicate place. The other choices use the wrong sound-alike words.

3. **The correct answer is (4): replace breaks with brakes** Choice (4) uses *brakes,* which stop cars. Choices (1) and (3) use the wrong sound-alike words, and choice (2) is incorrect because *neither* is an exception to the *ie* rule.

4. **The correct answer is (2): change already to all ready** *Already* means *previously,* and *all ready* means *entirely ready.* Choice (1) is incorrect because we use a comma only before a quotation. Choice (3) is the wrong verb tense, and there is no reason to capitalize the words in choice (4).

Exercise 12 (page 124)

1. **The correct answer is (1): change the spelling of sychology to psychology** Choice (1) shows the correct spelling of *psychology. Seminar* is spelled correctly in the original sentence.

2. **The correct answer is (2): change the spelling of sholder to shoulder** Choice (2) is the only one that doesn't misspell a word.

3. **The correct answer is (5): change the spelling of predjudice to prejudice** Choice (5) is the only one that doesn't misspell a word. Choice (1) also uses the wrong sound-alike word.

Unit 4: Essay Writing

Exercise 1 (page 129)

Answers will vary. Answer these questions to check your work:

- Is your introduction one paragraph?

- Does it start with a hook?

- Does it contain your thesis?

If you can answer *yes* to each of these questions, you have done the work correctly. Here's one possible introduction:

> Many Americans are worried about the rising cost of health care, and they want the government to do something about it. To keep medical costs down, however, people must accept responsibility for their own health. They need to stay informed about the latest health trends and take a look at their diet and exercise habits. They should also create a safe home environment to prevent injury.

The first sentence is the hook. The rest of the paragraph is the thesis.

Exercise 2 (page 130)

Answers will vary. Answer these questions to check your work:

- Do your conclusions restate the thesis?

- Do they contain a closing thought?

- Do they stick to the subject of the essay?

If you can answer yes to each of these questions, you have done the work correctly. Here is one possible conclusion for this essay:

> If I can forget my own problems and be thrilled by terrifying special effects, I will always enjoy horror movies. I like the fun of a good scare when I know I can't really be harmed. People who don't go to horror movies are missing a great escape.

The first two sentences restate the thesis. The last sentence is the closing thought.

Exercise 3 (page 130)

Your GED essay will be given a ranking on a scale of 1 through 6. The essay score, together with your score on Part I of the test, becomes your GED Writing Skills Test score. The merging of the two scores is done on a special grid used by the GED test scorers.

If your essay makes a point, has a clear structure, uses logical examples, and is relatively free from errors in sentence structure, usage, and mechanics, it will fall in the upper half of the point range with a score of 4 to 6. An essay that is not legible or not clearly related to the topic will receive no points.

ESSAY SCORING GUIDE

- A *6 essay* develops ideas clearly, uses particularly sophisticated and vivid examples, flows smoothly, and has almost no errors.

- A *5 essay* develops ideas fairly well, but the writing is not as smooth, the examples are not as good, and the essay has noticeably more errors than a 6 essay.

- A *4 essay* develops ideas adequately, but the writing is a bit more awkward, the examples less extensive and less effective, and the essay has noticeably more errors than the 5 essay.

- A *3 essay* shows some evidence of planning, but the examples are weak or underdeveloped. It also contains repeated errors in sentence structure, usage, and mechanics.

- A *2 essay* is weak in organization or inadequate in the development of ideas. It contains many errors.

- A *1 essay* lacks structure, purpose, and control. It contains many errors.

   Use the following sample essays to evaluate the essay you have written.

A SAMPLE 6 ESSAY

Hook and thesis, with three subjects stated

Advertisers spend billions of dollars each year persuading consumers to buy their products. To sell products, they exploit human desires to be healthy, to save money, and to be happy.

First subtopic, example

Explanation

It's pretty hard to resist a product that promises health and long life. Actors posing as doctors appear in advertisements to sell cold medicines, headache remedies, and even health insurance. These actors look authentic and authoritative, so we pay attention to what they say. They use charts and graphs, along with testimonials from "ordinary people," to convince us that one product is more beneficial to our health than another.

Second subtopic, example
Explanation

Just as we all want to be healthy, most of us also want to save money. With free samples, coupons, and low prices, advertisers urge us to try a product. If it costs less, we might try it. Then we might continue to buy it, get used to it, and keep buying it even if the price goes up a little.

Third subtopic
Example, and explanation

When an ad shows people having fun or falling in love, it suggests that a particular product brings happiness. Advertisers would like us to believe that the right toothpaste, drink, car, perfume, or aftershave is all that is needed to find true love and happiness.

Conclusion, with thesis implied

As consumers, we must be careful shoppers if we are to avoid the awesome power and influence of advertisers.

A 6 essay has a clear structure, develops the topic with excellent examples, and concludes neatly. The conclusion does not repeat the three-point thesis but implies it in the closing sentence.

A SAMPLE 5 ESSAY

Hook and thesis with two subtopics

Consumers are influenced in many ways by advertisers who have billions of dollars to spend on radio, television, newspapers, magazines, and billboards. The most vulnerble consumers are the ones with children, and advertisers that sell toys and food are quick to take advantage of that.

First subtopic

Most kids watch television, and TV bombards them with commercials that show how much fun they could have if they owned a particlar toy. Maybe it's the latest movie character, a dinosaur, or a mermaid. It could even be a character they see on television, but not necessarily in commercials. The television shows themselves serve as advertisements because often the characters in the programs are available as dolls in toy stores. If children see enough ads for a particlar product, there desire to have it will increase. On top of advertisements, kids can apply plenty of their own pressure on parents.

Several examples
Example and explanation

Second subtopic

Kids play with toys, but they eat food too, especially cereal. One cereal commercial actually states that "unless your kids are weird, they'll eat it." This implies that kids who don't like this cereal are not normal. Most parents, sure that their own kids are perfectly normal, probly will buy this particlar brand of breakfast food.

Examples and explanation

Advertisers count on parents to buy anything it takes to keep their children happy and normal.

This essay is a 5 because the second subtopic is not developed as completely as the first. There are also a few misspellings.

Hook and thesis with
two subtopics

Weak development,
confusing sentence structure

Example is developed, but
writing contains too
many errors

Example needs more
explanation

Thesis is restated, but
sentence structure is weak

A SAMPLE 4 ESSAY

Wherever we turn, we see advertisements. Ads are on television, on the radio, in the papers, everywhere. Sometimes they try to get us to buy products by pretending to be scientific. Other times they try to make us think we'll change for the better if we have the product, sometimes they just pressure us with time limits.

Sometimes advertisers try to get us to buy products by they'll pretend to be real science. They use charts and make it look like they're in a laboratory or a doctors office or something like that.

Some ads try to make us think we'll be better if we have the product. For example, sleep on a certain kind of mattress, the ad says you did a better job at work or school the next day. Another is use the right car for a happy picnic in the woods or some place.

Some ads just pressure us with time limits. They say a special price is over by some date pretty soon. They'll say hurry, don't wait, and they make you feel like you better run right out this very minute or you'll be sorry.

Pressure, pretend science, and promising to change us is how advertisements influence consumers.

This essay is a 4 because the support is weak and there are errors in sentence structure and mechanics. However, it does develop a thesis with a clear structure.

Thesis is stated, but it is
not logical

A SAMPLE 3 ESSAY

Its pretty hard to avoid the pressures of advertisers. Because they use athleets and movie stars to sell products and ordnary people.

Everybody reconizes athleets and movie stars, so you shouldn't be surprized that they appear in ads on television and elsewhere. Take Michael Jordan. hes a great basketball player, so he wears shoes anybody would like to buy them when they see him wearing them on television.

The same with movie stars. If you see Al Pacino or somebody like that useing a credit card in Europe on vacation, who wouldn't want to use that same credit card?

Sometimes it's just regular people in advertisements. Well, they they look like regular people, but you know there just actors. Anyway, you see them having fun with their familys, so you buy that kind of film, too.

Weather there famous or ordinary, consumers buy things that athletes and movie stars say to buy because we look up to them. Regular people can make us buy things, too. But only if the product seem to make them happy.

This essay is a 3 because the support is weak and errors in sentence structure confuse the reader.

A SAMPLE 2 ESSAY

Television is where most advertising is on. Kids programs, sports, news, everything has it. Then kids nag there parents all day to buy the stuff they seen on television this just gets parents mad and the kids wont get anything. Which serve them right if they act bratty like that.

Sports is another thing. You cant even watch a football or baseball without too many commercals. Why do they have to ruin a perfectly good ballgame with those dumb commercals. Then they use the same guys to brake into other programs, I mean sport guys who get millions of dollars I bet just to tell you to buy some kind of razer and you cant even see them play there game. Because the ads ruin the game right in the middle.

So in conclusion, I think there's too many commercals in the cartoons and the sports. News, too.

This essay is a 2 because it lacks a clear thesis, the support details wander from the topic, the conclusion doesn't match the thesis, and there are many errors.

A SAMPLE 1 ESSAY

I think advertising is horrible. Because they lie and you waist your hard earned money. I can't think of any place where you dont see ads there everywhere and all they do is lie and tell you to buy stuff you don't need and you cant aford to anyway so it's kind of rotten to do that. Besides that stuff isnt ture anybody knows that.

So how do they do it? Well, there is alot of ways. Television for example. People just leave the room when the comershal come on, because it gets loud and its like their yelling at you to buy something. Who wants to listen to stuff like that. That why remote controls are good. Because you can just change the chanel or turn off the sound. The best thing is to go get something to eat, and it probly wont even be what they advertise. Which shows you that the ads just lie anyway.

This essay is a 1 because the ideas are jumbled together. It lacks a clear thesis, subtopics, and examples to support them. The writer has no control over the topic.

Part 2
SOCIAL STUDIES

WHAT WILL I FIND ON THE SOCIAL STUDIES TEST?

The GED Social Studies Test is not a measurement of how much you know about specific social studies facts and concepts. Most questions will ask you to think logically about a passage or illustration related to a social studies topic.

CONTENT AREAS

Social Studies is Test 2 of the GED Tests and consists of five content areas. The percent for each area is given in parentheses.

History: (25 percent) The study of the American past, including major formative experiences such as the Civil War and national issues like slavery.

Geography: (15 percent) The study of location, physical environment, the earth and its people, geographic regions, and major themes such as agriculture.

Political science: (20 percent) The study of world political systems, especially political systems and beliefs in the United States.

Economics: (20 percent) The study of production and consumption of goods, foreign trade, and labor.

Behavioral science: (20 percent) The study of people as individuals and as members of groups.

TYPES OF QUESTIONS

When you take the GED Social Studies Test, you will have 85 minutes to answer 64 multiple-choice questions. Each question or set of questions will refer to a written passage or an illustration. To answer these questions, you will need to comprehend, apply, analyze, or evaluate the information presented. Of the social studies questions, 30 percent will be application questions, 30 percent will be analysis questions, 20 percent will be comprehension questions, and 20 percent will be evaluation questions.

Comprehension questions ask you to identify, restate, or summarize information and ideas that are stated directly or indirectly in a passage, drawing, or chart. The following question is an example of a comprehension question that asks you to summarize information.

1. Which of the following best summarizes the cartoonist's meaning?

    (1) The original concept of the U.S. presidency has stayed pretty much the same for more than 200 years.
    (2) The executive branch is one of the three branches of the federal government.
    (3) Too many people in the executive branch have held their jobs for too long and aren't keeping up with the times.
    (4) The current powers of the executive branch have greatly outgrown the original concept of the U.S. presidency.
    (5) People in the judicial and legislative branches are jealous of the powers of the executive branch.

The correct answer is choice (4).

Application questions ask you to use information from a passage, drawing, or chart to solve a problem or to use data in a different situation. The following application question asks you to use the information given to solve a problem.

2. The three branches of the federal government are executive, legislative, and judicial. Each branch has specific duties, as set out in the Constitution of the United States. Which one of the following people is a part of the judicial branch of the federal government?

   (1) a law clerk for an associate justice of the Supreme Court
   (2) the legal counsel to the President
   (3) a congressman from Ohio
   (4) the legal counsel to a Senatorial subcommittee
   (5) the lawyer for a large corporation who argues a case before the Supreme Court

Choice (1) is the correct answer.

Analysis questions ask you to determine causes and effects, distinguish facts from opinions, and draw conclusions. The analysis question below asks you to distinguish facts from opinions.

In 1918 and 1919, about 2 billion people came down with an especially lethal strain of flu virus. Between 20 million and 40 million died. This pandemic, or international epidemic, killed as many people in one year as the Black Death (bubonic plague) did between 1347 and 1351. Today, many people feel that flu vaccines have made the disease basically harmless. Some scientists worry, however, that available treatments might be useless against a particularly virulent flu.

3. Which of the following statements is an opinion, not a fact?

   (1) The 1918–1919 flu epidemic caused widespread death.
   (2) A pandemic is a worldwide epidemic.
   (3) About 2 billion people were affected by the flu in 1918 and 1919.
   (4) Modern medicine could easily defeat even an especially strong strain of flu virus today.
   (5) Scientists don't know exactly how many people died in the pandemic of 1918–1919.

The correct answer is choice (4).

Evaluation questions ask you to judge the accuracy of information, recognize the role of values in decision making, assess documentation or proof, and recognize logical fallacies. The evaluation question below asks you to determine the role that values play in beliefs.

The failure of communism led to the breakup of the Soviet Union into fifteen separate nations, including Russia, Ukraine, and Belarus. All fifteen adopted a system of democracy and capitalism, but soon began to have economic troubles. The new nations argued over ownership of the Black Sea Navy Fleet and the Crimean Peninsula, as well as disputing who would pay which debts of the old Soviet Union.

4. Which would be the point of view held by someone in one of the fifteen new nations who believes that the old Soviet Union should be restored?

   (1) Ukraine and Belarus are causing all the problems.
   (2) Restoring communism will make the Soviet Union great again.
   (3) The West is not giving enough help to democratic leaders such as Russia's Boris Yeltsin.
   (4) Russia should give the Black Sea Fleet and the Crimea to Ukraine.
   (5) The breakup of the Soviet Union was its own fault because communism was an unworkable and unjust system.

The correct answer is choice (2).

HISTORY

Building a Nation

Between 1492 and 1763, Spain, France, the Netherlands, and England fought for control of North America. All four nations sought wealth from the untapped resources of the so-called New World. Many Europeans also wanted to convert the native inhabitants to Christianity, or to make important new discoveries of territory to claim for their countries. By 1763, the English had won the prize. Through war, they took over territory claimed by the Dutch and the French. The Spanish, with their interests spread throughout Central and South America and parts of Europe, posed little threat to the English colonies along the eastern seaboard. With English rule firmly established, the seeds of American democracy were planted in the colonies.

Early Democracies

The first English settlers believed strongly in individual liberty, religious freedom, and self-government. The colonists' beliefs were based in part on English law, which granted citizens certain rights and provided for a **representative government**.

The first successful English settlement, Jamestown, was established in 1607 in what would become Virginia. After several rocky years, the settlement began to profit from a valuable new crop, tobacco. In 1619, the Jamestown colonists began to govern themselves through the House of Burgesses, the first representative assembly in America.

A second group of English colonists, arriving in Massachusetts in 1620, was the Pilgrims, who were religious dissenters, or protesters. On their ship the *Mayflower*, before landing, they developed the Mayflower Compact, a plan of self-rule, which served as the basis for the colony's government. The compact contained the fundamental democratic principle that a government's power depends on the consent of the governed.

Were the colonial governments truly representative? Participation in government was reserved for men, usually landowners. Native Americans had no say in the settlement or affairs of Europeans. Enslaved Africans were considered property and therefore had no rights as citizens. Thus, we can see today that the colonial governments did not represent everyone who lived in the colonies.

representative government: a government in which an elected or chosen few act for (or represent) the many

Exercise 1

> **Directions**
> Choose the one best answer to each item.

> Items 1 and 2 refer to the following paragraph and map.

The colonies were founded primarily for religious or economic purposes. That is, the founders wanted to provide a haven for a specific religious group or for all worshippers, or they wanted to develop land, make money for a company, or develop trade with Indians. Sometimes colonies were founded for a combination of economic and religious reasons. The map shows the thirteen colonies and the primary reason for the founding of each one.

THE 13 COLONIES: PRIMARY REASONS FOR FOUNDING

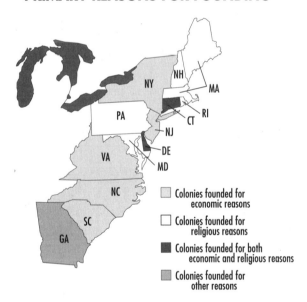

Colonies founded for economic reasons

Colonies founded for religious reasons

Colonies founded for both economic and religious reasons

Colonies founded for other reasons

1. According to the map, the colonies founded for <u>both</u> religious and economic reasons were

    (1) Connecticut, Delaware, and Georgia
    (2) New Jersey, Delaware, and Pennsylvania
    (3) Connecticut and Delaware
    (4) New Jersey and New York
    (5) Massachusetts, New Hampshire, Rhode Island, and Maryland

2. Which of the following conclusions could be drawn from the map?

    (1) Economic colonies were most successful in the South.
    (2) People living in religious colonies preferred to live in the North.
    (3) Colonies founded for both religious and economic reasons were the smallest ones.
    (4) Colonies founded for economic reasons tended to be large and located in the South.
    (5) Colonies were founded for two main reasons regardless of their size or location.

3. Read the following statement, made by John Winthrop, first governor of Massachusetts:

    "As for the Natives in New England, they inclose noe Land, neither have any setled habytation, nor any tame Cattle to improve the Land by, and soe have noe . . . Right to those Countries."

    Winthrop's statement reflects a common viewpoint held by New Englanders. Which item best summarizes this viewpoint?

    (1) Because Native Americans did not own land, they could not be represented in colonial governments.
    (2) Without improvements to the land, the Native Americans were not able to establish settlements.
    (3) Because Native Americans did nothing to show ownership of the land, they had no right to claim it.
    (4) Native Americans could claim any land they wanted, as long as they did not enclose it, settle on it, or graze cattle on it.
    (5) Because Native Americans had left the land as they found it—without fences or settlements—they had a greater claim to it than did the New Englanders.

To check your answers, turn to page 187

Revolution and Independence

Prior to 1776, each colony had developed in its own distinct way, and the independent-minded citizens preferred to maintain their differences. Events between 1754 and 1776, however, drew the colonies toward union with one another.

In 1754, conflict broke out between French and English settlers in areas north and west of the colonies. The conflict developed into a full-scale war—the French and Indian War—between France and Great Britain. In its hard-won victory in 1763, Britain gained virtually all French territory in North America, but at great cost.

To pay its debts and maintain control of the area, the British government began a series of restrictive measures. Colonists were required to pay taxes on imported goods such as sugar and were prevented from printing their own money. Under the Stamp Act, every paper document in the colonies was required to carry a stamp purchased from a government agent. The colonists protested with **boycotts** of English products. The colonists' outrage led to the First Continental Congress, a meeting of colonists, in 1774. In April 1775, the war now known as the American Revolution broke out and lasted until 1781, five years after the colonies had declared themselves free and independent of England. The Second Continental Congress began in May 1775. On July 4, 1776, Congress declared the colonies to be "free and independent States." You'll read more about the Declaration of Independence in Unit 3, Exercise 1.

Conflict and Compromise

During the first years of the new American nation, creating a national government was a matter of enormous conflict. Americans argued over issues such as states' rights, slavery, and the power of government as they worked out the details of running their country. After their experience with English rule, American citizens were determined to avoid a powerful, centralized government with broad powers over individuals and states. They believed in strong representation and individual freedoms.

The first national plan of government, the Articles of Confederation, provided a loose structure of union but made the federal government weak and ineffective. In 1787, a Constitutional Convention met for the purpose of revising the Articles. After nearly four months of debate and compromise, the United States Constitution was completed. It was not without flaws, but the framers thoughtfully provided a way to change it through **amendments** that can revise parts of the original document or add new provisions.

The next struggle was over **ratification**, or approval, by the states. In order to take effect, the Constitution had to be ratified by nine of the thirteen states. The nation divided itself into two opposing camps. The Federalists favored the Constitution and the strong central government it outlined. Anti-Federalists complained that it did not provide for individual rights and

liberties. The Anti-Federalists were persuaded to support the Constitution only after they were promised that a bill of rights would be added.

The first ten amendments to the United States Constitution form the Bill of Rights. They guarantee certain rights and freedoms to individuals; for example, the freedom to worship as we please, the freedom to express our opinions, and the right to a fair trial. These liberties, born of conflict, now form the cornerstone of the American democratic system.

Exercise 2

> **Directions**
> Choose the one best answer to each item.

1. Before 1774, the idea of a union of colonies was considered impossible. Which of the following is an objection the colonists would have had to a union?

   (1) They feared that the rights and freedoms of individuals would be overlooked.
   (2) They feared that their forms of self-government would be threatened.
   (3) They feared that their freedom to worship as they please would be lost.
   (4) They were afraid that a union would be easily overtaken by the British.
   (5) They were afraid that the Constitution could never be ratified.

2. In 1773, as colonial rebellion grew more daring, the British king said, "The colonies must submit or triumph." The British government passed strict, punishing laws intended to show the colonists that

   (1) they would not be allowed to raise their own taxes
   (2) it would make them pay for the repeal of the Stamp Act
   (3) Britain had complete authority over the colonies
   (4) Britain would win the Revolutionary War
   (5) the Declaration of Independence was null and void

boycott: a refusal to buy a product or service

amendment: a change or correction

ratification: formal approval, usually by the states

3. One possible disadvantage of a strong central government is that it may

    (1) give too many rights to states
    (2) give too many rights to individuals
    (3) limit the rights of individual citizens
    (4) prevent representative assemblies
    (5) limit the power of the Constitution

4. Which of the following situations is not protected by the Bill of Rights, a guarantee of individual rights and freedoms?

    (1) A white supremacy organization wants to hold a rally in a city park.
    (2) Mr. B., an avid sportsman, owns a variety of weapons.
    (3) A suspected drug dealer is arrested without a warrant.
    (4) A woman wants to run for the office of U.S. Senator but has not reached the minimum age of thirty.
    (5) A Jewish man wishes to wear his yarmulke, a cap with religious significance, at work.

To check your answers, turn to page 187.

GROWTH AND DIVISION

Was the Civil War fought over slavery? Historians are still debating that question. Before 1861, when the war began, the issue of slavery had already driven a wedge between the North and the South. As the nation expanded west of the Mississippi, the states argued over whether to extend slavery into the new territories. The adventure of moving west became linked with the fierce debate over slavery.

Slavery and Free Speech

During the early 1800s, more and more people began to demand that slavery be abolished. These **abolitionists** formed organizations to fight for the end of slavery. To them, slavery was morally wrong and had no place in a democracy. As this movement gained strength, southern political leaders feared that it would lead to slave rebellions and would threaten the southern way of life, which depended on slavery. In the South, abolitionist literature was seized and abolitionists were attacked. Abolitionists began to flood Congress with petitions demanding the end of slavery.

In 1836, under pressure from southern members, the U.S. House of Representatives passed a **"gag rule"** blocking all petitions and forbidding all discussion of the slavery issue. John Quincy Adams, a former U.S. president and now a state representative, devoted himself to the cause of repealing the gag rule. The rule, he said, violated Americans' right to petition their government and violated his own right of free speech. He encouraged citizens to send him their petitions, and he tirelessly presented them to Congress. Finally, in 1844, the gag rule was overturned.

Resentments in both North and South grew as the slavery debate intensified. In 1857, a case before the U.S. Supreme Court promised to resolve the debate once and for all. The case involved a man, originally a slave, named Dred Scott. With his master, Scott had spent four years living in the free state of Illinois and the free territory of Wisconsin. After his master's death, Scott sued for his freedom, saying that because he had lived on "free soil," he was now a free man.

The Supreme Court's ruling in *Dred Scott v. Sanford* included the following main points:

- Dred Scott, as an enslaved African American, was not a citizen and therefore could not sue in a federal court.

- Congress could not outlaw slavery in territories because that would deprive slaveholders of their property and thus violate the Fifth Amendment.

- Therefore, Congress could not forbid slave owners to take their slaves into free territory.

- Previous restrictions on slavery in the territories were unconstitutional.

The decision was a victory for southerners, who had been fighting to extend slavery to the territories, and a blow to abolitionists, who had hoped to stop the spread of slavery.

---

abolitionists: people wishing to abolish, or end, slavery

"gag rule": a rule passed in the U.S. House of Representatives to forbid any discussion of slavery

Exercise 3

Directions

Choose the one best answer to each item.

Items 1 and 2 refer to information in the text and the following map.

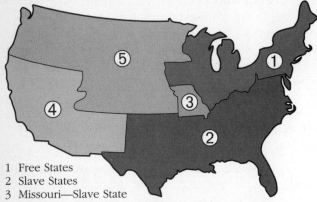

1 Free States
2 Slave States
3 Missouri—Slave State
4 California (Free State) and Utah and New Mexico territories (open to slavery by inhabitant's choice)
5 Northern territories

1. What generalization about slavery can you make from the map?

   (1) Slavery was not permitted in New Mexico and Utah territories.
   (2) The compromises of 1820 and 1850 created many new states.
   (3) Slavery tended to be limited to the southern states and territories.
   (4) People in the northern territories did not want slavery.
   (5) The proslavery people were gaining more and more territory.

2. According to the Dred Scott decision, which of the following states or territories would be off-limits to you if you were a slave owner?

   (1) California
   (2) Missouri
   (3) Utah Territory
   (4) Texas
   (5) Unorganized territory

3. John Quincy Adams said that with the gag rule, the southern representatives had equated the wrong of slavery with the right of petition. He meant that the southerners were trying to hold onto slavery by

   (1) disrupting Congress
   (2) denying free speech
   (3) only forbidding discussion
   (4) only blocking petitions
   (5) overturning the gag rule

4. In *Dred Scott v. Sanford*, the Supreme Court ruled that slavery could be extended into territories. In effect, this ruling

   (1) moved slavery from the states to the territories
   (2) forced slaves to move to the territories
   (3) allowed slavery anywhere in the United States
   (4) made slavery legal in the territories
   (5) forced slave owners to move to the territories

To check your answers, turn to page 187.

Expanding Westward

As soon as Americans had settled a country, they couldn't wait to explore it further. As if they were drawn by unseen forces, they began to pour over the Appalachians into the vast lands of the American West. During the first half of the nineteenth century, the United States expanded westward from the Mississippi River all the way to the Pacific Ocean. During these years, Americans believed they had a special mission to move into unexplored lands and "tame" them. In 1845, this mission was termed **"Manifest Destiny."**

GROWTH OF RAILROADS

Transportation was an essential part of westward expansion. Without a vast network of roads, canals, and railroads, Americans could not have reached the new lands so quickly and in such great numbers. In turn, the drive to move west spurred the rapid growth, development, and improvement of transportation systems.

Railroads in particular had a tremendous impact on westward expansion. The first steam-powered locomotives appeared in 1830, but railroad transportation did not boom for another twenty years. Between 1850 and 1860, the railroad network grew from 9,000 miles to 30,000 miles. Much of the new track connected the cities

---

"Manifest Destiny": the belief of Americans in the mid-nineteenth century that they had a special mission to explore the West

of the Northeast with the agricultural areas of the Middle West (the states along the Mississippi River). Manufactured goods from the Northeast and farm products from the West and Middle West could be shipped more easily and rapidly than ever before. Before 1860, people began to talk of a transcontinental railroad to link the vast resources of the West with the industrial centers of the East.

NATIVE AMERICANS: "YIELD OR PERISH"

After the Civil War ended in 1865, **migration** to the West increased. As waves of Americans crossed the Mississippi, seeking fortunes in the mines or homes on the prairies, they had a profound effect on the native peoples of the Great Plains and Far West. Railroad towns and farms took over the tribal homelands, which the Native Americans were expected to give up without protest. "The westward course of population is neither to be denied nor delayed for the sake of all the Indians that ever called this country their home," said a government report in 1873. "They must yield or perish."

Perhaps the most devastating effect of the railroad was the annihilation of the millions of buffalo that roamed the plains and served the Plains Nations' needs for food, shelter, and clothing. With the railroads came white hunters who killed the animals for food, for clothing, and for sport. The tracks split the herds and disrupted the Native Americans' hunting patterns. The end of the buffalo meant the end of the Plains Nations' way of life.

Exercise 4

Directions

Choose the one best answer to each item.

Item 1 refers to the following graph.

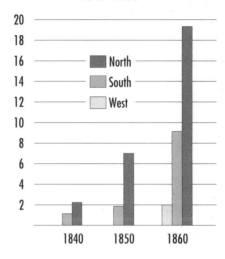

U.S. RAILROADS
1840–1860

1. What general conclusion can you draw from the graph?

   (1) The South showed very little railroad growth between 1840 and 1850.

   (2) Railroads grew at a phenomenal rate between 1840 and 1860.

   (3) Railroads did not appear in the West until 1860.

   (4) By 1860, the North had about 19,500 miles of railroads.

   (5) In spite of a boom in growth from 1850 to 1860, southern railroads could not catch up with northern railroads.

2. A person who believed in Manifest Destiny in the 1800s would most likely want to

   (1) preserve the natural environment
   (2) respect the rights of others
   (3) acquire more land and power
   (4) rule foreign lands
   (5) preserve peace at all costs

migration: movement of great numbers of people from one place to another with the intention of settling in the new area

3. In 1860, just before the Civil War began, the South had less than half the railroad mileage of the North. This deficiency placed the South at a disadvantage during the war. Which of the following items was not a disadvantage caused by a deficiency of railroad mileage?

   (1) Supplies and troops could not be transported quickly.

   (2) Many areas were not served by the railroad.

   (3) Railroad tracks in the South were wider than tracks in the North.

   (4) No alternate routes existed in case tracks were destroyed.

   (5) Many key cities had no direct connections.

4. Which of the following statements best summarizes the U.S. government's attitude toward Native Americans in the West?

   (1) They were no longer entitled to kill buffalo for food, shelter, and clothing.

   (2) They could live where they wanted as long as they did not interfere with settlers.

   (3) They were required to show the settlers how to live on the land.

   (4) They were a barrier to civilization and therefore had to move or be moved.

   (5) They were skillful buffalo hunters, but their towns were located on land desired by settlers.

To check your answers, turn to page 187.

GROWTH OF INDUSTRIAL POWER

The period 1870–1920, often known as the Industrial Revolution, was marked by tremendous economic growth, a boom in industry, and a flood of new inventions. These developments caused profound changes in American life. Locomotives, power looms, harvesting combines, and other machines turned factories and farms forever from small, home-based businesses into huge, profit-oriented companies. By 1900, the United States was the leading industrial nation in the world.

The Automobile Revolution

In finding a way to produce cars that the average person could afford, Henry Ford revolutionized American industry. To bring down the cost of building a car, Ford introduced a method of production, the assembly line, in 1913. As the chassis of a car passed by each worker, he or she performed a single, specialized job, repeating it as quickly as possible. Assembly-line methods cut production time for one car from 14 to 6 hours and allowed Ford to lower the price of a car from $600 in 1912 to $360 in 1916. At the same time, Ford doubled his employees' wages and reduced the working day from 9 hours to 8.

In other industries, standard business practice had been to keep wages as low as possible and prices as high as the market would allow. To the surprise of his critics, Henry Ford got rich by doing the opposite. By 1927, when the Model A replaced his original design, the Model T Ford had sold 15 million cars.

Hard Times in the Factory

Those who lived with the reality of factory work saw a less pleasant side of the industrial boom. Profits ruled, and workers became commodities, like flour or cloth, to be bought at the cheapest price. Immigrants, pouring into the cities looking for jobs, provided an endless source of cheap labor. Most factory workers labored long hours for low pay at jobs that were repetitive and often dangerous.

Even worse than the factories were the tenement sweatshops. Entire families, including young children, made artificial flowers, rolled cigars, or sewed garments at home, working late into the night for very low pay.

These terrible working conditions gave rise to labor unions. Individuals believed that if they organized into groups, their complaints would be heard by company owners and managers. Labor unions did win many improvements for workers, such as shorter workdays, fair pay, and safety measures, but often workers were reluctant to join. Changing economic conditions, strikes and angry employers kept unions from gaining a firm hold until 1886, when the American Federation of Labor (AFL) was formed. The AFL was successful partly because it was a collection of separate unions, each one representing a craft or skill. Each union operated independently but worked with the AFL for the benefit of all workers.

Exercise 5

> **Directions**
>
> Choose the one best answer to each item.

1. A labor union would be concerned with all of the following items except

   (1) regular inspection and repair of machinery

   (2) number and duration of rest breaks

   (3) vacation and insurance plans

   (4) overhead lighting in the workplace

   (5) how workers get to and from work

Items 2 and 3 refer to the following circle graphs.

EMPLOYMENT BY OCCUPATION

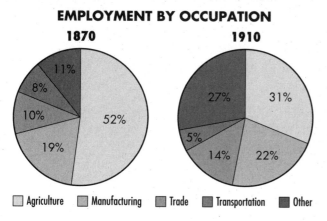

1870

1910

☐ Agriculture ☐ Manufacturing ☐ Trade ■ Transportation ■ Other

2. Many of the people who moved to the cities worked in factories—sewing, assembling, sorting, and so on. These workers fit into which category?

    (1) agriculture
    (2) manufacturing
    (3) trade
    (4) servants
    (5) transportation

3. What trend do the two graphs together show for agricultural workers between 1870 and 1910?

    (1) Due to increasing urbanization, fewer agricultural workers were needed in 1910 than in 1870.
    (2) The proportion of agricultural workers dropped from about half of all workers in 1870 to less than one-third in 1910.
    (3) Although the percentage of agricultural workers decreased between 1870 and 1910, the actual number increased.
    (4) In 1910, agricultural workers preferred to join the rush to the cities to work in trade and manufacturing jobs.
    (5) Agricultural workers were less in demand in 1910 than in 1870.

To check your answers, turn to page 187.

Imperialism

"Remember the *Maine!*" In 1898, Cubans were in the midst of a rebellion against Spanish rule. The U.S.S. *Maine*, docked in the port of Havana to protect Americans in Cuba, exploded. Exaggerated rumors of Spanish atrocities against the rebels had angered Americans for several years. Now American lives had been lost. "This means war!" screamed newspaper headlines.

The three-month Spanish-American War began a period of American **imperialism**, or expanding the country's influence in foreign lands. American railroad builders, steel makers, and bankers had conquered the American West and established the United States as a major industrial power. Now they were looking beyond the country's borders for new opportunities—new trade markets, mineral wealth, land for cash crops, and cheap labor.

U.S. imperialist policy during this period was characterized by increasing **intervention**. Under Theodore Roosevelt, president from 1901 to 1909, the United States took on the role of a political police force to protect the Americas from European powers. The U.S. government had long relied on the Monroe Doctrine to maintain power in the Americas. In 1823, President Monroe had warned European nations not to try to establish colonies in the Americas. Gradually the doctrine also came to mean that European nations should avoid interfering in Latin American independence movements. Under Roosevelt, the United States claimed the right to intervene in Latin American affairs.

The following political cartoon from 1901 depicts the United States as a protector of Latin American countries. Would you say the cartoonist approved of or meant to criticize U.S. imperialism?

---

imperialism: the policy of one country to extend its influence to other countries, seeking to gain economic and political control

---

intervention: interference; an active role in someone else's affairs

President Roosevelt pursued a policy called "Big Stick" diplomacy, which used the threat of military force to influence events in foreign nations. The U.S. government claimed to be maintaining regional stability, but many people believed these actions were more to protect American business interests in Latin American countries. More and more, these nations resented American interference.

The years 1900–1917 are also referred to as the *Progressive Era*, during which significant economic, social, and political reform took place in the United States. Public disapproval of the growth of big business was widespread. A group of journalists, dubbed *muckrakers* by Roosevelt, wrote detailed accounts of corruption caused by big business.

Exercise 6

Directions

Choose the one best answer to each item.

1. The United States fought the Spanish-American War not just to help Cubans liberate themselves from Spanish rule but to break up Spain's worldwide empire as well. Which of the following facts best supports this statement?

   (1) Spain was having trouble holding onto its empire.
   (2) While attention was focused on Cuba, American forces attacked the Philippines, a Spanish holding in the Pacific.
   (3) President McKinley offered conditions to Spain for avoiding war.
   (4) The explosion of the battleship *Maine* was blamed on the Spanish, some say falsely.
   (5) Before helping the Cubans, the United States promised not to claim control over Cuba once it was free.

2. Politician Carl Schurz argued that U.S. expansion into foreign lands violated American democratic principles. Which democratic ideal in particular would be violated by imperialism, a policy that allows one country to interfere in the government and business of another country?

   (1) "All men are created equal."
   (2) All men and women possess "certain unalienable Rights, . . . among these are Life, Liberty and the pursuit of Happiness."
   (3) Governments draw their powers "from the consent of the governed."
   (4) "Whenever any Form of Government becomes destructive of these ends, it is the Right of the People to alter or to abolish it."
   (5) "The people have a right to institute a new Government [that will] effect their Safety and Happiness."

3. In the cartoon in the passage, what do the hens represent?

   (1) Latin American countries
   (2) Latin American countries under U.S. protection
   (3) various U.S. imperialistic policies in Latin America
   (4) Latin American colonies of European nations
   (5) Latin American countries that refused U.S. protection

4. In the cartoon, what does the "European coop" marked "Monroe Doctrine" represent?

   (1) Latin American countries being protected ("cooped up") from European nations
   (2) U.S. policies restricted ("cooped up") by European imperialism
   (3) European nations in closed-door meetings ("cooped up") about Latin American independence movements
   (4) European countries restricted ("cooped up") by the Monroe Doctrine
   (5) European nations hiding in the chicken coop in fear of U.S. power

To check your answers, turn to page 188.

CRISES AT HOME AND ABROAD

In 1933, the nation was in the depths of the Great Depression. Thirteen million people were out of work. Banks closed daily, taking people's life savings with them. The Depression ended only after the United States entered World War II. Despite its toll in lost lives and destruction, the war, with its plentiful jobs, provided a great boost to the nation's economy.

The New Deal

To help Americans recover from the depression, President Franklin D. Roosevelt promised a "new deal." His New Deal programs attacked the Depression on all fronts. For example, the Securities and Exchange Commission (SEC) regulated the sale of stocks, the Tennessee Valley Authority (TVA) managed the natural resources of a seven-state region, and the National Recovery Administration (NRA) set guidelines for fair competition in business.

Two programs that helped put people back to work were the Civilian Conservation Corps (CCC) and the Works Progress Administration (WPA). The CCC, also called Roosevelt's "Tree Army," employed over two million young men who planted trees, fought forest fires, and performed other conservation tasks. The WPA, formed in 1935, is best remembered for the jobs it provided for teachers, artists, and writers who lent their creative talents to many projects.

World War II: The Home Front

In 1939, war broke out in Europe, with Great Britain and France allied (joined) against Germany. Americans supported the Allies in spirit, but the United States remained uninvolved in the war until December 7, 1941, when Japanese bombers made a surprise attack on a U.S. base in Pearl Harbor, Hawaii. The United States declared war on Japan. Two days later, Japan's allies, Germany and Italy, declared war on the United States.

As U.S. soldiers fought overseas, the nation supported the war effort with massive production of airplanes, weapons, and supplies. Americans scrimped and saved, sharing a patriotic desire to help the cause of American victory. But Japanese Americans were seen as a threat to national security. As a result, more than 120,000 Japanese Americans, two thirds of them American citizens, were imprisoned in camps throughout the country.

The Cold War and the Cuban Missile Crisis

World War II ended in 1945 with the first use of atom bombs, causing the most destructive bomb blasts in history over Hiroshima and Nagasaki, Japan. World power was divided between the United States and the communist Soviet Union. The icy tensions between the two powers and their allies came to be known as the Cold War. Many Americans considered **communism** wrong because it denied economic and political freedom. They wanted communism kept as far away as possible, an idea referred to as **containment**.

On October 22, 1962, President Kennedy announced that Soviet missile bases were being built in Cuba. Kennedy planned a two-part approach: a naval blockade (a shutting off of a port by linking up ships) to prevent Soviet ships from reaching Cuba, and a demand that the Soviet Union dismantle and remove the bases.

American warships surrounded Cuba. The nation held its breath as Soviet ships carrying missiles approached. The first of the ships reached the blockade and abruptly turned back. After two days of secret negotiations, the Soviets agreed to remove the Cuban bases. In return, the United States promised not to invade Cuba. War had been narrowly avoided.

communism: an economic and political system characterized by a classless society, equal distribution of economic goods, state control of the economy, and an emphasis on the state's needs rather than on individual liberties

containment: the policy of attempting to prevent the spread of a political system, such as communism

Exercise 7

Directions

Choose the one best answer to each item.

Item 1 refers to the following passage.

The Great Depression was brought about in part by reckless spending and wild speculation, or taking risks in hopes of quick profits. The wild mood of the 1920s was fueled by tremendous business growth and dreams of great wealth. Then, in the midst of plenty, the economy collapsed.

1. An example of speculation would be

    (1) buying a car on a four-year credit plan
    (2) selling a used computer at a profit
    (3) moving a successful restaurant to a new, larger location
    (4) investing in an uncertain business venture with borrowed money
    (5) using a credit card

2. In 1988, the U.S. government formally apologized to Japanese Americans and awarded the families of those who had been imprisoned modest monetary compensation for their losses. By this action, the United States acknowledged that

    (1) Japanese Americans were citizens
    (2) Japanese Americans posed no security threat to the United States
    (3) the civil rights of Japanese Americans had been violated
    (4) the conditions in the detention camps were unsatisfactory
    (5) the property of Japanese Americans should have been protected

3. Critics have said that Kennedy took a huge and terrible risk in the Cuban Missile Crisis. What did Kennedy risk?

    (1) loss of America's lead in the arms race
    (2) a Soviet invasion of the United States
    (3) destruction of the U.S. naval fleet
    (4) the possibility of nuclear war
    (5) the destruction of Cuba

To check your answers, turn to page 188.

The Civil Rights Movement

Many people date the beginning of the civil rights movement—the fight for equal rights for people of all races—from the Montgomery, Alabama, bus boycott of 1955-1956. In the fight against **segregation**, or formal separation of the races, the Montgomery boycott had special significance. The boycott began after a woman, Rosa Parks, was arrested for refusing to give up her bus seat to a white man. At that time in many cities of the South, African Americans were forced to sit in the backs of buses or to stand.

In response to Mrs. Parks' arrest, Montgomery's bus-riding black citizens boycotted—refused to use—the bus system. In spite of a constant harassment and acts of violence, they held on for more than a year. Finally, the U.S. Supreme Court ordered an end to segregated buses.

The Montgomery boycott mobilized African Americans into an organized resistance movement for the first time. From this movement emerged a leader who promoted peaceful means for protesting injustice—Dr. Martin Luther King Jr.

For the rest of the 1950s and through the 1960s, Americans fought for racial justice. Unfortunately, violence often erupted as civil rights groups became more demanding and racist resistance gained strength.

A Changing Population

For nearly two centuries, American culture was dominated by the values of whites of European descent, who held virtually every important position of political, economic, and social power. Since 1965, however, the American population has been shifting toward more ethnic diversity. By the end of the century, Americans with European ancestry will no longer be a majority.

These population changes have been caused by shifts in immigration patterns. In the past, most immigrants came from Europe. Between 1924 and 1965, U.S. immigration policy favored entry by northern Europeans and set quotas, or limits, on entry by others. The Immigration Act of 1965, which ended the quota system, had a great impact on the future face of America. By the 1980s, only 17 percent of the immigrants were European; 75 percent were from Asian and Latin American countries.

These immigrants have contributed enormous cultural diversity to the country. Their struggle to make a place for themselves in America has also provoked tensions between minorities and the established population. Cultural differences can be barriers to understanding, and many Americans now resent the flood of immigrants entering the country. They argue that immigrants take away jobs or, even worse, they burden our welfare system. "Stem the tide of illegal immigration!" is the rallying cry of some Americans.

---

segregation: formal separation of races, such as in schools, churches, and restaurants

The United States—Global Cop?

The United Nations, or UN, was created after World War II as an international peacekeeping organization. Member nations voluntarily join and uphold its goals and ideals. In general, the organization has intervened only in situations with international implications, such as war involving two or more nations. The policy has been one of national **sovereignty**, or freedom from external control. A country could do whatever it wanted within its own borders. But since the end of the 1980s, the UN has had a new policy based on the idea that a country's internal problems are a threat to the global community. Intervention based on **humanitarianism**, or concern for human rights, is now considered a legitimate role of the UN. With the Cold War over, the UN has taken over the superpowers' role of enforcing peace and settling disputes.

Exercise 8

Directions

Choose the one best answer to each item.

Item 1 refers to the following map.

SCHOOL INTEGRATION: 1960

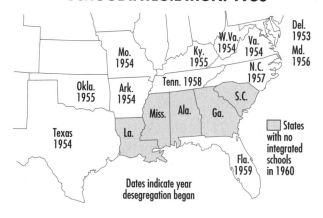

Dates indicate year desegregation began

1. The map shows that
   - **(1)** most southerners did not believe in integration but were forced by law to integrate their schools
   - **(2)** five states in the Deep South closed their schools rather than integrate
   - **(3)** five states in the Deep South had no intention of ever integrating their schools
   - **(4)** five states in the Deep South had not begun to integrate their schools by 1960
   - **(5)** most southern states, except those in the Deep South, agreed to integrate schools

2. For more than 100 years, the Statue of Liberty has been a beacon of hope and welcome to immigrants. The immigration restrictions of 1924 through 1965 reflected a view that
   - **(1)** agreed totally with the statue's message
   - **(2)** completely contradicted the statue's message
   - **(3)** applied the statue's message to northern European immigrants
   - **(4)** applied the statue's message to Latin American and Asian immigrants
   - **(5)** applied the statue's message to illegal immigrants only

3. UN intervention in response to public outcry usually is based on
   - **(1)** television coverage
   - **(2)** international peacekeeping
   - **(3)** concern for human rights
   - **(4)** national sovereignty
   - **(5)** the new code of international relations

To check your answers, turn to page 188.

---

sovereignty: a government's freedom from external control by another country

---

humanitarianism: concern for the well-being of all humanity

GEOGRAPHY

Global Mapping

Every place on earth has a unique location. The relative location of a place is its location in relation to other places. When you describe your town as a few miles south of another city or just beyond a bend in the river, you are describing its relative location. The absolute location of a place is its exact position on the planet. We find this position on a map by looking at a grid of lines that crisscross the surface of the globe to pinpoint the location of any place on earth.

Mapmakers measure distances north and south by drawing parallels of **latitude** north and south of the equator. (Parallel lines never meet; they are always the same distance apart.) The **equator** is an imaginary line that circles the earth exactly halfway between the North Pole and the South Pole. Because the equator is the starting point for measuring latitude, it is labeled 0°. The North Pole, which is as far north as one can go on earth, is exactly 90° north of the equator and is called 90° north latitude. All other parallels north of the equator lie between 0° and 90° north latitude.

A second set of lines measures **longitude**, distances east and west. These semicircular lines, which run between the North Pole and the South Pole, are known as meridians of longitude. The **prime meridian**, the starting point for measuring longitude, passes through an observatory in Greenwich, England. Mapmakers label each meridian as so many degrees east or west of the prime meridian until they reach the 180° meridian, which is halfway around the world from the prime meridian.

Every line of latitude or longitude can be thought of as a complete circle, which can be divided into 360 parts, or degrees, represented by the symbol °. Each degree can be divided into 60 minutes, represented by the symbol ′, and each minute into 60 seconds, represented by the symbol ″. The absolute location of Washington, D.C., is at 38.5° north latitude and 77.0° west longitude.

latitude: the position of a point on the earth's surface expressed as its distance (up to 90°) north or south of the equator

equator: an imaginary line that circles the earth exactly halfway between the North Pole and the South Pole

longitude: the position of a point on the earth's surface expressed as its distance (up to 180°) east or west of the prime meridian

prime meridian: the standard (0°) meridian of the earth, passing through Greenwich, England, from which longitude is measured

ROBINSON PROJECTION

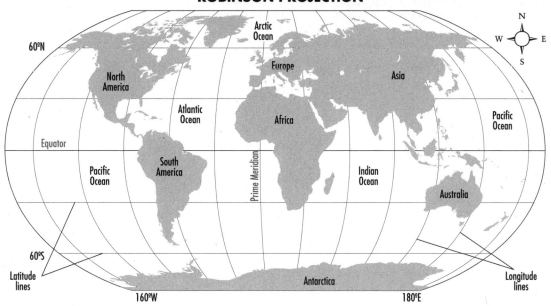

Exercise 1

Directions
For Item 1, fill in the blanks as instructed below. For Items 2 to 5, choose the <u>one best answer</u> to each item.

1. Write a **P** beside each sentence that describes parallels of latitude and an **M** beside each sentence that refers to meridians of longitude.

____ **(a)** These lines never meet.

____ **(b)** These lines meet at the North and South poles.

____ **(c)** These lines are always the same distance apart.

____ **(d)** These lines measure distances east and west.

____ **(e)** These lines measure distances north and south.

____ **(f)** These lines go no higher than 90°.

____ **(g)** These lines measure distances from the equator.

Items 2 to 4 refer to the map at the top of this page.

2. Where do the equator and the prime meridian cross?

   (1) Europe
   (2) the Arctic Ocean
   (3) Antarctica
   (4) Africa
   (5) the Atlantic Ocean

3. The longitude of the prime meridian is

   (1) 090° west
   (2) 000°
   (3) 180° west
   (4) 090° east
   (5) 090° north

4. In what direction is North America from the prime meridian?

   (1) east
   (2) west
   (3) north
   (4) south
   (5) southwest

5. To provide information about the absolute location of your seat at a ball game, you would

    (1) give the row number
    (2) give the seat number
    (3) give the row number and the seat number
    (4) explain how far back the seat is from the playing field
    (5) explain where the seat is in relation to the main gate

To check your answers, turn to page 188.

Latitude and Climate

Climate is the usual weather pattern found at a particular place on earth. Temperature, wind, and rain are elements of climate. So are seasonal changes. Why do different places have different climates? The main reason is **latitude**—the distance north or south of the equator.

Exactly how much sunlight most places receive varies from season to season. As the earth makes its yearly journey around the sun, it is tilted. The northernmost latitude to receive direct sunlight is 23° 30′ north. This parallel is called the Tropic of Cancer. The sun is directly overhead at the Tropic of Cancer on June 21 or June 22. As you might expect, the southernmost latitude to receive the direct rays of the sun is 23° 30′ south. The sun is directly overhead at this parallel, known as the Tropic of Capricorn, on December 21 or 22. Places between the Tropic of Cancer and the Tropic of Capricorn are known as the **tropics**, or low latitudes, and they generally have warm climates.

The Arctic Circle is located at latitude 66° 30′ north, and the Antarctic Circle at latitude 66° 30′ south. The regions between the Arctic Circle and the North Pole and between the Antarctic Circle and the South Pole are called the **polar regions**, or high latitudes. These areas receive no sunshine for part of the year and only slanting rays the rest of the year. The climate is cold, with short summers.

Between the tropics and the polar regions are the middle latitudes. Here, the sun's rays reach the earth at a high angle for part of the year and at a lower angle (greater slant) for the remaining months. Average temperatures are cooler than in the tropics but warmer than in the polar regions. These regions of earth, including the United States, are often called the **temperate zones**. Within these zones, temperatures vary greatly from place to place and from one season to another.

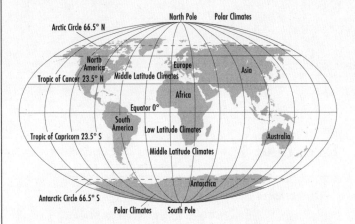

Geographers group areas with similar climate into regions. Temperature and rainfall in different regions are affected by features such as nearness to the ocean, wind patterns, and elevation, as well as latitude. Humid tropical climates, for example, exist in the low latitudes and can be either wet tropical (hot and very rainy all year) or wet-and-dry tropical (hot all year with wet and dry seasons). The rain forests of South America are wet tropical; the Caribbean Islands are wet-and-dry tropical.

---

climate: the weather pattern, including temperature, rain, snow, and wind conditions, that prevails in a region

---

latitude: the distance north or south of the equator

---

tropics: low-latitude areas that generally have warm climates year-round

---

polar regions: high-latitude regions, near the North Pole or South Pole, with the coldest temperatures

---

temperate zones: middle-latitude regions that are cooler than the tropics and warmer than the polar regions

Exercise 2

Item 4 refers to the following information.

Directions

Choose the <u>one best answer</u> to each item.

1. June 21 or 22, when the sun shines directly on the Tropic of Cancer, marks the beginning of summer in the northern hemisphere (the half of the earth north of the equator). In the southern hemisphere, June 21 or 22 marks the

   (1) beginning of winter
   (2) beginning of summer
   (3) end of summer
   (4) end of winter
   (5) spring equinox

2. Temperatures in the tropics are always hot, rarely falling below 70°F. Temperatures in the polar regions are always cold, rarely exceeding 30°F. Northern and southern temperate zones are found between the tropics and the polar regions. In these zones, temperatures are more moderate and usually fluctuate with the seasons. The continental United States lies within the

   (1) tropics
   (2) northern polar zone
   (3) southern polar zone
   (4) northern temperate zone
   (5) southern temperate zone

3. The equator divides the earth into the northern and southern hemispheres. At the equator,

   (1) the average temperature is 0°C
   (2) the latitude is 0°
   (3) the longitude is 0°
   (4) the temperate zones and the tropics meet
   (5) the sun is directly overhead all year

This climate graph shows average rainfall and temperature for a region. The bar graph shows rainfall; the line graph shows temperature. Rainfall is shown in inches on the right; temperature is shown in degrees on the left. The months of the year are shown along the bottom.

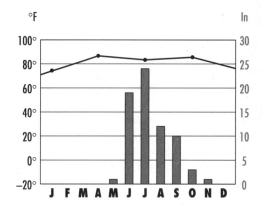

4. The graph above shows a place that is probably located between

   (1) the North Pole and the Arctic Circle
   (2) the Arctic Circle and the Tropic of Cancer
   (3) the Tropic of Cancer and the Tropic of Capricorn
   (4) the Tropic of Capricorn and the Antarctic Circle
   (5) the Antarctic Circle and the South Pole

To check your answers, turn to page 188.

NATURAL AND HUMAN-MADE RESOURCES

An environment is made up of all of the living and nonliving things in a place. People, plants, and animals all count on their environment for their survival. Plants and animals adapt physically to their environment. People adapt physically, but also use technology to change their environment. Consequently, they can survive in almost any environment on earth.

A **resource** is any part of the environment that people use to meet their wants and needs. Only a few resources, such as water, sunlight, and air, are used in their original forms. Most are changed before they can be used. Resources that can be made into a product are called **raw materials**. Trees, iron, and oil are all raw materials. For example, trees are used to make paper.

People's ideas about the value of resources often change as their way of life changes. Whales, for example, were an important resource in the early 1800s. Americans relied on whale oil to light their homes. By the late 1800s, however, whales were becoming harder to find, so people began to replace whale oil with kerosene, a by-product of oil. As a result, whales became a less important resource to Americans—many of whom now work to keep whales from dying out.

Electric lights replaced kerosene lamps, but the demand for oil continued to grow. Now it is used to heat homes, to lubricate machines, and to make fuel for automobile engines. In addition, oil has become an important source of chemicals for making plastics, dyes, and a variety of other products. Today so much oil is used that many fear that supplies will run out. Oil is a **nonrenewable resource**: once it is used up, it is gone forever. In contrast, trees are a **renewable resource**. As long as they are replanted, there will always be trees.

Is a field of corn a part of the natural environment? The answer is more tricky than you might expect. Unlike wheat, rice, and most other food crops, corn does not grow in the wild. It must be planted and tended. Corn originated over 10,000 years ago in the highlands of Mexico, where farmers cross-cultivated two wild plants. Over the years, they improved the seeds so the plant produced more food. The natural environment, therefore, cannot always be separated from the environment we have made for ourselves.

As corn became more plentiful, it was traded throughout North and South America. By the time Columbus arrived in the Americas, corn was grown as far north as Canada and as far south as Argentina. Corn was taken to Europe after 1492 and spread throughout southern Europe and into northern Africa.

Most of the corn grown today is fed to livestock (farm animals). People eat only a tiny percentage of corn in its natural state. Much is processed into oils, syrups, and starches. Factories use corn by-products to make glue, shoe polish, fireworks, crayons, ink, batteries, aspirin, paint, and cosmetics. Corn may also help power your car. Ethanol, a fuel derived from cornstarch, is often combined with gasoline to reduce air pollution from car engines. Scientists can now also make a plastic-type film and packing material from cornstarch.

---

resource: anything that people value and use

---

raw material: a natural resource in a state close to its original form in nature

---

nonrenewable resource: a nautral resource that cannot be recycled or recreated

---

renewable resource: any resource that can be regrown or remade in its original form

Exercise 3

> **Directions**
>
> For Item 1, fill in the blanks as instructed. For Items 2 to 5, choose the <u>one best answer</u> to each item.

1. Write an **R** beside each example of a renewable resource. Write an **N** beside each example of a nonrenewable resource.

   ____ **(a)** coal

   ____ **(b)** natural gas

   ____ **(c)** water

   ____ **(d)** corn

   ____ **(e)** iron

   ____ **(f)** wood

2. The text implies that some resources are more highly valued than others. This is probably because people tend to value resources that are

   (1) in scarce supply
   (2) in plentiful supply
   (3) nonrenewable
   (4) a source of food as well as fuel
   (5) of the greatest use to them at a given time

3. What is the main advantage in substituting a renewable resource for a nonrenewable one?

   (1) It conserves supplies of the nonrenewable resource.
   (2) It conserves supplies of both resources.
   (3) It encourages recycling.
   (4) It protects the environment.
   (5) It guards against pollution.

4. Many people are interested in replacing plastic made from petroleum with plastic made from cornstarch because

   (1) corn is a plant created by people
   (2) corn is a raw material and petroleum is not
   (3) corn can be recycled and petroleum cannot
   (4) corn is a renewable resource and petroleum is not
   (5) petroleum is a renewable resource and corn is not

5. The fact that corn is now used throughout the world can best be explained by the fact that

   (1) people need food
   (2) useful products tend to be used widely
   (3) corn is a nonrenewable resource
   (4) corn had religious significance for Aztecs
   (5) corn was used to feed African slaves

To check your answers, turn to page 188.

The Great American Desert

For generations, people from the United States regarded the Great Plains as the "Great American Desert." They saw only a flat land covered with shrubs and short grass. Hot, dry winds blow frequently across the plains during the summer months. In winter, sudden blizzards bury the region deep in snow.

The first people from the United States to settle on the Great Plains were ranchers. They herded their cattle and sheep on the grassy plains and shipped the animals to eastern markets. In the late 1800s, farmers also began to settle on the plains. By the 1920s, farms and ranches on the plains were booming. As more Americans moved to cities, the markets for beef, corn, and wheat reached increasingly high levels. Even the weather cooperated. Not realizing that rainfall on the plains comes in cycles, many farmers were convinced that "rain follows the plow."

In 1932, a drought began. Crops withered and died in the fields. That fall, farmers plowed and planted again. In doing so, they exposed more soil to the dry winds. With no plants to hold the soil in place, huge, black, billowing clouds of dust and dirt formed. These clouds settled and buried fields and farm buildings, blocked roadways, clogged water supplies, and killed animals.

Many people left the Great Plains during the dust storms, but some stayed on. Working with the federal government, they learned to practice **conservation**—careful and wise use of the environment. They repaired the damage they had done and slowly rebuilt the land around them. As a result, the Great Plains are more productive today than the most hopeful farmer could have imagined in the early 1900s.

conservation: using resources in the environment carefully and wisely

THE WATER CYCLE

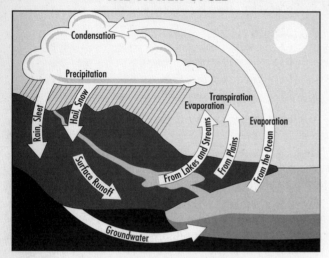

Water, Water Everywhere

There is as much water on earth today as there ever was or ever will be. This is because water is a **recyclable resource**. That is, it is a resource that is continually reused. The diagram above explains how.

Although the supply of water has not changed over the centuries, the demand for water has increased. Today the average American household uses between 140 and 168 gallons of water a day, or over 50,000 gallons a year. But individuals are responsible for only about 10 percent of the total demand. By far the largest users of water in the United States are farmers who irrigate their crops. It takes 652,000 gallons of water to produce just one acre of wheat. Cotton and other crops require even more water. Industry accounts for much of the rest of the nation's water use.

If water is a recyclable resource, why does it matter how much we use? For one thing, many Americans are using water more quickly than it can be replaced. Another cause for concern is pollution. Thousands of factories and communities dump waste material into oceans, rivers, and lakes. Farmers add to the problem by using chemicals to fertilize the soil and to keep away insects and other pests. Such chemicals pollute the water. Scientists have found evidence of fertilizers, pesticides, industrial chemicals, and sewage throughout the water cycle. They pollute the water not only in the community where it is originally contaminated but also in communities thousands of miles away.

Exercise 4

Directions
Choose the <u>one best answer</u> to each item.

1. Which of the following conclusions does the text support?

   (1) A change in one part of an environment affects all the other parts.
   (2) There are no limits to what technology can accomplish.
   (3) Farmers cannot protect themselves from drought.
   (4) Human activity always makes environments more productive.
   (5) It was a mistake to settle on the Great Plains.

2. The text suggests that the most important long-term effect of the dust storms of the 1930s was

   (1) a reduction in the number of farmers on the plains
   (2) an increased interest in conservation
   (3) the destruction of livestock
   (4) the destruction of water supplies
   (5) the destruction of crops

3. Which of the following statements is correct?

   (1) Condensation causes transpiration.
   (2) Surface runoff is groundwater.
   (3) Precipitation includes rain and snow.
   (4) Evaporation comes from groundwater.
   (5) Transpiration leads to evaporation.

4. Each step in the water cycle works to

   (1) increase the amount of water on earth
   (2) decrease the amount of water on earth
   (3) balance the amount of water that evaporates
   (4) balance the amount of water plants give off
   (5) balance other steps of the cycle

5. The passage suggests that people affect the water cycle, not the water supply, by

   (1) using too little water
   (2) using too much water
   (3) contaminating water supplies
   (4) building factories
   (5) irrigating their land

To check your answers, turn to page 188.

recyclable resource: a resource that is continually reused instead of being thrown away

POLITICAL SCIENCE

Democracy

Since its founding in 1776, the United States of America has been a **representative democracy**. That is, its citizens elect people to represent them and their wishes in governmental decisions. America's democratic system has attracted many immigrants from countries with more restrictive political systems.

Before the United States became a nation, the original thirteen states were **colonies** that belonged to England. King George III of England and his parliament believed that the colonies existed only to benefit England. Between 1763 and 1775, they instituted laws and taxes that helped England's economy at the expense of the American colonies. The colonists complained bitterly about the injustices of the following policies:

- Control over colonial settlement and government

- The large army England maintained in the colonies in peacetime

- Taxes imposed on the colonies to raise money for England

- The King's refusal of colonists' requests for more economic and political freedom

During these years, the colonists engaged in increasingly rebellious acts. In 1775, the colonies sent representatives to a meeting in Philadelphia, the Second Continental Congress. In June 1776, Thomas Jefferson, a Virginia delegate who later served as the third president, was chosen to write a statement of rights and grievances. In elegant and carefully reasoned language, Jefferson's Declaration of Independence explained why the colonies should separate from England.

Jefferson began with a statement of the rights of citizens, following closely the principles of the great philosopher John Locke. He wrote that "all men are created equal" and possess "certain unalienable Rights . . . Life, Liberty and the pursuit of Happiness." To secure these rights, "Governments are instituted . . . deriving their just powers from the consent of the governed." The Declaration ends by saying that the colonies owe no allegiance to England and are free and independent in every way.

representative democracy: a type of democracy in which citizens elect a few people to represent them in government

colony: a territory settled by people who remain governed by their native country

Exercise 1

Directions

Choose the one best answer to each item.

1. The fundamental idea behind democracy is
   (1) rule by the people
   (2) representative government
   (3) independence
   (4) rule by the few
   (5) unalienable rights

2. Which two roles were performed by Thomas Jefferson?
   (1) President of the United States and author of the Constitution
   (2) author of the Declaration of Independence and the Constitution
   (3) President of the United States and chief justice of the Supreme Court
   (4) author of the Declaration of Independence and President of the United States
   (5) chief justice of the Supreme Court and speaker of the House of Representatives

3. Although Thomas Jefferson wrote the Declaration of Independence, other delegates helped him, and the Second Continental Congress as a body made numerous changes. What does this process say about democracy?
   (1) Democratic decisions are usually a process of compromise, or give and take.
   (2) Most decisions are made by the few individuals who have the most knowledge.
   (3) Most democratic decisions are made in secret.
   (4) The most powerful people usually get their way.
   (5) Democracy is an inefficient way to govern.

4. Every citizen has a say in a New England town meeting, a tradition dating from the 1620s. Thomas Jefferson called town meetings "schools of political liberty." What did he mean?
   (1) The town meeting is a textbook example of direct democracy.
   (2) Town meetings are of questionable value politically.
   (3) A town meeting allows every participant to learn firsthand about self-government.
   (4) The town meeting is a free-for-all and thus teaches citizens about the dog-eat-dog world of politics.
   (5) Each participant in a town meeting must learn to fight for his or her freedom to speak.

5. Jefferson wrote that "all men are created equal" and possess "certain unalienable rights. . . ." Although he was a great thinker, which statement below is a logical inconsistency in Jefferson's reasoning?
   (1) England taxed the colonies without representation.
   (2) Government officials were appointed, not elected.
   (3) Plantations continued to exist in the South.
   (4) Slavery continued to exist in the colonies.
   (5) The colonies suffered economically when ties with England were severed.

To check your answers, turn to page 189.

The Federal Government

The **Constitution** of the United States, adopted in 1787, provides for a **federal system** of government, with powers divided between the national government and the states. The federal government is divided into three branches, each with specific roles and responsibilities.

The **legislative branch**—the U.S. Congress—is made up of two houses (bicameral). The House of Representatives now has 435 members. Each represents a particular geographic area of one of the fifty states. All members of the House stand for reelection every two years. Exactly how many representatives each state is allowed is determined by the population of that state. The Senate, the second house of Congress, has 100 members, two from each state, elected for terms of six years.

A suggested law, called a **bill**, can be introduced into either the House or the Senate. Majorities of both houses must vote in favor of a bill for it to pass. The bill then is sent to the White House for the president's signature. If the president signs the bill, it becomes a law. If not, the House and the Senate can still make it a law if two thirds of the members of each house vote again in favor of it.

SYSTEM OF CHECKS AND BALANCES

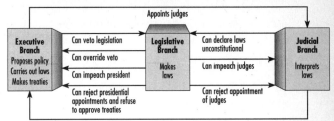

The **executive branch** includes the offices of the president and vice president of the United States. The president is commander in chief of the U.S. armed forces (army, navy, marines, air force) and political leader of the world's largest economy. With the "advice and consent" of the Senate, the president makes treaties and appoints ambassadors, many judges, and members of the cabinet (group of advisers).

Abroad, the president is the voice of the nation, carrying out foreign policy and making treaties. At home, the president is the nation's leader as well as the head of his or her political party, either Republican or Democratic. As party leader, the president often speaks out in favor of a bill (legislation), while members of Congress from the opposite party may take an opposing view.

The **judicial branch**—the Supreme Court of the United States, the nation's highest court—consists of nine justices who, once appointed, hold their jobs for life. There are now two women justices on the Court, and there has been an African American on the Court continuously for almost three decades. The Chief Justice acts as head of the Supreme Court. The job of the Supreme Court is to interpret the Constitution, which is

constitution: a written or unwritten structure setting out the principles, duties, and limits of government

federal system: a type of government in which power is shared between a central government and state governments

legislative branch: the part of government responsible for making laws

bill: a proposed law introduced to or in a legislature; when a bill is passed by the legislature, it becomes a law

executive branch: the segment of government responsible for executing, or carrying out, laws passed by the legislative branch

judicial branch: the court system of the U.S. government

now two centuries old. The United States has changed greatly in ways the authors of the Constitution could never have envisioned. Today the court must find ways to apply the Constitution to the problems of modern life.

The Supreme Court plays a very important part in the system of checks and balances. Through a process called **judicial review**, the Supreme Court can determine that laws passed by Congress and signed by the president are unconstitutional and therefore invalid.

Exercise 2

Directions
Choose the one best answer to each item.

1. Which state—Arkansas or Wyoming—has more representatives in the House of Representatives, and why?

	Arkansas	Wyoming
Size	52,078 sq. mi.	96,989 sq. mi.
Population	2.4 million	454,000
Votes cast in 1992	925,000	199,000
Date admitted to Union	1836	1890

(1) Wyoming, because its geographic size is larger
(2) Arkansas, because it was admitted to the union 54 years before Wyoming
(3) Arkansas, because its population is larger
(4) Wyoming, because it sends two senators to Congress
(5) Arkansas, because President Bill Clinton is from that state

2. How many senators represent each state?
(1) 50
(2) 2
(3) 100
(4) 435
(5) 6

3. Which statement best describes the duties of the President of the United States?
(1) The president represents the United States abroad and leads either the Democrats or the Republicans, as well as the armed forces and the nation as a whole, at home.
(2) The president leads the judicial branch.
(3) The president speaks as a military leader for the United States abroad.
(4) The president enforces the laws of the nation.
(5) The president serves as Secretary of State.

4. The three branches of the federal government are
(1) the judicial branch, the executive branch, and the system of checks and balances
(2) the legislative branch, the executive branch, and the judicial branch
(3) the legislative branch, the House of Representatives, and the Senate
(4) the executive branch, the judicial branch, and the House of Representatives
(5) the House of Representatives, the Senate, and the system of checks and balances

To check your answers, turn to page 189.

Federal Programs and Agencies

Ideas about the role of national government have changed greatly during the past sixty years. Before the 1930s, the U.S. government played a relatively small role in the lives of individual citizens. There were no federal programs to provide financial help to people who were unemployed, housing for poor people, or medical care for elderly people. The government did little to aid people after disasters or to support major arts groups.

The Great Depression of the 1930s was caused by many factors, including the extremely uneven distribution of the country's wealth after World War I; wild speculation in the stock market, which crashed in 1929; and the faulty belief of many Americans that the economy was self-regulating and that the government would cut back expenditures in difficult economic times. The Depression drastically changed the role of the federal government. In 1932, Franklin D. Roosevelt was elected president because of his promises to address the problems of the Depression through the creation of government programs. Roosevelt's "New Deal" covered a wide variety of needs. For example:

judicial review: the power of the courts to determine the constitutionality of laws and government actions

- The Federal Emergency Relief Act sent money to the states to supply food and clothing to aged, ill, or unemployed citizens.

- The Banking Act of 1933 created the Federal Deposit Insurance Corporation (FDIC), which established a system for protecting people's bank accounts if the banks failed.

- The Social Security Act, passed in 1935, provided pensions for retired workers and their spouses if they and their employers participated in the program. The act also included death benefits and support for surviving children up to the age of eighteen.

These programs and others often are referred to as **entitlements**, government programs that offer assistance to specific categories of citizens in need.

Agencies of the U.S. government deal with a wide range of issues of national concern—for example, highway safety, environmental protection, use of federal lands, and working conditions. The heads of these agencies, called secretaries, form the president's **cabinet**, a group of advisers who play an important role in running the government. Fourteen agencies make up the president's cabinet: the Departments of Defense, the Treasury, State, Justice, Labor, Agriculture, Commerce, Health and Human Services, Education, Transportation, Energy, Housing and Urban Development, Interior, and Veterans' Affairs.

The U.S. Postal Service is an independent government agency. Another independent agency is the National Aeronautics and Space Administration (NASA), which was created in 1958 and put the first men on the moon in 1969. The Selective Service System, created in 1940, registers all American men at age 18 for possible service in the U.S. military in case of war.

The Bureaucracy, Lobbyists, and PACs

Three entities or groups that affect the lives and futures of Americans are U.S. government **bureaucracy**, lobbyists, and PACs. The bureaucracy, or the organization of the government, is characterized by a formal structure of authority and specialization of tasks. More than three million civilians work in the federal bureaucracy today. Many of them are part of the **civil service**, where jobs are awarded to qualified workers who must first pass an official, task-related exam. These jobs are not awarded based on people's political views or someone else's recommendation. Civil service employees implement the laws and policies established by the government.

Although the bureaucracy is supposed to be regulated by elected officials, its sheer scope and size make regulation difficult. In addition, bureaucrats sometimes are caught between two sets of conflicting demands—for example, to lower the cost of a department's overall work and increase the number and range of tasks to be done.

Many private groups try to influence lawmakers about which bills to pass and which policies to establish. Although such groups sometimes are viewed negatively, they have legitimate interests and can sometimes influence governmental decisions toward a positive outcome for all Americans. These groups range from the well-known and powerful American Medical Association and National Rifle Association to lesser-known groups such as the Association of American Publishers and the American Agriculture Movement.

Most organizations employ **lobbyists**, people who represent an organization's interests to the appropriate elected officials and government agencies. Many lobbyists are former members of Congress or the executive branch. Such experiences help them understand the complexities of government and gain entry into administrative agencies.

---

entitlements: government programs that help specified groups of people

cabinet: presidential advisory body

bureaucracy: a large, complex administrative structure characterized by specialization of tasks and hierarchy of authority

civil service: body of employees who have passed specialized exams and are now employed in government service jobs

lobbyists: people attempting to influence government officials on behalf of interest groups

Political action committees, or **PACs**, are groups of individuals, associations, or businesses that work together to raise election money for candidates they feel will support their points of view in future governmental actions.

Exercise 3

1. What is the general purpose of federal agencies?

   (1) to fill the president's cabinet
   (2) to run the public schools
   (3) to deal with issues of safety, regulation, and welfare on the national level
   (4) to make scientific advancements
   (5) to nominate candidates for judgeships, Congress, and law enforcement

2. The phenomenal growth of America's urban population—people living in cities of one million or more—has led to the creation of several new cabinet departments over the years. Which of the following pairs would be most likely to deal with urban issues?

   (1) Department of State and Department of Justice
   (2) Department of Housing and Urban Development and Department of Transportation
   (3) Department of Agriculture and Department of Energy
   (4) Department of the Treasury and Department of Defense
   (5) Department of Agriculture and Department of Justice

3. An underlying value in government entitlement programs is the belief that all people

   (1) are created equal
   (2) have a right to certain basics in life such as a job, shelter, and food
   (3) are entitled to the same level of income and quality of life
   (4) should work if they are able
   (5) must contribute to the well-being of society

4. In the early years of the United States, jobs in government were awarded to supporters of the elected representatives through what was called the "spoils system." How does today's civil service system differ from the spoils system?

   (1) Employees are appointed by political action committees.
   (2) Employees work at highly specialized tasks.
   (3) Employees earn their jobs through their skill rather than by political appointment.
   (4) Employees are hired by political appointment rather than skill.
   (5) Employees work their way up through a hierarchy of authority.

Items 5 and 6 refer to the following cartoon.

5. Which statement best describes the cartoon?

   (1) The bureaucracy is operating in the dark.
   (2) The bureaucracy is an essential part of government.
   (3) The bureaucracy is too politicized to be effective.
   (4) The bureaucracy seems to be taking over the whole government.
   (5) The bureaucracy is not efficient at the national level.

PACs: political action committees—special interest groups that attempt to influence public policy

6. With which of the following statements would the cartoon's creator be most likely to agree?

 (1) Getting a job in the bureaucracy is easy to do.
 (2) The executive branch has gained too much power.
 (3) The bureaucracy should try to hire people with more experience.
 (4) Reducing the overall size of the bureaucracy would be good for the nation.
 (5) Most bureaucrats are poor workers.

7. Many lobbyists are experts in their fields, and their views are often sought by bureaucrats when new policies are being planned. Officials writing new federal guidelines for the inclusion of students with special needs in regular elementary classrooms would probably want to hear the views of lobbyists for which group?

 (1) American Association of Retired Persons
 (2) National Association of Realtors
 (3) National Education Association
 (4) National Rifle Association
 (5) American Agriculture Movement

Items 8 and 9 refer to the following cartoon.

8. The woman in the cartoon represents

 (1) the American people
 (2) consumers
 (3) food processors
 (4) farmers
 (5) the government

9. Which of the following statements best reflects the cartoonist's opinion?

 (1) There ought to be more government regulation of the food industry.
 (2) Government regulations have made canned goods safer to eat.
 (3) There is too much government regulation of the food industry.
 (4) Government regulations have made food more expensive.
 (5) Government regulations cost more than they are worth.

To check your answers, turn to page 189.

State and Local Governments

Like the national government, all fifty states have governments divided into executive, legislative, and judicial branches. State governments levy taxes to raise money for necessary services. Some states have sales taxes, other states have income taxes, and still other states have both. States also collect fees for various kinds of licenses—marriage licenses and drivers' licenses; fishing and hunting permits; and licenses for professionals such as lawyers, doctors, and dentists.

States use the tax money they collect to provide services and meet citizens' needs. States have primary responsibility for building and maintaining roads and highways within their borders. States set licensing and operating standards for beauty parlors, restaurants, and many other types of businesses and employ inspectors to check that the standards are maintained. States also pass laws to safeguard the health and welfare of their citizens.

Local governments are almost as varied as the communities they serve. Big cities such as Chicago, Denver, and Houston have very large local governments that provide a huge number of services for their residents—police departments, fire protection, street maintenance, social services, public libraries, and so on. Small towns often have part-time officials such as mayors who serve without pay. Many cities and towns have elected mayors as well as city councils. Others are run by city managers who are hired by the elected city councils.

One form of local government is the **special district**, which usually provides a single service such as flood control, fire protection, recreation, or, most commonly, education. Special districts may or may not have the same boundaries as other local government units such as cities.

---

special district: a local government unit set up to address a problem or provide a service in a specified area

Perhaps the most confusing unit of local government is the **county**, the major local division in most states. Counties vary considerably in their types of government and in their relationships to citizens, cities, and states. Typical county responsibilities include law enforcement, highway construction, courts, schools, and libraries.

Exercise 4

> **Directions**
>
> Choose the one best answer to each item.

1. Both state and national governments

 (1) have three main branches
 (2) make treaties with foreign nations
 (3) issue passports
 (4) have a legislature with one or more houses
 (5) establish qualifications for citizenship

2. Why do states require doctors and dentists to be licensed?

 (1) to generate revenue through the sale of the licenses
 (2) to maintain an acceptable level of quality of medical services for their citizens
 (3) to limit the number of doctors or dentists in the state
 (4) to regulate the prices that doctors and dentists charge their patients
 (5) to prevent doctors and dentists from other states from moving into the area

3. School systems are one type of

 (1) state agency
 (2) special district
 (3) federal agency
 (4) lobbying group
 (5) legislature

4. Which of the following would not be a reason to establish a special district?

 (1) to provide a service in an area larger than a city or town
 (2) to provide a service in an area smaller than a county
 (3) to provide a service such as fire protection in an isolated rural area
 (4) to streamline government by combining city governments within a district
 (5) to solve a problem such as pollution in an area that crosses city, county, or state boundaries

To check your answers, turn to page 189.

The United States in the World

For most of the last half-century, the United States was one of the world's two superpowers. Our major foreign policy goal was to resist the other superpower, the Soviet Union, and the communist system it promoted.

In the early 1990s, the Soviet Union and its communist system collapsed. At first, Americans cheered because the cold war between the superpowers was over. Soon, however, Americans realized that changes abroad meant changes at home. One of these changes involved spending newly available tax dollars. For decades, the national government had maintained a huge military presence at home and in Germany, Japan, the Philippines, Spain, Turkey, England, and elsewhere. It was generally agreed that this force level could be cut back, but disagreements arose about how much and what type of reduction there should be.

Cutbacks involved not just soldiers but also the businesses that supplied food, uniforms, shoes, weapons, ships, airplanes, and tanks to the U.S. military. Cities and towns that depended on these businesses for tax dollars and employment had to look for new businesses to attract to their areas.

Then came other questions:

- How should the saved military tax dollars be spent?

- What help, if any, should be given to people who lost their jobs in the cutbacks?

- What is the proper speed for cutbacks to maximize savings but minimize the problems for American workers and communities?

The answers to these questions will be determined by new leaders, new world events, and the American people.

county: the major unit of local government in most states

Exercise 5

> **Directions**
> Choose the <u>one best answer</u> to each item.

1. What was the major foreign policy goal of the United States for most of the last half-century?

   (1) to maintain military bases around the world
   (2) to contain communism
   (3) to reduce government spending
   (4) to elect new government leaders
   (5) to be the leader of nations such as Germany and the Philippines

2. After the Soviet Union broke up into fifteen separate nations, the United States began sending economic aid to the new republics. What good do American policy makers hope will come from this practice?

   (1) It will reduce inflation in the United States.
   (2) It will ensure that the new noncommunist nations become friendly to the United States and not slide back into communism.
   (3) It will prevent other nations from sending aid there.
   (4) It will create an easy way for the government to spend the money it saves on military cutbacks at home.
   (5) It will show the world that the United States is the only remaining superpower.

3. Now that communism has apparently lost its grip on Eastern Europe, some people say the United States should retreat from world affairs. What is the best argument against such a policy?

   (1) The United States should stay prepared for another wave of communism.
   (2) A superpower should never back down.
   (3) The United States should maintain a mighty military presence among nations.
   (4) Isolation is not possible in today's world, where Americans are affected by events in every corner of the earth.
   (5) The U.S. budget is committed to foreign intervention until the year 2000.

4. The secretary of state has been called the president's "right arm" in dealing with other nations. Which of the following is not a function of the State Department?

   (1) diplomacy
   (2) occupational health and safety
   (3) foreign policy
   (4) issue of passports
   (5) management of overseas bureaus

To check your answers, turn to page 189.

ECONOMICS

Consumption and Production

Think about the many economic choices you have made during the past week. How did you spend your money amid a vast array of goods and services? How much, if any, did you put away in savings? On a much broader scale, economics has to do with the production, exchange, and consumption of goods and services in a whole society.

In a modern economy, satisfying people's wants is a very complex process. Here is a model to help you picture how all kinds of goods and services are produced and distributed by the millions of people in our economy.

THE WANT-SATISFACTION CHAIN

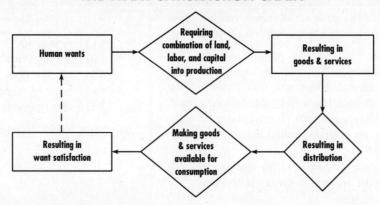

Consumption and Demand

One of the basic concepts in economics is demand. **Demand** is the amount of a product that consumers are both willing and able to buy at each price among a set of possible prices over a given time period. Look at the table and graph below.

DEMAND FOR MOVIES

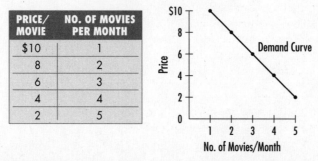

PRICE/ MOVIE	NO. OF MOVIES PER MONTH
$10	1
8	2
6	3
4	4
2	5

The table shows how many movies consumers attend per month at certain prices. The information in the table has been put on a graph to show what economists call a demand curve. The law of demand tells us that the higher the price of a movie, the lower the number of movies people will attend. For example, at $10 per movie, people will see only one movie per month.

demand: the amount of product consumers buy

Exercise 1

1. Ed and Linda have just eaten delicious platters of spaghetti at their favorite Italian restaurant. They have reached which stage in the want-satisfaction chain?

   (1) distribution
   (2) production
   (3) self-fulfillment
   (4) want satisfaction
   (5) choice making

2. What would be the result if distribution did not occur in the want-satisfaction process?

   (1) Goods and services produced could not be consumed.
   (2) Consumers would not be able to produce goods and services.
   (3) The process would go from production directly to consumption.
   (4) The process would be disrupted at the want-satisfaction stage.
   (5) The production resources of land, labor, and capital would not be needed.

3. Which of the following statements summarizes the want-satisfaction chain?

   (1) Land, labor, and capital all go into want satisfaction.
   (2) Wants recur, no matter how well or how often they are satisfied.
   (3) People are never satisfied.
   (4) Want satisfaction is a complex process involving production, distribution, and consumption of goods and services.
   (5) Want satisfaction is a complex process involving the consumption of goods and services.

4. According to the demand curve presented in the text, how many movies will the consumer attend at a price of $8.00?

   (1) one
   (2) two
   (3) three
   (4) four
   (5) five

5. Which price policy of a movie theater is likely to result in the highest attendance at movies? (Assume the demand curve shown in the text.)

   (1) charging $3.00 for the first movie on weekdays
   (2) charging $10.00 for first-run movies
   (3) charging $6.00 for the first movie on weekdays
   (4) charging $8.00 for first-run movies
   (5) charging $2.00 for the first movie on weekends

6. Researchers know that people will spend more for entertainment if their incomes increase. Which statement below supports this conclusion?

   (1) When moviegoers' incomes increase, the supply of movies increases.
   (2) When moviegoers' incomes increase, the supply of movies decreases.
   (3) When moviegoers' incomes increase, the price of a movie increases.
   (4) When moviegoers' incomes increase, the demand for movies decreases.
   (5) When moviegoers' incomes increase, the demand for movies increases.

To check your answers, turn to page 189.

Productivity

The **law of diminishing returns** states that at a certain point the addition of one resource (such as labor, for example, workers who pick apples) to a fixed resource (such as land, for example, an apple orchard) will result in less product being contributed by each individual worker. For example, 50 workers picking apples in a 20-acre orchard will result in a higher level of productivity *per worker* than 100 workers picking apples in the same orchard.

Fortunately, modern producers of goods and services have figured out ways to combine scarce resources to increase productivity. In addition, the resources have improved. Education has improved human resources (labor), technology and new inventions have improved capital (money available for business development or business transactions), and modern farming methods have improved.

Supply

Supply is the amount of a product that sellers (producers) are both willing and able to sell at each price among a set of possible prices over a given time period. Look at the table and graph below.

SUPPLY OF MOVIES

PRICE/ MOVIE	NO. OF MOVIES PER MONTH
$10	1
8	2
6	3
4	4
2	5

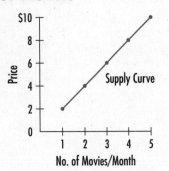

The table shows the numbers of movies that sellers (theater owners) are willing and able to offer at certain prices. The information in the table has been put on a graph to show what economists call a supply curve.

The Law of Supply and Demand

The law of supply and demand states that in a market economy, the interaction of supply and demand determines the prices and quantities of all kinds of goods and services—haircuts, auto repairs, bananas, computers, and movies. Look at the table and the graph below. The demand data and graph from page 172 and the supply data and graph from this lesson have been combined.

SUPPLY AND DEMAND FOR MOVIES

PRICE/ MOVIE	NO. OF MOVIES DEMANDED	NO. OF MOVIES SUPPLIED
$10	1	5
8	2	4
6	3	3
4	4	2
2	5	1

Price affects the quantity demanded and the quantity supplied in opposite ways. At higher prices, more of a product will be supplied, but less will be demanded. At lower prices, more of a product will be demanded, but less will be supplied. This is because buyers and sellers have different goals; buyers want the lowest possible prices and sellers want the highest possible prices. Through a process of bargaining, buyers and sellers reach a market price, the price at which they agree to trade. In the movie example, at a market price of $6.00 per movie, suppliers will offer three movies and buyers will attend three movies. At this price, the movie market is in balance. Unless some factor affects either supply or demand, the price is not likely to change.

---

law of diminishing returns: the idea that at a certain point, additional resources fail to increase output (results) or profit (money above and beyond the cost of production)

---

supply: the amount of product sellers make available

Exercise 2

Directions

Choose the <u>one best answer</u> to each item.

1. Which of the following statements best describes the law of diminishing returns?

   (1) As workers are added, total output increases.
   (2) As workers are added, total output decreases.
   (3) As additional workers are added, additions to output decrease.
   (4) As additional workers are added, additions to output increase.
   (5) As additional workers are added, additions to output stay the same.

2. Which policy is likely to result in movie suppliers being willing to show more movies at all possible prices?

   (1) a theater tax of $100.00 per movie shown
   (2) an advertising campaign for movies
   (3) a subsidy of $1.00 per customer paid to movie theaters
   (4) a city council ban on movies shown after midnight
   (5) a decrease in the price of popcorn

3. In the table presented in the text, what is the difference between the quantity supplied and the quantity demanded at a price of $2.00?

   (1) one
   (2) two
   (3) three
   (4) four
   (5) five

To check your answers, turn to page 190.

Government Taxation and Spending

Americans have to pay taxes for the government services they want. Government at all levels has the power to levy a wide range of taxes—on income, on sales, and on property—and to charge fees for a variety of things, such as building permits and marriage licenses.

In the United States today, there are three major types of taxes: regressive, progressive, and proportional. A **regressive tax** takes a larger percentage of income from people with lower incomes than from those with higher incomes. For example, a sales tax, especially on food, takes a larger percentage of lower-income earners' budgets because these people spend a greater share of their incomes on food than do people who earn more. A **progressive tax** is based on a person's ability to pay. Taxpayers at higher income levels pay larger portions of their incomes in taxes than people at lower income levels. Ideally, federal income taxes on both businesses and households are progressive. A **proportional tax** takes the same percentage of everyone's income. Some school taxes and many real estate taxes are proportional.

To understand the role of government in the U.S. economy, we need to know an important economic measure, the **gross domestic product (GDP)**. The GDP is the total annual value of goods and services produced by individuals, government, and business firms in the United States. In 1994, the GDP of the United States was about $6.7 trillion. Local, state, and federal expenditures combined amounted to about $2 trillion. With government involved in about one third of all economic activity, it is reasonable to ask what the government does and whether its involvement is too much or too little.

Historically, Americans have looked to the government for help with the following kinds of economic problems: 1) price-fixing among businesses; 2) unsafe/inhumane working conditions; 3) unsafe products and medications; 4) unemployment and disability; 5) unstable economic conditions; and 6) environmental pollution.

The following circle graphs show the percentages of their total budgets that the three levels of government

---

regressive tax: a tax rate that is higher for lower incomes than for higher incomes

progressive tax: a tax rate that increases as income increases

proportional tax: a tax rate that stays the same regardless of income

gross domestic product (GDP): the total annual value of goods and services produced in the United States

LOCAL GOVERNMENT

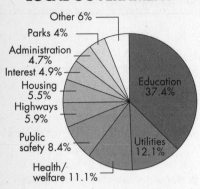

Other 6%
Parks 4%
Administration 4.7%
Interest 4.9%
Housing 5.5%
Highways 5.9%
Public safety 8.4%
Health/welfare 11.1%
Education 37.4%
Utilities 12.1%

STATE GOVERNMENT

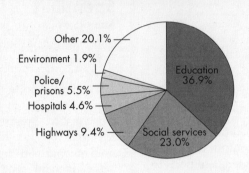

Other 20.1%
Environment 1.9%
Police/prisons 5.5%
Hospitals 4.6%
Highways 9.4%
Education 36.9%
Social services 23.0%

FEDERAL GOVERNMENT

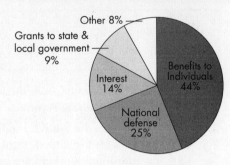

Other 8%
Grants to state & local government 9%
Interest 14%
Benefits to Individuals 44%
National defense 25%

spent in 1990 on activities such as national defense (federal government only), education, highways, and social services.

The federal government uses two kinds of policy to manage the economy: fiscal and monetary. **Fiscal policy** involves decisions related to government spending and taxation. **Inflation** and unemployment are two economic events the government watches. Inflation, defined as a general rise in prices, causes people to lose buying power. To correct inflation, the federal government may cut back on its own spending or try to raise taxes to control consumer spending.

Monetary policy involves decisions by the Federal Reserve Bank, the nation's central bank, to control the supply of money in the economy. The supply of money is directly related to interest rates. At higher rates of interest, people and businesses tend to borrow less money; at lower interest rates, people and businesses tend to borrow more money. The Federal Reserve controls the money supply by changing the interest rate. In inflationary times, the Federal Reserve may raise the interest rate to slow down economic activity. If the Federal Reserve wants to stimulate the economy, it will lower interest rates.

Exercise 3

> **Directions**
> Choose the one best answer to each item.

1. The federal withholding tax taken from your paycheck is an example of

   (1) a regressive tax
   (2) a sales tax
   (3) an income tax
   (4) a property tax
   (5) a license fee

2. Suppose that in a given year, the value of goods and services produced in the United States is divided as follows: $4.2 trillion produced by individuals; $2.1 trillion produced by government; $1.7 trillion produced by business firms. For the year, what will be the gross domestic product (GDP)?

   (1) $7.8 trillion
   (2) $7.9 trillion
   (3) $8.0 billion
   (4) $8.0 trillion
   (5) $8.1 trillion

fiscal policy: actions of the federal government related to taxing and spending

inflation: a general rise in prices

monetary policy: actions of the Federal Reserve Bank that affect interest rates and the supply of money

Items 3 and 4 refer to the graphs presented on the previous page.

3. The greatest percentage of federal government expenditures is for

(1) interest payments
(2) public safety
(3) benefits to individuals
(4) grants to states and localities
(5) education

4. Which of the following conclusions is best supported by the graphs?

(1) State and local governments bear most of the cost of education.
(2) The amount of interest paid by the federal government is too high.
(3) National defense accounts for 25 percent of federal expenditures.
(4) States are responsible for most highway expenditures.
(5) Government spending accounts for 30 percent of GDP.

Items 5 and 6 refer to the following graph.

THE NATIONAL DEBT 1981–1991
(Rounded)

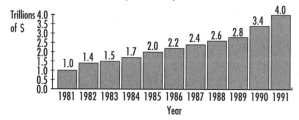

Source: *Economic Report of the President, 1991*

5. Between 1981 and 1985, the national debt

(1) stayed the same
(2) doubled
(3) tripled
(4) increased fourfold
(5) decreased

6. Which statement best summarizes the graph?

(1) The national debt can be controlled by wise monetary policy.
(2) The national debt is an accumulation of annual deficits.
(3) The national debt doubled between 1985 and 1991.
(4) The national debt increased fourfold between 1981 and 1991.
(5) The national debt is a serious problem for future generations.

7. What would be the most effective monetary policy in a time of severe inflation?

(1) encouraging banks to lend money
(2) raising interest rates and encouraging banks to stop lending
(3) encouraging banks to stop lending
(4) lowering interest rates
(5) raising interest rates

To check your answers, turn to page 190.

BEHAVIORAL SCIENCE

People and Cultures

Culture refers to the behavior, beliefs, and traditions of groups of people. Culture is influenced by physical environment (climate, terrain, and plant and animal life), social environment (groups of people with whom you come in contact), and technological environment (the tools that a society invents or uses).

Every society has two types of culture: material and nonmaterial. Material culture consists of those things that a society makes from its resources. Disneyland, movies, and denim jeans are part of the American material culture. Nonmaterial culture includes the beliefs and values that a society thinks are important. America's nonmaterial culture includes freedom of religion, equal rights, and democracy.

How Culture Is Learned

Through **socialization**, mostly through the influence of family members, friends, and schooling, people learn their religious beliefs, political attitudes, and outlook on the world. Two types of learning may occur during socialization. Trial-and-error learning takes place when a person tries out one kind of behavior after another in a new situation until he or she succeeds. In contrast, social learning occurs when a person imitates other people or communicates with them to gain knowledge. A toddler who is learning to talk is engaged in social learning.

Whenever information about what works in a certain situation is shared between humans, a form of cultural transmission takes place. Socially transmitted knowledge can and must be passed on to new generations if a culture is to be maintained. Through this process, called enculturation, the young people in a society learn about and share the culture of the older people.

Enculturation transmits negative as well as positive elements of a culture. For example, **prejudices** are judgments made about other people before all the facts are known, such as being afraid of a person of another race; **stereotypes** are assumptions that nearly everyone in a group of people has a certain characteristic—for example, that all women are bad drivers.

---

culture: the behavior, patterns, and artifacts that are made and shared by a group of people

---

socialization: the process during which members of a society learn to participate in that society, are taught their roles, and develop a self-image

---

prejudice: judgment made before all the facts are known

---

stereotype: an exaggerated belief that assumes nearly everyone in a group of people has a certain characteristic

How Culture Changes

As individuals change, their culture changes too. How do these changes happen? A cultural change may come from many sources, some originating within the society. The source of a change that comes from inside the society is called an **endogenous source**. The endogenous sources of the U.S. Civil Rights Act were the activists who demonstrated in America against open and deliberate racial and sexual discrimination.

The source of a change that originates outside the society is called an **exogenous source**. The exogenous sources that destroyed the hunting-and-gathering lifestyle of some Native Americans were the groups of European settlers who came to the Americas.

The following sources of cultural change can be endogenous or exogenous; sometimes the origin of a change is not clear.

1. An **innovation**—a new tool, technology, idea, or method—may be developed. *Example:* The invention of the microwave oven was an American innovation because it happened in the United States.
2. A custom, belief, or invention may spread from one culture to another through **diffusion**, or contact between societies. *Example:* Early Native Americans believed that bragging about a future accomplishment or event brought bad luck that could be neutralized by knocking on the base of an oak tree. This belief is evident when people knock on wood to keep a boast from backfiring.
3. Changes in the physical environment can cause a group of people to adjust accordingly. *Example:* As land is cleared and water is polluted in the Amazon rain forest, the native peoples of the rain forest must either move away or adapt their ways of living, hunting, and fishing.
4. An **internal conflict**, or struggle within a society because of opposing ideas, needs, wishes, or basic instincts, may cause change. *Example:* The Civil War in the United States led to freedom and new legal rights for African Americans.
5. A **revolution** may change the form of government and the structure of an entire society. *Example:* In 1979, a revolution in Iran led to the creation of an Islamic state based on strict enforcement of Shi'ite Islamic law.

endogenous source: a source of cultural change in a society that originates from within the society

exogenous source: a source of cultural change in a society that originates from outside the society

innovation: a new tool, technology, idea, or method that is developed within a society

diffusion: the process through which a custom, belief, or object spreads from one culture to another

internal conflict: a struggle within a society resulting from opposing ideas, needs, or basic instincts

revolution: an attempt to change the form of government and restructure society

Exercise 1

Items 4 and 5 refer to the following information.

Directions
Choose the one best answer to each item.

1. Which one of the following statements does not describe trial-and-error learning?

   (1) Solutions to problems are discovered.
   (2) Behaviors are tried until a successful one is found.
   (3) The sharing of solutions does not occur.
   (4) Technological and social progress occurs.
   (5) The knowledge others have learned is unimportant.

2. When Jiang first began to learn English on her own, she made many mistakes. Later, she became less self-conscious and asked for help with her grammar and sentences. Jiang's language learning involved which two processes?

   (1) enculturation and cultural transmission
   (2) trial-and-error learning and enculturation
   (3) social learning and enculturation
   (4) trial-and-error learning and social learning
   (5) prejudices and stereotypes

3. The changes in most Americans' views on the rights of racial and ethnic groups resulted from endogenous sources and

   (1) innovation
   (2) revolution
   (3) enculturation
   (4) the physical environment
   (5) internal conflict

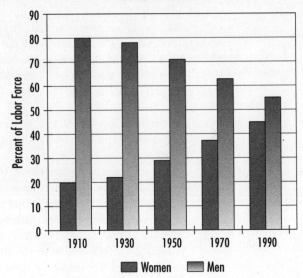

U.S. LABOR FORCE
1910–1990

Before the Industrial Revolution began in England around the year 1760, women played a major role alongside men in economic production. Because most goods were made in and sold from the home, women were not isolated from economic production. Technology from the Industrial Revolution eventually spread to the United States, and both women's and men's roles began to change. Men went to work outside the home, and women took on primary responsibility for raising children and keeping house.

4. According to the passage, what sources caused American women to withdraw from economic production?

   (1) innovation and diffusion
   (2) diffusion and the physical environment
   (3) physical environment and internal conflict
   (4) internal conflict and revolution
   (5) revolution and innovation

5. According to the graph, the proportions of men and women in the labor force since 1910 have

   (1) remained at about the same levels
   (2) both increased
   (3) both decreased
   (4) almost equalized
   (5) shown no change

To check your answers turn to page 190.

Influences on Human Behavior

Psychologists have found that the following factors influence human behavior:

- **Heredity** The genes you inherited from your parents control the development of your brain and other body structures that affect traits or behaviors such as intelligence, anxiety, and sociability.

- **Experiences** Experiences reflect the opportunities you have had to explore and learn about your world. You do not have exactly the same experiences as anyone else—even an identical twin.

- **Motives** Most of the things you do are motivated by your basic needs for food, warmth, and companionship. Other motives are based on goals valued by your culture, such as being rich, important, famous, or well educated.

- **Social relationships** Other individuals and groups influence your behavior. Your family, your religion, and the people with whom you work and play dictate your behavior in many different situations.

Personality

Your **personality** consists of the combination of ways you act, think, and feel that make you different from any other person. When a friend describes you as generous or shy, she or he is describing a personality trait that is typical of you. Why do you have your particular personality? Behavioral scientists rely primarily on three theories to explain this aspect of human behavior.

Psychoanalytic theory was developed by Sigmund Freud, a physician in Vienna who treated patients with emotional problems. Freud believed that much of human personality is controlled by forces in the unconscious mind and that those forces may be linked to childhood experiences and sexual motives.

Ivan Pavlov, who originated the **behaviorist theory**, believed that personality is learned through reward and punishment—that is, through the pleasant or unpleasant results of one's own behavior. In studies that he conducted on digestion, Pavlov started the stimulus of a clicking metronome every time he gave dogs powdered meat to eat. The dogs eventually learned to salivate when they heard the metronome alone. This simple form of learning is called **conditioning**.

Abraham Maslow was one of several psychologists who developed the **humanistic theory**, the idea that people determine their own destiny through an inner force that pushes them to grow, improve, and make decisions. According to Maslow, a person who reaches the highest level of personal development and fully realizes his or her potential has achieved self-actualization. Although very few people achieve full self-actualization, most people are partially actualized.

personality: the ways you act, think, and feel that make you different from others

psychoanalytic theory: Sigmund Freud's theory that much of human behavior is controlled by forces in the unconscious mind that may be linked to childhood experiences and sexual motives

behaviorist theory: a theory of personality developed by Ivan Pavlov that is based on the belief that human behavior is learned through experience

conditioning: a simple form of learning that can be used to change human behavior as well as to shape it

humanistic theory: a theory of personality based on the belief that people strive to achieve their fullest potential

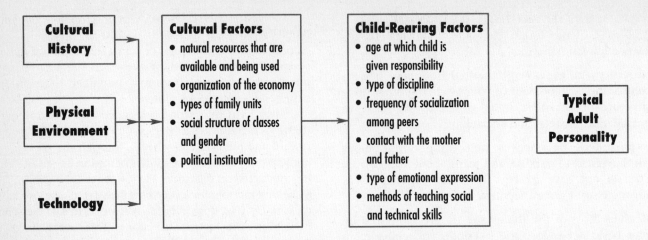

Exercise 2

Directions

Choose the one best answer to each item.

1. No one is around when Carlos notices that the door of the snack machine is open. Carlos still deposits his money in the machine and selects his snack. According to the

   (1) psychoanalytic theory, Carlos' selfish and aggressive tendencies prevented him from stealing the snack

   (2) psychoanalytic and behaviorist theories, the positive influence of society prevented Carlos from stealing the snack

   (3) behaviorist theory, Carlos' exposure to inappropriate behaviors in society prevented him from stealing the snack

   (4) humanistic theory, the destructive forces of society prevented Carlos from stealing the snack

   (5) humanistic theory, Carlos' low self-concept prevented him from stealing the snack

Items 2 and 3 refer to the following passage.

Studies of twins have shown that identical twins have almost identical IQ (intelligence quotient) test scores. The IQ scores of fraternal twins who grow up in a similar environment are just a little more similar than those of other pairs of siblings who are not twins. Similarly, studies of adopted children show that their IQs are more similar to those of their biological parents than to those of their adoptive parents.

2. The studies of twins and adopted children focused on

   (1) motivation
   (2) reactions to family members
   (3) similarity of twins
   (4) heredity
   (5) intelligence

3. Because identical twins have the same genes but fraternal twins share only about 50% of their genes, what conclusion can be drawn from the study of twins?

   (1) Identical twins look exactly alike, but fraternal twins only resemble each other.
   (2) A stimulating intellectual environment makes children bright like their parents.
   (3) Twins share the same experiences.
   (4) Intelligence is determined in part by heredity.
   (5) Both types of twins are equally intelligent.

To check your answers, turn to page 190.

Culture and Personality

When was the last time you and someone who was angry with you picked up rocks and took turns beating each other across the chest? This behavior may seem strange to you, but it is quite normal for the Yanomamo people of the Amazon. The culture in which people are raised plays an important role in shaping behavior and personality.

The child-rearing practices of a culture are especially important in the development of a culture's typical personality. How you were nursed, weaned, toilet trained, and nurtured; which aspects of your behavior were rewarded and which were punished; and how you were given attention and the amount of attention you were given as a child are some of the experiences that influence your personality as an adult.

Some cultures believe that physical punishment is an important and necessary part of the discipline of

SOME COMMON PSYCHOLOGICAL CONCEPTS

defense mechanism: any behavior or thought process a person uses to protect himself against painful or anxious feelings *(see examples below)*

repression: a defense mechanism of unconsciously holding back feelings or memories about unpleasant or painful experiences

projection: a defense mechanism in which a person unconsciously "projects" one's own ideas, impulses, or emotions onto another person, as if projecting film onto a screen; for example, saying someone else looks or feels sad when you really feel sad yourself

displacement: a defense mechanism in which a person transfers an emotion to another, more acceptable object

depression: an emotional condition characterized by feelings of hopelessness or inadequacy

subconscious: part of a person's mind in which thoughts or feelings occur while the person is not fully aware of them

children. Many other cultures disagree and have found other ways to correct children's behavior. The Hopi of the American Southwest discipline children who seriously misbehave by threatening them with *kachinas*. These masked dancers, who represent spiritual beings, pretend to steal the children, only to have the attempts thwarted by the parents. The children, of course, are so thankful to their parents for saving them that they behave—at least for a while.

How much emotion you show, how you display it, and even what emotions you feel (and when) also depend on your upbringing. Some cultures, such as the Zuni villagers of the North American Southwest, teach their members to control their emotions; other cultures encourage the free expression of emotions.

Even though you have close relationships with people outside your family, people who give you emotional support, you probably feel a stronger bond with family members and turn to them when you are sad, happy, or upset. You probably express those emotions in a manner similar to the way they were modeled in your family. The diagram on the preceding page shows the various factors that influence an individual's personality as an adult.

Exercise 3

Directions
Choose the <u>one best answer</u> to each item.

1. Which of the following is <u>not</u> a factor that may influence behavior and personality?

    (1) being raised in the Catholic faith
    (2) growing up in a wealthy family
    (3) crying easily
    (4) attending military school for grades 6 through 12
    (5) being the youngest in a family of ten

2. Children within a single culture develop different personalities because

    (1) the parents have different personalities
    (2) the child-rearing practices were the same
    (3) parents and other adults teach and treat their children differently
    (4) the forms of discipline were different
    (5) the children have different ways of showing emotion

Items 3 and 4 refer to the diagram presented in the passage on the previous page.

3. What would be the best title for the diagram?

    (1) The Organization of Society
    (2) How Children Learn
    (3) The Survival of Society
    (4) Influences on Adult Personality
    (5) Technology in the Modern World

4. According to the diagram, which of the following does not affect adult personality?

    (1) how the children are cared for when both parents work outside the home
    (2) how the adult personality affects the culture
    (3) how old the child is when he or she starts doing chores around the house
    (4) how the people gather and use the resources from the environment
    (5) how the child is encouraged in or discouraged from showing emotions

Item 5 refers to the following passage.

Conditioning shapes your behavior through three types of consequences. Positive reinforcement is any consequence you enjoy, so that you increase the frequency of your behavior. In negative reinforcement, your behavior is encouraged, or reinforced, because an unpleasant experience stops or is prevented when you behave that way. Punishment causes you to decrease the frequency of your behavior.

5. Learning occurs with conditioning because of

    (1) your understanding of the stimulus
    (2) positive reinforcement, negative reinforcement, and punishment
    (3) your determination to learn from every encounter
    (4) the way you were trained to deal with stress
    (5) the bell or metronome that operates with another stimulus

To check your answers, turn to page 190.

People as Members of Groups

A group is two or more people who interact regularly for a specific purpose. You probably have a closer relationship with some groups than you do with others. Your relationships with your family and close friends are probably very important to you. In fact, the main reason you spend time with these people is most likely because you value the relationships you have with them. A group whose members interact because they value one another is called a primary group. Such groups tend to be small because people typically do not develop close personal relationships with the many members of a large group.

A secondary group is one whose main purpose is something other than the development of personal relationships. The main purpose of your work group, for example, is to get a job done—although you may develop a primary group of friends within the work group. Our society today develops more secondary groups than primary groups, possibly because many families are geographically separated.

Behavioral scientists have found that groups influence behavior. For instance, you are more likely to voice your opinion among friends who hold the same values than with members of a group whose views differ from yours. In a group you are more likely to **conform**, or to go along with what the majority wants, even if they have not tried to pressure you. Another way people are influenced by groups is through **modeling**, or by observing the behavior of other group members.

Norms, Values, and Roles

The norms and values of your culture are your code for behavior. You have learned the **norms** of your culture, or how people expect you to act in certain situations. Some norms are expressed as laws with severe penalties for people who break them. For example, a person who is caught robbing a store is sent to jail. When we disregard other norms, however, the punishments are less severe—possibly just looks of disapproval.

conform: to give in to or follow what the majority of the people want, even if they have not tried to pressure you

modeling: shaping behavior based on observed behavior of others

norms: how a culture expects people to act in a certain situation

value: an idea or standard that the people of a culture think is important

role: a person's expected behavior based on social position, gender, and race

A **value** is an idea or standard that the people of a culture think is important. Americans, for example, share a common value that all people should have equal opportunity. Racism, sexism, and poverty may work against it, but equal opportunity is an ideal that most Americans think is important.

Each **role** that you have in society also includes certain expected behaviors. A person's gender, marital status, job, economic status, and ethnic background are all linked to certain expectations. Your role at work might be to act courteously, dress neatly, and perform specific tasks. Sex or gender roles are those that our society expects you to play because you are a male or a female.

Exercise 4

> **Directions**
> Choose the one best answer to each item.

1. Which of the following is <u>not</u> a group?
   (1) players in a softball game
   (2) people standing in line for movie tickets
   (3) workers brainstorming solutions to a problem
   (4) people picketing outside a factory
   (5) a family eating dinner

2. Many years ago a woman was beaten and stabbed to death in her New York City neighborhood while thirty-eight of her neighbors watched from their windows. No one came to her assistance or called the police. According to the rules of group behavior, one person coming forward to help probably would have caused other neighbors to
   (1) fear becoming involved
   (2) feel relief that someone did something
   (3) dislike the person who helped
   (4) offer their help as well
   (5) pretend nothing was happening

3. At the 1991 Tailhook Association convention in Las Vegas, a group of male Navy aviators reportedly fondled eighty-three female aviators, whom they forced to run between two lines of groping men in a hallway. Some of the men probably attacked the women because
   (1) the men had bad attitudes toward women
   (2) everyone else was doing the same thing
   (3) the men were prejudiced against the women
   (4) the women asked for it
   (5) the men and women evaluated the situation differently

4. Gender roles are shaped by group values. What value (belief) is behind the idea that women should be teachers, not presidents?
   (1) Men are the natural leaders of the human race.
   (2) A majority of teachers are women.
   (3) Women fill many clerical positions.
   (4) Sports provides men with leadership positions.
   (5) Men and women are equal in all respects.

To check your answers, turn to page 190.

Ethnicity and Multiculturalism

Almost every citizen or resident of the United States also belongs to one or more socially recognized ethnic and racial groups. Your ethnicity may include cultural traditions, religion, and history based on your ancestry. Your race, however, is based on physical characteristics such as skin color and facial features that may categorize you as a white American, a Native American, an African American, or an Asian American. You share your racial and national ancestry with other people, who may come from all classes of society. Your ethnic identity joins you with members of your ethnic group (or groups) and also separates you from other ethnic groups.

Many countries have homogeneous populations, that is, people with a single culture. The United States, by contrast, has a multicultural population; American citizens claim ancestry of over 100 nationalities, making this country one of the most culturally diverse nations of the world. The following graph indicates the racial origins of Americans.

RACIAL COMPOSITION OF THE U.S. POPULATION, 1990

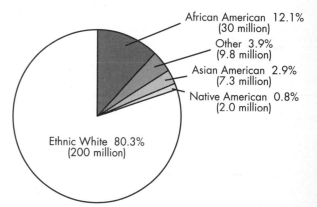

African American 12.1% (30 million)
Other 3.9% (9.8 million)
Asian American 2.9% (7.3 million)
Native American 0.8% (2.0 million)
Ethnic White 80.3% (200 million)

By a different measurement, 9 percent of Americans are of Hispanic origin; that is, their families come from Mexico, Cuba, Puerto Rico, or South America.

In spite of the United States' great diversity, many of its citizens suffer from racial and ethnic inequality. Most white Americans are descendants of immigrants from

Northern and Western Europe who entered the United States voluntarily. Whites have always occupied an advantaged position in American society. The ancestors of other groups, such as African Americans, some Hispanics, and Native Americans, were either forcibly brought to this country or forced from their lands through conquest and colonization. These groups have experienced exploitation, social inequality, prejudice, discrimination, and poverty. Although most Asian Americans came to this country voluntarily, they too have suffered from prejudice and discrimination by other ethnic groups who view them as competitors for jobs and other resources.

Exercise 5

Directions
Choose the one best answer to each item.

Items 1 and 2 refer to the following graphs.

U.S. HOUSEHOLDS, 1990

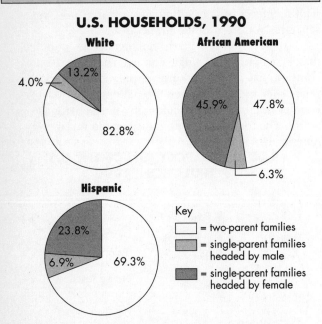

Key

☐ = two-parent families

▨ = single-parent families headed by male

▩ = single-parent families headed by female

1. In 1991, the average median incomes were $30,143 for white households, $22,586 for African-American households, and $20,885 for Hispanic households. From this information and the graphs, you can infer that

   (1) two-parent households are likely to be poor
   (2) single-parent, male-headed African-American families make up the largest group of poor

households

   (3) single-parent, male-headed Hispanic families make up the smallest group of poor households
   (4) the proportion of single-parent, female-headed households is lowest among the poor
   (5) a high proportion of poor households is likely to be headed by single females

2. Behavioral scientists might use the information in the graphs to make a case for

   (1) decreased social services for single-parent white families
   (2) increased health services for single-parent families
   (3) increased social services for single-parent African-American families
   (4) increased bilingual programs for Hispanic households
   (5) increased multicultural training for minority households

3. What does the circle graph on the preceding page indicate about racial and ethnic diversity in the United States?

   (1) Native Americans suffer more discrimination than any other group.
   (2) The proportions of Asian Americans and African Americans in the total population are growing.
   (3) Nonwhite groups make up about one fifth of the population.
   (4) Ethnic whites include people from many different cultural backgrounds.
   (5) Asian Americans are the smallest racial group in the country.

4. Which phrase best defines the term *multicultural nation*?

   (1) a nation of many cultures, each of which claims its own nationality
   (2) a country of many nationalities, all claiming the same geographic region
   (3) a culture of many ethnic groups, each of which strictly maintains its ancestral nationality
   (4) a country of many ethnic groups, each of which claims the same nationality
   (5) a country of many ethnic groups, each of which seeks political independence

To check your answers, turn to page 190.

Answers and Explanations
SOCIAL STUDIES

Unit 1: History

Exercise 1 (page 145)

1. **The correct answer is (3): (Comprehension)** Only Connecticut and Delaware are identified on the map as colonies founded for both economic and religious reasons.

2. The correct answer is (5): (Evaluation) The only conclusion that could be drawn from the map is choice (5). The map itself indicates no relationship between size or location and reason for founding as suggested by choices (3) and (4). The map does not explain colonists' preferences for a particular location or indicate which colonies were successful, so choices (1) and (2) are incorrect.

3. **The correct answer is (3): (Analysis)** The passage indicates that since the land does not show the usual signs of ownership—fences, dwellings, and cattle—the "natives" have no right to the land. The passage does not mention government as in choice (1). Choice (2) misses the point of the passage. Choices (4) and (5) are contradicted by the passage.

Exercise 2 (page 146)

1. **The correct answer is (2): (Analysis)** The importance of self-government is indicated in the previous section and in the idea that the colonists were very "independent minded."

2. **The correct answer is (3): (Analysis)** The text gives some clues (e.g., Britain's "restrictive measures") that, together with the king's statement, lead to the conclusion that Britain wanted complete authority. The issue of taxes was over British, not American, taxes; the Stamp Act was not an immediate memory in a long series of events; the Revolutionary War had not yet started; and the Declaration of Independence had not yet been written, so the other choices can be eliminated.

3. **The correct answer is (3): (Application)** A strong central government may limit individual rights. Such a government would not be likely to give too many rights to states, as suggested by choice (1), or to individuals, as in choice (2). There is no reason to suppose that representative assemblies would be prevented or that the Constitution's power would be limited by a strong central government, so choices (4) and (5) are incorrect.

4. **The correct answer is (4): (Application)** A senator's qualifications are not a matter of individual rights and freedoms. Choice (1) is protected by Amendment 1, the right of free speech and assembly; choice (2) by Amendment 2, the right to keep and bear arms; choice (3) by Amendment 4, freedom from unreasonable searches and seizures; and choice (5) by Amendment 1, freedom of religion.

Exercise 3 (page 148)

1. **The correct answer is (3): (Evaluation)** Choice (3) is the only choice that can be supported by the map. Choices (1) and (2) are not factually correct, and choices (4) and (5) are not indicated by information on the map.

2. **The correct answer is (1): (Application)** Missouri and Texas, choices (2) and (4), were already slave states, and the territories in choices (3) and (5) were opened to slavery by the Dred Scott decision. California entered the Union as a free, or nonslavery, state, and the Dred Scott decision affected only territories, which were under federal control.

3. **The correct answer is (2): (Analysis)** The right of petition is one of the rights guaranteed in the First Amendment, by the free speech clause. Forbidding discussion, choice (3), and blocking petitions, choice (4), are specific actions that deny free speech, but choice (2) is a better answer because it encompasses the concept that Adams was communicating.

4. **The correct answer is (4): (Comprehension)** The only answer that can be supported by the text is choice (4).

Exercise 4 (page 149)

1. **The correct answer is (2): (Evaluation)** Choices (1), (3), (4), and (5) are statements of fact, not conclusions.

2. **The correct answer is (3): (Evaluation)** People who believed in Manifest Destiny believed the United States had a right and duty to settle the North American continent. They did not care if this destroyed the environment (1) or infringed on the rights of the Native Americans who already occupied the territory (2). Manifest Destiny did not extend to territory off the continent (4). People who believed in the doctrine did not value peace because they were willing to fight the Native Americans for their territory.

3. **The correct answer is (3): (Analysis)** Differences in railroad width (or gauge) caused problems later in the building of nationwide rail networks, but they cannot be blamed for the difficulties caused by the inadequate rail system in the South. The rest of the choices describe real disadvantages.

4. **The correct answer is (4): (Comprehension)** Choice (4) is the only one supported by the text.

Exercise 5 (page 150)

1. **The correct answer is (5): (Analysis)** Labor unions had and have broad concerns about workplace safety such as choices (1) and (4), workers' well-being (2), and workers' benefits (3), but getting to and from work is up to the workers.

2. **The correct answer is (2): (Application)** Factory workers were part of the manufacturing segment.

3. **The correct answer is (2): (Comprehension)** The only change represented in the graphs is the decrease in the actual proportion of agricultural workers. The graphs do not show the effect of urbanization (1), changes in numbers of workers (3), workers' preferences (4), or changes in demand for workers (5).

Exercise 6 (page 152)

1. **The correct answer is (2): (Evaluation)** The fact that American forces attacked one of Spain's Pacific colonies indicates that Cuban liberation was not the only reason for engaging in the war. None of the other choices supports or suggests an American motive for the war.

2. **The correct answer is (3): (Analysis)** The definition of imperialism in the question strongly hints that imperialism would interfere with a nation's self-determination.

3. **The correct answer is (1): (Comprehension)** The cartoon depicts the hens as all Latin American countries, not necessarily countries protected (2) or by choice not protected (5) by the United States or colonized by Europe (4).

4. **The correct answer is (4): (Application)** European nations are locked in the coop (that is, away from Latin America) by the Monroe Doctrine, which restricts their activities.

Exercise 7 (page 154)

1. **The correct answer is (4): (Application)** Choices (1), (3), and (5) all contain some risk, but not on the scale of investing in an uncertain business venture with borrowed money. Choice (2) does not contain a risk.

2. **The correct answer is (3): (Evaluation)** Camp conditions (4), loss of property (5), and suspicion (2) were all part of the main violation, civil rights. Japanese citizenship (1) was not an issue.

3. **The correct answer is (4): (Evaluation)** The Cuban Missile Crisis went down in history as the closest the world ever came to nuclear war. The passage hints in several places at the gravity of the situation ("the nation held its breath," "war had been narrowly avoided").

Exercise 8 (page 155)

1. **The correct answer is (4): (Evaluation)** Only choice (4) can be supported by the map. The map does not show beliefs (1), intentions (3), or agreement (5) and does not indicate whether schools were closed (2).

2. **The correct answer is (3): (Analysis)** The immigration policy from 1924 to 1965 specifically welcomed immigrants from northern Europe.

3. **The correct answer is (3): (Application)** Humanitarianism is the main justification for intervention in a nation's affairs.

Unit 2: Geography

Exercise 1 (page 157)

1. **The correct answer is (Comprehension)** (a) P, (b) M, (c) P, (d) M, (e) P, (f) P, (g) P

2. **The correct answer is (5): (Application)** Europe (1) and the Arctic Ocean (2) are north of the equator. Antarctica (3) is south of it. Although both lines pass through Africa (4), they meet just west of the continent.

3. **The correct answer is (2): (Comprehension)** The prime meridian is the starting point for measuring longitude. Choice (5) is a parallel of latitude. All other choices are various degrees of longitude.

4. **The correct answer is (2): (Application)** North America lies west of the prime meridian.

5. **The correct answer is (3): (Comprehension)** Choices (1) and (2) are incomplete. Choices (4) and (5) refer to the seat's relative location.

Exercise 2 (page 159)

1. **The correct answer is (1): (Analysis)** The passage suggests that summer begins south of the equator on December 21 or 22, when the sun shines directly on the Tropic of Capricorn. Therefore, winter begins a half-year later.

2. **The correct answer is (4): (Evaluation)** Since temperatures in the United States fluctuate dramatically, it cannot lie within the tropics or a polar zone. The passage states that there are two temperate zones, north and south of the equator. Since the forty-eight contiguous states (states that share their borders with other states) lie north of the equator, this is the only choice the passage supports.

3. **The correct answer is (2): (Comprehension)** The map on page 158 shows the equator at 0° latitude, dividing the earth into northern and southern hemispheres. This region would not be cold (choice 1), and longitude divides the earth into eastern and western hemispheres (choice 3). The temperate zones meet the tropics at the Tropic of Cancer and the Tropic of Capricorn (choice 4). The passage states that the sun is directly overhead at the Tropic of Cancer in June and the Tropic of Capricorn in December, eliminating choice (5).

4. **The correct answer is (3): (Application)** The graph shows a place with hot temperatures all year long and a rainy season in the summer and dry for the remainder of the year. This is typical of wet-and-dry tropical weather, found only in the tropics.

Exercise 3 (page 161)

1. **The correct answer is (Application)** (a) N, (b) N, (c) R, (d) R, (e) N, (f) R

2. **The correct answer is (5): (Evaluation)** The passage shows how people have placed value on different resources throughout history depending on what their needs were. Examples are given to show that at any given time, the most valued resources were those that had the most varied or most important uses.

3. **The correct answer is (1): (Analysis)** Any action that conserves a nonrenewable resource is important. By its very nature, a renewable resource does not need to be conserved (2). Using a renewable resource does not specifically affect recycling (3) or pollution (5). It does protect the environment, but choice (1) is more specific and therefore a better answer.

4. **The correct answer is (4): (Analysis)** Because corn can be replanted, it is a renewable resource and therefore a better one to use than nonrenewable petroleum. Choices (2), (3), and (5) are not true. Choice (1) is not relevant.

5. **The correct answer is (2): (Analysis)** Although answers (1), (4), and (5) are true, they do not explain the spread of corn throughout the world. Choice (3) is not true.

Exercise 4 (page 162)

1. **The correct answer is (1): (Evaluation)** The other choices are not supported by the text.

2. **The correct answer is (2): (Analysis)** Choices (1), (3), (4), and (5) were all effects of the dust storms, but they were not as important in the long run as the increased interest in conservation.

3. **The correct answer is (3): (Application)** Rain and snow are precipitation; all other statements are incorrect.

4. **The correct answer is (5): (Analysis)** Choices (1) and (2) are incorrect because the supply of water is fixed. Choices (3) and (4) focus on one aspect of the cycle rather than the cycle as a whole.

5. **The correct answer is (3): (Comprehension)** The only way that people can affect the cycle is by contaminating it. Other activities may result in shortages in some areas or flooding in others but will not affect the overall supply.

Unit 3: Political Science

Exercise 1 *(page 164)*

1. **The correct answer is (1): (Comprehension)** The word democracy means "rule by the people."

2. **The correct answer is (4): (Application)** Jefferson is said to be the main author of the Declaration of Independence and was President of the United States from 1801 to 1809.

3. **The correct answer is (1): (Analysis)** Because all people participate in democratic decisions, compromises often must be made.

4. **The correct answer is (3): (Analysis)** Jefferson was remarking that the best way to learn about political freedom is to participate directly in a self-governing political unit, such as the town meeting.

5. **The correct answer is (4): (Evaluation)** Slaves and women were not included in the dictum that "all men are created equal," even though, of course, they are people. The other choices are true but are not logically inconsistent with Jefferson's premise.

Exercise 2 *(page 166)*

1. **The correct answer is (3): (Application)** The number of representatives that a state sends to the House is determined by its population.

2. **The correct answer is (2): (Comprehension)** Each state, regardless of its size, has only two U.S. senators.

3. **The correct answer is (1): (Analysis)** Choice (3) is true, but choice (1) is the best summary of the president's overall and most important duties while in office. The other choices are untrue.

4. **The correct answer is (2): (Comprehension)** The three main branches of government are legislative, executive, and judicial.

Exercise 3 *(page 168)*

1. **The correct answer is (3): (Comprehension)** Federal agencies deal with issues of national concern.

2. **The correct answer is (2): (Analysis)** The increasing urbanization of America has meant that the government must devote more and more energy to dealing with transportation, housing, and other issues common to urban growth.

3. **The correct answer is (2): (Evaluation)** Entitlement programs are designed to provide basic assistance to people in need so that no one will be destitute. Choices (1) and (4) are not underlying values in entitlement programs. Choice (3) is untrue. Choice (5) is a tenet of a communist society more than of a democratic one.

4. **The correct answer is (3): (Analysis)** Civil service replaced the spoils system as a fairer method for choosing government employees. Today, civil service workers must have skills that qualify them for their jobs.

5. **The correct answer is (4): (Analysis)** The power and size of the bureaucracy are portrayed as being out of control and not capable of being administered by the elected leaders of government.

6. **The correct answer is (4): (Evaluation)** The cartoonist clearly feels that the bureaucracy is too large, so it can be assumed that reducing the size of the bureaucracy would meet with the cartoonist's approval.

7. **The correct answer is (3): (Application)** Because the National Education Association is made up of classroom teachers, this group could provide the guideline writers with firsthand information about dealing with students who have special needs.

8. **The correct answer is (2)** The purse and the grocery cart suggest a shopper. There is no indication that she represents all Americans (choice 1). The cartoon criticizes government regulations, so she is unlikely to represent the government (choice 5). There is also no hint in her appearance that she is a food processor or a farmer (choices 3 and 4).

9. **The correct answer is (3)** Choices (1) and (2) are not supported by the cartoon. Choices (4) and (5) are hinted at but not directly addressed in the cartoon.

Exercise 4 *(page 170)*

1. **The correct answer is (1): (Application)** Both federal and state governments are divided into three main branches—legislative, executive, and judicial. Choices (2), (3), and (5) refer to rights and responsibilities given to the federal government alone. Choice (4) is incorrect because one state, Nebraska, has a legislative branch with only one house.

2. **The correct answer is (2): (Comprehension)** Through licensing, states maintain the quality of services supplied to their citizens.

3. **The correct answer is (2): (Comprehension)** Schools make up the majority of all special districts in the nation.

4. **The correct answer is (4): (Analysis)** Special districts are set up to deal with particular problems or provide services within specified areas, regardless of other governmental boundaries. They do not replace other governments.

Exercise 5 *(page 171)*

1. **The correct answer is (2): (Comprehension)** After the end of World War II in 1945, the main goal of American foreign policy became the containment of communism around the globe.

2. **The correct answer is (2): (Analysis)** Having nations friendly to the United States in other parts of the world means America can spend less time, energy, and money on defense against possible enemies. Such an outcome in the former Soviet Union will allow the United States to spend available resources on domestic needs rather than on military superiority.

3. **The correct answer is (4): (Evaluation)** The United States, a world leader, cannot suddenly isolate itself from the rest of the world, particularly when events elsewhere can have a tremendous impact on the American economy and foreign policy. Foreign policy should not be decided on the basis of possible future events (1) or pride (2). Today, the ideal is cooperation among nations, not aggression (3). No evidence exists of budget commitment to intervention (5).

4. **The correct answer is (2): (Application)** Occupational health and safety is the responsibility of the Labor Department. All other duties listed deal with foreign relations and therefore are part of the State Department.

Unit 4: Economics

Exercise 1 *(page 173)*

1. **The correct answer is (4): (Application)** Ed and Linda are temporarily satisfied in their desire to eat dinner, so they have reached the stage of want satisfaction.

2. **The correct answer is (1): (Analysis)** Without distribution, which is required between the production and consumption stages of the want-satisfaction process, any goods and services produced would not reach consumers.

3. **The correct answer is (4): (Analysis)** Choices (1), (2), (3), and (5) are true but tell only part of the story, so they are not adequate as conclusions drawn from the entire process.

4. **The correct answer is (2): (Comprehension)** Both the table and the graph indicate that at a price of $8.00, consumers will attend two movies per month.

5. **The correct answer is (5): (Analysis)** Choices (2), (3), and (4) won't result in any additional movie attendance. A $3.00 price (1) may increase weekday attendance, but the $2.00 price (5) is likely to yield the greatest attendance, because more people attend movies on weekends than on weekdays.

6. **The correct answer is (5): (Evaluation)** If people spend more on entertainment when they have more money, it makes sense that the demand for movies will increase when incomes increase. The number of movies made is not directly tied to moviegoers' incomes (1 and 2), nor is the price of a movie (3). Choice (4) would support the opposite conclusion from the one in the question.

Exercise 2 (page 175)

1. **The correct answer is (3): (Comprehension)** The key to understanding diminishing returns is to examine additional contributions of additional workers. Although total output can increase, it does so at a decreasing rate once the law of diminishing returns sets in.

2. **The correct answer is (3): (Analysis)** A subsidy lowers costs and is likely to increase supply. Taxes (1) raise costs. Advertising (2) is designed to affect demand. A ban on late movies (4) or a decrease in the price of popcorn (5) affects demand.

3. **The correct answer is (4): (Application)** Reading both the table and graph across from a $2.00 price shows that five movies will be demanded and one will be supplied, for a difference of four movies.

Exercise 3 (page 176)

1. **The correct answer is (3): (Application)** Federal withholding taxes are income taxes by definition.

2. **The correct answer is (4): (Comprehension)** The sum of 4.2, 2.1, and 1.7 trillions of dollars is $8.0 trillion.

3. **The correct answer is (3): (Comprehension)** Benefits to individuals, such as social security, unemployment compensation, and Medicare, make up 44 percent of the federal government budget.

4. **The correct answer is (1): (Analysis)** By far, education takes the greatest percentages of both state and local government expenditures; it is not included as a major category under federal expenditures. The graphs contain no information to support choices (2), (4), and (5). Choice (3) is true, but choice (1) is better supported by all three graphs.

5. **The correct answer is (2): (Application)** Between 1981 and 1985, the national debt doubled, from $1 trillion to $2 trillion.

6. **The correct answer is (4): (Analysis)** Choice (4) is the only statement that accurately sums up the information on the graph. Choice (3) is incomplete because it includes only the years 1985–1991. Choice (2) is a definition of the term national debt and says nothing about the graph. Choices (1) and (5) are opinions that cannot be supported by the graph.

7. **The correct answer is (2): (Evaluation)** Inflation is a general rise in the price level, which erodes the spending power of money. A way to slow inflation, especially if it is severe, is to discourage people from spending by raising interest rates and encouraging banks to stop lending.

Unit 5: Behavioral Science

Exercise 1 (page 180)

1. **The correct answer is (4): (Analysis)** Although an individual may achieve a certain amount of technological success through trial-and-error learning, there can be no social progress unless social learning and cultural transmission also occur.

2. **The correct answer is (4): (Application)** Jiang first tried out the language on her own and made many errors; later, she relied on others to help her. Choices (1) to (3) are only partially correct; prejudices and stereotypes (choice 5) did not enter into Jiang's learning at all.

3. **The correct answer is (5): (Comprehension)** Americans' beliefs about the rights of racial and ethnic groups changed after some groups within our society created internal conflict to bring social injustices to the attention of the majority.

4. **The correct answer is (1): (Application)** New technology applied to manufacturing outside the home forced the many women who remained at home to be separated from economic development. The technology was an English innovation that diffused from England to the United States.

5. **The correct answer is (4): (Comprehension)** The numbers have almost equalized. In 1990, there were only 10.2 percent more men in the labor force than women, compared with a 60.2 percent difference in 1910.

Exercise 2 (page 182)

1. **The correct answer is (2): (Analysis)** Carlos was able to resist the temptation to steal the snack because of society's positive influence. Choice (1) is not the best answer because Carlos' selfish tendencies would have encouraged him to steal the snack. According to the behaviorist theory, Carlos' exposure to inappropriate behaviors would have encouraged him to steal the snack (choice 3). The destructive forces of society in the humanistic theory would have led to Carlos' stealing the snack (choice 4). Choice (5) is not the best answer because Carlos' low self-concept probably would have led to his stealing the snack.

2. **The correct answer is (5): (Comprehension)** Choices (3) and (4) are partly true, but the studies also examined children who were not twins, and were concerned with only one trait, intelligence—not with inherited traits like height or eye color. There is no evidence for choices (1) and (2).

3. **The correct answer is (4): (Analysis)** Choice (4) is the only one that explains the focus of the passage.

Exercise 3 (page 183)

1. **The correct answer is (3): (Application)** Choice (3) is a behavior, not an influence.

2. **The correct answer is (3): (Analysis)** Even within one culture, parents raise their children differently enough for the children to develop different personalities.

3. **The correct answer is (4): (Analysis)** Choice (4) is the best title. Each of the other titles describes only part of the diagram.

4. **The correct answer is (2): (Comprehension)** The diagram does not show how the adult personality affects the culture, although there is a connection between the two.

5. **The correct answer is (2): (Comprehension)** Conditioning relies on reinforcers and punishment to shape behavior.

Exercise 4 (page 185)

1. **The correct answer is (2): (Application)** Members of a group interact with each other on a fairly regular basis.

2. **The correct answer is (4): (Analysis)** Groups can influence individual behavior through modeling. Seeing one person help, some of the other neighbors most likely would have helped, too.

3. **The correct answer is (2): (Analysis)** Some of the aviators may have been influenced by the behavior they saw modeled.

4. **The correct answer is (1): (Evaluation)** Choices (2), (3), and (4) are facts, not values. Choice (5) is a value but is contradicted by the message of the role.

Exercise 5 (page 186)

1. **The correct answer is (5): (Comprehension)** Most single-parent households are headed by poor African-American and Hispanic women.

2. **The correct answer is (3): (Evaluation)** The graphs show that African-American single-parent families outnumber two-parent African-American families. Assuming that many single parents, especially those who are poor, have trouble managing their households, the information indicates a pressing need for social services in that group.

3. **The correct answer is (3): (Evaluation)** The graph indicates nothing more than the proportions of racial groups at a given time. It does not show discrimination (1), growth (2), or cultural backgrounds (4). Choice (5) is incorrect because the graph shows Native Americans to be the smallest minority group.

4. **The correct answer is (4): (Analysis)** A multicultural nation, such as the United States, is a nation of many ethnic groups that retain some of their ancestors' cultures but all claim the same nationality (American).

Part 3
SCIENCE

RED ALERT

The GED Science Test is *not* a measurement of how much you know about specific scientific facts and concepts. Most questions on this test will ask you to think logically and carefully about a passage or illustration on a scientific topic.

CONTENT AREAS

Science is Test 3 of the GED Tests. It consists of the following four content areas. The percent for each area is given in parentheses.

Life science: (50%) The study of life processes and patterns and the study of humans and the environment

Earth science: (20%) The study of the earth's structure, its atmosphere and weather, and its natural resources

Chemistry: (15%) The study of the structure, states, and reactions of matter

Physics: (15%) The study of matter, motion, and energy

TYPES OF QUESTIONS

When you take the GED Science Test, you will have 95 minutes to answer 66 multiple-choice questions. Each multiple-choice question or set of multiple-choice questions will refer to a passage or to a chart or other illustration. These questions will ask you to comprehend, apply, analyze, or evaluate the scientific information presented. Of the science questions, 20 percent will be comprehension questions, 30 percent will be application questions, 30 percent will be analysis questions, and 20 percent will be evaluation questions.

COMPREHENSION

Comprehension questions ask you to identify, restate, or summarize information and ideas that are stated directly or indirectly in a passage, chart, or diagram. The following question is an example of a comprehension question. It asks you to decide on the best way to restate some information.

1. The Environmental Protection Agency conducted a study of indoor air pollution in the average American home. Findings of the study revealed that indoor air contains two to five times more poisonous chemicals than outdoor air. Household cleaning products are often the sources of these poisonous chemicals. As a result, people who use many of these chemicals can experience symptoms such as headaches, dizziness, and nausea.

    Which of the following best restates the purpose of the study conducted by the Environmental Protection Agency?

    (1) to cite the main hazards of outdoor air pollution
    (2) to analyze the amounts of chemicals in the indoor air of the average home
    (3) to explain the health effects of harmful chemicals
    (4) to ban commercial products that cause air pollution
    (5) to find the amounts of poisonous chemicals in household cleaning products

    The correct answer for Example 1 is choice (2). To answer this question correctly, you must restate the information presented in the first and second sentences of the paragraph. The other choices are inaccurate restatements of the information given.

APPLICATION

Application questions ask you to use information and ideas from a passage or illustration to solve a problem or make a prediction in a different situation. Below is an example of an application question. It asks you to apply the information it provides to another situation.

2. A lever is a simple machine consisting of a rigid object, such as a metal bar, that pivots on a fixed point, called the fulcrum.

Which of the following is an example of a lever?

(1) an oar on a rowboat
(2) the ramp of a building entrance
(3) the blades of a ceiling fan
(4) the conveyor belt in an assembly line
(5) the handle of a water faucet

Choice **(1)** is the correct answer for Example 2. The oar on a rowboat is a lever because it consists of a long pole made of a rigid material that pivots on a fulcrum (the oarlock). None of the items in the other choices is bar-shaped and functions according to the definition of a lever described in the sample question.

ANALYSIS

Analysis questions ask you to determine causes and effects, distinguish facts from opinions, and draw conclusions. The question below is an example of an analysis question that requires you to distinguish facts from opinions.

3. Supplies of fossil fuels—coal, oil, and natural gas—are dwindling. As a result, some scientists are experimenting with plants in an attempt to find a substitute for these fossil fuels. However, some people feel that using plants for fuel is not a wise alternative. They believe that this practice might result in a decrease of growing plants to feed people and livestock, and could thus contribute to the already existing problem of world hunger.

Which of the following statements is an opinion, not a fact?

(1) Coal, oil, and natural gas are fossil fuels.
(2) Scientists are investigating the possibility of using plants for fuel.
(3) Plants are raised to supply food for people and livestock.
(4) World hunger is a problem that already exists.
(5) Growing plants for the purpose of increasing fuel supplies is not a good idea.

The correct answer for Example 3 is choice **(5)**. The words "feel" and "believe" in the paragraph are clues that this statement is an opinion—a belief that cannot be proved true or false. All the other choices are facts because they contain information that can be proved true.

EVALUATION

Evaluation questions ask you to judge the accuracy and adequacy of information, as well as the methods and results of scientific experiments and studies. The question below is an example of an evaluation question.

4. Which of the following data would provide the best evidence of the effectiveness of a new drug for patients with AIDS?

(1) interviews with AIDS patients
(2) opinions of doctors
(3) successful results from several human studies
(4) experiments with laboratory rats
(5) analysis of the drug by chemists

The correct answer for Example 4 is choice **(3)**. AIDS patients who showed improvements in their health after being treated with a new drug would provide the strongest evidence that the drug was effective. Choices (1) and (2) are incorrect because this evidence would be based on personal attitudes and opinions, not proven results. Choice (4) is incorrect because humans' reactions to the drug might not be identical to rats' reactions. Choice (5) is incorrect because a chemical analysis of the drug would not be useful in judging the drug's effectiveness with patients.

LIFE SCIENCE

The Cell

Your body—like the bodies of all animals and plants—is made up of many individual living units. These tiny living units are called **cells.** Within an animal or plant, each cell carries on its own life processes: it takes in food, gets rid of waste products, and reproduces. There are an estimated 100 trillion cells in the human body.

All cells have three basic parts:

- the *cell membrane*, which is the outer covering that keeps the cell together

- the *nucleus*, which is the cell's control center—a self-contained body that directs the cell's activity from within the cell. The nucleus also contains **chromosomes**, the genetic blueprints for new cells.

- the *cytoplasm*, which makes up the rest of the cell—parts outside the nucleus but within the cell membrane. The cytoplasm contains the cell's internal organs, called *organelles*. Most of the cell's day-to-day activities are carried out by the organelles.

Each organelle has a specific job:

- The *endoplasmic reticulum* is a series of pathways through the cytoplasm. Proteins made by the cell move through these pathways.

- *Ribosomes*—make proteins. They are found in two places within the cell—in the endoplasmic reticulum membrane and scattered throughout the cytoplasm.

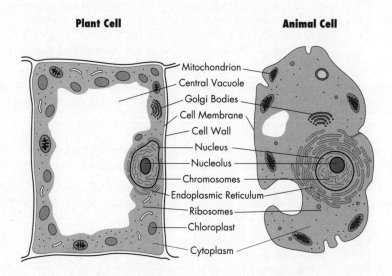

Plant Cell   Animal Cell

Mitochondrion
Central Vacuole
Golgi Bodies
Cell Membrane
Cell Wall
Nucleus
Nucleolus
Chromosomes
Endoplasmic Reticulum
Ribosomes
Chloroplast
Cytoplasm

cell: the smallest unit of life; the building block of larger plants and animals

chromosome: the carriers of genetic information within a cell nucleus

- *Golgi bodies*—groups of baglike organelles—also serve to transport proteins and other cell products. Their main function is storage and packaging of chemicals.

- *Mitochondria*—generate the energy to do all this work inside the cell.

Both plant and animal cells have **vacuoles.** A vacuole is a bubblelike structure inside the cytoplasm. Animal cells may have a few small vacuoles used primarily to store water, liquids, food, and waste material. Each plant cell, on the other hand, usually has one large central vacuole that occupies 80 to 90 percent of the cell's volume.

In addition to the cell membrane, the plant cell has a **cell wall.** The cell wall is thicker and tougher than the cell membrane. The cytoplasm of a plant cell also contains bodies called **chloroplasts,** which animal cells do not have. Chloroplasts contain the green pigment chlorophyll. They use light energy to manufacture food for the plant through a complex process called **photosynthesis.**

Cell Reproduction

Plant and animal cells reproduce by splitting into two. The largest and most complex animal or plant begins as a single cell that splits into two—and the two cells split into four, and the four split into eight, and so on.

Most cells reproduce through a process called **mitosis.** When one cell undergoes mitosis, the end product is two cells with the same components as the original cell—the same organelles, the same number of chromosomes, and so on.

Biologists have divided the process of mitosis into four stages, or phases.

Phase 1: Prophase During the prophase stage, the boundary between the nucleus and the cytoplasm disappears.

Phase 2: Metaphase In the metaphase stage, the pairs of chromosomes line up across the center of the cell.

Phase 3: Anaphase In the anaphase stage, each chromosome pair separates, and its members move toward opposite sides of the cell.

Phase 4: Telophase During the telophase stage, a separate nucleus forms around each group of chromosomes, the cytoplasm divides, and two separate cells form.

Interphase The interphase stage of mitosis is actually *the entire period between the end of the last cell division and the beginning of the next one.* During interphase, the chromosomes in the nucleus duplicate themselves. Each chromosome stays connected to its double.

vacuole: bubblelike structure in the cell's cytoplasm for storage of water, wastes, or nutrients

cell wall: a tough membrane outside the cell membrane of a plant cell

chloroplast: the body within a plant cell that creates energy through photosynthesis

photosynthesis: the process by which plant cells make food for themselves using energy from light

mitosis: the process by which a cell makes a copy of itself

Exercise 1

Directions

Choose the <u>one best answer</u> to each item.

---

1. In order to keep the heart pumping constantly, the cells of the heart use large amounts of energy. Which of the following bodies would you expect to be quite plentiful in heart cells?

   (1) cell membranes
   (2) chromosomes
   (3) Golgi bodies
   (4) mitochondria
   (5) nucleoli

2. Which of the following statements could be offered as evidence that Golgi bodies help "export" material that the cell manufactures?

   (1) Golgi bodies are formed from parts of the endoplasmic reticulum.
   (2) Nucleoli are most prominent in cells that are most active in protein production.
   (3) Golgi bodies manufacture proteins often used by other parts of the body.
   (4) Cells that make saliva, mucus, and other similar substances have more Golgi bodies than cells that do not perform these functions.
   (5) Golgi bodies travel freely through the cytoplasm.

Items 3 and 4 refer to the following information.

Reproduction is a normal part of a cell's activity. A cell that has just been formed by mitosis soon begins preparing to undergo mitosis itself. The following diagram represents the life cycle of a typical cell.

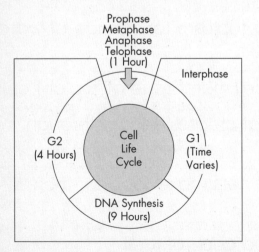

In this diagram, G1 and G2 are gaps in the process. During these gaps, the size of the cell doubles, and certain organelles double in number; no reproduction-related activity takes place.

3. Which of the following statements best expresses the main idea of the diagram?

   (1) A cell is always involved in the process of reproduction.
   (2) After a long period of preparation, the major stages of mitosis happen within a relatively short period of time.
   (3) Mitosis takes 1 hour from start to finish.
   (4) The average animal cell lives about 18 hours.
   (5) A cell's life cycle is equally balanced between dividing and synthesizing energy for the next cell division.

4. The diagram gives average amounts of time for each of the phases of the cell's life cycle. If you drew life cycle diagrams for many different types of cells, which section would vary most from diagram to diagram?

   (1) G1
   (2) synthesis
   (3) G2
   (4) interphase
   (5) prophase/metaphase/anaphase/telophase

To check your answers, turn to page 230.

Photosynthesis

Plant cells use energy from the sun to convert raw materials into the food they need. This process is known as *photosynthesis*. The main ingredients in photosynthesis are oxygen and carbon dioxide (two gases that are available in the atmosphere) and water (drawn up from the ground). The diagram below describes the process of photosynthesis, which occurs in two main phases: *light reactions* and *dark reactions*.

PHOTOSYNTHESIS

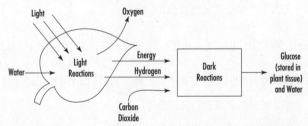

In light reactions, light energy is captured by chloroplasts in the plant cell. Some of the captured light energy is used to separate water into hydrogen and oxygen. The rest of the energy is stored for later use. The oxygen from the water is released into the atmosphere;

the hydrogen is then available for use in the dark reactions.

In dark reactions, hydrogen from the light reactions is brought together with carbon dioxide. Some of the hydrogen combines with some of the oxygen from the carbon dioxide and is released as water. The rest of the carbon, hydrogen, and oxygen are combined to form glucose. Energy stored during the light reactions helps this process along.

Glucose is the ideal food for both plant and animal cells. Some of the glucose produced during photosynthesis is used immediately by the plant. The rest is stored for later use. Eventually, the glucose is used either by the plant or by an animal that eats the plant.

Cell Respiration

Both plant and animal cells convert glucose to energy through a process called **cell respiration.** Like photosynthesis, respiration takes place in two stages. The first stage is called **glycolysis.** In this stage, glucose is broken down into pyruvic acid. Some energy is released at this stage.

The second stage of respiration requires oxygen. In this stage, called **aerobic respiration,** pyruvic acid and oxygen go through a complex series of reactions. The end products are carbon dioxide, water, and a lot of energy. The carbon dioxide and water are released from the cell.

To keep each cell functioning, a person's body must provide constant supplies of glucose and oxygen. Oxygen is always coming in through the lungs, where it is absorbed by red blood cells and delivered to the cells through the body's blood vessels. Our bodies get glucose by breaking down the food that we eat. Blood vessels carry the glucose to the cells. When the body gets more glucose than the cells need, the extra is converted into fat or starch and stored in the body.

Exercise 2

Directions

Choose the one best answer to each item.

1. What is the source of energy used for photosynthesis?

   (1) cellulose
   (2) chloroplasts
   (3) light
   (4) vacuoles
   (5) water

2. Which of the following inferences can you make based on the account of photosynthesis in the lesson?

   (1) Glucose is necessary for photosynthesis.
   (2) Plants need light to grow.
   (3) Animals do not benefit from photosynthesis.
   (4) Plants make all the water they need.
   (5) Plants are responsible for all oxygen.

Items 3 and 4 refer to the following passage.

Anaerobic respiration is another process that takes place in plants, animals, and one-celled organisms called yeast cells. It occurs when aerobic respiration is prevented by a lack of oxygen. When anaerobic respiration takes place in plants and yeast cells, it produces alcohol and carbon dioxide gas and is called fermentation. It is used to make bread and alcoholic beverages such as beer and wine.

3. Which of the following could prevent fermentation from occurring?

   (1) exercise
   (2) light
   (3) oxygen
   (4) pyruvic acid
   (5) yeast

cell respiration: the process by which animal and plant cells manufacture energy by breaking down molecules of glucose

glycolysis: the first stage of cell respiration, in which glucose is broken down into pyruvic acid

aerobic respiration: the second stage of cellular respiration, which produces carbon dioxide, water, and a lot of energy

4. Based on the information above, which of the following best explains why bread rises when it is baked?

(1) The bread dough expands as it fills up with alcohol.

(2) The heat of baking causes the added yeast cells to multiply.

(3) Lactic acid builds up in the bread dough.

(4) Lactic acid reacts with pyruvic acid, causing small explosions within the dough.

(5) The fermenting yeast releases bubbles of carbon dioxide gas, which expand the dough.

To check your answers, turn to page 230.

Reproduction and Development

All plants and animals reproduce. In flowering plants, the flower is specially designed to ensure that an egg cell will be **fertilized,** or joined with a sperm cell to produce an embryo (an organism in the early stage of development). Most animals reproduce when the male and female of a species bring the sperm and egg cells together.

Plant Reproduction and Development

A flowering plant's male sex organ is called a stamen. A *stamen* produces pollen—tiny grains that contain plant sperm cells. One plant may have several stamens. The flowering plant's female sex organ is a tubelike structure called a *pistil.* The female egg cells are in the **ovary** at the bottom of the tube. Each egg is enclosed in an *ovule.*

The pistil is at the center of the flower, with the stamens forming a ring around it. The flower's appearance and/or smell attracts an insect, which then lands on the flower, looking for food. If the insect has been dusted with pollen from another flower, and if this pollen comes into contact with the pistil, pollen can make its way down into the ovary to fertilize the egg.

Once an egg is fertilized, the flowering plant changes rapidly. The flower falls away. The ovules turn into seeds, and the ovary starts developing into a **fruit.** The fruit surrounds the seeds of the plant; its purpose is to carry the seed as far away as possible. This happens when animals carry fruits off and eat them, or when spiky coverings cause fruits to stick to the coats of passing animals.

Left to itself, a fruit ripens and falls apart; then the seeds fall to the ground. Eventually, the seeds *germinate*—put out roots and a stalk. The new plant grows to maturity, and the cycle begins again.

Animal Reproduction and Development

Animal reproduction and development can vary greatly from species to species; but each species has to go through the same basic stages—and deal with the same problems—in order to produce new offspring.

Fertilization. Union of a sperm cell and an egg cell from the same species can take place inside or outside the body:

- **Outside the body.** This method does not ensure success, but the animal's behavior can help. In some fish species, the male and female swim around in a circular mating dance. The female releases her eggs into the water, and the male then releases sperm in the same area.

- **Inside the female's body.** This method of fertilization is the surest way of bringing the sperm and egg together. In many species—from earthworms to lions—the male delivers the sperm directly to the egg by inserting his sex organ into a specific orifice, or opening, in the female's body.

Incubation. Animals have many ways of *incubating* their eggs, or ensuring that their fertilized eggs have a chance to develop. The most effective way to protect and nourish the embryo is to keep it close to the mother's body. Different animals' methods of incubation are outlined below:

- **Insects.** Most insects do nothing to protect their eggs; the insect strategy is to lay thousands of fertilized eggs and leave the eggs to fend for themselves.

- **Reptiles and birds.** A female reptile may lay dozens of fertilized eggs at a time. A female bird may lay only one

---

fertilization: the union of a sperm and an egg cell

ovary: the organ in an animal or plant that generates female egg cells for sexual reproduction

fruit: the structure into which a plant's ovary develops after one of its eggs is fertilized

or two. The eggs of these species are protected by hard or leathery shells. Inside the shell, the embryo develops safely, drawing food from the egg yolk.

- **Marsupials.** A female marsupial, such as a kangaroo, has a pouch to carry the young. Among marsupial mammals, at a certain stage the embryo crawls into its mother's pouch, where it continues to develop, drawing milk from a teat inside.

- **Placental mammals.** In placental mammals, including lions, squirrels, and humans, the fertilized egg never leaves the mother's body. It attaches itself to the inner wall of the womb and draws food directly from the mother through the umbilical cord. Only when incubation is complete does the offspring leave the mother's womb.

     Birth and Maturation. After incubation come birth and maturation. At maturity, an animal is ready to carry on the cycle of reproduction.

Human Reproduction and Development

Reproduction and development follow the same patterns in human beings as in other placental mammals. The female's egg is fertilized in the body. The fertilized egg attaches inside the mother's womb and incubates there. A protective sac called the **placenta** forms around the embryo, drawing food directly from the mother through the umbilical cord. After incubation, the baby emerges from the womb to start a thirteen- to sixteen-year process of maturation.

Exercise 3

Directions

Choose the <u>one best answer</u> to each item.

Items 1 and 2 refer to the following diagram.

GERMINATION OF A SEED

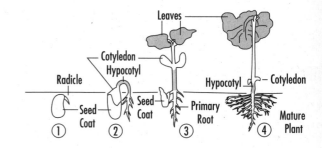

1. Which of the following parts of the seedling becomes the stem or stalk of the plant?

   (1)   cotyledon
   (2)   hypocotyl
   (3)   primary root
   (4)   radicle
   (5)   seed coat

2. In the mature plant, the cotyledons become

   (1)   the plant's first leaves
   (2)   the plant's primary root
   (3)   the plant's seed coat
   (4)   the seeds produced by the mature plant
   (5)   small, withered tissues on the stem

3. A dandelion starts out as a small yellow flower, but at some point it suddenly changes to a ball of white wisps that are easily blown away by the wind. Which of the following statements best explains this change?

   (1)   The dandelion has reached the end of its natural life cycle and died.
   (2)   The dandelion seed has germinated.
   (3)   The dandelion has dried up for lack of water.
   (4)   An egg cell within the dandelion's pistil has been fertilized by a grain of pollen.
   (5)   The dandelion has reacted to weed killer in the soil.

placenta: the protective sac in which a placental mammal's fetus develops

Item 4 refers to the following table.

REPRODUCTION AND DEVELOPMENT
AMONG VERTEBRATES[1]

	Fish	Amphibians	Reptiles	Birds	Mammals
Habitat[2]	water	water/land	land	land	land
Fertilization[3]	external	external	internal	internal	internal
Egg Size[4]	small	small	large	large	small
Development[5]	external	external	external	external	internal
Larval Stage?[6]	yes	yes	no	no	no

[1] animals with backbones
[2] type of environment in which animal lives
[3] inside or outside mother's body
[4] large or small; large have built-in food supply
[5] inside or outside mother's body
[6] first part of life spent in an immature form, as a tadpole is an immature frog

4. The table above lists the methods of reproduction and development of different animals. Which of the following pairs of vertebrates have all the same factors of reproduction and development?

   (1) fish and amphibians
   (2) amphibians and reptiles
   (3) reptiles and birds
   (4) birds and mammals
   (5) mammals and fish

Item 5 refers to the following table.

SELECTED METHODS OF BIRTH CONTROL

Method	Description	Failure Rate (%)
1. Surgical Sterilization	vasectomy or tubal ligation	0.003
2. Contraceptive Pill	pill that prevents ovulation	0.5–1.0
3. Diaphragm	physical barrier to sperm	10–12
4. Condom	physical barrier to sperm	15
5. Rhythm Method	abstinence from sex during woman's fertile period	25
6. Intercourse with no contraception		75–100

5. According to the table, which of the following is the most reliable method of birth control?

   (1) condom
   (2) contraceptive pill
   (3) diaphragm
   (4) rhythm method
   (5) surgical sterilization

To check your answers, turn to page 230.

Heredity

How can a newborn baby have "his father's nose" or "her mother's eyes"? Why are such attributes as sharp eyesight passed from one generation of a family to another? Somehow, parents pass on a code or set of instructions that guide the child's development.

Scientists began to study this code during the nineteenth century, when they first used the word *gene* to refer to each individual instruction in the code. The study of how the code worked was called *genetics*. Because in sexual reproduction *both* parents contribute genes to the code, the offspring's genetic code is a combination of the parents' codes.

According to the genetic theory of heredity, a person's *traits*—well-defined characteristics such as hair color or eye color—can be traced back to individual genes. For example, there is a human gene that controls the shape of the ear—whether the earlobe is attached to the side of the head or detached, forming a rounded shape at the bottom. If both parents have attached earlobes, their children's earlobes will be similar. If either parent has detached earlobes, it's very likely that their children will have detached earlobes too. And yet it's possible for a mother and father with detached earlobes to produce a child with attached earlobes. How can this happen?

The answer is that it actually takes a *pair* of genes—one contributed by each parent—to determine how a particular trait develops. In our example, each parent has a pair of genes that determines the shape of the earlobe. The father passes one of his two earlobe genes along to the baby, and the mother does the same with one of her two earlobe genes.

But if there are *two* genes for each trait, which gene is *expressed*—that is, which gene actually controls how the ear develops? When there are two types of genes for a trait, one of them is *dominant* and one is *recessive*. If either one of the gene pair is the dominant gene, that gene will be expressed; the recessive gene is expressed only when both genes in the gene pair are recessive. In the example about earlobes, the detached gene is the dominant gene. The only way the baby could be born with attached earlobes is if both parents pass along the attached gene.

The genes that are passed from parents to offspring during sexual reproduction are actually segments of *chromosomes*. An ordinary human cell has 46 chromosomes. Each chromosome is a molecule of a chemical called *deoxyribonucleic acid*, or *DNA*.

The special cells used in the process of sexual reproduction reproduce through a process called *meiosis*. Early in the process, each chromosome links up with another similar chromosome in a chromosome pair. Later, the pairs separate: one chromosome from each pair goes into each daughter cell—the sperm in males or the egg

cells in females. During sexual reproduction, a sperm cell unites with an egg cell to form one cell called a *zygote*. In the human zygote, 23 chromosomes from the sperm cell combine with 23 chromosomes from the egg cell. The result is 23 pairs, or 46 chromosomes—a complete set.

Genetic Engineering

A DNA molecule is a long chain with four different kinds of *bases*. Like beads on a string, the bases are repeated in different patterns along the chain. A particular gene is one particular section along the chain. Scientists have developed a process called *gene splicing*, in which they alter genes directly by making changes in the DNA itself. This process involves the following steps, illustrated by the following diagrams:

1.

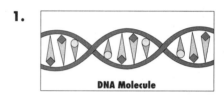

DNA Molecule

2.

Break in DNA Molecule

3.

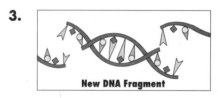

New DNA Fragment

4.

Recombining Ends

5.

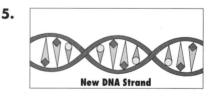

New DNA Strand

1. Identifying the site of the gene to be added or altered
2. Breaking the DNA chain at that point
3. Inserting the new genetic material at the break
4. Joining the separated ends of the original strand with the new material
5. Replacing the recombined DNA strand in the organism

The repaired DNA molecule still functions normally but contains new genetic information. DNA that is changed through the process of gene splicing is called *recombinant DNA*. When the cell with the recombinant DNA divides, the genetic change is carried over to the new cells.

Here are some examples of the uses of this kind of genetic engineering:

- **Corn:** Genetic engineering has produced strains of corn that are higher in nutritional value and more resistant to insects than previous strains.

- **Animals:** In one experiment, human growth genes were inserted into the DNA of mice. The mice grew to twice their normal size.

Evolution

In 1859, Charles Darwin published a book called *The Origin of Species*. This book put forth the view that nature is in a constant state of change—that animal and plant species are always developing in response to changes in their environment. Darwin's ideas are referred to as the theory of **evolution**.

Charles Darwin began developing his theory while on an around-the-world sea voyage aboard a British surveying ship. In the jungles of South America and on the Galapagos Islands, Darwin found an amazing variety of animal and plant life. He found many cases in which separate populations of a species in different places were different in important ways. Darwin also saw that very similar species differed according to how each animal lived in its environment.

As he tried to work out an explanation for these observations, Darwin formulated the following key ideas of evolution:

1. **Not all members of a species are exactly alike.** Darwin found local variations in species of birds, lizards, turtles, many other animals, and many plants.
2. **All living things compete for natural resources.** In order to survive, living things need resources such as food and shelter. If there are not enough of these resources to go around, some living things will survive and some will not.
3. **The conditions of the environment determine which living things will survive.** The animals or plants whose special features help them survive and reproduce in the environment are the ones that will

compete successfully and thrive. Darwin called this idea *natural selection*.

The process of evolution also involves other factors, including:

Change in the environment. New conditions may require new adaptations.

Migration. Over time, members of a population will adapt to their environment. If new members of the species move in and mix with the local population, the genetic makeup of the population will change. This will result in further evolutionary development.

Isolation. If part of a population gets separated from the rest of the group, the two groups will develop different features over time (*divergent evolution*).

Mutation. A *mutation* is a sudden change in the genetic makeup of an organism. If the change hinders the survival or reproduction of an organism, the mutation dies off. On the other hand, a mutation may help the offspring better survive in their environment. In that case, over time, the mutation might become standard for the species.

Exercise 4

Directions
Choose the one best answer to each item.

Items 1 and 2 refer to the following information.

Mutations occur when chromosomes separate imperfectly or break during cell reproduction. Mutations that occur in sex cells—that is, in sperm or egg cells—are called germ cell mutations. Mutations that occur in other cells are called somatic mutations.

1. Based on what you know from this lesson, you can infer that germ cell mutations

    (1) can affect the offspring of the plants or animals in which they occur
    (2) occur during mitosis
    (3) cause the sperm or egg cells to have half as many chromosomes as normal cells
    (4) are the cause of recessive genes
    (5) determine the sex of the animal's or plant's offspring

evolution: the changing of the genetic makeup of plants and animals over time

2. Where in the human body would a germ cell mutation occur?

    (1) bone marrow
    (2) brain
    (3) lung
    (4) ovary
    (5) skin

3. Which of the following problems are scientists most likely to try to solve with genetic engineering?

    (1) a broken arm
    (2) an abnormal gene that slows the body's protein production
    (3) the harmful effects of poison ivy
    (4) a rare recessive gene that causes a child to be born with six fingers on each hand and six toes on each foot
    (5) a child's loss of appetite

4. Which of the following pieces of evidence would best support the theory that evolution has been going on for millions of years?

    (1) fossils from different millennia showing that species had changed over time
    (2) members of a modern species that differ from each other
    (3) fossils of dinosaurs that have been extinct for millions of years
    (4) animal specimens from the 1800s that differ from the same species today
    (5) different animal species that live in the same environment that have come to look alike

5. Which of the following statements best explains why competition for resources is a necessary part of the process of natural selection?

    (1) Competition ensures that only the strongest, best-adapted species survive.
    (2) Competition increases the number of variations of a species.
    (3) Competition ensures that there are enough resources to go around.
    (4) Competition provides animals with a means of finding mates.
    (5) Evolution would fail without competition.

To check your answers, turn to page 230.

Human Body Systems and Nutrition

The systems of your body work together, day and night, to keep you alive and healthy. For example, you have a gas-exchange system that supplies you with oxygen and disposes of carbon dioxide. You also have a transportation system that carries blood around your body, and a factory system that processes the food you eat. *Nutrition* is the study of how that food affects the human body.

What exactly is a body system? In your body, cells with similar structures combine to form different types of *tissues* such as muscle, skin, and bone. The tissues are arranged into *organs*—body parts, such as your heart and your lungs, that perform certain functions. These organs are joined together to form your *body systems*. All your body systems interact with one another. The breakdown of one system often causes damage in another.

Body Systems

THE RESPIRATORY SYSTEM

The purpose of the *respiratory system* is to absorb oxygen from the air you breathe and pass it along to the blood. The respiratory system consists of the body parts that are used in breathing.

THE HUMAN RESPIRATORY SYSTEM

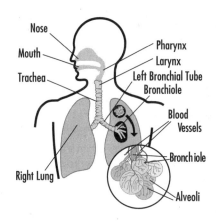

In the respiratory system, the nose, mouth, and trachea filter dust particles and other impurities from the air. Air then travels through the bronchial tubes, which branch out from the trachea. The bronchial tubes transport air to the lungs through smaller passages called bronchioles. From the bronchioles, air moves to millions of tiny air sacs called alveoli, whose chief job is to extract oxygen and deliver it to the bloodstream. At the same time, carbon dioxide is extracted from the blood and enters the lungs, from which it is exhaled into the air.

Breathing is regulated by the amount of oxygen you need and the amount of carbon dioxide you produce. When you exercise, your body's muscles use more oxygen and produce more carbon dioxide, which accumulates in the blood. To dispose of this carbon dioxide, you breathe harder, supplying active muscles with more oxygen.

THE CIRCULATORY SYSTEM

The *circulatory system* consists of three main parts—the heart, the blood vessels, and blood. The function of this system is to transport blood, which carries oxygen and nutrients throughout your body.

The heart is the center of the circulatory system. Study the diagram below. Notice that the heart actually consists of two adjacent pumps, each of which contains upper and lower chambers. The right atrium receives blood transported from the body. Blood moves from this receiving chamber to the right ventricle, where it is pumped to the lungs. The lungs supply the blood with oxygen in a process called pulmonary circulation. This oxygen-rich blood moves to the left atrium and then is pumped into the left ventricle. The left ventricle pumps the blood to the aorta, which supplies blood to arteries throughout the body.

THE HEART

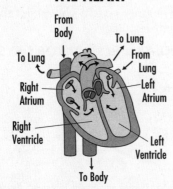

The blood vessels that carry the oxygen-rich blood *away* from the heart are called arteries. Blood vessels that carry blood containing carbon dioxide back *to* the heart are called veins. How does blood move from the arteries into the veins? Capillaries—very tiny blood vessels—join these two sets of tubes together. Blood flows from the arteries to the veins through the capillaries.

THE DIGESTIVE SYSTEM

The *digestive system* works somewhat like an assembly line in reverse. A chain of body parts disassembles, or breaks down, food into chemicals as the food travels slowly through the digestive tract—a long, winding food tube. Each body part along the way performs a special job. The diagram (top right) illustrates the stages of this process. As you study the diagram, follow the journey of food through the digestive tract.

THE HUMAN DIGESTIVE SYSTEM

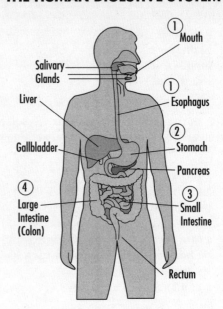

1. **Mouth and Esophagus:** The teeth chew and mash food. Saliva, a watery substance, breaks down the starches in food. Saliva also moistens and softens food. Swallowed food then enters the esophagus, a tube leading to the stomach.

2. **Stomach:** Contracting stomach muscles churn the food as it is mixed with stomach acid and other digestive juices. These juices help break down the proteins in food. Chyme, a soupy mixture of broken-down food from the stomach, enters the intestine.

3. **Small Intestine:** The small intestine, a coiled tube over 20 feet long, squeezes the food mixture along. Powerful digestive juices, some of which come from the liver, pancreas, and gallbladder, speed up the chemical breakdown of food. Some of the broken-down food is absorbed into the bloodstream. The remaining food particles enter the large intestine.

4. **Large Intestine (Colon):** The large intestine, or colon, a tube about 5 feet long, stores the waste, or unusable food particles. The waste thickens as water is absorbed. Eventually, solid waste products are pushed out of the body through the rectum.

Nutrition

Suppose you ate a grilled cheese sandwich, a cup of vegetable soup, and a fruit salad for lunch. Your meal contained five essential nutrients—carbohydrates, protein, fat, vitamins, and minerals.

Carbohydrates (starches and sugars) supply quick energy needed for physical activity and other body functions. Proteins repair and build body tissues. Fats provide the body's main source of energy during rest and light activity. In addition, fats are an important component of cell membranes. Vitamins and minerals regulate body functions.

In addition to these nutrients, you need fiber. Fiber consists of food particles that your body is unable to digest; it helps to push food along the intestines and to eliminate wastes from the body.

FOOD GUIDE PYRAMID
A Guide to Daily Food Choices

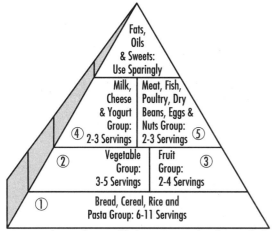

A serving refers to each portion of food eaten. For example, a cheese sandwich consists of 1 serving of cheese (Group 4) and 2 servings of bread (Group 1).

The United States Department of Agriculture (USDA) has published guidelines for good eating habits. Examine the model above, called the Food Guide Pyramid, which consists of five food groups.

Study the main nutrients in each of the food groups. Food Group 1 forms the base of the pyramid. Bread, cereal, rice, and pasta are excellent sources of carbohydrates. Food Groups 2 and 3—vegetables and fruits—are also high in carbohydrates, and they form the pyramid's second level. According to the diagram, the majority of foods you eat every day should come from these three groups.

The third level of the Food Guide Pyramid consists of Food Groups 4 (milk, cheese, and yogurt) and 5 (meat, fish, poultry, dry beans, eggs, and nuts). Foods from these two groups furnish your body with protein. Many dairy and meat products are also high in fat. Fats, oils, and sweets form the top level of the Food Guide Pyramid. These foods should be eaten sparingly because they contribute few nutrients to your diet and can be harmful to your health.

Exercise 5

Directions

Choose the one best answer to each item.

1. Which of the following shows the correct airflow sequence when a person inhales?

   (1) nose and mouth, bronchioles, bronchial tubes, trachea, lungs

   (2) bronchial tubes, trachea, bronchioles, lungs, nose and mouth

   (3) lungs, nose and mouth, trachea, bronchial tubes, bronchioles

   (4) nose and mouth, trachea, bronchial tubes, bronchioles, lungs

   (5) trachea, nose and mouth, lungs, bronchioles, bronchial tubes

Item 2 refers to the following graph.

AVERAGE HEARTBEAT RATE OF HUMANS

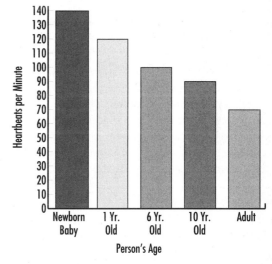

2. Which of the following statements is based on data shown in the graph?

   (1) A newborn baby's heartbeat is about twice as fast as an adult's heartbeat.

   (2) A one-year-old's heartbeat is about twice as fast as a ten-year-old's heartbeat.

   (3) A ten-year-old's heartbeat is faster than a six-year-old's heartbeat.

   (4) An adult's heartbeat is the same as a ten-year-old's heartbeat.

   (5) A newborn baby's heartbeat is slower than a one-year-old's heartbeat.

3. Which of the following body parts is a direct pathway to the stomach?

    (1) liver
    (2) esophagus
    (3) large intestine
    (4) small intestine
    (5) rectum

4. Constipation occurs when waste products are not passed through the large intestine and out of the body. To relieve these symptoms, a person should eat foods that are high in

    (1) carbohydrates
    (2) protein
    (3) fat
    (4) vitamins
    (5) fiber

5. Based on the Food Guide Pyramid, which of the following is the best choice for breakfast?

    (1) fried eggs, bacon, buttered toast
    (2) French toast with maple syrup, sausage
    (3) doughnut, coffee with cream and sugar
    (4) bran flakes with sliced bananas and skim milk
    (5) biscuits and gravy, ham steak

To check your answers, turn to page 231.

Ecosystems and the Environment

Our planet is sometimes referred to as Spaceship Earth—one giant system in which all living and nonliving things are interconnected. On Spaceship Earth, no single organism exists in isolation. The entire planet can be viewed as one **ecosystem:** a community of living things sharing a common space. All living things interact with one another, as well as with the nonliving things in their physical surroundings.

The term *ecosystem* also describes the interactions occurring within a specific environment on our planet.

Prairies, ponds, forest preserves, and city parks are all examples of ecosystems. The place in an ecosystem where an organism lives is called a **habitat.** Within an ecosystem, energy in the form of food is transferred from plants to a series of animals that feed on each other.

Think of a habitat as an organism's address—its residence within an ecosystem. Besides physical shelter, a habitat provides organisms with other life requirements. Most plants and animals need sunlight, soil, minerals, water, and suitable temperatures in order to survive. Animals also depend on the types of plants that can provide food and shelter. For example, many birds build nests in trees and feed on seeds and berries. Some animals rely more on other animals as their source of food.

Most organisms rarely stray from the borders of their own habitats. For example, you would not find polar bears living in a tropical jungle. Plants and animals have specialized needs for food and shelter. Over time, they have adapted to specific habitats where those needs are met.

As ecosystem resources are exploited by humans, changes are introduced into the ecosystem. These changes often interrupt or damage the **food chain**. A food chain shows the order in which energy from food is passed from plants to a hierarchy of animal life.

The Vanishing Rain Forest

A **tropical rain forest** is an ecosystem dominated by plants. It has average temperatures over 68° and more than 70 inches of rain each year. Under these conditions, thousands of species of plants compete for sunlight. In fact, much of the plant and animal life of the rain forest is in the upper level of the trees, called the *canopy,* close to the sunlight.

Tropical rain forests cover only 7 percent of the earth's surface, but their importance is much greater than that figure suggests. During the process of photosynthesis, rain forest plants absorb huge amounts of carbon dioxide from the atmosphere and give off large quantities

---

ecosystem: the interaction among living and nonliving things within a specific environment

---

habitat: the type of place where an organism lives

---

food chain: the order in which energy from food is passed from plants to a series of animals

---

tropical rain forest: a warm, rainy ecosystem with a huge quantity and variety of plant and animal life

of oxygen. Thus rain forests help maintain the balance of these gases in the atmosphere. Without the proper balance, the atmosphere would warm up, and this change in climate could harm plants and animals throughout the world.

Perhaps more important than the sheer quantity of tropical plant and animal life is the variety. Over half of the world's species of plants and animals are found in rain forests. Many industries, including medicine and pharmaceuticals, depend on the rain forests for resources. Unfortunately, many species of rain forest plants and animals are disappearing as their homes are destroyed. Logging roads open the forests to development. Lumber companies, farmers, and ranchers clear large areas and exhaust the nutrients in the soil. Even when the overused areas are abandoned, they are so large that the rain forest does not return.

Exercise 6

Directions
Choose the one best answer to each item.

Items 1 and 2 refer to the following diagram.

FOOD CHAIN WITHIN A POND

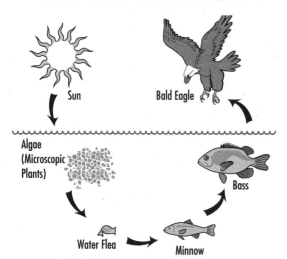

1. Which of the following links in the food chain can produce its own food?

   (1) algae
   (2) water flea
   (3) minnow
   (4) bass
   (5) bald eagle

2. The purpose of the diagram is most likely to

   (1) show the order in which energy from food is passed from plants to animals
   (2) illustrate the plants and animals that live in a specific habitat
   (3) show that photosynthesis can occur under-water as well as on land
   (4) explain the adaptations that occur in plants and animals living underwater
   (5) show an ecosystem in which organisms use the energy from sunlight

3. Both people and nature can destroy the delicate balances within an ecosystem. Which of the following is an example of a natural event that changes an existing habitat?

   (1) a housing development covering grassland
   (2) a dam flooding a canyon
   (3) a forest fire started by lightning
   (4) an oil spill polluting a beach
   (5) a strip mine destroying a hillside

4. One rain forest plant is the source of curare, which was used by South American natives on the tips of their arrowheads. When the arrowhead pierced the flesh of an animal or person, it caused temporary paralysis. The most likely medical application of curare is

   (1) a drug to relieve muscle aches caused by overexercise
   (2) a decongestant to relieve symptoms of respiratory diseases
   (3) a cure for breast cancer
   (4) a muscle relaxant for use during setting of fractured bones
   (5) a drug to firm and tone muscles

5. Arguments that rain forest destruction will cause global warming and eventual loss of the forests have little effect on the actions of people in tropical rain forest countries. Which of the following statements best explains this?

   (1) These people are not aware of global warming and rain forest destruction.
   (2) The short-term benefits of using the forests outweigh the long-term global benefits of conserving them.
   (3) The economic benefit of using up the forests will last for generations.
   (4) Most of these people live in large cities far away from the rain forests.
   (5) These people believe the rain forests will come back even though huge areas are cleared.

6. The lion-tailed macaque is almost gone from the rain forest of southern India. However, these monkeys have been successfully bred at the San Diego Zoo. The zoo is now training them to fight off predators, find their own food, and decrease their reliance on people. What is the purpose of such training?

   (1) to cut the expense of feeding the macaques at the zoo
   (2) to decrease the number of zookeepers who take care of the macaques
   (3) to prepare the macaques to return to the rain forest of southern India
   (4) to increase the number of macaques bred at the zoo
   (5) to decrease the number of macaques bred at the zoo

To check your answers, turn to page 231.

EARTH SCIENCE

The Solar System

For thousands of years, people have gazed at the sky and wondered about the vastness of the universe. In the past, people believed that the positions of the sun, moon, and planets in relation to the stars influenced events on the earth. *Astronomy*, the scientific study of space and the objects in it, has given today's scientists a much better understanding of the **universe**. We have even explored some of our near neighbors in the universe—the sun, planets, and moons—which, together with the earth, make up the **solar system.**

In its 4 to 6 billion years of existence, the earth has undergone tremendous changes. The material of which it is made has settled into layers all the way down to the core. Erosion, the wearing away of the earth's surface, has flattened mountains and cliffs and has created huge gorges such as the Grand Canyon. Volcanic eruptions on the ocean floor have built the islands of Hawaii and Japan and even now are creating new ocean floor. Perhaps the most far-reaching changes in the earth's surface are caused by **continental drift,** a process in which the earth's continents travel slowly over the surface of the planet.

More has been learned about the solar system in the last thirty years than in all of our previous history. The ancient Greeks called Mercury, Venus, Mars, Jupiter, and Saturn "planets," or wanderers, because these heavenly bodies moved in relation to the stars. The Greeks believed that the earth was the center of the universe, and that the sun, the stars, and the other planets moved around it.

Over time, however, the Greeks' theory was proved false. In 1543, Polish astronomer Nicolaus Copernicus observed the movements of the planets and concluded that all planets, including the earth, moved in **orbits,** or circular paths, around the sun. In the early 1600s, the German astronomer Johannes Kepler showed that each planet moved in an oval-shaped orbit called an *ellipse*. About the same time, the Italian astronomer Galileo was the first to study the planets through a telescope. His discovery of moons orbiting Jupiter was the first proof that not all heavenly bodies revolve around the earth. Three more planets were discovered with the help of the telescope—Uranus in 1781, Neptune in 1846, and Pluto in 1930.

At the center of our solar system is the sun, which, like all **stars,** is a ball of glowing, hot gas. The sun appears large and bright to us because it is relatively nearby—only 93 million miles away.

Much of our recent knowledge of the solar system has come from spacecraft that have collected and sent back information about, and spectacular photos of, the sun, moon, and planets. Currently, NASA's Hubble Space Telescope is obtaining data that will add greatly to scientists' knowledge and understanding of the universe.

universe: space and everything in it

solar system: the sun and the objects that revolve around it

continental drift: the slow movement of the continents over the surface of the earth as described by the theory of plate tectonics

orbit: the elliptical, or oval-shaped, path taken by a planet or other object around a star

star: an object in space that shines because it is giving off energy; a glowing ball of hot gas

Exercise 1

Directions

Choose the one best answer to each item.

Items 1 and 2 refer to the following information.

Term	Definition	Diagram
rotation	the spinning of a body on its axis, like a top	(globe with axis)
revolution	the movement of a body around another body	(earth orbiting sun)

1. Which of the following is a result of the rotation of the earth?

   (1) day and night
   (2) winter and summer
   (3) spring and fall
   (4) the movement of the continents
   (5) different stars being visible in the Northern and Southern Hemispheres

2. The farther a planet is from the sun, the longer it takes to complete a revolution. The farthest planet, Pluto, takes 248 years to complete a revolution around the sun. The earth takes 1 year. Based on this information, how long would you guess that it takes Jupiter, which is between the earth and Pluto, to revolve around the sun?

   (1) 1 day
   (2) 6 months
   (3) 1 year
   (4) 12 years
   (5) 250 years

3. Except for several moon landings by astronauts between 1969 and 1972, all exploration of the solar system has been done by unmanned spacecraft. Which of the following statements best explains why most spacecraft have explored the solar system without humans on board?

   (1) Unmanned spacecraft cost less and are easier to build and run than manned spacecraft because life-support systems do not have to be included.
   (2) It would take more than a year to get to Mars.
   (3) Astronauts have been unwilling to take the risks involved in traveling to the planets of the solar system.
   (4) Most space officials are not interested in exploring farther than the moon.
   (5) The moon missions provided all the information we need to know about the solar system.

To check your answers, turn to page 231.

Earth's Layers

Most scientists today believe that the earth, like all bodies in the solar system, originally formed from a nebula—a cloud of gas and dust. Over a period of more than a billion years, gravity caused the earth's materials to contract. In a process called *differentiation,* the materials that made up the forming planet sorted themselves by density. Heavier materials sank to the center, and lighter materials rose to the surface.

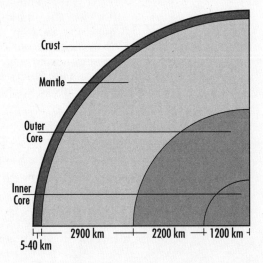

The result of differentiation is that the earth has four major layers, as shown in the diagram above.

- The outer layer, the *crust*, is made of rock that is between 5 and 40 kilometers (3 to 25 miles) thick.

- The second layer, the *mantle*, is about 2,900 kilometers (1,800 miles) thick. It is made of solid rock that under extreme pressure can flow like a thick plastic.

- The third layer, the *outer core*, is made mostly of molten iron. It is about 2,200 kilometers (1,370 miles) thick.

- The center of the earth, the *inner core*, is made mostly of solid iron.

Earthquakes and Volcanoes

According to the *plate tectonics theory*, the earth's outer layer consists of a number of thin crustal plates that fit together like a poorly made jigsaw puzzle. The plates slowly move across the earth's surface, carrying the continents and the oceans with them. The area where two plates meet is called a *plate boundary*. Most earthquake and volcanic activity occurs along these long, narrow boundaries of the earth's crustal plates. For example, the west coast of the United States is located along the boundary between the Pacific and North American plates.

Earthquakes have two main causes. The most common cause of earthquakes is an abrupt movement of rock along a *fault*, a crack in the earth's crust. Rock along the two sides of a fault may press together, causing strain on the fault. When the strain becomes too great, the rock ruptures abruptly, releasing pent-up energy in outward bursts called **seismic waves.** These waves move outward from the earthquake's *epicenter*, the point on the ground directly above the focus of the rupture. Imagine a rock thrown into a pond. The waves sent out by the rock's impact resemble a seismic wave front moving from a quake's epicenter. Waves are strongest near the epicenter and weaken as they move outward.

The second main cause of earthquakes is volcanic activity. Vibrations that lead to earthquakes have been observed in a series of highly active volcanoes, known as the "Ring of Fire," that circles the Pacific Ocean.

A volcano is the site where magma—melted rock and other material from within the earth's mantle—escapes through a hole in the surface known as a vent. Magma that reaches the surface is called lava. If large quantities of gases have built up in the underground magma chamber, the eruption may be powerfully explosive. If little gas has accumulated, the eruption may be less dramatic, mainly consisting of a flow of lava.

Exercise 2

Directions

Choose the <u>one best answer</u> to each item.

Items 1 and 2 refer to the following information.

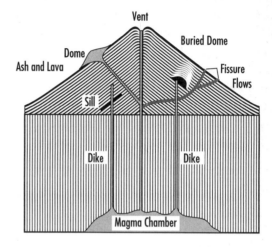

Volcanic explosions may be calm or violent. If the vent is clear, the lava flows through it calmly. If the vent is capped by debris or by a volcanic dome, tremendous pressure builds and is released in a powerful explosion. If the cap is located deep inside the volcano, magma shoots through the cap, up the long cylinder, and straight up into the air. If the cap is near the surface, the eruption expands both up and out into a large blast cloud.

1. Lava and ash on the outer layer suggest that the volcano

    (1) has erupted previously
    (2) is located near other volcanoes
    (3) does not emit these materials
    (4) has never erupted
    (5) will soon erupt

---

seismic wave: a form of energy, released during earthquakes, that moves through the earth's crust in outward bursts

2. Which of the following hypotheses best explains the existence of the dome?

   (1) Magma is pushed out from the center, building a dome on the surface.
   (2) Lava accumulates in one location after the eruption, building a dome above the surface.
   (3) Gas escapes from the fissure flows, creating a chamber just beneath the surface.
   (4) Debris from the surface accumulates in one area and tunnels down to the center.
   (5) Magma flows down from the dome into the central cylinder.

3. The crust gets hotter as you dig down into the earth from the surface. Which of the following supports the conclusion that the temperature of the crust rises as you get deeper?

   A. Oil pumped from deep wells is very warm.
   B. Air is hot at the bottoms of deep mines.
   C. Wells draw water from rock layers in the crust.

   (1) A only
   (2) B only
   (3) C only
   (4) A and B
   (5) B and C

4. Which layer of the earth contains material of the lowest density?

   (1) inner core
   (2) outer core
   (3) mantle
   (4) crust
   (5) nebula

To check your answers, turn to page 231.

EARTH'S RESOURCES

The earth's crust contains several natural resources that we depend on. Ore is used in manufacturing and construction. Fossil fuels are a source of energy. These natural resources are limited. As supplies decline, their value increases. As these resources become more scarce, people will have to rely on alternative forms of energy.

Ore Minerals

A *mineral* is a substance or combination of substances that occurs in rocks or soil. Some minerals, called **ores,** are useful because they contain metals. Ores are mined underground, quarried from the surface, or dredged from lakes or rivers, and then crushed. The crushed ore is then smelted—melted or fused—to separate the metal. Sometimes metals are used in pure form, but often they are combined with other metals to produce **alloys.** Much gold jewelry, for example, is actually made of an alloy of gold and copper.

Gold, silver, and copper were among the first metals used by humans. People made beads, coins, pins, food vessels, and jewelry from them. Later, tin and iron were also used. These are harder metals that are good for making tools and other items that must withstand long, hard use.

Today we use a wide variety of metals, a few of which are shown in the table below. But because the highest-quality ore deposits have been used up, most metals are now processed from low-grade ores.

Common Ore(s)	Metal	Uses
Bauxite	Aluminum	power lines, construction, cars, pots, pans, cans
Chalcopyrite Bornite	Copper	electrical and electronic components, water pipes
Hematite	Iron	construction industry, especially steelmaking
Nickeline	Nickel	stainless steel
Cassiterite	Tin	solder, cans, and pewter (tin combined with lead)

ore: a mineral that contains a useful metal

alloy: a combination of two or more metals (such as pewter, an alloy of tin and lead)

Fossil Fuels

Remains or traces of prehistoric life are called *fossils*. Coal, oil, and natural gas are **fossil fuels**—fuels that formed over millions of years from the remains of living organisms. These fuels are described in greater detail below.

Coal. About 270 to 350 million years ago, swamps covered much of the land. When plants died, they became waterlogged and did not decay completely. Instead, they formed a compact layer of soft material called peat. When peat is buried, it changes under pressure to lignite, a soft, brown coal. As heat and pressure increase, lignite changes to a harder, more compact form called bituminous coal. Where heat and pressure are the greatest, an even harder type of coal, anthracite, is formed.

The mining and burning of coal cause problems. Strip mining on the earth's surface can leave wastelands. Underground mining does less damage but poses safety and health risks for miners. Accidents and black lung disease are common among coal miners. In addition, most coal burned is bituminous coal. As it burns, it gives off sulfur particles that react with substances in the atmosphere to form air pollutants and acid rain.

Oil and Natural Gas. Oil and natural gas formed in shallow ocean areas from plant and animal remains. In time, the remains were covered with sediments that later became sedimentary rock. Over millions of years, the remains changed into petroleum, or oil, and natural gas.

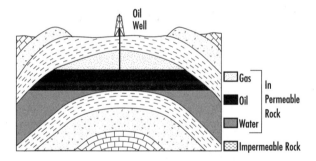

Oil Well

Gas
Oil — In Permeable Rock
Water
Impermeable Rock

Because oil and natural gas are fluids, they seep into layers of sedimentary rocks that are permeable. Since they are also lighter than water, they rise upward through water-filled layers of rock. Unless something stops them, they rise to the surface and evaporate. In some areas, oil and natural gas are trapped by rock formations that are not permeable. These oil traps have several structures, the simplest of which is shown in the graphic on this page.

Like burning coal, burning oil and natural gas cause air pollution. There are fewer known reserves of oil than there are of coal. The United States has already used much of its largest oil deposits on land.

Alternative Energy Resources

Fossil fuels are *nonrenewable resources:* when they're used up, they're gone. Most alternative sources of energy are *renewable resources:* they do not run out. Among the energy sources that are being used more and more are nuclear power, water power, solar energy, wind power, and geothermal power.

Nuclear Power. Basically, **nuclear power** uses the energy released by splitting uranium atoms to make steam. This steam drives a turbine, which operates a generator to make electricity. Unfortunately, high-quality uranium, which is scarce, is needed to fuel most nuclear reactors—nuclear power is a nonrenewable resource. There is also the potential for nuclear accidents such as those at Three Mile Island and Chernobyl. Furthermore, no one has discovered a safe way to dispose of the radioactive waste created by nuclear power plants.

Water Power. Water power, also known as hydroelectric power or hydropower, uses energy from running water to generate electricity. Water power has the advantage of being clean. However, it can be generated only where water flows from a high level to a low level, such as from a dam or waterfall.

Solar Energy. Have you noticed that on sunny winter days your house or apartment is warmer than on cloudy days? Even homes without special equipment use **solar energy** from the sun for warmth. Some homes have roof panels that collect solar energy for use in heating water and heating the house. Utility companies are experimenting with ways to use solar energy commercially to generate electricity.

Wind Power. Using the power of the wind to produce electricity is another promising way to cut down on the use of fossil fuels. Modern windmills that generate electricity are almost 100 feet tall with 50-foot blades.

---

fossil fuels: sources of energy—coal, oil, and natural gas—that formed over millions of years from the remains of living creatures

---

nuclear power: the splitting of uranium atoms in a reactor to make steam that is used to generate electricity

---

solar energy: energy from the sun

Although wind is a promising source of energy, at present it provides less than 1 percent of our electricity.

Geothermal Power. Heat energy from deep beneath the earth's surface can be used to generate electricity, or **geothermal power**. San Francisco, for example, makes about half its electricity using the steam produced by geysers—hot groundwater. Another source of geothermal energy is called *hot dry rock energy*. In this system, water is pumped down into the hot rock, where it is heated beyond the boiling point. The heated water is piped back up to the surface as steam, which is used to generate electricity. Because geothermal power depends on extreme heat underground, it is useful only in areas of volcanic and earthquake activity.

Exercise 3

Directions

Choose the <u>one best answer</u> to each item.

1. The fossil fuels we now use started forming millions of years ago. Which of the following is a true statement about fossil fuels?

   (1) Fossil fuels will continue to form, although it will be millions of years before they are usable.
   (2) Because of changes in the earth's crust, fossil fuels are no longer forming.
   (3) Once our store of fossil fuels is depleted, people will have to stop using energy in their homes and factories.
   (4) Fossil fuels are renewable resources.
   (5) Fossil fuels are preferable to alternative sources of energy because they produce little pollution comparatively.

2. In Ireland, farmers collect and dry peat for use as fuel. Which of the following statements is supported by the information given about fossil fuels?

   (1) About 300 million years ago, parts of Ireland were covered by swamps.
   (2) Thousands of years ago, parts of Ireland were covered by swamps.
   (3) Ireland has rich deposits of anthracite coal.
   (4) Ireland was once covered by a shallow ocean.
   (5) Ireland uses peat to generate electricity.

3. What is an ore?

   (1) a type of building stone
   (2) a valuable gemstone
   (3) a combination of metals
   (4) the pure form of a metal
   (5) a mineral that contains metal

4. Titanium is a metal that is lightweight and very strong. In which of the following items would titanium most likely be used?

   (1) storage batteries
   (2) electrical wires
   (3) aircraft frames
   (4) jewelry
   (5) coins

Items 5 and 6 refer to the following diagram.

SOLAR ENERGY PLANT HEATS OCEAN WATER

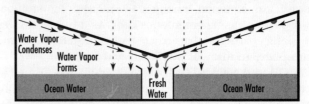

5. What is the purpose of the plant shown in the diagram?

   (1) using solar energy to boil water to make steam
   (2) using solar energy to produce fresh water from seawater
   (3) using solar energy to extract useful minerals from seawater
   (4) using water vapor to increase the humidity of the air
   (5) using water vapor to increase the temperature of the air

6. Which of the following is the most likely use of such a plant?

   (1) to produce a large city's drinking water
   (2) to produce part of a coastal city's drinking water
   (3) to process the wastewater of a city and release it as sewage into the ocean
   (4) to use solar energy to heat the homes and buildings of a city
   (5) to use solar energy to provide hot water to the homes and buildings of a city

To check your answers, turn to page 231.

geothermal power: heat energy from below the earth's surface; used to generate electricity

CHEMISTRY

Elements and Compounds

A cup of tea with lemon and sugar is a mixture of four unique substances: water, tea, sugar, and lemon juice. A *mixture* is a combination of substances that are not chemically united. In a mixture, each ingredient retains its unique chemical properties, or characteristics. The proportions of the substances in a mixture can vary. You can separate the components of a mixture by mechanical means such as adding heat. If you boil off the water, for example, you will be left with a sticky residue of lemon juice, sugar, and tea.

An *element* is a substance that cannot be broken down chemically into a simpler form. Chemists think of elements as the building blocks of more complicated chemicals called compounds. Unlike mixtures, *compounds* are made of two or more elements chemically united in an exact proportion.

Carbon and oxygen are both elements. The combination of these elements is a chemical compound, carbon dioxide. Chemical compounds such as carbon dioxide are expressed in chemical formulas. Formulas use symbols (letter groups representing each element) and subscripts (numbers representing how many atoms of each element there are in each molecule of the compound). For example, each molecule of carbon dioxide consists of one atom of carbon (C) and two atoms of oxygen (O). The formula for carbon dioxide is CO_2. The subscript 2 indicates two oxygen atoms. The formula for water, H_2O, indicates two atoms of hydrogen (H) and one atom of oxygen.

Atomic Theory

An *atom* is the smallest possible piece of an element that preserves the properties of the element. If you could look inside an atom, you would find that it is mostly empty space and that it contains smaller particles called protons, neutrons, and electrons. A *proton* is a heavy particle with a positive electrical charge. A *neutron* is a heavy particle that is electrically neutral. Together, the protons and neutrons make up the *nucleus*, the heavy center of every atom. Moving within a specific region around the nucleus are smaller, lighter, electrically negative particles called *electrons*. The positive charges of the protons and the negative charges of the electrons attract each other. These opposing charges hold the atom together.

A *molecule* is a group of two or more atoms and is the smallest part of an element or compound that retains characteristics of the element or compound. A molecule may be the smallest *stable* piece of an element. Hydrogen and oxygen do not exist as single atoms on the earth. Both of these elements form molecules made of two atoms: the hydrogen molecule is H_2 and the oxygen molecule is O_2. Molecules can also be combinations of more than one element: a water molecule (H_2O) consists of two atoms of hydrogen and one atom of oxygen.

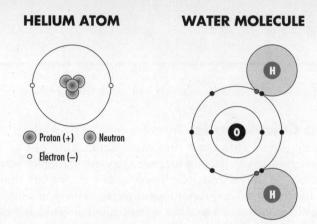

HELIUM ATOM   **WATER MOLECULE**

● Proton (+)   ● Neutron
○ Electron (−)

Electrons form a cloud around the nucleus; they do not follow set paths. An element or compound is stable when its outermost shell is full of electrons. If sharing or transferring electrons will make an atom more stable, it will join together with one or more other atoms to form a molecule. For example, each hydrogen atom has one electron on its outer shell but would be more stable if it had two. An oxygen atom has six electrons on its outermost shell but would be more stable if it had eight. When hydrogen and oxygen combine to form water, each atom has a full outer shell.

Each element has an *atomic number*, which tells you the number of protons in the nucleus. For example, the atomic number of carbon is 6. The higher the atomic number, the more protons the element has and the heavier it is.

There are also particles even more basic than protons, neutrons, and electrons. *Quarks* are the strongly interacting particles that make up the central part, or nucleus, of the atom. The particles scientists have called protons and neutrons are made up of quarks. *Leptons* are particles that interact more weakly and are found orbiting the nucleus. In fact, electrons are a type of lepton. In orbit around the nucleus, leptons hook atoms together to make everything we can see.

States of Matter

Most substances exist in one of three *states*, depending on temperature and pressure:

Solids have a definite shape, like the chair you are sitting in.

Liquids flow and take the shapes of their containers, such as a glass of lemonade.

Gases take the shapes of their containers only when confined; otherwise, they will spread out (expand) as far as they can. Gases can therefore be compressed into smaller spaces. The air you breathe is a gas.

All solids share certain characteristics. They tend to keep their shape and resist forces that otherwise would break or squeeze them. Because the molecules of a solid are close together and orderly, most solids are relatively dense and heavy. Generally, the molecules of solids keep to themselves.

To enter the solid state, a chemical substance goes through a process of becoming hard. The freezing point of water is the temperature at which liquid water begins to change into solid ice. You may have looked out on a cold morning and noticed both water and ice on the ground. The temperature 32° is both the freezing point of water and the melting point of ice. Water or any other chemical must get even colder than its freezing point to enter the solid state.

Liquids mix easily with other liquids. A liquid can be compressed, but only very slightly. Adding the right amount of heat to a solid chemical will turn it into a liquid. Most chemical compounds are lighter and take up more space in liquid form than in solid form because their molecules spread out.

Because gas molecules tend to move far away from each other, a gas consists mostly of empty space. This characteristic of gases makes it very possible to squeeze a gas into a much smaller space. Also, gases can mix freely with each other. Air is a mixture of many types of gases.

To change a liquid to a gas, you must add heat. Look at the motion of boiling water as it turns to steam. The turmoil you observe is the result of water molecules literally leaping into the air as the gas molecules move rapidly in three dimensions.

Exercise 1

Directions
Choose the <u>one best answer</u> to each item.

1. Which of the following is an example of a compound?

    (1) tea with sugar
    (2) hydrogen (H_2)
    (3) helium (He)
    (4) oil and vinegar dressing
    (5) ammonia (NH_3)

2. A chemical change occurs only when chemical bonds are made or broken. A physical change involves a change in a physical characteristic of a substance such as its size or appearance. A physical change doesn't affect the chemical makeup of the substance. Each of the following examples is a physical change EXCEPT:

    (1) a tailor making a cuff on a pair of trousers
    (2) a dent in a car body
    (3) a piece of cheese being cut into three slices
    (4) a new seat cover being added to a car seat
    (5) carbon and oxygen joining to form carbon dioxide

3. Each element differs from each other element because it

    (1) has different kinds of subatomic particles
    (2) has a different number of shells
    (3) is different in appearance
    (4) can be broken down differently
    (5) has a different number of protons

Items 4 to 6 refer to the following information.

The diagram below demonstrates the change in molecular behavior that occurs when a gas or a liquid is heated or cooled.

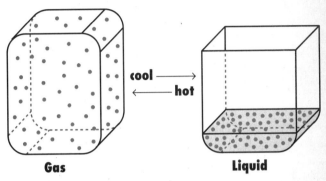

4. Which of the following statements best summarizes the main idea of the diagram?

    (1) Elements change from gas to liquid when they are heated.
    (2) Compounds are formed when a gas is cooled or heated.
    (3) Heat can change a liquid into a gas, and cooling can change a gas into a liquid.
    (4) Cooling can change a liquid into a gas, and heating can change a gas into a liquid.
    (5) Gas molecules repel each other.

5. A change in state caused by cooling is demonstrated by each of the following examples EXCEPT:

    (1) the accumulation of dew on the ground in the early morning
    (2) the freezing of water into ice
    (3) the condensation of gas into liquid at −194°C
    (4) the formation of steam in a boiling tea kettle
    (5) the formation of hailstones in the atmosphere

6. In an experiment designed to analyze what caused changes in state in certain substances, which of the following scientific instruments would be most helpful?

    (1) a microscope
    (2) a glass beaker
    (3) a magnifying glass
    (4) a scale
    (5) a thermometer

7. Protons have positive electrical charges and electrons have negative electrical charges. These opposite charges attract each other and hold an atom together. Although a neutral atom should have no effect on a passing electron, the positively charged nucleus does attract outside electrons, which aids in the formation of molecules. Which of these statements best describes molecular interaction?

(1) A neutral atom does not have any effect on a passing electron.

(2) Atoms of the same element always repel each other.

(3) There is no reason why chairs or atoms attract each other.

(4) Atoms of the same element always attract each other.

(5) Electrons can be influenced by other atoms and have a prime role in chemical behavior.

8. At what point on the thermometer would you expect to find that <u>all</u> the water lying in puddles in the street or on the sidewalk is frozen solid?

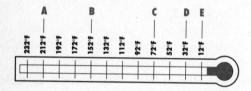

(1) A
(2) B
(3) C
(4) D
(5) E

To check your answers, turn to page 232.

Chemical Bonds

You may think that most chemicals are kept on laboratory shelves. Actually, almost every chemical element can be found right under your feet. Soil is a natural mixture of chemicals. When gardeners use fertilizers or insecticides, they add even more chemicals to the mix. This rich supply of elements and compounds makes the soil a hidden chemical factory.

Exactly what happens underground depends on how the raw materials interact with each other. Some elements react or interact with other elements easily, whereas others tend to keep to themselves. Chemists categorize the chemical elements in a chart called the *periodic table*, in which elements are listed according to weight and chemical behavior.

Common table salt, also known as sodium chloride or NaCl, is a harmless substance you probably keep in the kitchen. However, in elemental form, sodium and chlorine are not substances you would want to keep around the house. Sodium is a soft, silvery metal that reacts violently with water. Chlorine is a nonmetal and a highly poisonous yellow-green gas. These two dangerous elements become harmless when their atoms bond together to make salt.

Chemical bonds are the forces that hold atoms together. Atoms of some elements bond with each other to form a molecule of that element, such as O_2. Atoms of many elements bond with atoms of one or more other elements to form a chemical compound, such as NaCl.

Bonding always involves electrons. There are two types of chemical bonds: ionic bonds and covalent bonds.

Ionic bonds. An *ion* is an atom or group of atoms with an electrical charge. By losing an electron, an atom becomes positively charged. When an atom gains an electron, it becomes negatively charged. In the process of forming an *ionic bond*, one atom *transfers* electrons to another. The attraction between the charged particles holds the compound together. The compound is electrically neutral.

IONIC BOND   COVALENT BOND

For example, when sodium atoms and chlorine atoms combine to form salt, electrons are exchanged. The sodium atom loses an electron to chlorine and becomes positively charged. By gaining an electron, chlorine becomes negatively charged. The salt crystal is held together by the attraction between these positive and negative charges.

Covalent bond. A *covalent bond* forms when two or more atoms *share* electrons. The chemical bond holding water (H_2O) together is a covalent bond. The oxygen atom has six electrons in its outermost shell. Each hydrogen atom has one electron. When the three atoms share electrons, the molecule that is formed has a total of eight electrons, the number needed to fill the outermost shell. The negatively charged electrons orbiting both the hydrogen and oxygen atoms are attracted to the positively charged atomic nuclei. The resulting compound in this case is also electrically neutral. The diagram above represents the covalent bond in a water molecule.

Exercise 2

> **Directions**
>
> Choose the one best answer to each item.

1. Which of the following phrases best describes a chemical bond?

    (1) the loss of an electron
    (2) the force that holds atoms together
    (3) the attraction between negatively charged particles
    (4) the positive electrical charge of an atom
    (5) the negative electrical charge of an atom

2. Which of the following is a charged particle?

    (1) ion
    (2) atom
    (3) element
    (4) compound
    (5) molecule

3. Which of the following statements best explains how elements form compounds?

    (1) Gravity holds compounds together.
    (2) Some elements use magnetic forces to attract others.
    (3) The hardening of atoms holds chemical compounds together.
    (4) The attraction between charged particles holds chemical compounds together.
    (5) Shared atomic nuclei hold chemical compounds together.

4. The diagram below shows H_2, the hydrogen molecule, which is an example of a covalent bond. Each hydrogen atom by itself has one electron.

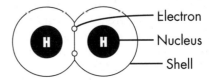

    Which of the following statements best describes H_2?

    (1) One hydrogen atom transfers its electron to another hydrogen atom.
    (2) The two bonding electrons are attracted to the two hydrogen nuclei.
    (3) Protons in the two hydrogen nuclei attract each other.
    (4) The two hydrogen atoms repel each other.
    (5) The two hydrogen atoms form multiple bonds with each other.

To check your answers, turn to page 232.

Chemical Reactions

In *chemical reactions*, chemical bonds are made or broken and new substances are formed. These new substances have unique characteristics and chemical behaviors that differ from those of the elements and compounds that made them.

Oxidation is a chemical reaction that occurs when a substance combines with oxygen. In a car's engine, gasoline oxidizes so quickly that the force of the reaction moves your car. On the other hand, rust forming on a piece of iron is an example of oxidation that can occur over a period of months or years. **Chemical kinetics** is the study of the factors that affect the speed of chemical reactions. Several such factors are:

Bonding behavior. Specific elements and compounds have typical behaviors, which are governed by the numbers of electrons they have. You already know that some elements tend to form ionic bonds, whereas others tend to form covalent bonds. When electrically charged atoms or ions are present in a chemical solution—a mixture of liquid chemicals—reactions occur more quickly than when atoms with covalent bonds are involved.

States of matter. A particular element or compound may react at a different speed, depending on whether it is in solid, liquid, or gas form. For example, a

---

chemical kinetics: the study of how outside forces affect the rate at which a chemical reaction takes place

mixture of dry powdered potassium sulfate and barium nitrate can sit around in a jar forever without reacting. However, when these two chemicals are mixed in a liquid **solution,** a chemical reaction occurs. The substance that results, or the *product*, is barium sulfate.

Size of the reactants. *Reactants* are substances that combine chemically to make a product. A reactant will combine chemically more quickly if it is introduced in powdered or liquid form than it will if it is put into the solution in one large piece.

Concentration of the reactants. The **concentration** of a solution is the amount of a dissolved substance in a measured amount of water or other solvent. A solution of one teaspoon of potassium sulfate and one teaspoon of barium nitrate in a gallon of water is very weak. Very little reaction would occur between these chemicals. As you added more reactants, the reaction would speed up as more molecules collided. Not all collisions result in chemical reactions, but when more molecules are present, they collide with other molecules much more often. Thus, the reaction occurs more quickly.

Temperature. Temperature affects chemical reaction rates because molecules need energy in order to react. The energy that is necessary to start a chemical reaction is called *activation energy*. Heat is a familiar source of activation energy. Heat used in cooking speeds up chemical reactions because at higher temperatures more molecules have the activation energy they need to start reacting. On the other hand, keeping food in the refrigerator slows down the chemical reactions we know as spoilage.

Adding a catalyst. *Catalysts* are chemicals that are added to chemical reactions to make them proceed faster. A catalyst encourages a chemical reaction to occur in some alternative way that will allow the reaction to move more quickly or, occasionally, more slowly than normal. During this process, the catalyst does not change or react.

You may have a catalytic converter in your car. It is an antipollution device that contains powdered inert metals and metal oxides. These substances encourage unburned fuel and carbon monoxide to burn completely.

Exercise 3

1. Each of the following is an example of a chemical reaction <u>except</u>

   (1) boiling water
   (2) frying an egg
   (3) bleaching fabric
   (4) burning charcoal
   (5) food spoilage

2. In certain pea and bean plants, chemicals called enzymes allow the plants to obtain nitrogen from the atmosphere and convert it to ammonia. The plants use ammonia to manufacture proteins. The enzymes in this process are an example of

   (1) oxidation at low speed
   (2) ions increasing the rate of a reaction
   (3) an increased concentration of reactants speeding a reaction
   (4) a catalyst making a reaction possible
   (5) temperature affecting the rate of a reaction

3. Fermentation is the chemical reaction that produces alcohol in wine or beer. In a winery, a fermenting tank of wine is sheathed in a metal jacket containing coolant. Often, the tank is equipped with a thermometer that gives a continuous digital readout of the temperature. Which of the following is the best explanation for this attention to temperature?

   (1) Wine should be chilled.
   (2) The wine maker wants to control the rate of fermentation.
   (3) A catalyst is acting on the wine.
   (4) Cool temperatures increase the quantity of wine.
   (5) The grape juice gets more concentrated when it is cool.

solution: a liquid or a gas that contains another substance with which it is not chemically united

concentration: the amount of a substance in a measured amount of another substance

4. The graph below describes the change in the quantity of chemical reactants during a chemical reaction.

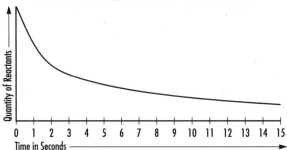

REACTANT QUANTITY OVER TIME

According to the graph, the quantity of reactants

(1) decreases over time
(2) increases over time
(3) increases and then decreases
(4) does not change
(5) increases halfway through the reaction

To check your answers, turn to page 232.

Solutions

Ocean water is a solution. A *solution* is a uniform mixture of one substance with another. In seawater, solid salt particles *dissolve*, or combine with water, so completely that they are invisible. Water is the *solvent*, the liquid that does the dissolving. Salt, the dissolved substance, is the *solute*.

Water is so good at dissolving other substances that chemists call it a universal solvent. As water travels over land and through rivers, it dissolves mineral salts that are naturally part of the soil and carries them out to sea.

In a solution, two or more distinct chemicals exist together in a uniform mixture. The salt in ocean water exists in the form of ions: positively charged sodium (Na) ions and negatively charged chlorine (Cl) ions. When the water evaporates, the positive and negative ions attract each other. They rejoin to form solid salt crystals known as sea salt. People collect sea salt by sending ocean water into shallow ponds and letting the water evaporate.

A solid dissolved in a liquid is a common type of solution; however, other types of solutions exist. A gas can dissolve in a liquid to form a solution. Picture the bubbles in a glass of soda pop. A soda drink is a solution of carbon dioxide gas dissolved in a flavored liquid. The bubbles are actually carbon dioxide surrounded by a thin film of liquid.

COMPOSITION OF AIR

Gas	Percent
Nitrogen (N_2)	78%
Oxygen (O_2)	21%
Argon (Ar)	0.93%
Neon (Ne)	0.002%
Helium (He)	0.0005%
Methane (CH_4)	0.0002%
Krypton (Kr)	0.0001%
Hydrogen (H_2)	0.00005%
Nitrous oxide (N_2O)	0.00005%
Xenon (Xe)	0.000009%

Many familiar mixtures are solutions. Air is actually a solution consisting of a mixture of gases. The chart above lists the individual elements and compounds in air. Notice that over 99 percent of air is a mixture of nitrogen, oxygen, and argon. The other chemicals are present in extremely tiny amounts.

Any time a GED question mentions a mixture or a solution, the parts of that substance are not chemically united. No chemical bonds are made or broken in a solution or mixture. Your understanding of the difference between a mixture and a chemical compound will help you answer the question.

Equilibrium

Chemists describe chemical reactions by writing chemical equations. The left side of an equation shows the *reactants*, the substances that undergo chemical change. The right side shows the *products*, the substances that are formed as a result of the chemical change. In the equation below, the reactants hydrogen and chlorine form the product hydrogen chloride.

$$H_2 + Cl_2 \rightarrow 2HCl$$
Reactants   Product

Most chemical reactions are reversible: the reactants do not completely change into products, and the products can change back into the reactants. When the reactants form products at the same rate that the products form reactants, the system is in **chemical equilibrium.** Reversible reactions are shown with double arrows. An example is shown below.

$$A + B \rightleftharpoons C + D$$
Reactants   Products

---

chemical equilibrium: the point at which a chemical reaction occurs at the same time and at the same rate as its opposing reaction

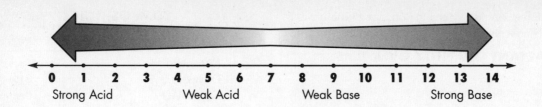

| 0 | 1 | 2 | 3 | 4 | 5 | 6 | 7 | 8 | 9 | 10 | 11 | 12 | 13 | 14 |

Strong Acid   Weak Acid   Weak Base   Strong Base

Chemical equilibrium can be upset in any of the following ways:

Changing the concentrations of the chemicals. If you add more *reactants* to a chemical system in equilibrium, the reaction will flow more quickly in the direction of the products. If you add more *products*, the reaction will flow in the direction of the reactants.

Increasing pressure on a gas. Gas molecules tend to spread out as far as they can, leaving lots of empty space between molecules. Chemists increase pressure on a gas by forcing it into a smaller container. Increasing the pressure on a gas makes the formation of *reactants* occur more quickly. Decreasing pressure, by allowing the gas to occupy a larger volume, makes the formation of *products* occur more quickly.

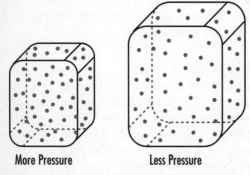

More Pressure   Less Pressure

Adding heat. A chemical reaction that gives off heat while it forms chemical products is called an *exothermic reaction*. Most chemical reactions are exothermic. Adding heat to an exothermic chemical reaction causes it to form more reactants. Lowering the temperature in an exothermic reaction causes an increase in products.

A chemical reaction that takes in heat while it forms chemical products is called an *endothermic reaction*. Heating an endothermic reaction causes it to form additional products. Cooling causes an endothermic reaction to form more reactants.

Introducing a catalyst. A catalyst changes the amount of time it takes to establish equilibrium. Although a catalyst changes the rate of the reaction, it does not favor either the forward direction (toward products) or the reverse direction (toward reactants).

Acids and Bases

You may have heard of hydrochloric acid, sulfuric acid, or nitric acid. **Acids** are chemicals with very special characteristics, including the ability to dissolve substances. **Bases** are chemicals that can neutralize acids.

Acids are known for their sour taste and for dissolving many substances. When put in solutions with water, acids dissolve and form *hydrogen ions* ($H+$). Bases have a bitter taste and are slippery to the touch. In a solution with water, bases form *hydroxide ions* ($OH-$). The *pH scale* measures the strength of an acid or a base. The entire pH scale ranges from 0 to 14. On the pH scale, water is neutral, with a pH of 7. Acids give readings below 7. Acids can be strong or weak. A pH of 1 or 2 designates a strong acid, whereas a pH of 5 or 6 indicates a weak acid. Bases have pH readings greater than 7.

Acetic acid, commonly called vinegar, is an example of a weak acid that may be a part of your diet. Hydrochloric acid is a very strong acid that is naturally present in your stomach and helps you digest food.

The word *hydroxide* in a chemical name indicates that the substance is a base. Bases are actually a bigger part of your life than you might suspect. Soaps are mild bases, and bleach is an even stronger base. (See the figure at the top of this page.)

When your stomach hurts, you may take an antacid. An antacid is a base that neutralizes excess stomach acid. When acids and bases react chemically, salt, a neutral compound, is formed. Water—also neutral—is produced as well. Here's an example of an acid/base reaction.

HCl	+	$NaOH$	→	$NaCl$	+	H_2O
Hydrochloric		Sodium		Sodium		Water
Acid		Hydroxide		Chloride		

acid: a substance which, when in solution, has a pH less than 7

base: a substance which, when in solution, has a pH greater than 7

Exercise 4

> **Directions**
> Choose the <u>one best answer</u> to each item.

1. Which of the following solutions is an example of a solid dissolved in a liquid?

   (1) carbonated water
   (2) champagne
   (3) sugar water
   (4) vinegar
   (5) ammonia

2. Which of the following terms best describes the role of water in salt water?

   (1) solvent
   (2) ion
   (3) atom
   (4) element
   (5) solute

3. Study this chemical equation:

   $$H_2 + I_2 \rightleftharpoons 2HI$$

   Which of the examples below does this equation represent?

   (1) an upset in equilibrium
   (2) a reversible reaction
   (3) increased concentration of reactants
   (4) decreased volume of reactants
   (5) increased pressure placed on reactants

> Item 4 refers to the following information.

The pH readings of certain substances are listed below.

Substance	pH
stomach acid	2
soda	2.3
coffee	2.8
beer	4.8
pond water	8
ammonia	11

4. Which of the following substances is the strongest acid?

   (1) stomach acid
   (2) soda
   (3) coffee
   (4) beer
   (5) ammonia

5. Which of the following substances is a base?

   (1) orange juice
   (2) calcium hydroxide
   (3) aspirin
   (4) vinegar
   (5) silver chloride

6. Which of the following factors would have the <u>least</u> effect on the equilibrium of a chemical reaction involving liquid reactants?

   (1) increasing the concentration of a reactant
   (2) adding heat
   (3) introducing a catalyst
   (4) increasing pressure
   (5) cooling

7. Which of the following situations occurs when you have a fever?

   (1) The chemicals in your body stop reacting.
   (2) The chemicals in your body become less concentrated.
   (3) The pressure increases on the reactants in your body.
   (4) The chemical changes in your body happen more slowly.
   (5) The chemical changes in your body happen more quickly.

8. An acid can be neutralized by adding a base. An indicator is a chemical that changes color at a specific pH. In an experiment, an indicator changes color to tell the experimenter when an acid has been neutralized.

   At the beginning of an experiment, an indicator is added to an acid solution, and the solution is clear. When a drop of base is added to the acid solution, the solution turns red. However, the flask is bumped, and the red color goes away. Which of the following conclusions best explains this phenomenon?

   (1) The indicator is not working correctly.
   (2) The bump on the flask has the effect of bleaching the indicator.
   (3) The quantity of base added is insufficient.
   (4) The indicator came apart when the flask was bumped.
   (5) The acid has gone out of the solution.

To check your answers, turn to page 232.

PHYSICS

Motion and Work

A roller coaster can never go as high or travel as fast later in the ride as it does on that first hill. A roller coaster is a good model of how energy, work, and motion interact.

Energy is the ability to do work. *Work* is the use of force to move something over a distance. Energy exists in many forms and can change from one form to another, but the total amount of energy always stays the same.

At the start of a roller-coaster ride, you are sitting still in a car. **Inertia** will keep you there all day unless an outside force intervenes. The motor that drags you up the hill provides the work you need to get started. A *force* is a push or a pull. You need to apply force to get the roller coaster up the hill. You can calculate the force you need by multiplying the mass you need to lift (the cars and the people) by the *acceleration* (the roller coaster's change of speed).

Sir Isaac Newton, the seventeenth-century English physicist, said that for every action there is an equal and opposite reaction. While the engine pulls the roller coaster up the hill, the roller coaster exerts its own downward force on the engine.

At the top of the first hill, the electrical energy of the motor changes into a stored force called **potential energy.** As the roller coaster screams downhill, the stored or potential energy changes to **kinetic energy.** This exchange between potential energy and kinetic energy keeps the roller coaster moving up and down over the tracks. As the wheels rub against the steel rails, **friction** slows the cars to an eventual halt.

Sir Isaac Newton developed these three laws of motion.

1. Every body (object) remains in a state of rest or of uniform motion in a straight line unless acted on by an outside force.
2. Force equals mass times acceleration. (F = M × A)
3. For every action there is an equal and opposite reaction.

Heat can be used to do work. It is a type of energy that comes from the vibration or movement of molecules. More vibration creates more heat.

Thermodynamics is the study of the movement of heat. The *first law of thermodynamics* states that heat energy cannot be created or destroyed. Instead, the energy changes form. In a steam, turbine, or jet engine, heat energy is changed to mechanical energy.

The *second law of thermodynamics* states that heat naturally flows from a hot place to a cold place. The temperature difference between the hot place and the cold place represents the energy available to power the engine. Engine designers would love it if all this heat energy could be turned into work. This never happens, however, because some heat is lost through the friction of engine parts rubbing against each other and some heat escapes to the outside world.

---

inertia: the tendency of an object to remain either at rest or in motion

---

potential energy: energy that is stored and is capable of being changed into another form of energy

---

kinetic energy: the energy of motion

---

friction: resistance to motion due to surface rubbing

Exercise 1

Directions

Choose the one best answer to each item.

1. During the launching of a rocket, the exploding fuel leaves the rocket and exerts a force on the rocket that sends it skyward. Which of the following statements best explains this phenomenon?

   (1) An object tends to remain at rest or in motion.
   (2) Potential energy is the capacity to do work.
   (3) For every action, there is an equal and opposite reaction.
   (4) Movement energy can dissipate in the form of heat.
   (5) You can use the position and velocity of an object to calculate its future position and velocity.

2. According to the laws of physics, which person is doing the most work?

   (1) a stranded motorist trying to push a truck that will not move
   (2) a construction worker moving a load of bricks
   (3) a doctor listening to a patient's heartbeat
   (4) an artist making an illustration
   (5) a cashier making change

3. According to the second law of thermodynamics, heat moves from a hot place to a cold place. Given this law, which of the following is most likely to occur as you make a snowball?

   (1) The snowball gets colder as it is compacted.
   (2) The warmth from your hands transfers to the snow.
   (3) The movement of your hands causes vibration of the frozen water molecules.
   (4) The temperature of the snow limits the amount of work your body can do.
   (5) Heat is lost through friction.

To check your answers, turn to page 233.

Waves

A wave is a disturbance in a liquid or a gas. Wave behavior is most noticeable on the surface of a liquid. Sound and light also travel in waves.

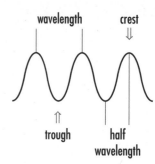

When children toss pebbles into a lake, the resulting pattern in the water is a wave. Although the wave spreads outward, the water moves only up and down when a wave passes. It does not move horizontally. The *crest* of a wave is the point at the top, and the *trough* of a wave is the point at the bottom. *Wavelength* is the distance between the crest of one wave and the crest of the next one. The distance between a crest and the next trough is a half wavelength.

Waves and sound. The number of crests passing a point in one second is called the *frequency* of the wave. Sound waves have high and low frequencies. A high-frequency sound has more waves per second and creates a high sound (like a dog whistle). A low-frequency sound has fewer waves per second and makes a low sound (like a bass drum). The frequency of a wave is measured in hertz. One *hertz* equals one wave per second. The human ear can hear sounds with frequencies ranging from 20 to 20,000 hertz. The range of sounds that a stereo system can reproduce is measured in hertz.

Waves and light. Light also travels in waves. The varying frequency of light waves causes varying colors. Human eyes can detect colors only within a certain frequency range. This range is called the *visible spectrum*, and it includes colors from low-frequency waves (red) to high-frequency waves (violet).

REFLECTION

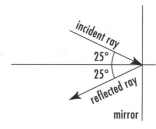

Light normally travels in straight lines or *rays*. When a beam of light hits a flat surface such as a mirror, the light is reflected back. The light ray moving toward the mirror is called the *incident ray*. The ray of light that bounces back is called the *reflected ray*. The angle of the incident ray equals the angle of the reflected ray. The *law of reflection* states that the angle of incidence equals the angle of reflection, as shown in the diagram above.

Exercise 2

> **Directions**
> Choose the <u>one best answer</u> to each item.

1. Which is a true statement?

    (1) The trough is the highest point of the wave.
    (2) Wavelength is the number of crests passing a point in one second.
    (3) The human ear can detect a sound with a frequency of 200 hertz.
    (4) The distance between a crest and the next trough is a wavelength.
    (5) A high-frequency sound has few waves per second.

> Item 2 refers to the diagram below.

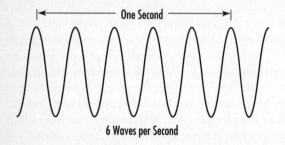

One Second

6 Waves per Second

2. Which of the following terms best describes the wave property illustrated in this diagram?

    (1) compression
    (2) frequency
    (3) visible spectrum
    (4) kinetic energy
    (5) hertz

3. Which of the following statements best explains what happens as the frequency of a wave increases?

    (1) Wave crests and troughs cancel each other.
    (2) Wavelengths become longer.
    (3) Wavelengths become shorter.
    (4) Crest and trough are 0 wavelength apart.
    (5) Frequency cannot be measured in hertz.

4. Which statement best explains why you look taller or thinner in a fun house mirror?

    (1) The mirror reflects the light.
    (2) The curves in the mirror distort the light rays returning to you.
    (3) Light does not travel in a straight line.
    (4) Air is a different medium than glass.
    (5) Light echoes back and forth between the mirror and the walls.

To check your answers, turn to page 233.

Magnetism

Magnetism is the ability of a substance to attract iron and other iron-based metals. The earth is a giant magnet. Like all magnets, it has two *magnetic poles*—north and south ends where the magnetic force is very strong.

The behavior of magnets can be described by the phrase "Opposites attract; likes repel," as shown in the diagram below. The north pole of one magnet attracts the south pole of another magnet. Two north poles move away from or repel each other.

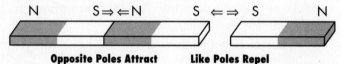

N   S⇒⇐N   S ⇐ ⇒ S   N

Opposite Poles Attract   **Like Poles Repel**

The poles of a magnet exert magnetic force in a *magnetic field*, the area subject to the influence of magnetism. If you sprinkle iron filings around a magnet, the filings line up in the area of the magnetic field. A common example of a magnetic field at work is in a tape recorder. In a tape recorder, a magnetic field aligns particles of metal on a cassette tape to record sound.

Electricity

Electricity is the energy produced by the movement of electrons between atoms. Most people use and experience electricity every day. Electricity takes two forms: **static electricity** and **electric current.**

Static electricity. Static electricity exists when an electric charge rests on an object. You're probably familiar with the small shock caused by static electricity when you shuffle across a carpet or pull off a wool sweater.

Electric current. When electrons flow, they produce an electric current. Electrons can move through solids (especially metals), gases, and liquids such as water. Substances (such as water) that allow an electric charge to flow easily are called *conductors*. Substances that do not conduct electricity, such as glass, porcelain, and plastic, are called *insulators*.

Electricity moves through wires much as water moves through pipes. You can measure the flow of a river by measuring how much water moves past a particular point. The strength of an electric current is measured in *amperes* (amps). An ampere measures how much electric charge moves past a point in one second.

Electric Circuits

An *electric circuit* is a path for electricity. A circuit begins at a power supply, goes through wires and/or electronic devices, and then returns to the power supply. You can think of an electric circuit as a complete circle. If current doesn't pass through the entire circle, the electricity doesn't flow.

SERIES CIRCUIT

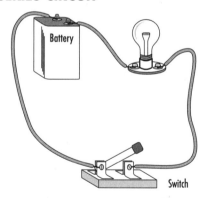

MORE RESISTANCE
Long wire
Narrow wire

LESS RESISTANCE
Short wire
Wide wire

As electricity moves along a wire, it meets electrical resistance, which slows down the flow. Electrical resistance is measured in *ohms*. A metal that is a good conductor has low electrical resistance. Some substances, however, have insulating qualities that offer a lot of resistance to electricity. In some cases, a particular electrical component requires a reduced flow of current, and the manufacturer intentionally puts a resistor in the circuit to control the flow. Resistance differs according to the length and width of the wire.

PARALLEL CIRCUIT

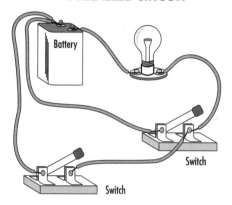

A circuit usually consists of a power source, wires, a switch, and the item you want to power. In a *series circuit*, current must flow through every part of the electrical pathway in order to return to power.

In a *parallel circuit*, the main current is divided into two or more individual pathways, and part of the current goes through each pathway. If any part of a parallel circuit is disconnected, the design of the circuit permits the current to flow through other paths. After following independent pathways, the separate parts of the current are rejoined to complete the circuit.

---

electricity: the occurrence of positively and negatively charged particles of matter at rest and in motion

---

static electricity: an electric charge at rest on an object

---

electric current: the movement of electrons through a wire

Exercise 3

1. You run a comb through your hair on a dry autumn day and hear a crackling sound. Which of the following terms best applies to this phenomenon?

   (1) magnetism
   (2) low humidity
   (3) static electricity
   (4) conductor
   (5) chemical energy

2. The strength of a current is calculated by the following formula:

   $$amps = \frac{quantity \ of \ charge \ (coulombs)}{time \ (seconds)}$$

   Which of the following situations would produce a charge of 100 amps?

   (1) 10 coulombs pass in 1,000 seconds
   (2) 100 coulombs pass in 10 seconds
   (3) 1,000 coulombs pass in 5 seconds
   (4) 1,000 coulombs pass in 10 seconds
   (5) 10,000 coulombs pass in 1,000 seconds

3. While standing at the most northern place on the earth, an explorer takes out her compass and notices that the needle points northeast. She asks her companion to check this by looking at his compass. It also points northeast. Which explanation best accounts for this?

   (1) The temperature is too cold for a compass to work.
   (2) The magnetic north pole is at a different location from the geographic North Pole.
   (3) The compass is too far away from the South Pole for it to detect the earth's magnetic field.
   (4) A compass lines up correctly only at the Equator.
   (5) The earth's magnetic field cannot be detected.

4. A few nails hang in a chain from a magnet. If you pull the magnet away, the nails fall to the ground. Which of the following statements best accounts for this?

   (1) Each nail has become a permanent magnet.
   (2) The magnetic field of the earth is stronger than the field around the magnet.
   (3) Nails tend to repel each other.
   (4) As the magnet moves farther away, its magnetic field becomes stronger.
   (5) As the magnet moves farther away, its magnetic field becomes weaker.

5. Resistance is measured in ohms. You can calculate the resistance in a circuit using the following formula.

   $$resistance = \frac{volts}{amps}$$

   Which of the following circuits has a resistance of 11 ohms?

   (1) a current of 10 amps on a 220-volt line
   (2) a current of 10 amps on a 110-volt line
   (3) a current of 10 amps on a 2,200-volt line
   (4) a current of 8 amps on a 12-volt line
   (5) a current of 16 amps on a 24-volt line

6. Which of the following terms is best defined as opposition to the flow of electric current?

   (1) ampere
   (2) volt
   (3) resistance
   (4) circuit
   (5) current

7. Which of the following conditions would decrease the resistance of a circuit?

   (1) lengthening the wire
   (2) replacing a thin wire with a thicker one
   (3) replacing a conductor with an insulator
   (4) adding a resistor to the circuit
   (5) breaking the circuit

Items 8 and 9 refer to the following information.

Five concepts important to electricity are defined below.

Static electricity: an electric charge resting on an object

Electric current: an electric charge in motion

Conductor: a substance through which an electric charge can flow freely

Insulator: a substance that does not conduct electricity

Earth ground: a safety device that diverts an electric current into the ground

8. Electrical wires are usually coated with plastic. This best illustrates which electrical concept?

    (1) static electricity
    (2) electric current
    (3) conductor
    (4) insulator
    (5) earth ground

9. You start your car and the needle on the gauge marked amps moves to the + sign. This best illustrates which electrical concept?

    (1) static electricity
    (2) electric current
    (3) conductor
    (4) insulator
    (5) earth ground

To check your answers, turn to page 233.

Part 3

Answers and Explanations
SCIENCE

Unit 1: Life Science

Exercise 1 (page 196)

1. **The correct answer is (4): (Comprehension)** Choice (4) is correct because mitochondria are the organelles responsible for energy production.

2. **The correct answer is (4): (Evaluation)** Choice (4) is the only one that establishes a direct link between export of material and the presence of Golgi bodies.

3. **The correct answer is (2): (Comprehension)** Choice (2) best sums up the main idea of the diagram.

4. **The correct answer is (1): (Application)** According to the diagram, the most variable phase of the life cycle is the gap between the end of mitosis and the beginning of DNA synthesis; this interval is labeled G1.

Exercise 2 (page 197)

1. **The correct answer is (3): (Comprehension)** Light energy is used to separate water into hydrogen and oxygen. This begins the process of photosynthesis.

2. **The correct answer is (2): (Comprehension)** Choice (2) is the best answer. Choice (1) is the reverse of what the lesson says; choice (3) is contradicted by the text; choice (4) is not true; choice (5) is too general to be a good answer.

3. **The correct answer is (3): (Analysis)** Since fermentation is a form of anaerobic respiration, we know from the passage that it takes place only when the cell cannot get enough oxygen for aerobic respiration. It follows that fermentation could not take place if choice (3), oxygen, were present.

4. **The correct answer is (5): (Application)** Of all the choices, (5) is the most plausible. Choice (1) does mention one of the products of fermentation, but it contradicts what we know about bread—that it is not filled with alcohol. There is not enough information to support choice (2). Choices (3) and (4) refer to lactic acid, which is produced by anaerobic respiration in animals, not in plants. Only choice (5) is a sensible explanation involving one of the products of fermentation.

Exercise 3 (page 199)

1. **The correct answer is (2): (Analysis)** The diagram shows that the hypocotyl first breaks through the ground and then straightens up to become the stem of the plant.

2. **The correct answer is (5): (Analysis)** The drawing shows that the cotyledons wither away once they are no longer needed.

3. **The correct answer is (4): (Application)** Sudden changes can accompany fertilization in a flowering plant. Choice (4) refers to fertilization.

4. **The correct answer is (3): (Comprehension)** Of the five types of vertebrates listed in the chart, reptiles and birds are the only two with all of the same factors in their reproduction and development methods.

5. **The correct answer is (5): (Comprehension)** According to the table, surgical sterilization has the lowest failure rate, which means that this method is the most reliable in preventing pregnancy.

Exercise 4 (page 202)

1. **The correct answer is (1): (Comprehension)** Because germ cell mutations occur in the cells used for sexual reproduction, it follows that these mutations would show up in the offspring. Choice (2) is incorrect: mutations that occur during mitosis are called somatic. Choices (3), (4), and (5) are incorrect based on the information given.

2. **The correct answer is (4): (Application)** A germ cell mutation would take place only in the part of the body where sex cells are produced. The ovary is the only body part listed that is involved in sexual reproduction.

3. **The correct answer is (2): (Application)** Of the choices presented, choices (1), (3), and (5) have nothing to do with genetics; choice (4) is caused by a genetic disorder but is not a life-threatening problem. Only choice (2) seems a likely candidate.

4. **The correct answer is (1): (Evaluation)** Because the key concept of the theory of evolution is that species change over the years, the best evidence would be evidence of long-term change. The ages of the fossils would prove that this kind of change has been taking place for millions of years.

5. **The correct answer is (1): (Comprehension)** Choice (1) best restates the role of competition in the process of natural selection. Choices (2) and (3) contradict the text. Choice (4) is wrong about the role of competition. Choice (5) is too vague a statement to be a good answer.

Exercise 5 *(page 205)*

1. **The correct answer is (4): (Comprehension)** Correctly following the sequence as described and shown in the diagram on page 203 should lead you to select choice (4). The other choices trace the airflow in incorrect order.

2. **The correct answer is (1): (Comprehension)** The bar on the graph for a newborn baby's heartbeat rises to the number 140. The bar for an adult's heartbeat rises to the number 70: $2 \times 70 = 140$. The other choices are all based on inaccurate readings of the graph.

3. **The correct answer is (2): (Comprehension)** Close study of the text and the illustration of the digestive system should lead you to select choice (2). None of the other choices accurately answers the question.

4. **The correct answer is (5): (Application)** The information in the text about the function of fiber should lead you to select choice (5). Fiber helps push food along the intestines and eliminate wastes from the body.

5. **The correct answer is (4): (Application)** The breakfast in choice (4) contains whole-grain cereal, a fruit, and a nonfat dairy product. The other choices are high in fat, which is not recommended in the Food Guide Pyramid. In addition, doughnuts and maple syrup are loaded with sugar. Coffee has no nutritional value.

Exercise 6 *(page 207)*

1. **The correct answer is (1): (Comprehension)** The diagram shows that algae—microscopic plants in the first link of the food chain—produce their own food by capturing energy from the sun (photosynthesis). All the other choices are animals that are unable to produce their own food.

2. **The correct answer is (1): (Analysis)** This is the only choice that analyzes the food relationships and distribution of energy within a food chain. Choice (2) describes the illustration but does not analyze the food relationships. Choice (3) is an incomplete analysis, because it focuses on just the first link in the food chain. Choice (4) mentions only part of the chain. Choice (5) is incomplete, because it does not separate the organisms into plants and animals.

3. **The correct answer is (3): (Analysis)** A forest fire started by lightning is the only choice that begins with an act of nature. The other choices are all results of human activities.

4. **The correct answer is (4): (Application)** Curare relaxes the muscles and makes them incapable of moving, so it would be useful in setting broken bones; the patient would be unable to move and disturb the position of the bone. Choices (1) and (5) are incorrect because in these situations one would not want muscle paralysis to occur. Choices (2) and (3) refer to parts of the body that are not affected by curare.

5. **The correct answer is (2): (Evaluation)** In underdeveloped tropical rain forest countries, the rain forests are the basic sources of land, food, and various products for the poor people. When present economic survival depends on using the rain forests, the long-term benefits of not using them seem far less important. None of the other choices is true.

6. **The correct answer is (3): (Analysis)** Because they have been bred and raised in captivity, the macaques are not used to life in the wild. To prepare them for release in the wild, the zoo is teaching them skills they will need to fend for themselves. Choices (1) and (2) may or may not be by-products of such training, but they are not its purpose. Choices (4) and (5) are not related to the teaching of wilderness skills.

Unit 2: Earth Science

Exercise 1 *(page 210)*

1. **The correct answer is (1): (Analysis)** As the earth rotates, it is day on the part facing the sun, and it is night on the part facing away from the sun. Choices (2) and (3) are incorrect because the seasons do not depend on the daily rotation of the earth. Choice (4) has nothing to do with the rotation of the earth. Choice (5) is incorrect because the fact that different stars are visible in the two hemispheres is a result of their facing different areas of the galaxy.

2. **The correct answer is (4): (Analysis)** According to the information given in the question, the time it takes Jupiter to revolve around the sun must be greater than the time it takes the earth (1 year) and less than the time it takes Pluto (248 years), because Jupiter is farther from the sun than earth but closer than Pluto. The only choice between those times is choice (4), or 12 years.

3. **The correct answer is (1): (Evaluation)** Unmanned spacecraft are more practical than manned spacecraft. Because they do not have to keep people alive in the vacuum of space, they cost less to design, build, and operate.

Exercise 2 *(page 211)*

1. **The correct answer is (1): (Analysis)** The volcano must have previously erupted for the lava and ash to accumulate on the outside. The other choices are not logical.

2. **The correct answer is (1): (Evaluation)** The diagram shows that some magma moves out from the central cylinder. It makes sense that the magma builds up and creates a dome. Choice (2) is not probable based on the diagram. Choices (3), (4), and (5) are not possible.

3. **The correct answer is (4): (Analysis)** Of the reasons given, only A and B involve heat. Warm oil and hot air deep in the earth are evidence that the temperature rises with depth.

4. **The correct answer is (4): (Comprehension)** According to the text, the lightest materials moved to the surface when the earth was taking shape, and the heaviest sank. The surface layer of the earth is the crust.

Exercise 3 *(page 214)*

1. **The correct answer is (1): (Analysis)** Although our store of fossil fuels may soon be depleted, the process that formed them continues.

2. **The correct answer is (2): (Evaluation)** Peat is the first stage of coal formation. Because farmers are now finding peat in Ireland, the conditions under which coal starts to form must have existed in the past. If choice (1) were true, it is likely that coal, not peat, would be found in Ireland. Choices (3) through (5) may or may not be true, but the information given does not support them.

3. **The correct answer is (5): (Comprehension)** According to the lesson, an ore is a mineral that contains metal.

4. **The correct answer is (3): (Application)** Because titanium is lightweight and very strong, it is useful in aircraft frames. The other choices are incorrect because in these objects the properties of light weight and strength are not particularly important.

5. **The correct answer is (2): (Comprehension)** The diagram shows solar energy being used to produce water vapor from sea water. When the vapor condenses, fresh water flows into a catch basin.

6. **The correct answer is (2): (Application)** Although the system produces fresh water, it appears too small to supply a large city. Also, to use ocean water, the plant must be on a coast. Choices (3) through (5) are incorrect because they do not involve the production of fresh water.

Unit 3: Chemistry

Exercise 1 (page 217)

1. **The correct answer is (5): (Application)** To form ammonia, nitrogen and hydrogen are chemically united.

2. **The correct answer is (5): (Analysis)** The formation of carbon dioxide is the only example of a chemical change. Carbon dioxide has chemical properties that are different from those of the elements carbon and oxygen which combine to form it. Choices (1), (2), and (4) are clearly physical changes. Choice (3) is a physical change—a smaller piece of cheese is still cheese and not some other substance.

3. **The correct answer is (5): (Analysis)** Every element has a unique number of protons, which is indicated by the atomic number.

4. **The correct answer is (3): (Comprehension)** The addition of heat can change a liquid to a gas. The removal of heat can change a gas to a liquid.

5. **The correct answer is (4): (Application)** Choices (1), (2), (3), and (5) all demonstrate changes in state caused by cooling. Choice (4) demonstrates a change in state caused by warming.

6. **The correct answer is (5): (Evaluation)** Matter changes state in response to temperature changes. A thermometer would be most useful in determining the temperatures at which substances underwent changes in state.

7. **The correct answer is (5): (Evaluation)** The interactions of electrons with other atoms explain chemical reactions and many of the physical properties of matter. The way that an atom interacts with other atoms depends on the number of electrons in its outermost shell.

8. **The correct answer is (5): (Application)** Water must be colder than 32° to freeze solid, because 32° is also the melting point of ice.

Exercise 2 (page 219)

1. **The correct answer is (2): (Comprehension)** Choice (2) correctly defines a chemical bond. No other choice is accurate.

2. **The correct answer is (1): (Comprehension)** An ion is a particle with an electrical charge.

3. **The correct answer is (4): (Analysis)** The attraction between charged particles influences both ionic and covalent bonds. Choices (1), (2), and (3)—gravity, magnetic forces, and hardening—are ways in which *objects* might be held together, but they do not relate to the atom. Atomic nuclei, choice (5), do not hold compounds together.

4. **The correct answer is (2): (Evaluation)** In a covalent bond, the shared electrons are attracted to the positively charged atomic nuclei. This attraction holds the molecule together. Choice (1) describes an ionic bond. Choices (3), (4), and (5) do not explain covalent bonding.

Exercise 3 (page 220)

1. **The correct answer is (1): (Application)** Boiling causes a physical change in water, transforming it from a liquid to a gas (steam). Chemical reactions involve at least two substances that react so that a new substance, or product, is formed. Choices (2), (3), (4), and (5) are all examples of chemical reactions.

2. **The correct answer is (4): (Analysis)** The enzymes function as catalysts: they enable the plant to convert nitrogen to ammonia. The other choices do not correctly identify the function of the enzymes.

3. **The correct answer is (2): (Analysis)** Temperature is one factor that affects the rate of a chemical reaction. The use of coolant and continuous temperature readout indicate the importance of temperature in the process of fermentation.

4. **The correct answer is (1): (Evaluation)** The downward slope over time shows that the reactants are used up as time progresses during a chemical reaction.

Exercise 4 (page 223)

1. **The correct answer is (3): (Application)** To make the solution sugar water, the solid sugar is dissolved in water.

2. **The correct answer is (1): (Comprehension)** Water is the solvent in salt water. Choices (2), (3), and (4) refer to other chemical concepts. Choice (5), *solute*, defines the role of salt in salt water.

3. **The correct answer is (2): (Comprehension)** The double arrow in this equation shows that this reaction is reversible. The other answers all refer to situations that might cause a reaction to reverse.

4. **The correct answer is (1): (Application)** Since stomach acid is the substance with the lowest pH on the chart, it is the strongest acid listed.

5. **The correct answer is (2): (Comprehension)** As stated in the text, the term *hydroxide* in the name of the chemical categorizes it as a base. The other substances are mostly acids; silver chloride, choice (5), is a salt.

6. **The correct answer is (4): (Analysis)** Liquids cannot be compressed very much, and increasing pressure should have no great effect on chemical equilibrium. All of the other choices describe techniques that would upset equilibrium in a reaction involving liquid reactants.

7. **The correct answer is (5): (Analysis)** When you have a fever, your body temperature increases. Added heat causes the chemical changes in your body to occur more quickly. None of the other choices has any basis in fact.

8. **The correct answer is (3): (Evaluation)** When enough of the base has been added to achieve the pH that the indicator detects, the color change will be permanent.

Unit 4: Physics

Exercise 1 *(page 225)*

1. **The correct answer is (3): (Application)** The downward force of the exploding fuel produces an equal and opposite reaction—the skyward movement of the rocket. Although the other statements are true explanations of situations in physics, they do not apply to this example.

2. **The correct answer is (2): (Analysis)** The construction worker is moving the heaviest load and, according to the laws of physics, is doing the most work. None of the others is moving as heavy a load. The stranded motorist is not moving anything and thus is doing no work.

3. **The correct answer is (2): (Comprehension)** Heat flows from warm to cold. None of the other choices reflects the second law of thermodynamics.

Exercise 2 *(page 226)*

1. **The correct answer is (3): (Comprehension)** The human ear can detect sounds with frequencies from 20 to 20,000 hertz.

2. **The correct answer is (2): (Application)** The diagram illustrates frequency. Hertz is the unit used to measure frequency. The other terms are concepts in physics but are not related to the diagram in any way.

3. **The correct answer is (3): (Analysis)** High-frequency waves have shorter wavelengths. None of the other statements is accurate.

4. **The correct answer is (2): (Evaluation)** Curves in a mirror distort the reflected light rays. None of the other answers provides an explanation of the distortion.

Exercise 3 *(page 228)*

1. **The correct answer is (3): (Application)** Static electricity causes the crackling sound you hear when you comb your hair on a dry day. Choices (1), (4), and (5) have nothing to do with this phenomenon. There is low humidity in the air on a dry day, but low humidity does not make the crackling sound as suggested in choice (2).

2. **The correct answer is (4): (Evaluation)** A charge of 1,000 coulombs divided by 10 seconds equals 100 amps. None of the other situations would produce this answer.

3. **The correct answer is (2): (Analysis)** The magnetic north pole is at a slightly different location from the geographic North Pole, so even when standing at the most northern place on the earth, you would not see the magnet pointing straight down. Neither temperature nor distance from the pole would affect this. Choices (4) and (5) are not true.

4. **The correct answer is (5): (Analysis)** The nails fall to the ground because the magnetic field of the magnet becomes weaker as it is pulled away from the nails. There is no evidence to support choice (1). The force of gravity pulls the nails to the floor—not the magnetic field of the earth, as described in choice (2). Choices (3) and (4) are not true.

5. **The correct answer is (2): (Evaluation)** A potential difference of 110 volts divided by 10 amps = 11 ohms. All of the other circuits have different resistance values.

6. **The correct answer is (3): (Comprehension)** Resistance is the term that means opposition to the flow of electric current. The other terms, although relevant to the subject of electricity, have different meanings.

7. **The correct answer is (2): (Comprehension)** Thick wire offers less resistance than thin wire. When you replace a thin wire with a thicker one, the resistance in the circuit goes down. Choices (1), (3), and (4) would increase the resistance. Choice (5) would stop the flow of electricity.

8. **The correct answer is (4): (Application)** The plastic coatings insulate the wires so that electricity is confined to the wires. In preventing the electric current from passing through alternate paths, the plastic covering acts as an insulator.

9. **The correct answer is (2): (Application)** The amp gauge measures electric current. Starting your car initiates the flow of electricity from the battery to the starter, which is a drain on electric current from the battery. Once the alternator begins working, it feeds electric current back to the battery, and you see the amp gauge move to "+."

Part 4

INTERPRETING LITERATURE AND THE ARTS

RED ALERT

WHAT WILL I FIND ON THE INTERPRETING LITERATURE AND ARTS TEST?

The GED Interpreting Literature and the Arts Test—Test Four on the GED—measures your ability to understand, analyze, and respond to ideas found in works of literature. In other words, you will interpret thoughts and feelings expressed in writing by other people. The following information will help you understand what you will find on the Interpreting Literature and the Arts Test.

The GED Interpreting Literature and the Arts Test is *not* a measurement of how much you know about literary history, techniques, or writers. It does *not* ask you to identify writers or remember when a work of literature was written. Finally, it does *not* contain trick questions designed to make you doubt your impressions and opinions about a literature passage. Most questions on the test ask you to think logically and carefully about what a writer is communicating to you.

The Interpreting Literature and the Arts Test uses material taken from three types of literature: popular literature, classical literature, and commentary on the arts.

- **Popular literature** is recent literature, written in the past few decades.

- **Classical literature** is older literature, most often written more than fifty years ago. It is generally of high quality.

- **Commentary on the arts** may include a book or movie review, or a newspaper article about the work of an artist. A commentary is simply one person's thoughts about another person's artistic expression.

When you take the test, you will have 65 minutes to answer forty-five multiple-choice questions. Each set of multiple-choice questions relates to a literature passage that is 200–400 words in length (generally no longer than half a page). To give you an idea of what each passage is about, each passage begins with a *purpose question*. For example, a passage about someone's experiences on the first day of a new job might ask as its purpose question, "Why is This Day Important?" or "What Happens at This New Job?"

Each of the forty-five questions on the test is multiple choice. These questions will ask you to *comprehend, apply,* or *analyze*. For example, you will be asked to identify main ideas, apply information to new situations, and analyze the tone or mood of a passage.

Comprehension questions comprise 60 percent of the Interpreting Literature and the Arts Test. These items are split evenly between two types of comprehension questions: literal comprehension and inferential comprehension. Literal comprehension questions ask you to restate and summarize information and ideas that are directly stated in a passage. *Inferential comprehension* questions ask you to identify implications, understand consequences, and draw conclusions about information that is stated only indirectly.

Read the following passage, then take a look at the literal comprehension and inferential comprehension questions that follow.

WHAT DISCOVERY WILL AFFECT BUCK'S LIFE?

Line Buck did not read the newspapers, or he would
have known that trouble was brewing, not
alone for himself, but for every tidewater dog,
strong of muscle and with warm, long hair,
5   from Puget Sound to San Diego. Because men,
groping in the Arctic darkness, had found a
yellow metal, and because steamships and
transportation companies were booming the
find, thousands of men were rushing into the
10   Northland. These men wanted dogs, and the
dogs they wanted were heavy dogs, with strong
muscles by which to toil, and furry coats to
protect them from the frost.
                         —From *The Call of the Wild* by Jack
15   London

1. Based on the information in this passage, which of the following best describes Buck?

    (1) a strong man who does not read newspapers
    (2) a supporting character who loves dogs
    (3) the owner of dozens of sled dogs
    (4) a character who happens to be a dog
    (5) one of thousands of men rushing north to find work

Lines 2-4 reveal the answer to this literal comprehension question: ". . . trouble was brewing, not alone for himself, but for every tidewater dog, strong of muscle and with warm, long hair. . . ." This tells you directly that Buck is a dog. The other choices imply that Buck is a person, so choice (4) is correct.

2. Based on lines 5-9, you can infer that the "yellow metal" is most likely

    (1) bronze
    (2) gold
    (3) silver
    (4) copper
    (5) diamonds

This question asks that you make an inference, or a logical judgment, about a phrase in this passage. In lines 5-9, you read that thousands of men are rushing north to mine a "yellow metal." From this information, you could infer that this metal must be extremely valuable. The only precious "yellow metal" mentioned in the choices is gold, but the speaker never states this fact directly. You use the information you have to make an inference. Choice (2) is correct.

Application questions comprise 15 percent of the test. These items ask you to use information and ideas from a passage in a different situation. For example, you might be asked how a certain character might behave in an entirely different situation based on the information in this passage.

HOW DOES BUCK BEHAVE AT HOME?

And over this great demesne Buck ruled. Here he was born, and here he had lived the four years of his life. It was true, there were other dogs. There could not but be other dogs on so vast a place, but they did not count.
                         —From *The Call of the Wild* by Jack London

3. Based on this description of Buck's behavior, which of the following people is most similar to Buck?

    (1) a man who fears his environment
    (2) a person who moves from place to place
    (3) a cruel, feared ruler
    (4) the owner of an animal shelter
    (5) a strong, confident leader

This passage tells us that Buck "ruled" the place where he had spent his whole life. He did not doubt his right to rule—other dogs "did not count"—but fear and cruelty are not mentioned. Therefore, choice (5) is correct.

Finally, **analysis** questions comprise 25 percent of the test. These questions ask you to examine the style or structure of a passage and decide what effect these elements have on the ideas that are expressed.

NONFICTION

In this unit, you'll practice reading and interpreting **nonfiction**, or factual writing about real people, places, and events. A sports magazine article about Shaquille O'Neal, a newspaper story that takes a behind-the-scenes look at a popular TV show, and a biography of John F. Kennedy are all examples of nonfiction.

Finding a Topic and Main Idea

Whether you're reading a memo from your boss, a letter from a friend, or a literature passage on the GED Test, one of the first questions you'll probably ask is *What is this about?*—in other words, *What is the topic?* The topic of an article or story is simply its subject. Identifying the topic of a passage will lead you to the writer's main idea. The **main idea** is the central point or idea that the writer wants to communicate. A main idea may be stated directly, or it may be unstated but strongly suggested.

Like a *stated* main idea, an *unstated* or *implied* main idea is also the writer's most important point. To identify an unstated main idea on the GED Test, ask yourself these questions:

• What is the topic? How can I tell?

• What do the supporting details say about that topic?

• What central idea or point do the details make clear?

If a main idea is stated directly, it often appears in the first or last sentence of a passage. The rest of the sentences in a passage are **supporting details** that give more information about the main idea.

---

nonfiction: writing about real people, places, and events (such as journals, newspaper stories, biographies, essays)

---

main idea: the point or idea that a writer wants to communicate

---

supporting detail: fact that provides more information about a main idea

Exercise 1

> **Directions**
>
> Items 1 and 2 refer to the following passage. As you read this passage, ask yourself: What is the author's topic? Then answer the questions.

WHAT HAS THIS DAD LEARNED?

Line Ruben Garcia wishes that, just once, someone would compliment him on his newly polished floor, his freshly ironed shirts, and his tasty pot roast.

5   One of an increasing number of stay-at-home dads, Garcia says he wants a little respect. He cooks, cleans and car-pools for his three children full time with no complaints—and receives little or no recognition for a hard day's work. . .

10   Garcia, 39, a former airline mechanic, was injured on the job in 1985, and has been unable to find similar work. With his wife working as a secretary, he has become a stay-at-home dad.

"I had to adjust to a new way of thinking,"
15 he says. "I had to rearrange my priorities. I was forced to become a mother and a father. By staying at home, I have learned what most men don't learn in a lifetime. When a child first learns to walk, talk, count or dress himself, it's a joyful
20 thing. And when you're away from home all day, you miss it."

—From "Home Bodies" by Pamela Stone

1. Which growing group of people does Ruben Garcia represent?

   (1) dads who work outside the home
   (2) out-of-work airline mechanics
   (3) dads who work two jobs
   (4) dads who stay at home and take care of children
   (5) grandfathers who babysit

2. Which of the following is the best restatement of Garcia's thoughts?

   (1) Working outside the home is exciting.
   (2) Parents who don't work outside the home are lonely.
   (3) Staying at home can be an isolating experience.
   (4) Fathers with nine-to-five jobs don't know their children well.
   (5) Staying at home is simple compared to airline work.

To check your answers, turn to page 267.

Identifying Diction and Tone

The term **diction** refers to word choice. Just as you change your spoken words to make them appropriate for different situations, writers change their diction to clarify and strengthen their ideas. Diction can be casual, formal, informal, conversational, or even full of slang.

As writers make decisions about their diction, they are developing the tone of their writing. **Tone** means the attitude, or feeling, that a passage conveys. The tone of a passage can be funny, scary, impersonal, passionate—anything a writer wants it to be.

The following two sentences show how making different word choices can change the tone of a sentence.

Sentence 1: Chandra listened with *quiet surprise* to her supervisor's *words*; then she *put* down the phone and *walked* into the hall.

Sentence 2: Chandra listened with *stunned astonishment* to her supervisor's *lecture*; then she *slammed* down the phone and *stormed* into the hall.

Another tone that you will find in literature is **irony**. Irony in literature—and in life—happens when there is a startling difference between what you expect to happen and what *actually happens*.

---

diction: word choice; the types of words used by a writer in different situations

tone: the attitude or feeling that a piece of writing conveys

irony: a situation in which there is a startling difference between what is expected to happen and what actually does happen

Exercise 2

Directions

Items 1 to 4 refer to the following passage. It comes from a speech that was given by Lucy Stone at a women's rights convention in 1855. At this time, women were fighting for the right to vote and to be well educated. What is the tone of this speech? What is the writer's attitude toward women's rights? Think about these questions as you read the passage. Then answer the questions.

WHY DOES LUCY STONE FEEL DISAPPOINTED?

Line   The last speaker alluded to this movement as being that of a few disappointed women. From the first years to which my memory stretches, I have been a disappointed woman. When, with my
5   brothers, I reached forth after the sources of knowledge, I was reproved with "It isn't fit for you; it doesn't belong to women." Then there was but one college in the world where women were admitted, and that was in Brazil. I would have
10   found my way there, but by the time I was prepared to go, one was opened in the young State of Ohio—the first in the United States where women and negroes could enjoy opportunities with white men. I was disappointed when I came
15   to seek a profession worthy of an immortal being—every employment was closed to me, except those of the teacher, the seamstress, and the housekeeper. In education, in marriage, in religion, in everything, disappointment is the lot of
20   woman. It shall be the business of my life to deepen this disappointment in every woman's heart until she bows down to it no longer. I wish that women, instead of being walking showcases, instead of begging of their fathers and brothers the
25   latest and gayest new bonnet, would ask of them their rights.

—From "A Disappointed Woman"
by Lucy Stone

1. Based on lines 1–2, you know that Stone

   (1) was the first speaker of the day
   (2) was furious with the previous speaker
   (3) was one of many speakers
   (4) was not listening to the other speakers
   (5) was the most popular speaker

2. Which of the following best restates Stone's statement in lines 2–4?

   (1) She has achieved many of her childhood goals.
   (2) She is on bad terms with her family.
   (3) She had an extremely unhappy childhood.
   (4) She has faced frustrations.
   (5) She does not believe that women will fight for more rights.

3. The tone of this passage could best be described as

   (1) encouraging
   (2) determined
   (3) outraged
   (4) uncertain
   (5) sympathetic

4. By choosing the expression "a profession worthy of an immortal being" (lines 15–16), Stone

   (1) challenges the views of the previous speaker
   (2) expresses her dislike of people who work at "lowly" jobs
   (3) encourages her listeners to set high goals for themselves
   (4) reminds her listeners that women and men are spiritual equals
   (5) says that women are superior to men

To check your answers, turn to page 267.

Recognizing Setting: Time and Place

When you read nonfiction, keep in mind that you're reading about *real* times, places, and events. A nonfiction passage about American pioneers might describe what a frontier town looked like in 1830, whereas a passage about the *Apollo 11* moon landing might describe the astronauts' equipment in 1969. Writers use details like these to tell us about the **setting**—the time and place—in which events occurred.

Distinguishing Fact from Opinion

When a writer of nonfiction wants you to believe something, he or she will almost always include a combination of facts and opinions. A **fact** is something that can be proved beyond the point of reasonable argument. For example, the statement "John F. Kennedy was the first Catholic president of the United States" is a fact. It can be verified, and no one can argue with it. In contrast, the statement "We need a female president" is an **opinion**. Some people might argue against this statement, and their opinions would also be valid. You could support either position, but you could not prove it conclusively.

Identifying Perspective

A **perspective** is the standpoint from which a person views something. Because your life experiences are different from everyone else's, your perspective will also be different. When you read, try to identify the perspective of each person who is mentioned. For example, if you're reading a newspaper story about a grocery store that was robbed, imagine how different the owner's perspective is from the perspective of the robber.

Finding Cause-and-Effect Relationships

In a cause-and-effect relationship, one event (the cause) leads to another event (the effect). For example, smoking (a cause) can lead to health problems (an effect). Furthermore, health problems (a cause) can lead to missing time from work (an effect). Life is filled with causes, or reasons, and effects, or consequences.

Exercise 3

Directions

Items 1 to 3 refer to the following passage. As you read this passage, think about how events changed Harriet Jacobs' life. Then answer the questions.

HOW DOES THIS GIRL'S LIFE CHANGE?

Line When I was nearly twelve years old, my kind mistress sickened and died. As I saw the cheek grow paler, and the eye more glassy, how earnestly I prayed in my heart that she might live!
5 I loved her; for she had been almost like a mother to me. My prayers were not answered. She died, and they buried her in the little churchyard, where day after day, my tears fell upon her grave.

I was sent to spend a week with my
10 grandmother. I was now old enough to begin to think of the future; and again and again I asked myself what they would do with me. I felt sure I should never find another mistress so kind as the one who had gone. She had promised my dying
15 mother that her children should never suffer for anything; and when I remembered that, and recalled her many proofs of attachment to me, I could not help having some hopes that she had left me free. My friends were almost certain it
20 would be so. They thought she would be sure to do it, on account of my mother's love and faithful service. But, alas! we all know that the memory of a faithful slave does not avail much to save her children from the auction block.
25 After a brief period of suspense, the will of my mistress was read, and we learned that she had bequeathed me to her sister's daughter, a child of five years old. So vanished our hopes. My mistress had taught me the precepts of God's Word: "Thou
30 shalt love thy neighbor as thyself." "Whatsoever ye would that men should do unto you, do ye even so unto them." But I was her slave, and I suppose she did not recognize me as her neigh-

---

setting: the time and place in which the action occurs

---

fact: something that can be proved to be true

---

opinion: a belief that cannot be proved absolutely but that can be supported

---

perspective: a way of looking at people, places, and events

bor. I would give much to blot out from my
35 memory that one great wrong. As a child, I loved
my mistress; and, looking back on the happy days
I spent with her, I try to think with less bitterness
of this act of injustice. While I was with her, she
taught me to read and spell; and for this privilege,
40 which so rarely falls to the lot of a slave, I bless
her memory.

—From *Incidents in the Life of a Slave Girl*
by Harriet Jacobs (Linda Brent)

1. One consequence of the reading of the will (lines
25–28) is that the speaker

(1) proves that she is able to read
(2) must go to live with her grandmother
(3) realizes that she is not free
(4) grows to hate her mistress
(5) discovers that she is free

2. Because of this mistress's basic kindness, the
speaker

(1) became an excellent seamstress
(2) was allowed to sit at her mother's deathbed
(3) will never go hungry
(4) must think of the future
(5) can read and spell

3. Which of the following most resembles the
speaker's situation at the end of this passage?

(1) a young mother who is diagnosed with
cancer
(2) a person who accepts certain inevitabilities—
like growing old or dying
(3) an employee who has worked hard but who
has been passed over for a promotion
(4) a high-school graduate on the day of
receiving his or her diploma
(5) a teacher whose students are failing

To check your answers, turn to page 267.

Drawing Conclusions

When you draw a **conclusion** about something, you use
inferential comprehension skills to make a judgment.
When you read, you use information about people,
places, and events to arrive at an idea not directly stated
in the passage. For example, a recently divorced woman
might discuss her ex-husband in a negative light. She
would probably want you to draw the conclusion that her
decision to end her marriage was correct.

Considering New Situations

On the GED Test, certain questions will ask you to apply
information and ideas from a nonfiction passage to new
situations. **Remember:** Application means using knowledge, skills, or information in a new way. One of the best
ways to practice for questions like these is to think about
how you might apply an author's ideas, point of view, or
experiences to your own life.

---

conclusion: a judgment or opinion based on information an author
provides

Exercise 4

Directions

Items 1 to 3 refer to the following passage, in which a Native American leader is speaking to a group of white missionaries. As you read, think about how his thoughts could be applied to more recent situations. Then answer the questions.

WHAT DO RED JACKET'S IDEAS MEAN TODAY?

Line   Brother, listen to what we say. There was a time when our forefathers owned this great island. Their seats extended from the rising to the setting sun. . . .

5   But an evil day came upon us. Your forefathers crossed the great water and landed on this island. Their numbers were small. They found friends and not enemies. . . . They asked us for a small seat. We took pity on them, granted their

10 request, and they sat down among us. We gave them corn and meat; they gave us poison in return. . . .

      At length their numbers had greatly increased. They wanted more land; they wanted our

15 country. Our eyes were opened and our minds became uneasy. Wars took place. . . . They also brought strong liquor among us. It was strong and powerful, and has slain thousands.

      Brothers, our seats were once large and

20 yours were small. You have now become a great people, and we have scarcely a place left to spread our blankets. You have got our country, but are not satisfied; you want to force your religion upon us.

      —From "On the White Man's and Red Man's Religion" by Sagoyewatha (Red Jacket)

1. Which of the following best describes Red Jacket's tone?

   (1) outraged and condescending
   (2) angry, yet polite and in control
   (3) understanding
   (4) frustrated and violent
   (5) patient, yet scared

2. If Red Jacket were living today, he would be most likely to give a speech about

   (1) the importance of preserving Native American culture
   (2) the importance of education in inner cities
   (3) why people of different ages cannot get along
   (4) the federal deficit crisis
   (5) the prevention of AIDS

3. Which of the following would Red Jacket most enjoy seeing today?

   (1) a Native American reservation
   (2) Native Americans in Congress
   (3) the monuments of Washington, D.C.
   (4) environmental activity in the United States
   (5) conflicts among white religious leaders

To check your answers, turn to page 267.

FICTION

The people, places, and events of **fiction** are *imaginary*, created for entertainment and to communicate something about life. Though fiction can be *based* on real people's lives or real events, it is different from nonfiction. A writer of fiction might also add details or exaggerate qualities in people, whereas a writer of nonfiction would not.

Recognizing Setting and Mood

When you begin to read a passage of fiction, you're entering a new world that an author has imagined. You'll want to discover the place you're reading about . . . what it looks like . . . how it makes you feel.

Often the first thing you learn about is the *setting*, the place and time of the story. Knowing the setting helps you analyze the characters' words and actions and understand what's happening.

The setting also helps you recognize the **mood**, or atmosphere, the author creates. Atmosphere is the way a place *feels*. It is the emotional effect created by the setting. For example, think about the feeling each of these settings creates:

- a sunrise in the mountains (hope; expectation)
- a bleak, crumbling castle during a thunderstorm (mystery; horror)
- a cozy fireside in a cabin in the woods (relaxation; romance)

Setting is important to what characters do and say. When you identify a setting, think about how it might influence the events of the story. For example, if the setting is a funeral, the action and events may reflect people's feelings about the person who died and how that death will affect them. Whatever the setting, you can be sure that the writer chose it for a reason.

Understanding Characterization

Sometimes you may hear a comment like, "Oh, my Uncle Frank is such a character!" By this, the person speaking probably means that Uncle Frank is a particularly interesting person with many memorable qualities and habits. In much the same way, **characters** in fiction writing are distinct people with specific qualities of personality and physical appearance. The characters' appearance or basic traits may be based on those of real people, but the characters never actually existed. They come to life through the written word.

Writers describe characters in two ways: by telling us *what the person looks like* and *by showing how the person behaves, or acts*. Both kinds of description help to create a picture of the character in the reader's mind.

fiction: writing about imaginary people and events

mood: the feeling or atmosphere that a piece of writing conveys

characters: the people portrayed in a novel, short story, or drama

Identifying Narrator and Point of View

Perspective is a way of looking at people, events, or issues. In nonfiction, the perspective is usually that of the writer. In fiction, however, the person who tells the story is called the **narrator**. The narrator's perspective is called **point of view**.

For example, if a character named Lee is telling his own story, he might say "I went on a date last Friday" or "I felt lost and worried." In this story, Lee is the narrator, and the story is told from his point of view. We say the story is told in the *first person*. If someone else (an outside observer) is telling the story, however, that person might say "*Lee* went on a date last Friday" or "*He* felt lost and worried." Then the author is telling the story in the *third person*. First person and third person are the two main narrative *voices* in fiction.

narrator: the person or character who tells a story

point of view: the perspective of the narrator

Exercise 1

HOW MIGHT THIS PLACE AFFECT THIS COUPLE'S LIFE?

Line   Although it was only four o'clock, the winter day
was fading. The road led southwest, toward the
streak of pale, watery light that glimmered in the
leaden sky. The light fell upon the two sad young
5   faces that were turned mutely toward it: upon the
eyes of the girl, who seemed to be looking with
such anguished perplexity into the future; upon
the sombre eyes of the boy, who seemed already
to be looking into the past.
10   The little town behind them had vanished as
if it had never been, had fallen behind the swell of
the prairie, and the stern frozen country received
them into its bosom. The homesteads were few
and far apart; here and there a windmill gaunt
15   against the sky, a sod house crouching in a
hollow. But the great fact was the land itself,
which seemed to overwhelm the little beginnings
of human society that struggled in its sombre
wastes. It was from facing this vast hardness that
20   the boy's mouth had become so bitter; because he
felt that men were too weak to make any mark
here, that the land wanted to be let alone, to
preserve its own fierce strength, its peculiar,
savage kind of beauty, its uninterrupted mournful-
25   ness.

          —From *O Pioneers!* by Willa Cather

1. Which of the following best describes this landscape?

    (1) wealthy and luxurious
    (2) sunny and bright
    (3) barren and powerful
    (4) green and flowering
    (5) warm and nurturing

2. Based on this description, which of the following would be most likely to happen?

    (1) The pioneers will be able to cultivate this land easily.
    (2) A tornado will destroy everything the pioneers have worked for.
    (3) The pioneers will nearly starve during a fierce winter storm.
    (4) The land will challenge the pioneers as they try to build their town.
    (5) The young couple will die before completing their prairie home.

WHAT DOES IGNATIUS LOOK LIKE?

Line   A green hunting cap squeezed the top of the
fleshy balloon of a head. The green earflaps, full of
large ears and uncut hair . . . stuck out on either
side like turn signals indicating two directions at
5   once. Full, pursed lips protruded beneath the
bushy black moustache and, at their corners, sank
into little folds filled with disapproval and potato
chip crumbs. In the shadow under the green visor
of the cap Ignatius J. Reilly's blue and yellow eyes
10   looked down upon the other people waiting
under the clock at the Holmes department store.

          —From *A Confederacy of Dunces*
            by John Kennedy Toole

3. Comparing the green earflaps to turn signals effectively creates a vivid image of

    (1) ears that lie flat to the head
    (2) a handsome man
    (3) ears that stick straight out
    (4) Ignatius's good driving skills
    (5) Ignatius's warm personality

4. In this description, Ignatius seems to be

    (1) part of the crowd around him
    (2) hiding under his cap while observing people
    (3) dressed to go somewhere formal
    (4) aware that he looks somewhat out of place
    (5) angry at the shoppers in the store

5. Which of the following best describes the narrator's tone?

    (1) humble
    (2) suspenseful
    (3) uncertain
    (4) comical
    (5) angry

To check your answers, turn to page 268.

Studying Plot

Every work of fiction has a **plot**. The plot is simply the sequence of events in the story—the answer to the question, *What happened?*

Usually, the plot follows a simple pattern of rising action, crisis, and falling action. The meaning of these terms is explained in Figure 1.

FIGURE 1

A plot usually follows the sequence of rising action, crisis, and falling action

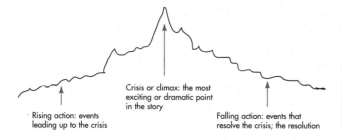

Rising action: events leading up to the crisis

Crisis or climax: the most exciting or dramatic point in the story

Falling action: events that resolve the crisis; the resolution

Recognizing Figurative Language

In the description of Ignatius J. Reilly on page 246, the author describes Ignatius's head as a "fleshy balloon." Of course, the author doesn't mean that Ignatius's head is actually a balloon. Instead, he uses **figurative language** to create a humorous, vivid **image**, or mental picture, of the size and shape of Ignatius's head.

When you read figurative language, remember that the words aren't supposed to be taken literally. They're meant to capture your imagination and help you see new relationships between things. Compare these types of figurative language:

> **Sentence 1:** Juanita's sparkling eyes are like gemstones. (simile)
>
> **Sentence 2:** Juanita's smile is dynamite. (metaphor)

A **simile** is a comparison. You can always recognize a simile because it contains the words *like* or *as*. A **metaphor** takes a comparison one step further: two things are described as if they are one and the same. The words *like* or *as* do not appear. For example, to make a stronger point about Juanita's powerful smile, the writer of sentence 2 says that her smile actually *is* dynamite.

Another type of figurative language is the symbol. A **symbol** is something that is used to *represent* another thing. For example, a flag is a symbol of a country. The dove symbolizes peace.

---

plot: the sequence of events in a story

---

figurative language: imaginative words and phrases that create a vivid image

---

image: a mental picture created for the reader by a skillful choice of words

---

simile: a figure of speech in which two things are compared through the use of the words *like* or *as*

---

metaphor: a comparison in which two things are described as the same—without the use of the words *like* or *as*

---

symbol: something used to represent something else

Exercise 2

Directions

Item 1 refers to the following passage. Read the passage and answer the question.

WHAT HAPPENS TO DEERSLAYER?

Line When about a hundred yards from the shore,
Deerslayer rose in the canoe . . . then quickly
laying aside the instrument of labor, he seized that
of war. He was in the very act of raising the rifle,
5 when a sharp report was followed by the buzz of
a bullet that passed so near his body, as to cause
him involuntarily to start.
　　　The next instant Deerslayer staggered, and
fell his whole length of the bottom of the canoe.
10 A yell—it came from a single voice—followed, and
an Indian leaped from the bushes upon the open
area of the point, bounding towards the canoe.
This was the moment the young man desired. He
rose on the instant, and leveled his own rifle at his
15 uncovered foe; but his finger hesitated about
pulling the trigger on one whom he held at such a
disadvantage. This little delay, probably, saved the
life of the Indian, who bounded back into the
cover as swiftly as he had broken out of it.
20 　　In the meantime Deerslayer had been swiftly
approaching the land, and his own canoe reached
the point just as his enemy disappeared. . . . [He]
did not pause an instant, but dashed into the
woods and sought cover.

　　　　　　　—From *The Deerslayer*
　　　　　　　by James Fenimore Cooper

1. The climax, or most dramatic point, of this
   passage is when

   (1) Deerslayer paddles toward land
   (2) the Indian takes cover in the woods
   (3) Deerslayer takes cover in the woods
   (4) Deerslayer's canoe touches ground
   (5) Deerslayer raises his rifle and takes aim

Item 2 refers to the following passage. Read the passage and answer the question.

HOW DOES THE BOY INTERPRET HIS SURROUNDINGS?

Line The mist was heavier yet when I got out upon the
marshes, so that instead of my running at everything, everything seemed to run at me. This was
very disagreeable to a guilty mind. The gates and
5 dykes and banks came bursting at me through the
mist, as if they cried as plainly as could be, 'A boy
with Somebody-else's pork pie! Stop him!' The
cattle came upon me with like suddenness, staring
out of their eyes, and steaming out of their
10 nostrils, 'Holloa, young thief!' One black ox, with
a white cravat on—who even had to my awak-
ened conscience something of a clerical air—fixed
me so obstinately with his eyes, and moved his
blunt head round in such an accusatory manner as
15 I moved round, that I blubbered out to him, 'I
couldn't help it, sir! It wasn't for myself I took it!'

　　　　　　　—From *Great Expectations*
　　　　　　　by Charles Dickens

2. In this excerpt, what do the cattle, the mist, the
   gates, and banks all symbolize to the boy as they
   "seemed to run at [him]"? (line 3)

   (1) his fear of being lost in the mist
   (2) the boy's guilty conscience
   (3) the boy's love of nature
   (4) his fear of the outdoor world
   (5) his joy at having something to eat

To check your answers, turn to page 268.

Identifying Theme and Main Idea

The **theme** of a passage is the belief about life that the author is expressing through a story. Themes in literature are often taken from universal issues such as aging, love, fear, and time.

　　　The theme of a work is closely related to its **main ideas**. For example, if the theme of a passage is "eagerness to grow up," the main idea could be "Young people are too quick to become adults." If the theme is "the beauty of old age," the main idea might be "A lifetime of overcoming hardship can make elderly people beautiful." To identify a writer's theme, ask yourself,

theme: a statement or belief about life

main idea: a writer's most important point

What does this passage say about life and about how people live?

On the GED Test, certain questions ask you to apply information and ideas from a passage to new situations. Keep in mind that the answers to application questions are never directly stated in a passage—only the clues are stated. To arrive at the correct answer, you will search for details in the passage that can be *related* to the question and then draw a logical conclusion.

Exercise 3

> **Directions**
>
> Choose the <u>one best answer</u> to each item.

> Items 1 to 4 refer to the following excerpt from a novel.

WHAT IS MRS. BENNET HOPING?

Line It is a truth universally acknowledged, that a single man in possession of a good fortune, must be in want of a wife.

5 However little known the feelings or views of such a man may be on his first entering a neighbourhood, this truth is so well fixed in the minds of the surrounding families, that he is considered as the rightful property of some one or other of their daughters.

10 "My dear Mr. Bennet," said his lady to him one day, "have you heard that Netherfield Park is let at last?"

Mr. Bennet replied that he had not.

"But it is," returned she, "for Mrs. Long has just been here, and she told me all about it."

15 Mr. Bennet made no answer.

"Do you not want to know who has taken it?" cried his wife impatiently.

"You want to tell me, and I have no objection to hearing it."

20 This was invitation enough.

"Why, my dear, you must know, Mrs. Long says that Netherfield is taken by a young man of large fortune from the north of England; that he

25 came down on Monday in a chaise and four to see the place, and was so much delighted with it that he agreed with Mr. Morris immediately; that he is to take possession before Michaelmas, and some of his servants are to be in the house by the end

30 of next week."

"What is his name?"

"Bingley."

"Is he married or single."

"Oh! Single, my dear, to be sure! A single

35 man of large fortune; four or five thousand a year. What a fine thing for our girls!"

—From *Pride and Prejudice* by Jane Austen

1. Where is the main idea of this passage stated?

   (1) in the middle of the excerpt
   (2) in the first sentence
   (3) nowhere, except indirectly
   (4) in the last sentence
   (5) nowhere, because there is none

2. In this conversation, Mrs. Bennet assumes that

   (1) Netherfield Park has been rented
   (2) her husband is interested in her story
   (3) her oldest daughter will fall in love with Bingley
   (4) Mr. Bingley is looking for a wife
   (5) her husband is an interfering man

3. Based on this passage, if Mrs. Bennet worked in an office instead of keeping a home, she could be expected to

   (1) fight for employees' rights
   (2) quickly become the office manager
   (3) be the most industrious worker in the office
   (4) consistently arrive late for work, without an excuse
   (5) pry into the personal lives of her coworkers

4. Why is Mrs. Bennet interested in Mr. Bingley?

   (1) He is a wealthy man.
   (2) His goal is to get married.
   (3) He is the son of a politician.
   (4) He is a poor man.
   (5) He has a promising career.

To check your answers, turn to page 268.

POETRY

A **poem** is a piece of writing that communicates an intense and often emotional message. Generally, poems are different from other literary forms in two ways: (1) Poems are often shorter pieces of writing, and (2) they have a different structure. A poet usually divides the lines of a poem into stanzas, which are like the verses of a song.

Poets often express ideas indirectly through rhyme, rhythm, and figurative language. The rhyme and rhythm help set the mood of a poem. They stem from a time when poems were sung out loud before they were written down.

Rhyme and Rhythm

A writer of prose uses paragraphs to break up a passage, making it easier to understand. Similarly, a poet breaks a poem into **stanzas**, or sections. Stanzas can do more than make a poem simpler to read, however. With each new stanza, the poet may introduce a new setting or speaker, a plot element, or a change in mood or tone.

Think about the song you have heard on the radio most recently. In popular songs, rhyme and rhythm make the words and the message more powerful. Poets use rhyme and rhythm in much the same way.

Rhyme is the sound likeness of two words. Rhyming words are effective in poetry because their sounds complement each other. Sometimes those sounds are exactly alike (as in *cat/hat* and *alive/survive*); at other times (as in *pound/pond*), the sounds are not exactly the same but are close enough to give the effect of a rhyme.

Rhyming words are also used to link ideas. In addition, rhyme may determine the structure of a poem. For example, a stanza in which the last words in lines 1 and 2 rhyme and the last words in lines 3 and 4 rhyme has a **rhyme scheme** of *aabb*.

Rhythm is the sound patterns that words make when placed together. Think about dancing. When you dance, your body moves to the rhythm of the music. In many poems, words do the same thing. Sometimes the rhythm is so strong and regular you can clap your hands to it. At other times, the rhythm is purposely uneven. A poet may want to capture dissimilar ideas or keep the reader's attention. Instead of rhythm, a poet may use *repetition*—the repeated use of a word or phrase—to make a point.

Although stanzas, rhyme, and rhythm can be important elements in a poem, some poems do not use all these techniques. When a poem contains irregular rhythm and rhyme, or no rhyme, the structure is called **free verse**. Many modern poets write free verse.

poem: relatively brief, often intense and emotional work of literature

stanza: two or more lines of poetry grouped together

rhyme: the use of words with endings that sound alike

rhyme scheme: a pattern of rhyming sounds that gives structure to a poem

rhythm: the pattern of sounds formed by words

free verse: poetry that contains little or no rhyme or rhythm

Exercise 1

> **Directions**
>
> Items 1 and 2 refer to the following poem. As you read this poem, think about how free verse makes the poem effective. Then answer the questions.

WHAT THOUGHTS COME TO THE SPEAKER'S MIND?

Line Do not boast of your speed,
O blue-green stream running by the hills:
Once you have reached the wide ocean,
You can return no more.
5   Why not stay here and rest,
When moonlight stuffs the empty hills?
Mountains are steadfast but the mountain streams
Go by, go by,
And yesterdays are like the rushing streams,
10   They fly, they fly,
And the great heroes, famous for a day,
They die, they die.
Blue mountains speak of my desire,
Green waters reflect my lover's love:
15   The mountains unchanging,
The waters flowing by.
Sometimes it seems the waters cannot forget me,
They part in tears, regretting, running away.
His guests are merry and joking.
20   A distant voyage is like chewing sugar cane,
Sweetness mixed with bitterness.
Return, soon I shall return to my home—
Though beautiful, this is not my land.
          —"Do Not Boast of Your Speed"
                    by Hwang Chin-i

1. This poem is primarily about

    (1) marriage
    (2) an athletic event
    (3) the birth of a child
    (4) the love of nature
    (5) the passage of time

2. Lines 7–12 differ from the rest of the poem because they

    (1) do not contain any figurative expressions
    (2) use rhyme and rhythm to describe the speaker's ancestors
    (3) address the ocean directly, as if it were a person
    (4) use rhyme and rhythm to describe the passage of time
    (5) contain no rhyme or rhythm and quote a different speaker

To check your answers, turn to page 268.

Recognizing Alliteration

"Who is the bravest, boldest, and best leader that our beloved country has ever seen?" This question contains four words that begin with *b*. Read it out loud, and notice how the words beginning with *b* catch your attention. Think, too, about how the sound links the leader with the country. Poets often place words that start with the same letter near each other to create this kind of effect. This technique is called alliteration.

Understanding Figurative Language: Personification and Symbolism

Like other writers, poets sometimes depend on figurative language to communicate ideas and observations. Figurative language is not meant to be taken literally; rather, it compares things in an unusual way. It creates mental images that help readers see ideas in new ways, too.

Symbolism and personification are two more types of figurative language. **Symbolism** is figurative language in which an object, a person, or an event represents something else. For example, a country's flag usually symbolizes its pride and its people. A wedding ring symbolizes long-lasting love. Black clothing often symbolizes mourning. **Personification** takes symbolism one step further. When an object is personified, it is given human qualities. (Just remember: *person*ification = like a *person*.) For example, a building doesn't experience feelings and emotions. Still, a writer might say, "The old building stood its ground bravely against the wrecking ball."

symbolism: figurative language in which an object, person, or event represents a larger, more abstract idea

personification: figurative language in which something that is not human is given human characteristics

Exercise 2

> **Directions**
>
> Items 1 to 3 refer to the following poem. As you read this poem, consider what new ideas the poet suggests. Then answer the questions.

HOW IS DEATH PERSONIFIED?

Line Because I could not stop for Death,
He kindly stopped for me;
The carriage held but just ourselves
And immortality.
5   We slowly drove, he knew no haste,
And I had put away
My labor, and my leisure too,
For his civility.
      We passed the school where children played
10 At wrestling in a ring;
We passed the fields of gazing grain,
We passed the setting sun.
      We paused before a house that seemed
A swelling of the ground;
15 The roof was scarcely visible,
The cornice but a mound.
      Since then 'tis centuries; but each
Feels shorter than the day
I first surmised the horses' heads
20 Were toward eternity.
          —"Because I Could Not Stop for Death"
                by Emily Dickinson

1. In this poem, death is personified in the form of

   (1) an elderly grandfather
   (2) a frightening old woman
   (3) a courteous carriage driver
   (4) an energetic young man
   (5) a silent young boy

2. "We slowly drove, he knew no haste,/And I had put away/My labor, and my leisure too,/For his civility." (lines 5-8)

   Which of the following best restates these thoughts?

   (1) We drove quickly because I was eager to return home.
   (2) Because the driver was rude, I asked to be taken home.
   (3) I was impressed by his politeness but soon felt ready to get back to work.
   (4) We drove hastily toward the setting sun as I enjoyed my leisure.
   (5) I no longer required work or rest, so I was content to move slowly.

3. The house to which the speaker refers in the fourth stanza (lines 13-16) symbolizes

   (1) the earth
   (2) a small apartment
   (3) her birthplace
   (4) a gravesite
   (5) a mansion

To check your answers, turn to page 268.

Identifying Theme and Main Idea

As in other kinds of writing, the main idea of a poem is its central point. The theme of a poem, however, is a broader statement or belief about life, relationships, feelings, or behavior. In a poem about reapers, for example, the poet's subject might be "work." The poet's theme might be "the monotony of physical labor." The poet's main idea might be "People can be hypnotized by the routine of their work, becoming blind to the world around them."

Exercise 3

> **Directions**
>
> Items 1 to 4 refer to the following poem. As you read, think about the tone of the poem and how you would state its theme. Then answer the questions.

WHERE IS THE SPEAKER GOING?

Line Farewell, my younger brother!
From the holy places the gods come for me.
You will never see me again; but when the showers pass and the thunders peal,
5 "There," you will say, "is the voice of my elder brother."
And when the harvest comes, of the beautiful birds and grasshoppers you will say,
"There is the ordering of my elder brother!"
          —"Farewell, My Younger Brother,"
              a traditional Navajo poem

1. Based on line 2, you can assume that the speaker

   (1) is near death
   (2) is not religious
   (3) has a brother who is dying
   (4) wants to leave town
   (5) is afraid

2. The speaker mentions being remembered in all of the following except

   (1) grasshoppers
   (2) rain
   (3) springtime flowers
   (4) thunder
   (5) the time of harvest

3. Which of the following best states the main idea of this poem?

   (1) Every harvest is beautiful.
   (2) Nature should be revered.
   (3) An elder brother is a good teacher.
   (4) A person's spirit carries on after death.
   (5) Brothers should be lifelong friends.

4. If the younger brother applied the theme of this poem to his life, he would most likely become a

   (1) loving parent
   (2) nature photographer
   (3) big-game hunter
   (4) skilled lumberjack
   (5) fiery preacher

   > Items 5 to 8 refer to the following sonnet.

As you read this sonnet, think about how this classical work of literature provides a timeless record of human emotion and about the ways in which you could apply Browning's images and ideas to life today. Then answer the questions.

WHAT STRONG EMOTIONS DOES THIS SPEAKER EXPRESS?

Line How do I love thee? Let me count the ways.
I love thee to the depth and breadth and height
My soul can reach, when feeling out of sight
For the ends of Being and ideal Grace.
5 I love thee to the level of every day's
Most quiet need, by sun and candlelight.
I love thee freely, as men strive for Right;
I love thee purely, as they turn from Praise.
I love thee with the passion put to use
10 In my old griefs, and with my childhood's faith.
I love thee with a love I seemed to lose
With my lost saints, I love thee with the breath,
Smiles, tears, of all my life!—and, if God choose,
I shall but love thee better after death.
       —Sonnet XLIII by Elizabeth Barrett Browning

5. The speaker connects her feelings of love with all of the following except

   (1) purity
   (2) freedom
   (3) passion
   (4) fear
   (5) faith

6. Which of the following literary techniques is used most often in this sonnet?

   (1) repetition
   (2) falling action
   (3) stage directions
   (4) foreshadowing
   (5) personification

7. If this sonnet were reviewed in a modern-day magazine, the reviewer would most likely characterize it as

   (1) emotionless
   (2) dramatic
   (3) dull
   (4) manipulative
   (5) inexpressive

8. Which of the following song titles best summarizes the main idea of this sonnet?

   (1) "Tears of a Clown"
   (2) "We Are the World"
   (3) "We Are Family"
   (4) "Tracks of My Tears"
   (5) "I Will Always Love You"

To check your answers, turn to page 268.

DRAMA

A **drama** is a play that can be read or performed on stage by actors.

When you watch a play, you can see how the actors react to each other. You can see that time passes. A **playwright** has other ways to help you picture these things when you read a play.

Understanding Setting and Stage Directions

Plays are divided into acts, which are further divided into *scenes*. Each scene advances the time and/or place of the action—that is, changes the setting. The *setting* of a drama is the time and place in which the action occurs. Identifying a play's setting might help you anticipate the action, since time and place can influence what happens. For example, if the setting is a small, cold Alaskan town, the action might focus on how people in the town cope with the long winter.

A playwright provides other clues through **stage directions**, which often appear in *italics*. Stage directions describe how the stage looks and how the actors should stand, move, look, or speak.

Recognizing Foreshadowing

Foreshadowing is the technique of suggesting an event that will occur later in the play. The foreshadowing may be found in stage directions or in a character's words or actions. For example, if a character wonders out loud when another character might come home after a long absence, the playwright may be foreshadowing this character's return. Watching for foreshadowing helps you understand what is happening—and what will happen—in a drama.

Analyzing Characters, Dialogue, and Conflict

Dialogue, or conversation, is the most important element in a play. By listening closely to dialogue between characters, you can gather information.

---

drama: a play that can be read or performed

---

playwright: the author of a drama

---

stage directions: information that describes the stage setting and the movements of the characters in a drama

---

foreshadowing: a technique used to suggest what will happen later

---

dialogue: a conversation between characters

A **monologue** is a long speech by one character when another character is on stage. A soliloquy occurs when the character is alone on stage. Monologues and soliloquies are important because characters reveal important feelings or experiences during these long and usually emotional speeches.

As you read, keep in mind that each character in a play has a different perspective to express. The different perspectives often result in a **conflict**, or problem.

The most common types of conflict in drama (and in all types of literature) are:

- conflict between people (such as friends or family members)

- conflict between a person and society (such as a person who opposes prejudice)

- conflict between a person (or people) and an element of nature (such as a hurricane)

- internal conflict—a spiritual or moral disturbance within one character

monologue: a long and often emotional speech by one character, often revealing important feelings or events, when another character is present

conflict: a clash of ideas, attitudes, or forces

Exercise 1

Directions

Items 1 and 2 refer to the following passage. As you read this passage, use the stage directions to imagine the scene and the action. Then answer the questions.

Items 3 to 6 refer to the following passage. Read the passage. Then answer the questions.

WHAT BRINGS THESE CHARACTERS TOGETHER?

Line *The stage is empty except for a few pale stars. Calorías and Julio enter. Calorías carries the cello on his shoulder.*

Guicho: (*Out of sight*) CA-LO-RIIIIAAS! CAAA-
5   LOOOO-RIIIIAAS!

Guicho appears over a dune. Calorías and Julio stand looking at each other. Guicho takes out his knife.

Julio: Hey Guichito.
10   Calorías: Why Guicho, you comin' with us?
Guicho: No.
Calorías: Ah yes. I see now. You have a knife.
         (*Approaching*) Perhaps you're angry. Did
         I hurt a friend of yours? (*He laughs*) Have
15   you come to kill me, little boy?
Guicho shakes his head. He is terrified.
Guicho: I want the guitarrón.
Julio: Ay Guichito. Go away.
Calorías: (*Picking up the cello*) This. Ah yes. It is
20   this you want.
Guicho: Just give it to me.
Calorías: If only it were so simple . . . eh? But I
         can't give it to you. I have to destroy it.
         —From *The Guitarrn* by Lynne Alvarez

1. The setting of this passage is

    (1) backstage at an orchestra hall
    (2) early morning in a Latin American city
    (3) nighttime in a desert-like place
    (4) a junkyard
    (5) late afternoon at the seashore

2. The stage directions in lines 13–19 show that Calorías is

    (1) foolish
    (2) eager to make friends with Guicho
    (3) afraid but hopeful
    (4) cruel
    (5) easily misled by Julio

WHY DO THESE CHARACTERS DISAGREE?

Line Troy: Your mama tells me you got recruited by a
           college football team? Is that right?
      Cory: Yeah. Coach Zellman say the recruiter
           gonna be coming by to talk to you. Get you
5   to sign the permission papers.
      Troy: I thought you supposed to be working
           down there at the A&P. Ain't you supposed
           to be working down there after school?
      Cory: Mr. Stawicki say he gonna hold my job for
10   me until after the football season. Say
           starting next week I can work weekends.
      Troy: I thought we had an understanding about
           this football stuff. You suppose to keep up
           with your chores and hold that job down at
15   the A&P. Ain't been around here all day on
           a Saturday. Ain't none of your chores done
           . . . and now you telling me you done quit
           your job.
      Cory: I'm gonna be working weekends.
20   Troy: You damn right you are! Ain't no need for
           nobody coming around here to talk to me
           about signing nothing.
      Cory: Hey, Pop, you can't do that. He's coming all
           the way from North Carolina.
25   Troy: I don't care where he coming from. The
           white man ain't gonna let you get nowhere
           with that football no way. You go and get
           your book-learning where you can learn to
           do something besides carrying people's
30   garbage.
                 —From *Fences* by August Wilson

3. Which of the following best describes Cory's perspective?

    (1) He wants to own the A&P.
    (2) He wants to give up football.
    (3) He wishes that he were better at football.
    (4) He can work and still play football.
    (5) He does not like the recruiter.

4. Which of the following best describes Troy's perspective?

    (1) He thinks Cory should continue working.
    (2) He is worried about his wife's reaction.
    (3) He wishes that Cory were a better player.
    (4) He admires and respects the recruiter.
    (5) He is jealous of Cory's athletic skill.

5. As a father, Troy could best be described as

    (1) sympathetic
    (2) wise
    (3) cruel
    (4) strict
    (5) easygoing

6. Which of the following is not clear by the end of this passage?

    (1) Coach Zellman's perspective
    (2) Cory's desire to play football
    (3) Cory's talent as a football player
    (4) Troy's perspective
    (5) whether Cory will play college football

To check your answers, turn to page 269.

Understanding Comedy and Tragedy

Many plays are categorized as either comedies or tragedies. In a **tragedy** a major character may suffer great misfortune or ruin, especially as a result of a choice he or she has made. Often the tragic choice involves a moral weakness. Tragedies are designed to evoke strong feelings of sadness and empathy in the audience.

A **comedy** is intended to amuse. It may be lighthearted or hilarious and it usually has a happy ending. Humor is used for many reasons; to break up the tension and conflict in drama, to reveal a character's personality, or to make an audience more receptive to the ideas being presented. Humor is also an important part of life, and drama is usually meant to remind us of elements of our own lives.

Two kinds of comedy are farce and satire. A **farce** contains humorous characterizations and improbable plots. For example, in a farce, two women might dress as men and never be recognized as women. A **satire** makes fun of human characteristics (such as pride or jealousy) or failings (such as being unable to communicate with one's children or being a fool for love). Irony and clever language are often used in satire. In both farce and satire, the characters and their actions are exaggerated to make the drama more entertaining and as a comment on society.

Exercise 2

Directions

Items 1 to 4 refer to the following passage. As you read, look for universal themes and situations. Then answer the questions.

WHAT PAST PROBLEMS DO LOLA AND DOC DISCUSS?

Line

Lola: You were so nice and so proper, Doc; I thought nothing we could do together could ever be wrong—or make us unhappy. Do you think we did wrong, Doc?

5 Doc: (*consoling*) No, Baby, of course I don't.

Lola: I don't think anyone knows about it except my folks, do you?

Doc: Of course not, Baby.

Lola: (*follows him in*) I wish the baby had lived,

10   Doc. . . . If we'd gone to a doctor, she would have lived, don't you think?

Doc: Perhaps. . . . We were just kids. Kids don't know how to look after things.

Lola: (*sits on couch*) If we'd had the baby she'd be

15   a young girl now; and then maybe you'd have saved your money, Doc, and she could be going to college—like Marie.

Doc: Baby, what's done is done.

Lola: It must make you feel bad at times to think

20   you had to give up being a doctor and to think you don't have any money like you used to.

Doc: No . . . no, Baby. We should never feel bad about what's past. What's in the past can't be

---

tragedy: drama that ends in great misfortune or ruin for a major character, especially when a moral issue is involved

---

comedy: drama that is intended to amuse through its lighthearted approach and happy ending

---

farce: a comedy that contains humorous characterizations and improbable plots

---

satire: a comedy that makes fun of human characteristics or failings

25   helped. You . . . you've got to forget it and
live for the present. If you can't forget the
past, you stay in it and never get out.

                —From *Come Back, Little Sheba*
                      by William Inge

1. Based on Doc's words in lines 23–26, with which
of the following proverbs would he be most likely
to agree?

   (1) Waste not, want not.
   (2) A stitch in time saves nine.
   (3) Count your pennies.
   (4) Don't cry over spilled milk.
   (5) Little wealth, little care.

2. Which of the following would be the best title for
this passage?

   (1) A Happy Marriage
   (2) Secrets of the Past
   (3) Saving for College
   (4) How to be a Good Doctor
   (5) A Scary Future

3. Which of the following best describes the tone of
this conversation?

   (1) whining
   (2) bitter
   (3) challenging
   (4) apologetic
   (5) understanding

4. What does the dialogue between Lola and Doc
suggest about their relationship?

   (1) It is strained and awkward.
   (2) They enjoy being silly together.
   (3) It is a close, loving relationship.
   (4) Everything they say and do seems rehearsed.
   (5) It is full of frustration.

To check your answers, turn to page 269.

COMMENTARY ON THE ARTS

Understanding Book Reviews

When a new book is published, critics write **reviews** that describe the new book and state their opinions about its quality. Book reviews help people make decisions about which books they want to read.

Some basic facts that are often included in a book review are:

- the book's title, author, and subject matter

- the author's reason for writing the book

- the author's background, qualifications, and experiences

- the reviewer's summary of the book's story or contents

- the reviewer's opinion of the book, whether it is worth reading and why

In discussing the worth of a book, a review often refers to such features as an interesting plot or logical structure, the writer's originality, and the believability of the material presented.

Analyzing Film and Television Reviews

Every day, your local newspaper prints reviews of TV shows and movies. Critics write reviews that offer their opinions of a new work. Film reviews help people decide whether they will buy a movie ticket, wait to rent a video, wait until the movie airs on network TV, or not bother seeing the movie at all. Television reviews not only help people decide which shows to watch but also help determine ratings—and which shows stay on the air.

Film critics write reviews after seeing an advance showing of a new movie. To support their opinions, they often recall specific scenes or quote lines of dialogue from the film. Like book reviewers, they may comment on plot, originality, and believability.

Television and film reviewers describe the topic of a show or film, identify the actors, and mention when and where it can be seen. They may explain whether they think the work is successful and why. For example, if a new show is a comedy, the reviewer might address questions such as: *Is it funny? Is the story original or predictable? Are the laughs natural? Do the actors have good comedic timing?*

---

review: commentary about a work or performance; may be favorable, unfavorable, or mixed

Exercise 1

> **Directions**
>
> Items 1 to 3 refer to the following passage. In this passage, the reviewer analyzes the roots of 12 stories by Gabriel García Márquez. Read the reviewer's comments. Then answer the questions.

ARE THESE NEW SHORT STORIES EFFECTIVE?

Line In his introduction to *Doce cuentos peregrinos [12 Traveling Tales]*, [Gabriel] García Márquez explains why there are exactly twelve stories and in what sense they are [traveling or] "wandering":

5 He once had a dream that he was attending his own raucous funeral. At the end everyone got to go home except him. "It was only then," he writes, "that I realized that dying means having to leave your friends forever."

10   The dream provoked a new awareness of his identity as a Latin American living abroad. He began to take notes for stories about Latin Americans living in Europe. Over the years some were lost, then retrieved, then lost again. The

15 stories, like the people they describe, were "wanderers." Finally, after a long process of unearthing or recreating some and eliminating others, he wound up with twelve.

      The best of these stories feature the combi-

20 nation of fantasy and reality and tongue-in-cheek hyperbole [exaggeration] that are the hallmarks of García Márquez's style. They capture beautifully the anguish of the transplanted Latin American, accustomed to the color and sensuality of his

25 native land, and seeking new magic in his unfamiliar surroundings. . . .

      Quite a few of these twelve wandering stories flop at the end; they depict interesting characters and weave intricate plots, only to lead

30 up to "so-what?" conclusions. But the best more than make up for the worst, and the collection proves that García Márquez is still a consummate story-teller.

          —From "Wanderers and References"
                by Barbara Mujica

1. From the reviewer's descriptions, you can infer that the short stories of García Márquez often

   (1) explore issues of death and dying
   (2) focus on Americans living in Latin America
   (3) contain a great deal of humor
   (4) blend imaginary or exaggerated events with real happenings
   (5) become dull after interesting beginnings

2. What is the main reason that the stories in this new book are described as "wandering" (lines 4 and 27)?

   (1) They describe characters who travel.
   (2) Their narrator cannot speak clearly.
   (3) Márquez wrote them while at home.
   (4) They are about exploring familiar places.
   (5) They have no structure whatsoever.

3. Which of the following groups is most similar to the characters in *Doce cuentos peregrinos*?

   (1) Americans on a short trip to India
   (2) Californians visiting Washington, D.C.
   (3) Americans living in India
   (4) Latin Americans who never leave home
   (5) business executives who attend a conference in Mexico City

To check your answers, turn to page 269.

Interpreting Comments on the Visual Arts

Visual arts are the kinds of art that you look at and examine. They include painting, photography, sculpture, and architecture. People enjoy the visual arts because they believe such works show them something new about themselves or society.

    Some basic facts that appear in comments on the visual arts often include:

- the title of the work of art

- where it can be seen

- the names of artists who have contributed

- the reviewer's opinion: whether the work of art is of value and why

visual arts: kinds of art, such as sculpture, painting, and photography, that people look at and examine

Interpreting Comments on the Performing Arts

Music, drama, and dance are **performing arts**. Critics of the performing arts publicize the work of different artists. Their commentaries help people decide whether they'd like to go see a play, a concert, or a dance troupe. They also explain the significance of a particular performance.

Some basic facts that often appear in comments on the performing arts include:

- the title and creator of the work

- where it played or is playing

- the names of the performers who appear

- the names of the director and producer

- the reviewer's opinion of the production and why it is or is not a success

A person reviewing a live show, such as a play or concert, has an advantage over a TV or book critic. This reviewer can include descriptions of actual audience reaction to the show being performed. For example, the reviewer could describe standing ovations, yawns, or other evidence of success or failure.

Exercise 2

Directions

Items 1 and 2 refer to the following passage. In this passage, the writer discusses the life work of a painter named Ted De Grazia. As you read, think about what De Grazia says about himself and his art. Then answer the questions.

WHAT WAS TED DE GRAZIA'S VISION?

Line To best appreciate the work and lifestyle of Ted
      De Grazia, one must visit his Gallery in the Sun in
      Tucson, Arizona—the artist's museum, gallery,
      workshop, former home and gravesite. His
5   philosophy was direct and simple: "Years ago
      galleries wouldn't show my work, so I built my
      own gallery. Later, when the work was beginning
      to get established, museums wanted nothing to do
      with it, so I built my own museum. All artists have
10   to believe in what they do."

De Grazia is best known for his paintings of Southwest Indians whom he depicted with stylistic brilliance and in a dazzling palette of colors, often with faces left blank; you fill in the emotions
15 yourself—joy, sorrow, fear, anger. . . .

Like most artists, De Grazia was often moody and introspective. Nothing upset him more than the changing face of the Indian scene. "All over the Southwest our Indians are changing," he said
20 shortly before his death on September 17, 1982. "Call it progress, if you will, to bring the Indians a better way of life. But it saddens me to see a jukebox in a Hopi trading post, and it saddens me to learn a mammoth supermarket is being built at
25 Window Rock, capital of the Navajo Nation. The Apaches, the Papagos, the Pimas, the Pueblo Indians along the Rio Grande—they are all changing. If God gives me the strength and time, I hope to capture on canvas what vestiges still exist
30 of their old and colorful ways."
      —From "The Color Between Earth and Sky"
                                    by Ron Butler

1. According to this reviewer, why did De Grazia often leave the faces in his paintings blank?

    (1) to show that an artist's work was never done
    (2) to give viewers' imaginations greater freedom
    (3) to emphasize that Indian culture was changing
    (4) because his subjects wanted privacy
    (5) because he was impatient to start a new work

2. Based on this passage, what advice would De Grazia most likely have given a friend?

    (1) "Never own your own business."
    (2) "Stick to the traditions of your family."
    (3) "Believe in what your work can accomplish."
    (4) "Do what you love as often as you can."
    (5) "Pay attention to newsworthy events."

To check your answers, turn to page 270.

---

performing arts: forms of artistic expression in which people perform, usually on stage and in front of an audience (such as music, dance, and drama)

Techniques of Commentary

Reviewers and critics use common writing techniques to emphasize and illustrate their main ideas. For example, they state their views clearly; support those views with relevant information; and use dramatic, descriptive language to express how specific works of art looked or sounded.

A reviewer's **perspective** is the way in which he or she views something. For example, when you speak from your own perspective about a new movie, you state whether you liked it, why you liked it, and why you think others should see it.

To identify a writer's perspective as you read commentary passages, ask yourself such questions as: *Who is speaking?* and *How do this person's experiences and opinions affect what he or she is saying and doing?*

Writers of commentary want to persuade you that a work of art is successful or not successful. They want you to see a movie—or they try to persuade you not to see it. To express their views, reviewers often use a combination of facts and opinions.

A fact is something that can be proven beyond a reasonable doubt. An opinion can be supported, but it cannot be proven conclusively. It is simply one person's belief. The statement "A new movie called *Menace II Society* just opened" is a fact. It is also an objective statement. **Objectivity** means that the person who made the statement is not influenced by emotion.

The statement "*Menace II Society* is a great work of art," however, is an opinion that could also contain a bias. A **bias** is a personal belief or attitude that prevents a person from being objective. For example, if the person who voiced this opinion were the director's sister, she might not be objective about the film. She may already have a personal bias in support of the movie, since it represents a family member's work. As you can see, bias isn't necessarily negative. A person can be biased either for or against something.

Diction means word choice, or the words used to express a thought. Examples of different types of diction include *casual, formal, informal, slang,* and *conversational*. Writers of commentary often depend on informal, conversational diction because they're communicating their personal opinions. Writers are also careful in their use of **descriptive language**—the words and phrases that show how something looks, sounds, feels, and so on. In commenting on the arts, writers often use **jargon**. Jargon is a specialized language that relates only to one topic.

Exercise 3

Directions
Choose the one best answer to each item.

Items 1 to 4 refer to the following excerpt from a magazine article.

WHAT DID DIZZY GILLESPIE REPRESENT?

Line   If you ever wanted to send Dizzy Gillespie a Christmas or birthday card, his address was a cinch to remember. All you had to scribble was "Diz, 07631." The post office always knew just
5   what to do.

    That was the nature of the fame commanded by the reigning monarch of the Land of Oo-Bla-Dee. In the last decade of his life, he had become the most recognizable single personification of jazz

---

perspective: the way the writer views something

objectivity: the ability to present information without being influenced by emotion or personal opinions

bias: a personal belief or attitude (either positive or negative) that prevents a person from being objective

diction: word choice

descriptive language: words and phrases that describe something

jargon: terminology related to only one area of interest (such as computers or medicine)

10 since Louis Armstrong. More than that even, he
reached beyond that insular world and became
an emblem of Americana, beloved the world
over. . . .

People who didn't know "A Night in
15 Tunisia" from "A Night at the Opera" still knew
Gillespie and his tilted trumpet, if not from any
record then from a turn on *The Tonight Show* or
The Cosby Show. His persona transcended jazz
without disassociating from it. In the last years of
20 his life the biggest bopper of them all lived to see
his original musical values largely vindicated
[cleared from criticism] and restored by a new
generation of whiz-bang wunderkinds (Jon Faddis,
Wynton Marsalis, et al.) who were willing to be
25 considered his spiritual proteges. He went out, as
much as ever, the quintessential [ultimate]
modern-jazz musician.

No musician ever roamed the world with a
more open musical mind or with fewer musical
30 prejudices about what his music should be. Unlike
fans and critics, who prefer purity of form,
Gillespie was ready to mix and match anything
that moved or excited him. This curiosity led him
into the world of Cuban and Brazilian music. . . .
35 Gillespie's diversions into other realms, however,
never supplanted his most seminal achievement,
which was to help define the fundamental
revisions of jazz grammar that became bebop.

—From "Remembering Dizzy"
by John McDonough

1. "No musician ever roamed the world with a more
open musical mind or with fewer musical prejudices about what his music should be." (lines
28–30)

This statement could best be described as

(1) a fact
(2) an opinion
(3) a bias
(4) a joke
(5) a criticism

2. Which of the following best summarizes this
reviewer's perspective?

(1) an admirer of Gillespie
(2) a lover of rock and roll
(3) Gillespie's best friend
(4) a fellow musician
(5) a relative of Gillespie

3. Based on lines 32–34, Gillespie is most similar to a
filmmaker who

(1) includes animation in a live-action film
(2) focuses on one filmmaking style
(3) never went to film school
(4) received extensive formal training
(5) builds a career on remaking classic movies

4. The first paragraph of this passage is effective
because it

(1) reveals Gillespie's spirituality
(2) documents Gillespie's birth date and age
(3) gives evidence of Gillespie's wealth
(4) illustrates Gillespie's worldwide fame
(5) shows that the U.S. Postal Service is
generous

> Items 5 and 6 refer to the following passage.

WAS MCCARTNEY'S CONCERT SUCCESSFUL?

Line [Most] of McCartney's new material fared well
against the Beatles classics—and deserved better
than the indifferent response the audience
afforded it. Excepting the early performance of the
5 rocker "Looking for Changes," the Silverdome
crowd used the new songs as an opportunity to
hit the rest rooms or perhaps buy a T-shirt—
which McCartney could well consider a reasonable
alternative.
10 Ultimately, however, McCartney's show was
lost in the cavernous Silverdome. Unlike the
roaring excitement of his pair of 1990 concerts at
the Palace, Friday's show seemed hollow—
pleasant, but lacking the visceral punch that's
15 essential for a truly thrilling concert.
That's a shame, because there was a lot to
like: a wonderful song selection; solid musical
performances; and a dazzling visual presentation.
But when they're put together in a place that's
20 just too big, the result is underwhelming. It's not
that big a thrill to be within the same square mile
as a Beatle.

—From "A Blast from the Past, Muffled"
by Gary Graff

5. According to lines 5–9, one effect of McCartney's new songs was that the audience

(1) rose to their feet to applaud
(2) became nostalgic for the 1960s
(3) went to the rest rooms
(4) bought so many T-shirts that they sold out
(5) went to buy tickets to McCartney's next concert

6. The reviewer was somewhat disappointed in the concert primarily as a result of

(1) a performance space that was too small
(2) McCartney's lackluster performance
(3) the poor service at the food and T-shirt stands
(4) the enormous stadium
(5) the audience's indifferent reaction

To check your answers, turn to page 270.

Purposes of Commentary

One role of commentary is to serve as an enduring record of art in history. Through commentary, we can read about plays that are no longer being performed, paintings that were destroyed in a war, or the philosophy of a painter who lived centuries ago.

Writers of commentary also serve another important purpose: to document changing trends in the arts and explain why those trends exist. A **trend** is a tendency of thought that can reflect just about anything—ideas about fashion, political opinions, fads, or a society's fears and beliefs. For example, a commentator might write an article about the trend among artists to document the AIDS epidemic through photography, drama, and film.

Another important role of commentary writers is to examine how social issues and trends are expressed through art. For example, some social questions and issues include:

• How are different ethnic groups portrayed on television?

• Do books today emphasize the importance of family?

• Why do people idolize movie stars?

Writers of commentary also invite their readers to draw conclusions. A **conclusion** is an observation or decision made after you have considered all the facts. When you draw conclusions, you use inferential comprehension skills such as finding unstated main ideas, identifying implications, understanding cause-and-effect relationships, and identifying consequences. You take all of the information that an author presents and reach a logical conclusion.

Exercise 4

> **Directions**
> Choose the one best answer to each item.

> Items 1 to 4 refer to the following excerpt from a newspaper article.

WHAT DOES THIS COMIC BOOK TEACH?

Line Money, the smooth-talking hunk, is dating Feather, but he gets sidetracked by Camille and Coco, who are impressed with his good looks and BMW. Feather is consoled by sweet—but chunky—
5 Steamboat, while idiot Homeboy and politically correct Malcolm have a showdown on the dance floor.

After his fling with the girls, Money tries to make up with Feather, who lets him have it for
10 ditching the dance without her. "You listen here, Money! Just because you got a nice car and think you're good lookin' doesn't mean jack! I saw you ride off with those . . . skunks! We're finished, ya dig? So get lost before you get thumped!"
15 That's how the story goes in the premiere issue of "Hip Hop Heaven," a comic book by Rex Perry, a Chicago fashion illustrator-turned-cartoonist who believes the time is ripe for black cartoon characters to enter the mainstream. . . .
20 From the get-go, Perry, 34, has aimed his comics at the head and the funnybone of his audience, which he defines as 12- to 20-year-old, multiracial hip-hoppers, by blending slapstick humor, soap-opera story lines and soapbox
25 sermonizing. "I decided 'Hip Hop Heaven' was a

trend: a person's or society's tendencies or patterns of thought (such as ideas about fashion, political opinions, or fads)

conclusion: an observation or decision made after a reasonable number of facts is known

way to reach kids and deliver a message and still incorporate fashion and music," he says. . . .

"It's important to me to let the kids know about ethnic pride, of showing them how to cope
30 in an urban environment. Life is not just about dancing and rap music and what kind of clothes you're wearing or how your hair is cut. It's more than that.

"It's getting your act together, and realizing
35 there's a big world you're going to have to deal with eventually."

—From "Life After Fashion" by Hugh Hart

1. Lines 1-7 illustrate the fact that "Hip Hop Heaven"

   (1)   won't ever be a successful comic book
   (2)   does not depict male characters
   (3)   is always set on a dance floor
   (4)   depicts a range of colorful, quirky characters
   (5)   does not contain realistic dialogue

2. According to this passage, Rex Perry's objective with "Hip Hop Heaven" is to teach

   (1)   better reading skills
   (2)   the history of African civilization
   (3)   success and ethnic pride
   (4)   dance and rap music
   (5)   how to develop a career

3. The goals that Rex Perry wants to achieve are most similar to the goals of

   (1)   a high school counselor
   (2)   an engineer
   (3)   a poet
   (4)   a basketball star
   (5)   an actor

4. "Hip Hop Heaven" represents a response to which of the following social trends?

   (1)   the increase in teenage pregnancies
   (2)   the emphasis on being "fashionable"
   (3)   the decline in movies about city life
   (4)   the desire to succeed in school
   (5)   the focus on a high-school diploma

Items 5 to 9 refer to the following passages.

WHAT ISSUES DOES JOHNNY CRESCENDO ADDRESS IN HIS MUSIC?

Line I don't want your charity
      or you to be paid to care for me
      I want choices and rights in my life
      I don't want to be in your care
5   Or put someplace "out there"
      I want choices and rights in my life
                —"Choices and Rights"

The music of British singer Johnny Cre-scendo is unlike anything on today's U.S. pop
10 charts, but it would strike a familiar chord with most Americans. Forget for a moment that Crescendo is disabled—his songs, with their rousing folk and blues aspects, recall a social protest tradition in music that stretches from the
15 1960s back to the 1930s and before.

In listening, however, it is impossible to "forget" Crescendo's disability. He doesn't allow you to. His disability informs his creative vision to the point of becoming inseparable from it, and his
20 militant, even angry lyrics are torn from the lives, struggles and triumphs of all disabled people. . . .

And empowerment is what links Crescendo's activism with his art. "Disability art is very powerful. If done right, it is a very powerful
25 force—primarily for the disabled but also for non-disabled people. Disabled people have got a lot to teach the world."

On a more personal level, he says, his work provides a sense of wholeness. The question, he
30 says, is, "Are you a whole person? For a long time I went around saying, 'I'm a non-disabled person with a bad leg.'" In this sense, integration is the central goal, and the heart of his creative vision, making his disability a full part of who he is as a
35 person. In the larger world, empowerment—both artistically and politically—is what he believes will make this wholeness available to all persons with disabilities.

—From "Johnny's Song" by Douglas Lathrop

5. "His disability informs his creative vision to the point of becoming inseparable from it. . . . " (lines 18–19)

   Based on this statement, what is probably true about Crescendo's lyrics?

   (1) They do not focus on his disability.
   (2) They imagine a life without disability.
   (3) They are remarkably creative.
   (4) They focus on concerns of the disabled.
   (5) They are not effective or moving.

6. Based on this passage, which of the following pairs of words best describes Johnny Crescendo?

   (1) nervous and high-strung
   (2) proud and strong
   (3) helpless and tentative
   (4) angry and cruel
   (5) happy and carefree

7. By beginning this essay with song lyrics by Johnny Crescendo, the reviewer

   (1) illustrates Crescendo's energetic concerts
   (2) critiques Crescendo's last album
   (3) proves how talented Crescendo is
   (4) emphasizes Crescendo's narrow vision
   (5) shows one of Crescendo's central themes

8. From the tone of this excerpt, you can assume that this reviewer

   (1) admires Crescendo's work
   (2) wants to meet Crescendo
   (3) is tired of Crescendo's subject matter
   (4) does not realize that Crescendo is disabled
   (5) wishes that he could sing

9. Which of the following is the best definition of the word *empowerment* as it is used in this passage?

   (1) a decrease in power and authority
   (2) embarrassment in front of one's peers
   (3) well-earned success
   (4) the ability to achieve a goal
   (5) a belief in law and order

To check your answers, turn to page 270.

Answers and Explanations
LITERATURE AND THE ARTS

Part 4

Unit 1: Nonfiction

Exercise 1 (page 239)

What Has This Dad Learned?

1. **The correct answer is (4): (Literal comprehension)** Lines 5-6 state that Garcia is part of "an increasing number of stay-at-home dads." Garcia is a former airline mechanic; but since this is not a growing group according to the passage, choice (2) is incorrect. Choices (1) and (3) can be eliminated, respectively, because Garcia does not work outside the home and does not have two jobs. There is no support for choice (5).

2. **The correct answer is (4): (Inferential comprehension)** Garcia suggests this point most strongly in lines 16–21; it takes only a small step to draw the conclusion. Choice (3) is addressed in the passage, but not as clearly as choice (4). The other choices are not supported by the passage.

Exercise 2 (page 240)

Why Does Lucy Stone Feel Disappointed?

1. **The correct answer is (3): (Inferential comprehension)** Lucy Stone makes a reference to "the last speaker," so she is probably one of many speakers. Choice (1) contradicts this fact. She may be furious, but her diction does not support this idea, so choice (2) can be eliminated. Since Stone quotes the previous speaker, she was interested and was listening, so choice (4) is incorrect. There is no evidence for choice (5).

2. **The correct answer is (4): (Literal comprehension)** The speaker says that she has always felt disappointed, or unfulfilled. Choice (1) contradicts this statement. She does not refer specifically to her family or childhood, so choices (2) and (3) are incorrect. Choice (5) is not related to this statement.

3. **The correct answer is (2): (Analysis)** Choice (4) is incorrect because Stone speaks as if she were quite sure of herself. Choice (3) can be eliminated because her diction indicates that she remains in control of her emotions. Later in the speech, she may be encouraging as choice (1) suggests; here, though, she speaks of her struggles. There is no evidence for choice (5).

4. **The correct answer is (4): (Analysis)** The context verifies that Stone is referring to times when she has been denied the opportunities that men enjoy. She is asking for equality, not superiority; thus, choice (5) can be eliminated. Choice (3) is incorrect because she is speaking solely of her own experiences. Choice (2) can be eliminated because she is expressing dislike for having no other work but that—not dislike of others who do such work. There is no evidence for choice (1).

Exercise 3 (page 241)

How Does This Girl's Life Change?

1. **The correct answer is (3): (Literal comprehension)** Lines 26-27 state, "we learned that she had bequeathed me to her sister's daughter." Choice (5) contradicts this fact. The speaker does not read the will, so choice (1) can be eliminated. The speaker will live with a relative of her mistress, not her own grandmother, so choice (2) is incorrect. The speaker tries to "blot out from [her] memory" this act, so choice (4) is incorrect.

2. **The correct answer is (5): (Literal comprehension)** Line 39 states that the mistress "taught me to read and spell." None of the other choices is supported in the passage.

3. **The correct answer is (2): (Application)** Like a person who accepts certain inevitabilities, the speaker has resigned herself to the outcome of her mistress's will. Choices (1) and (3) can be eliminated because they do not describe these feelings of acceptance and resignation. Choice (4) describes a happy occasion and can be eliminated. The speaker is not in a position of authority, so choice (5) is incorrect.

Exercise 4 (page 243)

What Do Red Jacket's Ideas Mean Today?

1. **The correct answer is (2): (Application)** Red Jacket is angry and frustrated by the events that he describes, yet his tone remains polite and in control.

2. **The correct answer is (1): (Application)** Red Jacket is upset by changes and threats to his people's religion and land, so he probably would work to preserve Native-American culture. Choices (2) and (3) are incorrect because he does not speak of education or of different generations. The passage offers no reason to believe that Red Jacket would take special interest in the federal deficit or AIDS, so choices (4) and (5) can be eliminated.

3. **The correct answer is (2): (Application)** Red Jacket would probably be gratified to see Native-Americans in Congress where they could take part in guiding the future. Choices (1) and (5) are incorrect because he probably would be sad to see the problems that reservation life can cause, and he would not want to see even more religious strife than there was in his day. There is no evidence for the other choices.

Unit 2: Fiction
Exercise 1 (page 246)

How Might This Place Affect This Couple's Life?

1. **The correct answer is (3): (Literal comprehension)** Lines 12 and 17-18 describe the landscape as frozen and overwhelming, respectively. It is a place of "vast hardness" (line 19) and of a "savage kind of beauty" (line 24). All of the other choices present positive descriptions.

2. **The correct answer is (4): (Inferential comprehension)** According to lines 16-19, "the great fact was the land itself, which seemed to overwhelm the little beginnings of human society that struggled in its sombre wastes." Thus, it is likely that the pioneers will face many challenges as they try to tame this land. Choice (1) contradicts this likelihood. There is no evidence for the other choices, although such events could take place.

What Does Ignatius Look Like?

3. **The correct answer is (3): (Analysis)** Ignatius's ears stick out from his head, much like turn signals. Choice (1) suggests the opposite. Choices (2), (4), and (5) all suggest a positive impression of Ignatius's appearance or behavior, which the passage does not support.

4. **The correct answer is (2): (Inferential comprehension)** Ignatius seems to be hiding under his cap and observing the other people from a distance. Choice (1) suggests the opposite, that he is part of the crowd. Ignatius is casually dressed, so choice (3) is incorrect. There is no evidence to support choices (4) and (5).

5. **The correct answer is (4): (Inferential comprehension)** The best choice is comical. The author's images suggest that there may be morbid or absurd elements to the story. That is a literary genre known as *black humor*.

Exercise 2 (page 248)

What Happens to Deerslayer?

1. **The correct answer is (5): (Analysis)** The most exciting, dramatic moment is when Deerslayer takes aim at the Indian. This moment of tension is followed by events that result from his decision not to fire. The other choices are all events that either lead up to or follow this climax.

How Does the Boy Interpret His Surroundings?

2. **The correct answer is (2): (Analysis)** Everything that the boy sees reminds him that he has stolen something. Choices (1), (3), and (4) are incorrect because he does not state his fear of being lost, love of nature, or fear of the outside world. He probably is happy to have some food, as choice (5) states; in this passage, however, what he thinks about is his guilt.

Exercise 3 (page 249)

What Is Mrs. Bennet Hoping?

1. **The correct answer is (2): (Literal comprehension)** The main idea of this passage, that " . . . a single man in possession of a good fortune, must be in want of a wife," is stated directly in the first sentence. The rest of the conversation serves to illustrate this belief.

2. **The correct answer is (4): (Inferential comprehension)** Mrs. Bennet is assuming that Bingley actually does want a wife. Choice (1) is incorrect because the reader knows for a fact that Netherfield Park has been rented. There is no mention of Mrs. Bennet's older daughter in particular, as choice (3) indicates. Lines 16-21 suggest that Mrs. Bennet does not care whether her husband is interested, so choice (2) can be eliminated. There is no evidence for choice (5).

3. **The correct answer is (5): (Application)** Mrs. Bennet's main characteristic in this passage is her nosiness into the lives of those around her. Choices (3) and (4) can be eliminated because the passage does not indicate how hardworking or lazy she might be. Ambition, which is suggested in choices (1) and (2), is hinted at, but it is not nearly as strong a characteristic in Mrs. Bennet as are curiosity and love for gossip.

4. **The correct answer is (1): (Inferential comprehension)** Mrs. Bennet's references to Mr. Bingley's yearly salary and his having rented Netherfield Park indicate that she is impressed by his wealth. Choice (4) states the opposite, that he is poor. She does not know for certain who his father is or that he wants to marry, so choices (3) and (2) are incorrect. There is no discussion of his career, so choice (5) can be eliminated.

Unit 3: Poetry
Exercise 1 (page 251)

What Thoughts Come to the Speaker's Mind?

1. **The correct answer is (5): (Inferential comprehension)** The reference to a voyage refers to the poet's impending death. The poet is reflecting on the passing of time.

2. **The correct answer is (4): (Analysis)** By repeating the phrases "Go by," "They fly," and "They die," the speaker uses rhyme, rhythm, and repetition to make the point that time passes. Line 10 contains a simile, so choice (1) is incorrect. Choice (2) can be eliminated because the speaker mentions great heroes, not his own ancestors. Choices (3) and (5) are incorrect because the speaker does not mention the ocean in these lines and because he does use rhyme and rhythm.

Exercise 2 (page 252)

How Is Death Personified?

1. **The correct answer is (3): (Literal comprehension)** Lines 2-5 introduce Death as a courteous carriage driver. There is no evidence of his age, as choices (1), (4), and (5) suggest. Because Death is characterized as male, choice (2) is incorrect.

2. **The correct answer is (5): (Literal comprehension)** The speaker has "put away" her labor and leisure (work and rest) because her life is over; Death is kind, she is content to move slowly. Choices (1), (2), and (3) are incorrect because they imply that the speaker wants to be taken home. Choice (4) can be eliminated because the speaker says that they drove slowly (line 5).

3. **The correct answer is (4): (Analysis)** The "house" is a gravesite. Choices (2) and (5) are incorrect because the speaker is using a figurative image. It is more specific than the earth as a whole, so choice (1) can be eliminated. There is no evidence to suggest she is at her place of birth, as choice (3) indicates.

Exercise 3 (page 252)

Where Is the Speaker Going?

1. **The correct answer is (1): (Inferential comprehension)** From the phrase "the gods come for me" (line 2), it can be assumed that the speaker is near death. The references to "holy places" and "gods" mean the speaker is likely a religious person, so choice (2) can be eliminated. There is no evidence for the other choices.

2. **The correct answer is (3): (Literal comprehension)** Choice (1) is mentioned in line 8, choices (2) and (4) appear together in line 4, and choice (5) is the subject of line 7.

3. **The correct answer is (4): (Inferential comprehension)** The speaker's point is that his spirit will live on in nature after death. The speaker might agree with the other choices, but these do not relate to the speaker's beliefs about death and spirituality.

268

4. **The correct answer is (2): (Application)** If the younger brother believes the speaker, he will probably have a greater respect for nature, since the speaker's spirit is a part of nature. Choices (3) and (4) can be eliminated because they suggest a disregard for nature. Choices (1) and (5) are incorrect, respectively, because nothing is suggested about the younger brother's children or about spreading the speaker's message to others.

What Strong Emotions Does This Speaker Express?

5. **The correct answer is (4): (Literal comprehension)** The speaker never compares her strong feelings to fear or any negative emotion. In lines 7-9, the speaker compares her love to the other choices.

6. **The correct answer is (1): (Analysis)** The speaker repeats the phrase "I love thee . . ." in lines 1, 2, 5, 7, 8, 9, 11, 12, and 14. This brief sonnet does not follow any strict narrative pattern of rising action, crisis, and falling action, so choice (2) is incorrect. Stage directions are used only in drama, so choice (3) can be eliminated. The speaker states that her love will continue after death. This statement does not stand out from the rest of the poem as a foreshadowing of her own death, so choice (4) is not the best answer. The speaker does not personify inanimate objects to describe her feelings, so choice (5) can be eliminated.

7. **The correct answer is (2): (Application)** Phrases such as "I love thee to the depth and breadth and height/My soul can reach . . ." (lines 2-3) and "I love thee with the breath,/Smiles, tears, of all my life!" (lines 12-13) are dramatic statements, full of emotion and exaggeration. Choices (1), (3), and (5) suggest the opposite and can be eliminated. The speaker's tone is one of honesty, not deceit or manipulation, so choice (4) can be eliminated.

8. **The correct answer is (5): (Application)** The speaker states her undying love, so choice (5) is the best answer. Choices (1) and (4) suggest a sad or negative theme and can be eliminated. The speaker is declaring her unity with one other person. Because choices (2) and (3) suggest connection with a larger group of people, they are incorrect.

Unit 4: Drama

Exercise 1 *(page 256)*

What Brings These Characters Together?

1. **The correct answer is (3): (Literal comprehension)** According to line 1, "a few pale stars" are shining, so choice (5) is incorrect. The fact that Guicho enters over a dune (line 6) suggests a desert or desert-like setting, thus eliminating the other choices.

2. **The correct answer is (4): (Inferential comprehension)** These stage directions call for Calorías to confront Guicho, laugh at him, and then put his hands on Guicho's cello. These actions—especially when added to his words at this point—show his pleasure at causing Guicho distress. There is no evidence for the other choices.

Why Do These Characters Disagree?

3. **The correct answer is (4): (Literal comprehension)** Cory's perspective, or opinion, is that he will be able to play football and continue working on the weekends. The clearest statement of this is in lines 9-11. There is no evidence for the other choices.

4. **The correct answer is (1): (Literal comprehension)** Troy's perspective is that football is not practical and won't make Cory a success. In lines 25-27 Troy states, "The white man ain't gonna let you get nowhere with that football no way." There is no evidence for the other choices.

5. **The correct answer is (4): (Inferential comprehension)** Statements such as, "You damn right you are! Ain't no need for nobody coming around here to talk to me about signing nothing" (lines 20-22) show that Troy is a strict parent. Choice (5) states the opposite. Cruel is too strong a word to describe Troy, so choice (3) is incorrect. Troy may be sympathetic sometimes, but not in this situation, so choice (1) can be eliminated. Troy may be trying to pass along wise advice, as choice (2) suggests, but his emotion undercuts his wisdom.

6. **The correct answer is (5): (Inferential comprehension)** The passage does not resolve what Cory will choose to do. All the other choices describe information that is directly stated or strongly suggested in the passage.

Exercise 2 *(page 257)*

What Past Problems Do Lola and Doc Discuss?

1. **The correct answer is (4): (Application)** Doc believes that "what's in the past can't be helped" (lines 24-25)—a good restatement of the proverb about spilled milk. Choices (1), (2), and (3) apply to being frugal and efficient, not to thoughts about the past. The passage indicates that Doc and Lola do not have a lot of money, as choice (5) suggests, but that choice can be eliminated because they have seen a good bit of care in the past.

2. **The correct answer is (2): (Inferential comprehension)** Lola and Doc are discussing secret events in their past. They seem to have a good marriage, but these memories are sad, so choice (1) is not the best answer. Doc "had to give up being a doctor . . ." (line 20), but they do not discuss this profession, so choice (4) is incorrect. References to college and the future do not suggest ways to succeed, so choices (4) and (5) are not logical.

3. **The correct answer is (5): (Analysis)** The stage direction in line 5 indicates that Doc is "consoling." Lola refers to how Doc must feel at times because he had to give up being a doctor and doesn't have the money he once had (lines 19-22). Both try to be understanding. Doc affectionately refers to Lola as "Baby." Neither whines, so choice (1) is incorrect. Although Lola has regrets (lines 9-11), there is no indication that either she or Doc is bitter, so choice (2) is incorrect. There are no challenges or apologies, so choices (3) and (4) are incorrect.

4. **The correct answer is (3): (Analysis)** Doc and Lola discuss their past problems in a loving manner. She asks him what he thinks (lines 3-4, 6-7, and 10-11). He calls her "Baby," consoles her (lines 5, 8, and 12-13), and encourages her to "live for the present" (line 26). There is no evidence for choices (1) and (4). Although Doc calls Lola "Baby," there is no indication of their acting silly together, so choice (2) is incorrect. They are discussing past problems. There is no evidence that their current relationship is full of frustration, so choice (5) is incorrect.

Unit 5: Commentary on the Arts

Exercise 1 *(page 260)*

Are These New Short Stories Effective?

1. **The correct answer is (4): (Literal comprehension)** Lines 19-22 state that one of this writer's "hallmarks" is to combine "fantasy and reality and tongue-in-cheek hyperbole," or exaggeration. Though choices (1) and (5) may be true, there is no evidence that any of Garcia Marquez's other books explore death or "flop at the end" (line 28). There is no evidence for the other choices.

2. **The correct answer is (1): (Inferential comprehension)** Lines 14-16 state that the stories are "wanderers" like the traveling characters they describe. There is no mention of where Garcia Marquez wrote them, so choice (3) can be eliminated. The stories are about traveling and about living in new places, so choice (4) can be eliminated. Though the reviewer criticizes only some of the stories' endings, choice (5) is not fully supported. There is no evidence for choice (2).

3. **The correct answer is (3): (Application)** Since the stories focus on Latin Americans living abroad, a group of Americans living in India would be similar. Choices (1), (2), and (5) involve groups of people visiting other places rather than living there. Choice (4) is incorrect since it describes a person who never leaves home.

Exercise 2 *(page 261)*

What Was Ted De Grazia's Vision?

1. **The correct answer is (2): (Literal comprehension)** Line 14 states that the blank faces enable viewers to "fill in the emotions." This is an artistic decision, not one based on time constraints, so choices (1) and (5) can be eliminated. Though choices (3) and (4) may be true, the stated reason is to enable viewers to participate creatively in the paintings.

2. **The correct answer is (3): (Application)** In lines 9-10, De Grazia states, "All artists have to believe in what they do." De Grazia has had success creating his own gallery and museum and focusing on a different culture, so choices (1) and (2) are unlikely. De Grazia would probably agree with choices (4) and (5), but they are not the focus of his statements.

Exercise 3 *(page 262)*

What Did Dizzy Gillespie Represent?

1. **The correct answer is (2): (Literal comprehension)** Since this statement cannot be proven to be true, and because not everyone would agree with it, it is an opinion. Choice (1) is the opposite of an opinion. Though this statement reveals a bias toward Gillespie, the statement itself is an opinion—and choice (3) is incorrect. The statement is serious and supportive, so choices (4) and (5) can be eliminated.

2. **The correct answer is (1): (Inferential comprehension)** The reviewer praises Gillespie's philosophy and music, so he is probably an admirer of Gillespie. There is no mention of rock and roll, so choice (2) is incorrect. The reviewer reveals no information about his own life or possible relationship to Gillespie, so the other choices can be eliminated.

3. **The correct answer is (1): (Application)** Gillespie mixed and matched any art forms that he liked. So, he is similar to a filmmaker who mixes live action and animation, or cartoons. Choices (2) and (5) suggest the opposite of creative mixing and matching. There is no reference to Gillespie's training or education, so choices (3) and (4) can be eliminated.

4. **The correct answer is (4): (Analysis)** These lines effectively illustrate that Gillespie was so famous that no address was needed on letters to him. Choices (1), (2), and (3) can be eliminated because the lines do not reveal Gillespie's spiritual beliefs, his age, or his wealth. In choice (5), efficient would be a better description than generous; in fact, no hint of generosity is given. Thus, choice (5) can be eliminated.

Was McCartney's Concert Successful?

5. **The correct answer is (3): (Literal comprehension)** Lines 6-7 state that the crowd "used the new songs as an opportunity to hit the rest rooms . . ." Since the audience lost interest, choice (1) is not logical. Though choices (2) and (4) may be true, they do not explain the effect of the new songs. There is no mention of a future show by McCartney, so choice (5) is incorrect.

6. **The correct answer is (4): (Literal comprehension)** Lines 10-11 state that the show "was lost in the cavernous Silverdome." Choice (1) implies the opposite. The reviewer describes McCartney's performance as "pleasant" (line 14), so choice (2) is incorrect. There is no mention of the service, and the audience's reaction was a result of the mediocre show, so choices (3) and (5) can be eliminated.

Exercise 4 *(page 264)*

What Does This Comic Book Teach?

1. **The correct answer is (4): (Inferential comprehension)** The first paragraph presents seven of the lively and interesting characters in "Hip Hop Heaven." There is no evidence that the comic book won't succeed, as choice (1) suggests. Choice (2) is incorrect because the characters Money, Steamboat, Homeboy, and Malcolm are male. A dance floor is mentioned as just one setting, so choice (3) is unlikely, and there is no evidence for choice (5).

2. **The correct answer is (3): (Literal comprehension)** In lines 28-30, Perry says that it is important to "let the kids know about ethnic pride, of showing them how to cope. . . ." The other choices are all goals that he might want his readers to achieve, but they are not directly addressed by Perry in the passage.

3. **The correct answer is (1): (Application)** Like a high school counselor, Perry wants to instill self-confidence and a desire to succeed in the "big world" (line 35). The other choices do not apply to a person who is directly helping students or young people.

4. **The correct answer is (2): (Inferential comprehension)** Lines 30-33 reveal that Perry is responding to the importance of fashion and fads in society: "Life is not just about dancing and rap music and what kind of clothes you're wearing. . . ." There is no mention of choices (1) or (3) in the passage. Choices (4) and (5) are the opposite of what Perry sees happening in society.

What Issues Does Johnny Crescendo Address in His Music?

5. **The correct answer is (4): (Inferential comprehension)** If Crescendo's creative vision is guided by his disability, then his lyrics probably focus on issues related to being disabled. Choices (1) and (2) suggest the opposite. There is no comment on whether the lyrics are creative, effective, or moving; thus, choices (3) and (5) can be eliminated.

6. **The correct answer is (2): (Inferential comprehension)** Lines 1-6 and lines 17-21 reveal a strong and powerful person and philosophy. Crescendo seems calm and confident, and so choices (1), (3), and (4) are incorrect. Crescendo may be a happy person, but his physical challenge means that he is not carefree as choice (5) suggests.

7. **The correct answer is (5): (Analysis)** These lyrics reveal a strong theme in Crescendo's work and vision—that he wants choices and rights for himself. There is no mention of a concert or album, as choices (1) and (2) suggest. Six lines of lyrics aren't enough to prove Crescendo's talent to everyone, or to argue that his vision is narrow, so choices (3) and (4) can be eliminated.

8. **The correct answer is (1): (Inferential comprehension)** The reviewer's tone is respectful, and he states that Crescendo's art is "unlike anything on today's U.S. pop charts" (lines 9-10). The reviewer does not reveal any personal wishes, so choices (2) and (5) can be eliminated. The commentary is positive, so choice (3) is incorrect. Lines 16-17 state, ". . . it is impossible to 'forget' Crescendo's disability," so choice (4) is incorrect.

9. **The correct answer is (4): (Literal comprehension)** The final paragraph explains that empowerment provides people with a sense of wholeness. Choices (1) and (2) describe negative events. The author might agree with the sentiment of choice (3), but that explanation does not fit the context of the paragraph. The article does not mention government or police, so choice (5) can be eliminated.

Part 5
MATHEMATICS

RED ALERT

The GED Math Test has 56 multiple-choice questions, each with five choices. You will have 90 minutes to complete the test. It measures how well you can apply your problem-solving skills in everyday experiences. It tests whether you know how to solve problems, not whether you can do tricky computations.

ARITHMETIC

Fifty percent of the items on the GED Math Test focus on your understanding of arithmetic. In the arithmetic items, you will perform basic operations using whole numbers, fractions, and decimals. Your understanding of ratio, percent, number relationships, and measurement will also be tested.

Look at the following sample.

Example 1

For her work, Maggie has to drive 500 miles from Charleston to Atlanta. In the morning, she drives 143 miles to Wytheville and stops for gas. Then she drives another 48 miles before stopping for lunch. How many miles does she have left to drive?

(1) 191
(2) 309
(3) 357
(4) 452
(5) 691

One way to solve this problem is to add the miles driven. Then subtract the total from 500.

$143 + 48 = 191 \qquad 500 - 191 = 309$

The correct answer is choice (2).

In Example 2, facts are presented using a graph. About 1 out of every 3 problems on the GED Math Test refers to some kind of graph, table, or diagram.

Example 2

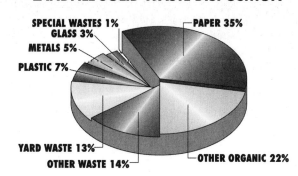

A landfill in California is estimated to hold 80 tons of solid waste. Which of the following expressions could be used to find what part of the waste is plastic?

(1) 0.07(80)

(2) 7(80)

(3) 7(0.08)

(4) $\dfrac{0.07(80)}{100}$

(5) $\dfrac{80}{0.07}$

In this problem, you are asked to read a graph and use the information to show how you would set up the problem. About 25% of the problems on the GED Math Test are set-up problems.

The graph shows that 7% of a landfill is made up of plastic. The problem asks about a particular landfill that holds 80 tons of solid waste. You need to find 7% of 80 to solve the problem. The correct answer is choice (1).

ALGEBRA

What about algebra? Algebraic skills are tested by about 30 percent of the items on the GED Math Test, but don't worry. You probably know more about algebra than you think. Look at this sample problem.

Example 3

Art bought 6 unopened wax packs of baseball cards for $3. At the same rate, what would he pay for 50 wax packs?

(1) $18

(2) $25

(3) $59

(4) $100

(5) Not enough information is given.

This kind of problem tests your understanding of ratio and proportion. You can solve it by writing a proportion, using x to represent the unknown amount.

$$\frac{6 \text{ packs}}{\$3} = \frac{50 \text{ packs}}{x}$$

$$6x = \$150$$

$$x = \frac{\$150}{6}$$

$$x = \$25$$

Choice (2) is the correct answer.

GEOMETRY

About 20% of the GED Math Test is about geometry. The geometry concepts tested on the GED Math Test are useful ones. In fact, you can probably already solve many of the geometry problems using your understanding of arithmetic. Try this problem.

Example 4

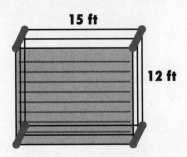

Su Ji plans to fence off an area of her yard for a vegetable garden. She stakes out a rectangular plot that is 15 feet long and 12 feet wide. How many feet of fencing will she need to enclose the garden?

(1) 24
(2) 27
(3) 30
(4) 54
(5) 180

You can use a formula to solve the problem. When you take the GED Math Test, you will be given a page of formulas that you can refer to at any time. One of the formulas is for finding the perimeter of a rectangle.

PERIMETER (*P*) OF A RECTANGLE
$P = 2l + 2w$; *where* l = length, and w = width

To use the formula, put in the values from the problem and solve.

$P = 2(15) + 2(12)$
$\quad = 30 + 24$
$\quad = 54$

Choice (4) is the correct answer.

In this section, you will learn how to use all the formulas on the formulas page of the GED Math Test. Formulas can be useful reminders of how to solve a problem. You will also learn how to solve problems using common sense and your understanding of life situations.

ARITHMETIC

Whole Numbers

The population of the world increases every second. At one point in 1992, the population was recorded as this.

BILLION	HUNDRED MILLION	TEN MILLION	MILLION	HUNDRED THOUSAND	TEN THOUSAND	THOUSAND	HUNDRED	TENS	ONES
5 ,	7	7	8 ,	9	0	7 ,	5	4	3

When reading or writing whole numbers, use a comma to mark the end of each group. Read each number group from left to right as if it were a number in the hundreds. Then at the comma, read the group name of *billion, million,* or *thousand.* Do not use the word *and* when reading whole numbers.

The zero in the ten thousands column is a *placeholder.* A placeholder fills the column, but it is not read.

5,	778,	907,	543
5 billion,	778 million,	907 thousand,	543

In words, the population of the world in 1992 is written *five billion, seven hundred seventy-eight million, nine hundred seven thousand, five hundred forty-three.*

The following symbols are used to compare numbers.

>	Greater than	$5 > 3$	Five is greater than three.
<	Less than	$3 < 5$	Three is less than five.
=	Equal to	$3 = 2 + 1$	Three is equal to two plus one.

Examples:

$13 < 17 \qquad 20 > 5$

smaller ←   → smaller

NOTE: When using > or < symbols, remember that the arrow points to the *smaller* number.

To compare whole numbers, first count the number of digits. The whole number with more digits is always greater. $60,000 > 6,000$

If the number of digits is the same, compare the digits in both numbers working from left to right. $652 > 642$ because $5 > 4$

Exercise 1

Directions

For Items 1 to 8, write the whole number in words.

1. 504

2. 1,420

3. 7,060

4. 34,000

5. 201,900

6. 1,450,323

7. 257,005,009

8. 6,000,000,000

Directions

For Items 9 and 10, solve as directed.

9. The following chart shows population figures for some cities for both 1980 and 1990. Compare the figures for the two years shown. Then complete the chart by adding > (greater than) or < (less than) symbols.

City	1990	> or <	1980
Phoenix	1,003,800		789,704
Chicago	2,852,041		3,005,072
Milwaukee	642,860		636,212
Philadelphia	1,608,942		1,688,210
Detroit	1,056,180		1,203,339
Jacksonville	649,437		540,920

10. Four businesses made donations to the Mt. Vernon Community Center this year. The amounts are shown in the table below.

Company	Amount Donated
Kids Plus Fashions	$1,060
The Toy Box	$1,580
The Playroom	$1,805
Kids First	$1,295

Which of the companies gave the greatest amount to the community center?

To check your answers, turn to page 379.

Rounding Whole Numbers

Rounding makes it easier to work with numbers.

Whole numbers can be rounded to the nearest ten or the nearest trillion or to any place value column in between. How a number is rounded depends on your needs.

For example, suppose a problem on the GED Math Test asks you to round 338 to the nearest hundred. When you round 338 to the nearest hundred, you are actually finding out whether 338 is closer to 300 or 400.

To round whole numbers:		Example:
Step 1	Underline the digit in the place to which you are rounding	Round 338 to the hundreds place. 3̲38
Step 2	Circle the number to its right.	3③8

Now look at the circled number.

Step 3

If the circled number is:		Example:
0, 1, 2, 3, or 4	Replace the circled digit and any digits to its right with zeros.	3③8 rounds to 300.
5, 6, 7, 8, or 9	Add 1 to the underlined digit and replace the circled digit and any digits to its right with zeros.	But 3⑤8 rounds to 400.

Examples:

- Round 67,149 to the nearest ten thousand.

  Underline the ten thousands place 6 and circle the ⑦.
  6⑦,149

  Since 7 > 5, add 1 to the 6 and replace the digits to the right with zeros. The nearest ten thousand is 70,000.

- Round 67,149 to the nearest thousand. 67,①49

  Since 1 < 5, replace 1 and the digits to the right with zeros. The nearest thousand is 67,000.

- Round 67,149 to the nearest hundred thousand.
  ⎽⑥7,149

  There isn't a digit in the hundred thousands column because the number 67,149 is less than 100,000. The column to the right of the hundred thousands column contains a 6. Since 6 > 5, write 1 in the hundred thousands column and replace the digits to the right with zeros. The nearest hundred thousand is 100,000.

Exercise 2

> **Directions**
> Round each number.

1. Round 586 to the nearest hundred.

2. Round 5,280 to the nearest thousand.

3. Bob is filling in a purchase authorization form at his work. His boss wants him to order a bookcase for the office. Bob has to list prices on the form to the nearest $10. If the price for the bookcase he wants is $98, what amount should he write on the form?

   (1) $10
   (2) $90
   (3) $98
   (4) $100
   (5) $110

4. A newspaper covering the beach cleanup reported the total number of volunteers rounded to the nearest ten. If there were 288 volunteers present, what number did the newspaper report?

   (1) 200
   (2) 250
   (3) 280
   (4) 290
   (5) 300

5. Arlington Stadium, the prior home of the Texas Rangers, had a maximum seating capacity of 43,508. What was the stadium's seating capacity to the nearest thousand?

   (1) 40,000
   (2) 43,000
   (3) 43,500
   (4) 44,000
   (5) 50,000

6. In 1991 there were about 5,641,000 cars registered in the state of Michigan. To the nearest hundred thousand, how many cars were registered in Michigan?

   (1) 6,000,000
   (2) 5,700,000
   (3) 5,650,000
   (4) 5,640,000
   (5) 5,600,000

To check your answers, turn to page 379.

Adding Whole Numbers

To add whole numbers, line up the numbers starting from the right so that each column has digits with the same place value.

When a column of digits has a sum equal to or greater than 10, you need to carry to the next column on the left.

Example:

Add: 14, 130, and 56.

$$
\begin{array}{r}
{}^{1} \\
{}_{1}14 \\
130 \\
+86 \\
\hline
230
\end{array}
$$

Aligning numbers allows you to add ones to ones, tens to tens, and so on.

The sum is 230. The answer to an addition problem is called the **sum**. You will usually use addition when a problem asks you to combine figures or to find a sum or a total.

Addition Tip: You can add more quickly if you look for numbers that go together to make 10, 100, and 1,000.

$$
\begin{array}{r}
2 \\
16 \\
74 \\
32 \\
+28 \\
\hline
150
\end{array}
$$

You can easily see that the sum of the ones column is 20.

277

Exercise 3

Directions

For Items 1 to 10, find the sums. For Item 11, solve as directed.

1. 728 + 1,113

2. 15 + 408 + 2,638

3. 13 + 21 + 47 + 19

4. 1,409,275 + 54,400

5. 28,490 + 102,117 + 5,063

6. 25 + 180 + 250 + 75 + 120

7. 2,509,800 + 14,750 + 300,500

8. 22 + 54 + 40 + 38 + 16

9. 206 + 1,414 + 320 + 145 + 2,800

10. 589,752 + 605,578 + 110,915

11. The Fairfax Cinema recently added a 10 a.m. showing for all children's features. Attendance at the morning showings for the last four weekends was 228, 276, 300, and 249. How many people attended the early matinees on those weekends?

    (1) 953
    (2) 1,043
    (3) 1,053
    (4) 1,063
    (5) 1,153

To check your answers, turn to page 379.

Subtracting Whole Numbers

To subtract whole numbers, align the numbers at the right with the greater number on top. Then subtract working from right to left.

In the example below, you need to **borrow** in order to subtract in the ones column. Borrow "ten" from the column to the left and add it to the digit you are subtracting from.

Example:

Subtract 1,395 from 5,024.

$$
\begin{array}{r}
4\,9^{1}1_{1} \\
5{,}0\not{2}4 \\
-1{,}395 \\
\hline
3{,}629
\end{array}
$$

The answer to a subtraction problem is called the **difference**. You will usually use subtraction when a problem asks you to separate or compare two numbers.

You can easily check subtraction using addition. Add the difference (the answer) to the number you subtracted. The result should be the number you subtracted from.

$$
\text{Subtract:}\quad
\begin{array}{r}
5{,}024 \\
-1{,}395 \\
\hline
3{,}629
\end{array}
\qquad
\text{Check:}\quad
\begin{array}{r}
3{,}629 \\
+1{,}395 \\
\hline
5{,}024
\end{array}
$$

Exercise 4

Directions

For Items 1 to 10, find the differences. Check your work using addition. For Item 11, solve as directed.

1. 184 − 61

2. 1,697 − 538

3. 2,359 − 1,769

4. 13,504 − 8,755

5. 200 − 112

6. 10,000 − 5,425

7. 50,914 − 49,358

8. 190,325 − 88,500

9. 3,532,500 − 1,975,250

10. 8,000,000 − 5,425,680

11. When Angela left Los Angeles to drive home to visit her brother in Nashville, the odometer of her car read 45,964 miles. When she got back to Los Angeles, the odometer read 50,066 miles. How many miles did she put on her car on the trip?

    (1) 4,002
    (2) 4,102
    (3) 5,002
    (4) 5,102
    (5) 14,102

To check your answers, turn to page 379.

Multiplying Whole Numbers

There are several ways to indicate multiplication. All these examples are read "six times five."

$$6 \times 5 \qquad 6 \cdot 5 \qquad 6(5)$$

The GED Math Test often uses parentheses to indicate multiplication.

To multiply whole numbers, align the numbers at the right. After the multiplication is done, decide where the commas belong in the answer by counting from the right in groups of three.

Example:

Multiply 542 by 23.

$$
\begin{array}{r}
542 \\
\times\ \ 23 \\
\hline
1626 \\
1084 \\
\hline
12466 \\
\end{array}
$$

Count in three places from the right and place the comma: 12,466

The answer to a multiplication problem is called the **product**. Use multiplication whenever a problem asks you to combine, join, or add the same amount several times.

Exercise 5

> ### Directions
> For Items 1 to 4, find the products. For Items 5 and 6, solve as directed.

1. 8 × 27

2. 25(140)

3. 60 × 36

4. 29(3,016)

5. Mark put $100 down on a stereo system. He agrees to pay $55 each month for 10 months to pay the balance he owes. What is Mark's total cost for the new system?
   - (1) $550
   - (2) $650
   - (3) $1,550
   - (4) $5,500
   - (5) $5,600

6. Kim's new job pays $280 per week. How much should she expect to earn in one year (52 weeks)?
   - (1) $3,360
   - (2) $8,900
   - (3) $11,860
   - (4) $14,460
   - (5) $14,560

To check your answers, turn to page 379.

Dividing Whole Numbers

Division is used to find out how many times one number goes into another number. A division problem can be written three ways. Each of these examples means "2,436 divided by 12."

$$2{,}436 \div 12 \qquad 12\overline{)2{,}436} \qquad \frac{2{,}436}{12}$$

On the GED Math Test, division is usually shown with a fraction bar, such as $\frac{198}{7}$. To divide whole numbers, we use a process called long division.

Example:

Since 12 will not divide into 3, put a 0 in the answer and bring down the next digit.

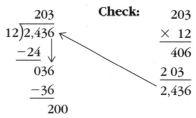

The answer to a division problem is called the **quotient**. You will usually use division when a problem asks you to separate an amount into groups or pieces of equal size. Check division by using multiplication.

Exercise 6

Directions

For Items 1 and 2, find the quotients. Check your work using multiplication. For Items 3 and 4, solve as directed.

1. $\dfrac{288}{9}$

2. $3,045 \div 15$

3. Cassady has a collection of 6,000 baseball cards. He plans to put his collection into albums. If each album page can hold 12 cards, how many album pages will he need?

   (1) 50
   (2) 200
   (3) 250
   (4) 400
   (5) 500

4. Laura is in charge of ordering supplies for the word processing pool at her work. The word processors use diskettes that come in boxes of 10. If Laura needs 200 diskettes, how many boxes should she buy?

   (1) 10
   (2) 20
   (3) 50
   (4) 100
   (5) 200

To check your answers, turn to page 379.

UNDERSTANDING WORD PROBLEMS

As an adult, you use common sense to solve most math situations in your life. You analyze a problem, choose a strategy for solving it, and carry out your plan.

The problems on the GED Math Test are drawn from everyday life experiences, but because the situations are not happening to you, word problems can seem difficult. The following plan can help you make sense of word problems.

PROBLEM-SOLVING PLAN

- Read and Restate the Question

- Find the Facts You Need

- Choose a Problem-Solving Method

- Estimate

- Compute and Check

Read and Restate the Question: One of the critical factors in doing well on the math portion of the GED Test is reading the problem and the questions carefully. A good way to make sure you understand what you have read is to put the question in your own words.

Find the Facts You Need: Some of the problems on the GED Math Test have too many facts. Some do not have enough information. Sometimes you will have to do an extra step to find one of the facts you need. Whatever the situation, before you begin any calculations, think about what facts you need to answer the question asked in the problem. You need the *right* facts to find the *right* answer.

Choose a Problem-Solving Method: Once you understand the question and find the facts, you need to choose a method to solve the problem. You will probably use one or more of the four arithmetic operations (addition, subtraction, multiplication, and division). At times, you may want to make a sketch, table, or a list.

Estimate: Over one-half of the items on the GED Math Test can be solved by estimation alone. To estimate, work with simpler numbers. For example, instead of dividing 384 by 48, think 400 divided by 50. A good estimate will often give you enough information to choose the correct answer from the choices. If it does, you have finished that item. If it doesn't, continue with the problem-solving plan.

Compute and Check: Perform the calculations you have chosen to find the exact answer. Then check to see if your answer makes sense. The answer should be reasonably close to your estimate. You can also use addition to check subtraction and multiplication to check division.

All GED Math Test items are multiple-choice with five answer choices. The choices on the Math Test are arranged in order from smallest to largest or from largest to smallest.

Exercise 1

1. The Wilkinsons' gas bill for December was $64. Their bills for January and February were $78 and $62, respectively. What was their average monthly bill for the three winter months?

   (1) $64
   (2) $68
   (3) $80
   (4) $102
   (5) $204

2. Liza supervises packing at a manufacturing company. Today her crew must pack videotapes into cartons. Each carton holds 22 videos. How many cartons must Liza have on hand to pack 5,720 videotapes?

   (1) 306
   (2) 260
   (3) 240
   (4) 214
   (5) 205

To check your answers, turn to page 379.

Solving Problems with Extra or Missing Information

The GED Math Test writers recognize that problems in life often have too little information, too much information, or both. They write problems to test your ability to figure out which facts you need to solve a problem.

Example:

Mei wants to buy a sweater originally priced at $62. The sweater is now on sale for much less. Mei plans to use a $35 gift certificate to help pay for the sweater. How much more does she owe?

   (1) $97
   (2) $37
   (3) $27
   (4) $17
   (5) Not enough information is given.

This problem seems easy enough. You have two amounts: $62 and $35. The words "how much more" suggest subtraction.

$62 − $35 = $27. Choice **(3)** is correct, right? Wrong!

Read carefully. You have two facts, but they aren't the facts you need. You are trying to find the difference between the sale price of the sweater and the amount of the gift certificate. But you don't know the sale price of the sweater. The original price was $62.

The correct answer is **(5)** Not enough information is given.

Not enough information is given will be the fifth choice on several of the items you will see on the GED Test. Some of the time that option will be the correct choice. Always read carefully, and think about which facts you need to solve the problem.

Example:

The Vision Center is offering a two-week special. You can buy 2 pair of eyeglasses (regularly priced at $59 each) for only $79. You can also save $20 on any pair of designer eyeglasses. How much would it cost to buy a pair of designer eyeglasses that originally cost $139?

   (1) $39
   (2) $98
   (3) $119
   (4) $158
   (5) Not enough information is given.

This problem has more than enough information. You are asked to figure out how much a pair of designer eyeglasses will cost. You need two facts: the original price of the glasses ($139) and the amount the glasses are marked down ($20).

Subtract to find the answer: $139 − $20 = $119
Choice **(3)** $119 is the correct choice.

You don't need to know that you can buy 2 pair of eyeglasses for $79 or that those glasses usually cost $59 per pair.

Exercise 2

1. Sarom is paying his bills. His rent is $450, his electric bill is $32, and his phone bill is $42. Because he recently switched long-distance companies, he has a $25 coupon that will reduce his phone bill. How much should Sarom pay the phone company?

   (1) $10
   (2) $17
   (3) $67
   (4) $499
   (5) Not enough information is given.

2. Aida and Ralph are buying baby furniture at a sale at Baby Blocks. They buy a crib (originally priced at $229) for only $139. They also buy a changing table that usually sells for $78. How much did they save on the changing table?

(1) $151
(2) $90
(3) $61
(4) $12
(5) Not enough information is given.

3. In 1992, the Mayor of Los Angeles was paid a salary of $117,884. By contrast, the Mayor of San Diego earned only $65,300. The San Diego City Manager was paid more, earning $126,375 for the year. What was the difference in salaries for the mayors of Los Angeles and San Diego?

(1) $183,184
(2) $61,075
(3) $52,584
(4) $8,491
(5) Not enough information is given.

4. In 1990, the U.S. Government estimated that 34,719,000 people did not have any type of health insurance. Even North Dakota, which ranked first in health coverage, had 40,000 people without insurance. The state with the greatest number of uninsured was California with 5,693,000 people uninsured. How many people in California have health insurance?

(1) 5,653,000
(2) 5,733,000
(3) 29,026,000
(4) 34,679,000
(5) Not enough information is given.

To check your answers, turn to page 379.

Solving Set-Up Problems

Set-up problems measure your ability to see a way to solve a problem. Instead of solving the problem, you are asked to choose which of the given expressions would be a right way to *set up* the problem.

Example:

For three days in August, the daily high temperatures for Fayetteville, North Carolina, were 93, 96, and 108 degrees. Which expression could be used to find the average high temperature for the three-day period?

(1) $93 + 96 + 108$
(2) $3(93 + 96 + 108)$
(3) $\dfrac{93 + 96 + 108}{3}$
(4) $93 + 96 + \dfrac{108}{3}$
(5) $\dfrac{108}{3} + (93 + 96)$

You already know how to find an average. To solve this problem, you need to add the temperatures and divide by 3 (the number of temperatures). Which of the answer choices does that? Choice (3) shows the correct set-up.

To solve set-up problems, you must know the order of operations. These rules help you translate a problem-solving method from words into numbers and symbols.

THE ORDER OF OPERATIONS
1. Do any operations in parentheses first.
2. Working from left to right, do any multiplication or division.
3. Working from left to right, do any addition or subtraction.

Examples:

$5 + 6(4)$	Do the multiplication step first.
$5 + 24$	Then do the addition step.
29	The correct answer is 29.
$7(6 + 2) - \dfrac{4}{2}$	Do the operations in parentheses.
$7(8) \quad - \dfrac{4}{2}$	Multiply, then divide.
$56 \quad - 2$	Subtract.
54	The correct answer is 54.

Sometimes you know how to solve a set-up problem, but you can't find your answer among the answer choices. That doesn't mean that you are wrong. Many problems can be solved in more than one way. These two expressions look different, but they have the same result.

$$2(15) + 2(8) = ? \qquad 2(15 + 8) = ?$$
$$30 + 16 = 46 \qquad 2(23) = 46$$

Exercise 3

Directions
Solve the following problems using the correct order of operations.

1. $7(8 - 6)(5 + 7)$

2. $\dfrac{36}{4} - 5 + 2(10)$

3. $10(5 + 2) - \dfrac{36}{4}$

4. $10(5) + \dfrac{36}{2} - 4$

Directions
Choose the one best answer to each item.

5. Software Shack is taking inventory. Vanna counts 12 boxes of high-density diskettes on the shelf in the store. She also finds a carton containing another 30 boxes in the storeroom. If each box holds 10 disks, which expression can Vanna use to compute how many high-density disks to list on the inventory form?

   (1) 12(30)(10)
   (2) 10(12 + 30)
   (3) 30(10) + 30(12)
   (4) 12(10 + 30)
   (5) 12(10) + 12(30)

6. On the way home from work, Gerry picked up two $8 pizzas for his family. When he got home, he found out his sister and her children would be staying for dinner. He went back to the restaurant and bought a large pizza for $12. Which expression can be used to figure out how much the pizzas cost altogether?

   (1) 2($8) − $12
   (2) 2($8) + 2($12)
   (3) 2($8 + $12)
   (4) 2($8)($12)
   (5) 2($8) + $12

7. Linda used to earn $9 an hour. She recently got a new job that pays $13 an hour. Linda worked 40 hours a week at the old job, but she will work only 35 hours per week on the new job. Which expression could be used to figure out how much more Linda will earn a week on her new job than she earned at her old job?

   (1) $9(40) + $13(35)
   (2) (40 − $9) + (35 − $13)
   (3) $13(35) − ($9 + 40)
   (4) $13(40) − $9(35)
   (5) $13(35) − $9(40)

To check your answers, turn to page 380.

Working with Item Sets

Item sets are groups of problems that use the same set of information. Sometimes the information is given in a paragraph. Because tables and graphs are often used to organize large amounts of facts, they are also used frequently to make item sets.

To avoid mistakes when solving item sets:

- Read all titles on the table, graph, or figure before you read the problems.

- On a graph, read the key and any markings along the sides.

- Read the direction line that tells you exactly which test items are based on the table, graph, or figure.

- Work the problems one at a time.

- Make sure you understand the question the item is asking.

- Make sure you find the right facts before you compute.

284

Exercise 4

Directions
Choose the <u>one best answer</u> to each item.

Items 1 and 2 are based on the following table.

Location	Elevation
Mount Everest	29,028 feet above sea level
Mount McKinley	20,320 feet above sea level
Mount Whitney	14,491 feet above sea level
Mount Hood	11,239 feet above sea level
Eagle Mountain	2,301 feet above sea level

1. What is the difference in elevation between Mount Hood and Mount McKinley?

    (1) 5,829 feet
    (2) 9,081 feet
    (3) 9,991 feet
    (4) 14,537 feet
    (5) Not enough information is given.

2. Which location is approximately twice the elevation of Mount Whitney?

    (1) Mount Everest
    (2) Mount McKinley
    (3) Mount Hood
    (4) Eagle Mountain
    (5) Not enough information is given.

Items 3 to 5 are based on the following graph.

THE ELECTRONIX TOY CO., VIDEO GAMES SOLD
First Year Sales, 1995

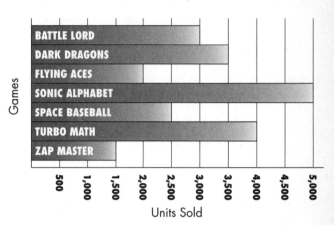

3. About how many game units were sold during the first year of sales for Battle Lord, Dark Dragons, and Flying Aces?

    (1) Between 4,000 and 5,000
    (2) Between 5,000 and 6,000
    (3) Between 6,000 and 7,000
    (4) Between 7,000 and 8,000
    (5) Between 8,000 and 9,000

4. Sonic Alphabet was the company's best selling educational game during the year. About how many more Sonic Alphabet games did the company sell than Space Baseball games?

    (1) Between 1,000 and 2,000
    (2) Between 2,000 and 3,000
    (3) Between 3,000 and 4,000
    (4) Between 4,000 and 5,000
    (5) Not enough information is given.

5. Electronix Toys hopes to sell three times as many units of Flying Aces and Zap Master next year. Which expression can be used to find how many units of those games the company hopes to sell?

    (1) 2,000 + 1,500 + 3
    (2) 3(2,000) − 3(1,500)
    (3) 3(2,000)(1,500)
    (4) 3(2,000 + 1,500)
    (5) 3(2,000 − 1,500)

Items 6 to 8 are based on the following graph.

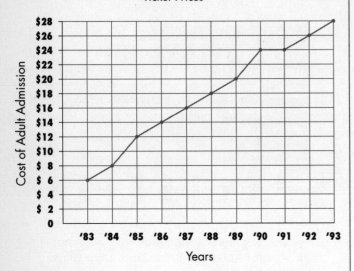

ADVENTURE PARK
Ticket Prices

Cost of Adult Admission

Years

6. The price of a ticket to Adventure Park increased every year but one. In which year did ticket prices remain the same?

  (1) 1988
  (2) 1989
  (3) 1990
  (4) 1991
  (5) Not enough information is given.

7. To celebrate the 25th anniversary of the park's opening, Adventure Park owners have decided to reduce the price of a ticket to $12 on weekdays only. In what year was $12 the regular price of admission to the park?

  (1) 1984
  (2) 1985
  (3) 1986
  (4) 1987
  (5) Not enough information is given.

8. Which expression can be used to find out how much more it costs two adults to enter the park in 1993 than it did in 1983?

  (1) $2(\$28) - 2(\$6)$
  (2) $\$28(\$6 - 2)$
  (3) $\$28 + \$28 + \$6 + \$6$
  (4) $2(\$6)(\$28)$
  (5) $\dfrac{\$28}{2} - \dfrac{\$6}{2}$

To check your answers, turn to page 380.

DECIMALS

Place Value

Decimals name parts of the whole. Decimal parts are written to the right of the whole number after a decimal point. The decimal point indicates the end of the whole number *and* the beginning of the decimal part.

A **mixed decimal** is a whole number *and* a decimal part. For this reason, when we read a mixed decimal we say "and" at the decimal point, just as we do when we read $5.75 as five dollars *and* seventy-five cents.

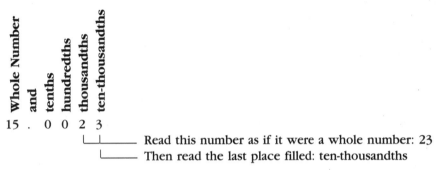

This mixed decimal would be read **15 *and* 23 ten-thousandths.**

Rounding and Comparing Decimals

Some problems ask you to round the answer to a certain decimal place.

Example:

Using a calculator, Jenna finds that the interest she will owe on her school loan this month is $23.626875. To the nearest cent, how much interest does Jenna owe?

Follow these steps to round decimals:

Step 1	Underline the digit in the place to which you are rounding.	$23.6<u>2</u>6875
Step 2	Circle the number to its right.	$23.6<u>2</u>⑥875
Step 3	If the circled number is:	

          0, 1, 2, 3, or 4   Drop the circled digit and any digits to its right.

          5, 6, 7, 8, or 9   Add 1 to the underlined digit, then drop the circled digit and any digits to its right.

Since $6 > 5$, add 1 to the 2 in the hundredths place, and drop the digits to the right. Jenna owes $23.63 in interest.

To compare decimals, add zeros after the last decimal place of the number with fewer decimal places so that the number of decimal places in both numbers is the same.

A special bolt manufactured for use in a communications satellite is supposed to measure 15.1 centimeters in length. Instead, each of the bolts in the last hour's production run measures 15.09 centimeters. Are these new bolts too long or too short?

You can easily see that 15.10 (or 15.1) is greater than 15.09. $15.1 > 15.09$ The bolts are too short.

Exercise 1

1. Thirteen and 5 hundredths is written as _____.
   (1) 13.005
   (2) 13.05
   (3) 13.5
   (4) 13.50
   (5) 13.500

2. Which of the following values are arranged in descending order (greatest to smallest)?
   (1) 0.2, 0.23, 0.235, 0.25, 0.255
   (2) 0.255, 0.25, 0.235, 0.23, 0.2
   (3) 0.2, 0.23, 0.235, 0.255, 0.25
   (4) 0.235, 0.255, 0.23, 0.25, 0.2
   (5) 0.2, 0.23, 0.25, 0.235, 0.255

3. Hugh Duffy of Boston holds the record for the highest season batting average in baseball. In 1894, he had 236 hits in 539 times at bat for an average of 0.43784786642. To the nearest thousandth, what is Duffy's record average?
   (1) 0.436
   (2) 0.437
   (3) 0.4378
   (4) 0.43785
   (5) 0.438

4. The foreign currency exchange rates change daily. If the daily rate of exchange for the British pound is 1.598 U.S. dollars, what is the exchange rate rounded to the nearest hundredth?
   (1) 1.598
   (2) 1.58
   (3) 1.59
   (4) 1.60
   (5) 2.00

5. Which of the following is greater than 23.46?
   (1) 23.0419
   (2) 23.358
   (3) 23.409
   (4) 23.460
   (5) 23.5

6. On a calculator, sales tax on an item priced at $5.75 is displayed as 0.474375. To the nearest whole cent, what is the amount of the sales tax?
   (1) $0.38
   (2) $0.40
   (3) $0.47
   (4) $0.48
   (5) $0.75

To check your answers, turn to page 380.

Adding and Subtracting Decimals

When adding or subtracting decimal numbers, first line the numbers up at the decimal point. Lining up the decimal points keeps the whole number and decimal place value columns in line.

Then add zeros after the decimal part of each number so that all the numbers in the problem have the same number of decimal places.

Examples:

Add: $77.23 and $88

$$\$\ 77.23$$
$$+88.00$$
$$\$165.23$$

16.2 + 90 + 7.043

$$16.200$$
$$90.000$$
$$+7.043$$
$$113.243$$

Adding zeros is particularly important when you are subtracting. The example below shows a common mistake people make when working with decimals.

	Incorrect	Correct
Subtract:	$88.	$88.00
	−77.23	−77.23
	$11.23	$10.77

The zeros in the examples above fill a place value column without changing the value of the number. Add zeros only to the right of the rightmost digit after the decimal point. Inserting a zero between the decimal point and a digit changes the value of the number.

5.2 = 5.20   5.2 ≠ 5.02   (≠ means *is not equal to*)
  five and   five and
two tenths   two hundredths

Addition and subtraction are *inverse*, or *opposite*, operations. To check a subtraction problem, use the inverse operation addition.

Solve: $125.63   Check: $ 58.18
       − 67.45   +67.45
       $ 58.18 $125.63

Exercise 2

> **Directions**
> Solve the following problems.

FIND THE SUMS.

1. 13.4 + 4.56 + 789.2
2. 134 + 1.456 + 78.92
3. $62.59 + $123.98 + $568
4. 5.00076 + 15.9 + 7.2309
5. $6,000 + $349.07
6. 0.98 + 0.89 + 0.0098

FIND THE DIFFERENCES.

7. 76.9 − 48.37
8. 76.9 − 4.083
9. 10,000 − 34.89
10. $56 − $34.75
11. $100 − $23.67
12. 23.45 − 23.045

13. Luisa stopped at several stores this afternoon. She spent $52.35 at Hardy's Hardware, $123.67 at Sheer's Market, and $16.98 on a prescription at Wen's Pharmacy. How much did she spend altogether?

   (1) $140.65
   (2) $176.02
   (3) $192.99
   (4) $193.00
   (5) $196.02

14. On Thursday the French franc was worth 0.1865 U.S. dollar. On Friday the rate was 0.1849 U.S. dollar. By how much did the value of the franc go down?

   (1) 0.0016
   (2) 0.0024
   (3) 0.016
   (4) 0.16
   (5) 0.3714

15. Kareem stopped at the grocery store on his way home to pick up five items for $2.59, $3.89, $1.32, $0.89, $1.29. What was the total cost of his purchases?

   (1) $5.24
   (2) $6.84
   (3) $7.79
   (4) $9.98
   (5) $12.98

16. Joretta, a technician, has a cable that is 1.6 cm in diameter. She needs a cable that is 0.85 cm in diameter. How many centimeters too large is the diameter of the cable she has?

   (1) 0.075
   (2) 0.21
   (3) 0.75
   (4) 0.975
   (5) 2.45

To check your answers, turn to page 380.

Multiplying Decimals

FOLLOW THESE STEPS TO MULTIPLY DECIMAL NUMBERS:

Example: (0.542)(2.3)

Step 1 Line the numbers up at the right just as you do with whole numbers.

$$\begin{array}{r} 0.542 \\ \times\ 2.3 \end{array}$$

Step 2 Multiply as you would with whole numbers.

$$\begin{array}{r} 0.542 \\ \times\ 2.3 \\ \hline 1626 \\ 1084\ \\ \hline 12466 \end{array}$$

Step 3 To place the decimal point in the answer, add up the total number of decimal places in the original problem. Then count in that number of places from the right, and place the decimal point in the answer.

$$\begin{array}{rl} 0.542 & \text{(3 decimal places)} \\ \times\ 2.3 & \text{(1 decimal place)} \\ \hline 1.2466 & \text{(4 total decimal places)} \end{array}$$

(0.542)(2.3) = **1.2466**

The number you get when you multiply two or more numbers together is called the **product**.

Exercise 3

Directions

Find the products in the following problems.

1. (5.24)(2.16)

2. (1.23)(23.4)

3. 21(22.2)

4. 0.004(1.2)

5. 15($3.07)

6. Bonita's weekly take-home pay is $279.25. What is her take-home pay for the year? (Use 52 weeks equals 1 year.)
   - (1) $1,452.10
   - (2) $3,351.00
   - (3) $10,367.75
   - (4) $13,962.50
   - (5) $14,521.00

7. Herb bought 2.8 pounds of ground turkey at $2.95 a pound. How much will the turkey cost?
   - (1) $0.826
   - (2) $5.75
   - (3) $8.26
   - (4) $9.26
   - (5) $82.60

8. Penny works as a courier for a small business. She uses her own car and is reimbursed for mileage at the rate of $0.42 a mile. Last week she drove 37 miles each day for 3 days. How much money will she be reimbursed?
   - (1) $1.26
   - (2) $15.54
   - (3) $46.62
   - (4) $93.24
   - (5) $139.86

To check your answers, turn to page 380.

Dividing Decimals

The division steps for decimal numbers are the same as for whole numbers, but there are special rules for placing the decimal point in the quotient.

$$\text{divisor} \rightarrow \quad 5\overline{)125} \quad \begin{array}{l} \leftarrow \text{quotient} \\ \leftarrow \text{dividend} \end{array}$$

with 25 as quotient above 125.

Examples:

$1.25 \div 5$	$2.436 \div 0.12$	$24.36 \div 0.012$
0.25	20.3	$2,030$
$5\overline{)1.25}$	$.12\overline{)2.436}$	$.012\overline{)24.360}$

If there is no decimal point in the divisor, move the decimal point straight up into the quotient.

If there is a decimal point in the divisior, move it as far as you can to the right. Then move the decimal point in the dividend **an equal number of places.**

If there are not enough places in the dividend, **add zero(s) in the dividend.**

To check your division, multiply the quotient (answer) by the divisor.

Examples:

0.25	20.3	2030
× 5	× .12	× .012
1.25	406	4 060
	2 03	20 30
	2.436	24.360 ←

Notice that the end zero in the last answer is crossed out. Because the zero isn't needed as a place holder, it is usually dropped from the answer.

Exercise 4

> **Directions**
> Find the quotients in the following problems.

1. $1.75 \div 7$

2. $332.2 \div 1.1$

3. JB Machine charges $0.08 for each T-4 toggle bolt. If a customer paid $64 for toggle bolts, how many did he buy?

   (1) 8
   (2) 80
   (3) 800
   (4) 8,000
   (5) Not enough information is given.

4. Kwon Manufacturing Company gives each of its 250 employees a quarterly bonus. At the end of the first quarter, the company has $9,876.47 to distribute equally among the employees. To the nearest cent, how much will each employee receive?

   (1) $39.51
   (2) $37.41
   (3) $35.34
   (4) $34.00
   (5) $30.68

To check your answers, turn to page 380.

Estimating with Decimals

Estimating is a useful tool for solving GED math problems containing decimals. To use estimation, you round some or all of the numbers in the problem to make the numbers easier to use. The shortcuts below are useful for making estimates involving a power of ten (10, 100, 1,000, and so on).

To multiply a decimal by a power of 10:
Move the decimal point one place to the *right* for every zero.

Examples:

$$0.024 \times 10 \rightarrow 0.024 = 0.24$$

$$0.024 \times 100 \rightarrow 0.024 = 2.4$$

$$0.024 \times 1000 \rightarrow 0.024 = 24$$

To divide by a power of 10:
Move the decimal point one place to the *left* for every zero.

Examples:

$$45 \div 10 \rightarrow 45 = 4.5$$

$$45 \div 100 \rightarrow 45 = 0.45$$

$$45 \div 1000 \rightarrow 045 = 0.045$$

Exercise 5

> **Directions**
> Choose the one best answer to each item.

1. St. John's sold 1,000 raffle tickets for a color TV at $2.50 each. How much money did they receive from ticket sales?

   (1) $2.50
   (2) $25.00
   (3) $250.00
   (4) $2,500.00
   (5) $25,000.00

2. Michelle and her nine coworkers bought an engraved pendant for $125.40 as a retirement gift for their supervisor. How much money will each person chip in as his or her share?

   (1) $1,254.00
   (2) $125.40
   (3) $12.54
   (4) $1.25
   (5) $0.13

3. Midtown Daily News estimates that one in every hundred newspapers is not delivered on time. If their daily distribution is 25,000 newspapers, how many newspapers are probably delivered late?

   (1) 2,500
   (2) 250
   (3) 25
   (4) 2.5
   (5) Not enough information is given.

4. Continental Cellular Telephone charges $0.95 per minute for calls made during the peak hours of 7 a.m. to 6 p.m. What will a caller be charged for a 5-minute call made at 3 p.m.?

   (1) $2.85
   (2) $4.75
   (3) $5.70
   (4) $6.65
   (5) $14.25

To check your answers, turn to page 380.

FRACTIONS

Unit 4

Fractions name part of the whole. The **denominator** of the fraction tells us how many equal parts there are in the whole. The **numerator** tells how many of those parts are shaded.

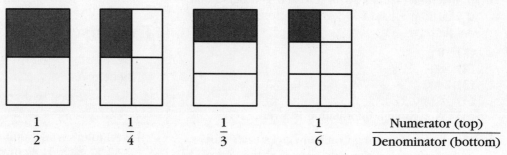

$$\frac{1}{2} \qquad \frac{1}{4} \qquad \frac{1}{3} \qquad \frac{1}{6}$$

Numerator (top)
Denominator (bottom)

Fractions can also name part of a group or set.

- Five months is $\frac{5}{12}$ of a year.

- Two feet is $\frac{2}{3}$ of a yard.

The fractions we have looked at so far have been *proper fractions*. A proper fraction represents part of a whole. In a proper fraction, the numerator is less than the denominator.

Examples:

$$\frac{1}{3} \qquad \frac{7}{8} \qquad \frac{5}{16}$$

In an **improper fraction**, the numerator is equal to or greater than the denominator.

$$\frac{3}{3} \qquad \frac{5}{4} \qquad \frac{8}{8} \qquad \frac{7}{2}$$

A **mixed number** is a whole number with a fraction. It represents one or more wholes *and* part of a whole.

$$1\frac{2}{3} \qquad 13\frac{1}{4} \qquad 2\frac{5}{6}$$

RENAMING FRACTIONS AND MIXED NUMBERS

Sometimes you need to change how a fraction is written. For example, when the answer to a problem is an improper fraction, the fraction should be renamed as a whole or mixed number.

To change an improper fraction to a whole or mixed number, divide the numerator by the denominator. If there is a *remainder*, or amount left over, write it over the denominator.

292

Examples:

$$\frac{3}{3} = 3\overline{)3} = 1 \qquad \frac{5}{3} = 3\overline{)5} \quad \frac{2}{3} = 1\frac{2}{3} \qquad \frac{15}{7} = 7\overline{)15} \quad \frac{1}{7} = 2\frac{1}{7}$$

To change a mixed number to an improper fraction, reverse the process above. Multiply the denominator by the whole number, and add the numerator.

Examples:

$1\frac{2}{3} = \frac{?}{3}$ Multiply 1 × 3. $1\frac{2}{3} = \frac{1 \times 3 + 2}{3} = \frac{5}{3}$
Then add 2.

$2\frac{1}{7} = \frac{?}{7}$ Multiply 2 × 7. $2\frac{1}{7} = \frac{2 \times 7 + 1}{7} = \frac{15}{7}$
Then add 1.

The fractions in the answer choices on the GED Math Test are always renamed in lowest terms. To rename a fraction in lowest terms, divide the numerator and the denominator by the *same* number. Renaming a fraction from higher numbers to lower numbers is called **reducing to lowest terms**.

Examples:

$$\frac{2}{4} \quad \frac{2 \div 2}{4 \div 2} = \frac{1}{2} \qquad \frac{4}{12} \quad \frac{4 \div 4}{12 \div 4} = \frac{1}{3} \qquad \frac{35}{42} \quad \frac{35 \div 7}{42 \div 7} = \frac{5}{6}$$

To rename to higher terms, multiply the numerator and denominator by the same number. Renaming a fraction from lower numbers to higher numbers is called **raising to higher terms.**

Examples:

$$\frac{2}{3} = \frac{?}{6} \quad \frac{2 \times 2}{3 \times 2} = \frac{4}{6} \qquad \frac{5}{6} = \frac{?}{42} \quad \frac{5 \times 7}{6 \times 7} = \frac{35}{42}$$

COMPARING FRACTIONS BY CROSS-MULTIPLICATION

Cross-multiplication means to multiply diagonally "across" the sign that links two fractions. You can use crossmultiplication to compare fractions.

- If two fractions are *equal*, you will get the same answer when you cross-multiply.

$$4(2) = 8 \qquad 8(1) = 8$$
$$\frac{1}{4} \diagdown \frac{2}{8} \qquad 8 = 8 \quad \text{These fractions are equal.}$$

If two fractions are *not equal*, when you cross-multiply you will get a greater number by the greater fraction.

$$8(1) = 8 \qquad 2(7) = 14$$
$$\frac{1}{2} \diagdown \frac{7}{8} \qquad 8 \text{ is less than } (<) 14 \text{ so } \frac{1}{2} < \frac{7}{8}$$

Exercise 1

> **Directions**
>
> Solve the following problems.

The directors of a community center invited area teenagers to help paint their building. The teens kept their own records. In order to compare their work, complete each column below.

Name	Paint Used (in quarter gallons)	Total Gallons Used
1. Nancy	$\frac{9}{4}$	
2. Tyrone		$3\frac{3}{4}$
3. Pava	$\frac{6}{4}$	
4. Carmen	$\frac{12}{4}$	
5. Hank		$4\frac{1}{4}$

Fill in each blank with <, >, or =.

6. $\frac{1}{3}$ _____ $\frac{7}{8}$

7. $\frac{2}{3}$ _____ $\frac{6}{9}$

8. $\frac{7}{9}$ _____ $\frac{4}{7}$

9. $\frac{6}{7}$ _____ $\frac{3}{8}$

> Items 10 and 11 refer to the following number line.

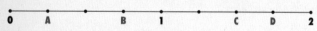

10. What is the value of Point A?

   (1) $\frac{1}{3}$

   (2) $\frac{1}{4}$

   (3) $\frac{1}{5}$

   (4) $\frac{1}{2}$

   (5) $\frac{1}{8}$

11. Which point represents the mixed number $1\frac{1}{2}$?

   (1) A
   (2) B
   (3) C
   (4) D
   (5) None of the above.

12. Which of the following pairs of fractions are equal?

   (1) $\frac{5}{10}$ and $\frac{5}{11}$

   (2) $\frac{9}{11}$ and $\frac{18}{23}$

   (3) $\frac{10}{20}$ and $\frac{5}{5}$

   (4) $\frac{3}{15}$ and $\frac{1}{5}$

   (5) $\frac{6}{8}$ and $\frac{2}{4}$

13. Which of the following is equal to $\frac{2}{3}$?

   (1) 5 inches as part of a foot
   (2) 15 minutes as part of an hour
   (3) $300 as part of Bun's $450 pay
   (4) 8 hours as part of a day
   (5) 500 Democrats as part of the 1,200 registered voters

14. Which of the following is equal to $\frac{3}{4}$?

   (1) $2 as part of $10
   (2) 9 eggs as part of a dozen
   (3) 2 weeks as part of a month
   (4) 90 points out of a possible 100 points
   (5) 24 inches as part of a yard

To check your answers, turn to page 381.

Estimating with Fractions

On the GED Math Test there may be times when you are asked to find an approximate fraction. At other times, you may find it helpful to use approximation to estimate an answer. There are two useful ways to find an approximate answer.

METHOD A

Round the numerator and denominator to the nearest 10 or 100 and rename.

Example:

The theater club has 80 members. 58 members have bought tickets to see "My Favorite Husband." This is approximately what fraction of the total members?

$\dfrac{58}{60}$ rounds to $\dfrac{60}{80}$ **Rename:** $\dfrac{60 \div 20}{80 \div 20} = \dfrac{3}{4}$

METHOD B

Check to see if one value is an approximate multiple of the other.

Example:

Of the 11 members of the student council, 6 voted "no" on the proposed fund-raiser. Approximately what fraction of the council voted "no"?

In this problem, $\dfrac{6}{11}$ of the council members voted against the proposal. The fraction $\dfrac{6}{11}$ is close to $\dfrac{6}{12}$, which reduces to $\dfrac{1}{2}$. So $\dfrac{6}{11}$ is approximately $\dfrac{1}{2}$.

Exercise 2

Directions

Choose an approximate fraction for each of the following items.

1. Eleven days is approximately what fraction of a month?

    (1) $\dfrac{1}{8}$

    (2) $\dfrac{1}{6}$

    (3) $\dfrac{1}{4}$

    (4) $\dfrac{1}{3}$

    (5) $\dfrac{1}{2}$

2. Uma collected $52 of the $100 promised by her office staff as a donation to "Toys for Tots." Approximately what fractional part has Uma collected?

    (1) $\dfrac{1}{8}$

    (2) $\dfrac{1}{6}$

    (3) $\dfrac{1}{4}$

    (4) $\dfrac{1}{3}$

    (5) $\dfrac{1}{2}$

3. The Belkakis Photo Club meets monthly. In June, 5 of the 42 members were absent. Approximately what fraction of the club was absent?

    (1) $\dfrac{1}{8}$

    (2) $\dfrac{2}{5}$

    (3) $\dfrac{1}{2}$

    (4) $\dfrac{5}{6}$

    (5) $\dfrac{7}{10}$

4. George has driven 72 of the 98 miles to Youngville. Approximately what fraction of the trip has he driven?

    (1) $\dfrac{1}{8}$

    (2) $\dfrac{2}{5}$

    (3) $\dfrac{1}{2}$

    (4) $\dfrac{5}{6}$

    (5) $\dfrac{7}{10}$

To check your answers, turn to page 381.

Adding and Subtracting Like Fractions

Values can only be added to or subtracted from like terms. Whole numbers are added to whole numbers. Decimal parts are subtracted from other decimal parts.

Fractions have **like terms** when they have the same denominator. When fractions have the same denominator, their numerators can be added or subtracted. The answer, if necessary, is renamed in lowest terms.

Examples:

$$\frac{3}{8} + \frac{1}{8} = \frac{4}{8} = \frac{1}{2}$$

$$\frac{2}{3} + \frac{2}{3} = \frac{4}{3} = 1\frac{1}{3}$$

$$\frac{3}{5} - \frac{2}{5} = \frac{1}{5}$$

$$\frac{5}{6} - \frac{1}{6} = \frac{4}{6} = \frac{2}{3}$$

To add mixed numbers with like denominators:

Step 1 Add the fractions together. Check to see if the fractional part can be reduced or renamed as a mixed number.

$$7\frac{3}{5}$$
$$+ 5\frac{4}{5}$$
$$\frac{7}{5} = 1\frac{2}{5}$$

Step 2 Add the whole numbers together, remembering to include any whole number from the simplified fraction.

$$7\frac{3}{5}$$
$$+ 5\frac{4}{5}$$
$$12 + 1\frac{2}{5} = 13\frac{2}{5}$$

To subtract mixed numbers with like denominators:

Step 1 Borrow, if necessary. Rename the 1 you borrowed as a fraction, using the denominator from the number you are subtracting.

$$7\frac{5}{12} = 6\frac{5 + 12}{12} = 6\frac{17}{12}$$
$$- 2\frac{7}{12}$$

Step 2 Subtract the fractions. Check to see if the difference can be reduced.

$$6\frac{17}{12}$$
$$- 2\frac{7}{12}$$
$$\frac{10}{12} = \frac{5}{6}$$

Step 3 Subtract the whole numbers.

$$6\frac{7}{12}$$
$$- 2\frac{7}{12}$$
$$4\frac{5}{6}$$

Exercise 3

Directions

Solve the following problems.

1. $\frac{1}{4} + \frac{3}{4}$

2. $\frac{7}{10} + \frac{5}{10}$

3. $4\frac{1}{3} + 2\frac{1}{3}$

4. $\frac{3}{4} - \frac{1}{4}$

5. $\frac{11}{12} - \frac{7}{12}$

6. $7 - \frac{1}{2}$

7. $12\frac{2}{5} - 7\frac{4}{5}$

8. Gabriela is happy that she has had time to jog three days this week. She ran $2\frac{1}{4}$ miles on Monday, $3\frac{1}{4}$ miles on Wednesday, and $3\frac{3}{4}$ miles on Friday. How many miles did she jog this week?

(1) $8\frac{1}{4}$

(2) $8\frac{1}{2}$

(3) $9\frac{1}{4}$

(4) $9\frac{1}{2}$

(5) 9

9. Before Karen left for the skiing trip, the gasoline tank of her car was $\frac{3}{4}$ full. When she returned, the gauge showed she had $\frac{1}{4}$ tank left. How much of a tank of gasoline did she use?

(1) $\frac{1}{8}$

(2) $\frac{1}{4}$

(3) $\frac{1}{3}$

(4) $\frac{1}{2}$

(5) $\frac{2}{3}$

10. The Garabedians have a wood-burning stove. They bought 2 cords of wood in November. They have used $\frac{2}{3}$ of a cord. How many cords of wood do they have left?

(1) $\frac{1}{2}$

(2) $\frac{3}{4}$

(3) $\frac{2}{3}$

(4) 1

(5) $1\frac{1}{3}$

11. Jack won an award that measures $6\frac{1}{4}$ inches on each side. He plans to mount the square award on a piece of wood so that the award has a $\frac{3}{4}$ inch border on all sides. What must the piece of wood measure in inches on each side to frame the award according to Jack's plan?

(1) $6\frac{3}{4}$

(2) 7

(3) $7\frac{1}{2}$

(4) $7\frac{3}{4}$

(5) $8\frac{1}{4}$

12. The Evergreen Landscaping Company has been hired to surround a golf course with drought-resistant plants. The company completed $\frac{1}{8}$ of the job last week and $\frac{3}{8}$ this week. What fraction of the job remains to be completed?

(1) $\frac{5}{8}$

(2) $\frac{1}{2}$

(3) $\frac{1}{4}$

(4) $\frac{1}{8}$

(5) Not enough information is given.

To check your answers, turn to page 381.

Adding and Subtracting Unlike Fractions

Fractions with different denominators (**unlike terms**) must be renamed before they can be added together or subtracted from each other.

What is $\frac{1}{2} + \frac{1}{3}$?

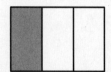

In order to add or subtract, the fractions must be renamed with the same or **common denominator**.

If we cut both rectangles into 6 pieces, we can see that $\frac{1}{2} = \frac{3}{6}$ and $\frac{1}{3} = \frac{2}{6}$.

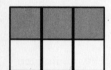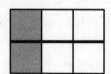

To add or subtract fractions with unlike denominators:

Step 1 Find a common denominator for the fractions.
Step 2 Rename the fractions in like terms.
Step 3 Add or subtract as you would like fractions.

$$\frac{1}{2} \quad \frac{1 \times 3}{2 \times 3} = \quad \frac{3}{6} \qquad \frac{1}{2} \quad \frac{1 \times 3}{2 \times 3} = \quad \frac{3}{6}$$
$$+\frac{1}{3} \quad \frac{1 \times 2}{3 \times 2} = +\frac{2}{6} \qquad -\frac{1}{3} \quad \frac{1 \times 2}{3 \times 2} = -\frac{2}{6}$$
$$\frac{5}{6} \qquad\qquad\qquad \frac{1}{6}$$

To find a common denominator, use these methods:

Check to see if one denominator is a multiple of the other.

- For $\frac{1}{2}$ and $\frac{3}{4}$ use 4 as the denominator.

- For $\frac{2}{3}$ and $\frac{7}{12}$ use 12 as the denominator.

If one denominator is not a multiple of the other, find a third number which is divisible by both denominators.

- For $\frac{2}{3}$ and $\frac{4}{5}$ use 15 as the denominator.

- For $\frac{1}{4}$ and $\frac{5}{6}$ use 12 as the denominator.

If all else fails, multiply one denominator by the other. This method will always give a common denominator, but the number may be higher than necessary, and it may be necessary to reduce the final answer.

- For $\frac{1}{5}$ and $\frac{3}{7}$ use 35 as the denominator.

- For $\frac{2}{3}$ and $\frac{5}{8}$ use 24 as the denominator.

Exercise 4

Directions
Solve the following problems.

1. $\frac{1}{2} + \frac{2}{3}$

2. $\frac{3}{5} + \frac{3}{4}$

3. $\frac{3}{4} - \frac{1}{3}$

4. $\frac{7}{8} - \frac{1}{2}$

5. Mike mailed two documents together, which weighed $\frac{2}{3}$ pound and $1\frac{1}{6}$ pounds respectively. How many pounds did his package weigh?

   (1) $1\frac{1}{2}$

   (2) $1\frac{3}{4}$

   (3) $1\frac{5}{6}$

   (4) $1\frac{7}{8}$

   (5) $2\frac{1}{6}$

6. The photo of Isaiah's son is $5\frac{11}{16}$ inches, just a little too wide for the $5\frac{1}{2}$ inch frame. What fraction of an inch should Isaiah cut off of the photo?

(1) $\frac{1}{18}$

(2) $\frac{1}{10}$

(3) $\frac{1}{8}$

(4) $\frac{3}{16}$

(5) $\frac{5}{18}$

7. Ricardo is biking $20\frac{2}{3}$ miles to Silver Lake. After he passes the $4\frac{1}{2}$ mile marker, how many more miles does he have to go?

(1) $15\frac{1}{6}$

(2) $16\frac{1}{6}$

(3) $16\frac{3}{8}$

(4) $16\frac{5}{8}$

(5) $17\frac{1}{6}$

8. The McKiernan family is getting together for Thanksgiving dinner at Betty's house. Betty bought a $12\frac{1}{2}$ pound turkey. Her sister-in-law Ann bought a $13\frac{3}{4}$ pound turkey. How many pounds of turkey will the family have altogether?

(1) $25\frac{1}{4}$

(2) $26\frac{1}{4}$

(3) $26\frac{3}{8}$

(4) $26\frac{1}{2}$

(5) $26\frac{3}{4}$

Items 9 and 10 refer to the following information.

Carlos told his children that he feels they watch too much television. His son Juan had watched TV for $1\frac{1}{2}$ hours that morning and $2\frac{1}{4}$ hours that afternoon. His daughter Luz had watched $\frac{1}{2}$ hour longer than Juan in the morning but only $1\frac{1}{2}$ hours total in the afternoon.

9. How many hours did Luz watch all together?

(1) $3\frac{1}{2}$

(2) $3\frac{3}{4}$

(3) 4

(4) $4\frac{1}{4}$

(5) $4\frac{3}{4}$

10. How many hours more did Juan watch TV than Luz?

(1) $\frac{1}{16}$

(2) $\frac{1}{12}$

(3) $\frac{1}{8}$

(4) $\frac{1}{6}$

(5) $\frac{1}{4}$

To check your answers, turn to page 381.

Multiplying and Dividing Fractions

Ramona works as an assistant for the County Clerk. She works $7\frac{1}{2}$ hours each day. Ramona estimates that $\frac{1}{3}$ of each day is spent processing voter registration records. How many hours per day does she work on voter records?

To solve this problem, you need to answer:

What is $\frac{1}{3}$ of $7\frac{1}{2}$?

To multiply fractions or mixed numbers:

Example: $7\frac{1}{2} \times \frac{1}{3}$

Step 1 Change mixed numbers to improper fractions. Write any whole number as a fraction.

$$7\frac{1}{2} \times \frac{1}{3} = \frac{15}{2} \times \frac{1}{3}$$

Step 2 Cancel where possible by dividing any numerator and any denominator by the same number.

$$\frac{\overset{5}{\cancel{15}}}{2} \times \frac{1}{\cancel{3}}$$
$$1$$

Step 3 Multiply numerator by numerator and denominator by denominator.

$$\frac{\overset{5}{\cancel{15}}}{2} \times \frac{1}{\cancel{3}} = \frac{5}{2}$$
$$1$$

Step 4 Rename, if necessary, changing improper fractions to mixed numbers or reducing.

$$\frac{5}{2} = 2\frac{1}{2}$$

Ramona spends 2½ hours per day on voter records.

Example:

How many $\frac{3}{8}$s are in $4\frac{1}{2}$? The strip below is $4\frac{1}{2}$ inches long. The strip is divided into twelve pieces, each $\frac{3}{8}$ inch long. $4\frac{1}{2} \div \frac{3}{8} = 12$

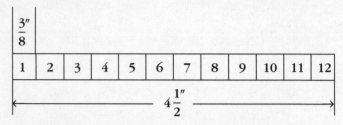

To divide with fractions or mixed numbers:

Example: $4\frac{1}{2} \div \frac{3}{8}$

Step 1 Write all numbers as fractions.

$$4\frac{1}{2} \div \frac{3}{8} = \frac{9}{2} \div \frac{3}{8}$$

Step 2 Rewrite the problem as multiplication by changing the ÷ sign to × and inverting (placing the top number on the bottom and the bottom number on the top) the fraction following the sign.

$$\frac{9}{2} \div \frac{3}{8} = \frac{9}{2} \times \frac{8}{3}$$

Step 3 Cancel where possible.

$$\frac{\overset{3}{\cancel{9}}}{\underset{1}{\cancel{2}}} \times \frac{\overset{4}{\cancel{8}}}{\underset{1}{\cancel{3}}}$$

Step 4 Multiply numerator by numerator. Then multiply denominator by denominator.

$$\frac{3}{1} \times \frac{4}{1} = \frac{12}{1}$$

Step 5 Rename, if necessary, changing improper fractions to mixed or whole numbers or reducing.

$$\frac{12}{1} = 12$$

Exercise 5

Directions

Choose the one best answer to each item.

---

1. Savita's car has a $13\frac{1}{2}$ gallon tank. It is $\frac{3}{4}$ full. How many gallons of gas are in her car's tank?

    (1) $9\frac{7}{8}$

    (2) 10

    (3) $10\frac{1}{8}$

    (4) $10\frac{1}{4}$

    (5) $10\frac{5}{8}$

2. How many feet of wood are needed to replace 5 staircase boards if each is $4\frac{2}{3}$ feet long?

    (1) 20

    (2) $20\frac{1}{3}$

    (3) $21\frac{1}{3}$

    (4) $22\frac{2}{3}$

    (5) $23\frac{1}{3}$

3. The Brownville PTA needs to cover 3 tables for the banquet. How many yards of fabric are needed if each tablecloth requires $2\frac{3}{4}$ yards?

    (1) $8\frac{1}{4}$

    (2) 8

    (3) $7\frac{3}{4}$

    (4) $7\frac{1}{2}$

    (5) $6\frac{3}{4}$

4. Richard's Farms has decided to allow the community to use $7\frac{1}{2}$ acres of their land for vegetable gardens this summer. If the town divides the area into 8 plots, how many acres will each plot be?

    (1) $\frac{7}{16}$

    (2) $\frac{1}{2}$

    (3) $\frac{15}{16}$

    (4) $15\frac{1}{2}$

    (5) 60

5. Mary is cutting $\frac{3}{4}$ inch strips from a piece of cardboard that is 12 inches wide. How many strips will she get?

    (1) 8
    (2) 9
    (3) 12
    (4) 16
    (5) 34

6. Jenkin's Market gives each worker a $\frac{1}{4}$ hour break every 3 hours. If only one worker takes a break at one time, how many workers can take a break during a 3-hour span?

    (1) 10
    (2) 11
    (3) 12
    (4) 13
    (5) 14

To check your answers, turn to page 382.

RATIO AND PROPORTION

Have you read articles in the newspaper lately that discuss hiring quotas or pupil-teacher ratios in over-crowded schools? You may have read or heard phrases such as inflation rate and per capita rise. These phrases, which are common in our everyday language, refer to mathematical patterns called ratios.

A **ratio** is a comparison of two numbers used to show a relationship or pattern.

A ratio can compare two similar values, such as men to women (both are people) and length to width (both are measures of length).

A ratio can also compare different units of measure: home runs per at bats, miles per hour, miles per gallon, and price per item. A ratio that compares different units of measure is called a **rate**.

A class has 5 women and 7 men. That ratio can be written three ways, each of which would be read 5 to 7.

With a Colon	Without a Colon	As a Fraction
5:7	5 to 7	$\dfrac{5}{7}$

The notation for ratios most often used on the GED Math Test is the fraction notation. The first number stated in the ratio is *always* written first or on top of the fraction bar!

Ratios communicate best when they are renamed in lowest terms. Like a fraction, you can rename a ratio. However, there is one important difference between ratios and fractions. Improper fractions are rewritten as whole or mixed numbers, but ratios are not.

Example:

Lorraine earns $400 weekly while her husband, Ron, earns $300. What is the ratio of Lorraine's earnings to her husband's earnings?

Write the ratio: $\dfrac{\$400}{\$300}$ **Rename** it: $\dfrac{\$400}{\$300} \div \dfrac{100}{100} = \dfrac{4}{3}$

The 4:3 ratio tells us that for every $4 Lorraine earns, Ron earns $3.

Sometimes you have to calculate one of the numbers in the ratio. How could you find the ratio of Lorraine's pay to their *total* weekly earnings?

Example:

First **add** their earnings to find the total.

$400 + $300 = $700

Then **write** the ratio and rename it:

$$\frac{\text{Lorraine's Earnings}}{\text{Total Earnings}} = \frac{\$400}{\$700} \div \frac{100}{100} = \frac{4}{7}$$

Exercise 1

Directions

For Items 1 to 5, write a ratio in lowest terms. For Items 6 to 8, choose the **one best answer** to each item.

1. The directions say to mix 5 cups water with 2 cups of cleaning solution. What is the ratio of water to solution?

2. The following statistics were given for Lisa's favorite team. What is their win:loss ratio?

Wins	Losses	Average	Streak
59	30	0.663	Win 1

3. Carolyn drove 375 miles to New York City. Her car used 15 gallons of gas. What was the rate of miles to gallons that she got on this trip?

4. The auto salesperson sold 36 cars last year. What is the ratio of cars sold per month?

5. Harry put $75 in his savings account and used the rest of his paycheck to pay bills totaling $325. What is the ratio of money saved to his *total pay*?

    (1) 3:16
    (2) 3:13
    (3) 1:4
    (4) 3:8
    (5) 1:2

6. On Monday, the Bijou Theater sold 120 children's tickets and 240 adults' tickets. What is the ratio of children's tickets to total tickets sold?

    (1) 3:1
    (2) 2:1
    (3) 1:2
    (4) 1:3
    (5) Not enough information is given.

Items 7 and 8 refer to the following information.

There are 25,000 registered voters in Big City. 15,000 voted during the last election.

7. What is the ratio of registered voters who *did not* vote to the total number of registered voters?

    (1) $\frac{2}{7}$

    (2) $\frac{2}{5}$

    (3) $\frac{3}{5}$

    (4) $\frac{5}{2}$

    (5) Not enough information is given.

8. What is the ratio of registered voters who did not vote to those who did vote?

    (1) $\frac{2}{5}$

    (2) $\frac{3}{5}$

    (3) $\frac{2}{3}$

    (4) $\frac{3}{2}$

    (5) Not enough information is given.

To check your answers, turn to page 382.

Proportion

A **proportion** represents two equal ratios. A variety of word problems can be solved by setting up a proportion.

Example:

Aida is preparing chicken diablo for the mayor's reception. She plans on using 6 pounds of chicken for every 9 guests. If the mayor has invited 150 guests, how many pounds of chicken will Aida need?

Carefully set up a proportion stating the values of both ratios. Write the known relationship as the first ratio. The second ratio must follow the pattern of the first *in the same order*.

$$\text{pounds} \quad \frac{6}{9} = \frac{n}{150} \quad \text{pounds}$$
$$\text{guests} \qquad\qquad \text{guests}$$

or

$$\text{guests} \quad \frac{9}{6} = \frac{150}{n} \quad \text{guests:}$$
$$\text{pounds} \qquad\qquad \text{pounds:}$$

Now you are ready to solve for the value of n.

To find the unknown value in a proportion (the value of n):

Step 1 Multiply the known denominator by the known numerator across from it.

$$\frac{9}{6} = \frac{150}{n} \quad 6(150) = 900$$

Step 2 Divide that answer by the numerator or denominator that remains.

$$\frac{9}{6} = \frac{150}{n} \quad 900 \div 9 = 100$$

$$\frac{9}{6} = \frac{150}{\textbf{100}}$$

Aida will need 100 pounds of chicken.

Exercise 2

1. The Murray Engraving Company prints formal invitations and announcements. Their standard price is $35 per 100 invitations. A company wants to purchase 1,200 announcements to advertise the grand opening of a new store. How much will the company be charged for the announcements?

    (1) $34
    (2) $210
    (3) $420
    (4) $525
    (5) $3,500

2. If 12 cans of oil cost $16.68, how much do 3 cans cost?

    (1) $1.39
    (2) $4.17
    (3) $8.34
    (4) $16.68
    (5) $50.04

3. Two quarts of oil cost $4.50. How much will 5 quarts cost?

    (1) $9.00
    (2) $9.50
    (3) $11.25
    (4) $22.50
    (5) Not enough information is given.

Items 4 and 5 refer to the following blueprint.

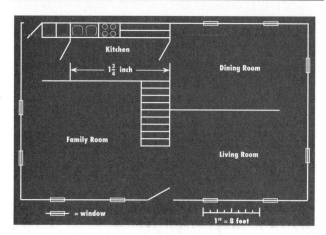

4. According to the architect's plan, how many feet wide will each living room window be?

(1) $\frac{1}{4}$

(2) $\frac{1}{2}$

(3) 1

(4) 2

(5) 3

5. According to the architect's plan, how many feet wide will the kitchen be?

(1) 8
(2) 10
(3) 12
(4) 13
(5) 14

6. Jerry works in the ticket office of the Community Theater. He mailed 5 tickets to the Higgins family, who sent a check for $77.50. At that rate, how many tickets should he send to MNG Offices, who sent a check for $232.50?

(1) 15
(2) 20
(3) 25
(4) 30
(5) 35

7. Carl drove 375 miles to New York City. His car used 15 gallons of gas. If he gets the same mileage on his next trip, how many miles can he drive on 25 gallons of gas?

(1) 225
(2) 500
(3) 625
(4) 825
(5) 9,375

Items 8 to 10 refer to the following information.

The Village School Committee is seeking to integrate all city schools. After gathering information about the community's ethnic distribution, the committee decides that in every group of 20 children, there should be 8 African-Americans, 6 Caucasians, 4 Hispanics, and 2 Asians.

8. If Green Elementary School has 750 students, how many Hispanic students are needed?

(1) 4
(2) 40
(3) 150
(4) 200
(5) Not enough information is given.

9. If Elm Middle School has 640 African-Americans, how many Asian students are needed to achieve full integration?

(1) 60
(2) 80
(3) 100
(4) 160
(5) Not enough information is given.

10. If South High School's enrollment of 5,000 is representative of the ethnic distribution within the community, how many of the students are Caucasian?

(1) 150
(2) 1,500
(3) 2,000
(4) 3,000
(5) Not enough information is given.

To check your answers, turn to page 382.

Proportions in Set-Up Problems

Some of the problems on the GED Math Test are set-up problems. In a set-up problem, you are asked to choose the correct way to solve the problem from the five answer choices you are given.

To choose the proper set-up for a proportion problem:

Step 1 Carefully set up a proportion to solve the problem.

Step 2 Write an expression for the cross products.

Step 3 Look carefully at the answer choices and choose the option that shows the correct multiplication and division set-up.

Test-Taking Tip: Always write the ratios in a proportion in the same order. Before writing a proportion to solve an item in the test, quickly jot down the labels in the order you want the numbers in the ratios to appear.

Example: $\dfrac{\text{miles}}{\text{hours}}$

Now try this GED Math Test problem.

Example:

The scale of miles on a map shows that 2 inches equals 400 miles. Which of the expressions below could be used to find how many miles are represented by 3 inches?

(1) $\dfrac{(2)(3)}{400}$

(2) $\dfrac{(3)(400)}{2}$

(3) $\dfrac{(3)(2)}{400}$

(4) $\dfrac{(3)(400)}{1}$

(5) Not enough information is given.

Step 1 Set up the proportion as you see it. $\qquad \dfrac{2}{400} = \dfrac{3}{x}$

Step 2 Write an expression. $\qquad \dfrac{400(3)}{2}$

Step 3 Now compare your expression to the answer choices.

Choice (2) shows 3 and 400 multiplied together and their product divided by 2 so answer choice (2) $\dfrac{(3)(400)}{2}$ is the correct set-up.

Exercise 3

Directions
Choose the one best answer to each item.

1. An ad on television says that 4 out of every 5 doctors interviewed recommended Vestamint antacid pills. If 500 doctors were interviewed, which of the following expressions represents the number of doctors who recommended Vestamint?

   (1) $\dfrac{5(500)}{4}$

   (2) $\dfrac{(4)500}{5}$

   (3) $\dfrac{4(5)}{500}$

   (4) $4(5)(500)$

   (5) Not enough information is given.

2. Franco's car gets 23 miles per gallon. If he drove 460 miles to San Francisco, which of the following expressions represents the gallons of gas he used?

   (1) $\dfrac{1(460)}{23}$

   (2) $\dfrac{23(460)}{1}$

   (3) $460(1)(23)$

   (4) $\dfrac{460(23)}{1}$

   (5) Not enough information is given.

3. Ned drove 23 miles in ½ hour. At the same rate, how far will he drive in 2 hours?

   (1) $\dfrac{23(2)}{\frac{1}{2}}$

   (2) $\dfrac{\frac{1}{2}(23)}{2}$

   (3) $\dfrac{2(\frac{1}{2})}{23}$

   (4) $2(\frac{1}{2})(23)$

   (5) $\dfrac{23}{\frac{1}{2}(2)}$

4. The Milton schools superintendent has announced that she will hire new teachers to bring the student-teacher ratio in the Milton schools to 20 to 1. If there are 12,000 students in Milton schools, which of the following expressions represents the number of additional teachers to be hired by the school superintendent?

(1) $\dfrac{1(12,000)}{20}$

(2) $\dfrac{20(12,000)}{1}$

(3) $\dfrac{1(20)}{12,000}$

(4) $1(20)(12,000)$

(5) Not enough information is given.

5. Carrie is making a dessert that calls for 6 ounces of chocolate chips to make 8 servings. Which of the following expressions could be used to figure out how many ounces she will need to make 12 servings?

(1) $\dfrac{6(12)}{8}$

(2) $\dfrac{8(12)}{6}$

(3) $\dfrac{6(8)}{12}$

(4) $6(8)(12)$

(5) $\dfrac{12}{6(8)}$

6. Steve earned $325 for 25 hours of work. At the same rate, which of the following expressions represents the amount (in dollars) he would earn for 40 hours of work?

(1) $40(325)(25)$

(2) $\dfrac{25(40)}{325}$

(3) $\dfrac{25(325)}{40}$

(4) $\dfrac{40(325)(25)}{50}$

(5) $\dfrac{40(325)}{25}$

To check your answers, turn to page 383.

PERCENT

Percent is a special rate or ratio meaning **per hundred**. 100% of something is all of it. 100% of a dollar is a dollar. 100% of a figure is the whole figure or one figure. When a percent is greater than 100, it represents more than one. For example, when profits are 200%, it means that they doubled.

Percents (per hundred) can be written as fractions or decimals. In many problems, you may find it helpful to change percent values into decimals or fractions or vice versa.

PERCENT AND FRACTION EQUIVALENTS

TO CHANGE A FRACTION TO A PERCENT

Write a proportion with the fraction as one ratio and $\frac{x}{100}$ as the other ratio.

Solve for the unknown by:

Raising the fraction to higher terms	Or	Using cross products

$\frac{1}{5}$ $\quad$ $\frac{1}{5}=\frac{x}{100}$ $\quad$ $\frac{1}{5}\times\frac{20}{20}=\frac{20}{100}$ $\quad$ 20% $\qquad$ $\frac{1}{3}$ $\quad$ $\frac{1}{3}=\frac{x}{100}$ $\quad$ $\frac{1(100)}{3}$ $\quad$ 33⅓%

$\frac{12}{25}$ $\quad$ $\frac{12}{25}=\frac{x}{100}$ $\quad$ $\frac{12}{25}\times\frac{4}{4}=\frac{48}{100}$ $\quad$ 48% $\qquad$ $\frac{5}{8}$ $\quad$ $\frac{5}{8}=\frac{x}{100}$ $\quad$ $\frac{5(100)}{8}$ $\quad$ 62½%

TO CHANGE A PERCENT TO A FRACTION

Write the percent over 100 and drop the % sign. Rename the fraction in lower terms or as a mixed number, if possible.

6% $\qquad$ $\frac{6}{100}$ $\qquad$ $\frac{3}{50}$

250% $\qquad$ $\frac{250}{100}$ $\qquad$ $\frac{5}{2}=2\frac{1}{2}$

PERCENT AND DECIMAL EQUIVALENTS

Percent means *per hundred*, so the % sign and two decimal places have the same meaning.

TO CHANGE A DECIMAL TO A PERCENT

Move the decimal point two places to the right and add a % sign.

0.02 $\qquad$ 0.02 $\qquad$ 2%

0.13 $\qquad$ 0.13 $\qquad$ 13%

3.6 $\qquad$ 3.60 $\qquad$ 360%

TO CHANGE A PERCENT TO A DECIMAL

Move the decimal point to the left and drop the % sign.

6% $\qquad$ 06 $\qquad$ 0.06

30% $\qquad$ 30 $\qquad$ 0.3

250% $\qquad$ 250 $\qquad$ 2.5

Exercise 1

> **Directions**
> Complete the tables below. For Items 15 and 16, choose the <u>one best answer</u>.

	Percent	Fraction		Decimal	Percent
1.		⅛	**8.**		7%
2.	25%		**9.**		10%
3.	40%		**10.**	0.18	
4.		½	**11.**	0.65	
5.		⅗	**12.**		125%
6.	70%		**13.**		180%
7.	75%		**14.**	2.5	

15. 25% equals $\frac{1}{4}$. Which of the following can you do to find 25% of a number quickly?

   (1) Divide the number by 10.
   (2) Divide the number by 4.
   (3) Divide the number by 2.
   (4) Multiply the number by 2.
   (5) Don't do anything; the number doesn't change.

16. Which of the following can you do to find 200% of a number quickly?

   (1) Divide it by 10.
   (2) Divide it by 2.
   (3) Multiply by 4.
   (4) Multiply by 2.
   (5) Don't do anything; you cannot find 200% of a number.

To check your answers, turn to page 383.

Solving Percent Problems Using Proportion

One of the best ways to solve percent problems is to use your knowledge of ratio and proportion. You can write a proportion using percent as a ratio to solve percent problems.

$$\frac{\%}{100} = \frac{\text{Part}}{\text{Whole}}$$

Examples:

What is 8% of 900?

   Write a proportion using the elements from the problem. Use a variable for the unknown part.

$$\underset{100}{\overset{\%}{}} \quad \frac{8}{100} = \frac{x}{900} \quad \underset{\text{(of) Whole}}{\overset{\text{(is) Part}}{}}$$

Solve:

$$\frac{8(900)}{100} = \frac{7{,}200}{100} = 72$$

72 is 8% of 900.

   You can also use proportion to solve for the unknown whole.

Eighty is 50% <u>of what number</u>?

   The question "of what number" indicates that the whole is missing.

$$\underset{100}{\overset{\%}{}} \quad \frac{50}{100} = \frac{80}{x} \quad \underset{\text{(of) Whole}}{\overset{\text{(is) Part}}{}}$$

Solve:

$$\frac{100(80)}{50} = 160$$

Eighty is 50% <u>of what number</u>? Eighty is 50% <u>of 160</u>.

   You can also use proportion to solve for the unknown percent.

Four hundred is <u>what percent</u> of 500?

   The question "what percent" indicates that the percent is missing.

$$\underset{100}{\overset{\%}{}} \quad \frac{x}{100} = \frac{400}{500} \quad \underset{\text{(of) Whole}}{\overset{\text{(is) Part}}{}}$$

Solve:

$$\frac{100(400)}{500} = 80$$

400 is 80% of 500.

   Remember that to solve percent problems using proportion:

- Figure out what element in the problem is missing.
- Set up the proportion.
- Solve for the missing element.

Exercise 2

Directions
Solve the following percent problems.

1. <u>What is</u> 90% of 180?

   $$\frac{\%}{100} \quad \underline{\quad} = \underline{\quad} \quad \frac{\text{(is) Part}}{\text{(of) Whole}}$$

2. <u>What percent</u> of 250 is 50?

   $$\frac{\%}{100} \quad \underline{\quad} = \underline{\quad} \quad \frac{\text{(is) Part}}{\text{(of) Whole}}$$

3. 100% of <u>what number</u> is 20?

   $$\frac{\%}{100} \quad \underline{\quad} = \underline{\quad} \quad \frac{\text{(is) Part}}{\text{(of) Whole}}$$

4. 70% of <u>what number</u> is 35?

   $$\frac{\%}{100} \quad \underline{\quad} = \underline{\quad} \quad \frac{\text{(is) Part}}{\text{(of) Whole}}$$

5. The Suttons are planning a vacation in Cancun. Their travel agent tells them that they can purchase a travel package for seven nights' lodging for $1,950. The agent offers them a 15% discount if they make their reservations today. How much will they save if they take advantage of the discount?

   (1) $19.50
   (2) $146.25
   (3) $195.00
   (4) $292.50
   (5) Not enough information is given.

6. Last year Monica earned $54 interest on her savings account. The interest rate was 4.5%. How much money was in her account before the interest was added?

   (1) $120
   (2) $1,200
   (3) $1,500
   (4) $7,500
   (5) $12,000

Items 7 and 8 refer to the following information.

Reggie's union negotiated a 6% cost of living increase. Reggie makes $29,500 a year.

7. By how much will Reggie's pay increase?

   (1) $17.70
   (2) $177
   (3) $1,070
   (4) $1,770
   (5) $2,770

8. What will Reggie's yearly salary be after the cost of living increase?

   (1) $29,577
   (2) $29,677
   (3) $31,270
   (4) $47,200
   (5) Not enough information is given.

9. Louise went shopping and bought a blouse for $24, slacks for $31.99, and shoes for $42.49. All her purchases are subject to a 5% sales tax. What is the total cost of her purchases including tax?

   (1) $4.92
   (2) $98.48
   (3) $103.40
   (4) $147.68
   (5) $149.24

10. Marylee works on commission. This month she has earned $325 for the first week, $480 for the second week, and $275 this week. What is the rate, or percent, of commission that she earns?

    (1) 2%
    (2) 4%
    (3) 5%
    (4) 6%
    (5) Not enough information is given.

To check your answers, turn to page 383.

Percent of Increase and Decrease

The **percent of increase or decrease** measures the change from one price or amount to another. Articles in the newspaper inform us that the value of real estate, for example, changes from time to time depending on factors in the economy. A person who buys a home one year finds its value has usually increased or decreased by the next year.

A different proportion can be used to find the percent of increase or decrease.

$$\frac{\% \text{ of Increase or Decrease}}{100} = \frac{\text{Change in Amount}}{\text{Original Amount}}$$

The change in amount is found by subtracting to find the difference between the original or earlier amount and the newer amount. This difference is compared to the original amount.

Example:

American Cinema has raised the price of admission from $6 per person to $7.50 per person. What is the percent of increase?

Step 1 Subtract to find the change between the original and the newer amount.

$$\begin{array}{r} \$7.50 \\ -6.00 \\ \hline \$1.50 \end{array}$$

Step 2 Put this amount over the original or earlier amount in a proportion.

$$\frac{\%}{100} = \frac{1.50}{6}$$

Step 3 Solve for percent.

$$\frac{100(1.50)}{6} = 25$$

The percent of increase is **25%**.

Example:

The Lunville High School had an enrollment of 1,050 students in 1994. This was less than the 1993 enrollment of 1,200. What was the percent of decrease in enrollment from 1993 to 1994?

Step 1 Subtract to find the change between the original and the newer amount.

$$\begin{array}{r} 1,200 \\ -1,050 \\ \hline 150 \end{array}$$

Step 2 Put this amount over the original or earlier amount in a proportion.

$$\frac{\%}{100} = \frac{150}{1,200}$$

Step 3 Solve for percent

$$\frac{100(150)}{1,200} = 12.5$$

The percent of decrease was **12.5%**.

Exercise 3

Directions

Choose the one best answer to each item.

1. During the 1990s many companies have reduced their work force. TGH Electronics employed 15,000 workers in 1992. By 1994 their work force was cut to 7,500. By what percent did their work force decrease?
   - **(1)** 5%
   - **(2)** 10%
   - **(3)** 20%
   - **(4)** 50%
   - **(5)** 100%

2. Tresses and Dresses Fashion Salon posted a notice that as of February 1, its prices will increase. A wash, cut, and blow dry will be $25, a tint will be $60, and a permanent will be $95. What is the percent of increase in the price for a permanent?
   - **(1)** 5%
   - **(2)** 10%
   - **(3)** 20%
   - **(4)** 25%
   - **(5)** Not enough information is given.

3. Fly-Us Airlines has lowered the economy fare from Chicago to Los Angeles from $264 to $212. To the nearest whole percent what is the percent of decrease in airfare?
   - **(1)** 16%
   - **(2)** 18%
   - **(3)** 20%
   - **(4)** 25%
   - **(5)** Not enough information is given.

4. Guiseppi's Pizza raised the price of a plain cheese pizza from $6.70 to $7.37. By what percent did the price for a plain cheese pizza increase?
   - **(1)** 5%
   - **(2)** 10%
   - **(3)** 20%
   - **(4)** 25%
   - **(5)** Not enough information is given.

5. Jody received a notice from the manager of Windsor Apartments that all rents will be increased by 8% effective June 1. Jody's rent is $450 a month now. How much will his rent be, effective June 1?

   (1) $486
   (2) $496
   (3) $500
   (4) $550
   (5) $586

6. In order to avoid lay-offs at Niki Computers, each assembler is being asked to take a 3% cut in pay. This would mean a loss of $420 a year to Maureen. What is her present salary before the paycut?

   (1) $1,400
   (2) $12,000
   (3) $14,000
   (4) $16,000
   (5) Not enough information is given.

7. Captive breeding of the Wild California Condor has increased the population from 20 to 64 birds. What is the percent of increase in the number of condors?

   (1) 31%
   (2) 44%
   (3) 69%
   (4) 220%
   (5) 320%

8. The regular price of a camera is $199. The sale price is $171. About what percent is the camera discounted?

   (1) 14%
   (2) 25%
   (3) 30%
   (4) 86%
   (5) Not enough information is given.

To check your answers, turn to page 384.

Solving Simple Interest Problems

When you have money in a savings account, the bank pays you interest. When you buy something on credit, you must pay interest. **Interest** is a percent paid for using someone else's money.

A formula for finding simple interest (i) is given on the GED list of formulas.

$i = prt$; where p = principal, r = rate, t = time

The **principal** is the amount of money borrowed.

The **rate** is the percent of interest charged or paid yearly. The percent must be written as a decimal or fraction in order to multiply.

The **time** is the number of years or part of a year for which the money is borrowed. When the time is in months, it should be written as a fraction over the denominator 12 (months in a year).

Example:

Find the simple interest on a new car loan of $8,000 at 9% interest for 4 years.

$i = prt$ principal is $8,000

rate 9% as a fraction $\left(\dfrac{9}{100}\right)$, or a decimal (0.09)

time is 4 years

$$i = \$8,000 \times \frac{9}{100} \times 4 \quad \textbf{or} \quad i = \$8,000(0.09)(4)$$

$$\frac{8,000}{1} \times \frac{9}{100} \times \frac{4}{1} = \$2,880$$

```
  $8,000
×   0.09
_____
$  720.00
×       4
_____
$2,880.00
```

PARTS OF A YEAR

Example:

Find the simple interest earned on a savings account of $250 at 3% interest for 4 months.

$i = prt$ **p**rincipal is $250

rate 3% as a fraction $\left(\dfrac{3}{100}\right)$, or a decimal (0.03)

time is 4 months, or $\dfrac{4}{12}$ of a year

The rate is annual. If the time includes months, the months are placed over 12 and reduced, if possible.

$$\dfrac{4 \text{ months}}{12 \text{ months}} = \dfrac{1}{3}$$

$$i = \$250\left(\dfrac{3}{100}\right)\left(\dfrac{1}{3}\right) \quad \textbf{or} \quad i = \$250\,(0.03)\left(\dfrac{1}{3}\right)$$

$$\dfrac{\$250}{1} \times \dfrac{3}{100} \times \dfrac{1}{3} = \dfrac{\$5}{2} = \$2.50 \qquad \begin{array}{r} \$\,2.50 \\ \times\ 0.03 \end{array}$$

$$\$\,7.50 \times \dfrac{1}{3} = \$2.50$$

AMOUNT TO REPAY

Example:

Stacy and Bob bought a new living room set for $2,400, which they agreed to pay for over 2 years at a 10% interest rate. How much money will they pay for the living room furniture?

This is a two-step problem.

Step 1 Find the amount of interest.

$$i = \$2,400\left(\dfrac{10}{100}\right)(2) \quad \textbf{or} \quad i = \$2,400\,(0.1)(2)$$

$$\dfrac{\$2,400}{1} \times \dfrac{10}{100} \times \dfrac{2}{1} = \$480 \qquad \begin{array}{r} \$\ 2,400 \\ \times\ \ 0.1 \\ \hline 240.0 \\ \times\ \ \ \ 2 \\ \hline \$480.00 \end{array}$$

Step 2 Add the interest to the principal to find the final cost.

$$\begin{array}{r} \$2,400 \\ +\ \ \ 480 \\ \hline \$2,880 \end{array} \text{ Amount to repay}$$

Exercise 4

> **Directions**
>
> Use the formula $i = prt$ to solve for the interest in the following problems.

1. Peter borrowed $2,000 from the Carpenter's Credit Union for 2 years at 9% interest. How much interest must he pay?

2. Carlos bought a new sofa for $599 at 10% interest with 6 months to pay. How much interest must he pay?

3. The Pepicellis want to buy a new home at a mortgage rate of 8.5%. Which expression below shows the interest that they will pay if they get a $125,000 mortgage for 25 years?
   - **(1)** $125,000(8.5)(25)
   - **(2)** $125,000(0.085)
   - **(3)** $125,000(0.085)(25)
   - **(4)** 25(0.085)
   - **(5)** $125,000(25)

4. Voeurn financed his $8,800 car at 7% for 5 years. What is the total amount that Voeurn must repay?
   - **(1)** $3,080
   - **(2)** $8,800
   - **(3)** $9,108
   - **(4)** $11,880
   - **(5)** $12,880

5. Angela put a $1,000 down payment on a used car costing $4,200. She got a simple interest loan from her bank for the remaining amount. The loan is for 3 years at an annual interest rate of 8%. What is the total amount Angela will repay the bank?
   - **(1)** $768
   - **(2)** $1,008
   - **(3)** $3,968
   - **(4)** $4,948
   - **(5)** $5,208

To check your answers, turn to page 384.

DATA ANALYSIS

Tables

Many important decisions depend on our ability to interpret data. Bits of information are easier to understand and use when they are well organized.

In a **table**, information is organized in columns and rows. **Columns** go up and down. To remember this, think of columns on buildings, such as the Lincoln Memorial in Washington, D.C. **Rows** go across. Think about finding your seat in a row at a sporting event. Columns and rows have labels that indicate what information will be found within them.

The title of the table indicates what information is included in the table as a whole.

LIVING ARRANGEMENTS OF YOUNG ADULTS IN 1990
Shown in Percents

	Males 18–24	Females 18–24	Males 25–34	Females 25–34
Child of Householder	58.1	47.7	15.0	8.1
Family Householder	14.8	29.5	55.9	73.3
Nonfamily Householder	9.9	8.0	16.2	9.9
Other	17.3	14.8	13.0	8.7

Source: Bureau of the Census; U.S. Department of Commerce

In a table the place where a particular row and column meet is called a **cell**.

Examples:

What percent of men between the ages of 25 and 34 are family householders?

Look across the row which reads *Family Householder* to the number in the column under *Males 25-34*. You can see that the cell labeled 55.9% represents the percent of men in this age group who are family householders.

What are the living arrangements for the highest percent of females ages 18-24?

Look down the column labeled *Females 18-24;* the highest number is 47.7%. Look across the row that contains 47.7% to the heading *Child of Householder*. The greatest percent of women, ages 18-24, are children of the householder.

Some problems on the GED Math Test will ask you to work with the figures given on a table to solve problems. Carefully use the table to find the right facts. Then use the facts to calculate the answer.

MEDIAN PRICE OF EXISTING SINGLE-FAMILY HOMES

City	1988	1990	1992
Akron, OH	$ 59,900	$ 67,700	$ 75,500
Baltimore, MD	$ 88,700	$105,900	$111,500
Boston, MA	$181,200	$174,200	$168,200
Charleston, SC	$ 73,100	$ 76,200	$ 82,000
Daytona Beach, FL	$ 62,600	$ 64,100	$ 63,600
Honolulu, HI	$210,000	$352,000	$342,000
Louisville, KY	$ 54,500	$ 60,800	$ 69,700
New York, NY	$183,800	$174,900	$169,300
San Francisco, CA	$212,900	$259,300	$243,900
Spokane, WA	$ 51,100	$ 55,500	$ 71,300

Source: National Association of Realtors

Median means "middle." When a list of prices is arranged from least to most expensive, the median price is the price in the middle of the list. In this table, the median prices represent typical prices for homes in these cities.

Example:

In 1992, the median price of a home in Daytona Beach, Florida, was about what fraction of the median price of a home in San Francisco, California?

(1) $\frac{1}{5}$

(2) $\frac{1}{4}$

(3) $\frac{1}{3}$

(4) $\frac{1}{2}$

(5) $\frac{2}{3}$

The question asks for a comparison of prices in 1992. Be sure to look in the proper column. In 1992 the median price of a home in Daytona Beach was $63,600 and in San Francisco it was $243,900. Because the question uses the word "about," your answer does not need to be exact. Use rounding to make the work easier.

$\dfrac{\$63,600}{\$243,900}$ rounded to $\dfrac{\$6\cancel{0},\cancel{000}}{\$24\cancel{0},\cancel{000}}$ is about $= \dfrac{1}{4}$

Choice (2) $\dfrac{1}{4}$ is the correct answer choice.

Exercise 1

Items 1 to 4 refer to the following table.

NUMBER OF SICK DAYS PER YEAR
per 100 currently employed people

Illness or Injury	18–24 Years	25–44 Years	45–64 Years
Common Cold	30.3	15.5	15.8
Influenza	72.2	66.2	63.1
Acute Bronchitis	6.5	6.7	3.6
Pneumonia	3.8	1.5	4.3
Fractures/Dislocations	28.7	29.0	8.0
Sprains/Strains	43.7	39.8	17.3
Open Wounds	33.2	7.7	5.1

Source: National Center for Health Statistics

1. About how many sick days related to acute bronchitis will be taken in a year by 100 workers between the ages of 45 and 64?

   (1) 3–4 days
   (2) 5–6 days
   (3) 7–8 days
   (4) 8–9 days
   (5) Not enough information is given.

2. About how many sick days related to fractures or dislocations will be taken in a year by 100 workers between the ages of 18 and 24?

   (1) 1–2 days
   (2) 3–4 days
   (3) 6–7 days
   (4) 17–18 days
   (5) 28–29 days

3. Which illness or injury caused the fewest sick days for people between the ages of 25 and 44?

   (1) Acute Bronchitis
   (2) Open Wounds
   (3) Pneumonia
   (4) Common Cold
   (5) Influenza

4. Which illness or injury caused the greatest number of sick days to be taken by all age groups?

   (1) Common Cold
   (2) Influenza
   (3) Pneumonia
   (4) Sprains/Strains
   (5) Open Wounds

Items 5 and 6 refer to the following table.

AIRLINE ON-TIME PERFORMANCE RATINGS

Airline	Percent of Flights
Northeast	92.7
AirGo	91.6
Aero USA	87.5
EastAir	84.1
Pegasus	74.2

5. How many flights out of 1,000 could be expected to be on time for Pegasus Airlines?

   (1) 159
   (2) 258
   (3) 371
   (4) 742
   (5) 841

6. Of 750 WestAir flights, 94 arrived late. WestAir's on-time percent is nearest that of which of the following airlines?

   (1) Northeast
   (2) AirGo
   (3) Aero USA
   (4) EastAir
   (5) Pegasus

Items 7 to 9 refer to the following table.

REFEREE ANNUAL SALARY SCALES

Years of Service	NHL	NBA
0–4	$50,000	$ 57,000
5–9	$60,000	$ 75,000
10–14	$80,000	$ 94,000
15–19	$90,000	$116,000
20+	$90,000	$141,000

7. After 12 years of service, how much more do NBA referees earn than NHL referees?

  (1) $4,000
  (2) $14,000
  (3) $26,000
  (4) $37,000
  (5) Not enough information is given.

8. If the NHL gives a 50% increase in salary to referees who have served from 5 to 9 years, which expression can be used to find the new annual salary for those referees?

  (1) $\dfrac{\$60,000}{0.5}$

  (2) $\dfrac{\$60,000}{0.5} + \$60,000$

  (3) $0.5(\$60,000)$
  (4) $0.5(\$60,000) + \$60,000$
  (5) $50(\$60,000)$

9. The NHL plans to increase the annual salary of referees with 20+ years of service another $75,000. How much more will an NHL referee earn with 20+ years of service than an NBA referee with the same years of service if the proposed change takes place?

  (1) $24,000
  (2) $51,000
  (3) $66,000
  (4) $75,000
  (5) Not enough information is given.

Items 10 to 12 refer to the table "Median Price of Existing Single-Family Homes" given on page 315.

10. The median price of a home in Akron in 1988 was about what fraction of the approximate median price of a house in Akron in 1992?

  (1) $\dfrac{1}{4}$

  (2) $\dfrac{1}{3}$

  (3) $\dfrac{1}{2}$

  (4) $\dfrac{2}{3}$

  (5) $\dfrac{4}{5}$

11. Rose and Taesung Kim bought a median-priced house in Louisville, Kentucky, in 1988. In 1992, Rose was offered a position in Baltimore, Maryland. The raise in salary enabled them to buy a median-price home in Baltimore. Approximately how many times greater in value was their home in Baltimore in 1992 than their home in Louisville in 1988?

  (1) two
  (2) three
  (3) four
  (4) five
  (5) six

12. From 1988 to 1992, which cities showed a decline in value of a median-priced home?

  (1) San Francisco and Louisville
  (2) Boston and New York
  (3) Daytona Beach and Boston
  (4) Baltimore and Spokane
  (5) New York and Charleston

To check your answers, turn to page 384.

Line Graphs

When a newspaper article contains a great deal of statistical information, the newspaper often uses a graph to show the data. The graph helps people reading the article more easily see the values being compared.

A **graph**, like a table, is used to organize numerical data.

MICCA MOTORS MONTHLY SALES FOR 1993 & 1994

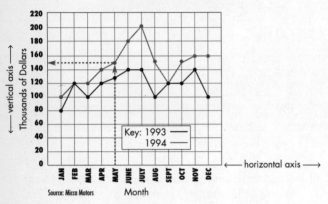

Source: Micca Motors   Month

On a **line graph**, a point is plotted at the intersection of the horizontal and vertical axes to show a value. After many values are plotted, the points are connected with a line.

Now use the graph to answer this question.

Example:

What were the monthly sales for May 1994?

The 1994 sales figures are shown by the screened line. The point for May is halfway between the lines for 140 and 160, or $140,000 and $160,000. Its value is 150. The sales for Micca Motors in May 1994 were $150,000.

Exercise 2

Directions

Complete the line graph by plotting the points given in Item 1. Then use the graph to answer Items 2 and 3.

AVERAGE WEEKDAY MILEAGE FOR DUNNE'S SALES PERSONNEL

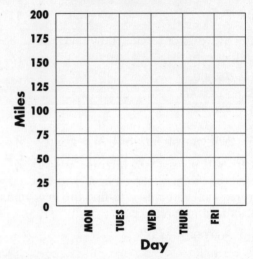

1. Plot and connect the following points on the graph above.

   - Monday   100 miles
   - Tuesday   50 miles
   - Wednesday   50 miles
   - Thursday   75 miles
   - Friday   150 miles

2. How many miles (total) does the average salesperson drive each week?

   (1) 85
   (2) 150
   (3) 425
   (4) 525
   (5) 600

3. How many more miles are driven from Wednesday through Friday than on Monday and Tuesday?

   (1) 50
   (2) 75
   (3) 100
   (4) 125
   (5) 275

318

Directions

Choose the one best answer to each item.

Items 4 and 5 refer to the following graph.

GASOLINE PRICE COMPARISON
November 24 to November 30

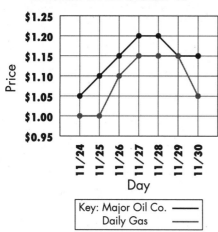

Key: Major Oil Co. ———
Daily Gas ———

4. What was Major Oil's price for 1 gallon of gasoline on November 27, the start of the Thanksgiving holiday?

   (1) $1.00
   (2) $1.05
   (3) $1.10
   (4) $1.15
   (5) $1.20

5. If each station had 200 customers on November 28, how many dollars more did Major Oil take in for gas purchases than Daily Gas?

   (1) $200
   (2) $100
   (3) $50
   (4) $10
   (5) Not enough information is given.

To check your answers, turn to page 385.

Bar Graphs

Bar graphs are also used to make comparisons. Like line graphs, bar graphs have two axis lines. Bars instead of points are used to show numerical values. The end of each bar on the graph corresponds to a value on the scale. Note: Sometimes you will see a break, or jagged line, in a graph. This is used to save space.

JUNK MAIL
Pieces of Direct Mail Rounded to the Nearest Ten

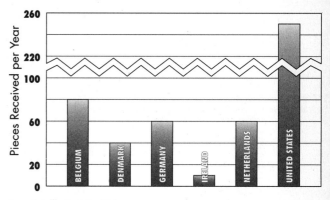

Source: Post offices in countries listed

Example:

How many pieces of junk mail does the average American receive each year? Find the bar that corresponds with the United States and follow the end of the bar to the numerical scale. The end of the bar falls halfway between 240 and 260, which is 250.

DOUBLE BAR GRAPHS

The following bar graph uses two bars. The top bar shows the percent of household work done by men. The bottom bar shows the percent of household work done by women. This is an effective way to show several comparisons on one graph.

PERCENT OF MEN AND WOMEN IN DUAL-EARNER FAMILIES WHO TAKE THE GREATER RESPONSIBILITY FOR HOUSEHOLD WORK

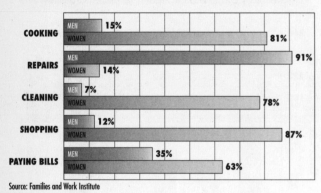

Source: Families and Work Institute

Exercise 3

Directions

Choose the one best answer to each item.

Items 1 to 3 refer to the double bar graph shown above.

1. If 2,500 individuals from dual-earner families participated in this study, how many were men who take the greater responsibility for shopping?

    (1) 12
    (2) 98
    (3) 256
    (4) 300
    (5) 550

2. Which of the following statements is supported by the graph?

    (1) About one-fourth as many men as women do the cooking.
    (2) More than ten times as many women than men do the cleaning.
    (3) About one-third as many women as men do the repair work.
    (4) More than ten times as many women than men do the shopping.
    (5) More than twice as many women than men pay the bills.

3. Based on the percents on the graph, out of 1,000 dual-earner couples, how many more women than men take a greater responsibility for doing the cleaning for the family?

    (1) 355
    (2) 425
    (3) 710
    (4) 850
    (5) Not enough information is given.

Items 4 and 5 refer to the following information.

U.S. HOMES WITH PERSONAL COMPUTERS

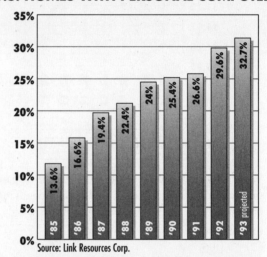

Source: Link Resources Corp.

4. By the end of 1992, 27 million homes had personal computers. At the time, about how many U.S. homes *did not* have computers?

    (1) 63 million
    (2) 105 million
    (3) 127 million
    (4) 150 million
    (5) Not enough information is given.

5. Using the projected figures, how many homes will own computers in 1993?

    (1) 32.7 million
    (2) 63 million
    (3) 198 million
    (4) 105 million
    (5) Not enough information is given.

To check your answers, turn page 385.

Circle Graphs

Pie or **circle graphs** are often used to show relationships between parts of the whole. The circle represents the whole amount being considered. When the sections of a circle graph are labeled as percents, the whole circle will total 100%.

The graph below shows the U.S. population by age. Notice that it does not give the population quantities in numbers. It gives only the percents of the total population that are within each age range.

U.S. POPULATION BY AGE, 1990

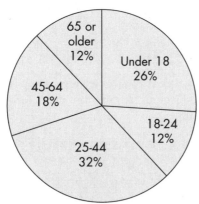

Source: Bureau of the Census, U.S. Department of Commerce, 1990 Census

Example:

What percent of the population is under 25 years of age?

(1) 12%
(2) 26%
(3) 32%
(4) 38%
(5) 50%

To answer this question, you need to add the percents for two age groups: those under 18 and those between 18 and 24.

Add: 26% + 12% = 38%

Choice **(4)** 38% is correct.

Some circle graphs show amounts instead of percents. The circle graph below shows how all of the Garcias' monthly income is spent. When the sections of the circle graph are added together, you have $1,700 which is the total monthly expenditures for the Garcia family.

GARCIA FAMILY MONTHLY BUDGET

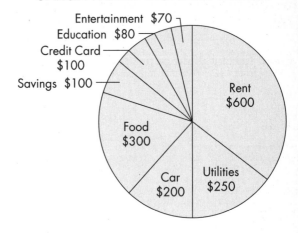

Example:

1. What <u>percent</u> of the whole budget goes to rent and utilities?

    (1) 10%
    (2) 20%
    (3) 25%
    (4) 50%
    (5) 75%

Rent and utilities add up to $850 of the $1,700. To find the percent, set up a proportion.

$$\frac{x}{100} = \frac{\$850}{\$1,700} \qquad \frac{100(\$850)}{\$1,700} = 50$$

Choice **(4)** 50% is correct.

Exercise 4

Items 1 and 2 refer to the graph "U.S. Population By Age" on page 321.

1. What fraction of the population is 45 years of age or older?

   (1) $\dfrac{3}{10}$

   (2) $\dfrac{1}{2}$

   (3) $\dfrac{2}{3}$

   (4) $\dfrac{3}{4}$

   (5) $\dfrac{7}{8}$

2. If the population of the United States is approximately 258 million, how many people are under 18 years of age?

   (1) 13,570,000
   (2) 26,000,000
   (3) 30,960,000
   (4) 52,098,000
   (5) 67,080,000

Items 3 and 4 refer to the graph of the "Garcia Family Monthly Budget" on page 321.

3. What is the *ratio* of entertainment to savings in the Garcias' budget?

   (1) $\dfrac{1}{17}$

   (2) $\dfrac{3}{17}$

   (3) $\dfrac{1}{2}$

   (4) $\dfrac{5}{8}$

   (5) $\dfrac{7}{10}$

4. Savings is what fraction of the total budget?

   (1) $\dfrac{1}{17}$

   (2) $\dfrac{3}{17}$

   (3) $\dfrac{1}{2}$

   (4) $\dfrac{5}{8}$

   (5) $\dfrac{7}{10}$

Items 5 and 6 refer to the following information.

During a recent beach cleanup, 800 pounds of refuse were collected. Refer to the chart for the quantity and type.

BEACH CLEANUP RESULTS

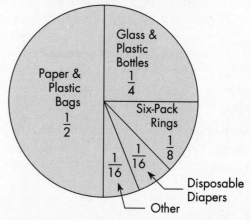

5. How many pounds of the garbage collected came from disposable diapers?

   (1) 400
   (2) 200
   (3) 100
   (4) 50
   (5) Not enough information is given.

6. What percent of refuse collected came from glass and plastic bottles?

   (1) 75%
   (2) 50%
   (3) 25%
   (4) 16%
   (5) Not enough information is given.

To check your answers, turn to page 385.

Finding The Mean

A very useful way to summarize information is to find the **mean**, or average.

Example:

The temperatures for a 7-day period in Boston in September were as follows: 63°, 62°, 70°, 80°, 61°, 58°, and 61°. The newspaper reported that the mean temperature was 65°.

To find the mean:

Step 1 Add the values listed.

$63° + 62° + 70° + 80° + 61° + 58° + 61° = 455°$

Step 2 Divide by the number of items in the list.

$\dfrac{455°}{7 \text{ days}} = 65°$ Weekly mean

A mean is a measure of central tendency. In other words, the mean is a measurement of the *center* value of a list of numbers. When you solve for the mean, check to see if your answer is a value between the highest and lowest values in the list.

Exercise 5

Directions

Choose the one best answer to each item.

---

1. Delia bowled in a 5-game tournament. Her scores were 134, 131, 147, 156, and 142. What was her mean score for the tournament?

    (1) 131
    (2) 134
    (3) 142
    (4) 147
    (5) 156

2. Lillian called eight offices in her area and asked each secretary who answered what was his or her yearly salary. What is the mean salary of the following replies: $15,200; $18,000; $14,500; $11,800; $21,500; $16,300; $10,900; and $17,400?

    (1) $10,000
    (2) $13,525
    (3) $14,500
    (4) $15,700
    (5) $21,500

To check your answers, turn to page 385.

Finding the Median

The median is another way to summarize a list of numerical data. When the values in a list are arranged in numerical order, the **median** is the middle value.

To find the median, arrange the values in order, and choose the value in the middle position.

Examples:

1. Find the median of the heights: 6 ft 2 in, 5 ft 11 in, and 6 ft.

    The median height is 6 feet.

    6 feet 2 inches ↑ 1 above

    (6 feet)

    5 feet 11 inches ↓ 1 below

2. The list of cars below has an even number of values. How can you find the median price?

Car Size	Price
Compact	$10,000
Mid-Sized	$13,400
Minivan	$18,300
Luxury	$35,000

    To find the median when there are an even number of values:

    Step 1 Identify the *two* values in the middle.

    $13,400
    $18,300

    Step 2 Find the *mean* of these two values.

    $\begin{array}{r} \$13{,}400 \\ +18{,}300 \\ \hline \$31{,}700 \end{array}$ $\begin{array}{r} \$15{,}850 \\ 2{\overline{)\$31{,}700}} \end{array}$

    The median price is $15,850.

Exercise 6

Directions

Choose the one best answer to each item.

Items 1 and 2 refer to the following table.

Church's Pizza	Small (12 inch)	Large (16 inch)
Cheese	$5.00	$ 7.75
Special	$8.75	$12.25
Vegetarian	$8.00	$11.75
Pepperoni	$5.75	$ 8.75
Hawaiian	$6.50	$ 9.75

1. What is the median price for a small pizza at Church's?

   (1) $5.00
   (2) $6.50
   (3) $6.80
   (4) $8.00
   (5) $8.75

2. What is the median price for a large pizza at Church's?

   (1) $7.75
   (2) $8.75
   (3) $9.75
   (4) $10.05
   (5) $11.75

3. Arthur's phone bills for the past four months were $42.65, $58.27, $70.01, and $68.43. What was the median amount of his phone service for those months?

   (1) $63.35
   (2) $67.89
   (3) $70.01
   (4) $237.55
   (5) $307.26

To check your answers, turn to page 385.

Simple Probability

"What chance do you have?" is another way of asking "What is the probability?" **Probability** is a ratio that compares the chances of a particular result with the total number of possibilities.

The probability that you will get heads when flipping a coin is 1 in 2. The probability ratio is often written as a fraction.

$$\frac{\text{chances of a particular result}}{\text{total possibilities}} \quad \frac{1 \text{ head}}{2 \text{ sides}} = \frac{1}{2}$$

The chances of winning a lottery might be given as 1 in 5,000,000. This is because approximately 5,000,000 tickets are sold and each ticket has one chance of winning.

$$\frac{1 \text{ chance to win}}{5,000,000 \text{ chances to win}}$$

Example:

The Flanagans made a trick-or-treat grab bag of candy. They put in 40 Milky Ways, 32 Hershey bars, and 24 Snickers. What is the probability that the first child will get a Milky Way?

Since all the candy is mixed together in the grab bag, you must add it to see the total number of possibilities.

40 Milky Ways + 32 Hershey bars + 24 Snickers = 96 candy bars

$$\frac{\text{the chance of a particular event (Milky Way)}}{\text{the total number of possibilities}} \quad \frac{40}{96}$$

Probabilities, like other ratios, are renamed in lowest terms.

$$\frac{40 \div 8}{96 \div 8} = \frac{5}{12}$$

The probability is 5 in 12, or $\frac{5}{12}$.

Exercise 7

> **Directions**
> Find the probability in each of the following problems.

1. Each multiple choice question has 5 answer choices. If you guess, what is the probability that you will be correct?

   (1) $\dfrac{3}{4}$

   (2) $\dfrac{2}{3}$

   (3) $\dfrac{1}{2}$

   (4) $\dfrac{2}{5}$

   (5) $\dfrac{1}{5}$

2. Terry bought 8 raffle tickets for a chance to win a trip to see a space shuttle launch. If 200 tickets are sold, what is the probability that Terry will hold the winning ticket?

   (1) $\dfrac{1}{8}$

   (2) $\dfrac{1}{16}$

   (3) $\dfrac{1}{25}$

   (4) $\dfrac{1}{50}$

   (5) $\dfrac{1}{200}$

3. If you choose a day of the week at random, what is the probability that it will be a Tuesday?

   (1) $\dfrac{3}{4}$

   (2) $\dfrac{2}{3}$

   (3) $\dfrac{1}{2}$

   (4) $\dfrac{1}{7}$

   (5) $\dfrac{1}{30}$

4. Betty Ann bought 12 tickets for the state lottery jackpot. One million tickets were sold. What is the probability that she will win?

   (1) $\dfrac{1}{1,000,000}$

   (2) $\dfrac{3}{250,000}$

   (3) $\dfrac{1}{62,500}$

   (4) $\dfrac{1}{100,000}$

   (5) $\dfrac{1}{1,000}$

5. With one roll of a six-sided die, what is the probability that Merilyn will roll a six?

   (1) $\dfrac{1}{6}$

   (2) $\dfrac{1}{3}$

   (3) $\dfrac{1}{2}$

   (4) $\dfrac{2}{3}$

   (5) $\dfrac{5}{6}$

6. With one roll of a six-sided die, what is the probability that Fred will *not* roll a three or four?

   (1) $\dfrac{1}{6}$

   (2) $\dfrac{1}{3}$

   (3) $\dfrac{1}{2}$

   (4) $\dfrac{2}{3}$

   (5) $\dfrac{5}{6}$

7. Sam has a fish tank that contains 40 female guppies and 40 male guppies. If Sam chooses a fish at random from the tank, what is the probability that it will be male?

   (1) $\dfrac{1}{2}$

   (2) $\dfrac{1}{4}$

   (3) $\dfrac{1}{8}$

   (4) $\dfrac{1}{10}$

   (5) $\dfrac{1}{40}$

8. Cathy's telephone has 18 numbers stored in its memory for speed dialing. Six of the numbers are long distance. If Cathy's son David accidentally dials one of the numbers, what is the probability that David has just made a long-distance call?

   (1) $\dfrac{1}{9}$

   (2) $\dfrac{1}{6}$

   (3) $\dfrac{1}{3}$

   (4) $\dfrac{2}{3}$

   (5) Not enough information is given.

9. A spinner has three sections colored red, yellow, and blue. The red section is twice the size of either the yellow or blue sections. What is the probability of the spinner landing on red?

   (1) $\dfrac{3}{4}$

   (2) $\dfrac{2}{3}$

   (3) $\dfrac{1}{2}$

   (4) $\dfrac{3}{8}$

   (5) Not enough information is given.

To check your answers, turn to page 386.

MEASUREMENT

Unit 8

U.S. System of Measurement

The U.S. system of measurement was brought by the colonists from England before the American Revolution. The United States still uses this system to measure length, weight, and volume. However, time is measured in the same way throughout the world.

Measurements are made using scales. Every scale is marked and labeled using some unit of measure. The diagram below is part of a one-foot ruler. Each numbered line represents one inch. The pencil measures 5 inches long.

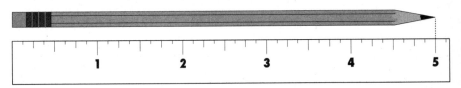

Weight (or mass) and volume are also measured using scales. Pressure-sensitive scales measure weight. Liquids are poured into calibrated containers.

The common units of the U.S. system are shown below.

Units of Length (Distance)

12 inches (in)	= 1 foot (ft)
3 feet (ft)	= 1 yard (yd)
36 inches (in)	= 1 yard (yd)
5,280 feet (ft)	= 1 mile (mi)

Units of Volume

8 fluid ounces (fl oz)	= 1 cup (c)
2 cups (c)	= 1 pint (pt)
2 pints (pt)	= 1 quart (qt)
4 cups (c)	= 1 quart (qt)
4 quarts (qt)	= 1 gallon (gal)

Units of Weight (Mass)

16 ounces (oz)	= 1 pound (lb)
2,000 pounds (lb)	= 1 ton (T)

Units of Time

1 year (yr)	= 365 days (d)
1 year (yr)	= 52 weeks (wk)
1 week (wk)	= 7 days (d)
1 day (d)	= 24 hours (hr)
1 hour (hr)	= 60 minutes (min)
1 minute (min)	= 60 seconds (sec)

Example:

How many minutes are in 5 hours? How many days are in 126 hours? These are questions that can be answered by renaming measurements. Use these steps to change to smaller or larger units of measure.

Multiply to change larger units to smaller units.	Divide to change smaller units to larger units.
5 hours = ? minutes	126 hours = ? days
1 hour = 60 minutes	24 hours = 1 day

$$\begin{array}{r} 60 \\ \times\ 5 \\ \hline 300 \text{ minutes} \end{array}$$

$$24)\overline{126} \quad 5\text{ R}6$$

126 hours = 5 days 6 hours

327

Exercise 1

Directions

Match the measure in Column A with an object or area in Column B which might have that measurement.

	Column A		Column B
_____	1. 6 inches	a.	one lap around a track field
_____	2. $\frac{1}{4}$ cup	b.	volume of a milk carton
_____	3. 1½ oz	c.	height of a 7-year-old girl
_____	4. 3 gal	d.	weight of a package of hamburger
_____	5. $\frac{1}{2}$ inch	e.	weight of a newborn baby
_____	6. $\frac{1}{4}$ mile	f.	weight of a jar of spices
_____	7. 1 pint	g.	amount of water in a bucket
_____	8. 4 feet	h.	thickness of a book
_____	9. 2 tons	i.	amount of vegetable oil in a cake recipe
_____	10. 2 qt	j.	height of a drinking glass
_____	11. 2 lb	k.	volume of a small container of ice cream
_____	12. 6 lb 12 oz	l.	weight of a freight car on a train

Directions

Solve the following as directed.

13. How many feet are in 36 inches?

14. 47 inches = _____ feet _____ inches

15. 20 ounces = _____ pounds _____ ounces

16. Change 34 ounces to pounds.

17. 36 hours = _____ days _____ hours

18. How many days are in 76 hours?

19. How many ounces are in 5.4 pounds?

20. Change 14 quarts to gallons.

21. 5,000 lb = _____ tons _____ pounds

22. Which of the following units would likely be used to state the weight of a baseball?

   (1) fluid ounces
   (2) pounds
   (3) inches
   (4) ounces
   (5) quarts

To check your answers, turn to page 386.

Metric System of Measurement

The metric system was developed in France in the late 1700s. Today it is the international measuring system of science throughout the world. The metric system is popular worldwide because it is a simple system to use and learn.

The metric system is a decimal system that uses prefixes to show whether a unit is *part* of the base unit or a *multiple* of the base unit.

For instance, a centimeter is part of a meter $\left(\frac{1}{100}\right)$, and a kilometer is a multiple of a meter (1,000 meters). The prefixes centi- and kilo- tell you how the unit of measure compares to a meter. Once you learn and understand the prefixes used in the metric system, it is easy to use.

The prefixes used in the metric system are shown in the chart below. The prefixes most commonly used are shown in boldface.

Prefixes for Multiples			Base Units	Prefixes for Parts		
Kilo-	Hecto-	Deka-	Meter Liter Gram	Deci-	**Centi-**	**Milli-**
1,000	100	10	1	0.1	**0.01**	**0.001**

The basic unit of length in the metric system is the **meter**. A meter is just a little longer than a yard. A kilometer (1,000 meters) is a little more than half a mile. It is about 0.6 mile.

The basic unit of weight in the metric system is the **gram**, but the kilogram is used more often. A kilogram, which equals 1,000 grams, is about 2 pounds, so kilograms are used in the metric system to measure quantities that we would measure in pounds. A gram is not very heavy. A paper clip weighs about 1 gram. Milligrams are used to measure very small quantities, for example, the amount of sodium in a potato chip.

The basic unit of liquid measure in the metric system is the **liter**. We buy soda in liter and 2-liter bottles. A liter is a little larger than a quart. Very small amounts of liquid are measured in milliliters. A teaspoon is equal to about 5 milliliters.

The common metric units are shown below.

Metric Units of Length

1 kilometer (km)	=	1,000 meters (m)
1 meter (m)	=	100 centimeters (cm)
1 centimeter (cm)	=	10 millimeters (mm)
1 meter	=	1,000 millimeters (mm)

Metric Units of Weight

1 metric ton (T)	=	1,000 kilograms (kg)
1 kilogram (kg)	=	1,000 grams (g)
1 gram (g)	=	100 centigrams (cg)
1 centigram (cg)	=	10 milligrams (mg)

Metric Units of Volume

1 kiloliter (kL)	=	1,000 liters (L)
1 liter (L)	=	100 centiliters (cL)
1 centiliter (cL)	=	10 milliliters (mL)

Follow these steps to rename metric units:

Step 1 Set up a proportion using the measurement fact you need.

Step 2 Solve the proportion.

Example:

How many liters are in 7 kiloliters? How many grams are in 8.5 centigrams? You can use what you know about metric prefixes to rename metric units.

Rename 7 kiloliters as liters.

Set up a proportion.

$$\frac{kL}{L} \quad \frac{1}{1,000} = \frac{7}{?} \quad \frac{kL}{L}$$

Solve the proportion.

$$\frac{1,000(7)}{1} = 7,000 \text{ L}$$

$$7,000 \text{ L} = 7 \text{ kL}$$

Rename 8.5 centigrams as grams.

Set up a proportion.

$$\frac{g}{cg} \quad \frac{1}{100} = \frac{?}{8.5} \quad \frac{g}{cg}$$

Solve the proportion.

$$\frac{1(8.5)}{100} = 0.085 \text{ g}$$

$$0.085 \text{ g} = 8.5 \text{ cg}$$

Exercise 2

Directions

Match the measure in column A with an object or area in column B which might have that measurement.

	Column A		Column B
_____ 1.	2 mm	**a.**	width of the cutting edge of a table knife
_____ 2.	3.5 kg	**b.**	amount in a bottle of vanilla extract
_____ 3.	2 km	**c.**	volume of a tankful of gasoline
_____ 4.	29 mL	**d.**	distance when walking 10 city blocks
_____ 5.	50 L	**e.**	weight of a newborn baby

Directions

For Items 6 to 8, rename the following metric units by proportion. For Items 9 and 10, choose the one best answer.

6. Rename 5 meters as centimeters.

7. Rename 60 kiloliters as liters.

8. Convert 8,762 grams to kilograms.

9. The New Wave Swim Team uses a 50-meter pool during the summer to prepare for long-course events. Josh competes in the 1,500 *meter*. How many *kilometers* are in this event?

    (1) 1.5
    (2) 15
    (3) 50
    (4) 150
    (5) 1,500

10. Which of the following units would likely be used to state a child's height?

    (1) kilometers
    (2) grams
    (3) centimeters
    (4) millimeters
    (5) milliliters

To check your answers, turn to page 386.

Addition and Subtraction of Measurements

When adding measurements in the U.S. system, you cannot carry as you would with whole numbers because the U.S. system is not based on units of 10.

Follow these steps to add measurements.

Step 1 Add the units separately.

Step 2 Simplify the answer, if necessary, by dividing to change the smaller units to larger units.

Example:

Add 2 lb 12 oz + 5 lb 7 oz.

$$\begin{array}{ll} 2 \text{ lb } 12 \text{ oz} & \text{Simplify the answer.} \\ + 5 \text{ lb } \ 7 \text{ oz} & \text{Use the fact: } 16 \text{ oz} = 1 \text{ lb.} \\ \hline 7 \text{ lb } 19 \text{ oz} & \text{Divide } 19 \text{ oz by } 16. \end{array}$$

$$16\overline{)19} \\ \underline{-16} \\ 3 \text{ oz}$$

Add this to the
pounds column.
1 lb 3 oz
+ 7 lb
8 lb 3 oz

The total is 8 lb 3 oz.

To subtract measurements in the U.S. system, you need to keep the common equivalents in mind. If borrowing is necessary, you cannot automatically borrow 10 as you do when working with whole numbers.

Follow these steps to subtract measurements.

Step 1 Subtract the smaller units first. If borrowing is necessary, borrow from the larger units and rename the one you borrowed in terms of the smaller unit.

Step 2 Subtract the larger units.

Example:

Subtract 6 ft 7 in from 11 ft 6 in.

$$\begin{array}{lll} 11 \text{ ft } 6 \text{ in} & \text{Borrow 1 foot,} & \overset{10}{\cancel{11}} \text{ft} \quad 6 \text{ in} + 12 \text{ in} = 18 \text{ in} \\ \underline{- \ 6 \text{ ft } 7 \text{ in}} & \text{rename it as} & \underline{- \ 6 \text{ ft}} \qquad \qquad \underline{- \ 7 \text{ in}} \\ & 12 \text{ inches, and} & 4 \text{ ft} \qquad \qquad 11 \text{ in} \\ & \text{add it to the} \\ & \text{inches column.} \end{array}$$

The difference is 4 ft 11 in.

Exercise 3

Directions
Solve as indicated. Simplify your answers if possible.

1. 11 in + 8 in

2. 3 ft 6 in − 2 ft 8 in

3. 1 hr − 24 min

4. 8 ft 7 in + 9 ft 5 in

5. 2 yd 2 ft + 3 yd 1 ft

6. 8 lb 12 oz + 10 lb 14 oz

7. 2 gal 1 qt − 1 gal 3 qt

8. 6 yd − 2 ft

9. 1 qt 3 c + 3 c

10. 4 lb 12 oz − 2 lb 2 oz

Directions
Choose the one best answer to each item.

11. Georgina wants to move her bookshelves from one room to another. One bookshelf is 42 inches wide, the other is 3 feet wide. When she puts the bookshelves end to end, how many feet and inches in length will they be?

    (1) 3 ft 6 in
    (2) 5 ft 10 in
    (3) 6 ft 6 in
    (4) 7 ft 6 in
    (5) 7 ft 0 in

12. Lael and Ryan both rented videos to watch on Friday night. Lael's is 135 minutes. Ryan's is 162 minutes. How much time would it take for them to watch both videos?

   (1) 3 hours 52 minutes
   (2) 4 hours 57 minutes
   (3) 5 hours
   (4) 5½ hours
   (5) 6 hours

13. Josie works at a fabric store. Each time she cuts fabric from a bolt, she must subtract it and write how much is left. The bolt had 12 yd 1 ft before she cut off 3 yd 2 ft. How much fabric is left on the bolt?

   (1) 7 yards 1 foot
   (2) 7 yards 2 feet
   (3) 8 yards
   (4) 8 yards 1 foot
   (5) 8 yards 2 feet

14. Luan has three suitcases for his flight to Vietnam. One weighs 24 lb 8 oz, the second weighs 12 lb 7 oz, and the third suitcase weighs 15 lb 10 oz. How many pounds over the weight allowance is Luan's luggage?

   (1) 10 lb
   (2) 12 lb 9 oz.
   (3) 20 lb
   (4) 42 lb 9 oz
   (5) Not enough information is given.

To check your answers, turn to page 386.

Multiplication of Measurements

Multiplication can be thought of as repeated addition. Instead of adding a number or measurement 4 times, you multiply by 4. Because multiplication and addition are related, the steps are similar for working with measurements.

Follow these steps to multiply measurements in the U.S. system.

   Step 1 Multiply the units separately.

   Step 2 Simplify the answer, if necessary, using division to change the smaller units to larger ones.

Example:

   5(6 gal 3 qt) = ?

Multiply:

$$\begin{array}{r} 6 \text{ gal} \quad 3 \text{ qt} \\ \times \qquad\qquad 5 \\ \hline 30 \text{ gal } 15 \text{ qt} \end{array}$$

Compare the units. Use the fact: 4 qt = 1 gal. Do you have more than 4 qt? Yes.

Divide: 15 qt by 4:
$$\begin{array}{r} 3 \text{ gal} \\ 4\overline{)15} \\ \underline{-12} \\ 3 \text{ qt} \end{array}$$

Add:
$$\begin{array}{r} 3 \text{ gal } 3 \text{ qt} \\ + 30 \text{ gal} \\ \hline \end{array}$$
Answer: **33 gal 3 qt**

Exercise 4

> **Directions**
>
> For Items 1 to 6, multiply the following. Simplify your answers when necessary. For Item 7, choose the one best answer.

1. 3(6 ft 5 in)

2. 3(4 d 15 hr)

3. 10(8 lb 12 oz)

4. 7(7 gal 3 qt)

5. 6(2 qt 3 pt)

6. 2(18 lb 10 oz)

7. Eileen is a window washer. She averages 5 minutes per window inside and out. About how many hours will it take her to complete the Finance Office Building, which has 60 windows?

   (1) 2
   (2) 3
   (3) 4
   (4) 5
   (5) 6

To check your answers, turn to page 386.

Division of Measurements

Janet needs to cut a board into 5 equal pieces. If the board measures 6 ft 8 in, how long will each piece be? (Disregard any waste.)

Follow these steps to divide measurements.

> **Step 1** Divide 5 into the larger unit of measure first.
>
> **Step 2** Change the remainder. Multiply to change the remaining larger units to smaller units.
>
> **Step 3** Add these smaller units to the smaller units in the original problem and divide.

Example: 6 ft 8 in ÷ 5

$$\begin{array}{r} 1\text{ft} \\ 5\overline{)6\text{ ft }8\text{ in}} \\ -5 \phantom{\text{ ft }8\text{ in}} \\ \hline 1\text{ ft} \end{array}$$

Change the remainder to smaller units.
1 ft(12) = 12 in

$$\begin{array}{r} 12\text{ inches} \\ +\ 8\text{ inches} \\ \hline 20\text{ inches} \end{array}$$

Add these smaller units to the smaller units in the original problem.

$$\begin{array}{r} 4\text{ in} \\ 5\overline{)20\text{ in}} \end{array}$$

6 ft 8 in ÷ 5 = **1 ft 4 in**

Exercise 5

> **Directions**
> Divide to solve the following.

1. 7 mi 4,362 ft ÷ 6

2. $\dfrac{13\text{ hr }30\text{ min}}{3}$

3. 4 gal 2 qt ÷ 3

4. 12 ft 9 in ÷ 3

5. What is the average height of the three Gonzalez children? Jose is 4 ft 7 in, Eva is 4 ft 9 in, and Rafael is 5 ft 2 in.
   - (1) 4 ft 10 in
   - (2) 4 ft 11 in
   - (3) 5 ft
   - (4) 5 ft 1 in
   - (5) 5 ft 2 in

6. Mickey has been hired to paint the exterior of a house, which would take him 12 eight-hour days to do alone. He has hired 2 workers to help him. Assuming that they all work at the same rate, how long will it take the three of them to complete the job?
   - (1) Three days
   - (2) Three days five hours
   - (3) Four 8-hour days
   - (4) Five 8-hour days
   - (5) Five days 6 hours

To check your answers, turn to page 387.

Operations with Metric Measurements

When metric measurements are expressed in the same units, they can be added and subtracted in the same way you add and subtract decimals. Meters can be added to meters. Kilograms can be subtracted from kilograms. Just line up the decimal points and carry out the operation.

Add: 4.5 m + 17.6 m

$$\begin{array}{r} 4.5\text{ m} \\ +17.6\text{ m} \\ \hline 22.1\text{ m} \end{array}$$

Carry the 1 just as in other decimal problems.

Subtract: 12.4 kg − 0.6 kg

$$\begin{array}{r} 12.4\text{ kg} \\ -0.6\text{ kg} \\ \hline 11.8\text{ kg} \end{array}$$

Borrow just as in other decimal problems.

Multiplication and division of metric measures are the same as in other decimal problems.

Examples:

Multiply 17.8 liters by 5.

Multiply, then place the decimal point in the answer.

$$\begin{array}{r} 17.8\text{ liters} \\ \times\ 5 \\ \hline 89.0\text{ liters} \end{array}$$

Divide 3.45 meters by 5.

Place the decimal point in the quotient and divide.

$$\begin{array}{r} 0.69\text{ meter} \\ 5\overline{)3.45\text{ meters}} \\ -3\ 0\phantom{5\text{ meters}} \\ \hline 45\phantom{\text{ meters}} \\ -45\phantom{\text{ meters}} \\ \hline \end{array}$$

Exercise 6

Directions

Solve as directed.

1. $9.9 \text{ L} + 99 \text{ L}$

2. $5.8 \text{ mm} + 7.2 \text{ mm}$

3. $13.4 \text{ km} - 500 \text{ m}$

4. $3.45 \text{ km} - 1.2 \text{ km}$

5. $4(5.6 \text{ cm})$

6. $9(5.450 \text{ kg})$

7. $\dfrac{1.6 \text{ km}}{4}$

8. $5.36 \text{ m} \div 4$

Directions

Choose the <u>one best answer</u> to each item.

9. When making a tablecloth for the banquet, Laurie trimmed 64 cm from a piece of fabric 220 cm long. How many centimeters long was the remaining fabric?

   (1) 156
   (2) 325
   (3) 460
   (4) 465
   (5) 523

10. Mary packaged her candied nuts in tins that weighed 2.5 kg each. She mailed 8 of these packages as holiday gifts. How many kilograms of nuts did she mail altogether?

    (1) 10.5
    (2) 12.5
    (3) 15
    (4) 20
    (5) 25.5

11. Jose and two friends are taking a 1,266-km trip that they hope to complete in two days. Which of the following expressions would be used to find the number of kilometers that they must drive each day?

    (1) $\dfrac{1,266}{3}$

    (2) $\dfrac{3(1,266)}{2}$

    (3) $\dfrac{1,266}{2}$

    (4) $\dfrac{2(1,266)}{3}$

    (5) $2(3)(1,266)$

12. Seong-Jin has two lengths of wire: 185 centimeters and 340 centimeters. What is the total length of the wire in meters?

    (1) 1.55 m
    (2) 5.25 m
    (3) 15.5 m
    (4) 52.5 m
    (5) 525 m

13. Caroline runs 5 kilometers every day. She carries a water bottle as she runs and drinks 2 ounces of water every 500 meters. If the bottle is full when she starts, how many ounces will remain when she completes her run?

    (1) 4
    (2) 7
    (3) 10
    (4) 20
    (5) Not enough information is given.

Items 14 and 15 refer to the following drawing.

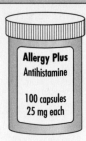

14. Baird takes two capsules of the medication shown four times a day for three days. How many milligrams of the medication does he take over the three-day period?

(1) 100 mg
(2) 200 mg
(3) 300 mg
(4) 600 mg
(5) Not enough information is given.

15. How many grams of medication are contained in 100 capsules?

(1) .25 g
(2) 2.5 g
(3) 25 g
(4) 250 g
(5) 2,500 g

To check your answers, turn to page 387.

Finding Perimeter

Perimeter is the linear distance around a flat figure. To put the finishing trim along the floor and ceiling edges of a room, you would need to find the perimeter of the room. The lengths of all the sides of a figure are added to find its perimeter.

The figures below show the addition used to find the perimeter of each.

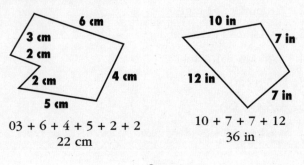

03 + 6 + 4 + 5 + 2 + 2
22 cm

10 + 7 + 7 + 12
36 in

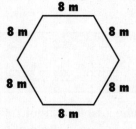

8 + 8 + 8 + 8 + 8 + 8
6(8) = 48 m

You can use formulas to find the perimeters of squares and rectangles.

A **square** has four equal sides. You can find the perimeter of a square by multiplying the length of one side by 4.

Square $P = 4s$; where s = side

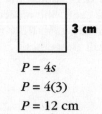

$P = 4s$
$P = 4(3)$
$P = 12$ cm

A **rectangle** has four sides also. The sides opposite each other are equal and parallel to each other. (One pair of sides = length, the other pair of sides = width.) You can find the perimeter by multiplying the length by 2 and the width by 2 and adding the products.

Rectangle $P = 2l + 2w$; where l = length, w = width

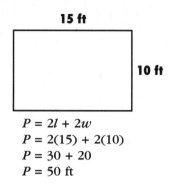

$P = 2l + 2w$
$P = 2(15) + 2(10)$
$P = 30 + 20$
$P = 50$ ft

Example:

What is the length of side CD in the figure below? To find the figure's perimeter, you need to find the missing segment length.

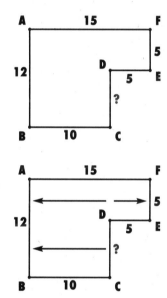

Look at the second figure. The arrows show that side CD is opposite side AB. You also see that the total of side EF and side CD must equal 12 units, the length of side AB. So side CD must equal 12 − 5, or 7 units.

On the GED Math Test, you can often find a missing length using the lengths of the sides you have been given.

Exercise 7

1.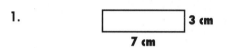

2.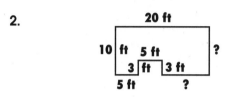

3.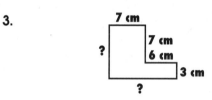

4.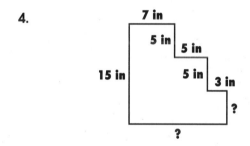

<table>
<tr><td>

Directions

Choose the <u>one best answer</u> to each item.

</td></tr>
</table>

5. Libby's house is on a square lot that measures 15 meters on each side. How many meters of fence does she need to enclose her lot?

   (1) 15
   (2) 30
   (3) 45
   (4) 60
   (5) 75

6. How many inches of framing are needed for an 8-inch by 11-inch photo?

   (1) 19
   (2) 27
   (3) 38
   (4) 88
   (5) 100

To check your answers, turn to page 387.

Finding Area

Area is the measure of the surface within a figure. Area is measured in square units. As you see in the figure below, a square that is 3 centimeters by 3 centimeters contains 9 *square* centimeters.

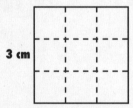

   The formula for finding the area of a square uses an exponent. In the expression 4^2, the 4 is called the **base** and ^{2} is called the **exponent**. The exponent tells you how many times to multiply the base by itself.

4^1	Multiply 4 one time	4	= 4
4^2	Multiply 4 two times	4(4)	= 16
4^3	Multiply 4 three times	4(4)(4)	= 64
4^4	Multiply 4 four times	4(4)(4)(4)	= 256

   To find the area of a square, take the measure of the side to the second power—or **square** it—as shown in the following formula.

Square $A = s^2$; where s = side

Example:

The area of the square in the figure below can be found by substituting 6 for s in $A = s^2$.

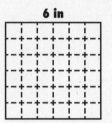

$A = 6^2 = 6(6) = 36$ square inches
$A = 36$ sq in, or 36 in^2

To find the area of a rectangle, multiply the length times the width as shown in the following formula.

Rectangle $A = lw$; where l = length, w = width

Example:

Now use the formula to find the area of this rectangle.

Substitute 12 for l and 4 for w and multiply.

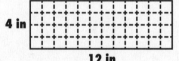

$A = 12(4)$
= 48 square inches
$A = 48$ sq in, or 48 in^2

Example:

The Goldhamers' kitchen (shown below) is L-shaped. To find the area of an irregular figure, divide the space into squares and rectangles. Find the area of each shape; then add them to find the total area. What is the area of the kitchen?

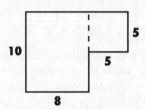

Find the area of the square.   Find the area of the rectangle.

$A = s^2$ $A = lw$
$A = 5^2$ $A = 10(8)$
$A = 25$ sq ft $A = 80$ sq ft

  Add: $25 + 80 = 105$ sq ft

  Answer: The total area of the Goldhamers' kitchen is 105 sq ft.

Exercise 8

Directions

Find the area of each figure below.

1.

3 cm

7 cm

2.

25 in

3.

1 ft

12 ft

4.

10 in

13 in

Directions

Choose the one best answer to each item.

Item 5 refers to the following information.

Sue Cheng has had a brick patio laid in her back yard as shown below. The rest of the yard is to be seeded with grass.

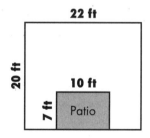

22 ft

20 ft

10 ft

7 ft

Patio

5. How many square feet of lawn will Sue have?
   (1) 84
   (2) 270
   (3) 300
   (4) 370
   (5) 440

6. Andrews Asphalt received an order to resurface a parking lot that is 188 meters long and 83 meters wide. What is the area to be resurfaced?
   (1) 22,493 m²
   (2) 15,604 m²
   (3) 11,025 m²
   (4) 542 m²
   (5) 459 m²

7. Tricia planted her vegetable garden in a square corner of her yard that measured 15 feet on each side. How many square feet were in Tricia's garden?
   (1) 15
   (2) 30
   (3) 60
   (4) 100
   (5) 225

8. How many square feet of butcher block are needed to cover a counter top that is 3 feet wide and 4 feet long?
   (1) 7
   (2) 10
   (3) 12
   (4) 14
   (5) 16

To check your answers, turn to page 387.

Finding Volume of Solid Figures

We have dealt with volume as the measure of how much liquid a container can hold. **Volume** is also the measure of how much space there is within a three-dimensional or solid figure. This volume is measured in cubic units.

A **rectangular container** is a three-dimensional figure with all right angles (90°). Picture a cardboard box. To find the volume, you are figuring out how many cubes (smaller boxes) will fit into the large box.

To find the volume of a rectangular container, multiply the length times the width times the height as shown in the following formula.

Rectangular Container $V = lwh$,

where l = length,

w = width,

h = height

337

Example:

Now find the volume of this rectangular container.

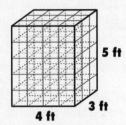

Put the values from the diagram in the formula.

$V = 4(3)(5) = 60$ cubic feet
$V = 60$ cu ft, or 60 ft^3

A **cube** is a solid figure in which all sides are of equal measure. The length, width, and height are the same in a cube. The figure below shows a cube with the measure of 3 inches on each side.

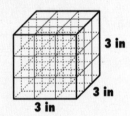

$V = 3(3)(3) = 27$ cubic inches
$V = 27$ cu in, or 27 in^3

To find the volume of a cube, take the measure of the side to the third power, or **cube** it, as shown in the following formula.

Cube $V = s^3$; where s = side

Example:

The volume of this cube is found by substituting 7 for s in $V = s^3$.

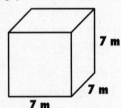

$V = 7(7)(7) = 343$ cubic meters
$V = 343$ cu m, or 343 m^3

Volume is used to solve problems in situations where you need to find the amount of space in a three-dimensional area. Some common applications in which you would need to find volume are air-conditioning a room, filling a swimming pool with water, and measuring the storage capacity of a closet or room.

Exercise 9

Directions
Find the volume of each of the following figures.

1.

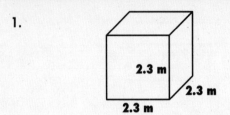

2.

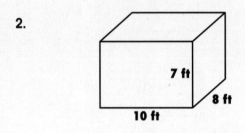

3.

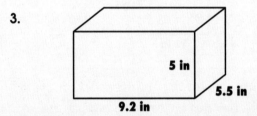

Directions
Choose the <u>one best answer</u> to each item.

4. Smart Moving and Storage decides to order new packing cartons that have a cube shape. What is the volume of one of the new cartons if each side of the carton measures 2 feet?

   (1) 4 cu ft
   (2) 6 cu ft
   (3) 8 cu ft
   (4) 12 cu ft
   (5) Not enough information is given.

5. The Abisi Photography Company sells photographic equipment. They pack photo albums in boxes that measure 1 cubic yard. How many boxes can they fit in a storage closet which measures 5 yards long, 3 yards wide, and 4 yards high?

(1) 20
(2) 60
(3) 180
(4) 200
(5) 240

6. When Tom decided to install air conditioning in his studio, the salesperson asked him how many cubic feet he wanted to cool. He measured the space and told the salesperson that it was 20 feet long, 16 feet wide, and 10 feet high. How many cubic feet does his studio measure?

(1) 2,000
(2) 2,500
(3) 2,800
(4) 3,200
(5) 3,600

To check your answers, turn to page 388.

ALGEBRA

Signed Numbers

Temperatures drop below zero; unfortunately, so do checking account balances on occasion. These numbers can be shown using **signed numbers**. Signed numbers are used to show how far a number is from zero.

Most numbers that you use are positive numbers. As you see on the number line below, **positive numbers** are all numbers greater than zero. **Negative numbers** are all numbers less than zero. Zero, itself, is neither positive nor negative.

On a horizontal number line (shown below), the values *increase* or are greater as you move to the right. Values *decrease* or are less as you move to the left.

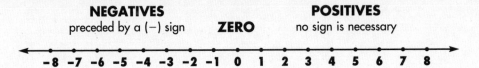

NEGATIVES
preceded by a (−) sign

ZERO

POSITIVES
no sign is necessary

−8 −7 −6 −5 −4 −3 −2 −1 0 1 2 3 4 5 6 7 8

Exercise 1

> **Directions**
> Choose the one best answer to each item.

> Items 1 to 3 refer to the following number line.

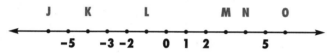

1. What is the value of point J?
   - (1) −8
   - (2) −7
   - (3) −6
   - (4) −5
   - (5) −4

2. What is the value of point M?
   - (1) −1
   - (2) 0
   - (3) 3
   - (4) 4
   - (5) 6

3. Which is a true statement?
   - (1) L < K
   - (2) K > 2
   - (3) N < 5
   - (4) 1 < −3
   - (5) −5 > L

To check your answers, turn to page 388.

Adding and Subtracting Signed Numbers

Example:

It was 3° at noon on a cold winter day. The temperature dropped 5° by 6 p.m. What was the temperature after it had dropped?

"Dropped 5°" can be written as −5. You need to add +3 and −5. Look at the number line. Begin at 3, then move down 5 points. The temperature dropped to −2°.

Rules for adding signed numbers:

- To add signed numbers with the <u>same sign</u>, use these steps.

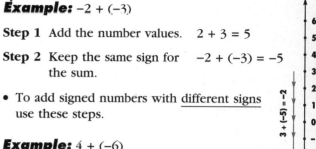

Example: −2 + (−3)

Step 1 Add the number values.   2 + 3 = 5

Step 2 Keep the same sign for   −2 + (−3) = −5
the sum.

- To add signed numbers with <u>different signs</u> use these steps.

Example: 4 + (−6)

Step 1 Subtract the number   6 − 4 = 2
values.

Step 2 Use the sign of the   6 is larger, so use a
larger number for   negative sign
the sum.   4 + (−6) = −2

Now let's take a look at a situation that requires subtraction.

Example:

On a cold winter day, the temperature in Smallville is 5°. The temperature in Metropolis is even colder at −1°. What is the difference between the two temperatures?

To find the difference, subtract the colder temperature from the warmer one. 5 − (−1)

You can solve this problem easily using the number line at the right. Count the places between the two points. There are 6. 5 − (−1) = 6

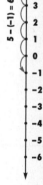

Rules for subtracting signed numbers:

Examples:

	$5 - (-1)$	$-2 - (-6)$
Step 1 Change the subtraction sign to an addition sign, *and* change the sign of the number to its right.	becomes $5 + 1$	becomes $-2 + 6$
Step 2 Complete the problem using the rules for adding signed numbers.	Add and keep the sign. $5 + 1 = 6$	Subtract and use the sign of the larger value. $-2 + 6 = 4$

Remember that you can always replace double-negative signs with an addition sign.

Exercise 2

Directions

Choose the <u>one best answer</u> to each item.

1. A volcano erupted 200 feet below sea level. Lava spurted 328 feet above the tip of the volcano. Which of the following expressions could be used to find the height above sea level that the lava reached?

   (1) $-200 - 328$
   (2) $-200 + 328$
   (3) $200 + 328$
   (4) $200 - 328$
   (5) $328 + 200$

2. What is the total of $-4 + (-23) + (-67) + (-1) + 45$?

   (1) -50
   (2) -49
   (3) 0
   (4) 49
   (5) 50

3. The elevation of the Caspian Sea is 92 feet below sea level. The elevation of Lake Torrens in Australia is 92 feet above sea level. How much higher in elevation is Lake Torrens than the Caspian Sea?

   (1) -184 feet
   (2) 0 feet
   (3) 184 feet
   (4) 368 feet
   (5) Not enough information is given.

4. The temperature on Tuesday was 22°. On Wednesday the temperature had dropped to 4 below zero ($-4°$). Which expression below would be used to show how many degrees the temperature dropped?

   (1) $22 + (-4)$
   (2) $22 - (-4)$
   (3) $(-4) + 22$
   (4) $(-4) - 22$
   (5) $22 - 4$

5. What is the sum of 9, -10, 11, and -49?

   (1) 39
   (2) 38
   (3) -38
   (4) -39
   (5) -40

6. Which of the following expressions is equal to $6 - (-3) + (-2)$?

   A. $6 + 3 - 2$
   B. $6 - 3 + 2$
   C. $6 + 3 + (-2)$

   (1) A and B
   (2) B and C
   (3) A and C
   (4) A, B, and C
   (5) None of the above

7. On Tuesday it was 5° above zero. By Wednesday morning the temperature had dropped 10°. Thursday's temperature was 10° above zero. Which expression below will give the difference in the temperature from Wednesday to Thursday?

   (1) $10 + (5 - 10)$
   (2) $10 - (5 + 10)$
   (3) $10 + (5 + 10)$
   (4) $10 - (5 - 10)$
   (5) $(5 - 10) - 10$

To check your answers, turn to page 388.

Multiplying and Dividing Signed Numbers

Rules for multiplying and dividing signed numbers:

Step 1 Multiply or divide just as if the numbers were all positive.

Step 2 Figure out the sign of the answer. Two numbers of the same sign will give a positive answer. Two numbers with different signs will give a negative answer.

Study the following examples.

Problem	**Operation and Rule**
$4(-2) = -8$	*Multiply.* Different signs yield a negative number.
$\dfrac{-8}{-2} = 4$	*Divide.* The same signs yield a positive number.
$-6(-5) = 30$	*Multiply.* The same signs yield a positive number.
$\dfrac{-15}{3} = -5$	*Divide.* Different signs yield a negative number.

We can draw a few shortcuts from these rules.

Example:

Find the product of $(-1)(-1)(-1)(-1)$.

The answer is 1.

An **even number of negatives multiplied** together will give a **positive** answer.

Example:

Find the product of $(-1)(-1)(-1)(-1)(-1)$.

The answer is −1.

An **odd number of negatives multiplied** together will give a **negative** answer.

Exercise 3

Directions
Find the product or quotient of the following.

1. $6(10)$

2. $-5(12)$

3. $-6(-7)$

4. $\dfrac{20}{-4}$

5. $\dfrac{-25}{5}$

6. $\dfrac{-45}{-9}$

7. What is the value of $4(-3)(-2)(1)$?
   - **(1)** −24
   - **(2)** −14
   - **(3)** −10
   - **(4)** 10
   - **(5)** 24

8. What is the value of $\dfrac{-7(6)}{-3}$?
   - **(1)** 14
   - **(2)** 12
   - **(3)** −10
   - **(4)** −10
   - **(5)** −14

To check your answers, turn to page 388.

Working with Expressions

In mathematics, an **expression** is a way of writing a number relationship using symbols instead of words. You can also write a number relationship when one or more of the numbers are unknown. Letters, called **variables**, represent the unknown numbers.

Algebraic expressions use variables, numbers, and symbols to express numerical relationships.

In Words	In Symbols
Some amount	n (any variable)
Two numbers	x and y (any two variables)
An amount increased by 10	$t + 10$
An amount minus 15	$b - 15$
An amount subtracted from 15	$15 - b$
The product of an amount and 7	$7y$
The quotient of an amount divided by 11	$\dfrac{n}{11}$
A number times itself	m^2

Study these next examples to see how words like quantity, total, and all are used to indicate the part enclosed within parentheses. The word quantity is most often used to indicate an operation in parentheses.

In Words	In Symbols
The quantity of an amount minus five	$(x - 5)$
Five times the quantity of six and four	$5(6 + 4)$
Seven times the total of an amount and seven	$7(n + 7)$
The product of eight and the quantity of fifteen plus a number	$8(15 + s)$
Twice an amount minus that amount plus four, all multiplied by ten	$10(2w - w + 4)$

To solve an algebra problem, the first step is to translate the words of the problem into mathematical symbols. On the GED Math Test, there will be set-up problems that test your ability to choose the correct algebraic expression to represent the situation in a word problem.

Exercise 4

Directions
Choose the one best answer to each item.

1. If b represents the number of items bought for $2 each, which expression would be used to represent the total cost?
   (1) $b - \$2$
   (2) $b + \$2$
   (3) $\$2b$
   (4) $\dfrac{b}{\$2}$
   (5) $(b - \$2)$

2. Last week Mary paid $35 more for groceries than she paid this week. If x is the amount she paid this week, which of the following expressions represents the amount she paid last week?
   (1) $\$35 - x$
   (2) $x - \$35$
   (3) $\$35x$
   (4) $x + \$35$
   (5) $\dfrac{x}{\$35}$

3. Mike bought 3 cassettes and paid with a $20 bill. If y represents the price of each cassette, which expression would be used to represent his change?
   (1) $\$20 - 3y$
   (2) $3y - \$20$
   (3) $\dfrac{\$20 - y}{3}$
   (4) $3(\$20 - y)$
   (5) $\$20 + 3y$

4. Which expression would be used to represent 15 subtracted from a number times itself?
   (1) $2p - 15$
   (2) $15 - 2p$
   (3) $15p^2$
   (4) $15 - p^2$
   (5) $p^2 - 15$

5. Nancy and five women from her office chipped in on a gift for their supervisor. If g represents the price of the gift, which expression would be used to represent Nancy's share of the gift?

(1) $5g$

(2) $6g$

(3) $g + 6$

(4) $\dfrac{g}{6}$

(5) $\dfrac{6}{g}$

6. The price of each pound of lobster has risen $1 since last week. If the price of one pound of lobster last week is represented by w, which expression represents the price of a two-pound lobster *this week*?

(1) $2w + \$1$

(2) $w^2 + \$1$

(3) $2(w + \$1)$

(4) $2(w^2 + \$1)$

(5) $2w^2 + \$1$

7. Harry runs 3 miles less each day than his brother Mike does. If m represents the number of miles that Mike runs, which of the following expressions represents the total miles that Harry runs in 6 days?

(1) $6m - 3$

(2) $6(m - 3)$

(3) $m - 6$

(4) $\dfrac{m - 3}{6}$

(5) $6(m + 3)$

8. Which expression could be used to find 43 minus the quantity of x plus $2y$?

(1) $(x + 2y) - 43$

(2) $-43 + (2y - x)$

(3) $43(x + 2y)$

(4) $43 - 2xy$

(5) $43 - (x + 2y)$

To check your answers, turn to page 388.

Finding Square Roots

A value taken to the second power is said to be *squared*.

The expression 3^2 is read *three squared*.

The symbol $\sqrt{}$ means **square root**. Finding the square root is the opposite of squaring. The square of 3 is 9, so $\sqrt{9}$ is 3.

To find the square root, think, "What number times itself will give this value?"

The following square roots are those most commonly found on the GED Math Test.

$\sqrt{1} = 1$	$\sqrt{64} = 8$	$\sqrt{225} = 15$
$\sqrt{4} = 2$	$\sqrt{81} = 9$	$\sqrt{400} = 20$
$\sqrt{9} = 3$	$\sqrt{100} = 10$	$\sqrt{900} = 30$
$\sqrt{16} = 4$	$\sqrt{121} = 11$	$\sqrt{1,600} = 40$
$\sqrt{25} = 5$	$\sqrt{144} = 12$	$\sqrt{2,500} = 50$
$\sqrt{36} = 6$	$\sqrt{169} = 13$	$\sqrt{3,600} = 60$
$\sqrt{49} = 7$	$\sqrt{196} = 14$	$\sqrt{10,000} = 100$

To find the square root of a value on the table, you can approximate an answer.

Example:

Find the square root of 72.

Step 1 Find which numbers the square root value falls between.

$\sqrt{64} = 8$
$\sqrt{72} = ?$
$\sqrt{81} = 9$

Step 2 The square root of the value is between their square roots.

$\sqrt{72}$ is between 8 and 9.

Exercise 5

Directions

Find the following square roots.

1. $\sqrt{100}$

2. $\sqrt{225}$

3. $\sqrt{196}$

4. $\sqrt{144}$

5. $\sqrt{49}$

6. $\sqrt{400}$

7. If the area of a square is 64 square meters, how many meters long is each side?

   (1) 4
   (2) 8
   (3) 16
   (4) 24
   (5) 32

8. $\sqrt{200}$ is

   (1) Between 10 and 11
   (2) Between 11 and 12
   (3) Between 12 and 13
   (4) Between 13 and 14
   (5) Between 14 and 15

To check your answers, turn to page 388.

Scientific Notation

Scientific notation is a method of writing a number that has many digits. Exponents as powers of 10 are used to abbreviate the number.

Multiplying or dividing by 10, 100, or 1,000 can be done quickly by moving the decimal point to the right or left. This is what is done in scientific notation. Remember that the exponent equals the number of places to move the decimal point. The exponent indicates place value.

In scientific notation, the number 45,678,000,000 is written 4.5678×10^{10}.

To write a number using scientific notation:

Step 1 Place the decimal point to the right of the first digit, and count how many places to the **left** you have moved the decimal point.   4.5678000000   *10 places*

Step 2 Drop the zeros in the number, and write it multiplied by 10 to the power equal to the number of places counted. 4.5678×10^{10}

To interpret a number using scientific notation:

Step 1 Move the decimal point to the right the number of decimal places indicated by the exponent. Add zeros as needed. $1.506 \times 10^6 = 1.506000.$

Step 2 Count from the right to put a comma after every group of three digits.   1,506,000

Exercise 6

Directions

Choose the one best answer to each item.

1. Which expression is 2,345,000 in scientific notation?

   (1) 23.45×10^2
   (2) 2.345×10^4
   (3) 2.345×10^6
   (4) 2.345×10^7
   (5) 234.5×10^2

2. The planet Pluto stays about 3.6×10^9 miles from the sun. How would that distance be written as a whole number?

   (1) 360,000
   (2) 3,600,000
   (3) 36,000,000
   (4) 360,000,000
   (5) 3,600,000,000

3. Which of the following statements is true?

(1) 4×10^3 is greater than 4,500.
(2) 4×10^3 is equal to 40,000.
(3) 4×10^3 is equal to 10,000.
(4) 4×10^3 is equal to 4,000.
(5) 4×10^3 is less than 400.

4. The distance from Mars to the Earth is about 56,000,000 kilometers. How would this distance be written in scientific notation?

(1) 5.6×10^8
(2) 5.6×10^7
(3) 5.6×10^6
(4) 5.6×10^5
(5) 5.6×10^4

To check your answers, turn to page 388.

Simplifying Algebraic Expressions

In algebra, terms are added and subtracted. A term has a **variable**, or letter part, and a **coefficient**, or number part.

In the expression $3t + 2c$
                          ↑   ↑

3 is the coefficient of t 2 is the coefficient of c

Simplifying an expression means combining like terms. To add or subtract like terms, combine their coefficients using the rules for signed numbers.

When there is no coefficient in front of a variable, the coefficient is 1.

$3t + 4t + 5t$	$3 + 4 + 5$	$= 12t$
$3t - 4t + 5t$	$3 - 4 + 5$	$= 4t$
$6s + 8s + s$	$6 + 8 + 1$	$= 15s$
$10b - 8b$	$10 - 8$	$= 2b$
$15y - 5y - (-y)$	$15 - 5 + 1$	$= 11y$

A **constant** is a number that does not have a variable. In the example below, 4 and 9 are constants. Constants can be combined as like terms.

$3n + 4 - 9 = 3n - 5$

Variables with different exponents (y, y^2, or y^3) are *not* like terms. To simplify any expression, combine like terms only.

$$3x^2 + 5x + 7 + 5x^2 - 2x - 3$$

x^2 terms	x terms	constants
$3x^2 + 5x^2$	$5x - 2x$	$7 - 3$
$8x^2$	$3x$	4 $= 8x^2 + 3x + 4$

You may need to remove parentheses to simplify an expression.

Example:

Ellen bought 2 bouquets of flowers for $8 each and 2 vases for $4 each. You can find the total she spent in two different ways.

1. Add the amounts and multiply by 2: $2(\$8 + \$4) = 2(\$12) = \$24$

2. Multiply each amount by 2, and then add: $2(\$8) + 2(\$4) = \$16 + \$8 = \$24$

Both ways are equal: $2(\$8 + \$4) = 2(\$8) + 2(\$4)$

This example illustrates the **distributive law** of multiplication, which states that when a number is multiplied by a sum or difference within a set of parentheses, you may do either of these things:

1. Do the operation in parentheses and then multiply.
2. Multiply each number in the parentheses by the value outside and then do the addition or subtraction operation.

This law is used in algebra to simplify an expression when the value for the variable is not known. To multiply a value by a variable expression, multiply the coefficient by each value within the parentheses.

Examples:

Simplify:

$6(x + 4)$	$10(3n^2 - 6n - 3)$	$-2(7y - 8)$
$6(x + 4)$	$10(3n^2 - 6n - 3)$	$-2(7y - 8)$
$6(x) + 6(4)$	$10(3n^2) - 10(6n) - 10(3)$	$-2(7y) + (-2)(-8)$
$6x + 24$	$30n^2 - 60n - 30$	$-14y + 16$

Exercise 7

> **Directions**
> Choose the one best answer to each item.

1. What is $7s + 6s + s + s + 4s$ in simplified form?

(1) $19s$
(2) 19
(3) $17s$
(4) $17s^2$
(5) $19s^2$

2. What is $0.8b + 1.7b$ in simplified form?

(1) $0.25b$
(2) $0.9b$
(3) $1.36b$
(4) $2.5b$
(5) $25.0b$

3. Which of the following is equal to $4(t - 7)$?

   (1) $4(t + 7)$
   (2) $4(t) - 7$
   (3) $4(t) - 4(7)$
   (4) $4(t) + 4(7)$
   (5) $4t - 11$

4. Which of the following expressions is equal to
$5(3t^2 + t - 2)$?

   (1) $15t^2 + t - 10$
   (2) $t^2 + 5t + 10$
   (3) $15t^2 + t + 10$
   (4) $15t^2 + 5t - 10$
   (5) $15t^2 - 5t - 10$

5. Which of the following expressions is equal to
$5r - 2(2r + 6)$?

   (1) $r + 12$
   (2) $r - 12$
   (3) $r - 6$
   (4) $20r + 12$
   (5) $20r + 6$

6. Which of the following expressions is equal to
$2(3a + 5b) + 3(5a - 3b)$?

   (1) $21a + b$
   (2) $21a + 7b$
   (3) $a + 7b$
   (4) $a + b$
   (5) $21a + 19b$

7. Which expression does $6(5a + 4b) + 2(2a - b)$
equal?

   (1) $26a + 26b$
   (2) $15a + 18b$
   (3) $34a + 26b$
   (4) $34a + 22b$
   (5) $56ab$

8. Which of the following expressions is equal to
$3a - 2(6a + 8)$?

   (1) $-9a + 16$
   (2) $15a - 16$
   (3) $-15a - 16$
   (4) $-9a - 16$
   (5) $-9a + 6$

To check your answers, turn to page 388.

Evaluating Expressions

A **variable** is a letter used in place of a number. Within the same expression or equation, the variable must represent the same value.

    In $n + n = 8$: both n's have the same value.

    To simplify an algebraic expression when the values of the variables are given:

Step 1 Substitute the values given for the variables.

Step 2 Follow the rules for order of operations.

To evaluate algebraic expressions correctly, operations must be done in the following order.

$$8 + 5(6 - 4)^3$$
$$\downarrow$$

P	Parentheses	$8 + 5(2)^3$
		$\downarrow$
E	Exponents or roots	$8 + 5(8)$
		$\downarrow$
M D	Multiplication or	$8 + 40$
	Division from left to right	
A S	Addition or Subtraction from	$\downarrow$
	left to right	48

Examples:

Find the value of the following.
$3x^2$ when $x = 7$ $2 + n^3$ when $n = 4$

Step 1 Substitute the values given for the variables.
    $3(7)^2$ $2 + (4)^3$

Step 2 Follow the rules for order of operations.
    Exponents $3(7)^2$ Exponents $2 + (4)^3$
                  $3(49)$ $2 + (64)$
    Multiply 147 Add 66

Unless there are parentheses grouping the values, only the number immediately in front of the exponent is raised to a power.

Example:

Find the value of $3x^2y$ when $x = 6$ and $y = 4$.

Step 1 Substitute the values given for the variables.
    $3(6)^2(4)$

Step 2 Follow the rules for order of operations.
    Exponents $3(6)^2(4)$
                      $3(36)(4)$
    Multiply 432

Example:

Find the value of $(2 + n)^3$ when $n = 4$.

Step 1 Substitute the values given for the variables.

$$(2 + 4)^3$$

Step 2 Follow the rules for order of operations.

Parentheses	$(2 + 4)^3$
	$(6)^3$
Exponents	216

Exercise 8

Directions

Simplify the following expressions given $x = 2$, $y = 3$, and $z = 1$.

1. x^2

2. z^2

3. $5y^2$

4. xy^2

5. $\dfrac{x^2}{4}$

6. x^2y

7. $x^2 + y^2$

8. $(x + y)^2$

9. $x^2 + y$

10. x^2y^2

Directions

Choose the one best answer to each item.

11. What is the value of $\dfrac{t^2 + s^2}{s}$ when $t = 6$ and $s = -4$?

    (1) 13
    (2) 7
    (3) 2.5
    (4) −5
    (5) −13

12. What is the value of the expression $3.14r^2h$ when $r = 10$ and $h = 2$?

    (1) 6.28
    (2) 62.8
    (3) 452.16
    (4) 628
    (5) 1,256

13. What is the value of the expression $5s^3$ when $s = 2$?

    (1) 30
    (2) 40
    (3) 100
    (4) 300
    (5) 1,000

14. Which of the following will give the value of the expression prt, when $p = \$2,000$, $r = 0.06$ and $t = 4$?

    (1) $\$2,000(0.06 + 4)$
    (2) $\dfrac{\$2,000(0.06)}{4}$
    (3) $\$2,000(0.06)(4)$
    (4) $\$2,000 - (0.06)(4)$
    (5) $\$2,000 + (0.06) + (4)$

To check your answers, turn to page 388.

Solving Equations

A father is ten times as old as his son. Their combined ages add to 33. Can you figure out their ages? One way to solve the problem is to guess ages and see if your guesses work. Trial and error is a legitimate way to solve a problem, but it does take time. You can most easily solve this problem by writing an equation and solving it.

An **equation** is a numerical statement in which one value is equal (=) to another.

$$2 + 2 = 4 \quad 7(2) = 14 \quad n + 7 = 9$$

Notice in the third equation n must equal 2 to make this statement true.

$m + 4 = 16$ What value for m will make this equation true? The variable m must equal 12. How do you get 12 using the numbers 16 and 4? Subtract: $16 - 4 = 12$.

$x - 8 = 10$ What value for x will make this equation true? The variable x must equal 18. How do you get 18 using the numbers 10 and 8? Add: $10 + 8 = 18$.

$3y = 30$ What value for y will make this equation true? The variable y must equal 10. How do you get 10 using the numbers 30 and 3? Divide: $30 \div 3 = 10$.

$\frac{r}{5} = 4$ What value for r will make this equation true? The variable r must equal 20. How do you get 20 using the numbers 5 and 4? Multiply: 5(4) = 20.

To solve an equation:

Step 1 Get the variable alone on one side by moving the number with it to the other (opposite) side of the equation.

Step 2 Do the inverse (or opposite) operation.

Examples:

Solve: $y + 3 = 9$

Step 1 Move the 3 to the other side, and change its sign.

$y + 3 = 9$
-3

Step 2 **Subtract** it from 9. $y = 6$

You can check your answer by substituting it for the variable in the original equation.

Check: $y + 3 = 9$
$(6) + 3 = 9$

Solve: $7m = 77$

Step 1 Move the 7 to the other side, and apply the inverse operation.

$7m = \frac{77}{7}$

Step **Divide** it into 77. $m = 11$

Check: $7m = 77$
$7(11) = 77$

You can check your answer by substituting it for the variable in the original equation.

Check: $y + 3 = 9$
$(6) + 3 = 9$

Solve: $\frac{b}{2} = 16$

Step 1 Move the 2 to the other side, and apply the inverse operation.

$\frac{b}{2} = 16(2)$

Step 2 **Multiply** it by 16. $b = 32$

Check: $\frac{b}{2} = 16$

$\frac{32}{2} = 16$

Exercise 9

Directions
Solve these equations using the inverse operation. Show each step.

	A.	B.	C.
1.	$n - 19 = 27$	$p + 27 = 46$	$7r = 56$
2.	$t + 15 = 19$	$\frac{c}{4} = 25$	$3f = 51$
3.	$\frac{a}{11} = 5$	$c + 26 = 32$	$n - 79 = 113$
4.	$\frac{x}{5} = 11$	$q + 9 = 97$	$\frac{n}{6} = 8$
5.	$9b = 90$	$72 = x - 48$	$\frac{s}{2} = 150$

6. Twelve people bought theater tickets for a total of $72. If t represents the price of each ticket, then the equation $12t = \$72$ can be used to find the price of one ticket. What does t, the price of one ticket, equal?

(1) $6
(2) $12
(3) $72
(4) $864
(5) Not enough information is given.

7. Lance plans to tile his kitchen floor. The area of the floor is 132 square feet, and the length of the room measures 12 feet. If w represents the width of the room, then the equation $12w = 132$ can be used to find the width. What is the width of the room?

(1) 8 feet
(2) 9 feet
(3) 10 feet
(4) 11 feet
(5) 12 feet

8. Ellen recently got a raise of $115 per month. She now earns $2,300 per month. If x represents her previous monthly salary, then the equation $x + \$115 = \$2,300$ can be used to find the amount she earned per month before her raise. What is that amount?

    (1) $2,080
    (2) $2,170
    (3) $2,185
    (4) $2,285
    (5) $2,415

To check your answers, turn to page 389.

Solving Multi-Step Equations

Some equations require more than one step to solve. Your task, however, is still the same. You need to find a way to isolate the variable on one side of the equation.

Test-Taking Tip

Since the GED Math Test is a multiple-choice test, you can choose to guess and check to solve some algebra problems. Select one of the answer choices and substitute it into the equation in the problem. Try each choice until you find the correct one. The guess-and-check method is a good choice if an equation looks long or difficult to solve.

To isolate the variable:

    Step 1 Remove any number added or subtracted by doing the inverse operation.

    Step 2 Remove any number multiplied or divided by doing the inverse operation.

Example:

    Solve: $3b + 7 = 28$

    Step 1 Remove the 7 by $3b + 7 = 28$
          subtracting. -7

    Step 2 Remove the 3 by $3b = 21$
          dividing. 3
                          $b = 7$

Substitute your answer into the original equation, and solve to check your answer.

    Check: $3b + 7 = 28$
                $3(7) + 7 = 28$
                  $21 + 7 = 28$

It may be necessary to simplify each side of an equation by combining like terms before solving by inverse operations. To simplify each side of the equation, remember to do the operation <u>as indicated</u> on the same side of the equation. You do the opposite or inverse operation only when you move a value to the opposite side of the equation.

Example:

    Solve: $8y - 10 - 2y = 10 - 8$
             On the same side, do the same (indicated) operation.

    Step 1 **Combine** like terms on $8y - 10 - 2y = 10 - 8$
          each side. $6y - 10 = 2$

          On the opposite side, do the opposite (inverse) operation.

    Step 2 Remove the 10 by $6y - 10 = 2$
          adding. $+ 10$

    Step 3 Remove the 6 by $6y = 12$
          dividing. 6
                          $y = 2$

When a variable appears on both sides of the equation, use inverse operations to get the variables together on one side of the equation and the constants together on the other side.

Example:

    Solve: $4(n - 6) = 3n$

    Step 1 **Multiply** 4 times each $4(n - 6) = 3n$
          number in the paren- $4n - 24 = 3n$
          theses.

    Step 2 Move the $3n$ to the op- $4n - 24 = 3n$
          posite side by $-3n$
          subtracting.

    Step 3 Remove the 24 by $n - 24 = 0$
          adding. $+ 24$
                          $n = 24$

Exercise 10

Directions
Solve each equation using inverse operations.

1. $4w + 6 = 34$

2. $28 = 12y - 8$

3. $\frac{s}{4} - 13 = 2$

4. $3r + 6 + 2r = 21$

5. $3v - 42 = 100 - 2(20)$

6. $7(g - 6) = 42$

7. $8t = 2t + 6$

8. $13m + 7 = 11m + 21$

9. $14s + 11 = 13s + 17$

10. If $v - 6.8 = 3.4$, then what is the value of v?
    (1) 2
    (2) 3.4
    (3) 8.5
    (4) 10.2
    (5) 23.12

11. If $0.5k + 2 = 11$, then what does k equal?
    (1) 5
    (2) 18
    (3) 49
    (4) 60.5
    (5) 71

12. If $3x + 2(5x - 8) = 11x - 4$, then what does x equal?
    (1) 2
    (2) 3
    (3) 4
    (4) 5
    (5) 6

13. If $b^2 = 400$, then what is the value of b?
    (1) 10
    (2) 20
    (3) 30
    (4) 40
    (5) 50

14. If $6n + 6 = 5n + 6$, then what is the value of n?
    (1) 0
    (2) 2
    (3) 6
    (4) 10
    (5) 12

15. If $12k + 14 = 2(k + 22)$, then what does k equal?
    (1) 0
    (2) 3
    (3) 6
    (4) 12
    (5) 15

To check your answers, turn to page 389.

Solving Inequalities

An **inequality** is a statement that two or more values are *unequal*.

The symbols of an inequality are:

>   Greater than
<   Less than
≥   Greater than **or** equal to
≤   Less than **or** equal to

In the statement $n - 3 = 10$, the only value which will satisfy the equation is $n = 13$.

In the statement $n - 3 > 10$, many values will satisfy the inequality. n can be 14, 15, 16, or any value greater than 13. The solution to the inequality can be written $n > 13$.

The solution set of an inequality consists of those values which will satisfy or make the statement true. The solution set can include whole numbers, fractions, and decimals.

Inequality	Solution Set
$x > 3$	x can be any number greater than 3
$y < 10$	y can be any number less than 10
$r \geq 7$	r can be 7 or any number greater than 7
$s \leq 5$	s can be 5 or any number less than 5

Inequalities, like equations, can be solved by inverse operations. The symbol of the inequality remains, unless a side is multiplied or divided by a negative quantity. Then the inequality symbol is reversed.

Example:

Solve: $3y - 7 \geq 11$

Step 1 Remove the 7 by **adding**. $3y - 7 \geq 11$
$\;+\;7$

Step 2 Remove the 3 by **dividing**. $3y \geq 18$
$\;3$

y can be 6 or any value $y \geq 6$
greater than 6.

Example:

Which of the following inequalities is true when x is replaced by 5?

A. $2x + 3 \leq 15$
B. $3x + 8 \geq 29$
C. $-7x + 2 < -19$

To answer this question, you can solve each inequality and check to see if 5 is in the solution set. Note the sign reversal in **C**.

A. $2x + 3 \leq 15$
$\;2x \leq 12$
$\;x \leq 6$ Yes $5 \leq 6$

B. $3x + 8 \geq 29$
$\;x \geq 21$
$\;x \geq 7$ No $5 \geq 7$

C. $-7x + 2 < -19$
$\;-7x < -21$
$\;x > 3$ Yes $5 > 3$

You may also answer the question by substituting 5 in each inequality to see if the statement is true.

A. $2x + 3 \leq 15$ $2(5) + 3 \leq 15$
$\;10 + 3 \leq 15$
$\;13 \leq 15$ Yes

B. $3x + 8 \geq 29$ $3(5) + 8 \geq 29$
$\;15 + 8 \geq 29$
$\;23 \geq 29$ No

C. $-7x + 2 < -19$ $-7(5) + 2 < -19$
$\phantom{C.\;-7x + 2 < -19}\;-35 + 2 < -19$
$\phantom{C.\;-7x + 2 < -19\;-35}\;-33 < -19$ Yes

Exercise 11

Directions

Use inverse operations to solve the following inequalities.

1. Which of the following is true for $w - 15 < 12$?
    (1) $w < 3$
    (2) $w < 27$
    (3) $w > 3$
    (4) $w = 27$
    (5) $w < 180$

2. Which of the following is true for $2x \leq 100$?
    (1) $x = 25$
    (2) $x \leq 25$
    (3) $x \geq 50$
    (4) $x \leq 50$
    (5) $x = 200$

3. Which of the following is true for $3g + 17 > 140$?
    (1) $g = 37$
    (2) $g \geq 37$
    (3) $g > 41$
    (4) $g = 41$
    (5) $g > 52$

4. Which of the following values is in the solution set of $-3y - 7 \geq -28$?
    (1) 7
    (2) 8
    (3) 10
    (4) 12
    (5) 20

5. Which of the following values is *not* in the solution set of $8b - 4 > 28$?
    (1) 4
    (2) 5
    (3) 6
    (4) 7
    (5) 8

6. Which of the following inequalities is true when x is replaced by 10?
    (1) $2x + 3 \leq 15$
    (2) $3x + 8 \geq 29$
    (3) $7x - 2 < 19$
    (4) $4x - 8 < 30$
    (5) $2x + 9 > 35$

To check your answers, turn to page 389.

Using Formulas

You have used formulas to find the perimeter and area of squares and rectangles. You can also use formulas as equations to solve for the length of a side when the perimeter or area is given.

Items A and B refer to the following figure.

12 in

Examples:

A. If the area of the rectangle is 84 square inches, what is the width of the rectangle?

Step 1 Substitute the values given for the variables in the appropriate formula

$A = lw$ *Length = 12*

$84 = 12w$ *Area = 84*

Step 2 Simplify each side of the equation, and use inverse operations to solve.

$$\frac{84}{12} = w$$

$7 = w$, the width of the rectangle

B. If the perimeter of the rectangle given is 36, what is the width of the rectangle?

Step 1 Substitute the values given for the variables in the appropriate formula.

$P = 2l + 2w$ *Length = 12*

$36 = 2(12) + 2w$ *Perimeter = 36*

Step 2 Simplify each side of the equation, and use inverse operations to solve.

$36 = 24 + 2w$

-24

$\dfrac{12 = 2w}{2}$

$6 = w$, the width of the rectangle

C. If the area of a square is 64 ft², what is the length of each side?

Step 1 Substitute the values given for the variables in the appropriate formula.

$A = s^2$ *Area = 64*

$64 = s^2$

When the variable in an equation is squared, or taken to the second power, the inverse operation is finding the square root of the number on the other side of the equation.

Step 2 Simplify each side of the equation, and use inverse operations to solve.

$$\sqrt{64} = s$$

$8 = s$, the side of the square

Exercise 12

> **Directions**
>
> Use the following formulas to solve Items 1 to 7.

Area (A) of a square or a rectangle

square	$A = s^2$; where s = side
rectangle	$A = lw$; where l = length, w = width

Perimeter (P) of a rectangle

$P = 2l + 2w$; where l = length, w = width

Volume (V) of a rectangular container

$V = lwh$;   where l = length, w = width,
                  h = height

1. How many inches is the length of a rectangle with an area of 68 cm² and a width of 4 cm?

   (1) 4
   (2) 9
   (3) 17
   (4) 34
   (5) 272

2. How many centimeters high is a rectangular container with a volume of 60 cm³, a length of 3 cm, and a width of 4 cm?

   (1) 2
   (2) 5
   (3) 6
   (4) 8
   (5) 10

3. Which equation below would be used to find the length of each side of a square with an area of 121 in²?

   (1) $121 = 4s$
   (2) $121 = s^3$
   (3) $121 = lw$
   (4) $121 = s^2$
   (5) Not enough information is given.

4. How many yards wide is Jill's front lawn with an area of 32 sq yd?

   (1) 4
   (2) 6
   (3) 8
   (4) 12
   (5) Not enough information is given.

5. Ron used 30 feet of fence to enclose a pen for his dog. If the pen is 5 feet wide, how many feet long is it?

   (1) 4
   (2) 6
   (3) 8
   (4) 10
   (5) Not enough information is given.

6. Which equation below would be used to find the width of a rectangular container with a volume of 600 cm^3, a length of 10 cm, and a height of 10 cm?

   (1) $600 = s^3$
   (2) $600 = 10(10)w$
   (3) $600 = 10(10) + 10w$
   (4) $600 = 10w$
   (5) Not enough information is given.

7. A rectangular yard has a perimeter of 144 feet. What is the width of the yard in feet if the length of the yard is 42 feet?

   (1) 72
   (2) 60
   (3) 36
   (4) 30
   (5) 24

To check your answers, turn to page 389.

Quadratic Equations

A **quadratic equation** is an equation in which the variable is raised to the second power or squared. Quadratic equations usually have two different solutions. There are two values for the variable that will **satisfy** the equation or make it true.

The two values that will satisfy $y^2 - 4y + 3 = 0$ are $y = 1$ and $y = 3$. When either of these values is substituted into the equation, it will be true.

$$y^2 - 4y + 3 = 0 \qquad y^2 - 4y + 3 = 0$$
$$(1)^2 - 4(1) + 3 = 0 \qquad (3)^2 - 4(3) + 3 = 0$$
$$1 - 4 + 3 = 0 \qquad 9 - 12 + 3 = 0$$

Since it is not likely that there will be more than one quadratic equation given on the GED Math Test, that one problem can be most easily solved by guessing and checking the multiple-choice answers in the equation. Use guess and check to solve this problem.

Example:

If $10t^2 - 15 = 235$, then t equals what numbers?

   (1) 0 and 5
   (2) 0 and −5
   (3) 5 and −5
   (4) 5 and 10
   (5) −5 and 10

Perhaps you may notice that the problem contains several multiples of 5 so you can try (3) 5 and -5. Substitute each of these values into the equation.

$$10t^2 - 15 = 235 \qquad 10t^2 - 15 = 235$$
$$10(5)^2 - 15 = 235 \qquad 10(-5)^2 - 15 = 235$$
$$10(25) - 15 = 235 \qquad 10(25) - 15 = 235$$
$$250 - 15 = 235 \qquad 250 - 15 = 235$$

Both of these values satisfy the equation, so choice (3) is the correct answer.

Exercise 13

Directions
Solve the following.

1. If $p^2 - 5p = 14$, then p equals what numbers?

   (1) 0 and −2
   (2) −2 and 7
   (3) 7 and −5
   (4) −5 and 4
   (5) 4 and 10

2. If $2r^2 + 2r - 60 = 0$, then what does r equal?

   (1) −5 and 6
   (2) −5 and 7
   (3) 5 and −6
   (4) 7 and −6
   (5) 8 and −9

3. If $z^2 - z - 56 = 0$, then z equals what numbers?

  (1) 2 and −3
  (2) −3 and 4
  (3) 4 and −5
  (4) −5 and 8
  (5) −7 and 8

To check your answers, turn to page 389.

Using Algebra to Solve Word Problems

Earlier in this unit you read a problem about a man and his son.

Example:

The father is ten times as old as his son. Their combined ages add up to 33. How old is the father?

Now let's see how an equation can be written to solve the problem.

Step 1 Use a variable to represent an unknown amount.

$$x = \text{son's age}$$

Step 2 Write a variable expression to represent other unknown quantities.

The father is ten times as old as his son.

father's age = $10x$

Step 3 Write an equation which restates the information in the problem using these expressions.

Their combined ages add to 33.

$$x + 10x = 33$$

Unknown Amounts	Variable Expressions	Equation
Son's age	x	$x + 10x = 33$
Father's age	$10x$	

Step 4 Solve the equation to find the value of the variable.

$$x + 10x = 33$$
$$11x = \frac{33}{11}$$
$$x = 3$$

Step 5 Use the value for the variable to *answer the question asked.*

How old is the father?
father = $10x$

Therefore the father is 10(3), or 30 years old.

A common kind of algebra word problem involves consecutive numbers. Consecutive numbers are numbers which follow each other in counting order. Examples: 5 and 6; 10 and 11; and 97, 98, and 99.

If one number is x, the next consecutive number is $x + 1$.

Example:

The sum of two consecutive numbers is 45. What are the numbers?

Steps 1-3 Make a table to represent the unknowns.

Unknown Amounts	Variable Expressions	Equation
First number	x	$x + x + 1 = 45$
Next number	$x + 1$	

Step 4 Solve the equation.
$$x + x + 1 = 45$$
$$2x + 1 = 45$$
$$2x = 44$$
$$x = 22$$

Step 5 Answer the question asked.

What are the numbers?
First number = x, or 22
Next number = $x + 1$, or 23
The numbers are 22 and 23.

Writing inequalities is done in the same way as writing equations. However, a symbol of inequality, $>$, $<$, $\geq$, or $\leq$, is used in place of the equal sign (=).

Example:

The sum of three consecutive even numbers is less than 0. Find the three highest possible values for these numbers.

Unknown Amounts	Variable Expressions	Equation
First number	x	$x + x + 2 + x + 4 < 0$
Second number	$x + 2$	
Third number	$x + 4$	

$$x + x + 2 + x + 4 < 0$$
$$3x + 6 < 0$$
$$3x < -6$$
$$x < -2$$

If x must be an even number less than −2, the highest possible value for x is −4.

If $x = -4$, $x + 2 = -2$, and $x + 4 = 0$.

Exercise 14

1. Carl and his wife Mary drove to the lake in separate cars. Carl's car used twice as much gasoline as his wife's car. Together they used six gallons. How many gallons of gasoline did *Carl's car* use?

Unknown Amounts	Variable Expressions	Equation
Mary's car		
Carl's car		

How many gallons of gasoline did *Carl's car* use?_____

2. The high temperature today was 72°. That is 20° warmer than yesterday's high. What was yesterday's high temperature?

Unknown Amount	Variable Expression	Equation
Yesterday's temperature		

What was yesterday's high temperature?_____

3. Consecutive odd or even numbers are separated by 2. The sum of two consecutive odd numbers is 96. What is the first number?

Unknown Amounts	Variable Expressions	Equation
First number		
Next number		

What is the first number?_____

4. Debbie is three times as old as her daughter Aisling. In 10 years she will be twice as old as Aisling. How old is Debbie now?

Unknown Amounts	Now	In 10 Years	Equation
Aisling's age			
Debbie's age			

How old is Debbie now?_____

5. Which of the following values is in the solution set for $5m + 15 > 30$?

   (1) 4
   (2) 3
   (3) 2
   (4) 1
   (5) 0

6. Twice as many women as men voted during the local election. If 3,600 individuals voted, how many women voted?

   (1) 1,200
   (2) 1,500
   (3) 2,000
   (4) 2,400
   (5) 3,000

7. An adult ticket to the movie cost $2 more than a child's ticket. A preschool spent $100 to pay for 10 children and 5 adults to see the movie. How much did each child's ticket cost?

   (1) $4
   (2) $6
   (3) $7.50
   (4) $8
   (5) $10

8. John wants to use a length of no more than 22 feet to install 3 bookshelves on a wall in his office. Which of the following lengths (in feet) of bookshelves can he use?

   (1) 7
   (2) 8
   (3) 9
   (4) 10
   (5) Not enough information is given.

9. Last week Carmen drove round-trip to work each day Monday through Friday. She also drove 74 miles round-trip on Wednesday evening to see a play. The car's odometer shows that Carmen drove a total of 324 miles last week. How many miles is her round-trip drive to work?

   (1) 12
   (2) 25
   (3) 50
   (4) 60
   (5) 72

10. The sum of three consecutive numbers is 159. What is the largest number?

   (1) 46
   (2) 47
   (3) 51
   (4) 52
   (5) 54

11. Sharon is 4 years younger than Kenny. In 5 years, three times Sharon's age will equal twice Kenny's age. How old is Sharon now?

   (1) 3
   (2) 7
   (3) 11
   (4) 15
   (5) 19

To check your answers, turn to page 390.

GEOMETRY

Lines and Angles

Parallel lines are lines on the same plane (a flat surface) that do not meet or intersect. Parallel lines remain an equal distance apart at every point. **Intersecting lines** are lines that *do* cross or intersect. Remember that when lines cross, they form angles. Those angles are measured in degrees (°).

A line that intersects two or more parallel lines is a **transversal**. In the figures below, lines A and B are parallel. Line C is a transversal. The intersecting lines form 8 angles.

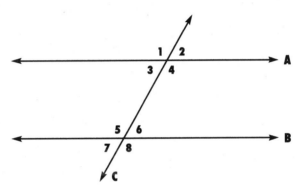

In the figure above, the following pairs of angles are equal:

Corresponding Angles	Vertical Angles	Alternate Angles
∠1 and ∠5	∠1 and ∠4	∠3 and ∠6
∠2 and ∠6	∠2 and ∠3	∠4 and ∠5
∠3 and ∠7	∠5 and ∠8	∠1 and ∠8
∠4 and ∠8	∠6 and ∠7	∠2 and ∠7

Another kind of angle is a straight angle. A **straight angle** is an angle whose sides lie on a straight line. A straight angle measures 180°.

If the sum of two angles is 180°, then the angles are **supplementary angles**. Angles 1 and 2 above are supplementary. If you know the measure of one of the angles, you can figure out the measure of the other.

Example:

If ∠1 = 100°, what is the measure of ∠2?   180° − 100° = 80°   ∠2 = 80°

When the sum of two angles is 90°, the angles are **complementary angles**. If you know the measure of one angle, you can find the measure of the other.

Example:

$\angle A = 40°$. What is the measure of $\angle B$?

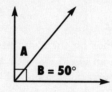

$90° - 40° = 50°$

Example:

Line AB is a transversal within two parallel lines.

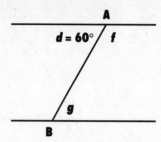

Find the measure of $\angle g$.

Angle g is an alternate angle to $\angle d$, so $\angle g$ is also 60°.

Find the measure of $\angle f$.

Angle f is a supplementary angle to $\angle d$, so $\angle f$ is 120°.
$(180° - 60°) = 120°$

Exercise 1

Directions

Items 1 to 4 refer to the following lines.

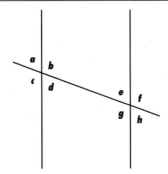

1. If ∠a is 70°, what is the measure of ∠b?

2. If ∠a is 70°, what is the measure of ∠e?

3. Name all the angles that equal ∠a.

4. Name all the angles that equal ∠b.

5. ∠X and ∠Y are complementary. If ∠X measures 35°, what is the measure of ∠Y?

    (1) 55°
    (2) 65°
    (3) 90°
    (4) 145°
    (5) Not enough information is given.

Item 6 refers to the following diagram.

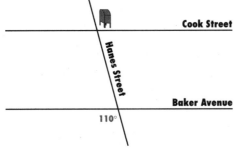

6. What is the angle of the intersection of Cook and Hanes Streets where the mailbox is to be installed?

    (1) 70°
    (2) 75°
    (3) 80°
    (4) 85°
    (5) 110°

7. ∠3 and ∠4 are supplementary angles. ∠4 measures 90°. Which is a true statement?

    (1) You cannot know the measure of ∠3.
    (2) ∠3 and ∠4 are complementary angles.
    (3) ∠3 and ∠4 are vertical angles.
    (4) ∠3 measures 90°.
    (5) The measures of ∠3 and ∠4 are not equal.

To check your answers, turn to page 390.

Area of a Parallelogram

A **parallelogram** is a four-sided figure whose opposite sides are parallel and equal to each other. The longer side of the parallelogram is called the **base**, similar to the length of a rectangle. A line perpendicular to the bases is called the **height**. In the parallelogram below, the base is 8 cm and the height is 4 cm.

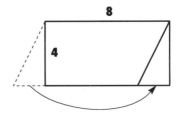

Use this formula to find the area:

Area (A) of a parallelogram:
$A = bh$; where b = base, h = height

Example:

Find the area of the parallelogram above.

Substitute 8 for b and 4 for h in $A = bh$.

$A = 8(4)$
$8(4) = 32$ square centimeters
32 sq cm, or 32 cm^2

The area of the parallelogram is 32 sq cm.

Exercise 2

Directions

Find the area of each parallelogram below.

1.
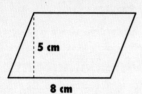
5 cm
8 cm

2.
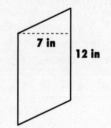
7 in
12 in

3.
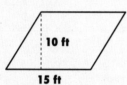
10 ft
15 ft

4.
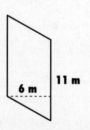
11 m
6 m

Directions

Item 5 refers to the parallelogram below.

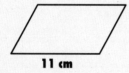
11 cm

5. Which of the following statements is true for the parallelogram shown?

   (1) $P = 32$ inches
   (2) $P = 44$ inches
   (3) $A = 44$ square inches
   (4) $A = 56$ in^2
   (5) Not enough information is given.

To check your answers, turn to page 390.

Types of Triangles

All **triangles** have 3 sides and 3 angles. The sum of the angles of any triangle is *always* equal to 180°. A triangle is defined by the measures of its angles and sides.

An **equilateral triangle** has 3 sides of equal length and 3 angles that measure 60° each. ∆ABC is an equilateral triangle.

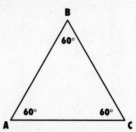

An **isosceles triangle** has two sides of equal length and two equal angles called base angles. The third angle of an isosceles triangle is called the **vertex angle**. ∆JKL is an isosceles triangle.

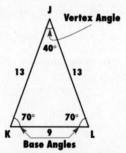

You know that a right angle measures 90°. A **right triangle** has one right (90°) angle. The longest side of a right triangle, called the **hypotenuse**, is directly across from the right angle. The other sides of a right triangle are called **legs**. ∆DEF and ∆GHI are right triangles.

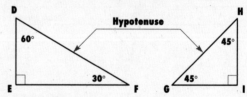

A **scalene triangle** has no equal sides and no equal angles. ∆PQR is a scalene triangle.

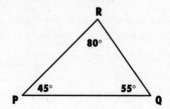

Exercise 3

Directions
Choose the <u>one best answer</u> to each item.

Item 1 refers to the following triangle.

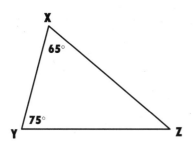

1. What kind of triangle is △XYZ?

   (1) Equilateral
   (2) Right
   (3) Scalene
   (4) Isosceles
   (5) Not enough information is given.

2. The measure of the angles of △RST are 30°, 60°, and 90°. What kind of triangle is △RST?

   (1) Equilateral
   (2) Right
   (3) Isosceles
   (4) Scalene
   (5) Not enough information is given.

Items 3 and 4 refer to the following triangle.

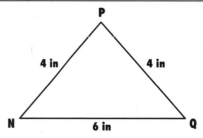

3. In △NPQ, NP and PQ each measure 4 inches. What kind of triangle is △NPQ?

   (1) Equilateral
   (2) Right
   (3) Scalene
   (4) Isosceles
   (5) Not enough information is given.

4. If ∠N and ∠Q each measure 65°, what is the measure of ∠P?

   (1) 30°
   (2) 50°
   (3) 65°
   (4) 130°
   (5) Not enough information is given.

To check your answers, turn to page 390.

Perimeter and Area of a Triangle

What is the perimeter of the triangle below? The perimeter of any triangle can be found by adding the measure of all the sides.

Perimeter (*P*) of a triangle:

$P = a + b + c$; where *a, b,* and *c* are the sides.

Example:

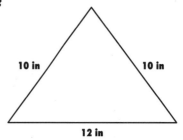

The perimeter of the triangle above is found by substituting the values given for the sides *a, b,* and *c* in $P = a + b + c$.

$P = 10 + 10 + 12$

$P = 32$ inches

When a rectangle, square, or other parallelogram is cut in half diagonally, two equal triangles are formed. How does this fact help you to find a triangle's area?

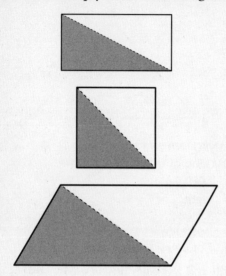

To find the area of each triangle in the figures above, you would find the area of the rectangle, square, or parallelogram and take half of it.

Area (A) of a triangle:

$A = \frac{1}{2}bh$; where b = base, and h = height

As in a parallelogram, the height of the triangle must be perpendicular to the base. Sometimes the height of the triangle appears outside the triangle itself.

Examples:

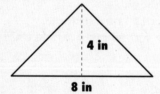

The height is shown within the triangle.

$A = \frac{1}{2}bh$

$A = \frac{1}{2}(8)(4)$

$A = 16 \text{ in}^2$

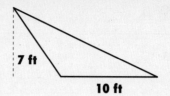

The height is shown outside of the triangle.

$A = \frac{1}{2}bh$

$A = \frac{1}{2}(10)(7)$

$A = 35 \text{ sq ft}$

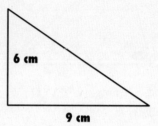

The height of a right triangle is the side that forms a right angle with the base.

$A = \frac{1}{2}bh$

$A = \frac{1}{2}(9)(6)$

$A = 27 \text{ cm}^2$

364

Exercise 4

Directions

Find the perimeter and area of each of the following triangles.

1.

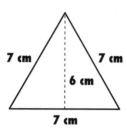

7 cm   7 cm

6 cm

7 cm

Perimeter = _____

Area = _____

2.

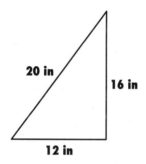

20 in   16 in

12 in

Perimeter = _____

Area = _____

Directions

Choose the one best answer to each item.

3. △GHJ is an equilateral triangle with a side of 6 inches. Which of the following statements is true based on the information given?

    (1) The height of △GHJ is also 6 inches.
    (2) The area of △GHJ can be found using
    $$A = \frac{1}{2}(6)(6).$$
    (3) The base of △GHJ is the longest side.
    (4) The perimeter of △GHJ can be found using
    $P = 6 + 6 + 6.$
    (5) The largest angle of △GHJ is a right angle.

4. How many square cm are enclosed in △MNO with a height of 14 cm and a base of 20 cm?

    (1) 70
    (2) 140
    (3) 200
    (4) 280
    (5) Not enough information is given.

5. How many cm are needed to go around △MNO with a height of 14 cm and a base of 20 cm?

    (1) 28
    (2) 34
    (3) 47
    (4) 54
    (5) Not enough information is given.

6. Smith City Hall has a triangular garden. The sides measure 6 ft, 10 ft, and 10 ft. The landscaper is going to install a trim around the edges. How many feet of trim does he need?

    (1) 26
    (2) 30
    (3) 52
    (4) 60
    (5) Not enough information is given.

7. One side of an equilateral triangle measures 12 inches. Find the perimeter of the triangle in inches.

    (1) 24
    (2) 36
    (3) 48
    (4) 72
    (5) 144

8. Two sides of a scalene triangle measure 18 inches and 13 inches. What is the perimeter of the triangle in inches?

    (1) 31
    (2) 44
    (3) 49
    (4) 62
    (5) Not enough information is given.

To check your answers, turn to page 390.

Right Triangles and the Pythagorean Relationship

A Greek mathematician, Pythagoras, discovered a relationship between the measure of the legs and the hypotenuse of a right triangle. The relationship known as the Pythagorean relationship is shown on the formula sheet.

Pythagorean relationship:
$c^2 = a^2 + b^2$; where c = hypotenuse, a and b are legs of a right triangle.

The hypotenuse is the longest side of the right triangle. It is across from the right angle and is always represented in the formula by c. In the figure below, $c =$ 25. Either leg may be a or b. When these values are substituted in the formula, you see that the Pythagorean relationship is true.

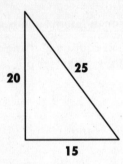

Example:

$$c^2 = a^2 + b^2$$
$$(25)^2 = (15)^2 + (20)^2$$
$$625 = 225 + 400$$

To find the unknown side of a right triangle, substitute the known values for the variables and solve the equation.

Example:

Find the hypotenuse of a right triangle with one leg = 9 cm and the other leg = 12 cm.

$$c^2 = a^2 + b^2$$
$$c^2 = (9)^2 + (12)^2$$
$$c^2 = 81 + 144$$
$$c^2 = 225$$

To solve for c, find $\sqrt{225}$. The value of c is 15.

Example:

Find the hypotenuse of a right triangle with legs that are 18 ft and 24 ft long.

Most Pythagorean problems on the GED Math Test utilize 3:4:5 or 5:12:13 ratios.

Look at the values for 3:4:5 right triangles shown in the table below.

Leg (a)		Leg (b)		Hypotenuse (c)	
3		4		5	
6	3(2)	8	4(2)	10	5(2)
9	3(3)	12	4(3)	15	5(3)
12	3(4)	16	4(4)	20	5(4)
15	3(5)	20	4(5)	25	5(5)

A shortcut to find the hypotenuse in the problem above is to check to see if the lengths given fit into a 3:4:5 ratio.

As 18 is 3(6) and 24 is 4(6), the hypotenuse must be 5(6), or 30.

You can check the answer using the Pythagorean formula.

$$c^2 = a^2 + b^2$$
$$30^2 = 18^2 + 24^2$$
$$900 = 324 + 576$$

Example:

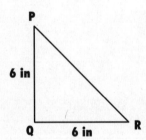

Find the length of the hypotenuse in $\triangle PQR$.

The solution to some problems, such as this one, may require estimating the square root.

$$c^2 = a^2 + b^2$$
$$c^2 = (6)^2 + (6)^2$$
$$c^2 = 36 + 36$$
$$c = \sqrt{72}$$

The square root of 72 is not a whole number. It is between $\sqrt{64}$ and $\sqrt{81}$. The square root of 72 is between 8 and 9, so the length of the hypotenuse is between 8 and 9 inches long.

Exercise 5

Directions

Find the missing side of the following right triangles.

	Leg A	Leg B	Hypotenuse
1.	3	4	_____
2.	6	_____	10
3.	8	8	_____
4.	_____	40	50

Directions

Choose the <u>one best answer</u> to each item.

5. Which expression equals the length in centimeters of the second leg of a right triangle with a leg that equals 48 cm and a hypotenuse that equals 60 cm?

(1) $\sqrt{1,024}$
(2) $\sqrt{1,296}$
(3) $\sqrt{1,600}$
(4) $\sqrt{2,304}$
(5) $\sqrt{2,916}$

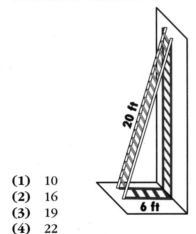

6. Tammy placed a 20-foot ladder against the house to reach the second-floor windows. The bottom of the ladder was 6 feet away from the house. About how many feet above the ground were the second-floor windows?

(1) 10
(2) 16
(3) 19
(4) 22
(5) Not enough information is given.

To check your answers, turn to page 391.

Congruent and Similar Triangles

Congruent triangles are identical figures. In congruent triangles, the three corresponding angles are equal and the three corresponding sides are equal.

Similar triangles are the same shape, but they may not be the same size. In similar triangles, all three corresponding angles are equal in measure, and the corresponding sides are in proportion to each other.

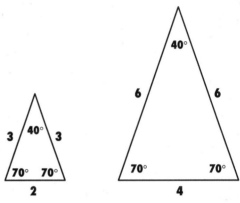

The triangles shown above are similar. All three corresponding angles are equal and the proportion of *corresponding* sides is true.

$$\frac{2}{3} = \frac{4}{6}$$

$$3(4) = 2(6)$$

$$12 = 12$$

If you know that two triangles are similar, you can solve for a missing angle or side using ratio and proportion. Study these common applications of similar triangles in word problems.

Shadow of objects at the same time of day

At 3 p.m. yesterday, a flagpole cast a shadow 10 feet long. At the same time a 3-foot stick placed perpendicular to the ground cast a 1-foot shadow. How many feet tall is the flagpole?

Sketch the situation. Both figures make a right angle (90°) with the ground, and the sun shines on both objects at the same angle. Therefore, the situation described is about similar triangles with two equal angles.

To find the length of the shadow, set up a proportion.

$$\frac{\text{object}}{\text{shadow}} \qquad \frac{3}{1} = \frac{x}{10} \qquad \frac{\text{object}}{\text{shadow}}$$

$$3(10) = 1(x)$$
$$30 = x$$

The flagpole is 30 feet tall.

Distance across a lake, pond, or river

What is the distance across the river?

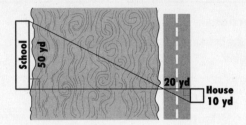

On the GED Math Test, a sketch is usually given with this type of problem. Notice that the lines form a large and small right triangle.

The intersection of the triangles are vertical angles. Vertical angles are equal, so those angles and the right angles are the two angles that prove that the triangles are similar.

To find the distance across the river, set up a proportion.

$$\frac{\text{long side}}{\text{base}} \qquad \frac{20}{10} = \frac{x}{50} \qquad \frac{\text{long side (across river)}}{\text{base}}$$

$$20(50) = 10(x)$$
$$1{,}000 = 10x$$
$$100 = x$$

It is 100 yards across the river.

Small triangle within a large triangle

What is the length of AB?

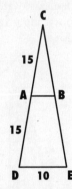

∠C is in both triangles. ∠A and ∠D are corresponding angles. They are in corresponding positions because a transversal (AD) crosses two parallel lines (AB and DE). Therefore ΔDEC and ΔABC are similar.

To find the length of AB, set up a proportion.

$$\frac{\text{CD}(15 + 15)}{\text{DE}} \qquad \frac{30}{10} = \frac{15}{x} \qquad \frac{\text{AC}}{\text{AB}}$$

$$10(15) = 30(x)$$
$$150 = 30x$$
$$5 = x$$

AB is 5 inches.

Exercise 6

Directions

Choose the <u>one best answer</u> to each item.

Item 1 refers to the following diagram.

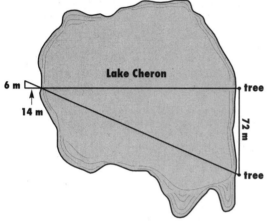

1. Surveyors are finding the distance in meters across Lake Cheron. First the distance between two trees on the opposite shore is measured. Then the surveyors stake out two similar right triangles. Using the measurements in the diagram, what is the distance in meters across the lake?

   (1) 84
   (2) 144
   (3) 168
   (4) 432
   (5) Not enough information is given.

2. At 5 p.m., an 8-foot signpost cast a shadow 12 ft long. At the same time, a tree cast a shadow 45 ft long. How tall in feet is the tree?

   (1) 20
   (2) 30
   (3) 45
   (4) 96
   (5) Not enough information is given.

Item 3 refers to the isosceles triangle below.

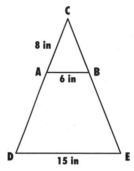

3. What is the length of side CE in inches?

   (1) 12
   (2) 14
   (3) 20
   (4) 27
   (5) 51

To check your answers, turn to page 391.

Finding the Circumference of a Circle

A **circle** is a curved line in which every point on the curve is an equal distance from another point called the **center**.

The distance across a circle through its center is called the **diameter**. The distance around a circle is called the **circumference**. The ancient Greeks discovered a relationship between diameter and circumference. They used the Greek letter **pi** (π) to name the amount by which the diameter must be multiplied to find the circumference. They soon learned to use pi to find the area of a circle and the volume of a cylinder.

The circumference of a circle is a little more than 3 times the diameter. This value is called pi (π). Archimedes *approximated* π to be between $3\frac{1}{7}$ and $3\frac{10}{71}$. On the formula sheet given with your GED Math Test, π is rounded off to 3.14. Sometimes it is expressed as $\frac{22}{7}$.

The formula for finding the distance around a circle is this.

Circumference (*C*) of a circle:

$C = \pi d$; where $\pi = 3.14$ and d = diameter

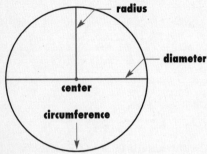

Example:

Find the circumference of a circle with a diameter of 5 cm.

$C = \pi d$

$C = 3.14(5)$

$C = 15.7$ cm

Exercise 7

Directions

Find the circumference of each of the following circles. Use the formula $C = \pi d$; where $\pi = 3.14$ and d = diameter.

1.

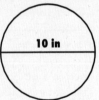

2.

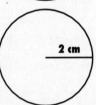

3. How many feet long is the circumference of a circle with a diameter of 6 feet?

   (1) 3.14
   (2) 9.46
   (3) 12.0
   (4) 18.84
   (5) 37.68

To check your answers, turn to page 391.

Finding the Area of a Circle

The area of a circle is also an estimate found by using 3.14 for the value of π.

The formula is:

Area (*A*) of a circle:

$A = \pi r^2$; where $\pi = 3.14$ and r = radius

To find the area of a circle, take the radius to the second power and multiply it by 3.14 for π.

Example:

Find the area of a circle with a radius of 8 in.

$A = \pi r^2$

Remember to simplify exponents first.

$A = 3.14(8)^2$

$A = 3.14(64)$

$A = 200.96$ square inches

Remember that the radius is half of the diameter. To find the radius when the diameter is given, divide the diameter by 2.

Exercise 8

Directions

Find the area of each of the following circles. Use the formula $A = \pi r^2$; where $\pi = 3.14$ and r = radius.

1.

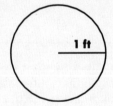

2.

3.

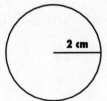

4. Which of these expressions would be used to find the area of a circle with a radius of 2.5 m?

   (1) 3.14(2.5)
   (2) 3.14(5)
   (3) 3.14(5)(5)
   (4) 3.14(2.5)(2.5)
   (5) Not enough information is given.

5. J'lene is very proud of her circular garden. She arranged plants and flowers in the center and a stone walkway around them as shown.

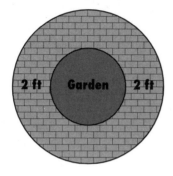

If the walkway is 2 feet wide, what is the area of the walkway?

   (1) 12.56
   (2) 15.7
   (3) 37.68
   (4) 50.24
   (5) Not enough information is given.

To check your answers, turn to page 391.

Finding the Volume of a Cylinder

A three-dimensional figure with a circular base is a **cylinder**. To find the volume of a cylinder, you must find the area of the base and multiply it by the height of the cylinder.

The formula is:

Volume (*V*) of a Cylinder:

$V = \pi r2h$; where $\pi = 3.14$, r = radius, and h = height

Remember to simplify the exponent before completing the other multiplication.

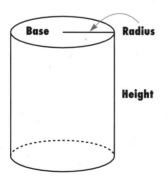

Example:

Find the volume of a cylinder with a height of 6 feet and a base with a 2-foot radius.

$$V = \pi r^2 h$$
$$V = 3.14(2)^2(6)$$
$$V = 3.14(4)(6)$$
$$V = 3.14(24)$$
$$V = 75.36$$

Volume is given in cubic units. The volume of the cylinder above is 75.36 cubic feet.

Example:

Which expression would be used to find how many cubic meters are contained in the cylinder below?

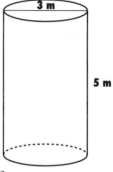

   (1) $3.14(3)^2(5)$
   (2) $3.14(1.5)^2(5)$
   (3) $3.14(5)^2(3)$
   (4) $3.14(5)^2(1.5)$
   (5) Not enough information is given.

The formula uses the radius, so the diameter must be divided by 2. $3 \div 2 = 1.5$ Then substitute this value for the radius (*r*) and 5 for the height (*h*) in the formula.
   $3.14(1.5)^2(5)$
Choice (2) is correct.

Exercise 9

1.

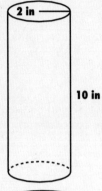

2.

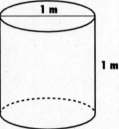

3.

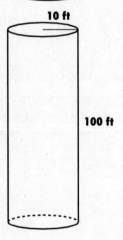

4. Which expression would be used to find the volume of a cylinder with a height of 500 cm and a radius of 100 cm?

    (1) $3.14(100)^2$
    (2) $3.14(500)^2$
    (3) $3.14(100)^2(500)$
    (4) $3.14(500)^2(100)$
    (5) $3.14(100)^2+(500)$

5. How many inches tall is a cylinder with a volume of 31.4 in^3 and a radius of 1 inch?

    (1) 1
    (2) 5
    (3) 8
    (4) 10
    (5) Not enough information is given.

Item 6 refers to the following cylinder.

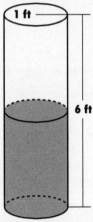

6. The water heater shown above is half full. How many cubic feet of water does it *now* hold?

    (1) 6.00
    (2) 9.42
    (3) 18.84
    (4) 37.68
    (5) 54.99

Item 7 refers to the following figures.

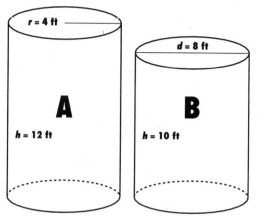

7. About how many more cubic feet does cylinder A hold than cylinder B?

(1) 20
(2) 100
(3) 200
(4) 230
(5) Not enough information is given.

To check your answers, turn to page 391.

Coordinate Geometry

The **coordinate plane** is formed from two number lines. The **x-axis** is horizontal. The **y-axis** is the vertical number line. This lesson combines algebra and geometry to show how the positive and negative values for variables x and y in an equation can be graphed as a line.

All points on the coordinate plane can be identified by counting from the point where the x- and y-axes cross, called the **origin**. First count right or left, then count up or down. These directions are indicated by the coordinates of a point (x, y). Each line in the grid represents a whole number distance.

The x-coordinate, given first, tells how many places to count right or left along the x-axis. The y-coordinate, given next, tells how many places to count up or down from the x-value. Count right or up for positive values and left or down for negative ones.

To plot the point $(3, -1)$ on a coordinate plane, place your pencil at the origin. Then move your pencil 3 lines to the right along the x-axis. From there, move 1 line down parallel to the y-axis. This is point $(3, -1)$.

Exercise 10

Directions

Write the correct letter next to the coordinates of each point listed below.

1. $(3, 4)$
2. $(3, -4)$
3. $(-3, -4)$
4. $(-3, 4)$
5. $(1, -2)$
6. $(-6, 0)$
7. $(0, 6)$
8. $(5, -4)$
9. $(-3, -3)$
10. $(5, 3)$
11. $(-1, 5)$
12. $(0, -4)$

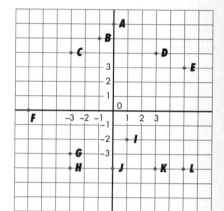

13. Plot the following points on the graph below, and label them with the correct letter name.

M $(1, 1)$
N $(-2, -2)$
P $(5, -2)$
Q $(-5, 5)$
R $(0, -4)$
S $(3, 0)$
T $(-3, -1)$
V $(4, -3)$
W $(0, 1)$
X $(4, 4)$
Y $(-3, 0)$
Z $(-4, 3)$

To check your answers, turn to page 392.

Graphing a Line

You know that in the equation $10 = x + 2$, x must equal 8 to make the equation true. In the equation $y = x + 2$, what value for x will make the equation true?

The value of y in the equation $y = x + 2$ depends on the value of x.

If . . .	Then . . .	Therefore . . .	Coordinates . . .
$x = 0$	$y = 0 + 2$	$y = 2$	$(0, 2)$
$x = 1$	$y = 1 + 2$	$y = 3$	$(1, 3)$
$x = 2$	$y = 2 + 2$	$y = 4$	$(2, 4)$
$x = 3$	$y = 3 + 2$	$y = 5$	$(3, 5)$
$x = -1$	$y = -1 + 2$	$y = 1$	$(-1, 1)$
$x = -4$	$y = -4 + 2$	$y = -2$	$(-4, -2)$

The x and y values become coordinates of points. The coordinates in the table above are plotted on the graph below. What do you notice about these points?

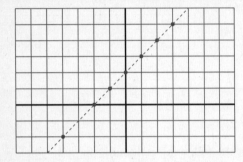

A straight line can be drawn through all of the points that satisfy the equation $y = x + 2$. Draw the line. This line, as other lines, goes on in both directions to infinity (with no end).

An equation with 2 variables is a **linear equation** because its solutions form a straight line. It is impossible to show all the possible combinations for x and y that would make this equation true, so the solution to the equation is a graph of the line.

TEST-TAKING TIP

It is recommended that you find at least three points on the line. If you find only two and make a mistake with either one, the line will be incorrect. However, if you find three points on a straight line, then you can be confident that it is correct.

Example:

Graph the solution to $y = 2x - 4$.

To find the line that is the solution to any equation:

Step 1 Make a table with a column for x-values and a column for y-values. List any three values for x in the x column. Any numbers will do.

x	y
0	
1	
2	

Step 2 Substitute each value for x into the equation and solve for y. Write these values for y in the y-column. Be sure to keep them in the correct order.

$y = 2x - 4$

	x	y
when $x = 0$, $y = 2(0) - 4 = -4$	0	-4
when $x = 1$, $y = 2(1) - 4 = -2$	1	-2
when $x = 2$, $y = 2(2) - 4 = 0$	2	0

Step 3 Plot the points, and draw a line through them.

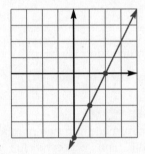

This is the graph of the equation $y = 2x - 4$.

Exercise 11

Directions

Complete a table for the following equation. Then plot the points to draw the graph of the line.

1. $y = x + 4$

x	y
−2	
−1	
0	
1	

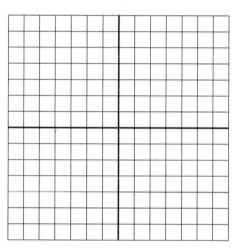

Items 2 and 3 refer to the following graph.

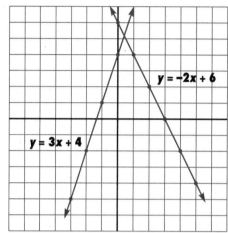

$y = -2x + 6$

$y = 3x + 4$

2. Benny was graphing the equation of the line $y = -2x + 6$. He made the following table for the coordinates.

Point	x	y
A	0	6
B	−1	4
C	−2	10

Which of the following statements is true?

(1) His table is correct and all three points are on the line $y = -2x + 6$.

(2) Point A is incorrect. It will not fall on the line $y = -2x + 6$.

(3) Point B is incorrect. It will not fall on the line $y = -2x + 6$.

(4) Point C is incorrect. It will not fall on the line $y = -2x + 6$.

(5) None of the points is correct.

3. Which of the following are coordinates of a point on the line $y = 3x + 4$?

(1) $(0, -4)$

(2) $(1, 7)$

(3) $(1, 4)$

(4) $(2, 2)$

(5) None of the above.

To check your answers, turn to page 392.

Using a Formula to Find the Distance Between Points

Example:

What is the distance between points *A* and *B* on the graph?

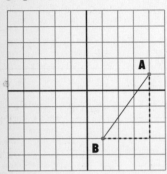

The dotted lines form a right triangle. The distance from *A* to *B* becomes the hypotenuse of the right triangle. If you count line spaces to find the lengths of the legs of the triangle, you can find the distance from *A* to *B* by solving for the hypotenuse.

$$c^2 = a^2 + b^2$$
$$c^2 = 3^2 + 4^2$$
$$c^2 = 9 + 16$$
$$c = \sqrt{25}$$
$$c = 5$$

Since the points are not on the same vertical or horizontal line, the distance cannot be counted simply by counting line spaces. To find the distance between any two points, you can use the formula given on the GED formula page.

The formula is stated:

Distance (*d*) between the two points in a plane:

$$d = \sqrt{(x_2 - x_1)^2 + (y_2 - y_1)^2}$$

where (x_1, y_1) and (x_2, y_2) are two points in a plane

Step 1 Use the coordinates of point *A* (4,1) as (x_2, y_2) and the coordinates of point *B* (1, −3) as (x_1, y_1).

Step 2 Substitute these into the formula.

$$d = \sqrt{(x_2 - x_1)^2 + (y_2 - y_1)^2}$$
$$d = \sqrt{(4 - 1)^2 + (1 - (-3))^2}$$

Step 3 Simplify and solve the equation.

$$d = \sqrt{(3)^2 + (1 + 3)^2}$$
$$d = \sqrt{(3)^2 + (4)^2}$$
$$d = \sqrt{9 + 16}$$
$$d = \sqrt{25}$$
$$d = 5$$

The distance between points *A* and *B* is 5.

Exercise 12

Directions

Find the distance between the points listed. Items 1 to 4 refer to the graph below.

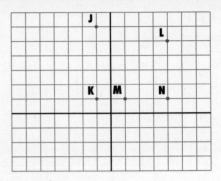

1. *J* (−1, 6) and *K* (−1, 1)

2. *M* (1, 1) and *N* (4, 1)

3. *L* (4, 5) and *N* (4, 1)

4. *L* (4, 5) and *M* (1, 1)

5. (5, 9) and (−1, 1)

To check your answers, turn to page 392.

Slope of a Line

The **slope** of a line is the measure of the slant or incline of the line.

Slope is written as a ratio that compares

$$\frac{\text{change in } y\text{-units}}{\text{change in } x\text{-units}} \quad \frac{\text{up or down}}{\text{right or left}}$$

The slope can also be found by using a formula given on the formula sheet.

Slope of a Line (m)

$$m = \frac{y_2 - y_1}{x_2 - x_1}$$

where (x_1, y_1) and (x_2, y_2) are two points in a plane

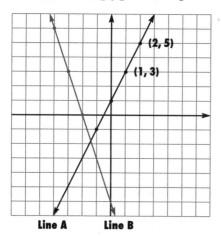

Line A   Line B

To use the formula to find the slope of Line A, $y = 2x + 1$:

Step 1 Choose any two points on the line.

x	y
1	3
2	5

Step 2 Substitute the values in the formula and subtract.

$$\frac{y_2 - y_1}{x_2 - x_1}$$

$$\frac{5 - 3}{2 - 1} = \frac{2}{1} = 2$$

The slope is 2.

each time count $\dfrac{\text{up 2 and}}{\text{over 1}}$

Lines that go up from left to right, such as line A, have a *positive slope*. Lines that go down from left to right, such as line B, have a *negative slope*.

Exercise 13

1. $y = 3x - 1$

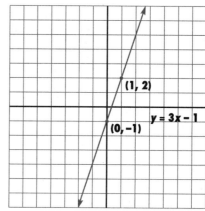

2. $y = 4$

3. Find the slope of the line that passes through the points $(4, 5)$ and $(8, 9)$.

4. Find the slope of the line that passes through the points $(-1, 3)$ and $(3, -1)$.

To check your answers, turn to page 392.

Equation of the Line (Slope and y-intercept)

In the equation of the line $y = 2x + 1$, the numbers 2 and 1 have special significance; in the equation $y = -4x - 3$, the numbers -4 and -3 have special significance.

Look at the graph of these lines below.

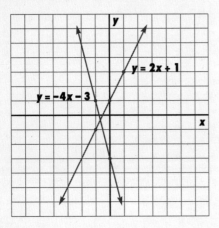

Notice that the line $y = 2x + 1$ crosses the y-axis at $(0, 1)$.

The line $y = -4x - 3$ crosses the y-axis at the point $(0, -3)$.

The point where the line crosses the y-axis is called the **y-intercept**. The value of x is 0 at the y-axis.

In any equation in the form: $y = mx + b$, the value added or subtracted from the x-value is equal to the y-intercept.

Example:

What are the coordinates of the y-intercept of the line $y = -2x - 7$?

The value of x is 0 at the y-intercept.

The y-intercept of the line $y = -2x - 7$ is -7.

Therefore the coordinates of the y-intercept are $(0, -7)$.

The slope of the line $y = 2x + 1$ is $\frac{2}{1}$.

The slope of the line $y = -4x - 3$ is $-\frac{4}{1}$.

In any equation in the form $y = mx + b$, **m (the coefficient of x) is equal to the slope of the line.** The formula for slope of a line uses m as slope.

$$m = \frac{y_2 - y_1}{x_2 - x_1}$$

Exercise 14

1. What are the coordinates of the y-intercept of the line $y = 4x - 6$?

   (1) $(0, 6)$
   (2) $(0, 4)$
   (3) $(-6, 0)$
   (4) $(4, 0)$
   (5) $(0, -6)$

2. What are the coordinates of the y-intercept of the line $y = 3x + 2$?

   (1) $(3, 0)$
   (2) $(0, 2)$
   (3) $(2, 0)$
   (4) $(0, 3)$
   (5) $(0, -2)$

3. The point with the coordinates $(0, -3)$ is the y-intercept of which of the following lines?

   (1) $y = -3x + 2$
   (2) $y = -2x + 3$
   (3) $y = -3x - 3$
   (4) $y = x$
   (5) Not enough information is given.

4. What is the slope of the line $y = 4x + 2$?

   (1) $\frac{2}{1}$

   (2) $-\frac{4}{1}$

   (3) $\frac{1}{4}$

   (4) $\frac{4}{1}$

   (5) Not enough information is given.

To check your answers, turn to page 392.

Answers and Explanations
MATHEMATICS

Unit 1: Arithmetic

Exercise 1 (page 276)

1. The correct answer is: Five hundred four
2. The correct answer is: One thousand, four hundred twenty
3. The correct answer is: Seven thousand, sixty
4. The correct answer is: Thirty-four thousand
5. The correct answer is: Two hundred one thousand, nine hundred
6. The correct answer is: One million, four hundred fifty thousand, three hundred twenty-three
7. The correct answer is: Two hundred fifty-seven million, five thousand, nine
8. The correct answer is: Six billion
9.

City	1990	> or <	1980
Phoenix	1,003,800	>	789,704
Chicage	2,852,041	<	3,005,072
Milwaukee	642,860	>	636,212
Philadelphia	1,608,942	<	1,688,210
Detroit	1,056,180	<	1,203,339
Jacksonville	649,437	>	540,920

10. The correct answer is (C): The Playroom Compare the four figures. The greatest is $1,805.

Exercise 2 (page 277)

1. The correct answer is: 600
2. The correct answer is: 5,000
3. The correct answer is (4): $100 Round 98 to the nearest 10.
4. The correct answer is (4): 290 Round 288 to the nearest 10.
5. The correct answer is (4): 44,000 Round 43,508 to the nearest thousand.
6. The correct answer is (5): 5,600,000 Round 5,641,000 to the nearest hundred thousand.

Exercise 3 (page 278)

1. The correct answer is: 1,841
2. The correct answer is: 3,061
3. The correct answer is: 100
4. The correct answer is: 1,463,675
5. The correct answer is: 135,670
6. The correct answer is: 650
7. The correct answer is: 2,825,050
8. The correct answer is: 170
9. The correct answer is: 4,885
10. The correct answer is: 1,306,245
11. The correct answer is (3): 1,053

Exercise 4 (page 278)

1. The correct answer is: 123
2. The correct answer is: 1,159
3. The correct answer is: 590
4. The correct answer is: 4,749
5. The correct answer is: 88
6. The correct answer is: 4,575
7. The correct answer is: 1,556
8. The correct answer is: 101,825
9. The correct answer is: 1,557,250
10. The correct answer is: 2,574,320
11. The correct answer is (2): 4,102

Exercise 5 (page 279)

1. The correct answer is: 216
2. The correct answer is: 3,500
3. The correct answer is: 2,160
4. The correct answer is: 87,464
5. The correct answer is (2): $650 $100 + ($55 × 10)
6. The correct answer is (5): $14,560 $280 × 52

Exercise 6 (page 280)

1. The correct answer is: 32
2. The correct answer is: 203
3. The correct answer is (5): 500 6,000 ÷ 12
4. The correct answer is (2): 20 200 ÷ 10

Unit 2: Understanding Word Problems

Exercise 1 (page 282)

1. The correct answer is (2): $68 Add the bills and divide by 3, the number of bills:

$$(\$64 + \$78 + \$62) \div 3 = \frac{\$204}{3} = \$68$$

2. The correct answer is (2): 260 Divide the number of videotapes by the number that will fit in a carton: $\frac{5,720}{22} = 260$

Exercise 2 (page 282)

1. The correct answer is (2): $17 You don't need to know the amount of the rent and the electric bill. Subtract: $42 – $25 = $17
2. The correct answer is (5): Not enough information is given. You need to know the sale price of the changing table. You don't need the information about the crib.
3. The correct answer is (3): $52,584 You don't need to know the city manager's salary. Subtract to find the difference: $117,884 – $65,300 = $52,584. Using estimation, you can solve this item more quickly. Think: $120,000 – $65,000 = $55,000
4. The correct answer is (5): Not enough information is given. You know how many people did not have health coverage in California in 1990. You need the population of California in 1990 in order to find an answer.

Exercise 3 *(page 284)*

1. **The correct answer is:** 7(8 − 6)(5 + 7)
   7(2)(12)
   14(12) = 168

2. **The correct answer is:** $\frac{36}{2} - 5 + 2(10)$
   9 − 5 + 20
   4 + 20 = 24

3. **The correct answer is:** $10(5 + 2) - \frac{36}{4}$
   $10(7) - \frac{36}{4}$
   70 − 9 = 61

4. **The correct answer is:** $10(5) + \frac{36}{2} - 4$
   50 + 18 − 4
   68 − 4 = 64

5. **The correct answer is (2): 10(12 + 30)** All the boxes have the same number of diskettes. You find the total number of boxes and then multiply by the number of diskettes in each box.

6. **The correct answer is (5): 2($8) + $12** Two pizzas cost $8 each and one cost $12. You could use addition: $8 + $8 + $12, but choice (5) has the same value.

7. **The correct answer is (5): $13(35) − $9(40)** To find out how much Linda earned at either job, multiply the number of hours by the hourly wage. Subtract the old job's wages from her weekly earnings on the new job.

Exercise 4 *(page 285)*

1. **The correct answer is (2): 9,081 feet Subtract:** 20,320 − 11,239 = 9,081. You can use estimation to solve this problem. **Think:** 20,000 − 11,000 = 9,000. No other answer choice is close to the estimate.

2. **The correct answer is (1): Mount Everest**
   Use estimation to solve it. **Round** 14,491 to 14,000 and Multiply by 2. 14,000(2) = 28,000. Only the elevation of Mount Everest is close to the estimate.

3. **The correct answer is (5): Between 8,000 and 9,000. Add** the amounts from the graph: 3,000 + 3,500 + 2,000 = 8,500

4. **The correct answer is (2): Between 2,000 and 3,000. Subtract:** 5,000 − 2,500 = 2,500

5. **The correct answer is (4): 3(2,000 + 1,500)** Probably the simplest way to solve the problem is to add the units sold for the two games and multiply by 3.

6. **The correct answer is (4): 1991** The line on the graph does not ascend from 1990 to 1991 so you know the price did not go up in 1991.

7. **The correct answer is (2): 1985** Find $12 on the scale, and follow it across to the line. The point on the line is directly over 1985.

8. **The correct answer is (1): 2($28) − 2($6)** One way to solve the problem is to find the total admission for the two adults for both years and then find the difference.

Unit 3: Decimals

Exercise 1 *(page 288)*

1. **The correct answer is (2): 13.05**
2. **The correct answer is (2): 0.255, 0.25, 0.235, 0.23, 0.2**
3. **The correct answer is (5): 0.438** 0.43$\overline{7}$84786642
   8 > 5, so 1 is added to 7.
4. **The correct answer is (4): 1.60** 1.5$\overline{9}$8
   8 > 5, so 1 is added to 9.
5. **The correct answer is (5): 23.5**
6. **The correct answer is (3): $0.47**

Exercise 2 *(page 289)*

1. **The correct answer is: 807.16**
2. **The correct answer is: 214.376**
3. **The correct answer is: $754.57**
4. **The correct answer is: 28.13166**
5. **The correct answer is: $6,349.07**
6. **The correct answer is: 1.8798**
7. **The correct answer is: 28.53**
8. **The correct answer is: 72.817**
9. **The correct answer is: 9,965.11**
10. **The correct answer is: $21.25**
11. **The correct answer is: $76.33**
12. **The correct answer is: 0.405**
13. **The correct answer is (4): $193.00** Add the amounts she spent to find the total.
14. **The correct answer is (1): 0.0016** Subtract 0.1849 from 0.1865 to find the difference.
15. **The correct answer is (4): $9.98** $2.59 + $3.89 + $1.32 + $0.89 + $1.29 = $9.98
16. **The correct answer is (3): 0.75** 1.6 − 0.85 = 0.75

Exercise 3 *(page 290)*

1. **The correct answer is: 11.3184**
2. **The correct answer is: 28.782**
3. **The correct answer is: 466.2**
4. **The correct answer is: 0.0048**
5. **The correct answer is: $46.05**
6. **The correct answer is (5): $14,521** 52($279.25)
7. **The correct answer is (3): $8.26** 2.8($2.95)
8. **The correct answer is (3): $46.62**
   3($0.42)(37) = $46.62

Exercise 4 *(page 291)*

1. **The correct answer is: 0.25**
2. **The correct answer is: 302**
3. **The correct answer is (3): 800** Divide $64 by $0.08.
4. **The correct answer is (1): $39.51 Divide:** $9,876.47 ÷ 250 = $39.50588
   Round to the nearest cent: $39.51

Exercise 5 *(page 291)*

1. **The correct answer is (4): $2,500.00** $2.50(1,000) Move the decimal point 3 places to the right.
2. **The correct answer is (3): $12.54** $125.40 ÷ 10. Move the decimal 1 place to the left.
3. **The correct answer is (2): 250** 25,000 ÷ 100. Move the decimal 2 places to the left.
4. **The correct answer is (2): $4.75** This problem contains extra information. You need to multiply $1 by 5. **Estimate:** $1(5) = $5.

Unit 4: Fractions

Exercise 1 (page 294)

Name	Paint Used (in quarter gallons)	Total Gallons Used
1. Nancy	$\frac{9}{4}$	$2\frac{1}{4}$
2. Tyrone	$\frac{15}{4}$	$3\frac{3}{4}$
3. Pava	$\frac{6}{4}$	$1\frac{1}{2}$
4. Carmen	$\frac{12}{4}$	3
5. Hank	$\frac{17}{4}$	$4\frac{1}{4}$

6. The correct answer is: $\frac{1}{3} < \frac{7}{8}$

7. The correct answer is: $\frac{2}{3} = \frac{6}{9}$

8. The correct answer is: $\frac{7}{9} > \frac{4}{7}$

9. The correct answer is: $\frac{6}{7} > \frac{3}{8}$

10. The correct answer is (2): $\frac{1}{4}$

11. The correct answer is (3): C

12. The correct answer is (4): $\frac{3}{15}$ and $\frac{1}{5}$

13. The correct answer is (3): $300 as part of Bun's $450 pay.
$$\frac{\$300}{\$450} = \frac{2}{3}$$

14. The correct answer is (2): 9 eggs as part of a dozen.
$$\frac{9}{12} = \frac{3}{4}$$

Exercise 2 (page 295)

1. The correct answer is (4): $\frac{1}{3}$ $\frac{11}{30}$ can be rounded to $\frac{10}{30}$ and renamed.

2. The correct answer is (5): $\frac{1}{2}$ $\frac{52}{100}$ can be rounded to $\frac{50}{100}$ and renamed.

3. The correct answer is (1): $\frac{1}{8}$ $\frac{5}{42}$ can be rounded to $\frac{5}{40}$ and renamed.

4. The correct answer is (5): $\frac{7}{10}$ $\frac{72}{98}$ can be rounded to $\frac{70}{100}$ and renamed.

Exercise 3 (page 296)

1. The correct answer is: 1 $\frac{4}{4} = 1$

2. The correct answer is: $1\frac{1}{5}$
$\frac{12}{10} = 1\frac{2}{10}$, which can be renamed $1\frac{1}{5}$.

3. The correct answer is: $6\frac{2}{3}$

4. The correct answer is: $\frac{1}{2}$ $\frac{2}{4}$ can be renamed $\frac{1}{2}$.

5. The correct answer is: $\frac{1}{3}$ $\frac{4}{12}$ can be renamed $\frac{1}{3}$.

6. The correct answer is: $6\frac{1}{2}$ $6\frac{2}{2} - \frac{1}{2}$

7. The correct answer is: $4\frac{3}{5}$ $11\frac{7}{5} - 7\frac{4}{5}$

8. The correct answer is (3): $9\frac{1}{4}$

9. The correct answer is (4): $\frac{1}{2}$
She had $\frac{2}{4}$, which can be renamed $\frac{1}{2}$.

10. The correct answer is (5): $1\frac{1}{3}$

11. The correct answer is (4): $7\frac{3}{4}$

12. The correct answer is (2): $\frac{1}{2}$

Exercise 4 (page 298)

1. The correct answer is: $1\frac{1}{6}$

$$\begin{array}{c} \frac{1}{2} \\ +\frac{2}{3} \\ \hline \frac{7}{6} \end{array} = \begin{array}{c} \frac{3}{6} \\ +\frac{4}{6} \\ \hline \frac{7}{6} \end{array} = 1\frac{1}{6}$$

2. The correct answer is: $1\frac{7}{20}$

$$\begin{array}{c} \frac{3}{5} \\ +\frac{3}{4} \\ \hline \frac{27}{20} \end{array} = \begin{array}{c} \frac{12}{20} \\ +\frac{15}{20} \\ \hline \frac{27}{20} \end{array} = 1\frac{7}{20}$$

3. The correct answer is: $\dfrac{5}{12}$

$$
\begin{array}{ccc}
\dfrac{3}{4} & & \dfrac{9}{12} \\[2mm]
-\dfrac{1}{3} & = & -\dfrac{4}{12} \\[2mm]
\hline
& & \dfrac{5}{12}
\end{array}
$$

4. The correct answer is: $\dfrac{3}{8}$

$$
\begin{array}{ccc}
\dfrac{7}{8} & & \dfrac{7}{8} \\[2mm]
-\dfrac{1}{2} & = & -\dfrac{4}{8} \\[2mm]
\hline
& & \dfrac{3}{8}
\end{array}
$$

5. The correct answer is (3): $1\dfrac{5}{6}$

$$\dfrac{2}{3} + 1\dfrac{1}{6}$$

6. The correct answer is (4): $\dfrac{3}{16}$

$$5\dfrac{11}{16} - 5\dfrac{1}{2}$$

7. The correct answer is (2): $16\dfrac{1}{6}$

$$20\dfrac{2}{3} - 4\dfrac{1}{2}$$

8. The correct answer is (2): $26\dfrac{1}{4}$

$$12\dfrac{1}{2} + 13\dfrac{3}{4}$$

9. The correct answer is (1): $3\dfrac{1}{2}$

$$1\dfrac{1}{2} + \dfrac{1}{2} + 1\dfrac{1}{2}$$

10. The correct answer is (5): $\dfrac{1}{4}$

$$3\dfrac{3}{4} - 3\dfrac{1}{2}$$

Exercise 5 (page 301)

1. The correct answer is (3): $10\dfrac{1}{8}$

$$\dfrac{3}{4} \times \dfrac{27}{2} = \dfrac{81}{8} = 10\dfrac{1}{8}$$

2. The correct answer is (5): $23\dfrac{1}{3}$

$$\dfrac{5}{1} \times \dfrac{14}{3} = \dfrac{70}{3} = 23\dfrac{1}{3}$$

3. The correct answer is (1): $8\dfrac{1}{4}$

$$\dfrac{3}{1} \times \dfrac{11}{4} = \dfrac{33}{4} = 8\dfrac{1}{4}$$

4. The correct answer is (3): $\dfrac{15}{16}$

$$7\dfrac{1}{2} \div 8 = \dfrac{15}{2} \times \dfrac{1}{8} = \dfrac{15}{16}$$

5. The correct answer is (4): 16

$$12 \div \dfrac{3}{4} = \dfrac{12}{1} \times \dfrac{4}{3} = \dfrac{48}{3} = 16$$

6. The correct answer is (3): 12

$$3 \div \dfrac{1}{4} = \dfrac{3}{1} \times \dfrac{4}{1} = 12$$

Unit 5: Ratio and Proportion

Exercise 1 (page 382)

1. The correct answer is: $\dfrac{5}{2}$

$$\dfrac{\text{water}}{\text{solution}}$$

2. The correct answer is: $\dfrac{59}{30}$

$$\dfrac{\text{win}}{\text{loss}}$$

3. The correct answer is: $\dfrac{25}{1}$

$$\dfrac{375 \text{ miles}}{15 \text{ gallons}}$$

4. The correct answer is: $\dfrac{3}{1}$

$$\dfrac{36 \text{ cars sold}}{12 \text{ months}}$$

5. The correct answer is (1): 3:16

$$\dfrac{\$75 \text{ savings}}{\$400 \text{ total pay}}$$

6. The correct answer is (4): 1:3

$$\dfrac{120 \text{ child's tickets}}{360 \text{ total tickets}}$$

7. The correct answer is (2): $\dfrac{2}{5}$

$$\dfrac{10{,}000 \text{ didn't vote}}{25{,}000 \text{ registered}}$$

8. The correct answer is (3): $\dfrac{2}{3}$

$$\dfrac{10{,}000 \text{ didn't vote}}{15{,}000 \text{ voted}}$$

Exercise 2 (page 304)

1. The correct answer is (3): $420

$$\dfrac{\$35}{100} = \dfrac{?}{1{,}200}$$

$$\dfrac{\$35(1{,}200)}{100} = \$420$$

2. The correct answer is (2): $4.17

$$\dfrac{12}{\$16.68} = \dfrac{3}{?}$$

3. The correct answer is (3): $11.25

$$\dfrac{2}{\$4.50} = \dfrac{5}{?}$$

4. The correct answer is (4): 2

$$\dfrac{\frac{1}{4}}{?} = \dfrac{1}{8}$$

5. The correct answer is (5): 14

$$\dfrac{1\frac{3}{4}}{?} = \dfrac{1}{8}$$

6. **The correct answer is (1): 15**

$$\frac{5}{\$77.50} = \frac{?}{\$232.50}$$

7. **The correct answer is (3): 625**

$$\frac{375}{15} = \frac{?}{25}$$

8. **The correct answer is (3): 150**

$$\frac{4}{20} = \frac{?}{750}$$

9. **The correct answer is (4): 160**

$$\frac{8}{2} = \frac{640}{?}$$

10. **The correct answer is (2): 1,500**

$$\frac{6}{20} = \frac{?}{5,000}$$

Exercise 3 *(page 306)*

1. **The correct answer is (2):** $\dfrac{4(500)}{5}$

2. **The correct answer is (1):** $\dfrac{1(460)}{23}$

3. **The correct answer is (1):** $\dfrac{23(2)}{\frac{1}{2}}$

4. **The correct answer is (5): Not enough information is given.** We are not told how many teachers are employed by the Milton schools at this time.

5. **The correct answer is (1):** $\dfrac{6(12)}{8}$

$$\frac{6 \text{ ounces}}{8 \text{ servings}} = \frac{x}{12 \text{ servings}}$$

$$\frac{6(12)}{8}$$

6. **The correct answer is (5):** $\dfrac{40(325)}{25}$

$$\frac{\$325}{25 \text{ hr}} = \frac{x}{40 \text{ h}}$$

$$\frac{40(325)}{25}$$

Unit 6: Percent

Exercise 1 *(page 309)*

	Percent	Fraction
1.	$12\frac{1}{2}\%$	$\frac{1}{8}$
2.	25%	$\frac{1}{4}$
3.	40%	$\frac{2}{5}$
4.	50%	$\frac{1}{2}$
5.	60%	$\frac{3}{5}$
6.	70%	$\frac{7}{10}$
7.	75%	$\frac{3}{4}$

	Decimal	Percent
8.	0.07	7%
9.	0.1	10%
10.	0.18	18%
11.	0.65	65%
12.	1.25	125%
13.	1.8	180%
14.	2.5	250%

15. **The correct answer is (2): Divide the number by 4.**

16. **The correct answer is (4): Multiply by 2.**

Exercise 2 *(page 310)*

1. **The correct answer is: 162 is the missing part.**

$$\frac{90}{100} = \frac{x}{180}$$

2. **The correct answer is: 20%**

$$\frac{x}{100} = \frac{50}{250}$$

3. **The correct answer is: 20 is the missing whole.** 100% of any number is that number.

$$\frac{100}{100} = \frac{20}{x}$$

4. **The correct answer is: 50 is the missing whole.**

$$\frac{70}{100} = \frac{35}{x}$$

5. **The correct answer is (4): $292.50**

$$\frac{15}{100} = \frac{x}{\$1,950} \quad \frac{\text{discount}}{\text{total price}}$$

6. **The correct answer is (2): $1,200**

$$\frac{4.5}{100} = \frac{\$54}{x} \quad \frac{\text{interest}}{\text{account balance}}$$

7. **The correct answer is (4): $1,770**

$$\frac{6}{100} = \frac{x}{\$29,500} \quad \frac{\text{increase}}{\text{original salary}}$$

8. **The correct answer is (3): $31,270** Add his cost of living increase to his previous salary.

$$\begin{array}{r} \$29,500 \\ + 1,770 \\ \hline \$31,270 \end{array}$$

9. **The correct answer is (3): $103.40**
   Step 1 Find total of purchases.

   $24.00
   31.99
   +42.49

   $98.48

   Step 2 Find 5% sales tax.

   $$\frac{5}{100} = \frac{tax}{\$98.48}$$

   tax = $4.924 or $4.92

   Step 3 Add tax to total.

   $98.48
   +4.92

   $103.40

10. **The correct answer is (5): Not enough information is given.** Commission is part of the total sales. To find the percent of commission, you need to know the amount of her total sales.

Exercise 3 *(page 311)*

1. **The correct answer is (4): 50%**

   $$\frac{x}{100} = \frac{7,500}{15,000} \quad \frac{change}{original\ number}$$

2. **The correct answer is (5): Not enough information is given.** The original amount is not given.

3. **The correct answer is (3): 20%**

   $$\frac{x}{100} = \frac{\$52}{\$264} \quad \frac{change}{original\ amount}$$

   19.6% rounded to the nearest whole % is 20%.

4. **The correct answer is (2): 10%**

   $$\frac{x}{100} = \frac{\$0.67}{\$6.70} \quad \frac{change}{original\ amount}$$

5. **The correct answer is (1): $486**

6. **The correct answer is (3): $14,000**

7. **The correct answer is (4): 220%**

   $$\frac{x}{100} = \frac{64 - 20}{20} \quad \frac{change}{original\ number}$$

8. **The correct answer is (1): 14%**

   $$\frac{x}{100} = \frac{\$28}{\$200} \quad \frac{discount}{price}$$

   Since the problem asks for an approximation, round $199 to $200.

Exercise 4 *(page 313)*

1. **The correct answer is: $360** $2,000(0.09)(2)

2. **The correct answer is: $29.95**

   $$\frac{\$599}{1} \times \frac{1}{10} \times \frac{1}{2}$$

   6 months is ½ year or $599(0.1)(0.5)

3. **The correct answer is (3): $125,000(0.085)(25)**

4. **The correct answer is (4): $11,880**

   $8,800(0.07)(5) = $3,080
   $3,080 interest
   +8,800 loan
   $11,880 total to be repaid

5. **The correct answer is (3): $3,968** Angela borrowed $3,200.
   $3,200(0.08)(3) = $768

   $768 interest
   +3,200 loan
   $3,968 total to be repaid

Unit 7: Data Analysis

Exercise 1 *(page 316)*

1. **The correct answer is (1): 3-4 days** Look across the row labeled "Acute Bronchitis" to the column labeled "45-64 Years." The amount 3.6 days falls between 3 and 4 days.

2. **The correct answer is (5): 28-29 days** Look across the row labeled "Fractures/Dislocations" to the column labeled "18-24 Years." The amount 28.7 falls between 28 and 29 days.

3. **The correct answer is (3): Pneumonia** Only 1.5 days are listed under the "25-44 Years" column.

4. **The correct answer is (2): Influenza** The number of sick days taken for influenza is the highest number listed in each column.

5. **The correct answer is (4): 742** Take 74.2% of 1,000.

6. **The correct answer is (3): Aero USA** Subtract 94 from 750 to find the number of WestAir flights that arrived on time. Divide the difference 656 by 750, the total number of flights. You need to carry out the division to only two places to see that Aero USA's percent is nearest.

7. **The correct answer is (2): $14,000** Look at the row for 10-14 years of service. Compare the two numbers, and find the difference.

8. **The correct answer is (4): 0.5($60,000) + $60,000** Find the amount of the raise by multiplying 0.5 by the current salary of $60,000. Then add the raise to the current salary.

9. **The correct answer is (1): $24,000** Add $90,000 and $75,000 to find the proposed salary for NHL referees with 20+ years of experience. Then subtract the NBA salary for the same range.

10. **The correct answer is (5): $\frac{4}{5}$**

    $$\frac{\$59,900}{\$75,500} \text{ rounded to } \frac{\$60,000}{\$75,000} = \frac{4}{5}$$

11. **The correct answer is (1): Two** Round each value.

    $$\frac{\$110,000}{\$50,000} = \text{about } 2$$

12. **The correct answer is (2): Boston and New York** Boston's price fell from $181,200 to $168,200 and New York's median price decreased from $183,800 to $169,300.

384

Exercise 2 *(page 318)*

1.

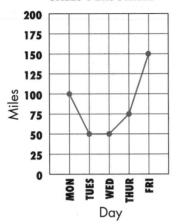

AVERAGE WEEKDAY MILEAGE FOR DUNNE'S SALES PERSONNEL

2. **The correct answer is (3): 425**
   Add the miles from each day 100 + 50 + 50 + 75 + 150

3. **The correct answer is (4): 125**
   (50 + 75 + 150) − (100 + 50)

4. **The correct answer is (5): $1.20** Beginning at 11/27 (November 27), look up the line to the corresponding point. Now look to the scale on the left where you see $1.20.

5. **The correct answer is (5): Not enough information is given.**
   You are not told how many gallons of gasoline were sold by each station.

Exercise 3 *(page 320)*

1. **The correct answer is (4): 300** 12% of 2,500 were men who take greater responsibility for shopping.

$$\frac{12}{100} = \frac{x}{2,500}$$

$$\frac{12(2,500)}{100} = 300$$

2. **The correct answer is (2): More than ten times as many women than men do the cleaning.** 7% of the cleaning is done by men. 78% done by the women is more than ten times that amount.

3. **The correct answer is (3): 710** 78% of the women take a greater responsibility versus 7% of the men. Subtract to find the difference: 78% − 7% = 71%; 71% of 1,000 is 710.

4. **The correct answer is (1): 63 million** 29.6% is about 30% of the 27 million homes with computers.

$$\frac{10}{100} = \frac{27 \text{ million}}{x}$$

$$\frac{100(27 \text{ million})}{30} = 90 \text{ million}$$

The *total number of homes* in 1992 was about 90 million. If approximately 30% of the 90 million homes had computers, then approximately 70% of the homes *did not* have computers.

$$\frac{70}{100} = \frac{x}{90 \text{ million}}$$

$$\frac{70(90 \text{ million})}{30} = 63 \text{ million}$$

5. **The correct answer is (5): Not enough information is given.**
   You are not given the projected figures for the total number of homes in 1993.

Exercise 4 *(page 322)*

1. **The correct answer is (1):** $\frac{3}{10}$ 18% + 12% = 30%, or $\frac{3}{10}$ of the population.

2. **The correct answer is (5): 67,080,000** Estimate: 26% is approximately 25%, so divide $\frac{258,000,000}{4}$, or solve by a proportion.

$$\frac{26}{100} = \frac{x}{258,000,000}$$

$$\frac{26(258,000,000)}{100} = 67,080,000$$

3. **The correct answer is (5):** $\frac{7}{10}$

$$\frac{\text{entertainment}}{\text{savings}} = \frac{\$70}{\$100} = \frac{7}{10}$$

4. **The correct answer is (1):** $\frac{1}{17}$

$$\frac{\text{savings}}{\text{total budget}} = \frac{\$100}{\$1,700} = \frac{1}{17}$$

5. **The correct answer is (4): 50** Multiply 800 by $\frac{1}{16}$.

6. **The correct answer is (3): 25%** The fraction in the section for glass and plastic bottles is $\frac{1}{4}$. The fraction $\frac{1}{4}$ is equal to 25%.

Exercise 5 *(page 323)*

1. **The correct answer is (3): 142**   710 ÷ 5

2. **The correct answer is (4): $15,700** $125,600 ÷ 8

Exercise 6 *(page 324)*

1. **The correct answer is (2): $6.50**

2. **The correct answer is (3): $9.75**

3. **The correct answer is (1): $63.35**
   Add the middle two values.
   $ 58.27
   +68.43
   ─────
   $126.70

   Divide this sum by 2.

   $63.35
   2)$126.70

Exercise 7 (page 325)

1. The correct answer is (5): $\frac{1}{5}$ One correct answer out of five choices.

2. The correct answer is (3): $\frac{1}{25}$ Terry has 8 chances out of 200 to win. The fraction $\frac{8}{200}$ equals $\frac{1}{25}$.

3. The correct answer is (4): $\frac{1}{7}$ There are only seven possibilities, the seven days of the week. Tuesday is one of seven.

4. The correct answer is (1): $\frac{3}{250,000}$

5. The correct answer is (1): $\frac{1}{6}$ One of the six faces is a 6.

6. The correct answer is (4): $\frac{2}{3}$ Four of the six faces are *not* 3 or 4. Rename $\frac{4}{6}$ as $\frac{2}{3}$.

7. The correct answer is (1): $\frac{1}{2}$ How many guppies are in the tank is not important as long as there are the same number of males and females. There are 2 possible outcomes and 1 is male.

8. The correct answer is (3): $\frac{1}{3}$ Six of the 18 numbers are long-distance calls. $\frac{6}{18}$ equals $\frac{1}{3}$.

9. The correct answer is (3): $\frac{1}{2}$ Yellow and blue must each occupy $\frac{1}{4}$ of the spinner.

Unit 8: Measurement

Exercise 1 (page 328)

1. The correct answer is: j
2. The correct answer is: i
3. The correct answer is: f
4. The correct answer is: g
5. The correct answer is: h
6. The correct answer is: a
7. The correct answer is: k
8. The correct answer is: c
9. The correct answer is: l
10. The correct answer is: b
11. The correct answer is: d
12. The correct answer is: e
13. The correct answer is: 3 ft
14. The correct answer is: 3 ft 11 in
15. The correct answer is: 1 lb 4 oz
16. The correct answer is: 2 lb 2 oz
17. The correct answer is: 1 d 12 hr
18. The correct answer is: 3 d 4 hr
19. The correct answer is: 86.4 oz
20. The correct answer is: 3 gal 2 qt, or $3\frac{1}{2}$ gal
21. The correct answer is: 2 T 1,000 lb, or $2\frac{1}{2}$ T
22. The correct answer is (4): ounces

Exercise 2 (page 329)

1. The correct answer is: a
2. The correct answer is: e
3. The correct answer is: d
4. The correct answer is: b
5. The correct answer is: c
6. The correct answer is: 500 cm

$$\frac{1}{100} = \frac{5}{?}$$

$$\frac{5(100)}{1} = 500 \text{ cm}$$

7. The correct answer is: 60,000 L

$$\frac{1}{1,000} = \frac{60}{?}$$

$$\frac{60(1,000)}{1} = 60,000 \text{ L}$$

8. The correct answer is: 8.762 kg

$$\frac{1}{1,000} = \frac{?}{8,762}$$

$$\frac{1(8,762)}{1,000} = 8.762 \text{ kg}$$

9. The correct answer is (1): 1.5
10. The correct answer is (3): centimeters

Exercise 3 (page 330)

1. The correct answer is: 1 ft 7 in
2. The correct answer is: 10 in
3. The correct answer is: 36 min
4. The correct answer is: 18 ft
5. The correct answer is: 6 yd
6. The correct answer is: 19 lb 10 oz
7. The correct answer is: 2 qt
8. The correct answer is: 5 yd 1 ft
9. The correct answer is: 2 qt 2 c, or $2\frac{1}{2}$ qt
10. The correct answer is: 2 lb 10 oz
11. The correct answer is: (3) 6 ft 6 in
12. The correct answer is: (2) 4 hr 57 min
13. The correct answer is: (5) 8 yd 2 ft
14. The correct answer is (5): Not enough information is given. You need to know the weight allowance.

Exercise 4 (page 331)

1. The correct answer is: 19 ft 3 in, or 6 yd 1 ft 3 in
2. The correct answer is: 13 d 21 hr
3. The correct answer is: 87 lb 8 oz
4. The correct answer is: 54 gal 1 qt
5. The correct answer is: 21 qt
6. The correct answer is: 37 lb 4 oz
7. The correct answer is (4): 5

Exercise 5 *(page 332)*

1. **The correct answer is: 1 mi 1,607 ft**
2. **The correct answer is: 4 hr 30 min**
3. **The correct answer is: 1 gal 2 qt, or $1\frac{1}{2}$ gal**
4. **The correct answer is: 4 ft 3 in**
5. **The correct answer is (1): 4 ft 10 in**
6. **The correct answer is (3): Four 8-hour days**

Exercise 6 *(page 333)*

1. **The correct answer is: 108.9 L**
    99.0
    +9.9
    ──────
    108.9
2. **The correct answer is: 13 mm**
    5.8
    +7.2
    ──────
    13.0
3. **The correct answer is: 12.9 km**   500 m = 0.5 km
    13.4
    −0.5
    ──────
    12.9
4. **The correct answer is: 2.25 km**
    3.45
    −1.20
    ──────
    2.25
5. **The correct answer is: 22.4 cm**
6. **The correct answer is: 49.05 kg**
7. **The correct answer is: 0.4 km**
8. **The correct answer is: 1.34 m**
9. **The correct answer is (1): 156**   220 − 64 = 156
10. **The correct answer is (4): 20**
11. **The correct answer is (3): $\frac{1,266}{2}$**
12. **The correct answer is (2): 5.25 m**
    Add: 185 + 340 = 525 cm
    Change to meters.
    $$\frac{525}{?} = \frac{100}{1}$$
    $$\frac{1(525)}{100} = 5.25 \text{ m}$$
13. **The correct answer is (5): Not enough information is given.**
    You would need to know how much the bottle holds to solve the problem. Don't waste time working with the numbers until you have read the whole problem. Make sure you have all the facts you need before you start any calculations.
14. **The correct answer is (4): 600 mg**
    2 capsules
    × 4 times per day
    8 capsules daily
    × 3 days
    24 capsules in 3 days
    24 × 25 mg = 600 mg
15. **The correct answer is (2): 2.5 g**
    25 mg × 100 = 2,500 mg = 2.5 g

Exercise 7 *(page 335)*

1. **The correct answer is: 20 cm** 2(7) + 2(3)
2. **The correct answer is: 66 ft**

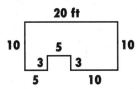

    20 + 10 + 10 + 3 + 5 + 3 + 5 + 10
3. **The correct answer is: 46 cm**

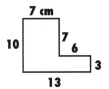

    7 + 7 + 6 + 3 + 13 + 10
4. **The correct answer is: 60 in**

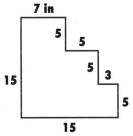

    7 + 5 + 5 + 5 + 3 + 5 + 15 + 15
5. **The correct answer is (4): 60**   perimeter of a square: 4(15)
6. **The correct answer is (3): 38**   perimeter of a rectangle: 2(11) + 2(8)

Exercise 8 *(page 337)*

1. **The correct answer is: 21 cm^2**   7(3)
2. **The correct answer is: 625 sq in**   25^2
3. **The correct answer is: 12 sq ft**   12(1)
4. **The correct answer is: 130 in^2**   13(10)
5. **The correct answer is (4): 370** Find the area of her backyard, and subtract the area of the patio. 22(20) − 10(7)
6. **The correct answer is (2): 15,604 m^2** Use the formula for finding the area of a rectangle.
    $A = lw$
    $A = 188(83)$
    $A = 15,604 \text{ m}^2$
    You can solve this problem more quickly using estimation.
    Instead of: 188(83)
    Think: 190(80) = 15,200
    Only choice (2) is close to the estimate.
7. **The correct answer is (5): 225**   15^2
8. **The correct answer is (3): 12**   4(3)

Exercise 9 (*page 338*)

1. The correct answer is: **12.167 m³**   2.3(2.3)(2.3)
2. The correct answer is: **560 ft³**   10(7)(8)
3. The correct answer is: **253 cu in**   9.2(5)(5.5)
4. The correct answer is (3): **8 cu ft** Use the formula for finding the volume of a cube.
   $V = s^3$
   $V = 2(2)(2) = 8$ cu ft
5. The correct answer is (2): **60**   5(3)(4)
6. The correct answer is (4): **3,200**   20(16)(10)

Unit 9: Algebra

Exercise 1 (*page 341*)

1. The correct answer is (3): **−6**
2. The correct answer is (3): **3**
3. The correct answer is (3): **N < 5**

Exercise 2 (*page 342*)

1. The correct answer is (2): **−200 + 328** 200 feet below sea level is −200 and the lava shot up 328 (a positive).
2. The correct answer is (1): **−50**
3. The correct answer is (3): **184 feet** You need to find the difference between the two numbers: 92 − (−92) = 184 feet.
4. The correct answer is (2): **22 − (−4)** The second temperature (−4) is subtracted from the first (22).
5. The correct answer is (4): **−39**
   Add: 9 + (−10) + 11 + (−49) = −39
6. The correct answer is (3): **A and C**
   −(−3) changes to + 3.
   +(−2) is the same as − 2.
7. The correct answer is (4): **10 − (5 − 10)** The operation in parentheses is used to find the temperature for Wednesday, which is subtracted from Thursday's temperature to find the change, or difference.

Exercise 3 (*page 343*)

1. The correct answer is: **60**
2. The correct answer is: **−60**
3. The correct answer is: **42**
4. The correct answer is: **−5**
5. The correct answer is: **−5**
6. The correct answer is: **5**
7. The correct answer is (5): **24**
8. The correct answer is (1): **14**

Exercise 4 (*page 344*)

1. The correct answer is (3): **$2b**
2. The correct answer is (4): **x + $35**
3. The correct answer is (1): **$20 − 3y**
4. The correct answer is (5): **p² − 15**
5. The correct answer is (4): $\frac{g}{6}$
6. The correct answer is (3): **2(w + $1)** The price of one pound of lobster this week is w + $1. Two pounds would be twice the sum of w + $1.
7. The correct answer is (2): **6(m − 3)** Harry runs m − 3 each day. In six days he runs 6 times that amount.
8. The correct answer is (5): **43 − (x + 2y)**

Exercise 5 (*page 346*)

1. The correct answer is: **10**
2. The correct answer is: **15**
3. The correct answer is: **14**
4. The correct answer is: **12**
5. The correct answer is: **7**
6. The correct answer is: **20**
7. The correct answer is (2): **8**
8. The correct answer is (5): **Between 14 and 15**

Exercise 6 (*page 346*)

1. The correct answer is (3): 2.345×10^6 Move the decimal point behind the first digit, which is 6 places to the left.
2. The correct answer is (5): **3,600,000,000** Move the decimal point 9 places to the right to change back to standard notation.
3. The correct answer is (4): 4×10^3 **is equal to 4,000** 10^3 is equal to 1,000.
4. The correct answer is (2): 5.6×10^7

Exercise 7 (*page 347*)

1. The correct answer is (1): **19s**
2. The correct answer is (4): **2.5h** Add the coefficients 0.8 + 1.7.
3. The correct answer is (3): **4(t) − 4(7)**
4. The correct answer is (4): $15t^2 + 5t - 10$
5. The correct answer is (2): **r − 12**   5r − 2(2r) − 2(6)
6. The correct answer is (1): **21a + b**
7. The correct answer is (4): **34a + 22b**
   6(5a + 4b) + 2(2a − b)
   30a + 24b + 4a − 2b
   34a + 22b
8. The correct answer is (4): **−9a − 16**

Exercise 8 (*page 349*)

1. The correct answer is: **4** $2^2 = 2(2)$
2. The correct answer is: **1** $1^2 = 1(1)$
3. The correct answer is: **45** $5(3)^2 = 5(9)$
4. The correct answer is: **18** $2(3)^2 = 2(9)$
5. The correct answer is: **1**
   $\frac{2^2}{4} = \frac{4}{4}$
6. The correct answer is: **12** $2^2(3) = 4(3)$
7. The correct answer is: **13** $2^2 + 3^2 = 4 + 9$
8. The correct answer is: **25** $(2 + 3)^2 = (5)^2$
9. The correct answer is: **7** $2^2 + 3 = 4 + 3$
10. The correct answer is: **36** $(2)^2(3)^2 = (4)(9)$
11. The correct answer is (5): **−13**
    $\frac{6^2 + (-4)^2}{-4} = \frac{36 + 16}{-4} = \frac{52}{-4}$
12. The correct answer is (4): **628** $3.14(10)^2(2) = 3.14(100)(2)$
13. The correct answer is: (2) **40**
14. The correct answer is (3): **$2,000(0.06)(4)**

Exercise 9 *(page 350)*

1. **A.** $n = 27 + 19 = 46$
   B. $p = 46 - 27 = 19$
   C. $r = 56 \div 7 = 8$
2. **A.** $t = 19 - 15 = 4$
   B. $c = 25(4) - 100$
   C. $f = 51 \div 3 = 17$
3. **A.** $a = 5(11) = 55$
   B. $c = 32 - 26 = 6$
   C. $n = 113 + 79 = 192$
4. **A.** $x = 11(5) = 55$
   B. $q = 97 - 9 = 88$
   C. $n = 8(6) = 48$
5. **A.** $b = 90 \div 9 = 10$
   B. $x = 72 + 48 = 120$
   C. $s = 150(2) = 300$
6. **The correct answer is (1): \$6**
   $12t = \$72$
   $\dfrac{\$72}{12} = \$6$
7. **The correct answer is (4): 11 ft**
   $12w = 132$
   $\dfrac{132}{12} = 11$
8. **The correct answer is (3): \$2,185**
   $x + \$115 = \$2,300$
   $x = \$2,300 - \$115 = \$2,185$

Exercise 10 *(page 352)*

1. **The correct answer is: $w = 7$** $w = \dfrac{34 - 6}{4}$
2. **The correct answer is: $y = 3$** $y = \dfrac{28 + 8}{12}$
3. **The correct answers is: $s = 60$** $s = 4(2 + 13)$
4. **The correct answer is: $r = 3$** $r = \dfrac{21 - 6}{5}$
5. **The correct answer is: $v = 34$** $v = \dfrac{60 + 42}{3}$
6. **The correct answer is: $g = 12$** $g = \dfrac{42 + 42}{7}$
7. **The correct answer is: $t = 1$**
   $8t - 2t = 6$
   $6t = 6$
8. **The correct answer is: $m = 7$**
   $13m - 11m = 21 - 7$
   $2m = 14$
9. **The correct answer is: $s = 6$**
   $14s - 13s = 17 - 11$
   $3s = 6$
10. **The correct answer is (4): 10.2** $v = 3.4 + 6.8 = 10.2$
11. **The correct answer is (2): 18**
    $k = \dfrac{11 - 2}{0.5} = 18$
12. **The correct answer is (5): 6**
    $3x + 10x - 16 = 11x - 4$
    $0 + 13x - 11x = -4 + 16$
    $2x = 12$
    $x = 6$
13. **The correct answer is (2): 20** $(20)^2 = 400$

14. **The correct answer is (1): 0**
15. **The correct answer is (2): 3**

Exercise 11 *(page 353)*

1. **The correct answer is (2): $w < 27$** $w < 12 + 15$
2. **The correct answer is (4): $x \leq 50$**
   $x \leq \dfrac{100}{2}$
3. **The correct answer is (3): $g > 41$**
   $g > \dfrac{140 - 17}{3}$
4. **The correct answer is (1): 7**
   $-3y - 7 \geq -28$
   $-3y \geq 21$
   $y \leq 7$
   $7 = 7$ so it is in the solution set.
5. **The correct answer is (1): 4**
   $8b - 4 > 28$
   $8b > 32$
   $b > 4$
   4 is not greater than 4. 4 is not in the solution set.
6. **The correct answer is (2): $3x + 8 \geq 29$**

Exercise 12 *(page 354)*

1. **The correct answer is (3): 17** $68 = 4l$
2. **The correct answer is (2): 5** $60 = 3(4)b$
3. **The correct answer is (4): $121 = s^2$**
4. **The correct answer is (5): Not enough information is given.**
   The length of the yard is not given.
5. **The correct answer is (4): 10** $30 = 2l + 2(5)$
6. **The correct answer is (2): $600 = 10(10)w$**
7. **The correct answer is (4): 30** $P = 2l + 2w$
   $144 = 2(42) + 2(w)$

Exercise 13 *(page 355)*

1. **The correct answer is (2): −2 and 7**
   $(-2)^2 - 5(-2) = 14$
   $4 + 10 = 14$
   $(7)^2 - 5(7) = 14$
   $49 - 35 = 14$
2. **The correct answer is (3): 5 and −6**
   $2(5)^2 + 2(5) - 60 = 0$
   $2(25) + 10 - 60 = 0$
   $50 + 10 - 60 = 0$
   $2(-6)^2 + 2(-6) - 60 = 0$
   $2(36) - 12 - 60 = 0$
   $72 - 12 - 60 = 0$
3. **The correct answer is (5): −7 and 8**
   $(-7)^2 - (-7) - 56 = 0$
   $49 + 7 - 56 = 0$
   $(8)^2 - 8 - 56 = 0$
   $64 - 8 - 56 = 0$

Exercise 14 *(page 357)*

1. **The correct answer is: 4 gallons** Carl's car is $2x$.

Unknown	Variable	Equation
Mary's car	x	$x + 2x = 6$
Carl's car	$2x$	

   $3x = 6$
   $x = 2$
   $2x = 4$ Carl's car

2. **The correct answer is: 52°** Yesterday's temperature was x.

Unknown	Variable	Equation
Yesterday's temperature	x	$72 = x + 20$

   $x = 52$

3. **The correct answer is: 47** The first number is x.

Unknown	Variable	Equation
1st no.	x	$x + x + 2 = 96$
2nd no.	$x + 2$	

   $2x + 2 = 96$
   $2x = 94$
   $x = 47$ First number

4. **The correct answer is: 30 years old** Debbie's age is $3x$.

Ages	Now	Now + 10	Equation
Aisling	x	$x + 10$	$3x + 10 = 2(x + 10)$
Debbie	$3x$	$3x + 10$	

   $3x - 2x = 20 - 10$
   $x = 10$
   $3x = 30$ Debbie's age

5. **The correct answer is (1): 4** Since the value of m must be greater than 3, only choice (1) can be correct.

6. **The correct answer is (4): 2,400** Women = $2x$

Unknown	Variable	Equation
Men	x	$x + 2x = 3,600$
Women	$2x$	

   $x = 1,200$
   $2x = 2,400$ Women

7. **The correct answer is (2): $6** Child's ticket = t

   $10t + 5t = \$100 - \$10$
   $15t = \$90$
   $t = \$6$ Child
   $t + \$2 = \$8$ Adult

8. **The correct answer is: 7** $3s \leq 22$

9. **The correct answer is (3): 50** Round-trip distance = x

Unknown	Variable	Equation
Dist. to work	x	$5x + 74 = 324$
Trips to work	$5x$	

   $x = \dfrac{324 - 74}{5}$
   $x = 50$

10. **The correct answer is (5): 54** Largest number = $x + 2$

Nos.	Variable	Equation
1st no.	x	
2nd no.	$x + 1$	$x + x + 1 + x + 2 = 159$
3rd no.	$x + 2$	

    $3x + 3 = 159$
    $x = \dfrac{159 - 3}{3}$
    $x = 52$
    $x + 2 = 54$ Largest number

11. **The correct answer is (1): 3** Sharon = $a - 4$

Ages	Now	Now + 5	Equation
Kenny	a	$a + 5$	
Sharon	$a - 4$	$a - 4 + 5$ or $a + 1$	$2(a + 5) = 3(a + 1)$

    $2a + 10 = 3a + 3$
    $2a - 3a = 3 - 10$
    $-a = -7$
    $a = 7$

Unit 10: Geometry

Exercise 1 *(page 361)*

1. **The correct answer is: $\angle b = 110°$** $180° - 70°$
2. **The correct answer is: $\angle e = 70°$** It corresponds with $\angle a$.
3. **The correct answer is: Angles d, e, and b**
4. **The correct answer is: Angles c, f, and g**
5. **The correct answer is (1): 55°** $90° - 35° = 55°$
6. **The correct answer is (5): 110°**
7. **The correct answer is (4): $\angle 3$ measures 90°**

Exercise 2 *(page 362)*

1. **The correct answer is: 40 cm²**
2. **The correct answer is: 84 in²**
3. **The correct answer is: 150 ft²**
4. **The correct answer is: 66 m²**
5. **The correct answer is (5): Not enough information is given.** The perimeter cannot be found without the length of the side. The area cannot be found without the length of the height.

Exercise 3 *(page 363)*

1. **The correct answer is (3): Scalene** A scalene triangle has no equal angles.
2. **The correct answer is (2): Right** Any triangle with a 90° angle is called a right triangle.
3. **The correct answer is (4): Isosceles** An isosceles triangle has two sides of equal length.
4. **The correct answer is (2): 50°** $180 - (65 + 65)$

Exercise 4 *(page 365)*

1. **The correct answer is: $P = 21$ cm** $A = 21$ cm²
2. **The correct answer is: $P = 48$ in** $A = 96$ in²
3. **The correct answer is (4): The perimeter of $\triangle$GHJ can be found using $P = 6 + 6 + 6$.** All three sides of an equilateral triangle have the same length.
4. **The correct answer is (2): 140** Square units are units of area.
   $\dfrac{1}{2}(20)(14)$
5. **The correct answer is (5): Not enough information is given.** You need the measure of all three sides to find the perimeter.
6. **The correct answer is (1): 26** $6 + 10 + 10$
7. **The correct answer is (2): 36** The sides of an equilateral triangle are equal. Add: $12 + 12 + 12 = 36$
8. **The correct answer is (5): Not enough information is given.** Since all sides of a scalene triangle are different, there is no way to know the length of the missing side.

Exercise 5 *(page 367)*

Leg A Leg B Hypotenuse

1. The correct answer is:

    3   4   **5**

    $c^2 = 3^2 + 4^2$

    $c = \sqrt{25}$

2. The correct answer is:

    6   **8**   10

    $(10)^2 = (6)^2 + b^2$

    $100 - 36 = b^2$

    $\sqrt{64} = b$

3. The correct answer is:

    8   8   **Between 11 and 12**

    $c^2 = 8^2 + 8^2$

    $c = \sqrt{128}$

4. The correct answer is:

    30   40   50

    $50^2 = a^2 + 40^2$

    $2{,}500 - 1{,}600 = a^2$

    $\sqrt{900} = a$

5. The correct answer is (2): $\sqrt{1{,}296}$

    $60^2 = 48^2 + b^2$

    $3{,}600 - 2{,}304 = b^2$

    $\sqrt{1{,}296} = b$

6. The correct answer is (3): 19

    $20^2 = 6^2 + b^2$

    $400 - 36 = b^2$

    $\sqrt{364} = b$

    Guess and check the answers.
    $19(19) = 361$

Exercise 6 *(page 369)*

1. **The correct answer is (3): 168** Because the angles are the same, the two right triangles are similar. Use a proportion to find the missing side (the distance across the lake).

    $$\frac{6\text{m (base)}}{14\text{ m (height)}} = \frac{72\text{ m (base)}}{x\text{ m (height)}}$$

    $$\frac{14(72)}{6} = 168$$

2. **The correct answer is (2): 30** The angle of the sun is the same on both the tree and the post, so you have two similar right triangles. Use a proportion to find the height of the tree.

    $$\frac{8\text{ ft post}}{12\text{ ft shadow}} = \frac{x\text{ ft tree}}{45\text{ ft shadow}}$$

    $$\frac{8(45)}{12} = 30\,ft$$

3. **The correct answer is (3): 20** Side *CE* is proportional to side *AC*. Set up a proportion.

    $$\frac{6\text{ in (base)}}{8\text{ in (side)}} = \frac{15\text{ in (base)}}{x\text{ in (side)}}$$

    $$\frac{8(15)}{6} = 20\,in.$$

Exercise 7 *(page 370)*

1. The correct answer is: **31.4 in**   3.14(10)

2. The correct answer is: **12.56 cm** $d = 2(2)$; then multiply by 3.14.

3. The correct answer is (4): **18.84 ft**   3.14(6)

Exercise 8 *(page 370)*

1. The correct answer is: **3.14 ft²** $3.14(1)^2 = 3.14(1)$

2. The correct answer is: **113.04 in²**

    $r = \frac{1}{2}(12) = 6$

    $3.14(6)^2 = 3.14(36)$

3. The correct answer is: **12.56 cm²** $3.14(2)^2 = 3.14(4)$

4. The correct answer is (4): **3.14(2.5)(2.5)**

5. **The correct answer is (5): Not enough information is given.** You need to know the diameter or radius of the garden to find the radius of the larger circle.

Exercise 9 *(page 372)*

1. The correct answer is: **125.6 cubic inches**

    $3.14(2)^2(10)$

    $3.14(4)(10)$

2. The correct answer is: **0.785 cubic meters** Half of the diameter is 0.5.

    $3.14(0.5)^2(1)$

    $3.14(0.25)(1)$

3. The correct answer is: **31,400 ft³**

    $3.14(10)^2(100)$

    $3.14(100)(100)$

4. The correct answer is (3): **3.14(100)²(500)**

5. The correct answer is (4): **10**

    $V = \pi r^2 h$

    $31.4 = 3.14(1)^2 h$

    Simplify the exponent and multiply.

    $31.4 = 3.14h$

    Divide by 3.14 to find *h*.

    $h = \frac{31.4}{3.14}$

6. The correct answer is (2): **9.42** $3.14(1)^2(6) \div 2$

    $\frac{3.14(1)(6)}{2} = 9.42$

7. **The correct answer is (2): 100** The radius for both figures is the same. Find the volume of each, and subtract to find the difference.

    Cylinder A: $(3.14)(4)^2(12) = 602.88$

    Cylinder B: $(3.14)(4)^2(10) = 502.4$

    The difference is nearly 100 cubic feet.

Exercise 10 (page 373)

1. The correct answer is: (3, 4) D
2. The correct answer is: (3, –4) K
3. The correct answer is: (–3, –4) H
4. The correct answer is: (–3, 4) C
5. The correct answer is: (1, –2) I
6. The correct answer is: (–6, 0) F
7. The correct answer is: (0, 6) A
8. The correct answer is: (5, –4) L
9. The correct answer is: (–3, –3) G
10. The correct answer is: (5, 3) E
11. The correct answer is: (–1, 5) B
12. The correct answer is: (0, –4) J
13.

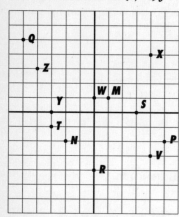

Exercise 11 (page 375)

1. The correct answer is: $y = x + 4$

x	y
–2	2
–1	3
0	4
1	5

2. The correct answer is (3): Point B is incorrect. It will not fall on the line $y = -2x + 6$.

$$-2(-1) + 6 = 2 + 6 = 8$$

3. The correct answer is (2): (1, 7)

$$y = 3x + 4$$
$$7 = 3(1) + 4$$

Exercise 12 (page 376)

1. The correct answer is: 5 Points on the same vertical line have the same x-coordinates. Count down from $J(-1, 6)$ to $K(-1, 1)$, or subtract the y-coordinates ($6 - 1$).

2. The correct answer is: 3 Points on the same horizontal line have the same y-coordinates. Count over from $M(1, 1)$ to $N(4, 1)$, or subtract the x-coordinates ($4 - 1$).

3. The correct answer is: 4 Points on the same vertical line have the same x-coordinates. Count down from $L(4, 5)$ to $N(4, 1)$, or subtract the y-coordinates ($5 - 1$).

4. The correct answer is: 5 Substitute the coordinates of the points into the distance formula.

$$d = \sqrt{(x_2 - x_1)^2 + (y_2 - y_1)^2}$$
$$d = \sqrt{(4 - 1)^2 + (5 - 1)^2}$$
$$d = \sqrt{3^2 + 4^2}$$
$$d = \sqrt{9 + 16}$$
$$d = 5$$

5. The correct answer is: 10 Substitute the coordinates of the points into the distance formula.

$$d = \sqrt{(x_2 - x_1)^2 + (y_2 - y_1)^2}$$
$$d = \sqrt{(5 - (-1))^2 + (9 - 1)^2}$$
$$d = \sqrt{36 + 64}$$
$$d = \sqrt{100}$$
$$d = 10$$

Exercise 13 (page 377)

1. The correct answer is: $\frac{3}{1}$, or 3 Count up and over on the graph, or substitute the values for the points in the formula for slope.

$$m = \frac{2 - (-1)}{1 - 0} = \frac{2 + 1}{1} = \frac{3}{1} = 3$$

2. The correct answer is: The slope of a horizontal line is zero.

3. The correct answer is: Slope = 1 Substitute the values for the points in the formula for slope.

$$m = \frac{9 - 5}{8 - 4} = \frac{4}{4} = 1$$

4. The correct answer is: Slope = –1 Substitute the values for the points in the formula for slope.

$$m = \frac{-1 - 3}{3 - (-1)} = \frac{-4}{4} = -1$$

Exercise 14 (page 378)

1. The correct answer is (5): (0, –6) In the equation $y = 4x - 6$, –6 is the y-intercept.

2. The correct answer is (2): (0, 2) In the equation $y = 3x + 2$, 2 is the y-intercept.

3. The correct answer is (3): $y = -3x - 3$ In the equation $y = -3x - 3$, –3 is the y-intercept.

4. The correct answer is (4): $\frac{4}{1}$ In the equation $y = 4x + 2$, the slope = 4.

Posttests

WRITING SKILLS

75 Minutes ❖ 55 Questions

PART I

Directions
Choose the one best answer to each item.

Items 1 to 6 refer to the following paragraphs.

(1) Some of the worlds largest cities depend on underground railway systems for urban transportation. (2) These underground trains called subways are powered by electricity and run through tunnels built beneath city streets. (3) The trains carry large numbers of people, thereby freeing the streets of a significant amount of traffic. (4) We who walk, drive or travel by bus on surface streets are unaware of the vast maze of tunnels and tracks transporting people continually beneath our feet. (5) Only the occasional rumble of a train through a tunnel reminds us of the underground transit system.

(6) Unfortunately, it costs millions of dollars to build a subway system. (7) Building a subway system tears up a city and creates even more traffic problems above ground until it's finished. (8) It can take months or even years to complete a system. (9) Then more government funds are needed to maintain the trains and stations and to provide security for travellers. (10) Some cities are building less expensive rail lines above ground these visible light-rail systems interfere with other traffic and usually cover a smaller area than do subways.

1. Sentence 1: **Some of the worlds largest cities depend on underground railway systems for urban transportation.**

   What correction should be made to this sentence?

   (1) change worlds to Worlds
   (2) change worlds to world's
   (3) change the spelling of cities to citys
   (4) insert a comma after cities
   (5) change systems for to systems. For

2. Sentence 2: **These underground trains called subways are powered by electricity and run through tunnels built beneath city streets.**

   Which of the following is the best way to write the underlined portion of this sentence? If you think the original is the best way, select choice (1).

   (1) underground trains called subways are powered
   (2) underground trains called subways are power
   (3) underground trains, called subways are powered
   (4) underground trains, called subways, are powered
   (5) underground trains, called subways, is powered

3. Sentence 3: **The trains carry large numbers of people, thereby freeing the streets of a significant amount of traffic.**

   What correction should be made to this sentence?

   (1) change carry to carries
   (2) insert a comma after numbers
   (3) change the spelling of significant to significant
   (4) change the spelling of amount to ammount
   (5) no correction is necessary

4. Sentence 4: **We who walk, drive or travel by bus on surface streets are unaware of the vast maze of tunnels and tracks transporting people continually beneath our feet.**

What correction should be made to this sentence?

(1) remove the comma after <u>walk</u>
(2) insert a comma after <u>drive</u>
(3) insert a comma after <u>streets</u>
(4) change the spelling of <u>continually</u> to <u>continualy</u>
(5) no correction is necessary

5. Sentence 7: **Building a subway system tears up a city and creates even more traffic problems above ground until it's finished.**

If you rewrote sentence 7 beginning with

<u>While a subway system is being built, traffic above ground</u> the next word should be

(1) tears
(2) creates
(3) increases
(4) decreases
(5) finishes

6. Sentence 10: **Some cities are building less expensive rail lines <u>above ground these visible light-rail systems</u> interfere with other traffic and usually cover a smaller area than do subways.**

Which of the following is the best way to write the underlined portion of this sentence? If you think the original is the best way, select choice (1).

(1) above ground these visible light-rail systems
(2) above ground while these visible light-rail systems
(3) above ground because these visible light-rail systems
(4) above ground if these visible light-rail systems
(5) above ground, but these visible light-rail systems

Items 7 to 12 refer to the following paragraph.

(1) Thirty-four million Americans who need dental treatment don't get it because they are afraid of pain. (2) Even though dentists can deaden pain with local anesthetics, many people become quiet anxious about dental work. (3) Now there is a new laser availeable for several dental procedures. (4) The new technology promise treatment with little or no pain. (5) The laser can, with little harm to the surrounding area, remove damaged gum tissue. (6) With laser treatment, neither fillings nor root canals are painful. (7) Cavities can be simply rinsed away, leaving the tooth more resistant to decay because the laser leaves a densely packed tooth surface. (8) Root canal procedures treat infected tissue around the roots of teeth and usually require two sessions. (9) In just one session, the laser destroys the damaged tissue and kills the bacteria that cause disease. (10) When the Federal Drug Administration approves laser treatment for all of these procedures, fearful people may be able to get the dental treatment they need.

7. Sentence 2: **Even though dentists can deaden pain with local anesthetics, many people become quiet anxious about dental work.**

What correction should be made to this sentence?

(1) insert a comma after <u>though</u>
(2) remove the comma after <u>anesthetics</u>
(3) change <u>become</u> to <u>became</u>
(4) change the spelling of <u>quiet</u> to <u>quite</u>
(5) change the spelling of <u>anxious</u> to <u>anxsious</u>

8. Sentence 3: **Now there is a new laser availeable for several dental procedures.**

What correction should be made to this sentence?

(1) change the spelling of <u>there</u> to <u>they're</u>
(2) change the spelling of <u>availeable</u> to <u>available</u>
(3) insert a comma after <u>availeable</u>
(4) change the spelling of <u>for</u> to <u>four</u>
(5) change the spelling of <u>several</u> to <u>sevral</u>

9. Sentence 4: **The new <u>technology promise treatment</u> with little or no pain.**

Which of the following is the best way to write the underlined portion of this sentence? If you think the original is the best way, select choice (1).

(1) technology promise treatment
(2) technology promised treatment
(3) technology promises treatment
(4) technology, promise treatment
(5) technology. Promise treatment

10. Sentence 5: **The laser can, with little harm to the surrounding area, remove damaged gum tissue.**

If you rewrote sentence 5 beginning with

The laser can remove damaged gum tissue without
the next word should be

(1) removing
(2) surrounding
(3) cleaning
(4) harming
(5) treating

11. Sentence 6: **With laser treatment, neither fillings nor root canals is painful.**

What correction should be made to this sentence?

(1) remove the comma after treatment
(2) change the spelling of neither to niether
(3) insert a comma after canals
(4) change is to be
(5) change is to are

12. Sentence 9: **In just one session, the laser destroys the damaged tissue and killed the bacteria that cause disease.**

What correction should be made to this sentence?

(1) change destroys to destroy
(2) change destroys to destroyed
(3) change killed to killing
(4) change killed to kills
(5) change cause to causing

Items 13 to 15 refer to the following paragraph.

---

(1) For more than a decade, Americans have worked conscientiously to change their eating habits. (2) Now it looks as though they may be slipping back into unhealthful behavior. (3) A nation concerned with wieght control, cholesterol levels, and blood pressure readings, America cut back its intake of high-fat foods. (4) Between 1970 and 1990, for example, consumption of red meat dropped twenty pounds per person. (5) Articles on heart-healthy dieting filled magazines; books on the subject appeared on bestseller lists. (6) Low-fat or nonfat foods appeared on grocery store shelves. (7) But it appear that some people are fed up with eating well and are indulging themselves with old-fashioned rich foods. (8) Ice-cream manufacturers find consumers eager to buy extra-rich flavors despite their high fat content. (9) Fast-food restaurants find it easier to sell high-calorie double burgers than the leaner meats they have tried to market. (10) This worries physicians, who

warn that high-fat, high-cholesterol food still poses serious health threats.

13. Sentence 3: **A nation concerned with wieght control, cholesterol levels, and blood pressure readings, America cut back its intake of high-fat foods.**

What correction should be made to this sentence?

(1) change nation to Nation
(2) change the spelling of wieght to weight
(3) insert a comma after and
(4) change its to it's
(5) change the spelling of intake to inntake

14. Sentence 7: **But it appear that some people are fed up with eating well and are indulging themselves with old-fashioned rich foods.**

What correction should be made to this sentence?

(1) change appear to appears
(2) change people are to people be
(3) insert a comma after well
(4) change indulging to indulge
(5) no correction is necessary

15. Sentence 10: **This worries physicians, who warn that high-fat, high-cholesterol food still poses serious health threats.**

Which of the following is the best way to write the underlined portion of this sentence? If you think the original is the best way, select choice (1).

(1) This worries physicians, who warn
(2) This worry physicians, who warn
(3) This worries physicians, that warn
(4) This worries physicians, who warns
(5) This change in eating habits worries physicians, who warn

---

Items 16 to 19 refer to the following paragraph.

---

(1) Is television a major source of the violence in our society? (2) The television industry says no—even though the average American child, while still in elementary school, saw 8,000 murders and 100,000 acts of violence on television. (3) Is it possible to curb television violence without governmental censorship? (4) Some people believe warning labels for violent programs, similar to the movie rating system, will solve the problem others advocate use of a computer chip that would allow viewers at home to program violent shows out of their television sets. (5) Still others say the best way to curbing violence is to stop watching the programs. (6) Refusing to patronize the sponsors of

violent programs is another possible solution. (7) The theory is that, if people stop buying products that are advertise on violent television shows, the sponsors will withdraw their support and the shows will go off the air. (8) Television may or may not be guilty of causing violence in our society. (9) If it is, the solution may lie in a combination of all of these ideas.

16. Sentence 2: **The television industry says no—even though the average American child, while still in elementary school, saw 8,000 murders and 100,000 acts of violence on television.**

What correction should be made to this sentence?

(1) insert a comma after even
(2) remove the comma after child
(3) remove the comma after school
(4) change elementary school to Elementary School
(5) change saw to sees

17. Sentence 4: **Some people believe warning labels for violent programs, similar to the movie rating system, will solve the problem others advocate use of a computer chip that would allow viewers at home to program violent shows out of their television sets.**

Which of the following is the best way to write the underlined portion of this sentence? If you think the original is the best way, select choice (1).

(1) solve the problem others advocate
(2) solve the problem, others advocate
(3) solve the problem that others advocate
(4) solve the problem. Others advocate
(5) solve the problem, so others advocate

18. Sentence 5: **Still others say the best way to curbing violence is to stop watching the programs.**

Which of the following is the best way to write the underlined portion of this sentence? If you think the original is the best way, select choice (1).

(1) to curbing violence is to stop watching
(2) to curbing violence is to stop watch
(3) to curbing violence is to stopping watching
(4) to curbing violence is to stopping watch
(5) to curb violence is to stop watching

19. Sentence 7: **The theory is that, if people stop buying products that are advertise on violent television shows, the sponsors will withdraw their support and the shows will go off the air.**

What correction should be made to this sentence?

(1) change is to being
(2) change advertise to advertised
(3) remove the comma after shows
(4) change the spelling of their to there
(5) change will go to went

Items 20 to 23 refer to the following paragraph.

(1) During the Great Depression, more than five thousand banks closed, which resulted in many people losing all there savings. (2) Wealthy people that had made fortunes in the stock market lost everything, and many of them committed suicide. (3) Unemployment reached 25 percent, with 15 million people out of jobs. (4) Many young people who were ready to go to work for the first time had no hope of employment, so they wandered around the country riding freight trains. (5) Because so many of these young wanderers sought shelter in freight cars, the railroads added empty cars to their trains to help them. (6) Years of drought in the part of the country known as the great plains drove people west. (7) Families abandoned their unproductive farms, loaded their possessions into their beat-up cars, and headed for California, hoping to find a better life. (8) However, they found no help when they got there. (9) *The Grapes of Wrath* is a great book by John Steinbeck, it tells the story of some of these people.

20. Sentence 1: **During the Great Depression, more than five thousand banks closed, which resulted in many people losing all there savings.**

What correction should be made to this sentence?

(1) change Great Depression to great depression
(2) remove the comma after Depression
(3) remove the comma after closed
(4) change the spelling of losing to loosing
(5) change the spelling of there to their

21. Sentence 2: **Wealthy people <u>that had made fortunes in the stock market lost</u> everything, and many of them committed suicide.**

    Which of the following is the best way to write the underlined portion of this sentence. If you think the original is the best way, select choice (1).

    (1) that had made fortunes in the stock market lost
    (2) whom had made fortunes in the stock market lost
    (3) who had made fortunes in the stock market lost
    (4) that had made fortunes in the stock market lose
    (5) that had make fortunes in the stock market lost

22. Sentence 6: **Years of drought in the part of the country known as the great plains drove people west.**

    What correction should be made to this sentence?

    (1) change <u>country</u> to <u>Country</u>
    (2) insert a comma after <u>country</u>
    (3) change <u>known</u> to <u>knowed</u>
    (4) change <u>great plains</u> to <u>Great Plains</u>
    (5) change <u>drove</u> to <u>drive</u>

23. Sentence 9: ***The Grapes of Wrath* is a great book by John Steinbeck, it tells the story of some of these people.**

    If you rewrote sentence 9 beginning with

    <u>In his great book, *The Grapes of Wrath*</u>, the next word should be

    (1) these
    (2) John
    (3) people
    (4) readers
    (5) you

Items 24 to 28 refer to the following paragraphs.

(1) Many Americans express concern about the declining ethics of their country's leaders. (2) They look at the federal government and see instances of sexual harassment, misspending of campaign money, and personal travel at the taxpayers' expense. (3) Federal officials are not the only ones who behave immorally.

(4) State and local officials also abused the power of their positions. (5) People have become used to wasteful, extravagant spending on the part of politicians. (6) Who claim to be eager to save money. (7) Our leaders say they are concerned about law and order nevertheless many of them break the laws they expect everyone else to obey.

(8) It is fortunate that reformers, public watchdogs, and the media keep an eye on public officials. (9) Newspapers and television especially try to keep people informed about political scandals. (10) Reporters publish probing articles about the behavior of political figures so that citizens can look at candidates carefully before they vote for them.

24. Sentence 4: **<u>State and local officials also abused the power of their positions.</u>**

    Which of the following is the best way to write the underlined portion of this sentence? If you think the original is the best way, select choice (1).

    (1) State and local officials also abused
    (2) State and local officials, also abused
    (3) State and local officials also, abused
    (4) State and local officials also abuse
    (5) State and local officials abused

25. Sentences 5 and 6: **People have become used to wasteful, extravagant spending on <u>the part of politicians. Who claim</u> to be eager to save money.**

    Which of the following is the best way to write the underlined portion of this sentence? If you think the original is the best way, select choice (1).

    (1) the part of politicians. Who claim
    (2) the part of politicians. Who claiming
    (3) the part of politicians who claim
    (4) the part of politicians. Who claims
    (5) the part of politicians who, claim

26. Sentence 7: **Our leaders say they are concerned about law and order nevertheless many of them break the laws they expect everyone else to obey.**

Which of the following is the best way to write the underlined portion of this sentence? If you think the original is the best way, select choice (1).

(1) law and order nevertheless many of them break

(2) law and order, nevertheless many of them break

(3) law and order; nevertheless, many of them break

(4) law and order nevertheless, many of them break

(5) law and order nevertheless. Many of them break

27. Sentence 9: **Newspapers and television especially try to keep people informed about political scandals.**

Which of the following is the best way to write the underlined portion of this sentence? If you think the original is the best way, select choice (1).

(1) Newspapers and television especially try

(2) Newspapers, and television especially try

(3) Newspapers and Television especially try

(4) Newspapers and television especially tries

(5) Newspapers and television, especially, try

28. Sentence 10: **Reporters publish probing articles about the behavior of political figures so that citizens can look at candidates carefully before they vote for them.**

If you rewrote sentence 10 beginning with

To help citizens vote wisely, the next word should be

(1) probing

(2) reporters

(3) politicians

(4) write

(5) voters

Items 29 to 31 refer to the following passage.

---

(1) With all the talk about weight loss, diets, exercise, cholesterol, and calories, one thing seems clear. (2) More and more people must cut fat from their diets. (3) To improve their health. (4) Grocery shelves are stocked with products labeled "light," "low-fat,"

and "cholesterol-free." (5) Government officials and health professionals are concerned about what these labels really mean, and for consumers, the prices are high. (6) It's not necessary to spend a lot of money to reduce fat in your diet. (7) In fact, low-fat eating is relatively inexpensive because it involves lots of fruit and vegetables rather than expensive red meat. (8) You can cut fat from your diet by eating more salads, using low-fat sauces, and don't use fat when you cook.

29. Sentences 2 and 3: **More and more people must cut fat from their diets. To improve their health.**

Which of the following is the best way to write the underlined portion of these sentences? If you think the original is the best way, select choice (1).

(1) diets. To

(2) diets To

(3) diets; to

(4) diets, to

(5) diets to

30. Sentence 5: **Government officials and health professionals are concerned about what these labels really mean, and for consumers, the prices are high.**

Which of the following is the best way to write the underlined portion of this sentence? If you think the original is the best way, select choice (1).

(1) and for consumers, the prices are high

(2) and for consumers, high prices

(3) and consumers are concerned about the high prices

(4) and for consumers, price is the issue

(5) and high prices worry consumers

31. Sentence 8: **You can cut fat from your diet by eating more salads, using low-fat sauces, and don't use fat when you cook.**

Which of the following is the best way to write the underlined portion of this sentence? If you think the original is the best way, select choice (1).

(1) don't use fat when you cook

(2) cooking without fat

(3) to cook without fat

(4) don't cook with fat

(5) watch fat in cooking

Items 32 to 40 refer to the following paragraphs.

(1) For several years, public knowledge about the hazards of cigarette smoking has increased, so one in four Americans smokes cigarettes. (2) Public health officials now express a growing concern for nonsmokers who are exposed involuntarily to the secondhand smoke of others. (3) They see a need to publicize the injurious effects of passively inhaling smoke, and are especially worried about children. (4) Because of diseases from passive smoke inhalation under eighteen months of age, between 7,500 and 15,000 children are hospitalized each year. (5) Becoming ill, our country faces a serious problem. (6) Even though they aren't all hospitalized. (7) Between 7,500 and 150,000 children get sick from secondhand smoke. (8) Exposed to cigarette smoke, children are likely to contract ear infections, pneumonia, bronchitis, and their lungs will get other diseases. (9) The Environmental Protection Agency (EPA) also estimates that every year 3,000 lung cancer deaths result from secondhand smoke.

(10) The EPA would like citizens to discourage smoking in their houses, legislators to pass antismoking laws, and steps taken to protect workers. (11) Government guidelines suggest ways to reduce illness from secondhand smoke. (12) They say bars and restaurants should check a building's ventilation capabilities before they allow smoking. (13) Air from designated smoking areas should be directed outside. (14) Instead of being recycled. (15) Employers should support programs that help their workers quit smoking. (16) People should not allow smoking in their homes, and the public should go only to restaurants and bars that ban smoking.

32. Sentence 1: **For several years, public knowledge about the hazards of cigarette smoking has increased, so one in four Americans smokes cigarettes.**

What correction should be made to this sentence?

(1) change years, public to years. Public
(2) change public knowledge to knowing about
(3) change increased, so to increased so
(4) replace so with yet
(5) no correction is necessary

33. Sentence 3: **They see a need to publicize the injurious effects of passively inhaling smoke, and are especially worried about children.**

What correction should be made to this sentence?

(1) change effects of to effects. Of
(2) replace smoke, and with smoke. And
(3) replace and with although they
(4) replace and with so
(5) remove the comma before and

34. Sentence 4: **Because of diseases from passive smoke inhalation under eighteen months of age, between 7,500 and 15,000 children are hospitalized each year.**

If you rewrote sentence 4 beginning with

Between 7,500 and 15,000 children the next word should be

(1) smoke
(2) under
(3) passive
(4) hospitalized
(5) age

35. Sentence 5: **Becoming ill, our country faces a serious problem.**

Which of the following is the best way to write the underlined portion of this sentence? If you think the original is the best way, select choice (1).

(1) Becoming ill
(2) To become ill
(3) Children being ill
(4) When children become ill
(5) Being ill

36. Sentences 6 and 7: **Even though they aren't all hospitalized. Between 7,500 and 150,000 children get sick from secondhand smoke.**

Which of the following is the best way to write the underlined portion of these sentences? If you think the original is the best way, select choice (1).

(1) hospitalized. Between
(2) hospitalized between
(3) hospitalized, between
(4) in the hospital. Between
(5) in the hospital between

37. Sentence 8: **Exposed to cigarette smoke, children are likely to contract ear infections, pneumonia, bronchitis, and their lungs will get other diseases.**

What correction should be made to this sentence?

(1) change <u>smoke, children</u> to <u>smoke. Children</u>
(2) change <u>infections, pneumonia</u> to <u>infections. Pneumonia</u>
(3) change <u>bronchitis, and</u> to <u>bronchitis. And</u>
(4) change <u>their lungs will get other diseases</u> to <u>other lung diseases</u>
(5) change <u>their lungs will get other diseases</u> to <u>they'll have other lung diseases</u>

38. Sentence 10: **The EPA would like citizens to discourage smoking in their houses, legislators to pass antismoking laws, and <u>steps taken to protect workers.</u>**

Which of the following is the best way to write the underlined portion of this sentence? If you think the original is the best way, select choice (1).

(1) steps taken to protect workers
(2) steps to protect workers
(3) employers to take steps to protect workers
(4) workers take steps to protect themselves
(5) workers to be protected

39. Sentence 14: **Instead of being recycled.**

What correction should be made to this sentence?

(1) replace <u>Instead of being</u> with <u>It shouldn't be</u>
(2) replace <u>Instead of</u> with <u>Air is</u>
(3) replace <u>of</u> with a comma
(4) replace <u>of being</u> with <u>it should be</u>
(5) replace <u>being recycled</u> with <u>recycling it</u>

40. Sentence 16: **People should not allow smoking in their homes, and the public should go only to restaurants and bars that ban smoking.**

What correction should be made to this sentence?

(1) change <u>allow smoking</u> to <u>allow. Smoking</u>
(2) change <u>homes, and</u> to <u>homes. And</u>
(3) replace <u>and</u> with <u>but</u>
(4) replace <u>and</u> with <u>so</u>
(5) no correction is necessary

Items 41 to 44 refer to the following paragraph.

(1) Teenagers need ways to assert their independence. (2) One way is to drive a car. (3) Unfortunately, they don't always realize how powerful and dangerous a car is. (4) They see a car as a source of power and freedom who can get them places fast. (5) They forget cars are like weapons that can cause serious injury or even kill. (6) Insurance companies charge high rates for teenage drivers. (7) Which suggests they are a high risk. (8) It might help if driver's licenses showed how well a person will understand the hazards of driving a car. (9) Then states could issue licenses only to those kids understand how serious driving is. (10) Teenagers must remember that you and your car are not the only ones on the road.

41. Sentence 4: **They see a car as a source of power and freedom who can get them places fast.**

What correction should be made to this sentence?

(1) replace <u>They</u> with <u>He or she</u>
(2) replace <u>They</u> with <u>We</u>
(3) replace <u>who</u> with <u>whom</u>
(4) replace <u>who</u> with <u>that</u>
(5) replace <u>freedom who</u> with <u>freedom. Who</u>

42. Sentences 6 and 7: **Insurance companies charge high rates for teenage drivers. Which suggests they are a high risk.**

If you rewrote sentences 6 and 7 beginning with

<u>Because insurance companies believe teenage drivers are a high risk,</u> the next word(s) should be

(1) charging
(2) you
(3) they
(4) the companies
(5) charges

43. Sentence 8: **It might help if driver's licenses showed how well a person will understand the hazards of driving a car.**

What correction should be made to this sentence?

(1) replace <u>It</u> with <u>They</u>
(2) replace <u>driver's licenses</u> with <u>they</u>
(3) replace <u>a person</u> with <u>they</u>
(4) change <u>will understand</u> to <u>understand</u>
(5) change <u>will understand</u> to <u>understands</u>

44. Sentence 10: **Teenagers must remember that you and your car are not the only ones on the road.**

Which of the following is the best way to write the underlined portion of this sentence? If you think the original is the best way, select choice (1).

(1) you and your car
(2) they and their cars
(3) other cars
(4) anyone else's car
(5) many cars

Items 45 to 48 refer to the following paragraph.

---

(1) The advent of railroads went hand in hand with the Industrial Revolution in England in the nineteenth century. (2) Although England had good transportation systems on water and roads, the Industrial Revolution increases the need to transport raw materials and manufactured goods. (3) The steam engine, a new power source that powered industrial machinery and ships, will help solve the transportation problem. (4) In 1825, George Stephenson built a steam locomotive that could carry heavy loads long distances by rail. (5) Rail transport was not new. (6) Horse-drawn cars that moved along rails had been use in British coal mines for a long time. (7) Stephenson's accomplishment was to combine the concept of rail transport with the steam engine. (8) The first railroad linked two English mining towns, but by 1845 rail lines linked all the large cities and industrial regions in Britain. (9) Its expansion enhanced the expansion of the Industrial Revolution.

45. Sentence 2: **Although England had good transportation systems on water and roads, the Industrial Revolution increases the need to transport raw materials and manufactured goods.**

What correction should be made to this sentence?

(1) change had to will have
(2) insert has before had
(3) change increases to increase
(4) change increases to increased
(5) change increases to increasing

46. Sentence 3: **The steam engine, a new power source that powered industrial machinery and ships, will help solve the transportation problem.**

If you rewrote sentence 3 beginning with

The steam engine was a new power source that

the next word should be

(1) helps
(2) helped
(3) will
(4) powerful
(5) powering

47. Sentence 6: **Horse-drawn cars that moved along rails had been use in British coal mines for a long time.**

What correction should be made to this sentence?

(1) replace that with who
(2) change moved to will move
(3) change been to be
(4) change use to used
(5) change use to using

48. Sentence 9: **Its expansion enhanced the expansion of the Industrial Revolution.**

Which of the following is the best way to write the underlined portion of this sentence? If you think the original is the best way, select choice (1).

(1) Its expansion
(2) Expanding this
(3) Expansion of rail lines
(4) To expand it
(5) Their expansion

Items 49 to 55 refer to the following paragraph.

---

(1) Workplace safety is an issue that interests Government officials and business owners. (2) Today's workers face substantial riskes from many more sources than just heavy machinery. (3) Everyone recognizes the dangers faced by roofers, miners, firefighters and police officers who don't work inside offices. (4) Now technology has brought new hazards to office workers. (5) People who work with computers for example can develop back problems from sitting in inappropriate chairs. (6) If the keyboard isn't at just the right level, computer operators can incur wrist injuries that could require surgery. (7) Fatigue and eyestrain, trouble workers who spend their day looking at computer monitors. (8) Ergonomics is a growing sciens that addresses these issues. (9) It deals with features of the

work enviorment, including office furniture design, office lighting, and use of space. (10) It's costly for everyone if a worker is injured on the job.

49. Sentence 1: **Workplace safety is an issue that interests Government officials and business owners.**

What correction should be made to this sentence?

(1) change the spelling of safety to safty
(2) change the spelling of interests to intrests
(3) change Government to government
(4) insert a comma after officials
(5) no correction is necessary

50. Sentence 2: **Today's workers face substantial riskes from many more sources than just heavy machinery.**

Which of the following is the best way to write the underlined portion of this sentence? If you think the original is the best way, select choice (1).

(1) Today's workers face substantial riskes from
(2) Todays workeres face substantial riskes from
(3) Today's workers, face substantial riskes from
(4) Today's workers face substantial risks from
(5) Today's workers' faced substantial riskes from

51. Sentence 3: **Everyone recognizes the dangers faced by roofers, miners, firefighters and police officers who don't work inside offices.**

What correction should be made to this sentence?

(1) change the spelling of recognizes to reconizes
(2) remove the comma after roofers
(3) remove the comma after miners
(4) insert a comma after firefighters
(5) change don't to dont

52. Sentence 5: **People who work with computers for example can develop back problems from sitting in inappropriate chairs.**

Which of the following is the best way to write the underlined portion of this sentence? If you think the original is the best way, select choice (1).

(1) computers for example can
(2) computers. For example can
(3) computers for, example can
(4) computers, for example, can
(5) computers for example, can

53. Sentence 7: **Fatigue and eyestrain, trouble workers who spend their day looking at computer monitors.**

What correction should be made to this sentence?

(1) change the spelling of Fatigue to Fatige
(2) remove the comma after eyestrain
(3) change trouble to troubles
(4) change their to there
(5) change their to they're

54. Sentence 8: **Ergonomics is a growing scients that addresses these issues.**

Which of the following is the best way to write the underlined portion of this sentence? If you think the original is the best way, select choice (1).

(1) growing scients that addresses these issues
(2) growing scients that address these issues
(3) growing science that addresses these issues
(4) growing scients who addresses these issues
(5) growing scients whom addresses these issues

55. Sentence 9: **It deals with features of the work enviorment, including office furniture design, office lighting, and use of space.**

Which of the following is the best way to write the underlined portion of this sentence? If you think the original is the best way, select choice (1).

(1) work enviorment, including
(2) works enviorment, including
(3) work enviornment, including
(4) work enviorment, including
(5) work enviorment, includeing

Part II
45 Minutes

Directions

Read carefully the directions and the essay topic given below. Plan your essay carefully before you write. Use scratch paper to make any notes. Read carefully what you have written and make any changes that will improve your essay. Check your paragraphs, sentence structure, spelling, punctuation, capitalization, and usage. Try to write your essay in 45 minutes, as that is the amount of time you will be given on the actual GED Test.

TOPIC

Telephone answering machines are becoming nearly as common in private homes as they are in offices. Some people appreciate these machines and rely on them to send and to receive telephone messages. Others resent answering machines and refuse to use them. They will neither have one in their home nor leave messages on one.

In an essay of about 200 words, tell whether you find answering machines a convenience, an annoyance, or both. Use examples from your own experience and observations.

SOCIAL STUDIES

85 Minutes ❖ 64 Questions

Directions

Choose the one best answer to each item.

Items 1 to 5 are based on the following three graphs.

GROWTH

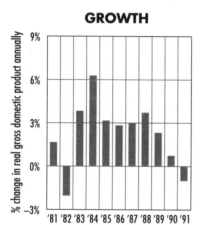

INFLATION

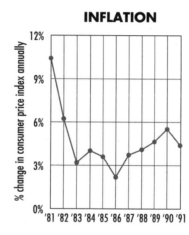

UNEMPLOYMENT

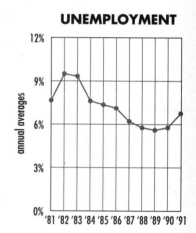

1. The two-year period with the greatest percent change in the rate of inflation was the period from

   (1) 1989 to 1991
   (2) 1981 to 1983
   (3) 1984 to 1986
   (4) 1988 to 1990
   (5) 1985 to 1987

2. Which statement best describes the relationship shown by the charts between the growth of the gross domestic product and the rate of unemployment?

   (1) A low rate of growth is often linked to high or rising unemployment.
   (2) A high rate of growth is often linked to high or rising unemployment.
   (3) A low or falling rate of unemployment is often linked to a low rate of growth.
   (4) A high or rising rate of unemployment is often linked to moderate growth.
   (5) A negative rate of growth is often linked to a low or falling rate of unemployment.

3. The greatest decrease in the growth of the gross domestic product was from
   (1) 1981 to 1982
   (2) 1984 to 1985
   (3) 1988 to 1990
   (4) 1988 to 1991
   (5) 1985 to 1987

4. These graphs could help a person determine the best time to look for a new job. Such a time would be when
   (1) inflation is rising, unemployment is falling, and economic growth is rising
   (2) inflation is falling, unemployment is rising, and economic growth is falling
   (3) inflation is falling, unemployment is falling, and economic growth is rising
   (4) inflation is falling, unemployment is falling, and economic growth is falling
   (5) inflation is rising, unemployment is rising, and economic growth is rising

5. The U.S. economy showed strong growth between 1983 and 1989. The most likely cause was
   (1) an increase in the number of immigrants to the U.S. between 1981 and 1990
   (2) the falling rate of inflation between 1981 and 1986
   (3) the reelection of President Ronald Reagan in 1984
   (4) the falling rate of unemployment between 1983 and 1989
   (5) the strengthening of the European Common Market in the 1980s

Items 6 to 10 refer to the following passage.

In June 1991, Mount Pinatubo in the Philippines began one of the most violent volcanic eruptions of the twentieth century. More than 200,000 acres were covered with a thick coat of volcanic ash, pumice, and debris. In some places the coating grew to 15 feet thick. More than 600 people died. Some were killed by the ash itself. Many others died from inhaling the deadly gases Mount Pinatubo gave off. Experts believe that the gases and ash thrown into the upper atmosphere were the cause of below-average worldwide temperatures the following year. Each year's monsoon season for the decade following the 1991 explosion is expected to cause avalanches. About half of the 7 billion cubic meters of volcanic material deposited on Mount Pinatubo's slopes is likely to wash down into the plains below.

6. What was the major worldwide effect of Mount Pinatubo's explosion in 1991?
   (1) avalanches
   (2) a thick coat of ash
   (3) monsoons
   (4) cooling temperatures
   (5) deadly gases

7. According to the passage, avalanches are predicted during each monsoon season until at least what year?
   (1) 1991
   (2) 1992
   (3) 1995
   (4) 2000
   (5) 2001

8. To prevent more death and destruction from Mount Pinatubo's mud slides, a reasonable policy would be to
   (1) plant grasses and crops
   (2) blow up the mountain
   (3) pray for dry weather
   (4) do nothing
   (5) relocate people to a safe area

9. The eruption created more than 60,000 refugees, many of them farmers and their families. The U.S. government sent $400 million in aid to help these people, but criticized the way some of it was spent by the Philippine government. Philippine officials used much of the money to build four-lane highways and tall concrete buildings. What was the probable reason for American criticism of this use of the money?
   (1) Not enough American contractors were used on the construction projects.
   (2) The $400 million was not enough to build all the highways that the Philippine officials wanted to construct.
   (3) The highways and tall buildings did not help the 60,000 refugees recover their lost farms and villages.
   (4) The highways were poorly constructed and were damaged in the next monsoon season.
   (5) American officials were not sure that the highways and tall buildings would withstand a possible future eruption of Mount Pinatubo.

10. According to the passage, people were killed by falling ash and

    (1) monsoons
    (2) cooling temperatures
    (3) avalanches
    (4) falling buildings
    (5) deadly gases

Items 11 to 13 are based on the following passage.

In the summer of 1991, construction workers preparing the foundation of a new federal office building at the southern tip of Manhattan found an archaeological treasure. The construction workers uncovered some human skeletons just 20 feet below the surface. Archaeologists were called in, and they quickly realized the area was an old graveyard.

By studying colonial maps, the archaeologists determined the graveyard to be one called "Negroes' Burial Ground," which from 1710 to 1790 was used as a burial site for an untold number of African-American slaves and a few white paupers. Within a year of the start of archaeological work at the site, the remains of more than 400 bodies were unearthed.

The archaeologists found evidence to suggest that the burial site—the only such site with any pre-Revolutionary use now known in the United States—is one of the most significant archaeological discoveries of the twentieth century. For example, studies of the children's skeletons found there have indicated that as many as half of the area's slaves died at birth or within the first few years of life.

At first, federal officials refused to halt construction at the site. However, numerous groups and individuals, including people in Congress, New York's City Hall, and various African-American organizations, protested. The construction project was cancelled, and plans were made to include the ancient graveyard in a proposed historic district.

11. Which of the following sentences best summarizes the most important points of the passage?

    (1) In 1991, one of the most significant archaeological discoveries of the century was made in Manhattan.
    (2) In the early 1990s, the federal government started construction of a new office building in Manhattan but later abandoned the project after receiving complaints.
    (3) Archaeologists believe that as many as half of all African Americans born in the area of Manhattan in the 1700s died within the first few years of life.
    (4) The remains of more than 400 bodies in an old African-American graveyard were unearthed in the early 1990s.
    (5) Archaeologists often find items of great historical value at construction sites in major American cities.

12. Which of the choices below would be a good clue to the archaeologists that the graveyard was used during colonial times in America?

    (1) a Civil War sword
    (2) an engraved ring that says "for King and country"
    (3) a pair of plastic sandals
    (4) a map of the United States showing the transcontinental railroad
    (5) a family photograph

13. What does the death rate of newborns and young children say about life in the 1700s as compared with life today?

    (1) Life in the 1700s was much like it is today.
    (2) Medical care and nutrition in the 1700s were poor by today's standards.
    (3) Parents in the 1700s did not take very good care of their children.
    (4) About as many people in the 1700s lived to adulthood as do today.
    (5) Life in the 1700s was much easier than it is today.

Item 14 refers to the following cartoon.

'What it says isn't always what it means'

14. This cartoon refers to which principle of American government?

(1) separation of church and state
(2) checks and balances
(3) judicial review
(4) equality before the law
(5) bill of rights

15. The nine justices of the U.S. Supreme Court all receive lifetime appointments. In which of the following ways are their decisions probably most affected by this fact?

(1) Because they have federal appointments, they probably favor the federal government over state governments when the two are on opposite sides of an issue.
(2) They work more slowly and carefully than they might if some oversight group could set the pace.
(3) They probably tend to follow the beliefs of the president who nominated them.
(4) They probably tend to become independent thinkers because they are not accountable to any politician or party.
(5) They probably rely more heavily on initial drafts of decisions that are written by their law clerks.

Items 16 to 19 refer to the following chart.

U.S. NATIONAL PARKS AND THEIR VISITORS

Year	No. of Parks	No. of Visitors (in thousands)
1970	35	45,879
1960	29	26,630
1950	28	13,919
1940	26	7,358
1930	22	2,775
1920	19	920
1910	13	119

16. How many visits were made to U.S. national parks in 1960?

(1) 29
(2) 26,630
(3) 12,711
(4) 26.63 million
(5) 29 million

17. The number of national parks almost tripled between 1910 and 1970, but the number of visits increased at a much higher rate. Two of the oldest parks, Yellowstone and Yosemite, continue to have among the largest numbers of visitors per year. What factors probably best account for this great increase in visits?

(1) a general increase in the U.S. population and more leisure time
(2) a vastly improved transportation system and more leisure time
(3) creation of new parks close to large metropolitan areas and a general increase in U.S. population
(4) better advertising about improved park facilities and an increased interest nationally in ecology and the environment
(5) improved security services within the parks and an increase in the amount of disposable income available to most Americans

18. Between which two years did the smallest actual increase in visits take place?

(1) 1960 and 1970
(2) 1920 and 1930
(3) 1910 and 1920
(4) 1950 and 1960
(5) 1930 and 1940

19. The factor that has contributed most to the growth in the number of national parks, as well as in the numbers of national historic sites, battlefields, and monuments, has been

   (1) the general growth of the federal government in the twentieth century

   (2) the growth of the amount of leisure time for most Americans in the twentieth century

   (3) a general American belief that national historic and natural sites of interest should be preserved for future generations to enjoy

   (4) the increasing number of states in the western United States that were admitted to the Union in the first half of the twentieth century

   (5) the inability of state governments to care adequately for various sites because of local financial problems

---

Items 20 to 22 are based on the following table.

PROJECTED POPULATION OF SOME GROUPS OF PEOPLE WITHIN THE UNITED STATES
(number in millions)

Group	Year 2000	Year 2050	Year 2080
Male, White	108.8	105.6	103.6
Female, White	112.7	116.2	108.7
Male, Black	16.7	22.4	22.6
Female, Black	18.3	24.7	25.0

20. According to the chart, which group will be the largest in the year 2050?

   (1) all females
   (2) all males
   (3) black males
   (4) white females
   (5) white males

21. Which group will show a decrease of 4 million between the years 2000 and 2080?

   (1) black females
   (2) all females
   (3) white females
   (4) white males
   (5) all males

22. Which statement best summarizes the content of the table?

   (1) The number of blacks in the United States will increase between the years 2000 and 2080.

   (2) The number of blacks in the United States will show the greatest percentage of increase between the years 2000 and 2050.

   (3) The number of white females in the United States will increase between the years 2000 and 2050.

   (4) The number of whites in the United States will be greater than the number of blacks in the years between 2000 and 2080.

   (5) The total number of blacks in the United States will increase between the years 2000 and 2080 both in actual numbers and in relation to the total number of whites.

Items 23 to 28 refer to the following passage.

Andrew Jackson (1767–1845) was elected president of the United States in 1828. Following are some highlights of his colorful life:

- At age thirteen, Jackson joined the Continental Army and fought the British in the Revolutionary War. When taken prisoner, Jackson refused to clean a British officer's boots, and the officer struck him in the head with a sword. The permanent scar became a lifelong reminder of his hatred for the British.

- In 1787, Jackson was admitted to the bar in North Carolina, where he practiced law for several years.

- In 1791, he married Rachel Donelson Robards, believing, as she herself believed, that she was legally divorced at the time. Three years later, this proved to be untrue and the couple had to remarry. The resulting scandal followed the pair for the rest of their lives.

- In 1796, Jackson was elected without opposition as Tennessee's first representative to the U.S. House of Representatives.

- In 1798, Jackson was elected to Tennessee's highest court, where he was noted for dispensing quick, fair justice.

- In 1806, he fought a duel. Both men were shot, and his opponent died, although Jackson could have honorably prevented this death.

- In the War of 1812, Jackson rose to the rank of general and became a war hero through his successful leadership of American troops at the Battle of

New Orleans. Later in his career, his political opponents charged him with murder for having approved the execution of several American soldiers for minor offenses during the war.

- As president, Jackson vetoed dozens of bills and grew powerful through the use of the spoils system.

- In 1835, he survived an assassination attempt. In 1837, he retired to his plantation after attending the inauguration of his handpicked successor, Martin Van Buren.

23. Jackson once said, "I believe that just laws can make no distinction of privilege between the rich and poor. . . ." What part of his life could he cite to prove that he followed this belief?

   (1) his marriage to Rachel Robards
   (2) his being charged with the murder of several American soldiers during the War of 1812
   (3) his time spent as a justice of the Tennessee Supreme Court
   (4) his use of the spoils system
   (5) his status as a hero of the War of 1812

24. Senator Henry Clay once described Jackson as "corrupt." What fact of Jackson's life might Clay have cited to prove his charge?

   (1) his manipulation of the spoils system
   (2) his joining of the Continental Army at age thirteen
   (3) the duel he fought in which both he and his opponent were shot
   (4) his almost lifelong hatred of the British
   (5) his election as Tennessee's first representative to the U.S. Congress

25. Jackson was known throughout his life for sometimes behaving in a rash manner. Which of his actions could be cited to support this point of view?

   (1) studying law and being admitted to the bar
   (2) marrying a woman whose marital status was later questioned
   (3) retiring to his plantation after his two terms as president and hating the British
   (4) joining the army at thirteen and fighting a duel
   (5) becoming a hero of the War of 1812 and serving on the Tennessee Supreme Court

26. In which two American wars did Andrew Jackson participate?

   (1) the Revolutionary War and the War of 1812
   (2) the Civil War and the Spanish-American War
   (3) World War I and World War II
   (4) the Korean War and the Vietnam War
   (5) the Crimean War and the Russo-Japanese War

27. In the Battle of New Orleans, British casualties numbered 2,000 whereas American casualties were only 21. What might be inferred about Jackson's military skills from this fact?

   (1) that the British troops were poorly trained
   (2) that the American troops had more and better weapons than the British did
   (3) that Jackson was an able military commander
   (4) that Jackson's infamous temper caused his chief military subordinates to do anything to win
   (5) that Jackson made a much better military leader than president

28. President Jackson vetoed the bill to recharter the Bank of the United States. As a result, "pet" banks began to print money and make new loans with little backing. Issuing new money and making loans in this way most likely resulted in

   (1) a severe depression
   (2) severe inflation
   (3) more unemployment
   (4) decreased spending
   (5) a trade deficit

Items 29 to 31 refer to the following passage.

What makes a good marriage? The collective efforts of numerous researchers are now beginning to develop an answer. A Florida study of marriages lasting twenty-five years or more showed that a key element of a successful relationship is the ability to solve problems jointly. The ability to listen constructively and nondefensively is another. The ability to have fun together—to be humorous and playful—is also important. The early results of a Michigan study point toward "affective affirmation" as a strong predictor of marital happiness. Affective affirmation is the unconditional approval of one's mate. This is such a powerful force in nonverbal communication, such as body language, that it can bring about a remarkable transformation in a relationship. In affective affirmation, each person moves toward his or her spouse's innermost ideal of a partner because of the existing positive indicators already being received.

29. Which sentence best summarizes this passage?

(1) People married for twenty-five years or more usually have happy marriages.

(2) Several basic factors seem to play important roles in determining how good a marriage is.

(3) Researchers in Florida and Michigan have studied the qualities that go into making a good marriage.

(4) The ability to have fun together is a key element needed to make a good marriage.

(5) Affective affirmation is the one essential quality needed to make a good marriage.

30. A married couple that argues a lot might best solve their problems by

(1) getting a divorce

(2) seeking counseling to learn how to solve problems jointly

(3) asking their friends for advice

(4) setting aside a special time each day to try to work out their differences in a calm, nonconfrontational way

(5) reading books that discuss how to deal with problems in relationships

31. Many people believe that most marital problems are caused by differences between people and by problem areas such as money, children, and sex. However, a Denver researcher has discovered that it is not the differences and problems themselves that are most important but how these differences and problems are handled, especially early in the marriage. This finding confirmed the importance of which key factor?

(1) the ability to provide affective affirmation for each other

(2) the ability to solve problems jointly

(3) the ability to listen constructively

(4) the ability to be playful with each other

(5) the ability to limit arguments to 10 minutes or less

Items 32 and 33 refer to the following passage.

From 1848 to 1919, American women fought for a constitutional amendment giving them suffrage, or the right to vote. Year after year, more and more women attended rallies and marched in the streets. In one parade, a reporter noted that "women doctors, women lawyers, women architects, women artists, actresses and sculptors; women waitresses, domestics; a huge division of industrial workers . . . all marched with an intensity and purpose that astonished the crowds that lined the streets." In 1919, Congress passed the Nineteenth Amendment, giving women the right to vote. A year later, the states ratified it, and female suffrage became the law of the land.

32. Attending speeches, rallies, and marches are activities that

(1) are protected by the First Amendment

(2) were unbecoming for women at the time

(3) convinced lawmakers to pass the Nineteenth Amendment

(4) did little to further the cause of suffrage

(5) showed how determined all women were

33. Which conclusion is best supported by the reporter's description of a suffragist parade?

(1) Only a handful of women wanted suffrage and were willing to take a stand.

(2) Only wealthy women had time to take part in marches and parades supporting suffrage.

(3) Voting was not a serious issue for most women.

(4) Women from many different walks of life took a stand in favor of women's suffrage.

(5) Working women were interested in voting because the stakes were higher for them.

Items 34 to 36 refer to the following passage.

The growth of industry and business led to several new ways of doing business. These new practices allowed owners of large companies to run their smaller competitors out of business by controlling supplies and prices. Once they had control of the market, these so-called "robber barons" could charge any prices they wished for their goods.

Trust: a combination of businesses in which one board of trustees controls the member companies

Monopoly: a business that has complete control over an industry or trade

Holding company: a combination of businesses in which one company owns stock in another company

Vertical integration: control of all steps of the production process in an industry

Horizontal integration: control of one area of production in an industry—for example, manufacturing or distribution

34. In 1873, John D. Rockefeller's Standard Oil Company bought several bankrupt oil refineries. This move, which gave Standard Oil control over the refining stage of oil production, is an example of

(1) a trust
(2) a monopoly
(3) a holding company
(4) vertical integration
(5) horizontal integration

35. By 1879, Standard Oil controlled nearly all of the means of transporting oil. The company now had the power to control oil prices. This situation is an example of

(1) a trust
(2) a monopoly
(3) a holding company
(4) vertical integration
(5) horizontal integration

36. Many Americans were against "big business" entities such as trusts, monopolies, and holding companies because they

(1) encouraged corruption and kept prices low
(2) encouraged competition and kept prices high
(3) killed competition and kept prices high
(4) killed competition and kept wages high
(5) kept prices low and wages high

37. During the Cold War, many Americans believed that communism, if allowed to spread, would threaten democracy. To prevent the spread of communism, the United States pursued a policy of

(1) intervention in the affairs of communist countries
(2) brinkmanship, or risking war to maintain peace
(3) containment, or keeping communism within its current borders
(4) massive retaliation against any threat or action by a communist country
(5) covert operations, or secret activities aimed at undermining communist governments

Items 38 to 40 refer to the following graph.

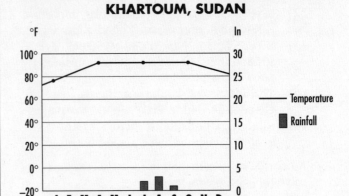

38. In what regions are you most likely to find a climate such as the one indicated in the graph?

(1) tropics
(2) polar regions
(3) temperate zones
(4) mountains
(5) deserts

39. Which phrase best describes this climate?

(1) hot and very rainy
(2) hot, humid summers and mild winters
(3) hot with very little rain
(4) varying temperatures with very little rain
(5) freezing temperatures with little or no precipitation

40. What kind of vegetation would you expect to find in this climate?

(1) rain forests
(2) forests
(3) tall grasses
(4) short grasses and shrubs
(5) little or no vegetation

Items 41 and 42 refer to the following passage.

During the 1970s, gasoline processed in the United States contained lead additives that boosted octane. When scientists discovered the health risks lead posed, they began to test children for lead content in their blood. They found that those who lived within 500 feet of a main road had dangerously high levels.

41. The main idea of the passage is that

(1) gasoline processed in the United States contained lead additives

(2) scientists tested children for lead content in their blood

(3) children who lived near a main road had dangerously high levels of lead in their blood

(4) location can put people at higher risk for lead poisoning

(5) living near a main road is dangerous

42. What conclusion can be reached from the passage?

(1) Gasoline processed in the United States is no longer dangerous.

(2) Location can put people at higher risk for lead poisoning.

(3) Location is often a vital factor in explaining health risk.

(4) Living too near a main road can cause lead poisoning.

(5) U.S. companies are responsible for the high levels of lead in children's blood.

43. George Washington set a precedent by not running for a third term as president. Later this practice became law. Why is a two-term limit a good policy for the country?

(1) Most people are too tired after two terms as president to be effective during a third term.

(2) Many people want to be president, and it's not fair to them if one person has the job too long.

(3) One person should not have so much power for such a long period of time.

(4) Members of Congress object to the predictable policies of one president.

(5) Most citizens get tired of listening to one leader after eight years and need to hear from someone else.

Items 44 and 45 refer to the following cartoon.

44. Whom do the men in the cartoon represent?

(1) the United Nations

(2) the secretaries of state, labor, and commerce and their aides

(3) American military leaders and policy makers

(4) Russian military leaders and policy makers

(5) military leaders of several nations

45. What underlying point of view is the cartoonist presenting?

(1) The Defense Department has too many generals.

(2) Military leaders have too many tax dollars to spend as they choose.

(3) Leaders of the Air Force, Army, Navy, and Marines spend too much time having meetings and not enough time fighting wars.

(4) The legislative and executive branches of government have given too much power to military leaders.

(5) Military spending is important to the economic well-being of the United States.

46. U.S. senators are elected for six-year terms. They are expected to represent the interests of their states and to take a long-range view of the needs of the entire country. Which qualities or experiences would be least useful for a U.S. senator to have?

(1) an ability to reach compromises on important issues

(2) a clear understanding of the meaning of the Constitution

(3) strong financial and business skills

(4) strong ties to a foreign government

(5) a good public speaking style

47. Medicare, which provides health care to elderly Americans, is an example of

(1) government bureaucracy
(2) Social Security
(3) an independent agency
(4) a political action committee
(5) a government entitlement program

Item 48 refers to the following cartoon.

48. What does this 1977 cartoon say about lobbyists?

(1) Lobbyists often drive expensive cars.
(2) Lobbyists have too strong a hold on Congress.
(3) Lobbyists are overpaid.
(4) Lobbyists are often former members of Congress.
(5) Lobbyists represent many different types of special interests.

49. For years, the United States took a hard-line stance against the communist Soviet Union. Now we are friendly and helpful toward Russia, the largest republic to result from the breakup of the Soviet Union. This change shows that U.S. foreign policy

(1) is flexible enough to change when circumstances change
(2) reflects a wishy-washy attitude toward world events
(3) is staunchly against communism
(4) is subject to the whims of the president
(5) has not changed for at least fifty years

50. The secretary of state has been called the president's "right arm" in dealing with other nations. Which of the following is not a function of the State Department?

(1) diplomacy
(2) occupational health and safety
(3) foreign policy
(4) issue of passports
(5) management of overseas bureaus

51. The consumer price index (CPI) is used to measure inflation, or a general rise in prices. The index measures the prices of a "typical consumer's market basket" of goods and services. Which of the following items would not be in this market basket?

(1) mortgage payment
(2) meat
(3) automobiles
(4) medical care
(5) wages

52. If the CPI increases 25 percent in a year, economists would probably agree that

(1) the economy is undergoing rampant inflation
(2) the economy is in a mild inflation
(3) the economy is in a slight recession, a period of general decline in economic activity
(4) the economy is in a depression, a severe economic downturn
(5) the economy is just fine

53. Suppose that home sales, as well as sales of automobiles, furniture, and appliances, are down. Large sellers of these and many other products announce massive layoffs. In this situation, the government should

(1) increase taxes to reduce consumer spending and increase government expenditures to stimulate investment
(2) lower interest rates to increase investment and raise taxes on the middle class
(3) lower interest rates to stimulate investment and decrease government expenditures to reduce inflation, or a rise in prices
(4) lower interest rates to stimulate investment and decrease taxes to stimulate consumer spending
(5) do nothing

54. Fiscal policy involves decisions related to government spending and taxation in response to changes in the economy. Which is the best example of a fiscal policy?

(1) encouraging people to spend more
(2) encouraging people to spend less
(3) giving business people tax credits for buying new equipment
(4) telling banks to lend more
(5) printing money

55. If the demand for automobiles increases, but the supply does not change, what will happen to the price and the quantity exchanged?

(1) They will stay the same.
(2) The price and the quantity exchanged will increase.
(3) The price will increase and the quantity exchanged will decrease.
(4) The price will decrease and the quantity exchanged will increase.
(5) The price will stay the same and the quantity exchanged will increase.

Items 56 and 57 refer to the following information.

The table below shows the number of widgets produced by ABC Widget Company if it adds workers without changing any other economic resource.

Number of Workers	Total Widgets Produced	Number Added
1	50	—
2	110	60
3	160	50
4	200	40
5	230	30

56. Based on the table, which added worker makes the greatest contribution to the total output of widgets?

(1) first
(2) second
(3) third
(4) fourth
(5) fifth

57. The law of diminishing returns takes effect with the addition of which worker?

(1) first
(2) second
(3) third
(4) fourth
(5) fifth

58. Jody is learning a new computer program by trying out the various key commands and screen options. She is engaging in

(1) social learning as she imitates and communicates with other people to gain knowledge
(2) socialization as she learns to participate in society
(3) role reversal as she fills a role that is not expected of her
(4) trial-and-error learning as she tries out a behavior without first knowing whether it will work
(5) enculturation as the knowledge she gains is passed on from generation to generation

Items 59 and 60 refer to the following graph.

MEDIAN AGE AT FIRST MARRIAGE

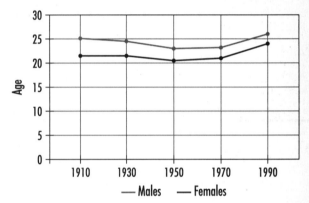

— Males — Females

59. Based on the graph, what seems to have been the trend since 1970?

(1) Men were older than the women they married in 1970.
(2) Women were older than the men they married in 1990.
(3) Men wed in 1990 were older than those wed in 1970.
(4) Women wed in 1970 were younger than those wed in 1990.
(5) Both men and women have been marrying somewhat later in life.

60. The post-1970 change in behavior shown in the graph most likely resulted from

(1) men wanting to marry older women
(2) more women pursuing careers before marrying
(3) many women choosing not to marry at all
(4) women wanting to marry older men
(5) men having difficulty finding jobs

61. Every culture has certain expectations about the way people should behave. These behavioral expectations are known as norms. Which one of the following examples is not a norm?

(1) Always excuse yourself when you bump into someone.

(2) Married persons should not have sexual relations with anyone but their spouses.

(3) Parents are to provide for their children before providing for themselves.

(4) Men are better than women at managing people.

(5) Children who get into mischief should be corrected by their parents.

Items 62 to 64 refer to the following passage.

Sigmund Freud, the father of psychoanalytic theory, believed that much of human behavior is controlled by forces in the unconscious mind and that those forces may be linked to childhood experiences and sexual motives. Freud distinguished three parts of the mind: id, ego, and superego. The id consists of the basic drives and instincts with which we are born and that urge us to obtain immediate pleasure and avoid pain. The ego helps the id meet its needs and drives safely and realistically, but not necessarily morally. The superego is a person's conscience; it determines what is morally right and wrong as learned from social influences.

62. According to Freud's theory,

(1) you are born with the ability to distinguish right from wrong

(2) the ego part of your mind determines your childhood experiences

(3) much of your personality is controlled by forces in your unconscious mind

(4) your personality influences your basic needs and drives

(5) the id and the ego control the superego

63. Nine-year-old Jarmon stole money from his mother's purse. Later, feeling guilty, he quietly returned the cash. According to Freud's theory, what caused Jarmon to put the money back?

(1) his id

(2) his emotions

(3) his superego

(4) his personality

(5) his ego

64. Which one of the following methods would Freud have recommended for dealing with emotional problems?

(1) Explore the unconscious mind through random thoughts and memories.

(2) Teach the unconscious mind to respond to a stimulus representing a positive feeling.

(3) Develop a means of inner growth and development.

(4) Develop a self-image.

(5) Explore conflicts arising from opposing ideas, needs, wishes, and instincts.

416

SCIENCE

95 Minutes ❖ 66 Questions

Items 1 to 4 refer to the following information.

Sound is produced by vibration. As an object vibrates, it produces sound waves in air or other substances. Sound can be described in terms of the characteristics defined below.

Speed: a measure of how fast sound travels through air, water, or a solid object

Reflection: the change in direction that occurs when a sound wave returns from an obstacle

Pitch: the highness or lowness of a sound

Intensity: the loudness of a sound

Resonance: the process of sound vibrations building up; a sound wave is produced in response to another sound wave

1. What causes sound?
   (1) the intensity of a sound wave
   (2) the vibration of an object
   (3) the movement of air
   (4) an echo
   (5) a change in pitch

2. A window pane rattles as an airplane goes by. Which of the following characteristics of sound does this situation best illustrate?
   (1) speed
   (2) reflection
   (3) pitch
   (4) intensity
   (5) resonance

3. A violin is tuned by tightening or loosening the strings. Which of the following characteristics of sound does this situation best illustrate?
   (1) speed
   (2) reflection
   (3) pitch
   (4) intensity
   (5) resonance

4. Sound travels through air at about 331 meters per second. If you see an airplane flying overhead but do not hear it until 4 seconds later, how far was the airplane from you when you first saw it?
   (1) 331 meters
   (2) 662 meters
   (3) 993 meters
   (4) 1,324 meters
   (5) 2,648 meters

Items 5 to 7 refer to the following information.

According to the theory of evolution, similar organisms are descended from the same type of ancestor. The organisms most fit to survive in an environment will reproduce most successfully, passing on their characteristics to the next generation. This process, known as natural selection, ensures that a species develops characteristics suited to survival in a particular environment.

While forming the theory of evolution, Charles Darwin observed many species of finches on different islands. Each species of finch was similar to the others in many ways. However, the beaks of these species differed, according to each species's which is method of getting the available food. Four types of beak are illustrated below.

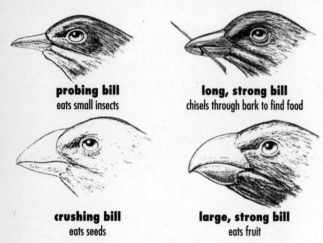

probing bill
eats small insects

long, strong bill
chisels through bark to find food

crushing bill
eats seeds

large, strong bill
eats fruit

5. Which of the following statements best summarizes the process of natural selection?

   (1) All organisms are descended from one ancestor.

   (2) Some organisms reproduce more successfully than others.

   (3) Characteristics are passed down from parents to offspring.

   (4) Some species are better adapted to an environment than other species.

   (5) Organisms best adapted to an environment survive and reproduce.

6. Which of the following statements best explains why finches developed a variety of beak shapes?

   (1) Different types of food were available on different islands.

   (2) All finches are descended from the same type of ancestor.

   (3) Finches with probing bills are most likely to eat insects.

   (4) Finches with crushing bills are most likely to eat seeds.

   (5) Beak shapes are passed on from parents to offspring.

7. In which of the following environments would a finch with a small probing bill be more likely to survive than other finches?

   (1) an open beach with small insects on the sand

   (2) a rocky area with numerous seeds deposited by the wind

   (3) a heavily wooded area with many fruit trees

   (4) a very dry area with a few trees

   (5) a grassland area with many grass seeds

8. Energy from sunlight is the essential fuel for photosynthesis. Protein compounds called enzymes accelerate the chemical reactions of a cell during photosynthesis. Without enzymes, the main chemicals involved in each phase of photosynthesis would react too slowly to perform this vital function. Which of the following processes most closely resembles the function of an enzyme?

   (1) a furnace blasting energy in the form of heat

   (2) a pair of bellows fanning the flames of a sluggish fire

   (3) a solar battery harnessing energy from sunlight

   (4) a bucket brigade passing pails of water to extinguish a fire

   (5) a locomotive losing speed because it is running out of fuel

> Items 9 and 10 refer to the following passage.

Animals are more likely to become extinct if their requirements for food or habitat are very specific. Some species can adapt to eating only one kind of food and living in only one kind of environment. The disappearance of their source of food or nesting site jeopardizes the survival of the species. For example, pandas used to make their homes in the bamboo forests of China. Pandas feed almost entirely on bamboo shoots. However, to accommodate the growing human population of China, the bamboo forests were cleared to make room for housing. In addition, humans used the bamboo from the forests for building materials, fuel, and food.

9. Which of the following was the most likely effect of bamboo forest destruction?

   (1) The panda population declined sharply.

   (2) Pandas migrated to a different habitat.

   (3) Pandas interacted more with humans.

   (4) Pandas became primarily meat eaters instead of plant eaters.

   (5) Pandas easily adapted to changes in their environment.

10. Which of the following groups would be most likely to protest against the destruction of the bamboo forests?

   (1) a development company wanting to build housing

   (2) government officials wanting to lower the population densities of the cities

   (3) food companies harvesting and selling bamboo shoots

   (4) health-care professionals warning about overcrowded conditions in the cities

   (5) animal rights groups trying to save the panda from extinction

> Items 11 and 12 refer to the following definitions.

   Change in the environment: a change in the conditions under which a population lives and competes

   Migration: movement of some members of a species into an environment where other members of the species already live

   Isolation: separation of some members of a species from the main group, and their entry into a different environment

   Mutation: sudden development in an animal or plant of a strange new feature resulting from a genetic accident

   Sexual selection: the way in which members of some species choose mates because of certain physical characteristics

11. The formation of a land bridge between two islands allows a group of monkeys from one island to travel to the other island, where monkeys of the same species also live. The factor for evolutionary change in this case is

   (1) change in the environment
   (2) migration
   (3) isolation
   (4) mutation
   (5) sexual selection

12. In a population of lizards living near a pond, one lizard is suddenly born with webbed hind feet. Such feet enable the lizard to swim fast enough so that it can catch insects in the water as well as on the shore. The factor for evolutionary change in this case is

   (1) change in the environment
   (2) migration
   (3) isolation
   (4) mutation
   (5) sexual selection

> Item 13 refers to the following information.

   An acid is a substance that yields positive ions when dissolved in water. A base is a substance that yields negative ions when dissolved in water. When acids and bases are combined, the properties of both are lost and water and a salt are formed. This is called neutralization.

13. Salicylic acid is the chemical packaged and sold as aspirin. Some people experience a side effect when taking this drug. Which side effect is the most likely result of ingesting salicylic acid?

   (1) headache
   (2) sore throat and cold
   (3) irritated stomach
   (4) sleepiness
   (5) nervousness

> Items 14 and 15 refer to the following information.

   A pulley is a machine that divides the weight of a load to provide a mechanical advantage. In the pulley system illustrated below, the man supports half the weight of the load, while the other half is supported by the rope attached to the ceiling. For each yard that the load is lifted, the man has to pull two yards of rope. In this system, the mechanical advantage is 2.

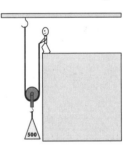

14. How does a pulley provide a mechanical advantage?

   (1) It helps reduce the effort needed by the man.

   (2) It takes all the weight of the load.

   (3) It decreases the distance the rope must be pulled.

   (4) It increases the friction that must be overcome.

   (5) It makes heavy objects light.

15. Which of the following statements is supported by the information given?

(1) To lift the load 2 yards, the man must pull 4 yards of rope.

(2) To lower the load 1 yard, the man must pull 2 yards of rope.

(3) The more pulleys, the greater the mechanical advantage.

(4) To lower the pulley wheel, the man must pull the rope.

(5) The fewer pulleys, the less the mechanical advantage.

16. In a photocopier, a metal drum has a negative electric charge. When an image of a document is projected onto the drum, the electric charge is deactivated wherever light hits the drum. The black toner powder is attracted to the areas of electric charge that remain. The photocopier deposits the toner powder on the paper, where it is melted in place. Which of the following is the most likely cause of getting blank pages instead of copies of a document from a photocopier?

(1) The paper jams inside the machine.

(2) The toner powder is melted unevenly.

(3) Static electricity attracts the toner powder to the paper.

(4) The supply of toner powder has run out.

(5) The electric power has been disconnected.

Items 17 to 19 refer to the following information.

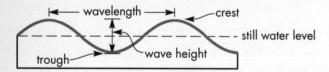

The height and wavelength of a water wave depend on several factors. The speed of the wind, the length of time the wind has blown, and the size of the area over which the wind blows all contribute to a wave's height and length. The largest water waves are produced by strong winds that blow for many hours over large areas.

17. In which of the following locations are waves likely to be highest?

(1) Pacific Ocean

(2) Lake Superior

(3) Mediterranean Sea

(4) Red Sea

(5) Gulf of Mexico

18. When a wave reaches shallow water, its wavelength gets shorter. The ocean bottom slows the wave down, but the crest continues to move forward. What is the result of this situation?

(1) A current pulls the wave back away from shore.

(2) The crest tumbles over and the wave breaks.

(3) The wave comes onto the beach at an angle.

(4) The crest gets higher.

(5) The trough moves faster.

19. Which of the following statements is supported by the given information?

(1) Calm seas are the result of light winds.

(2) The average height of an ocean wave is 3 meters.

(3) During a storm, wave height can reach 30 meters.

(4) The waves in a lake are as large, on average, as the waves in the ocean.

(5) The trough of a wave is as high as the crest.

Items 20 and 21 refer to the following information.

Miles below the surface of Los Angeles is a network of blind thrust faults, or breaks in the underlying rock. The faults are blind because they cannot be seen from the surface. They are called thrust faults because when they break, one side moves up over the other, pushing upward toward the surface. A sudden movement of a blind thrust fault under the San Fernando Valley caused a major earthquake in January 1994.

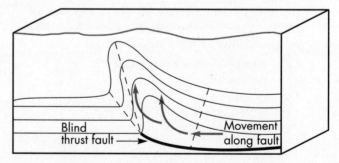

20. Which of the following is the most likely result if movement along a blind thrust fault occurs very gradually over thousands of years?

(1) the creation of a flat plain

(2) the formation of hills and mountains

(3) a severe earthquake

(4) the formation of a river valley

(5) a change in the local climate

21. Which of the following is most similar to the movement of a blind thrust fault?

    (1) sliding a carton up a ramp
    (2) rolling a ball down a bowling alley
    (3) sledding down a snowy hill
    (4) going up in an elevator
    (5) ice skating on a frozen pond

Items 22 to 24 refer to the following diagram.

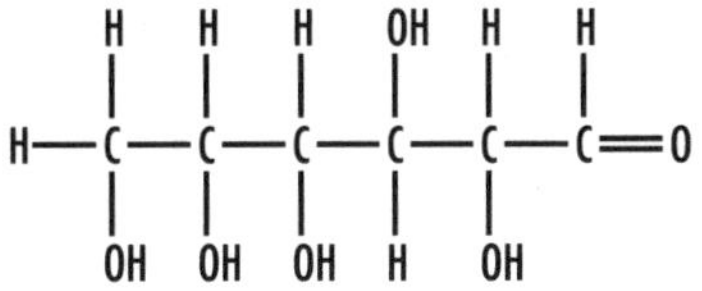

$$H-\overset{\overset{\displaystyle H}{|}}{\underset{\underset{\displaystyle OH}{|}}{C}}-\overset{\overset{\displaystyle H}{|}}{\underset{\underset{\displaystyle OH}{|}}{C}}-\overset{\overset{\displaystyle H}{|}}{\underset{\underset{\displaystyle OH}{|}}{C}}-\overset{\overset{\displaystyle OH}{|}}{\underset{\underset{\displaystyle H}{|}}{C}}-\overset{\overset{\displaystyle H}{|}}{\underset{\underset{\displaystyle OH}{|}}{C}}-\overset{\overset{\displaystyle H}{|}}{C}=0$$

22. Which of the following formulas corresponds to the structural formula above?

    (1) $C_{12}H_{22}O_{11}$
    (2) $C_4H_4N_2O_2$
    (3) $C_6H_{12}O_6$
    (4) COH_{24}
    (5) $C_6(OH)_2$

23. The diagram above shows the atoms in one molecule of glucose. How many atoms of carbon (C) would there be in two molecules of glucose?

    (1) 4
    (2) 6
    (3) 8
    (4) 10
    (5) 12

24. Which of the following statements is supported by the information in the diagram?

    (1) One molecule of glucose contains fourteen hydrogen (H) atoms.
    (2) One molecule of glucose contains eleven oxygen (O) atoms.
    (3) Glucose can dissolve in water (H_2O).
    (4) Glucose contains carbon (C), hydrogen (H), and oxygen (O).
    (5) Glucose contains carbon (C), hydrogen (H), nitrogen (N), and oxygen (O).

Items 25 to 27 refer to the following information.

Our bodies produce the energy we need through the process of respiration. In this process, oxygen burns and glucose, a type of sugar, breaks down. Carbon dioxide, water, and energy known as ATP are released. The following formula and illustration summarize the process of aerobic respiration:

Energy released during respiration is used for cell growth, cell division, and chemical transport. It is also used for the muscle contractions that cause movement and keep us warm. During physical exercise, the body must provide a steady supply of energy to muscle cells. When the muscles are depleted of ATP, they begin to feel heavy.

25. Which of the following is produced during respiration?

    (1) glucose
    (2) oxygen
    (3) carbon monoxide
    (4) ATP
    (5) carbon

26. Which of the following is most likely to result from a lack of oxygen?
    A. Cells cannot transport chemicals adequately.

    B. Cell growth is inhibited.

    C. Muscle movement becomes difficult.

    (1) A only
    (2) B only
    (3) C only
    (4) A and B only
    (5) A, B, and C

27. After the 15th round of a boxing match, Muhammad Ali, the former heavyweight champion, remarked, "My arms were so tired that I could barely lift them above my trunks." Which of the following is the best scientific explanation of Muhammad Ali's remark?

   (1) His lungs received an inadequate supply of oxygen.
   (2) His opponent had repeatedly punched his arm muscles.
   (3) The cells in his arm muscles ran out of ATP.
   (4) His diet lacked the glucose needed to fuel his muscle cells.
   (5) His muscle cells released huge amounts of energy.

28. Plants, like animals, develop defenses that protect them from their enemies and increase their chances of survival in their environment. Hemlock is a flowering plant that protects itself by producing a poisonous chemical. Which of the following plants also has a chemical defense system?

   (1) a golden barrel cactus covered with sharp spines
   (2) a stinging nettle that releases acid when touched
   (3) a rose with thorns on its stem
   (4) a cork oak tree with a protective bark
   (5) a palm tree surrounded by spiny fibers

Item 29 refers to the following graph.

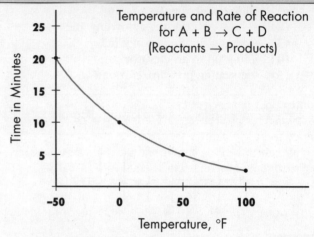

29. Which of the following statements is supported by the information given?

   (1) As the temperature increases, all reactions take more time.
   (2) As the temperature increases, most reactions take less time.
   (3) When A and B are combined in a chemical reaction, C and D are the products that result.
   (4) Although A and B are liquids, the product of their reaction is two gases.
   (5) At 50°F, it takes 10 minutes for A and B to combine and form C and D.

30. Litmus paper can be used to show the presence of an acid or a base. When a substance is neutral, it turns litmus paper purple. When the substance is an acid, litmus paper turns pink-red. When a base is present, litmus paper turns blue. In which of the following situations would litmus paper most likely be used?

   (1) to measure the temperature of a solution of vinegar and water
   (2) to test the chemical properties of the water in a fish tank
   (3) to measure the amount of rain that falls in 24 hours
   (4) to measure the amount of salt in ocean water
   (5) to determine the correct dose of aspirin for a patient

In our world today, machines do most of our heavy physical work, motor vehicles eliminate the need to walk, and food is readily available. This lifestyle has contributed to the fact that many Americans are overweight. Physical reasons, such as a genetic tendency to gain weight, also contribute to obesity. Being overweight is a risky condition: the risk of death from physical illness increases as the amount of extra weight increases. The graph below illustrates this risk.

PERCENT OF DEATHS ABOVE NORMAL

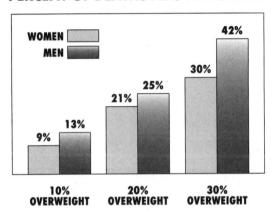

31. Which of the following hypotheses is supported by the data in the graph?

   (1) Overweight men have a greater risk of death from physical illness than overweight women.
   (2) The more overweight a person is, the less the risk of death from physical illness.
   (3) Women who are 10 percent overweight have the same risk of death as women of normal weight.
   (4) Overweight men have a greater risk of heart attack than overweight women.
   (5) Overweight women have a greater risk of stroke than overweight men.

32. Each of the following factors contributes to obesity except

   (1) lack of exercise
   (2) easily available food
   (3) a balanced diet
   (4) a genetic tendency to gain weight
   (5) lack of active work

A fruit is a seed-bearing structure that develops from the ovaries of a plant. The chart below classifies simple fruits into two main categories: fleshy fruits and dry fruits. In a fleshy fruit, the ovary and related flower parts form a fleshy structure around the seed. In a dry fruit, however, the ovary forms a protective hard coat around the seed.

		CHARACTERISTICS
FLESHY FRUITS	Drupes	Fleshy outer layer Hard stone or pit inside Single seed
	Berries	Fleshy tissue Many seeds embedded in flesh of most species
	Pomes	Fleshy outer layer Inner core More than one seed encased in core
DRY FRUITS	Dehiscent	Hard outer coat bursts open when ripe
	Indehiscent	Hard outer coat remains intact

33. Watermelons and tomatoes are both examples of

   (1) drupes
   (2) berries
   (3) pomes
   (4) dehiscents
   (5) indehiscents

34. In which of the following categories of fruit does an apple belong?

   (1) drupe
   (2) berry
   (3) pome
   (4) dehiscent
   (5) indehiscent

35. What type of fruit are cherries and plums?

   (1) drupe
   (2) berry
   (3) pome
   (4) dehiscent
   (5) indehiscent

36. A milkweed pod splits open, releasing airborne seeds. Milkweed is a kind of

   (1) drupe
   (2) berry
   (3) pome
   (4) dehiscent
   (5) indehiscent

37. Which of the following pieces of evidence would best support the theory that evolution has been going on for millions of years?

(1) fossils from different millenia showing that species had changed over time

(2) members of a modern species that differ from each other

(3) fossils of dinosaurs that have been extinct for millions of years

(4) animal specimens from the 1800s that differ from the same species today

(5) different animal species that live in the same environment that have come to look alike

Items 38 and 39 refer to the following passage.

People are born with one of the following four types of blood: A, B, AB, and O. Blood type is determined by genetic factors only. Transfusions of incorrect blood types result in serious complications.

In 1941, the U.S. War Department established a policy for collecting blood used for transfusions: the U.S. military would accept blood from white donors only. At that time, Dr. Charles Drew was supervising a nationwide program, sponsored by the American Red Cross, to collect blood. Drew, an accomplished African-American doctor and medical researcher, protested the War Department's policy: "No difficulties have been shown to exist between the bloods of different races, which would in any way counter-indicate the use of blood from an individual of one race in an individual of another race."

38. Which of the following factors most likely determined the U.S. War Department's blood-collection policy?

(1) personal observations
(2) racial prejudice
(3) proven facts
(4) chemical analyses of blood
(5) results of blood transfusions

39. Which of the following statements about blood is not supported by scientific evidence?

(1) Blood type is genetically determined.
(2) Certain procedures must be followed to ensure safe transfusions of blood.
(3) Blood types vary from individual to individual.
(4) Donated blood must be carefully typed before it is used.
(5) Any individual can safely give blood to any other individual.

Items 40 and 41 refer to the following graph.

BREAKDOWN OF SNACKS AMONG U.S. CHILDREN

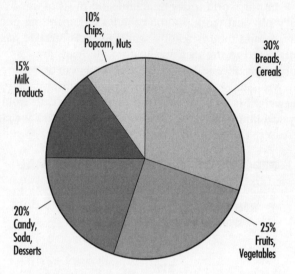

10% Chips, Popcorn, Nuts

15% Milk Products

30% Breads, Cereals

20% Candy, Soda, Desserts

25% Fruits, Vegetables

40. What percentage of children's snacks is accounted for by carbohydrates derived from grains?

(1) 10 percent
(2) 15 percent
(3) 20 percent
(4) 25 percent
(5) 30 percent

41. Which of the following groups of snacks has the least nutritional value?

(1) breads, cereals
(2) fruits, vegetables
(3) candy, soda, desserts
(4) milk products
(5) chips, popcorn, nuts

42. Sodium nitrate and sodium nitrite are added to foods to preserve them. These food additives are usually found in cured meats such as hot dogs, sausage, bologna, and bacon. Once digested in the stomach, nitrates and nitrites are changed into substances that cause cancer in laboratory animals. Which of the following would provide the strongest evidence in further studies to determine if nitrates and nitrites cause cancer in humans?

(1) public opinion surveys
(2) conclusive results from experiments with laboratory animals
(3) a decrease in the rate of stomach cancer
(4) results showing cancer in additional human and animal studies
(5) investigations of the meat-packing industry

Item 43 refers to the following diagram.

RAIN FOREST RESERVE

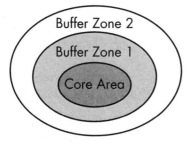

Core Area: Reserved for plants and animals only.
Buffer Zones 1 and 2: Reserved for human use (areas set aside for housing, scientific research, tourism, and agriculture)

43. Which of the following best explains the main purpose for creating the core area of a rain forest reserve?

    (1) to protect rain forest plants and animals from human activities
    (2) to conduct studies of an ecosystem
    (3) to develop exciting tourist attractions
    (4) to provide new housing developments for rain forest people
    (5) to improve methods of raising crops

44. The depth of the ocean can be measured by a ship's echo sounder, which bounces sound waves off the ocean floor. The sound waves travel from the ship to the ocean bottom and back. Because sound travels at 1,524 meters per second through ocean water, the depth can be calculated by timing the sending and return of the echo. If an echo is sent out and returns in 10 seconds, how deep is the ocean at that point?

    (1) 152.4 meters
    (2) 1,524 meters
    (3) 3,810 meters
    (4) 7,620 meters
    (5) 15,240 meters

45. According to the law of superposition, in a bed of undisturbed sedimentary rocks, each layer of rock is younger than the one below it. In which of the following situations would this law also apply?

    (1) the deposition of lava and ash from volcanic eruptions
    (2) the formation of mountains when land is uplifted
    (3) the cutting of a river valley through a plateau
    (4) the formation of a lake in the crater of a large meteor
    (5) the formation of sand from the weathering of rock

Items 46 and 47 refer to the following passage.

Most of the oil used in the United States comes from offshore drilling or is imported from other countries. The large oil deposits on U.S. land have already been used. However, there are extensive, untapped oil shale deposits in Colorado, Utah, and Wyoming. Oil shale is a fine-grained sedimentary rock that contains a substance called kerogen. Oil shale burns when lit with a match. When the shale is heated to about 480°C (900°F), kerogen decomposes and yields shale oil.

Pilot projects have shown that shale oil can be used in boilers or upgraded by expensive processing for other uses. However, shale oil production requires large amounts of water, which is scarce in the region in which it is found. In addition, it produces huge amounts of waste shale. For these reasons, shale oil has not yet been produced for commercial use.

46. What will be the result if scientists and engineers cannot find a way to process shale oil economically?

    (1) The oil shale deposits in Colorado, Utah, and Wyoming would be used in place of natural gas.
    (2) The United States will continue to depend on offshore drilling and other countries for its oil.
    (3) The oil shale deposits will be used for other purposes such as building materials.
    (4) The shale oil will be produced in spite of the problems associated with it.
    (5) The oil shale deposits will be used to produce natural gas.

47. Which of the following is the most important reason that shale oil has not been produced commercially?

(1) Scientists have not yet figured out how to get oil from oil shale.
(2) Oil from oil shale is more expensive than oil from offshore drilling and from other countries.
(3) The deposits of oil shale are too small to make processing them worthwhile.
(4) Large quantities of water are needed to produce shale oil.
(5) Waste shale is difficult to dispose of.

> Items 48 and 49 refer to the following information.

The calorie is the unit that measures the energy content of food. A machine called a calorimeter measures the number of calories in a food sample by burning the food and measuring the amount of heat energy it gives off. Fried foods such as french fries, potato chips, and doughnuts have a lot of fat and are relatively high in calories, compared with other dietary choices such as carbohydrates and proteins.

Fats differ from carbohydrates in that they have many more carbon and hydrogen atoms than oxygen atoms; one fat has a chemical formula of $C_{57}H_{110}O_6$. The following pie chart shows the balance of foods that makes up a healthy diet.

PIE CHART

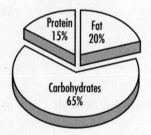

48. According to the graph, what percentage of your daily diet should consist of carbohydrates?

(1) 15 percent
(2) 20 percent
(3) 35 percent
(4) 65 percent
(5) 85 percent

49. In order to maintain a diet with the recommended percentages of protein, fat, and carbohydrates, which of the following pieces of information would be most valuable?

(1) data on how many grams of carbohydrates are in the foods you eat
(2) data on how much protein and fat are in the foods you eat
(3) information on the amounts of protein, fat, and carbohydrates in the foods you eat
(4) the number of calories in each of the foods you eat
(5) information on the amounts of carbohydrates, calories, and fat in the foods you eat

50. The chart below lists the calorie contents of various foods.

Food	Calories
asparagus with lemon dressing	65
low-fat blueberry mousse	46
grilled fish and vegetables	249
omelet	180
raspberry sherbet	230
salad	184
soup	150
stuffed tomatoes	345
sweet potatoes	190

To stay within a calorie limit of 400, which of the following foods could you eat?

(1) Asparagus with lemon dressing, grilled fish and vegetables, low-fat blueberry mousse
(2) Asparagus with lemon dressing, stuffed tomatoes, raspberry sherbet
(3) Omelet, salad, low-fat blueberry mousse
(4) Stuffed tomatoes, salad, raspberry sherbet
(5) Grilled fish and vegetables, sweet potatoes, low-fat blueberry mousse

51. The following formula can be used to calculate the amount of fat in ground beef.

$$\frac{\text{Weight of fat}}{\text{Weight of beef samples}} \times 100 = \text{percent fat}$$

Using this formula, which beef sample comes closest to a 15-percent fat content?

(1) 10 ounces of fat in a 25-ounce beef sample
(2) 5 ounces of fat in a 25-ounce beef sample
(3) 4 ounces of fat in a 25-ounce beef sample
(4) 15 ounces of fat in a 25-ounce beef sample
(5) 20 ounces of fat in a 25-ounce beef sample

52. Although fats are necessary for a healthy diet, fried foods are not recommended by many doctors. Which of the following statements best explains this?

    (1) Fats from fried foods are the only sources of fat from food.
    (2) Fried foods contain excessive amounts of carbohydrates.
    (3) Fats from fried foods burn more quickly than fats from other foods.
    (4) Fats from fried foods are less healthy than fats from other sources.
    (5) Fried foods contain excessive amounts of protein.

Items 53 to 56 refer to the following information.

The pH scale measures the strength of an acid or a base. Acids have pH values less than 7. Bases, which have the ability to neutralize acids, have pH values greater than 7. Water is considered neutral and has a pH of 7. The chart below lists the pH levels of several substances.

Substance	pH
lime	1.9
grapefruit juice	3
human blood	7.5
seawater	8.25
magnesium hydroxide	10.5
lye	13

53. Which of the following substances most closely matches the pH of pure water?

    (1) lime
    (2) grapefruit juice
    (3) human blood
    (4) seawater
    (5) magnesium hydroxide

54. Which of the following substances is the strongest base?

    (1) lime
    (2) grapefruit juice
    (3) water
    (4) human blood
    (5) lye

55. Which of the following characteristics of a substance could you predict based on its pH value?

    (1) how much the substance weighs
    (2) how the substance will react when combined with an acid or a base
    (3) whether the substance is a mixture or a chemical compound
    (4) what kind of chemical bond the substance will form
    (5) how much water the substance contains

56. The pH level of human saliva varies from 6.5 to 7.5. Which of the following statements best explains this variation?

    (1) Human saliva is pure water and contains no other chemicals.
    (2) Human saliva is an acid that begins dissolving food in your mouth.
    (3) Human saliva contains varying concentrations of several chemicals.
    (4) Human saliva is a base until a person eats acidic foods.
    (5) Salts found in human saliva vary its pH level.

57. A pendulum is a weight suspended on a string that is attached to a fixed point, as illustrated in the following diagram.

PENDULUM

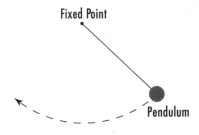

Gravity causes a pendulum to move. Which type of energy conversion occurs in a pendulum?

    (1) Electrical energy changes to light energy.
    (2) Kinetic energy changes to heat energy.
    (3) Chemical energy changes to electrical energy.
    (4) Potential energy changes to kinetic energy.
    (5) Sound energy changes to mechanical energy.

58. A machine is a device that transfers energy from one place to another or from one form to another. Which of the following statements best depicts the use of a machine to do work?

   (1) lifting a 50-pound barbell
   (2) running around a track
   (3) closing a door
   (4) lifting a baby
   (5) prying open a lid with a knife

59. Work is measured in foot-pounds (ft-lb). A foot-pound is the amount of work done by a force of one pound in moving an object one foot in the direction of the force. The formula for work is as follows.

Work = Force × Distance

In a weight lifting competition, an athlete raises a 100-pound barbell 6 feet. How much work has the athlete done?

   (1) 17 ft-lb
   (2) 60 ft-lb
   (3) 600 ft-lb
   (4) 100 ft-lb
   (5) 3,600 ft-lb

60. Water moves up and down when a wave passes. It does not move horizontally. Below, a toy boat is floating on the surface of a pond. A stone is thrown into the water.

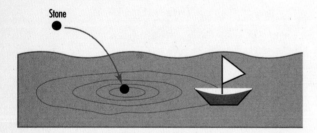

Which of the following statements best describes the resulting motion of the boat?

   (1) It moves horizontally with each successive wave.
   (2) It moves horizontally ahead of the waves.
   (3) Its motion is related to the water temperature.
   (4) It bobs up and down but does not move horizontally.
   (5) It vibrates long after the waves have passed.

61. Which of the following statements best explains why a 6-foot-tall man appears only 2 inches high in a photograph?

   (1) A camera reflects light back to the source of the image.
   (2) A camera refracts light and projects the man's image on film.
   (3) There are limits to the size of a photograph.
   (4) You can take photos only of distant objects.
   (5) You can adjust the amount of light entering a camera.

62. The following diagram shows a phrase written on paper and its reflection in a flat mirror.

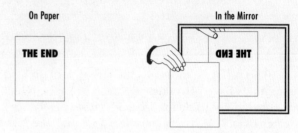

Which of the following statements best describes the relationship between the printed words and their mirror image?

   (1) The image is smaller than the object.
   (2) The mirror enlarges the image.
   (3) The mirror turns the image upside down.
   (4) The mirror image and the reflected object are identical in every way.
   (5) The mirror image is reversed.

63. Electric current will flow when there is an increase in electrical pressure (voltage) in one part of a circuit. Which of the following terms relates directly to this phenomenon?

   (1) insulator
   (2) conductor
   (3) static
   (4) ampere
   (5) potential difference

64. In a parallel circuit, electric current moves through at least two separate paths. If current cannot flow through one pathway, it still flows through other parts of the circuit. Which of the following situations could cause a current to change pathways?

(1) All of the appliances on the first pathway are being used.
(2) The electricity surges as a result of lightning.
(3) The first pathway is shorter than the other paths.
(4) The first pathway is longer than the other paths.
(5) A broken appliance is still plugged into the first pathway.

65. One volt of electricity is equal to 0.001 kilovolt. To convert volts to kilovolts, you should take the number of volts and

(1) divide by 1,000
(2) divide by 100
(3) divide by 10
(4) multiply by 100
(5) multiply by 1,000

66. George Ohm was a mathematician who studied electrical resistance. Ohm's law describes the following relationship among current, voltage, and resistance.

$$\text{current} = \frac{\text{voltage}}{\text{resistance}}$$

According to Ohm's law, what would happen if the resistance in a circuit remained the same and the voltage decreased?

(1) The amount of current would remain constant.
(2) The amount of current would increase.
(3) The amount of current would decrease.
(4) The circuit could not function.
(5) The current would change direction.

INTERPRETING LITERATURE AND THE ARTS

65 Minutes ❖ 45 Questions

> **Directions**
> Choose the one best answer to each item.

> Items 1 to 4 refer to the following excerpt from a play.

WHAT DOES THIS CONVERSATION REVEAL?

Line Laura: *(Rising)* Mother, let me clear the table.

Amanda: No, dear, you go in front and study your typewriter chart. Or practice your shorthand a little. Stay fresh and pretty!—It's almost time for our gentlemen callers to start arriving. *(She flounces girlishly toward the kitchenette)* How many do you suppose we're going

5 to entertain this afternoon?

(Tom throws down the paper and jumps up with a groan)

Laura: *(Alone in the dining room)* I don't believe we're going to receive any, Mother.

Amanda: *(Reappearing airily)* What? No one—not one? You must be joking! *(Laura nervously echoes her laugh. She slips in a fugitive manner through the half-open portieres and*

10 *draws them gently behind her. A shaft of very clear light is thrown on her face against the faded tapestry of the curtains.)* Not one gentleman caller? It can't be true! There must be a flood, there must have been a tornado!

Laura: It isn't a flood, it's not a tornado, Mother. I'm just not popular like you were in Blue Mountain . . . *(Tom utters another groan. Laura glances at him with a faint, apolo-*

15 *getic smile. Her voice catching a little)* Mother's afraid I'm going to be an old maid.

—From *The Glass Menagerie*
by Tennessee Williams

1. Which of the following best describes Laura's behavior toward her mother?

   (1) cruel
   (2) kind
   (3) flirtatious
   (4) mocking
   (5) impatient

2. According to this passage, what does Amanda expect is going to happen?

   (1) They will eat dinner.
   (2) Laura will practice her shorthand.
   (3) Tom will announce he is moving.
   (4) Male admirers will visit Laura.
   (5) Laura will become upset.

3. The stage directions in lines 6 and 14 suggest that Tom

(1) loves his sister
(2) is about to go out
(3) will finish reading the paper
(4) does not have a job
(5) is impatient with his mother

4. "A shaft of very clear light is thrown on [Laura's] face against the faded tapestry of the curtains." (lines 10–11)

In a live performance, the most important result of this stage direction would be that the audience could

(1) focus on Laura's face as Amanda speaks
(2) see that it is not yet dark
(3) see that Laura is hiding from Amanda and Tom
(4) focus on Tom's reaction to Amanda's words
(5) see that the family is not wealthy

Items 5 to 8 refer to the following excerpt from a short story.

WHAT KIND OF PERSON WAS JOSÉ MONTIEL?

Line When José Montiel died, everyone felt avenged
except his widow; but it took several hours for
everyone to believe that he had indeed died. Many
continued to doubt it after seeing the corpse in
5 the sweltering room, crammed along with pillows
and linen sheets into a yellow coffin, with sides as
rounded as a melon. He was very closely shaved,
dressed in white, with patent-leather boots, and he
looked so well that he had never seemed as alive
10 as at that moment. It was the same Mr. Chepe
Montiel as was present every Sunday at eight-
o'clock Mass, except that instead of his riding
quirt he had a crucifix in his hands. It took
screwing the lid on the coffin and walling him up
15 in the showy family mausoleum for the whole
town to become convinced that he wasn't playing
dead.

After the burial, the only thing which
seemed incredible to everyone except his widow
20 was that José Montiel had died a natural death.
While everyone had been hoping he would be
shot in the back in an ambush, his widow was
certain she would see him die an old man in his
bed, having confessed, and painlessly, like a
25 modern-day saint. She was mistaken in only a few
details. José Montiel died in his hammock, the
second of August, 1951, at two in the afternoon,

as a result of a fit of anger which the doctor had
forbidden. But his wife also was hoping that the
30 whole town would attend the funeral and that the
house would be too small to hold all the flowers.
Nevertheless, only the members of his own party
and of his religious brotherhood attended, and the
only wreaths they received were those from the
35 municipal government.

—From "Montiel's Widow"
by Gabriel Garcia Márquez

5. "When José Montiel died, everyone felt avenged except his widow . . ." (lines 1–2)

From this statement, what can you conclude about José Montiel?

(1) His death was violent.
(2) His last wish was never known.
(3) He was beloved.
(4) He had been married many times.
(5) He had many enemies.

6. " . . . the only thing which seemed incredible to everyone except his widow was that José Montiel had died a natural death." (lines 18–20)

Which of the following best restates this idea?

(1) Everyone but Montiel's wife believed that someone would kill him.
(2) No one could believe that Montiel had stayed married.
(3) Everyone believed that he would die a natural death.
(4) The town went into deep mourning over Montiel's death.
(5) Montiel's widow had wanted to kill him.

7. Based on the information in this passage, which of the following describes how Montiel's widow felt toward her husband?

(1) mocking and scornful
(2) angrily resentful
(3) confused and alone
(4) ashamed but brave
(5) respectful and loving

8. Based on the town's opinion, José Montiel would have been most likely to

(1) be kind to a stranger
(2) plant a garden
(3) lead a church service
(4) betray a friend
(5) adopt an orphaned child

Items 9 to 12 refer to the following excerpt from a book review.

WHAT MAKES THIS NOVEL SO INTERESTING?

Line Crime novel fans, check out the current crop of
thrillers written by women about women crime
solvers. A new breed of sleuth has burst on the
scene. She's professional, disciplined, and dedi-
5   cated. A hot date matters less to her than a hot
clue. She's also more ethical and humane than her
male counterparts—in fact, all-around nicer—and
must contend not only with the killer but with the
hostility she arouses in those who are threatened
10 by her strength.

     Patricia D. Cornwell produces such a heroine
in *Cruel & Unusual* (Scribner's, $21). Kay
Scarpetta is chief medical examiner of Virginia,
which means that her typical workday involves
15 carving up some hapless crime victim with a
Stryker saw and sorting through organs. . . .

     The pace is unrelenting; the suspense
nerve-jangling; the dialogue scalpel sharp. Characters are deftly drawn. The workaholic Kay has a
20 tragic love affair in her past ("Mark's death had
left a tear in my soul"). Her sidekick, Marino, a
police lieutenant, is both gruff and lovable. Kay's
precocious niece, Lucy, helps track the killer with
her computer savvy. The "love interest" in this
25 book is not romantic, but between the middle-
aged Kay and Lucy, a kind of surrogate daughter.

     Throughout, you're showered with info on
high-tech methods of crime detection, as in a
sequence in which Kay and colleagues return to
30 the scene of a ten-year-old murder and reenact it
through the latest chemical potions. I was
particularly moved by Kay's confrontation with a
former law school professor, whom she has
always resented. He browbeat her, he confesses,
35 because he didn't want her to lose herself in love.
"I was determined that you would not waste your
gifts and give away your power." Cornwell's Kay
Scarpetta is a woman functioning at the peak of
her powers. She is truly a heroine of our times.

          —From "Female Suspicions" by Erica Abeel

9. Based on lines 1–3, which of the following works
    is most similar to *Cruel & Unusual?*

    (1) a TV show about a police lieutenant and his
         niece
    (2) a documentary about female artists, pro-
         duced by a woman
    (3) a novel about a gruff law school professor
    (4) a movie written and directed by a woman
    (5) a magazine article about women's changing
         roles

10. According to the reviewer, the dialogue in *Cruel
    & Unusual* is

    (1) sappy and emotional
    (2) tired and dull
    (3) unrealistic and outdated
    (4) direct and concise
    (5) graphic and gruesome

11. According to the review, which of the following is
    not a part of this novel's plot?

    (1) crime reenactment
    (2) crime detection
    (3) relationships at work
    (4) family relationships
    (5) romantic love

12. Which of the following best restates the profes-
    sor's explanation in lines 36–37?

    (1) "I wanted you to become a professor."
    (2) "I wanted you to get married and have a
         family."
    (3) "You worked too hard in school."
    (4) "I knew you would never fall in love."
    (5) "I wanted you to achieve your full
         potential."

Directions Items 13 and 14 refer to the following poem.

IS THIS WEDDING RING STILL USEFUL?

Line My wedding-ring lies in a basket
      as if at the bottom of a well.
      Nothing will come to fish it back up
      and onto my finger again.
5   It lies
      among keys to abandoned houses,
      nails waiting to be needed and hammered
      into some wall,
      telephone numbers with no names attached,
10   idle paperclips.
            It can't be given away
      for fear of bringing ill-luck.
            It can't be sold
      for the marriage was good in its own
15   time, though that time is gone.
            Could some artificer
      beat it into bright stones, transform it
      into a dazzling circlet no one could take
      for solemn betrothal or to make promises
20   living will not let them keep? Change it
      into a simple gift I could give in friendship?
                    — "Wedding-Ring" by Denise Levertov

13. The tone and topic of this poem sound most similar to that of a

   (1) song
   (2) diary entry
   (3) newspaper advertisement
   (4) love letter
   (5) law document

14. "My wedding-ring lies in a basket/as if at the bottom of a well." (lines 1–2)

This figurative language is an example of

   (1) a symbol of the importance of marriage to the speaker
   (2) a metaphor that shows how unhappy the speaker was in her marriage
   (3) a metaphor that shows how lonely the speaker is without a spouse
   (4) a simile that suggests how distant the speaker's marriage now seems
   (5) a personification of the failure of the speaker's marriage

Items 15 to 17 refer to the following excerpt from an essay.

WHY IS MR. RANDOLPH REMEMBERED?

Line When I was a young boy I often went out to the Oklahoma State Capitol, where I assisted Mr. J. D. Randolph with his duties as custodian of the State Law Library. I was about eleven years old at the
5   time, quite impressionable, and very, very curious about the mysterious legal goings-on of the legislators. All the more so because while I was never able to observe the legislature in session, it was not at all unusual for me to look up from
10   pushing a broom or dusting a desk to see one of the legislators dash into the library to ask Jeff— Mr. Randolph was always addressed by his first name—his opinion regarding some point of law. In fact, I soon came to look forward to such
15   moments because I was amazed by the frequency with which Mr. Randolph managed to come up with satisfactory answers, even without consulting the heavy volumes which ranged the walls.
          I wasn't surprised that Mr. Randolph was a
20   janitor instead of a lawyer or legislator; Oklahoma was segregated at the time and Afro-Americans were strictly limited in their freedom to participate in the process of government. We could obey or break laws, but not make or interpret them. In
25   view of this, I was amazed that Mr. Randolph had come to know so much about the subject. . . .
          I was more impressed with the fact that Mr. Randolph could carry so many of the mysterious details of law and the laws which governed the
30   state of Oklahoma within his own head. Now, I knew he had been one of the first schoolteachers in the city and the state, and that he read and owned a large collection of books. But just how he had come to learn the law was part of an
35   experience about which I was never to hear him talk.

        —From "Perspective of Literature"
                by Ralph Ellison

15. ". . . it was not at all unusual for me to look up . . . to see one of the legislators dash into the library to ask . . . Mr. Randolph . . . his opinion regarding some point of law." (lines 9-13)

This description shows that

(1) politicians turned to Mr. Randolph for help and advice
(2) Mr. Randolph was becoming bored with his duties as custodian
(3) Mr. Randolph held strong opinions on every issue
(4) busy legislators often run behind schedule
(5) Mr. Randolph encouraged these kinds of questions

16. As a boy, Ellison was

(1) confident
(2) ambitious
(3) easily influenced
(4) easily amused
(5) admired

17. From the information in this passage, you can assume that Mr. Randolph

(1) knew more about Oklahoma law than many lawyers
(2) was proud of his private book collection
(3) treated the young Ellison like a son
(4) preferred custodial work to teaching school
(5) stayed after hours to read in the law library

Items 18 to 20 refer to the following excerpt from a play.

WHAT ISSUES IS WALTER STRUGGLING WITH?

Line Walter: Yeah. You see, this little liquor store we got in mind cost seventy-five thousand and we figured the initial investment on the place be 'bout thirty thousand, see.
5 That be ten thousand each. Course, there's a couple of hundred you got to pay so's you don't spend your life just waiting for them clowns to let your license get approved—
10 Ruth: You mean graft?
Walter: (*frowning impatiently*) Don't call it that. See there, that just goes to show you what women understand about the world. Baby, don't nothing happen for you in
15 this world 'less you pay somebody off!
Ruth: Walter, leave me alone! (*She raises her head and stares at him vigorously—then says, more quietly*) Eat your eggs, they gonna be cold.
20 Walter: (*straightening up from her and looking off*) That's it. There you are. Man say to his woman: I got me a dream. His woman say: Eat your eggs. (*Sadly, but gaining in power.*) Man say: I got to take hold of this
25 here world, baby! And a woman will say: Eat your eggs and go to work. (*Passionately now.*) Man say: I got to change my life, I'm choking to death, baby! And his woman say—(*In utter anguish as he brings his fists down on his thighs*)—
30 Your eggs is getting cold!
Ruth: (*softly*) Walter, that ain't none of our money.
Walter: (*not listening at all or even looking at
35 her*) This morning, I was lookin' in the mirror and thinking about it . . . I'm thirty-five years old; I been married eleven years and I got a boy who sleeps in the living room—(*Very, very quietly*)—and all
40 I got to give him is stories about how rich white people live . . .
Ruth: Eat your eggs, Walter.
Walter: Damn my eggs . . . damn all the eggs that ever was!
45 Ruth: Then go to work.
Walter: (*looking up at her*) See—I'm trying to talk to you 'bout myself—(*Shaking his head with the repetition*)—and all you can say is eat them eggs and go to work.
—From *A Raisin in the Sun* by Lorraine Hansberry

18. Walter becomes frustrated with Ruth because he believes that she

(1) is not listening to him
(2) wants to do something illegal
(3) loves their son more than him
(4) won't let him have dreams
(5) wants to leave him

19. Which of the following actions is most similar to the plan Walter proposes in lines 5-9?

(1) going to city hall to request permission to purchase a liquor license
(2) arguing with a family member over right and wrong
(3) purposely leaving a car in an illegal parking spot
(4) buying a used car with money earned at a weekend job
(5) giving someone with connections money to get good basketball seats

20. The stage directions in lines 20–30 enhance Walter's speech by revealing his

(1) financial security
(2) growing frustration
(3) emotional stability
(4) physical strength
(5) increasing happiness

> Items 21 and 22 refer to the following excerpt from a magazine article.

WHY IS STORYTELLING IMPORTANT?

Line Who tells the stories? It is a significant question. Who imagines the world for us, and how do they do it? As media critic George Gerbner notes, "Children used to grow up in a home where
5 parents told most of the stories. Today television tells most of the stories to most of the people most of the time."

When parents cease to be the primary storytellers, cease offering their children their own
10 versions of the world, a significant shift takes place. The power of describing the world passes into the hands of those who do not know the child personally and may have purposes other than the enrichment of his or her inner life. The
15 agenda of these non-parental, electronic storytellers is obvious: to sell merchandise.

This should make us ask: Whose imagination of reality are we and our kids being exposed to? Is it an imagination we can accept? Whose interest
20 does an acceptance of this world serve?
—From "Media and Values" by Michael Warren

21. Based on this passage, which of the following best states the author's main idea?

(1) TV shows today are imaginative.
(2) TV's main goal is to enrich children's lives.
(3) Telling stories is not the best way to teach children.
(4) TV is no substitute for caring parenting.
(5) Children can never watch too much TV.

22. The statement from George Gerbner in lines 4–7 is effective because it

(1) offers an opinion for the author to argue against
(2) provides statistics that support the author's beliefs
(3) causes readers to doubt their assumptions about TV
(4) symbolizes the author's own fear of TV
(5) provides support from an authority

> Items 23 and 24 refer to the following excerpt from a novel.

HOW DO KITCHENS MAKE THIS AUTHOR FEEL?

Line The place I like best in this world is the kitchen. No matter where it is, no matter what kind, if it's a kitchen, if it's a place where they make food, it's fine with me.
5 Ideally it should be well broken in. Lots of tea towels, dry and immaculate. White tile catching the light (ting! ting!)

I love even incredibly dirty kitchens to distraction—vegetable droppings all over the floor,
10 so dirty your slippers turn black on the bottom. Strangely, it's better if this kind of kitchen is large. I lean up against the silver door of a towering, giant refrigerator stocked with enough food to get through a winter. When I raise my eyes from the
15 oil-spattered gas burner and the rusty kitchen knife, outside the window stars are glittering, lonely.

Now only the kitchen and I are left. It's just a little nicer than being all alone.
20 When I'm dead worn out, in a reverie, I often think that when it comes time to die, I want to breathe my last in a kitchen. Whether it's cold and I'm all alone or somebody's there and it's warm, I'll stare death fearlessly in the eye. If it's a
25 kitchen, I'll think, "How good."
—From *Kitchen* by Banana Yoshimoto

23. "White tile catching the light (ting! ting!)" (lines 6–7)

With this statement, the narrator

(1) imagines a conversation with the reader
(2) describes how clean glassware sparkles in the light
(3) makes a joke about her silverware
(4) imagines the sound that light makes
(5) creates an image of herself cleaning the kitchen

24. Why is the image of dying in a kitchen (lines 20–25) surprising?

   (1) A kitchen is often the scene of death and violence.

   (2) The speaker does not seem at all afraid of death.

   (3) A kitchen generally symbolizes life and nourishment.

   (4) Earlier, the speaker stated she would prefer to die in bed.

   (5) A kitchen generally symbolizes rest and relaxation.

Items 25 to 27 refer to the following excerpt from a play.

HOW DOES THIS YOUNG WOMAN REACT?

Line Husband: Well, how are we today?
[*Young Woman—no response*]
Nurse: She's getting stronger!
Husband: Of course she is!
5   Nurse: [*Taking flowers*] See what your husband
      brought you.
    Husband: Better put 'em in water right away.
      [*Exit Nurse.*] Everything OK? [*Young
      Woman signs "No."*] Now see here, my
10   dear, you've got to brace up, you know!
      And—and face things! Everybody's got
      to brace up and face things! That's what
      makes the world go round. I know all
      you've been through but—[*Young
15   Woman signs "No."*] Oh, yes I do! I
      know all about it! I was right outside all
      the time! [*Young Woman makes
      violent gesture of "No." Ignoring*] Oh
      yes! But you've got to brace up now!
20   Make an effort! Pull yourself together!
      Start the uphill climb! Oh I've been
      down—but I haven't stayed down. I've
      been licked but I haven't stayed licked!
      I've pulled myself up by my own
25   bootstraps, and that's what you've got
      to do! Will power! That's what con-
      quers! Look at me! Now you've got to
      brace up! Face the music! Stand the
      gaff! Take life by the horns! Look it in
30   the face!—Having a baby's natural!
      Perfectly natural thing—why should—
      [*Young Woman chokes—points wildly
      to door. Enter Nurse with flowers in a
      vase.*]
35   Nurse: What's the matter?

Husband: She's got that gagging again—like she
      had the last time I was here. [*Young
      Woman gestures him out.*]
    Nurse: Better go, sir.
40   Husband: [*At door*] I'll be back.
[*Young Woman gasping and gesturing.*]
    Nurse: She needs rest.
    Husband: Tomorrow then. I'll be back tomor-
      row—tomorrow and every day—
45   goodbye.
        —From *Machinal* by Sophie Treadwell

25. Based on the setting of this passage and on the husband's comments, you can infer that this young woman

   (1) is resting quietly at home

   (2) has been through childbirth

   (3) is in love with her husband

   (4) will never be able to walk again

   (5) was in a serious car accident

26. The stage directions in lines 2, 8, 9, 17, and 18 show that this young woman is

   (1) upbeat and hopeful

   (2) sincere and well-intentioned

   (3) generous and noble

   (4) afraid and timid

   (5) depressed and upset

27. As the passage continues, the young woman becomes

   (1) increasingly uncertain

   (2) more dependent on her husband

   (3) more panic-stricken

   (4) increasingly ashamed

   (5) intensely serious

Items 28 to 32 refer to the following excerpt from a short story.

WHY WAS THIS LESSON MEANINGFUL?

Line I rose from my desk and walked to the window.
The light made my skin look orange, and I started
thinking about what Wickham had told us once
about light. She said that oranges and apples,
5   leaves and flowers, the whole multi-colored world,
was not what it appeared to be. The colors we
see, she said, look like they do only because of the
light or ray that shines on them. "The color of the
thing isn't what you see, but the light that's
10 reflected off it." Then she shut out the lights and
shone a white light lamp on a prism. We watched
the pale splay of colors on the projector screen;

some people ooohed and aaahed. Suddenly, she
switched on a black light and the color of
15 everything changed. The prism colors vanished,
Wickham's arms were purple, the buttons of her
dress were as orange as hot coals, rather than the
blue they had been only seconds before. We were
all very quiet. "Nothing," she said after a while,
20 "is really what it appears to be." I didn't really
understand then. But as I stood at the window,
gazing at my orange skin, I wondered what kind
of light I could shine on Marvin, Oakley, and me
that would reveal us as the same.

        —From "The Kind of Light That Shines
        on Texas" by Reginald McKnight

28. In lines 10-18, the narrator describes

  (1) a disagreement between himself and
     Wickham
  (2) a science experiment using apples
  (3) the friendship between Marvin and Oakley
  (4) a science experiment using light and color
  (5) what it is like to be in school

29. In lines 1-4, what event causes the narrator to
remember Wickham's lesson?

  (1) The light coming from the window makes
     his skin appear orange.
  (2) He has an argument with Marvin and Oakley.
  (3) Light hits a basket of apples and oranges.
  (4) He opens a picture album from school.
  (5) He goes to a reunion and sees old friends.

30. " . . . Wickham's arms were purple, the buttons of
her dress were as orange as hot coals, rather than
the blue they had been only seconds before."
(lines 16-18)

The author includes these details to show that

  (1) Wickham became very ill
  (2) the class was afraid of Wickham
  (3) heat can change the color of objects
  (4) Wickham's dress was ugly
  (5) colors can change under certain light

31. " . . . I wondered what kind of light I could shine
on Marvin, Oakley, and me that would reveal us as
the same." (lines 22-24)

From this statement, you can conclude that the
narrator

  (1) realizes that, under the skin, all people are
     the same
  (2) wants to perform an experiment with light
  (3) didn't understand the science lesson
  (4) wishes he could be better friends with
     Marvin
  (5) enjoyed Wickham's science lesson

32. Based on this passage, you can assume that
Marvin, Oakley, and the narrator probably are

  (1) from different ethnic backgrounds
  (2) first cousins
  (3) from different economic backgrounds
  (4) from similar ethnic backgrounds
  (5) best friends

Items 33 to 37 refer to the following poem.

WHAT DOES THIS SPEAKER FIND IN THE ATTIC?

Line A cat by the fireside, purring,
    But I don't stop there; I go
    through the living room and up the stairs.
    My little brother stirs in his crib.
5   My sister and I sleep in our tumbled rooms,
    and our parents sleep together,
    fingers intertwined.
    The second stairway's narrow.
    It darkens when I close the door
10 behind me. And I climb up to the attic,
    to the bustles and pantaloons
    hidden in trunks, the diaries and love-letters,
    the photographs, the rings,
    the envelopes full of hair.
15 Here's the old silverware
    Great Aunt Irene and Uncle Eric used.
    The fork is curved
    from her life-long habit
    of scraping the plate,
20 His knife is broader,
    the better for buttering bread.
    Here are the bookcases of discarded books:
    Tarzan, Zane Grey, a textbook Shakespeare,
    piles of *National Geographic, Look* and *Life*;
25 enough to last me a while.
    I sit on the dusty floor
    and open a book.
    Dream music fills the air
    like the scent of dried herbs.

        —"Herbs in the Attic" by Marilyn Waniek

33. In lines 1-7, what does the speaker describe?

  (1) her fear at being discovered
  (2) a musty attic
  (3) the family cat
  (4) a sleeping household
  (5) a haunted house

34. Which of the following does the list of objects in lines 11-14 suggest?

(1) a happy marriage
(2) the speaker's lifetime
(3) a time and people of the past
(4) the future
(5) how quickly children grow

35. Lines 15-25 imply that the speaker

(1) visits the attic often
(2) has read each of the books
(3) does not know where anything is
(4) thinks that these objects are valuable
(5) is not allowed in the attic

36. "Dream music fills the air/like the scent of dried herbs." (lines 28-29)

This figurative language is effective because it reveals

(1) how old and dusty the attic is
(2) how the speaker imagines past sounds and smells
(3) the speaker's excellent cooking skills
(4) that the speaker brought a radio with her
(5) the speaker's fear of the attic

37. With which of the following statements would the speaker be most likely to agree?

(1) Families shouldn't save old objects.
(2) Heirlooms have no emotional value.
(3) Snooping around is wrong.
(4) People's belongings are uninteresting.
(5) Every family has a rich and detailed history.

Items 38 to 42 refer to the following excerpt from a speech.

WHY IS THE WORD *NO* IMPORTANT TO THIS SPEAKER?

Line Brief, solid, affirmative as a hammer blow, this is
the virile word, which must enflame lips and save
the honor of our people, in these unfortunate days
of anachronistic imperialism. . . .

5   We do not know how to say "no," and we
are attracted, unconsciously, like a hypnotic
suggestion, by the predominant *si* of the word on
thought, of the form on essence—artists and weak
and kindly, as we have been made by the beauty

10   and generosity of our land. Never, in general
terms, does a Puerto Rican say, nor does he know
how to say "no": "We'll see," "I'll study the
matter," "I'll decide later"; when a Puerto Rican
uses these expressions, it must be understood that

15   he does not want to; at most, he joins *si* with the
no. . . .

We have to learn to say "no," raise our lips,
unburden our chest, put in tension all our vocal
muscles and all our will power to fire this *o* of *no*,

20   which will resound perhaps in America and the
world, and will resound in the heavens with more
efficacy than the rolling of cannons.
—From "No" by José De Diego

38. Based on this passage, you can infer that the speaker's heritage is

(1) African American
(2) Puerto Rican
(3) Haitian
(4) Mexican
(5) European

39. According to this speaker, in what manner does the Puerto Rican citizen say "no"?

(1) in a tone of voice that cannot be misunderstood
(2) with faith that justice will be done
(3) in a tone of voice that may offend others
(4) with expressions that might sound like "yes" to others
(5) with a firm, resounding voice that cannot be questioned

40. The speaker wishes that his people would learn to say "no" so that they might

(1) find better jobs
(2) be stricter parents
(3) save their environment
(4) help end political oppression
(5) increase their exports

41. Based on lines 8-10, the speaker believes that his homeland is

(1) cruel
(2) unattractive
(3) nurturing
(4) forgotten
(5) hopeless

42. "We have to learn to say no, . . . to fire this *o* of *no* . . . " (lines 17-19)

The speaker compares the sound of the word *no* to gunfire in order to

(1) stress that war is imminent
(2) encourage the Puerto Rican people to revolt
(3) support gun control
(4) show that he is not afraid
(5) emphasize the power of this word

Items 43 to 45 refer to the following excerpt from a newspaper article.

HOW WILL A NEW LAW AFFECT TELEVISION VIEWERS?

Line   Beginning Thursday, TV sets with screens 13 inches or larger made for sale in the USA must have closed-captioning devices.

5   While the move was hailed by advocates for the hearing impaired, the technology involved could help other viewers as well, strengthening reading skills or learning a new language.

       Currently, nearly all network prime-time TV is routinely captioned. "In terms of captioning, the
10   glass is three-quarters full," says Don Thieme of the National Captioning Institute. "Our priority is to make greater strides in cable and syndication."

       Senator Tom Harkin [Democrat from Iowa], sponsor of The Television Decoder Circuitry Act,
15   says the law brings the hearing impaired "fully into the mainstream of American life."

       L.A. Law's Richard Dysart, himself hearing impaired, says the move will "free" older Americans who "may resist getting a hearing aid
20   because of the stigma attached. We should all have the opportunity to increase the quality of our lives by hearing a little better," says Dysart.

       —From "More Closed Captions Open Communications" by Donna Gable

43. Which of the following social issues does this passage address?

  (1) the rights of the hearing impaired
  (2) the rights of all disabled people
  (3) employment rights
  (4) better representation of the hearing impaired on television
  (5) the conflict between TV executives and civil rights groups

44. Based on lines 13–16, it can be assumed that Senator Harkin

  (1) does not support closed captioning
  (2) approves of the new closed-captioning law
  (3) is a fan of Richard Dysart
  (4) is himself hearing impaired
  (5) has no interest in disabled people

45. Which of these laws would be most similar to the new closed-captioning law?

  (1) a law that restricts funding for new libraries
  (2) an act making Braille mandatory in public places
  (3) a law that increases funding for special education
  (4) an act to increase the number of public parks
  (5) a law that creates a curfew for children under age 12

MATHEMATICS

90 Minutes ❖ 56 Questions

Directions

Choose the <u>one best answer</u> to each item.

Items 1 and 2 refer to the following table.

SPORTS WAREHOUSE
Swimwear Specials

Quantity Discounts	1–9	10–19	20+
Team USA suits	$27 each	$24 each	$20 each
Slimstripe suits	$25 each	$22 each	$19 each
Solid-color suits	$22 each	$21 each	$18 each

1. The West Beach swim team plans to purchase 10 Team USA suits in July and 20 solid-color suits in September. Which of the following expressions could be used to find the team's total cost for the suits?

   (1) $20(\$18) - 10(\$24)$
   (2) $(10 + 20)(\$24 + \$18)$
   (3) $(10 + 20)(\$24)(\$18)$
   (4) $10(\$24) + 20(\$20)$
   (5) $10(\$24) + 20(\$18)$

2. Which of the following purchases would cost the least amount of money?

   (1) 11 Team USA suits
   (2) 13 Slimstripe suits
   (3) 9 Team USA suits
   (4) 11 Solid-color suits
   (5) 20 Solid-color suits

3. Ashley has a roll of velcro that is 4 meters long. How many 10-centimeter lengths can be cut from the roll?

   (1) 6
   (2) 14
   (3) 40
   (4) 100
   (5) 400

4. Which of the following is equal to 16?

   (1) 4^4
   (2) $(2 + 6)^2$
   (3) 8^2
   (4) $2^2 + 6^2$
   (5) 2^4

Items 5 and 6 refer to the following figure.

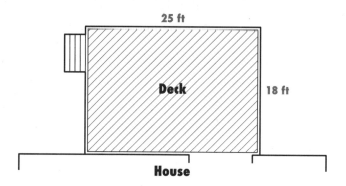

25 ft

Deck   18 ft

House

5. The Chastain family has hired a contractor to build a rectangular deck with the dimensions shown in the figure above. Which of the following expressions could be used to find the area of the deck in square feet?

(1) 2(18) + 2(25)
(2) 2(18)(25)
(3) 18 + 18 + 25 + 25
(4) 18(25)
(5) ½(18)(25)

6. The contractor budgets $200 to hire a painter to waterproof the deck. The painter charges $22.50 per hour. If the painter finishes the job in 5 hours, how much less than the estimate does the waterproofing job cost?

(1) $8.89
(2) $40.00
(3) $87.50
(4) $112.50
(5) $160.00

7. A factory pays $1,536 per 24-hour day for electrical power. Which of the following expressions could be used to find the factory's cost for 2 hours of electrical power?

(1) $\dfrac{2(1,536)}{24}$

(2) $\dfrac{1,536}{2(24)}$

(3) $\dfrac{12(1,536)}{24}$

(4) $\dfrac{24(1,536)}{2}$

(5) $\dfrac{24(2)}{1,536}$

Item 8 refers to the following diagram.

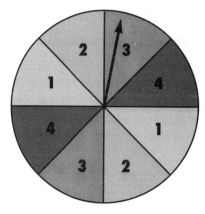

8. A spinner is divided into eight equal sections and numbered as shown. What is the probability of the pointer stopping on a number less than 3?

(1) $\dfrac{1}{1}$

(2) $\dfrac{1}{2}$

(3) $\dfrac{1}{3}$

(4) $\dfrac{1}{4}$

(5) Not enough information is given.

Item 9 refers to the following diagram.

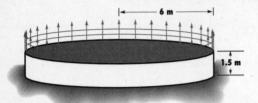

9. The Lincoln Children's Hospital recently added a circular goldfish pond for their young patients. The pond has a radius of 6 meters. The hospital decides to install an iron railing around the outside of the pond. About how many meters of railing will they need?

(1) 19
(2) 28
(3) 38
(4) 113
(5) Not enough information is given.

Items 10 and 11 refer to the following graph.

SNACK SHOP INVENTORY
Breakdown According to Dollar Value
August 31, 19__

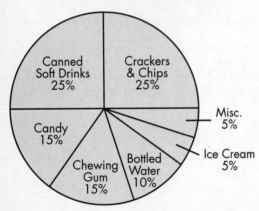

10. What percent of the dollar value of the snack shop's inventory does not come from ice cream, candy, and chewing gum?

(1) 25%
(2) 35%
(3) 45%
(4) 65%
(5) 85%

11. If the Snack Shop's total inventory is worth $3,400, which of the following expressions could be used to find the dollar value of the bottled water and canned soft drinks?

(1) $\dfrac{(10 + 25)(\$3,400)}{100}$

(2) $(0.10)(0.25)(\$3,400)$

(3) $\dfrac{(10)(25)(\$3,400)}{100}$

(4) $\dfrac{10 + 25 + \$3,400}{100}$

(5) $\dfrac{\$3,400}{(0.10 + 0.25)}$

12. The manager of a music store decides to reduce the price of an acoustic guitar by 35%. The original price of the guitar is $710. What is the sale price of the guitar?

(1) $685.15
(2) $675.00
(3) $461.50
(4) $248.50
(5) Not enough information is given.

Item 13 refers to the following diagram.

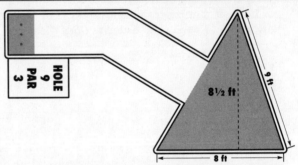

13. The owner of King Tut Putt, a miniature golf course, needs to replace the triangular piece of artificial turf on Hole #9 (the shaded portion in the diagram). Which of the following expressions could be used to find how many square feet of turf she will need to repair the hole?

(1) ½(8)(8½)
(2) 8 + 8 + 8½
(3) 2(8) + 2(8½)
(4) 8²
(5) (3.14)(8½)

14. After making a $1,000 down payment, Mavis wants to finance the remaining $9,600 on the purchase price of a new car. She will borrow the money for five years at an annual interest rate of 10%. How much will she pay in interest on the loan?

(1) $1,920
(2) $2,120
(3) $4,800
(4) $5,280
(5) $5,300

15. What is the value of $\dfrac{m^2 - n^2}{n}$ when $m = 4$ and $n = -2$?

(1) -2
(2) -3
(3) -4
(4) -6
(5) -10

Items 16 and 17 refer to the following diagram.

16. Main Street is perpendicular to State Boulevard. Riverside Drive is parallel to Parkview Road. Using the distances shown on the map, what is the distance to the nearest yard from the corner of State and Main to the corner of State and Parkview?

(1) 225
(2) 356
(3) 375
(4) 392
(5) 633

17. Which of the following expressions could be used to find the distance (c) from the corner of Main and Riverside to the corner of State and Riverside?

(1) $c^2 = 300^2 + 400^2$
(2) $c^2 = \sqrt{300 + 400}$
(3) $c^2 = (300 + 400)^2$
(4) $c = 300^2 + 400^2$
(5) $c = \sqrt{(300 + 400)^2}$

18. Cathy is six years younger than twice the age of her sister Robin. Robin is two years younger than her brother Brad. The total of their ages is 84. If x represents Brad's age, which of the following expressions could be used to represent Cathy's age?

(1) $2(x - 2) - 6$
(2) $2(x - 2 - 6)$
(3) $2x - 6$
(4) $2(x - 2) + 6$
(5) $2(x - 2)$

Item 19 refers to the following diagram.

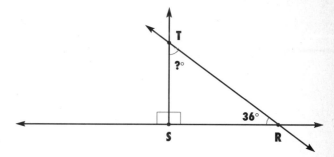

19. Line TR intersects lines ST and SR forming a triangle. If $\angle SRT$ measures 36°, what is the measure of $\angle STR$?

(1) 36°
(2) 54°
(3) 90°
(4) 126°
(5) 144°

Item 20 refers to the following table.

Dental Service	Time Required for Service
Adult Cleaning	¾ hour
Pediatric Cleaning	½ hour
Fluoride Treatment	¼ hour
Single-Surface Filling	⅓ hour
Multi-Surface Filling	½ hour
Crown	1¼ hour

20. Dr. Colleen Roberts performs two crown procedures immediately after lunch and then an adult cleaning. In the time remaining in her 4-hour afternoon schedule, which of the following procedures could she complete?

  (1) A fluoride treatment and a crown
  (2) Two multi-surface fillings
  (3) Two pediatric cleanings
  (4) An adult cleaning and a fluoride treatment
  (5) Two single-surface fillings

Items 21 and 22 refer to the following information.

David drove a moving van from Salt Lake City to Washington, D.C. His mileage figures for the five days of his trip are given in the following table.

Day	Distance
First	380 miles
Second	464 miles
Third	494 miles
Fourth	415 miles
Fifth	297 miles

21. If David drove an average of 11 miles per gallon of gasoline, approximately how many gallons of gasoline did David use on the last three days of his trip?

  (1) 33
  (2) 110
  (3) 362
  (4) 402
  (5) 1,206

22. What was the average distance in miles that David drove per day?

  (1) 396
  (2) 410
  (3) 415
  (4) 479
  (5) Not enough information is given.

23. To ship its products, a computer keyboard manufacturer wants to purchase rectangular boxes that are 2 feet wide and 3 feet long. The boxes must contain at least 15 cubic feet of space. What must be the minimum height of the box?

  (1) 2½ feet
  (2) 4½ feet
  (3) 6 feet
  (4) 9 feet
  (5) Not enough information is given.

24. A sculptor who is 6 feet tall casts a shadow 4 feet in length. At the same time, a sculpture's shadow is 20 feet in length. Which of the following is a true statement about the height of the sculpture?

  (1) The height of the sculpture cannot be calculated using the information given.
  (2) The width of the sculpture must be greater than its height.
  (3) The sculpture's height is five times the height of the sculptor.
  (4) The sculpture's height cannot be greater than the length of its shadow.
  (5) The height of the sculpture must be at least ten times the height of the sculptor.

25. The area of a square is nearly 1,500 square inches. Approximately what is the measure in inches of each side of the square?

  (1) Between 25 and 30
  (2) Between 30 and 35
  (3) Between 35 and 40
  (4) Between 40 and 45
  (5) Between 45 and 50

26. A color cartridge for the XT-100 inkjet printer is $5 more than twice the price of a black ink cartridge. If you can buy both cartridges for a total of $43.25, what is the cost of the color cartridge?

  (1) $8.25
  (2) $12.75
  (3) $22.30
  (4) $30.50
  (5) $38.75

27. At Hattie's Fabric Store, lace is sold by the yard. If Michelle spent $14.25 on lace that costs $3 per yard, how many yards of lace did she buy?

    (1) 3
    (2) 3½
    (3) 4¾
    (4) 42¾
    (5) Not enough information is given.

Item 28 refers to the following diagram.

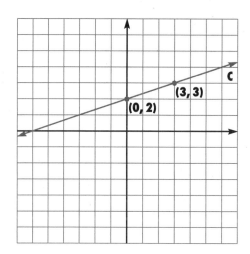

28. What is the slope of Line C?

    (1) $\dfrac{3}{1}$

    (2) $\dfrac{1}{3}$

    (3) $-\dfrac{1}{3}$

    (4) $-\dfrac{3}{1}$

    (5) Not enough information is given.

29. If a truck averages 10 kilometers per liter of gasoline, how many kilometers will the truck drive on a full tank of gas?

    (1) 40
    (2) 80
    (3) 110
    (4) 300
    (5) Not enough information is given.

30. Ms. Clark is making matching dressses for her twin daughters. Each dress requires 45 inches of lace trim. How many yards of lace should she buy?

    (1) 1¼
    (2) 2½
    (3) 3¾
    (4) 7½
    (5) Not enough information is given.

31. Ace Glassware recently began to manufacture two sizes of boxes to package its products. Both boxes are cube shaped. The smaller one measures 6 centimeters on each side. The larger one measures 10 centimeters on each side. How many cubic centimeters greater in volume is the larger box than the smaller one?

    (1) 784
    (2) 256
    (3) 216
    (4) 64
    (5) Not enough information is given.

Items 32 and 33 refer to the following diagram.

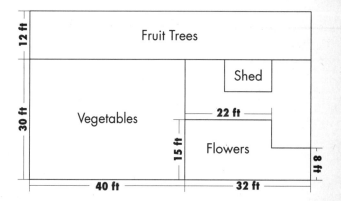

A civic group in Wasatch City has decided to turn an abandoned lot into a community garden. Their plan is shown in the figure above.

32. A local business offers to donate fencing for the garden. How many feet of fencing will they need to fence in the entire lot?

    (1) 84
    (2) 114
    (3) 144
    (4) 228
    (5) 3,024

33. The civic group decides to plant fruit trees in one area of the garden. Each tree will need 36 square feet of room. Which expression can be used to find out how many fruit trees can be planted in the area set aside for trees on the diagram?

(1) $2(72) + 2(12)$

(2) $\dfrac{(2)72 + 2(36)}{12}$

(3) $\dfrac{72 + 12}{36}$

(4) $12(72)(36)$

(5) $\dfrac{12(72)}{36}$

Items 34 and 35 refer to the following information.

The Far West Tent Company has a variety of tent sizes for different camping needs. The most popular models are shown below.

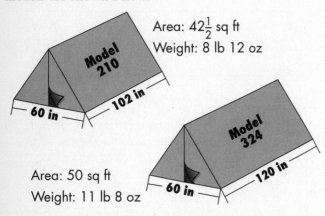

Model 210 — Area: $42\frac{1}{2}$ sq ft — Weight: 8 lb 12 oz — 60 in — 102 in

Model 324 — Area: 50 sq ft — Weight: 11 lb 8 oz — 60 in — 120 in

34. Both tents have the same width, but they differ in length. How much longer is Model 324 than the smaller tent?

(1) 2 ft 8 in
(2) 1 ft 8 in
(3) 1 ft 6 in
(4) 1 ft
(5) Not enough information is given.

35. How much less does the smaller tent weigh than the larger one?

(1) 2 lb 06 oz
(2) 2 lb 12 oz
(3) 3 lb 04 oz
(4) 3 lb 06 oz
(5) 3 lb 12 oz

Item 36 refers to the following information.

Radio Station KORB is donating plastic water bottles for a marathon. The Everpure Water Company will donate the drinking water to fill the 1-liter bottles.

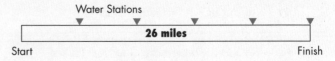

Water Stations

26 miles

Start   Finish

36. The radio station plans to have tables set up in 5 locations equally spaced along the 26-mile race course. Approximately how many miles will there be between water stations?

(1) Between 2 and 3 miles
(2) Between 3 and 4 miles
(3) Between 4 and 5 miles
(4) Between 5 and 6 miles
(5) Not enough information is given.

Items 37 to 39 refer to the following graph.

AVERAGE TICKET PRICES FOR ENTERTAINMENT EVENTS

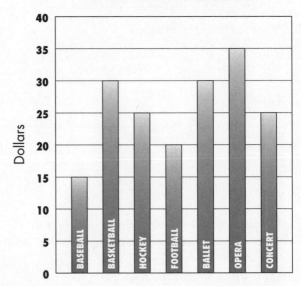

37. The average cost of a baseball ticket is what fraction of the average cost of a football ticket?

(1) ⅓
(2) ½
(3) ¾
(4) 1½
(5) 1¾

38. Approximately what is the mean price of a ticket to the entertainment events shown on the graph?

(1) $15
(2) $19
(3) $22
(4) $26
(5) $31

39. A family of four wants to buy tickets to a concert and a basketball game. Which of the following expressions can be used to find out how much the family will spend on tickets for the two events?

(1) $\dfrac{\$30 + \$25}{4}$

(2) $4(\$30)(\$25)$

(3) $\dfrac{\$30(\$25)}{4}$

(4) $4(\$30 - \$25)$

(5) $4(\$30 + \$25)$

Items 40 to 42 refer to the following information.

Julius works as an office assistant at a large real estate firm. Recently he made a graph showing his hourly wage for the years 1988 through 1994.

OFFICE ASSISTANT WAGES

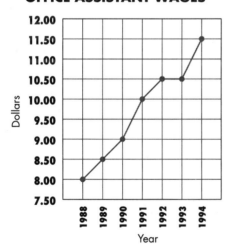

40. If Julius worked 2,080 hours in 1993, what was his annual salary for that year?

(1) $18,720
(2) $19,760
(3) $20,800
(4) $21,840
(5) $23,920

41. At the beginning of which two years did Julius receive a $1 per hour raise?

(1) 1991 and 1994
(2) 1993 and 1994
(3) 1990 and 1992
(4) 1989 and 1990
(5) Not enough information is given.

42. What percent raise did Julius receive at the beginning of 1992?

(1) 5%
(2) 10%
(3) 25%
(4) 50%
(5) 100%

43. Kevin and Kyle are playing a board game. To advance, a player rolls a six-sided die. The sides of the die are marked with color dots. Two sides are red, two are green, and two are black. On any given turn, what is the probability that a player will roll either red or green?

(1) ⅙
(2) ⅓
(3) ½
(4) ⅔
(5) Not enough information is given.

44. The Downtown Car Wash uses approximately 50,000 gallons of water daily. Of the total daily water usage, 93% is recycled and reused. How many gallons of the water used daily are not recycled?

(1) 538
(2) 3,500
(3) 5,376
(4) 46,500
(5) 71,429

45. Between the hours of 6 a.m. and 12 noon, 38,000 cars cross the Hammett River Toll Bridge. During these hours, 5 out of every 8 cars are traveling south. How many cars travel north between 6 a.m. and 12 noon?

(1) 4,750
(2) 7,600
(3) 14,250
(4) 23,750
(5) Not enough information is given.

46. Wilt Chamberlain's 1961–62 year yielded the highest points per game average of his career. He played in 80 games and scored a total of 4,029 points. What were his average points per game for the 1961–62 season to the nearest tenth?

(1) 19.6
(2) 40.3
(3) 50.4
(4) 80.0
(5) Not enough information is given.

47. At the end of October, Maggie figures out that 38 of the 180 school days have gone by. Approximately what fraction of the school year is over?

(1) ⅛
(2) ⅙
(3) ⅕
(4) ⅓
(5) ⅖

48. Using satellite photography, geologists have determined that the Channel Islands off the coast of California are moving along earthquake faults at the rate of 4.5 millimeters a year. If motion continues at this rate, how many millimeters will the islands move in 25 years?

(1) 5.5
(2) 11.25
(3) 20.5
(4) 29.5
(5) 112.5

49. Keith and Bernard assemble bicycle parts. Together they assembled 65 parts in one hour. Bernard assembled 9 more parts than Keith. How many parts did Bernard assemble?

(1) 28
(2) 37
(3) 56
(4) 74
(5) Not enough information is given.

50. Three consecutive numbers total 51. Which of the following equations could be used to find the three numbers?

(1) $3x = 51$
(2) $3x = \dfrac{51}{3}$
(3) $x + x + x = 51$
(4) $3(x + x + x) = 51$
(5) $x + (x + 1) + (x + 2) = 51$

51. A zoo ticket for an adult costs twice the price of a child's ticket. A senior ticket is $2 less than the price of an adult's ticket. If the Williams family spends $34 on tickets for two adults, six children, and one senior, what is the cost of a child's ticket?

(1) $1.50
(2) $3.00
(3) $4.00
(4) $6.00
(5) Not enough information is given.

52. Which of the following is true for
$5a - 2 \geq 6(4 - 1)$?

(1) $a > 4$
(2) $a < 3$
(3) $a > 5$
(4) $a \geq 1$
(5) $a \geq 4$

Item 53 refers to the following graph.

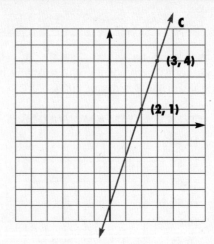

53. Line C is a graph of which of the following equations?

(1) $3y = x - 8$
(2) $y = 3x + 2$
(3) $y = 3x - 5$
(4) $2y = x - 1$
(5) $y = 2x + 4$

54. Katarina is retiling her kitchen floor. She is putting a circular design in the center that measures 6 feet in diameter. What is the area of the tile circle to the nearest square foot?

(1) 28
(2) 31
(3) 38
(4) 57
(5) Not enough information is given.

Items 55 and 56 refer to the following figure.

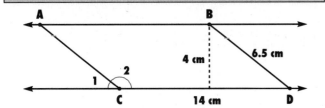

55. Lines *AB* and *CD* are parallel. Segments *AC* and *BD* are parallel. The distance from *C* to *D* measures 14 centimeters. What is the area of the parallelogram in square centimeters?

(1) 91
(2) 56
(3) 52
(4) 26
(5) 24.5

56. Angle 1 measures 40°. What is the measure of $\angle 2$?

(1) 20°
(2) 50°
(3) 80°
(4) 140°
(5) 320°

QUICK-SCORE ANSWERS

ANSWERS TO POSTTESTS 1-5

WRITING SKILLS

Part I

1. 2	40. 5
2. 4	41. 4
3. 5	42. 4
4. 2	43. 5
5. 3	44. 2
6. 5	45. 4
7. 4	46. 2
8. 2	47. 4
9. 3	48. 3
10. 4	49. 3
11. 5	50. 4
12. 4	51. 4
13. 2	52. 4
14. 1	53. 2
15. 5	54. 3
16. 5	55. 4
17. 4	
18. 5	**Part II**
19. 2	Turn to
20. 5	page 453.
21. 3	
22. 4	
23. 2	
24. 4	
25. 3	
26. 3	
27. 5	
28. 2	
29. 5	
30. 3	
31. 2	
32. 4	
33. 5	
34. 2	
35. 4	
36. 3	
37. 4	
38. 3	
39. 1	

SOCIAL STUDIES

1. 2	33. 4
2. 1	34. 5
3. 4	35. 2
4. 3	36. 3
5. 2	37. 3
6. 4	38. 1
7. 5	39. 3
8. 5	40. 5
9. 3	41. 4
10. 5	42. 3
11. 1	43. 3
12. 2	44. 3
13. 2	45. 2
14. 3	46. 4
15. 4	47. 5
16. 4	48. 2
17. 2	49. 1
18. 3	50. 2
19. 3	51. 5
20. 1	52. 1
21. 3	53. 4
22. 5	54. 3
23. 3	55. 2
24. 1	56. 2
25. 4	57. 3
26. 1	58. 4
27. 3	59. 5
28. 2	60. 2
29. 2	61. 4
30. 2	62. 3
31. 2	63. 3
32. 1	64. 1

SCIENCE

1. 2	34. 3
2. 5	35. 1
3. 3	36. 4
4. 4	37. 1
5. 5	38. 2
6. 1	39. 5
7. 1	40. 5
8. 2	41. 3
9. 1	42. 4
10. 5	43. 1
11. 2	44. 4
12. 4	45. 1
13. 3	46. 2
14. 1	47. 2
15. 1	48. 4
16. 4	49. 3
17. 1	50. 1
18. 2	51. 3
19. 1	52. 4
20. 2	53. 3
21. 1	54. 5
22. 3	55. 2
23. 5	56. 3
24. 4	57. 4
25. 4	58. 5
26. 5	59. 3
27. 3	60. 4
28. 2	61. 2
29. 3	62. 5
30. 2	63. 5
31. 1	64. 5
32. 3	65. 1
33. 2	66. 3

LITERATURE AND THE ARTS

1. 2	24. 3
2. 4	25. 2
3. 5	26. 5
4. 1	27. 3
5. 5	28. 4
6. 1	29. 1
7. 5	30. 5
8. 4	31. 1
9. 2	32. 1
10. 4	33. 4
11. 5	34. 3
12. 5	35. 1
13. 2	36. 2
14. 4	37. 5
15. 1	38. 2
16. 3	39. 4
17. 1	40. 4
18. 4	41. 3
19. 5	42. 5
20. 2	43. 1
21. 4	44. 2
22. 5	45. 2
23. 4	

MATHEMATICS

1. 5	29. 5
2. 4	30. 2
3. 3	31. 1
4. 5	32. 4
5. 4	33. 5
6. 3	34. 3
7. 1	35. 2
8. 2	36. 4
9. 3	37. 3
10. 4	38. 4
11. 1	39. 5
12. 3	40. 4
13. 1	41. 1
14. 3	42. 1
15. 4	43. 4
16. 5	44. 2
17. 1	45. 3
18. 1	46. 3
19. 2	47. 3
20. 5	48. 5
21. 2	49. 2
22. 2	50. 5
23. 1	51. 2
24. 3	52. 5
25. 3	53. 3
26. 4	54. 1
27. 3	55. 2
28. 2	56. 4

Answers and Explanations
POSTTESTS

Posttest 1: Writing Skills
PART I

1. **The correct answer is (2): change worlds to world's** Choice (2) uses an apostrophe to show possession. Choice (1) capitalizes a general word; choice (3) introduces a spelling error; choice (4) inserts an unneeded comma, which separates the subject from its verb; and choice (5) creates a sentence fragment.

2. **The correct answer is (4): underground trains, called subways, are powered** Choice (4) uses commas to set off an interrupting element. Choice (1) omits the commas, choice (2) uses an incorrect verb form for the past participle, choice (3) omits one of the required commas, and choice (5) lacks subject-verb agreement.

3. **The correct answer is (5): no correction is necessary**

4. **The correct answer is (2): insert a comma after drive** Choice (2) places a comma between items in a series of three. Choice (1) deletes the comma between items in the series, choice (3) incorrectly places a comma after the last item in the series, and choice (4) introduces a spelling error.

5. **The correct answer is (3): increases** Choice (3) captures the meaning of the original sentence: the building of a subway temporarily increases traffic above ground. The other choices change the meaning of the sentence.

6. **The correct answer is (5): above ground, but these visible light-rail systems** Choice (5) uses an appropriate connecting word to show the proper relationship between the independent clauses in this compound sentence. The other choices change the meaning of the sentence.

7. **The correct answer is (4): change the spelling of quiet to quite** Choice (4) correctly spells the intended word and maintains the sentence's meaning. Choice (1) places a comma in the middle of the dependent clause, choice (2) removes the comma required after the dependent clause, choice (3) shifts to the past tense, and choice (5) introduces a spelling error.

8. **The correct answer is (2): change the spelling of availeable to available** Choice (2) does not add an *e* before adding a suffix to *avail*. Choice (1) uses the wrong sound-alike word, there is no need for the comma in choice (3), choice (4) uses the wrong sound-alike word, and choice (5) introduces a spelling error.

9. **The correct answer is (3): technology promises treatment** Choice (3) corrects the error in subject-verb agreement. Choice (1) lacks subject-verb agreement, choice (2) shifts to the past tense, choice (4) incorrectly inserts a comma between the subject and its verb, and choice (5) creates sentence fragments.

10. **The correct answer is (4): harming** Choice (4) accurately introduces the rest of the sentence (harming the surrounding area).

11. **The correct answer is (5): change is to are** Choice (5) uses a plural verb, *are*, to agree with the singular plural subject, *neither fillings nor root canals*. Choice (1) omits the comma after an introductory phrase, choice (2) introduces a spelling error, choice (3) incorrectly inserts a comma between the subject and its verb, and choice (4) uses part of the infinitive alone as a verb.

12. **The correct answer is (4): change killed to kills** Choice (4) maintains the present tense. Choice (1) lacks subject-verb agreement, choice (2) shifts to the past tense, and choices (3) and (5) use the present participle alone as a verb.

13. **The correct answer is (2): change the spelling of wieght to weight** Choice (2) obeys the rule for words in which *ei* sounds like *a*. Choice (1) capitalizes a general word, choice (3) places a comma after the conjunction in a series, choice (4) uses the wrong sound-alike word, and choice (5) adds a letter to a prefix.

14. **The correct answer is (1): change appear to appears** Choice (1) uses a singular verb to agree with the singular subject (it). Choice (2) uses part of the infinitive as a verb, choice (3) uses a comma to separate the verbs in a compound verb, and choice (4) uses the wrong verb form for the present participle.

15. **The correct answer is (5): This change in eating habits worries physicians, who warn** Choice (5) is the only choice that does not use a pronoun with an unclear antecedent.

16. **The correct answer is (5): change saw to sees** Choice (5) keeps the verb in the present tense and maintains tense consistency throughout the paragraph. There is no need for the comma in choice (1), choices (2) and (3) omit commas that set off an interrupting element, and choice (4) capitalizes a general term.

17. **The correct answer is (4): solve the problem. Others advocate** Choice (4) corrects the run-on sentence by making two separate sentences. Choice (1) is a run-on, choice (2) is incorrect because a comma without a connecting word between two independent clauses still results in a run-on, choice (3) changes the meaning of the sentence, and choice (5) uses an inappropriate connecting word.

18. **The correct answer is (5): to curb violence is to stop watching** Choice (5) uses the correct verb form for the infinitive. The other choices have incorrect infinitives.

19. **The correct answer is (2): change advertise to advertised** Choice (2) uses the correct verb form for the past participle. Choice (1) uses a present participle alone as a verb, choice (3) omits the comma that follows a dependent clause, choice (4) uses the wrong sound-alike word, and choice (5) shifts to the past tense.

20. **The correct answer is (5): change the spelling of there to their** Choice (5) correctly uses the possessive *their*. Choice (1) fails to capitalize the name of a historical era, choice (2) omits the comma after an introductory phrase, choice (3) deletes a necessary comma, and choice (4) introduces a spelling error.

21. **The correct answer is (3): who had made fortunes in the stock market lost** Choice (3) uses the correct relative pronoun for antecedents that refer to people. Choices (1), (4), and (5) use the wrong relative pronoun for people, and choice (2) uses the wrong form of the pronoun for its role in the clause.

22. **The correct answer is (4): change great plains to Great Plains** Choice (4) capitalizes the name of a place. Choice (1) capitalizes a general word, there is no need for the comma in choice (2), choice (3) uses the wrong verb form for the past participle, and choice (5) shifts the tense to the present.

23. **The correct answer is (2): John** Choice (2) supplies the only word that logically refers back to the pronoun *his* in the introductory phrase.

24. **The correct answer is (4): State and local officials also abuse** Choice (4) maintains present tense and is consistent with the rest of the paragraph. The other choices do not correct the shift in tense. Choices (2) and (3) also insert unneeded commas.

25. **The correct answer is (3): the part of politicians who claim** Choice (3) corrects the sentence fragment by attaching it to the rest of the sentence. Choice (1) maintains the fragment, choice (2) uses the participle instead of the proper verb form, choice (4) lacks subject-verb agreement, and choice (5) inserts an unneeded comma.

26. **The correct answer is (3): law and order; nevertheless, many of them break** Choice (3) uses the correct punctuation with the connecting word nevertheless in a compound sentence. The other choices use incorrect punctuation.

27. **The correct answer is (5): Newspapers and television, especially, try** Choice (5) is the only one that uses commas to set off interrupting material. Choice (4) also lacks subject-verb agreement.

28. **The correct answer is (2): reporters** Choice (2) is the only choice that maintains the meaning of the original sentence.

29. **The correct answer is (5): diets to** When the modifier follows the main clause, there is no comma. The other choices use incorrect punctuation.

30. **The correct answer is (3): and consumers are concerned about the high prices** Choice (3) is the only choice that corrects the faulty parallel structure.

31. **The correct answer is (2): cooking without fat** Choice (2) is the only choice that corrects the faulty parallel structure.

32. **The correct answer is (4): replace so with yet** Choice (4) supplies the appropriate connecting word. Choice (1) creates a fragment. The other choices don't correct the connector.

33. **The correct answer is (5): remove the comma before and** Choice (5) corrects the unnecessary separation of two clauses. Choices (1) and (2) create fragments. Choices (3) and (4) use inappropriate connecting words.

34. **The correct answer is (2): under** Choice (2) rightly places the modifier next to the word it modifies. The other choices make no sense.

35. **The correct answer is (4): When children become ill** Choice (4) turns the modifier into a dependent clause and clarifies the sentence. The other choices don't correct the dangling modifier.

36. **The correct answer is (3): hospitalized, between** Choice (3) connects the dependent clause to the main clause with a comma to correct the fragment. The other choices don't correct the fragment or are not correctly punctuated.

37. **The correct answer is (4): change their lungs will get other diseases to other lung diseases** Choice (4) maintains parallel structure, unlike choice (5). Choice (1) creates a fragment. Choices (2) and (3) don't make sense.

38. **The correct answer is (3): employers to take steps to protect workers** Choice (3) maintains parallel structure. Choices (1), (2), and (5) don't. Choice (4) changes the meaning of the sentence.

39. **The correct answer is (1): replace Instead of being with It shouldn't be** Choice (1) provides a subject and verb to turn the fragment into a complete sentence. Choices (2) and (4) change the meaning of the sentence. Choices (3) and (5) don't correct the fragment.

40. **The correct answer is (5): no correction is necessary**

41. **The correct answer is (4): replace who with that** Choice (4) uses a pronoun that agrees with a nonhuman antecedent. Choice (1) shifts to a singular pronoun, choice (2) shifts to first person, choice (3) uses a relative pronoun that assumes a human antecedent, and choice (5) creates a fragment.

42. **The correct answer is (4): the companies** Choice (4) corrects the fragment and uses a clear subject. Choices (1) and (5) use verb forms inappropriately. Choice (2) shifts from third to second person, and choice (3) makes an unclear pronoun reference.

43. **The correct answer is (5): change will understand to understands** Choice (5) uses the present tense, which is consistent throughout the paragraph. Choice (1) changes an indefinite pronoun (*it*) to a third-person pronoun (*they*), choice (2) uses a pronoun without an antecedent, choice (3) uses a plural pronoun for a singular antecedent, and choice (4) lacks subject-verb agreement.

44. **The correct answer is (2): they and their cars** Choice (2) uses third-person pronouns to agree with the antecedent *teenagers*. Choice (1) shifts to second person; choices (3), (4), and (5) change the meaning of the sentence.

45. **The correct answer is (4): change increases to increased** Choice (4) uses the past tense, which is consistent throughout the paragraph. Choice (1) shifts to future tense, choice (2) uses a verb phrase to shift tense, choice (3) lacks subject-verb agreement, and choice (5) uses a participle as a verb.

46. **The correct answer is (2): helped** Choice (2) uses a past-tense verb that is consistent with the rest of the sentence and the paragraph. Choice (1) shifts to present tense; choice (3) shifts to future tense; choice (4) is an adjective, not a verb; and choice (5) uses a participle as a verb.

47. **The correct answer is (4): change use to used** Choice (4) uses the correct past participle for use. Choice (1) uses a pronoun that assumes a human antecedent, choice (2) shifts to future tense, choice (3) incorrectly uses *be* as a verb, and choice (5) uses a present participle as a verb.

48. **The correct answer is (3): Expansion of rail lines** Choice (3) gives the sentence a clear subject. The other choices use pronouns that don't have clear antecedents.

49. **The correct answer is (3): change the spelling of Government to government** Choice (3) is correct because there is no reason to capitalize government when it is a general term. Choices (1) and (2) are misspellings, and there's no reason for the comma in choice (4).

50. **The correct answer is (4): Today's workers face substantial risks from** Choice (4) adds an *s* to risk to make it plural. The other choices add *es*, and choice (2) also incorrectly spells *workers*. Choice (3) separates a subject from its verb, using a comma. Choice (5) shifts to the past tense.

51. **The correct answer is (4): insert a comma after firefighters** Choice (4) places a comma after the last item in a series. Choice (1) misspells a word, choices (2) and (3) omit commas in a series, and choice (5) omits the apostrophe in a contraction.

52. **The correct answer is (4): computers, for example, can** Choice (4) uses commas to set off an interrupting element. Choice (1) has no commas, choice (2) creates a fragment, and choices (3) and (5) use only one comma to set off an interrupter.

53. **The correct answer is (2): remove the comma after eyestrain** Choice (2) removes a comma that separates a subject from its verb. Choice (1) misspells a word, choice (3) lacks subject-verb agreement, and choices (4) and (5) use the wrong sound-alike word.

54. **The correct answer is (3): growing science that addresses these issues** Choice (3) spells *science* correctly. Choice (1) misspells *science*, choice (2) lacks subject-verb agreement, and choices (4) and (5) use incorrect relative pronouns.

55. **The correct answer is (4): work environment, including** Choice (4) spells *environment* correctly. Choice (2) misspells it, choice (3) continues to misspell *environment*, and choice (5) also misspells *including*.

PART II

The scoring information below will help you estimate a score for your essay. If you can, ask an instructor to read and score your essay. To help you decide which skills you need to work on, make a list of its strengths and weaknesses based on the checklist below.

With 6 as the top score and 1 as the bottom, rank your essay for each item in the checklist. Put a check in the box that you think reflects the quality of that particular part of your essay.

Does My Essay . . .	1	2	3	4	5	6
discuss the topic?						
have a clear, controlling idea that is developed throughout?						
have a clear structure (introduction, body, conclusion)?						
tell the reader in the introduction what the topic is and what I am going to say about it?						
use details and examples to support each point?						
sum up the essay in the conclusion?						
have few or no errors in sentence structure, usage, or punctuation?						

Posttest 2: Social Studies

1. **The correct answer is (2): (Application)** The greatest percent change in inflation was a decrease of approximately 7.5 percent from 1981 to 1983, making choice (2) the best answer.

2. **The correct answer is (1): (Analysis)** A low rate of growth often means that employers are not expanding their businesses and therefore not hiring additional employees, and the employers may actually be laying off some workers in response to sluggish sales.

3. **The correct answer is (4): (Application)** The greatest decrease—about 5 percent—was from 1988 to 1991.

4. **The correct answer is (3): (Evaluation)** The best time to look for a job would be when the economy was growing (so that businesses might be in need of additional workers), unemployment was falling (so that there would be fewer available workers for employers to choose from), and inflation was falling (so that businesses would not be afraid of future monetary problems).

5. **The correct answer is (2): (Analysis)** Falling inflation is good for both business and employment because business can better predict the costs of its materials and supplies and people have a consistent amount of money to spend. Choice (4) was an effect, not a cause, of economic growth. Choices (1), (3), and (5) represent factors not included in the graph.

6. **The correct answer is (4): (Comprehension)** All of the choices describe the effects of the Mount Pinatubo eruption, but only choice (4) describes an effect that touched the whole world.

7. **The correct answer is (5): (Application)** Because the effects of the 1991 eruption are expected to last for a decade, avalanches are predicted until at least the year 2001.

8. **The correct answer is (5): (Analysis)** The safest plan would be to move people out of the danger zone. Planting grasses and crops (choice 1) is often a good long-term solution to prevent mudslides on slopes, but plants are not likely to grow in volcanic ash. Meanwhile, the destructive slides would continue. Choices (2), (3), and (4) are not reasonable options.

9. **The correct answer is (3): (Evaluation)** Because most of those who were displaced were farmers from small towns and villages, the creation of highways and tall buildings clearly did not help them regain what they had lost.

10. **The correct answer is (5): (Comprehension)** The passage states that deadly gases and falling ash were the elements that killed the most people.

11. **The correct answer is (1): (Evaluation)** The major emphasis in the passage is on the importance of the archaeological discovery, so choice (1) is correct.

12. **The correct answer is (2): (Analysis)** The reference to ''King'' links the graveyard to colonial times, when most residents of New York were subjects of the King of England.

13. **The correct answer is (2): (Evaluation)** Because medical care and nutrition greatly affect the span of life and because many fewer than half of all newborns and young children die today in the United States, it can be surmised that today's levels of medical care and nutrition are superior to those of the 1700s.

14. **The correct answer is (3): (Application)** The power of the judicial system to review the constitutionality of laws is the principle of American government to which the cartoon refers.

15. **The correct answer is (4): (Evaluation)** This independence has led some justices, including some of the most famous, to follow their consciences, regardless of previous tilts toward liberal or conservative platforms.

16. **The correct answer is (4): (Comprehension)** The chart lists numbers of visits in thousands, and 26,630 times 1,000 equals 26.63 million.

17. **The correct answer is (2): (Evaluation)** The twentieth century has seen a great improvement in transportation systems worldwide. In addition, a shortened work week and more work-saving machines for both the home and the factory have led to an increase in leisure time. These two factors have allowed Americans to take more vacations and to visit national parks more frequently.

18. **The correct answer is (3): (Comprehension)** The smallest number of increased visits was 801,000, which occurred between 1910 and 1920.

19. **The correct answer is (3): (Analysis)** The belief in the preservation of valuable sites in America has contributed to the increase in the numbers of national parks, historic sites, battlefields, and monuments.

20. **The correct answer is (1): (Comprehension)** In the year 2050, the largest group will be females (white women and black women combined).

21. **The correct answer is (3): (Comprehension)** According to the chart, the number of white females will decrease from 112.7 million to 108.7 million, a difference of exactly 4 million.

22. **The correct answer is (5): (Analysis)** Choice (5) gives the most complete description of the relationship between the black population and the white population. Each of the other choices describes only one portion of the facts presented in the chart.

23. **The correct answer is (3): (Analysis)** Because the passage states that while a judge, Jackson was noted for his fairness, choice (3) is correct. None of the other choices is related to his beliefs about justice and fairness.

24. **The correct answer is (1): (Application)** Jackson's manipulation of the spoils system, which was in and of itself corrupt, would be a justification for Clay's description. The other four choices are in no way related to Jackson's corruptibility.

25. **The correct answer is (4): (Application)** Going off to fight a war as a youngster and becoming involved in a duel are clearly not well-thought-out actions. None of the other events, as described, could be called rash.

26. **The correct answer is (1): (Comprehension)** According to the passage, Jackson fought in the Revolutionary War in the late 1700s and in the War of 1812.

27. **The correct answer is (3): (Analysis)** The success of the Americans in the Battle of New Orleans and the extremely low number of American casualties are strong indicators that Jackson was a good military commander. Nothing in the passage supports any of the other four choices.

28. **The correct answer is (2): (Application)** Increasing the money supply and giving loans without increasing production would result in inflation.

29. **The correct answer is (2): (Comprehension)** Choice (2) best describes the overall meaning of the passage. All the other choices describe an individual part of the passage only.

30. **The correct answer is (2): (Analysis)** The passage points out the importance of joint problem solving, so seeking counseling to foster this ability would probably be the best way for the couple to reduce the number of arguments they have.

31. **The correct answer is (2): (Analysis)** The ability to solve problems jointly is directly tied to the Denver researcher's findings that the way in which problems are solved affects the likelihood of success in the marriage.

32. **The correct answer is (1): (Application)** The activities described are protected by the rights of free speech and assembly guaranteed in the First Amendment.

33. **The correct answer is (4): (Evaluation)** The description of the parade indicates that all sorts of women participated in pro-suffrage marches and other activities, so choice (4) is the best conclusion. The other choices assume that only certain groups of women marched or make incorrect assumptions about the womens' support of suffrage.

34. **The correct answer is (5): (Application)** By controlling at least one step in the oil production process—refining—Rockefeller had achieved horizontal integration.

35. **The correct answer is (2): (Application)** Standard Oil controlled nearly all of the oil production industry, making this a monopoly.

36. **The correct answer is (3): (Comprehension)** The passage states that the robber barons ran their competitors out of business and kept prices high.

37. **The correct answer is (3): (Analysis)** To prevent the spread of communism is to contain it, so containment (3) is the only possible choice. In its fight against communism, the United States has since pursued the other policies listed, except choice (4), massive retaliation.

38. **The correct answer is (1): (Application)** The temperatures shown on the graph indicate a warm tropical climate.

39. **The correct answer is (3): (Application)** The place shown on the graph receives only a few inches of rain each year. It is therefore an arid or desert climate. Choice (1) describes a tropical climate, choice (2) a subtropical climate, choice (4) a semiarid climate, and choice (5) a polar climate.

40. **The correct answer is (5): (Analysis)** The climate is so dry that it is unlikely there would be much vegetation.

41. **The correct answer is (4): (Comprehension)** Choices (1), (2), and (3) are details that support the main idea. Choice (5) is a false generalization. Only choice (4) expresses the main idea.

42. **The correct answer is (3): (Analysis)** The passage provides no support for choices (1) and (5). Choice (2) is the main idea of the passage. Choice (4) is supported by the passage, but is not broad enough to be a logical conclusion.

43. **The correct answer is (3): (Analysis)** The two-term limit is part of the system of checks and balances, which prevents any one group or individual from gaining too much power in the nation.

44. **The correct answer is (3): (Comprehension)** The figures in the cartoon represent U.S. military and political leaders.

45. **The correct answer is (2): (Analysis)** This cartoonist is pointing out the extremely high level of spending by the nation's military groups. Many Americans have criticized this level as being excessive and sometimes wasteful.

46. **The correct answer is (4): (Analysis)** Strong ties to a foreign government might make it impossible for an elected American official to operate with the best interests of the United States in mind.

47. **The correct answer is (5): (Application)** Medicare is an entitlement program that benefits millions of Americans over age 65.

48. **The correct answer is (2): (Analysis)** The cartoon's portrayal of lobbyists parking in spaces reserved for members of Congress expresses the idea that lobbyists may have too much influence over Congress.

49. **The correct answer is (1): (Analysis)** Foreign policy is meant to change with world events. After World War II, the United States allied itself with Japan and Germany, its enemies during that war, against the Soviet Union. Now that communism has collapsed, the U.S. can be friendly with the republics that once formed the Soviet Union.

50. **The correct answer is (2): (Application)** Occupational health and safety is the responsibility of the Labor Department. All other duties listed deal with foreign relations and therefore are part of the State Department.

51. **The correct answer is (5): (Analysis)** Housing (rent and mortgage payments), food, cars, and medical care are all goods or services purchased by typical consumers. Wages represent income, not spending.

52. **The correct answer is (1): (Analysis)** A 25-percent increase in the CPI means that prices are rising rapidly. The CPI measures overall prices, and an increase in prices means inflation.

53. **The correct answer is (4): (Evaluation)** The passage describes downturns in the housing and durable goods markets and resulting unemployment, which is clearly a situation of declining economic activity or recession. Lower interest rates will cause people to borrow and spend more, and decreased taxes will make more income available for spending. These two measures together would be likely to stimulate economic activity.

54. **The correct answer is (3): (Analysis)** The investment tax credit, which gives businesses a tax break when they buy new equipment, is a fiscal policy measure.

55. **The correct answer is (2): (Analysis)** An increase in demand means that more will be purchased at every possible price. Hence, if demand increases and supply does not change, the demand curve will shift outward from the price axis, resulting in a higher price and more quantity exchanged.

56. **The correct answer is (2): (Application)** The second worker adds 60 units to output; all other workers, including the first one, add fewer than 60 units.

57. **The correct answer is (3): (Application)** Total output increases, but the third worker adds 50 units, fewer than the 60 units added by the second worker.

58. **The correct answer is (4): (Application)** Trial-and-error learning involves trying a certain behavior without knowing what the outcome will be. If the behavior brings success, you use it again. Otherwise, you try a different behavior.

59. **The correct answer is (5): (Comprehension)** Choices (1), (3), and (4), although supported by the graph, are statements of fact related to specific years, not trends. Choice (2) is a statement related to a specific year and is also contradicted by the graph. Only choice (5) describes a trend that is supported by the graph.

60. **The correct answer is (2): (Analysis)** Between 1970 and 1990, an increasing number of women started professional careers, and thus more and more women put off marriage in order to succeed at their work before starting families.

61. **The correct answer is (4): (Application)** The statement "Men are better than women at managing people" is a role expectation that reflects a value or belief. It does not dictate a way of behaving.

62. **The correct answer is (3): (Comprehension)** Choice (3) is stated in the passage. All other choices are contradicted by the information in the passage.

63. **The correct answer is (3): (Application)** The superego is a person's conscience and guide to making moral decisions.

64. **The correct answer is (1): (Analysis)** Choice (1) is a simple description of psychoanalysis, Freud's method of therapy for emotional problems. Choice (2) describes a method of the behaviorist theory of personality. Choice (3) is a means of self-actualization, the goal of the humanistic theory. Choice (4) is a partial definition of socialization, and choice (5) describes internal conflict, one cause of cultural change.

Posttest 3: Science

1. **The correct answer is (2): (Comprehension)** According to the passage, sound is produced by the vibration of an object.

2. **The correct answer is (5): (Application)** The sound wave from the plane's engine causes the window to rattle. This is an example of resonance. None of the other choices applies to this situation.

3. **The correct answer is (3): (Application)** Tuning a violin requires adjustment of the pitch of each string. None of the other choices has to do with the highness or lowness of sound.

4. **The correct answer is (4): (Analysis)** Because it took 4 seconds for the sound to reach you, the airplane must have been 1,324 meters away (331 meters per second times 4 seconds).

5. **The correct answer is (5): (Comprehension)** The statement in choice (5) includes the most important elements of natural selection: survival and reproduction. Choice (1) is not true: similar organisms are believed to have the same type of ancestor. Choices (2), (3), and (4) are all true, but none of them includes enough information to be a good summary of the process.

6. **The correct answer is (1): (Comprehension)** Choice (1) restates the information given in the second paragraph of the passage: beaks differed according to each species' method of getting the available food. Choices (2), (3), (4), and (5) are all true, but none explains why the birds developed beaks of different shapes.

7. **The correct answer is (1): (Application)** A finch with a small probing bill could catch tiny insects in an open area more easily than finches with other types of bills.

8. **The correct answer is (2): (Application)** The air released from bellows makes a sluggish fire burn faster. Similarly, enzymes "fan the flames" of, or speed up, the chemical reaction of a cell during photosynthesis. None of the other choices presents a process in which something accelerates a reaction.

9. **The correct answer is (1): (Analysis)** Pandas are an example of a species that eats mainly one kind of food—bamboo shoots—and lives in one kind of area—bamboo forests. Therefore, destruction of their habitat and food source caused their population to decline sharply. Pandas are now an endangered species. The effects presented in the other choices could not have occurred, because pandas' requirements for food and habitat are very specific.

10. **The correct answer is (5): (Evaluation)** Of the groups mentioned, only animal rights activists would be likely to protest against the destruction of the bamboo forests. Each of the groups in choices (1) through (4) would have something to gain by allowing the destruction of the bamboo forests.

11. **The correct answer is (2): (Application)** The movement of the new monkey group into the existing monkey environment is an example of migration, so choice (2) is the correct answer.

12. **The correct answer is (4): (Application)** The lizard with webbed feet is a genetic mutation; in fact, this is an example of a mutation that might actually make the species better able to survive.

13. **The correct answer is (3): (Analysis)** Adding extra acid to an already acidic environment can result in an irritated stomach. None of the other choices describes symptoms related to additional acidity. A headache (1) or sore throat (2) may actually be relieved by aspirin.

14. **The correct answer is (1): (Comprehension)** According to the passage, the pulley divides the weight of the load, bearing half of it in this case.

15. **The correct answer is (1): (Evaluation)** Because the mechanical advantage of this pulley system is 2, the man must pull twice as far on the rope as the load is lifted. Choices (2) and (4) are contradicted by the passage and the diagram. Choices (3) and (5) may or may not be true, but they are not supported by the passage or the diagram.

16. **The correct answer is (4): (Analysis)** Because the toner forms the image of the document on the copies, blank pages must result from the machine running out of toner. Choices (1) and (5) would result in no output at all. Choice (2) would result in uneven, poor quality copies. Choice (3) simply describes how the machine functions.

17. **The correct answer is (1): (Application)** Because the Pacific Ocean is by far the largest body of water listed, it is likely that strong winds blowing over it will create higher waves than in any of the other choices.

18. **The correct answer is (2): (Analysis)** As the bottom of the wave is slowed, the crest continues to move forward at the same speed. Then the crest tumbles forward and the wave breaks. Choice (1) is incorrect because a current may or may not be acting on the waves in a given area. Choice (3) is true, but it is not the result of the slowing of the wave. Choices (4) and (5) are not true.

19. **The correct answer is (1): (Evaluation)** The passage states that very strong winds create large waves; therefore, you can infer that light winds result in calm seas. Choices (2) and (3) may or may not be true, but they are not supported by the information in the passage and diagram. Choices (4) and (5) are not true.

20. **The correct answer is (2): (Analysis)** The gradual upward movement of a blind thrust fault would slowly push up the surface, forming hills and mountains. Choices (1), (4), and (5) do not occur as the result of movements along faults. Choice (3) is incorrect because an earthquake is the result of sudden, not gradual, movement.

21. **The correct answer is (1): (Application)** An upward movement along a slope is characteristic of a blind thrust fault. Sliding a carton up a ramp is the only choice that has this characteristic.

22. **The correct answer is (3): (Comprehension)** There is a one-to-one correspondence between the numbers of atoms in a written formula and a structural formula. The other choices describe chemicals not shown in the structural formula.

23. **The correct answer is (5): (Analysis)** Because there are six atoms of carbon in one molecule of glucose, there are twelve atoms of carbon in two molecules ($6 \times 2 = 12$).

24. **The correct answer is (4): (Evaluation)** Choice (4) is the only answer supported by the diagram. Choices (1), (2), and (5) are contradicted by the diagram. Choice (3) may be true, but you cannot tell from the information provided.

25. **The correct answer is (4): (Comprehension)** ATP, carbon dioxide, and water are produced during respiration. Choices (1) and (2) are both reactants in this process. Choices (3) and (5) are not involved in the reaction.

26. **The correct answer is (5): (Analysis)** Oxygen is required for respiration. Energy released during respiration is used for chemical transport, cell growth, and muscle movement, as well as for cell division.

27. **The correct answer is (3): (Comprehension)** Muhammad Ali's remark is a restatement of the information in the concluding sentence of the passage: "When the muscles are depleted of ATP, they begin to feel heavy." The other choices do not accurately explain Muhammad Ali's comment.

28. **The correct answer is (2): (Application)** All choices are examples of plants with defense systems, but only the stinging nettle, which releases acid, has a chemical defense system.

29. **The correct answer is (3): (Evaluation)** This is stated by the equation in the graph. Choices (1), (2), and (4) are not supported by the information. Choice (5) is contradicted by the graph.

30. **The correct answer is (2): (Application)** Choice (2) is the only choice that involves testing for the presence of an acid or a base. The other choices involve measurement of quantities or temperature.

31. **The correct answer is (1): (Evaluation)** Only choice (1) is substantiated by the data in the graph. Choices (2) and (3) are not correct, according to the graph. Choices (4) and (5) can be neither proved nor disproved by the data provided.

32. **The correct answer is (3): (Analysis)** Choices (1), (2), (4), and (5) are all mentioned in the passage as possible causes of obesity. Choice (3) is more likely to help maintain a normal weight.

33. **The correct answer is (2): (Application)** Based on the illustration and explanation in the chart, watermelons and tomatoes are both classified as berries. These fruits have fleshy tissue in which several seeds are embedded.

34. **The correct answer is (3): (Application)** Like a pear, an apple is a pome: it has a fleshy outer layer and an inner core.

35. **The correct answer is (1): (Application)** A cherry or a plum, like a peach, is a drupe because it has a fleshy outer layer that encases a hard stone or pit.

36. **The correct answer is (4): (Application)** Like a pea pod, a milkweed pod holds seeds and also splits open, so it is a dehiscent.

37. **The correct answer is (1): (Evaluation)** Because the key concept of the theory of evolution is that species change over the years, the best evidence would be evidence of long-term change. The ages of the fossils would prove that this kind of change has been taking place for millions of years.

38. **The correct answer is (2): (Evaluation)** The policy excluding African Americans from donating blood to the U.S. military was based on racial prejudice. The other choices are factors that could have been used as evidence to show that the blood-collection policy was scientifically unsound.

39. **The correct answer is (5): (Evaluation)** Because transfusions of incorrect blood types result in complications, it is not true that any individual can safely give blood to any other individual. The donor and receiver must have matching or compatible blood types. The other choices are supported by scientific information given in the passage.

40. **The correct answer is (5): (Comprehension)** You have learned that breads and cereals are sources of carbohydrates derived from grains. The graph shows that breads and cereals account for 30 percent of children's snacks.

41. **The correct answer is (3): (Analysis)** You have learned how to analyze the nutritional value of food. Candy, soda, and desserts are high in sugar and very low in nutrients. The other choices are all better sources of important nutrients.

42. **The correct answer is (4): (Evaluation)** Findings from human and animal studies would provide the experimental evidence needed to determine the link between the two food additives and cancer in humans. The findings in choice (2) would not necessarily apply to human subjects. Choices (1) and (5) would not involve scientific testing of a hypothesis. The data from choice (3) would not explain the declining cancer rate.

43. **The correct answer is (1): (Analysis)** As the diagram illustrates, only native plants and animals live in the core area. This arrangement improves their chances for survival, because human activities tend to disturb wildlife. The other choices describe the purposes of creating buffer zones 1 and 2.

44. **The correct answer is (4): (Analysis)** The sound would travel 15,240 meters altogether (1,524 meters per second times 10 seconds). However, half the time would be spent going to the bottom, and half returning to the surface, so the depth would be 15,240 meters divided by 2, or 7,620 meters.

45. **The correct answer is (1): (Application)** The deposition of layers of lava and ash is similar to the deposition of sediment, in that each layer forms later, and thus is younger, than the one below it. None of the other choices involves deposition of substances in layers.

46. **The correct answer is (2): (Analysis)** If shale oil cannot be produced economically, the United States will remain dependent on offshore wells and other countries for its oil. Choices (1) and (5) are incorrect because oil shale cannot replace, and cannot be used to produce, natural gas. Choice (3) is incorrect because oil shale can burn—not a good quality for a building stone. Choice (4) might eventually come to pass, but it is unlikely while less costly means of obtaining oil exist.

47. **The correct answer is (2): (Evaluation)** Because there are still much less expensive sources of oil, shale oil production is not worth the expense. Choices (1) and (3) are not true. Choices (4) and (5) are true, but these factors contribute to the central problem, the high cost of production.

48. **The correct answer is (4): (Comprehension)** The section of the graph that represents carbohydrates indicates 65 percent.

49. **The correct answer is (3): (Evaluation)** To follow the recommended dietary percentages, you would need to know the protein, fat, and carbohydrate contents of the foods you eat. Although the other choices would be helpful, they are not as complete as choice (3).

50. **The correct answer is (1): (Comprehension)** Asparagus with lemon dressing (65 calories), grilled fish and vegetables (249 calories), and low-fat blueberry mousse (46 calories) add up to a 360-calorie dinner. All other meals listed exceed 400 calories.

51. **The correct answer is (3): (Evaluation)** A 25-ounce beef sample that contained 4 ounces of fat would have a fat content of 16 percent. This answer is closest to 15 percent. All other answers exceed 15 percent by larger amounts.

52. **The correct answer is (4): (Evaluation)** Choice (4) is the best explanation why doctors do not recommend fried foods. Choices (1), (2), (3), and (5) do not follow from the data provided.

53. **The correct answer is (3): (Application)** At 7.5, human blood most closely matches the pH of water, which is 7. The other choices are more strongly acidic or basic.

54. **The correct answer is (5): (Comprehension)** Bases have pH values greater than 7. Lye, with a pH of 13, is stronger than any other base listed.

55. **The correct answer is (2): (Evaluation)** The pH value indicates whether a substance is an acid or a base. Because bases have the ability to neutralize acids, you can predict what will happen when an acid is combined with a base or a base is combined with an acid. None of the other choices correctly identifies the purpose of the pH scale.

56. **The correct answer is (3): (Analysis)** The range suggests that human saliva contains varying concentrations of chemicals. Choices (1) and (5) are not logical. Choices (2) and (4) may be possible, but neither is the most logical explanation.

57. **The correct answer is (4): (Application)** A pendulum converts gravitational potential energy to kinetic energy. None of the other choices describes what a pendulum does.

58. **The correct answer is (5): (Application)** The knife used to pry up the lid is a machine. Although work is done in each of the other choices, no other choice involves the use of a machine.

59. **The correct answer is (3): (Evaluation)** The calculation is 100 lb × 6 ft = 600 ft-lb.

60. **The correct answer is (4): (Comprehension)** A wave will cause the boat to move up and down, but it will not push the boat horizontally. None of the other statements is true.

61. **The correct answer is (2): (Evaluation)** The lens of a camera refracts or bends the light and projects the image on film. Although choice (1) may be true to a small extent, it does not explain how the camera puts the small image of the tall man on film. Choices (3) and (4) are not true. Choice (5), although true, does not explain how the image gets onto the film.

62. **The correct answer is (5): (Analysis)** A mirror reverses an image. None of the other statements is true.

63. **The correct answer is (5): (Comprehension)** Potential difference is the reason that electric current flows. Although the other terms have to do with electricity, none of them is directly related to the flow of current.

64. **The correct answer is (5): (Analysis)** If an appliance is broken, the electricity in a parallel circuit will take another pathway. Choices (1) and (2) are not correct. Choices (3) and (4) have nothing to do with the description of a parallel circuit.

65. **The correct answer is (1): (Evaluation)** If 1 volt is equal to 0.001 kilovolt, conversion of volts to kilovolts requires division by 1,000.

66. **The correct answer is (3): (Evaluation)** The amount of current would decrease. None of the other choices would be in accordance with Ohm's law.

Posttest 4: Interpreting Literature and the Arts

What Does This Conversation Reveal? (page 430)

1. **The correct answer is (2): (Inferential comprehension)** In contrast to Tom, who becomes impatient, Laura responds kindly to Amanda's questions and worries. She is not cruel, mocking, or impatient with her mother, so choices (1), (4), and (5) are incorrect. It is Amanda, not Laura, who is described as flirtatious, so choice (3) can be eliminated.

2. **The correct answer is (4): (Literal comprehension)** In line 3, Amanda says, "It's almost time for our gentlemen callers to start arriving." Choice (1) is incorrect because they have just finished eating dinner. Amanda suggests that Laura practice shorthand, but this is not the focus of the passage, so choice (2) is not the best answer. There is no evidence to support choices (3) and (5).

3. **The correct answer is (5): (Inferential comprehension)** Tom throws down his paper and groans in response to things his mother says or in response to what Laura says about her. The other choices could be true, but they are not suggested by these stage directions.

4. **The correct answer is (1): (Analysis)** The most likely reason that the playwright includes directions for "very clear light" on Laura's face is because it is important to see her face and its expression at this moment. The light could be coming from a lamp, so choice (2) is incorrect. Laura may be evading her mother, but she has no reason to hide from Tom, so choice (3) can be eliminated. The light shines on Laura's face, not Tom's, so choice (4) can be eliminated. The "faded tapestry" may be related to the family's lack of money (5), but Laura's expression is more important.

What Kind of Person Was José Montiel? (page 431)

5. **The correct answer is (5): (Inferential comprehension)** If people felt *avenged*, they felt vindicated and relieved. This suggests that Montiel had many enemies who are glad he is gone. Choices (1), (3), and (4) are incorrect, respectively, because the term *avenged* does not suggest a violent death, love, or marriage. A last wish is not mentioned, so choice (2) is incorrect.

6. **The correct answer is (1): (Literal comprehension)** This statement suggests that everyone *but* Montiel's wife believed he would be killed, not die "a natural death." Choice (3) states the opposite. This statement does not mention Montiel's marriage, so choice (2) can be eliminated. Choice (4) is incorrect because the townspeople probably disliked him, although their emotions are not described. Montiel's widow thought she would "see him die an old man in his bed, . . ." so choice (5) is incorrect.

7. **The correct answer is (5): (Inferential comprehension)** Montiel's widow is the only one who does not feel "avenged" by his death. The passage suggests that she remained respectful and loving toward him. Choices (1), (2), and (4) are all negative emotions that are not suggested by the passage. While she may feel confused and alone, the passage does not address this possibility, so choice (3) is incorrect.

8. **The correct answer is (4): (Application)** The townspeople's opinions and anger suggest he would probably betray a friend. The other choices are incorrect since they are all good, positive actions. They suggest traits that would have made Montiel more loved than he was.

What Makes This Novel So Interesting? *(page 432)*

9. **The correct answer is (2): (Application)** One of the reviewer's central points is that this novel was written *by* a woman *about* a female detective, so a female-produced documentary about female artists is most similar. Though this novel contains a young niece and a law school professor, they are only supporting characters, so choices (1) and (3) can be eliminated. Choice (4) would be logical only if the movie's subject matter was about a female. Choice (5) could be logical only if the article was also written by a woman.

10. **The correct answer is (4): (Literal comprehension)** The dialogue is described as "scalpel sharp," which means it is direct and concise. Choices (1), (2), and (3) do not suggest crisp, razor-edged dialogue. Although Scarpetta's work might sometimes be described as "graphic and gruesome," it would be inappropriate to apply the term to the dialogue, so choice (5) can be eliminated.

11. **The correct answer is (5): (Literal comprehension)** Lines 24–25 state, "The 'love interest' in this book is not romantic. . . ." All of the other choices are directly stated as elements in Cruel & *Unusual.* Choice (1) is mentioned in lines 29–31, choice (2) is noted in line 28 and elsewhere, choice (3) is referred to in line 29, and choice (4) is mentioned in line 23.

12. **The correct answer is (5): (Literal comprehension)** The professor did not want Kay to "lose herself"—and her abilities—in love and not reach her full potential as an individual. Choice (2) is the opposite of what the professor wanted for Kay. There is no support for the other choices in the passage.

Is This Wedding Ring Still Useful? *(page 433)*

13. **The correct answer is (2): (Analysis)** This poem is free verse; it has no rhyme or rhythm. A song usually contains both rhyme and rhythm, so choice (1) is incorrect. Also, this poem addresses a very personal issue of a sort that might be confided in a diary. The speaker is describing the end of a love relationship, so choice (4) is incorrect. The subject matter of this poem would probably not be found in a newspaper advertisement or law document, so choices (3) and (5) can be eliminated.

14. **The correct answer is (4): (Analysis)** This simile (a comparison that contains *like* or *as*) is between a wedding ring and an object that has fallen to the bottom of a well. If the ring were really at the bottom of a well, it would be lost and far away. A metaphor does not use the words *like* or *as*, so choices (2) and (3) can be eliminated. The ring now seems diminished in importance; choice (1) can therefore be eliminated. Choice (5) is incorrect because the ring is not personified (given human traits).

Why Is Mr. Randolph Remembered? *(page 433)*

15. **The correct answer is (1): (Literal comprehension)** This statement reveals that the politicians and legislators depended on Mr. Randolph's vast knowledge. Choice (2) is incorrect because Mr. Randolph's feelings about his job are not related to the politicians' questions. Although choices (3) and (5) may be true, they do not pinpoint the most important reason for including this description: to show that Mr. Randolph's knowledge was important to the legislators. There is no evidence for choice (4).

16. **The correct answer is (3): (Inferential comprehension)** This passage suggests that, as a young boy, Ellison watched the goings-on carefully and was deeply influenced by Mr. Randolph; also, he describes himself as "impressionable." It is Mr. Randolph, not Ellison, who is depicted as an admired person, so choice (5) can be eliminated. There is no evidence for the other choices.

17. **The correct answer is (1): (Inferential comprehension)** The fact that the legislators turned to him for information and advice suggests that he knew more than they did. While the other choices could be true, the passage does not support them.

What Issues Is Walter Struggling With? *(page 434)*

18. **The correct answer is (4): (Inferential comprehension)** In lines 46–49, Walter complains to Ruth, "See—I'm trying to talk to you 'bout myself . . . and all you can say is eat them eggs and go to work." He believes that she won't let him dream about a better future. Choice (1) is incorrect because Walter knows that Ruth is listening—she just doesn't want to talk about his plans. It is Walter, not Ruth, who is considering doing something illegal; thus, choice (2) can be eliminated. There is no support in the passage for choices (3) and (5).

19. **The correct answer is (5): (Application)** Walter is proposing to bribe someone to get his liquor license approved quickly, much as a person might pay someone off to get choice tickets. Choice (2) describes what Walter and Ruth are doing but does not apply to Walter's plan. Choice (3) is not as similar as choice (5), since this action does not provide as clear an advantage. Choices (1) and (4) can be eliminated because they are perfectly legal and respectable.

20. **The correct answer is (2): (Analysis)** The stage directions in this passage indicate that Walter goes from sadness to passion to anguish—a range of emotions best summarized as "growing frustration." Choice (1) is incorrect because the friction in the conversation arises from Walter's need to feel financially secure; he does not feel that way yet. In this passage, Walter becomes angrier and less stable; thus, choices (3) and (5) can be eliminated. The stage directions suggest that his emotions trigger physical responses; however, physical strength—choice (4)—is not mentioned.

Why Is Storytelling Important? *(page 435)*

21. **The correct answer is (4): (Literal comprehension)** This passage is devoted to describing the dangers that occur "When parents cease to be the primary storytellers" (lines 9–10) and TV takes over that responsibility. Choices (1), (2), and (5) offer positive views of TV. Choice (3) contradicts the author's central belief.

22. **The correct answer is (5): (Analysis)** Media critic George Gerbner is an expert voice. In lines 4–8, he supports the author's belief that TV now tells the stories instead of parents. Choice (1) is incorrect since Gerbner supports the author's belief. Gerbner does not list any statistics to support his belief, so choice (2) can be eliminated. Choice (3) may be true for some readers, but not for all readers. The author has a bias against TV but is not afraid of TV, as choice (4) suggests.

How Do Kitchens Make This Author Feel? *(page 435)*

23. **The correct answer is (4): (Analysis)** The narrator is describing her fantasy of the sound of light striking the white tiles in a kitchen. Choices (1) and (2) are incorrect, respectively, because she is not speaking with another person, nor does she mention glassware. She is describing the beauty of the kitchen, not joking or cleaning, so choices (3) and (5) can be eliminated.

24. **The correct answer is (3): (Analysis)** Kitchens are usually associated with life, food, and activity, so the image of death in a kitchen is unusual. Choice (1) states the opposite. Though choice (2) is true, it does not explain why the pairing of a kitchen and death is unusual. Choice (4) is incorrect because the speaker never makes this statement. A bedroom or family room, not a kitchen, would symbolize rest and relaxation, so choice (5) can be eliminated.

How Does This Young Woman React? *(page 436)*

25. **The correct answer is (2): (Inferential comprehension)** In line 30, the husband states, "Having a baby's natural!" The young woman is in the hospital, so choice (1) is incorrect. She does not seem to want her husband there, so choice (3) is not necessarily true. There is no evidence for choices (4) and (5).

26. **The correct answer is (5): (Analysis)** These stage directions call for the young woman to indicate that she is not feeling better and that her husband doesn't understand. The best description of her to this point is depressed and upset. Choices (1) and (2) describe positive frames of mind. Choice (4) can be eliminated because the young woman does not express herself in a timid way. There is no evidence for choice (3).

27. **The correct answer is (3): (Inferential comprehension)** The young woman begins to gesture violently and points wildly to the door (lines 17–18 and 32–33). Both stage directions reveal her growing sense of panic. Choice (1) states the opposite. Choice (2) is incorrect because the woman does not want her husband in the room. Choices (4) and (5) are not supported in the passage.

Why Was This Lesson Meaningful? *(page 436)*

28. **The correct answer is (4): (Literal comprehension)** In lines 10–11, Wickham turns off the lights and shines a light on a prism. From this, you know that the class is watching an experiment with light and color. Apples and oranges are used as an example, but they are not the focus of the experiment; thus, choice (2) is incorrect. There is no evidence for the other choices.

29. **The correct answer is (1): (Literal comprehension)** When the narrator walks to the window, he notices the effect of light on his skin. Choice (3) can be eliminated because it refers to memories of the past. Choice (2) may be suggested, but only after the memory is shared. There is no evidence for choices (4) and (5).

30. **The correct answer is (5): (Analysis)** These details show how color can change when hit by a certain light. Choice (3) is incorrect because it states that heat, not light, causes the change. The other choices are not supported in the passage.

31. **The correct answer is (1): (Inferential comprehension)** With this statement, the narrator shows his realization that skin color only makes people look different—it doesn't make them different. Choices (2) and (5) may be true, but they do not summarize the narrator's main point. Choice (3) contradicts the passage; choice (4) is not supported in it.

32. **The correct answer is (1): (Inferential comprehension)** Because the narrator wonders what kind of light would make his and friends' skin color look the same, you can conclude that they are from different ethnic backgrounds. Choice (4) states the opposite. There is no evidence to suggest choices (2) or (3). Choice (5) may be true, but it is not relevant to the narrator's comment about skin tone.

What Does This Speaker Find in the Attic? *(page 437)*

33. **The correct answer is (4): (Literal comprehension)** The speaker describes her sleeping family as she walks past their rooms. She does not mention fear or thoughts that the house might be haunted, so choices (1) and (5) are incorrect. The cat is simply one detail in the stanza, so choice (3) is not the best answer. Since the attic is not described until the second stanza, choice (2) can be eliminated.

34. **The correct answer is (3): (Inferential comprehension)** Some of the items mentioned sound old-fashioned; all have been put away and are not in current use. Thus, choices (2) and (4) cannot be correct. Choices (1) and (5) are incorrect because they mention only a few of the details in these lines.

35. **The correct answer is (1): (Inferential comprehension)** The speaker seems familiar with the old silverware and the books and where they are in the attic, so she must have visited the attic often. Choice (2) is incorrect because the speaker says the books will "last [her] a while"; she must not have read them yet. She seems to know her way around, so choice (3) can be eliminated. There is no evidence for choices (4) and (5).

36. **The correct answer is (2): (Analysis)** The speaker is imagining the music of long ago, and the scent of the air when these old family members were alive. Choices (1), (3), and (4) are incorrect because the speaker is not literally referring to actual smells, to cooking, or to music. Choice (5) is not supported in the passage.

37. **The correct answer is (5): (Application)** The speaker is examining the evidence of her own family's past, so she probably would agree that most families have detailed, rich histories. The speaker enjoys looking at these old objects and knows quite a bit about Aunt Irene and Uncle Eric from them; thus, the other choices can be eliminated.

Why Is the Word *No* Important to This Speaker? *(page 438)*

38. **The correct answer is (2): (Inferential comprehension)** In lines 5 and 12–14, the speaker says that "We" do not know how to say "no" and that "Puerto Ricans" do not know how to say "no." By identifying himself with those who do not know how to say "no," he is also identifying himself with Puerto Ricans. Based on this association, the other choices are incorrect.

39. **The correct answer is (4): (Literal comprehension)** According to the speaker, Puerto Ricans may say, "We'll see," but mean "no." To many people, this expression may sound like "yes." Because this confusion exists, choices (1) and (5) are incorrect. The tone of voice described is accommodating, not offensive, so choice (3) is incorrect. There is no evidence for choice (2).

40. **The correct answer is (4): (Inferential comprehension)** In lines 1–5, the speaker explains that the word "no" is necessary to end "anachronistic imperialism," or an outdated system in which a country is ruled by outsiders. Though the speaker might want his people to find better jobs, save the environment, or increase exports, these goals are not the most direct result of the powerful word "no." The other choices are not discussed in this passage.

41. **The correct answer is (3): (Inferential comprehension)** The speaker describes his homeland as full of beauty and generosity. Of the choices, nurturing is closest to this description. Choices (1), (2), and (5) are negative descriptions, and the speaker's devotion to Puerto Rico means that the land is not forgotten, as choice (4) suggests.

42. **The correct answer is (5): (Analysis)** To the speaker, the sound of the *o* in *no* is as sharp and powerful as gunfire. He is referring figuratively to gunfire, so choices (1), (2), and (3) are incorrect. He is trying to motivate his people, not prove that he is brave; therefore, choice (4) can be eliminated.

How Will a New Law Affect Television Viewers? *(page 439)*

43. **The correct answer is (1): (Literal comprehension)** This passage discusses how the hearing impaired can come "fully into the mainstream of American life" (lines 15–16). Only the hearing impaired are mentioned, so choice (2) is incorrect. A hearing impaired actor is quoted, but is not the focus, as choice (4) suggests. There is no conflict mentioned, so choice (5) can be eliminated. There is no evidence for choice (3).

44. **The correct answer is (2): (Inferential comprehension)** Harkin praises the law and its positive effects for the hearing impaired. Choices (1) and (5) suggest the opposite. Harkin does not comment on Dysart, so choice (3) can be eliminated. Choice (4) is not supported by the passage.

45. **The correct answer is (2): (Application)** The closed-captioning law would enable hearing impaired people to watch TV, much as mandatory Braille in public places would enable blind individuals to read information. Choice (1) would decrease learning and special access for the disabled. Choice (3) does not concern the physically impaired. Choices (4) and (5) are not related to rights for the disabled.

Postest 5: Mathematics

1. **The correct answer is (5): 10($24) + 20($18)**

   Read the table to find the discount price for each type of suit. Each price is multiplied by the number to be purchased. The two products are added to find the total cost.

2. **The correct answer is (4): 11 Solid-color suits**

   Evaluate each of the answer choices using the discount prices from the table. Choice (4) will cost $231, the lowest price of any choice.

   $11 \times \$24 = \$264$

   $13 \times \$22 = \$286$

   $9 \times \$27 = \$243$

   $11 \times \$21 = \$231$

   $20 \times \$18 = \$360$

3. **The correct answer is (3): 40** 1 m = 100 cm, so 4 m contains 400 cm. Divide 400 by 10.

4. **The correct answer is (5): 2^4** 2(2)(2)(2) = 16

5. **The correct answer is (4): 18(25)** Use the formula:

   $A = lw$; where l = length and w = width.

6. **The correct answer is (3): $87.50** Multiply $22.50 by 5 hours to find the total owed to the painter. Subtract the total from $200 to find the difference between the total and the estimate.

7. **The correct answer is (1):** $\dfrac{2(1,536)}{24}$

   Set up a proportion and solve.

8. **The correct answer is (2): ½** Four of the 8 sections are labeled with a number less than 3 (either 1 or 2). ⁴⁄₈ = ½

9. **The correct answer is (3): 38** You need to find the circumference of the pond. Use the formula: $C = \pi d$; where π = 3.14 and d = diameter. Remember that the diameter is two times the radius.

   $C = 3.14(12)$

   $C = 37.68$ meters

10. **The correct answer is (4): 65%** Add the percents for items other than ice cream, candy, and chewing gum, or add the amounts for those items, and subtract from 100%.

11. **The correct answer is (1):** $\dfrac{(10 + 25)(\$3,400)}{100}$

    You need to add 10% and 25% and then multiply the total percent by $3,400.

12. **The correct answer is (3): $461.50** You can find 35% of $710 and then subtract that amount from $710, or you can subtract 35% from 100% to get 65%. Then find 65% of $710.

13. **The correct answer is (1): ½(8)(8½)** Use the formula for finding the area of a triangle:

    $A = \frac{1}{2}bh$; where b = base and h = height.

    $A = \frac{1}{2}(8)(8\frac{1}{2})$

14. **The correct answer is (3): $4,800** Use the formula for finding simple interest: $i = prt$; where p = *principal*, r = *rate*, and t = *time*.

    $i = \$9,600(0.10)(5)$

    $i = \$4,800$

15. **The correct answer is (4): −6** Substitute the values from the problem and solve.

16. **The correct answer is (5): 633** The triangles formed by the streets are similar. Use a proportion to solve for the missing distance.

17. **The correct answer is (1): $c^2 = 300^2 + 400^2$** You are solving for the hypotenuse of a right triangle. Use the Pythagorean relationship.

18. **The correct answer is (1): $2(x - 2) - 6$**

    Brad's age = x

    Robin's age = $x - 2$

    Cathy's age = $2(x - 2) - 6$

19. **The correct answer is (2): 54°** The total of the three angles in a triangle is 180°. Subtract the angles you have (90° and 36°) from 180°.

20. **The correct answer is (5): Two single-surface fillings** Find the amount of time needed to perform two crown procedures and an adult cleaning.

    $1\frac{1}{4} + 1\frac{1}{4} + \frac{3}{4} = 3\frac{1}{4}$

    Subtract from 4 hours: $4 - 3\frac{1}{4} = \frac{3}{4}$

    Evaluate each of the options to see which will take ¾ of an hour or less. Choice (5) will take ⅔ of an hour or 40 minutes.

21. **The correct answer is (2): 110** Add the number of miles for the last three days of the trip and divide by 11.

22. **The correct answer is (2): 410** Add the number of miles driven each day, and divide by 5 (the number of days driven).

23. **The correct answer is (1): 2½ feet** Use the formula for finding the volume of a rectangular container and solve for height.

    $V = lwh$

    15 cu ft ≤ 3(2)h

    $\dfrac{15}{6} \leq h$

    $\dfrac{15}{6} \leq 2\dfrac{1}{2}$

24. **The correct answer is (3): The sculpture's height is five times the height of the sculptor.** Set up a proportion and solve.

SCULPTOR		SCULPTURE
$\dfrac{height}{shadow}$	$\dfrac{6}{4} = \dfrac{x}{20}$	$\dfrac{height}{shadow}$

    $\dfrac{6(20)}{4} = 30\,ft$

    The sculpture is 30 feet high. Evaluate each statement.

25. **The correct answer is (3): Between 35 and 40** You need to find the square root of 1,500. The square of 40 is 1,600; the square of 30 is 900. Since 1,500 is near 1,600, you can estimate the square root is between 35 and 40. You can calculate the square of 35 to check your answer.

26. **The correct answer is (4): $30.50** Write an equation to solve the problem. Let x = the price of a black ink cartridge.

    Let $2x + 5$ = the price of a color cartridge.

    $x + 2x + 5 = \$43.25$

    $3x + \$5 = \$43.25$

    $3x = \$38.25$

    $x = \$12.75$

    Then substitute $12.75 into the expression for the price of a color cartridge: 2($12.75) + $5 = $30.50.

27. **The correct answer is (3): 4¾** Divide $14.25 by $3 to find the number of yards.

28. **The correct answer is (2): ⅓** Choose two points on line C and use the formula for finding slope.

    Think: the line runs 3 units for every 1 unit it rises.

29. **The correct answer is (5): Not enough information is given.** You need to know how much the gas tank holds to solve the problem.

30. **The correct answer is (2): 2½** Use the fact. 36 in = 1 yd
Multiply. 45(2) = 90 inches.
Ms. Clark needs 90 inches. Divide by 36 to find the number of yards.
$$\frac{90}{36} = 2\frac{1}{2}$$

31. **The correct answer is (1): 784** Find the volume of each box and subtract. Use the formula. $V = s^3$
$10^3 = 1,000$ and $6^3 = 216$. The difference is 784.

32. **The correct answer is (4): 228** The lot measures 42 ft by 72 ft. Use the formula.
$P = 2l + 2w$
$P = 2(72) + 2(42)$
$P = 144 + 84 = 228$ feet
To simplify the calculations, use rounding. 2(70) + 2(40)

33. **The correct answer is (5):** $\dfrac{12(72)}{36}$ You need to find the area of the space reserved for fruit trees and then divide by 36 sq ft, the number of sq ft needed for each tree.

34. **The correct answer is (3): 1 ft 6 in**
Use the fact. 1 ft = 12 in
Subtract the lengths.
120 − 102 = 18 in
Change 18 inches to feet and inches. 18 in = 1 ft 6 in

35. **The correct answer is (2): 2 lb 12 oz**
Use the fact. 1 lb = 16 oz
Subtract 8 lb 12 oz from 11 lb 8 oz. Change 1 pound to 16 ounces when you borrow.

36. **The correct answer is (4): Between 5 and 6 miles**
Divide 26 by 5. $\dfrac{26}{5} = 5.2$, or $5\dfrac{1}{5}$.

37. **The correct answer is (3):** $\dfrac{3}{4}$ The ratio of the price of a baseball ticket to the price of a football ticket is $\dfrac{15}{20}$, which equals ¾.

38. **The correct answer is (4): $26** Add the prices from the graph and divide by 7, the number of entertainment events shown. Round to the nearest whole dollar.

39. **The correct answer is (5): 4($30 + $25)** The concert tickets are $25 and the basketball tickets are $30. You could multiply each by 4 as in this expression: 4($30) + 4($25), or you can add the two amounts and then multiply by 4. Both expressions get the same result.

40. **The correct answer is (4): $21,840** Find the hourly wage for 1993 and multiply by 2,080.
10.50(2,080) = 21,840.

41. **The correct answer is (1): 1991 and 1994** The graph goes up in $0.50 increments. The only years when the line goes up two increments are 1991 and 1994.

42. **The correct answer is (1): 5%** Julius got a $0.50 increase. Divide the increase by his salary in 1991 ($10.00).

43. **The correct answer is (4): ⅔** There are four chances to get red or green and six sides on the die. $\dfrac{4}{6}$ renames to $\dfrac{2}{3}$.

44. **The correct answer is (2): 3,500** If 93% of the water used is recycled, 7% is not (100% − 93% = 7%). Find 7% of 50,000. You can also find 93% of 50,000 and then subtract the result from 50,000.

45. **The correct answer is (3): 14,250** Set up a proportion to find the number of cars traveling south; then subtract from 38,000.

46. **The correct answer is (3): 50.4** Divide 4,029 by 80. Carry the division out to the nearest hundredth and round. You can also use estimation: divide 4,000 by 80. Only choice (3) could be correct.

47. **The correct answer is (3): ⅕** You can divide 38 by 180, which gives you 0.21. Since $\dfrac{20}{100}$ equals $\dfrac{1}{5}$, you know $\dfrac{1}{5}$ is the best answer choice. You can also round $\dfrac{38}{180}$ to $\dfrac{40}{180}$ and rename. The renamed fraction $\dfrac{2}{9}$ is close to $\dfrac{2}{10}$, which rounds to $\dfrac{1}{5}$.

48. **The correct answer is (5): 112.5** Multiply 4.5 by 25. Estimate: Round 4.5 to 5, and multiply: 5(25) = 125. Your answer must be in the hundreds so only choice (5) can be correct.

49. **The correct answer is (2): 37**
x = the number Keith assembled
$x + 9$ = the number Bernard assembled
$x + x + 9 = 65$
$\quad 2x + 9 = 65$
$\quad\quad 2x = 56$
$\quad\quad\ x = 28$
Bernard assembled 28 + 9 = 37 parts.

50. **The correct answer is (5): $x + (x + 1) + (x + 2) = 51$**
Let x represent the first number in the series. The expressions $x + 1$ and $x + 2$ represent the next two numbers in the series.

51. **The correct answer is (2): $3.00** Let x represent the price of a child's ticket. $2x$ represents the price of an adult's ticket. $2x − 2$ represents the price of a senior's ticket. Multiply each expression by the number the Williams family bought as you set up the equation.
$2(2x) + 6x + (2x − 2) = \$34$
$4x + 6x + (2x − 2) = \$34$
$12x − 2 = \$34$
$12x = \$36$
$x = \$3$

52. **The correct answer is (5): $a \geq 4$**
$\quad 5a - 2 \geq 6(4 - 1)$
$\quad 5a - 2 \geq 24 - 6$
$\quad 5a - 2 \geq 18$
$\quad\quad 5a \geq 20$
$\quad\quad\ a \geq 4$

53. **The correct answer is (3): $y = 3x − 5$** The easiest way to solve this is to use the formula for finding the y-intercept. At this point, the value of x is always 0 and $y = b$.
$y = mx + b$
$y = m(0) + b$
$y = 0 − 5$
You can also find the coordinates of a point on line C. Then calculate the equations in the answer choices by substituting the values for x and y.

54. **The correct answer is (1): 28** The radius of the circle is ½ the diameter: $\dfrac{6}{2} = 3$.
Use the formula.
$A = \pi r^2$
$A = 3.14(3)^2$

55. **The correct answer is (2): 56** Use the formula for finding the area of a parallelogram.
$A = bh$
$A = 14(4)$

56. **The correct answer is (4): 140°**
Subtract: 180 − 40 = 140. Angles 1 and 2 are supplementary angles.

Practice Tests

WRITING SKILLS

75 Minutes ❖ 55 Questions

Part I

The multiple-choice section consists of paragraphs with numbered sentences. Some of the sentences contain errors in sentence structure, usage, or mechanics (spelling, punctuation, and capitalization). After reading the numbered sentences, answer the multiple-choice questions that follow. Some of the sentences are correct as written. The best answer for other questions is the one that leaves the sentence as originally written. The best answer for some questions is the one that produces a sentence that is consistent with the verb tense and point of view used throughout the paragraph.

You should spend no more than 75 minutes on the multiple-choice questions and 45 minutes on your essay. Work carefully, but do not spend too much time on any one question. You may begin working on the essay part of this test as soon as you complete the multiple-choice section.

Do not mark in this test booklet. Record your answers on the separate answer sheet provided. Be sure that all requested information is properly recorded on the answer sheet. To record your answers, mark one numbered space on the answer sheet beside the number that corresponds to the question in the test booklet.

Do not rest the point of your pencil on the answer sheet while you are considering your answer. Make no stray or unnecessary marks. If you change an answer, erase your first mark completely. Mark only one answer space for each question; multiple answers will be scored as incorrect. Do not fold or crease your answer sheet.

FOR EXAMPLE

Sentence 1: **We were all honored to meet governor Phillips.**
What correction should be made to this sentence?

(1) insert a comma after <u>honored</u>
(2) change the spelling of <u>honored</u> to <u>honered</u>
(3) change <u>governor</u> to <u>Governor</u>
(4) replace <u>were</u> with <u>was</u>
(5) no correction is necessary

① ② ● ④ ⑤

In this example, the word "governor" should be capitalized; therefore, answer space 3 would be marked on the answer sheet.

GED Test _____

Name _____

Date _____

- Use a No. 2 pencil.
- Mark one numbered space beside the number that corresponds to each question you are answering.
- Erase errors cleanly and completely

1. ① ② ③ ④ ⑤   20. ① ② ③ ④ ⑤   38. ① ② ③ ④ ⑤
2. ① ② ③ ④ ⑤   21. ① ② ③ ④ ⑤   39. ① ② ③ ④ ⑤
3. ① ② ③ ④ ⑤   22. ① ② ③ ④ ⑤   40. ① ② ③ ④ ⑤
4. ① ② ③ ④ ⑤   23. ① ② ③ ④ ⑤   41. ① ② ③ ④ ⑤
5. ① ② ③ ④ ⑤   24. ① ② ③ ④ ⑤   42. ① ② ③ ④ ⑤
6. ① ② ③ ④ ⑤   25. ① ② ③ ④ ⑤   43. ① ② ③ ④ ⑤
7. ① ② ③ ④ ⑤   26. ① ② ③ ④ ⑤   44. ① ② ③ ④ ⑤
8. ① ② ③ ④ ⑤   27. ① ② ③ ④ ⑤   45. ① ② ③ ④ ⑤
9. ① ② ③ ④ ⑤   28. ① ② ③ ④ ⑤   46. ① ② ③ ④ ⑤
10. ① ② ③ ④ ⑤   29. ① ② ③ ④ ⑤   47. ① ② ③ ④ ⑤
11. ① ② ③ ④ ⑤   30. ① ② ③ ④ ⑤   48. ① ② ③ ④ ⑤
12. ① ② ③ ④ ⑤   31. ① ② ③ ④ ⑤   49. ① ② ③ ④ ⑤
13. ① ② ③ ④ ⑤   32. ① ② ③ ④ ⑤   50. ① ② ③ ④ ⑤
14. ① ② ③ ④ ⑤   33. ① ② ③ ④ ⑤   51. ① ② ③ ④ ⑤
15. ① ② ③ ④ ⑤   34. ① ② ③ ④ ⑤   52. ① ② ③ ④ ⑤
16. ① ② ③ ④ ⑤   35. ① ② ③ ④ ⑤   53. ① ② ③ ④ ⑤
17. ① ② ③ ④ ⑤   36. ① ② ③ ④ ⑤   54. ① ② ③ ④ ⑤
18. ① ② ③ ④ ⑤   37. ① ② ③ ④ ⑤   55. ① ② ③ ④ ⑤
19. ① ② ③ ④ ⑤

Items 1 to 11 refer to the following paragraphs.

(1) The science of cryonics may offer a solution to people who would like to live forever. (2) Cryonics, the practice of freezing people in liquid nitrogen after they die. (3) Once a cure is found for the disease that killed a frozen body it is thawed, revived, and cured. (4) The procedure could have resulted, therefore, in near immortality for those who use it.

(5) Cryonics began in 1964 when the Physicist Robert Ettinger published a book that introduced cryonics as a means of living forever. (6) Since then, for example, few people have shown interest in having their bodies frozen for future revival. (7) Only about a dozen people have had their bodies frozen in cryonics centers in Michigan and California. (8) Many more claim to have considered cryonics as an option.

(9) Most people, therefore, say they would never freeze themselves for the future. (10) Some feel cryonics simply did not work. (11) After all, a person cannot legally be frozen until they are dead, and the chance of reviving a dead body is slim in any situation. (12) Many others claim they cannot afford to consider cryonics, it generally costs well over $100,000 for full-body preservation. (13) Other people unsure of what the future holds, say they would not want to be revived many years from now in a future they may not like.

1. Sentence 2: **Cryonics, the practice of freezing people in liquid nitrogen after they die.**

   What correction should be made to this sentence?

   (1) replace Cryonics, the with Cryonics is the
   (2) insert a comma after practice
   (3) insert a comma after people
   (4) replace after they die with once they are dead
   (5) no correction is necessary

2. Sentence 3: **Once a cure is found for the disease that killed a frozen body it is thawed, revived, and cured.**

   Which of the following is the best way to write the underlined portion of this sentence? If you think the original is the best way, select choice (1).

   (1) body it is
   (2) body that is
   (3) body, it is
   (4) body, that it is
   (5) body is

3. Sentence 4: **The procedure could have resulted, therefore, in near immortality for those who use it.**

   Which of the following is the best way to write the underlined portion of this sentence? If you think the original is the best way, select choice (1).

   (1) The procedure could have resulted, therefore, in
   (2) The procedure could result, therefore, in
   (3) The procedure will result, therefore, in
   (4) The procedure has resulted, therefore, in
   (5) The procedure will have resulted, therefore, in

4. Sentence 5: **Cryonics began in 1964 when the Physicist Robert Ettinger published a book that introduced cryonics as a means of living forever.**

   What correction should be made to this sentence?

   (1) change began to begins
   (2) change began to begun
   (3) change Physicist to physicist
   (4) insert a comma after Ettinger
   (5) no correction is necessary

5. Sentence 6: **Since then, for example, few people have shown interest in having their bodies frozen for future revival.**

   Which of the following is the best way to write the underlined portion of this sentence? If you think the original is the best way, select choice (1).

   (1) Since then, for example, few people
   (2) Since then, moreover, few people
   (3) Since then, as a result, few people
   (4) Since then, therefore, few people
   (5) Since then, however, few people

6. Sentences 7 and 8: **Only about a dozen people have had their bodies frozen in cryonics centers in Michigan and California. Many more claim to have considered cryonics as an option.**

The most effective combination of sentences 7 and 8 would include which of the following groups of words?

(1) California, many more
(2) California, so many more
(3) California since many more
(4) California, although many more
(5) California because many more

7. Sentence 9: **Most people, therefore, say they would never freeze themselves for the future.**

Which of the following is the best way to write the underlined portion of this sentence? If you think the original is the best way, select choice (1).

(1) Most people, therefore, say
(2) As a result, most people say
(3) Most people, however, say
(4) But most people say, therefore,
(5) However most people say

8. Sentence 10: **Some feel cryonics simply did not work.**

Which of the following is the best way to write the underlined portion of this sentence? If you think the original is the best way, select choice (1).

(1) simply did not work
(2) simply has not worked
(3) simply could have not worked
(4) simply will not work
(5) simply had not worked

9. Sentence 11: **After all, a person cannot legally be frozen until they are dead, and the chance of reviving a dead body is slim in any situation.**

Which of the following is the best way to write the underlined portion of this sentence? If you think the original is the best way, select choice (1).

(1) a person cannot legally be frozen until they are dead
(2) people cannot legally be frozen until he or she is dead
(3) a person cannot legally be frozen until he or she are dead
(4) a person cannot legally be frozen until he or she is dead
(5) people cannot legally be frozen until they is dead

10. Sentence 12: **Many others claim they cannot afford to consider cryonics, it generally costs well over $100,000 for full-body preservation.**

Which of the following is the best way to write the underlined portion of this sentence? If you think the original is the best way, select choice (1).

(1) cryonics, it generally costs
(2) cryonics, that generally costs
(3) cryonics, which generally costs
(4) cryonics, and it generally costs
(5) cryonics, generally it costs

11. Sentence 13: **Other people unsure of what the future holds, say they would not want to be revived many years from now in a future they may not like.**

What correction should be made to this sentence?

(1) insert a comma after people
(2) change future to Future
(3) remove the comma after holds
(4) insert a comma after revived
(5) insert a comma after now

Items 12 to 22 refer to the following paragraphs.

(1) Although crime is a huge social problem, the face of crime may be changing. (2) In the next century, fighting and preventing crime will require the police to know and use computers well. (3) More and more crimes will be committed not with guns but with computers. (4) This is a natural change, given the other ways in which our society is changing. (5) For example, as society does more business with computers and less with cash, crimes such as muggings, and armed robbery will wane. (6) Replacing them with crimes such as unauthorized electronic money transfers and credit card fraud committed by thieves using computers. (7) More than a trillion dollars are moved around the world with computers every day the potential for computer theft and fraud is great. (8) Computer criminals will also spy on rival companies and countries and disable there computer systems with viruses. (9) Terrorism and violence, including electronic hijackings, also appeared.

(10) But when the technology to commit these crimes exist, it will also exist to prevent the crimes. (11) The same technology that is available to criminals will be available to police. (12) Although this is true, companies and governments either have not foreseen the need and have been slow to invest in computer security. (13) So far, the loss of money and information due to such crimes has not even began to reach its potential. (14) Thus, they still tend to write off any loss as simply a cost of doing business. (15) However, even if computer security were to keep pace with the criminal computers will change the face of crime forever.

12. Sentences 2 and 3: **In the next century, fighting and preventing crime will require the police to know and use computers well. More and more crimes will be committed not with guns but with computers.**

The most effective combination of sentences 2 and 3 would include which of the following groups of words?

(1) well, more
(2) well, and more
(3) well while more
(4) well because more
(5) well even though more

13. Sentence 5: **For example, as society does more business with computers and less with cash, crimes such as muggings, and armed robbery will wane.**

What correction should be made to this sentence?

(1) change does to did
(2) change does to has done
(3) insert a comma after computers
(4) remove the comma after cash
(5) remove the comma after muggings

14. Sentence 6: **Replacing them with crimes such as unauthorized electronic money transfers and credit card fraud committed by thieves using computers.**

Which of the following is the best way to write the underlined portion of this sentence? If you think the original is the best way, select choice (1).

(1) Replacing them with crimes such as unauthorized electronic money transfers and credit card fraud committed
(2) Replacing them will be crimes such as unauthorized electronic money transfers and credit card fraud committed
(3) Replacing them will be crimes such as unauthorized electronic money transfers and credit card fraud will be committed
(4) Replacing them with crimes such as unauthorized electronic money transfers and credit card fraud will be committed
(5) Replace them with crimes such as unauthorized electronic money transfers and credit card fraud committed

15. Sentence 7: **More than a trillion dollars are moved around the world with computers every day the potential for computer theft and fraud is great.**

Which of the following is the best way to write the underlined portion of this sentence? If you think the original is the best way, select choice (1).

(1) every day the potential
(2) every day, the potential
(3) every day. Therefore, the potential
(4) every day because the potential
(5) every day, making the potential

16. Sentence 8: **Computer criminals will also spy on rival companies and countries and disable there computer systems with viruses.**

What correction should be made to this sentence?

(1) replace will also spy with have also spied
(2) insert a comma after companies
(3) insert a comma after countries
(4) replace there with their
(5) no correction is necessary

17. Sentence 9: **Terrorism and violence, including electronic hijackings, also appeared.**

What correction should be made to this sentence?

(1) remove the comma after violence
(2) remove the comma after hijackings
(3) change appeared to have appeared
(4) change appeared to had appeared
(5) change also appeared to will also appear

18. Sentence 10: **But when the technology to commit these crimes exist, it will also exist to prevent the crimes.**

What correction should be made to this sentence?

(1) insert a comma after commit
(2) change first exist to exists
(3) change first exist to existed
(4) change will also exist to exist
(5) change will also exist to existed

19. Sentence 12: **Although this is true, companies and governments either have not foreseen the need and have been slow to invest in computer security.**

What correction should be made to this sentence?

(1) change the spelling of companies to compannies
(2) change the spelling of governments to goverments
(3) change foreseen to foresaw
(4) replace the second and with or
(5) change have been to were

20. Sentence 13: **So far, the loss of money and information due to such crimes has not even began to reach its potential.**

What correction should be made to this sentence?

(1) change loss to lost
(2) replace due with do
(3) replace to with too
(4) insert a comma after crimes
(5) change began to begun

21. Sentence 14: **Thus, they still tend to write off any loss as simply a cost of doing business.**

What correction should be made to this sentence?

(1) replace they with money and information
(2) replace they with companies and governments
(3) change tend to tended
(4) change tend to will intend
(5) change the spelling of business to busness

22. Sentence 15: **However, even if computer security were to keep pace with the criminal computers will change the face of crime forever.**

What correction should be made to this sentence?

(1) insert a comma after security
(2) insert a comma after pace
(3) insert a comma after criminal
(4) insert a comma after computers
(5) no correction is necessary

Items 23 to 34 refer to the following paragraphs.

---

(1) The U.S. Constitution guarentees freedom of the press. (2) This freedom was viewed as vital by early Americans, who live with governments that restricted free speech. (3) Many of these early Americans had been forced to leave their native countries because their political views clashed with the views of their governments. (4) Thus, the U.S. press has operated under few legal limits and one major function of the press has been to watch our governments and report what they are doing.

(5) Not everyone agrees that the press should have such broad freedom. (6) Some people claim that there is no restrictions on what journalists may say or write. (7) Journalists will fail to verify the accuracy of information in their efforts to be the first to publish a story. (8) Also, some journalists may publish information they know to be false just because it makes a story interesting, because they dislike the person they are reporting on, they may want to hurt that person.

(9) Those who feel the press has treated them unfairly have always had access to the Courts. (10) Many journalists will be sued for libel, and a few of these suits have reached the Supreme Court. (11) Like the *New York Times* winning a Supreme Court case in 1964. (12) In this case, the Supreme Court ruled that libel means not only publishing false information but also to do so knowingly or without trying to verify the information. (13) Many people who disagree with this decision and claim it allows journalists to lie if they can show they did so unknowingly. (14) However, others claim that a strong press, not one weakened by lawsuits, can only be an effective source of information.

23. Sentence 1: **The U.S. Constitution guarentees freedom of the press.**

What correction should be made to this sentence?

(1) change U.S. to u.s.
(2) change Constitution to constitution
(3) change the spelling of guarentees to guarantees
(4) insert a comma after guarentees
(5) no correction is necessary

24. Sentence 2: **This freedom was viewed as vital by early Americans, who live with governments that restricted free speech.**

What correction should be made to this sentence?

(1) change was to is
(2) change live to lives
(3) change live to had lived
(4) insert a comma after governments
(5) change the spelling of speech to speach

25. Sentence 4: **Thus, the U.S. press has operated under few legal limits and one major function of the press has been to watch our governments and report what they are doing.**

Which of the following is the best way to write the underlined portion of this sentence? If you think the original is the best way, select choice (1).

(1) limits and one
(2) limits and, one
(3) limits, and, one
(4) limits, and one
(5) limits, one

26. Sentence 6: **Some people claim that there is no restrictions on what journalists may say or write.**

If you rewrote sentence 6 beginning with

Some people claim that no restrictions the next word should be

(1) is
(2) are
(3) will
(4) have
(5) what

27. Sentence 7: **Journalists will fail to verify the accuracy of information in their efforts to be the first to publish a story.**

Which of the following is the best way to write the underlined portion of this sentence? If you think the original is the best way, select choice (1).

(1) Journalists will fail
(2) Journalists may fail
(3) Journalists had failed
(4) Journalists have failed
(5) Journalists failed

28. Sentence 8: **Also, some journalists may publish information they know to be false just because it makes a story interesting, because they dislike the person they are reporting on, they may want to hurt that person.**

What correction should be made to this sentence?

(1) replace it makes with they make
(2) change the spelling of interesting to intresting
(3) replace interesting, because with interesting, or because
(4) replace they are with it is
(5) change may want to wanted

29. Sentence 9: **Those who feel the press has treated them unfairly have always had access to the Courts.**

What correction should be made to this sentence?

(1) insert a comma after those
(2) insert a comma after unfairly
(3) change always to all ways
(4) change Courts to courts
(5) no correction is necessary

30. Sentence 10: **Many journalists will be sued for libel, and a few of these suits have reached the Supreme Court.**

What correction should be made to this sentence?

(1) replace will be with have been
(2) remove the comma after libel
(3) insert a comma after suits
(4) replace have reached with will reach
(5) no correction is necessary

31. Sentence 11: **Like the *New York Times* winning a Supreme Court case in 1964.**

If you rewrote sentence 11 beginning with For example, the *New York Times* the next word should be

(1) winning
(2) win
(3) wins
(4) won
(5) has won

32. Sentence 12: **In this case, the Supreme Court ruled that libel means not only publishing false information but also to do so knowingly or without trying to verify the information.**

What correction should be made to this sentence?

(1) replace that with where
(2) insert a comma after means
(3) change to do to doing
(4) change trying to to try
(5) change to verify to verifying

33. Sentence 13: **Many people who disagree with this decision and claim it allows journalists to lie if they can show they did so unknowingly.**

What correction should be made to this sentence?

(1) remove Many people
(2) remove who
(3) insert a comma after decision
(4) insert a comma after lie
(5) insert a comma after show

34. Sentence 14: **However, others claim that a strong press, not one weakened by lawsuits, can only be an effective source of information.**

Which of the following is the best way to write the underlined portion of this sentence? If you think the original is the best way, select choice (1).

(1) that a strong press, not one weakened by lawsuits, can only be
(2) that a strong press, not one weakened only by lawsuits, can be
(3) that a strong press, not only one weakened by lawsuits, can be
(4) that a strong press, not one weakened by lawsuits, can be only
(5) that only a strong press, not one weakened by lawsuits, can be

---

Items 35 to 45 refer to the following paragraphs.

(1) Television seems to be offering more and more news shows every year. (2) But are these shows really giving us news? (3) According to television critics, television viewers have, in the past few years, saw a growth in the number of shows offering *infotainment*. (4) *Infotainment* is a combination of the words *information* and *entertainment* as suggested by this pairing, infotainment is a blend of factual information with elements of entertainment. (5) This blend reflected the media's efforts to report news in a more entertaining fashion or to report more entertaining news. (6) But when news shows attempt to deliver news and entertain to, viewers are not always sure what information is real.

(7) For example, if a U.S. senator is said to have met with drug dealers to buy illegal drugs, so a news show may recreate this meeting. (8) The show's producer and director hires someone to write a script (often based on partial and possibly distorted facts) and use professional actors to stage the meeting. (9) Often neither the actors nor an announcer on the show tell viewers that the meeting on the screen is fake. (10) After all, believing that they are seeing the meeting instead of merely hearing about it, may be more interesting to viewers. (11) Thus, the show's ratings are high, and its viewers are entertained.

(12) The problem is that this leaves some viewers believing that they witnessed the meeting and now know all the details. (13) Viewers have really not witnessed the meeting and have not even seen and heard clear, factual news.

(14) When television shows do not provide you with clear, factual news, those shows, critics claim, should not be promoted as news.

35. Sentence 3: **According to television critics, television viewers have, in the past few years, saw a growth in the number of shows offering *infotainment*.**

If you rewrote sentence 3 beginning with In the past few years, television viewers have the next word should be

(1) saw
(2) seen
(3) grown
(4) watched
(5) been

36. Sentence 4: *Infotainment* is a combination of the words *information* and *entertainment* as suggested by this pairing, infotainment is a blend of factual information with elements of entertainment.

What correction should be made to this sentence?

(1) replace *entertainment* as with *entertainment. As*

(2) replace *entertainment* as with *entertainment, as*

(3) replace pairing, infotainment with pairing. Infotainment

(4) replace pairing, infotainment with pairing while infotainment

(5) replace pairing, infotainment with pairing, and infotainment

37. Sentence 5: **This blend reflected the media's efforts to report** news in a more entertaining fashion or to report more entertaining news.

Which of the following is the best way to write the underlined portion of this sentence? If you think the original is the best way, select choice (1).

(1) This blend reflected the media's efforts to report

(2) This blend reflected the media's efforts, to report

(3) This blend reflects the media's efforts, to report

(4) This blend reflects the media's efforts to report

(5) This blend reflected, the media's efforts to report

38. Sentence 6: **But when news shows attempt to deliver news and entertain to, viewers are not** always sure what information is real.

Which of the following is the best way to write the underlined portion of this sentence? If you think the original is the best way, select choice (1).

(1) to deliver news and entertain to, viewers are

(2) to deliver news and entertain to viewers are

(3) to deliver news, and entertain to viewers are

(4) to deliver news and entertain too, viewers are

(5) to deliver news, and entertain too viewers are

39. Sentence 7: **For example, if a U.S. senator is said to have met with drug dealers to buy illegal drugs, so a news show may recreate this meeting.**

What correction should be made to this sentence?

(1) replace for example with however

(2) remove so

(3) replace so with and

(4) replace so with while

(5) no correction is necessary

40. Sentence 8: **The show's producer and director hires someone to write a script (often based on partial and possibly distorted facts) and use professional actors to stage the meeting.**

Which of the following is the best way to write the underlined portion of this sentence? If you think the original is the best way, select choice (1).

(1) The show's producer and director hires someone

(2) The show's producer and director hire someone

(3) The show's producer and director has hired someone

(4) The show's producer and director, hiring someone

(5) The show's producer and director had hired someone

41. Sentence 9: **Often neither the actors nor an announcer on the show tell viewers that the meeting on the screen is fake.**

Which of the following is the best way to write the underlined portion of this sentence? If you think the original is the best way, select choice (1).

(1) neither the actors nor an announcer on the show tell

(2) neither the actors nor an announcer on the show to tell

(3) neither the actors nor an announcer on the show has told

(4) neither the actors nor an announcer on the show told

(5) neither the actors nor an announcer on the show tells

42. Sentence 10: **After all, believing that they are seeing the meeting instead of merely <u>hearing about it, may be more</u> interesting to viewers.**

Which of the following is the best way to write the underlined portion of this sentence? If you think the original is the best way, select choice (1).

(1) hearing about it, may be more
(2) hearing about it may be more
(3) hearing about it. May be more
(4) hearing about, it may be more
(5) hearing about. It may be more

43. Sentence 12: **The problem is that this leaves some viewers believing that they witnessed the meeting and now know all the details.**

What correction should be made to this sentence?

(1) insert a comma after <u>is that</u>
(2) replace <u>this</u> with <u>the reenactment</u>
(3) change the spelling of <u>believing</u> to <u>beleiving</u>
(4) insert a comma after <u>meeting</u>
(5) no correction is necessary

44. Sentence 13: **Viewers have really not witnessed the meeting and have not even seen and heard clear, factual news.**

If you rewrote sentence 13 beginning with <u>Thus, viewers not only have not witnessed the meeting</u> the next word should be

(1) but
(2) and
(3) also
(4) they
(5) have

45. Sentence 14: **When television shows do not provide you with clear, factual news, those shows, critics claim, should not be promoted as news.**

If you rewrote sentence 14 beginning with <u>According to critics, television shows should not be promoted as news when they do not provide</u> the next word should be

(1) them
(2) you
(3) us
(4) our
(5) viewers

Items 46 to 55 refer to the following paragraphs.

(1) We are all interested in what the future holds for us. (2) By studying society and job trends, experts in the early part of the next century can tell you a lot about your work. (3) As a student, for example, you'll probably attend schools that run through the Summer. (4) More important, these schools will run under the leadership of business, will teach by simulating the workplace, and to emphasize workplace skills. (5) In these ways, schools will work more directly at preparing you for work.

(6) As a worker, you'll probably hold a job in which you'll collect transmit or retrieve, information stored on a computer. (7) Farming and factory jobs declined even more than they already have. (8) This does not mean, however, that you will be away from home more. (9) In fact, your likely to work out of your home in the future, communicating with your coworkers through a computer over telephone lines. (10) You'll be a more relaxed worker because you won't have to fight heavy traffic on side Streets and Boulevards to get to work. (11) Also, because many workers will not come into the office to work, work schedules will probably be more flexible. (12) If you do not celebrate Christmas, for example, you may prefer to work that day and take off a holiday of your choice. (13) Finally, your computer will have its own intellegence, and you will command it with your voice, not a keypad.

46. Sentence 2: **By studying society and job trends, experts in the early part of the next century can tell you a lot about your work.**

If you rewrote sentence 2 beginning with <u>Experts who study society and job trends</u> the next word should be

(1) can
(2) by
(3) early
(4) in
(5) about

47. Sentence 3: **As a student, for example, you'll probably attend schools that run through the Summer.**

What correction should be made to this sentence?

(1) remove the comma after <u>example</u>
(2) change the spelling of <u>probably</u> to <u>probally</u>
(3) change <u>run</u> to <u>ran</u>
(4) change <u>Summer</u> to <u>summer</u>
(5) no correction is necessary

48. Sentence 4: **More important, these schools will run under the leadership of business, will teach by simulating the workplace, and to emphasize workplace skills.**

What correction should be made to this sentence?

(1) replace will run with ran
(2) replace will teach with taught
(3) replace to emphasize with will emphasize
(4) change the spelling of emphasize to emphasis
(5) no correction is necessary

49. Sentence 6: **As a worker, you'll probably hold a job in which you'll collect transmit or retrieve, information stored on a computer.**

Which of the following is the best way to write the underlined portion of this sentence? If you think the original is the best way, select choice (1).

(1) you'll collect transmit or retrieve, information
(2) you'll collect, transmit or retrieve, information
(3) you'll collect transmit, or retrieve information
(4) you'll collect transmit or retrieve information
(5) you'll collect, transmit, or retrieve information

50. Sentence 7: **Farming and factory jobs declined even more than they already have.**

What correction should be made to this sentence?

(1) insert a comma after jobs
(2) insert have after jobs
(3) replace declined with will decline
(4) change declined to decline
(5) insert will after already

51. Sentence 9: **In fact, your likely to work out of your home in the future, communicating with your coworkers through a computer over telephone lines.**

Which of the following is the best way to write the underlined portion of this sentence? If you think the original is the best way, select choice (1).

(1) In fact, your likely to work out of your home
(2) In fact, your likly to work out of you're home
(3) In fact, you're likely to work out of your home
(4) In fact, you're likely to work out of you're home
(5) In fact, you're likly to work out of your home

52. Sentence 10: **You'll be a more relaxed worker because you won't have to fight heavy traffic on side Streets and Boulevards to get to work.**

What correction should be made to this sentence?

(1) insert a comma after worker
(2) change side Streets to Side Streets
(3) replace Streets and Boulevards with streets and boulevards
(4) insert a comma after Boulevards
(5) no correction is necessary

53. Sentence 11: **Also, because many workers will not come into the office to work, work schedules will probably be more flexible.**

What correction should be made to this sentence?

(1) change the spelling of because to becuase
(2) replace work, work with work. Work
(3) change the spelling of schedules to sckedules
(4) change will probably be with are probably be
(5) no correction is necessary

54. Sentence 12: **If you do not celebrate Christmas, for example, you may prefer to work that day and take off a holiday of your choice.**

What correction should be made to this sentence?

(1) change Christmas to christmas
(2) replace example, you with example. You
(3) insert a comma after day
(4) change holiday to Holiday
(5) no correction is necessary

55. Sentence 13: **Finally, your computer will have its own intelligence, and you will command it with your voice, not a keypad.**

What correction should be made to this sentence?

(1) replace its with it's
(2) change the spelling of intellegence to intelligence
(3) remove the comma after intellegence
(4) remove and
(5) change the spelling of voice to voise

To check your answers, turn to page 529.

Part II

45 Minutes

Directions

This part of the Writing Skills Test is intended to determine how well you write. You are asked to write an essay that explains something or presents an opinion on an issue. In preparing your essay, you should take the following steps.

1. Read carefully the directions and the essay topic given below.
2. Plan your essay carefully before you write.
3. Use scratch paper to make any notes.
4. Read carefully what you have written and make any changes that will improve your essay.
5. Check your paragraphs, sentence structure, spelling, punctuation, capitalization, and usage, and make any necessary corrections.

You will have 45 minutes to write on the topic below. Write legibly and use a ballpoint pen so that the evaluators will be able to read your writing.

TOPIC

A conflict has arisen near your home town. The state wants to build a new highway on the outskirts of town. However, a study of the area shows many endangered species of insects living in the area. Some groups want the highway to be built. Other groups want the area to be left alone for the insects. Which group do you agree with?

Write a letter of 200 to 250 words to the editor of your local newspaper, stating your opinion. Give reasons and specific examples to support your opinion.

To evaluate your essay, turn to pages 453 and 532.

SOCIAL STUDIES

85 Minutes ❖ 64 Questions

You should spend no more than 85 minutes answering the questions. Work carefully, but do not spend too much time on any one question. Be sure you answer every question. You will not be penalized for incorrect answers.

Do not mark in this test booklet. Record your answers on the separate answer sheet provided. Be sure all requested information is properly recorded on the answer sheet. To record your answers, mark the numbered space on the answer sheet beside the number that corresponds to the question in the test.

Do not rest the point of your pencil on the answer sheet while you are considering your answer. Make no stray or unnecessary marks. If you change an answer, erase your first mark completely. Mark only one answer space for each question; multiple answers will be scored as incorrect. Do not fold or crease your answer sheet.

FOR EXAMPLE

Early colonists of North America looked for settlement sites that had adequate water supplies and were accessible by ship. For this reason, many early towns were built near

(1) mountains
(2) prairies
(3) rivers
(4) glaciers
(5) plateaus

① ② ● ④ ⑤

The correct answer is "rivers"; therefore, answer space 3 would be marked on the answer sheet.

GED Test _____

Name _____

Date _____

- Use a No. 2 pencil.
- Mark one numbered space beside the number that corresponds to each question you are answering.
- Erase errors cleanly and completely

1. ① ② ③ ④ ⑤
2. ① ② ③ ④ ⑤
3. ① ② ③ ④ ⑤
4. ① ② ③ ④ ⑤
5. ① ② ③ ④ ⑤
6. ① ② ③ ④ ⑤
7. ① ② ③ ④ ⑤
8. ① ② ③ ④ ⑤
9. ① ② ③ ④ ⑤
10. ① ② ③ ④ ⑤
11. ① ② ③ ④ ⑤
12. ① ② ③ ④ ⑤
13. ① ② ③ ④ ⑤
14. ① ② ③ ④ ⑤
15. ① ② ③ ④ ⑤
16. ① ② ③ ④ ⑤
17. ① ② ③ ④ ⑤
18. ① ② ③ ④ ⑤
19. ① ② ③ ④ ⑤
20. ① ② ③ ④ ⑤
21. ① ② ③ ④ ⑤
22. ① ② ③ ④ ⑤

23. ① ② ③ ④ ⑤
24. ① ② ③ ④ ⑤
25. ① ② ③ ④ ⑤
26. ① ② ③ ④ ⑤
27. ① ② ③ ④ ⑤
28. ① ② ③ ④ ⑤
29. ① ② ③ ④ ⑤
30. ① ② ③ ④ ⑤
31. ① ② ③ ④ ⑤
32. ① ② ③ ④ ⑤
33. ① ② ③ ④ ⑤
34. ① ② ③ ④ ⑤
35. ① ② ③ ④ ⑤
36. ① ② ③ ④ ⑤
37. ① ② ③ ④ ⑤
38. ① ② ③ ④ ⑤
39. ① ② ③ ④ ⑤
40. ① ② ③ ④ ⑤
41. ① ② ③ ④ ⑤
42. ① ② ③ ④ ⑤
43. ① ② ③ ④ ⑤

44. ① ② ③ ④ ⑤
45. ① ② ③ ④ ⑤
46. ① ② ③ ④ ⑤
47. ① ② ③ ④ ⑤
48. ① ② ③ ④ ⑤
49. ① ② ③ ④ ⑤
50. ① ② ③ ④ ⑤
51. ① ② ③ ④ ⑤
52. ① ② ③ ④ ⑤
53. ① ② ③ ④ ⑤
54. ① ② ③ ④ ⑤
55. ① ② ③ ④ ⑤
56. ① ② ③ ④ ⑤
57. ① ② ③ ④ ⑤
58. ① ② ③ ④ ⑤
59. ① ② ③ ④ ⑤
60. ① ② ③ ④ ⑤
61. ① ② ③ ④ ⑤
62. ① ② ③ ④ ⑤
63. ① ② ③ ④ ⑤
64. ① ② ③ ④ ⑤

Directions

Choose the one best answer to each item.

Items 1 to 6 refer to the following information.

The terms defined below are some basic terms of economics.

Balance of trade: the difference between the total values of the goods and services flowing into and out of a country in relation to a specific trading partner over a set period of time

Inflation: a general rise in the level of prices

Monopoly: control of the available supply of a specific product or service by a single producer or seller

National debt: the amount of money the federal government has borrowed over time as a result of expenditures in excess of its revenues

Profit: the difference between the total cost of making and marketing a product and the total revenue that it yields

1. The amount of money a publicly held company sometimes distributes to its shareholders usually comes from what source?

   (1) the national debt
   (2) inflation
   (3) profit
   (4) the balance of trade
   (5) a monopoly

2. In many years, Japanese businesses earn more money from American customers than American businesses earn from Japanese customers. This imbalance in Japan's favor describes what fact of American economic life today?

   (1) a rising national debt
   (2) low inflation
   (3) high U.S. profits
   (4) an unfavorable balance of trade
   (5) an ineffectual monopoly

3. After World War I, defeated Germany saw its money become worthless. At one point, a person needed a wheelbarrow to carry all the currency required to purchase a single loaf of bread. In the early 1990s, the German government refused to lower the relatively high interest rate it paid to depositors. This policy negatively affected the economies of other nations in Europe and elsewhere, and many governments were very angry with the Germans. Nevertheless, the Germans continued the policy to protect themselves from the possibility of

   (1) a large national debt
   (2) runaway inflation
   (3) lowered profitability
   (4) an unfavorable balance of trade
   (5) foreign monopolies

4. The United States has laws to regulate monopolies. Some monopolies are forced to break up into several competing companies. Other monopolies—especially utilities, such as electric companies and gas companies—are allowed to operate but are carefully watched over by government officials. What is the advantage of allowing some monopolies to operate?

   (1) Businesses are able to take advantage of certain economies of scale and distribution so that the general sale price to customers can be kept low.
   (2) The government can control the basic supply of energy to citizens.
   (3) Government bureaucrats can play a role in the daily lives of people.
   (4) Businesses do not have to spend money on advertising and selling and can keep their costs to customers low.
   (5) Some businesses can make large profits.

5. A company whose cost of production increased while the selling price of its products stayed the same would probably experience

   (1) a favorable balance of trade
   (2) an unfavorable balance of trade
   (3) heightened profitability
   (4) lowered profitability
   (5) a monopoly

6. Under communism, the government controlled the means of production. Which business goal did the Soviet Union say was bad and therefore illegal?

(1) inflation
(2) profit
(3) national debt
(4) monopoly
(5) balance of payments

Items 7 to 10 refer to the following circle graph.

IMMIGRATION TO THE UNITED STATES 1900–1910

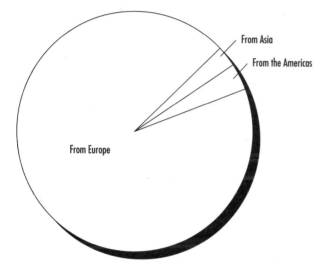

From Asia
From the Americas
From Europe

7. The period from the late 1800s to the early 1900s was a time of discrimination against people from Japan and China who wanted to immigrate to the United States. Which statement concerning the circle graph describes an effect of that discrimination?

(1) All of the immigrants to the United States came from Asia, the Americas, and Europe between 1900 and 1910.
(2) More immigrants came from Europe than from any other continent.
(3) According to the chart, no immigrants came from Africa or Australia.
(4) In the chart, "the Americas" refers to all those nations of the Western Hemisphere except the United States.
(5) Only a very small percentage of the total number of immigrants to the United States came from Asia, which includes China and Japan.

8. According to the graph, what percentage of the total number of immigrants came from Europe?

(1) about 10 percent
(2) about 30 percent
(3) about 50 percent
(4) about 70 percent
(5) about 90 percent

9. The early 1900s were a time when most immigrants traveled by boat to the United States. European immigrants landed at and were processed through Ellis Island in New York Harbor. Asian immigrants landed at and were processed through Angel Island in San Francisco Harbor. Based on the information in the circle graph, which of the following statements is true?

(1) Many more immigrants were processed through Ellis Island than through Angel Island in the early 1900s.
(2) Asian immigrants were often forced to live at Angel Island for several months when they first arrived.
(3) Ellis Island was the port of entry for passengers who did not travel first class.
(4) Immigrants at both Ellis Island and Angel Island had to pass brief medical examinations.
(5) Most immigrants from the rest of the Americas were refused entry to the United States between 1900 and 1910.

10. Racial tensions and the aftermath of the Civil War in the United States probably had what effect on immigration to the United States between 1900 and 1910?

(1) They led to heavier immigration from Europe.
(2) They led to virtually no immigration from Africa.
(3) They caused Asian immigrants to reconsider their decisions to move to the United States.
(4) They made available to immigrants from the Americas places for legal immigration to the United States.
(5) They caused the United States to follow the foreign policy of isolationism.

Items 11 to 13 refer to the following map.

TIME ZONES IN THE CONTINENTAL UNITED STATES

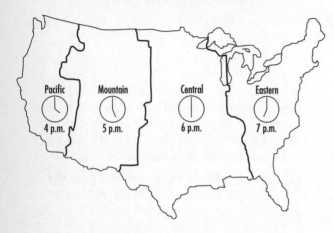

11. When it is 1:00 p.m. in San Francisco, what time is it in New York City?

    (1) 2 p.m.
    (2) 3 p.m.
    (3) 4 p.m.
    (4) 1 p.m.
    (5) 1 a.m.

12. A government worker in Washington, D.C., has to make a phone call to a Portland, Oregon, business that opens at 9:00 a.m. What is the earliest time in Washington, D.C., that the government worker can reach the Portland business?

    (1) 9 a.m.
    (2) 10 a.m.
    (3) 9 p.m.
    (4) 8 a.m.
    (5) noon

13. Time zones came into use in the United States in the late 1800s. What event or invention was the greatest cause of this innovation?

    (1) the end of the Civil War
    (2) the completion of the transcontinental railroad
    (3) the widespread use of tin cans for preserving food
    (4) the inauguration of the Pony Express
    (5) the growth in the number of European immigrants to the United States

Items 14 to 16 refer to the following information and graph.

PROFITS FOR GARCIA'S GOODIES

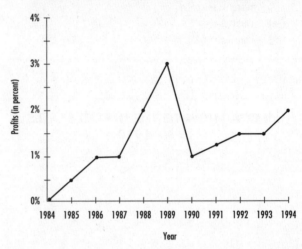

Mr. Antonio Garcia owns Garcia's Goodies, a gourmet grocery store he started in 1984. The line graph above shows the after-tax profits the store generated in each year of the first decade the store was in business.

14. According to the line graph, the year of highest profits was

    (1) 1984
    (2) 1987
    (3) 1989
    (4) 1993
    (5) 1990

15. When profits fell in 1990, Mr. Garcia could have successfully rectified the situation by

    (1) reducing the number of full-time store employees
    (2) getting a large loan from a nearby bank
    (3) asking some of the store's managers to take long paid vacations
    (4) giving cost-of-living salary increases to minimum-wage employees only
    (5) working with owners of similar, nearby stores to raise prices on most items

16. In which year did Mr. Garcia probably hire the most employees?

    (1) 1986
    (2) 1984
    (3) 1989
    (4) 1991
    (5) 1993

Items 17 and 18 refer to the following illustration.

LATITUDE AND LONGITUDE

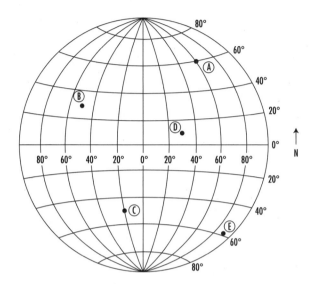

Items 19 and 20 refer to the following bar graph.

FEDERAL SPENDING ON EDUCATION 1965 AND 1971

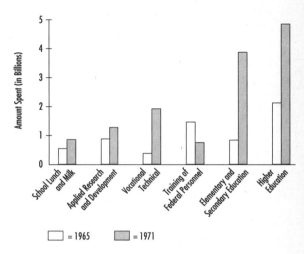

☐ = 1965   ▨ = 1971

17. According to the illustration, which of the lettered points is found at 50 degrees south latitude and 20 degrees west longitude?

(1) A
(2) B
(3) C
(4) D
(5) E

18. What direction is point B from point D?

(1) west northwest
(2) east southeast
(3) east northeast
(4) west southwest
(5) south

19. According to the bar graph, spending for which category declined between 1965 and 1971?

(1) school lunch and milk
(2) applied research and development
(3) vocational technical
(4) training of federal personnel
(5) elementary and secondary education

20. Which of the following statements can be verified by information in the graph?

(1) The federal government spent a relatively small amount of its funds on education in both 1965 and 1971.
(2) The food served in most school lunch rooms did not adequately meet federal nutrition guidelines.
(3) Applied research and development was a relatively small part of the overall education budget in both 1965 and 1971.
(4) In 1971, most Americans believed federal funds for education were not being wisely spent.
(5) The number of Americans in college included a greater percentage of African Americans in 1971 than in 1965.

Items 21 to 24 refer to the following information.

Listed below are five major present-day forms of government.

Aristocracy: government in which a small, privileged, hereditary group governs

Constitutional monarchy: government in which the real power is held by an elected parliament or congress but documents recognize a hereditary ceremonial king or queen

Dictatorship: government in which an individual and a small, trusted group of followers have all the power, usually to the detriment of the majority of citizens

Direct democracy: government in which all eligible citizens are entitled to participate in the process of making laws and setting policy

Representative democracy: government in which freely elected representatives of the great mass of citizens make laws and set policy

21. In Iraq, Saddam Hussein rules what type of government?

    (1) aristocracy
    (2) constitutional monarchy
    (3) dictatorship
    (4) direct democracy
    (5) representative democracy

22. Queen Elizabeth II of Great Britain and Northern Ireland is the head of

    (1) an aristocracy
    (2) a constitutional monarchy
    (3) a dictatorship
    (4) a direct democracy
    (5) a representative democracy

23. Although many others would disagree, the Irish Republican Army would probably describe the government of Northern Ireland as

    (1) an aristocracy
    (2) a constitutional monarchy
    (3) a dictatorship
    (4) a direct democracy
    (5) a representative democracy

24. People in the United States tend to oppose dictatorships because

    (1) most Americans have a basic belief in the rights of all people to have a say in their government
    (2) most known dictatorships have operated to the detriment of the majority of their citizens
    (3) most people in the United States know little about forms of government other than democracy
    (4) dictatorships often deny equal trading rights in their nations to U.S. companies
    (5) the United States has never been governed by a dictatorship

Items 25 to 27 refer to the following information.

Violence has become a major concern of many Americans in the 1990s. This violence includes child abuse, spousal abuse, random shootings, assaults, and abuse of the elderly.

25. A member of a child welfare league would probably be most involved with finding solutions to which type of violence?

    (1) child abuse
    (2) spousal abuse
    (3) abuse of the elderly
    (4) random shootings
    (5) assaults

26. A member of the American Association of Retired Persons would probably be most involved in finding solutions to which type of violence?

    (1) child abuse
    (2) spousal abuse
    (3) abuse of the elderly
    (4) random shootings
    (5) assaults

27. Street gangs are most often associated with which type of criminal activity?

    (1) anti-Semitic hate crimes
    (2) thefts of information from computer systems
    (3) retaliatory shootings
    (4) rape
    (5) credit card forgeries

Items 28 to 31 refer to the following map.

EXPANSION OF THE CONTINENTAL UNITED STATES

28. According to the map, the last part of the continental United States that was added was

(1) the Louisiana Purchase
(2) the Mexican Cession
(3) Oregon Country
(4) the Gadsden Purchase
(5) Florida

29. The Mexican War of 1846–1848 was ended by the Treaty of Guadalupe Hidalgo, which gave what large area of land to the United States?

(1) the Louisiana Purchase
(2) the Mexican Cession
(3) Oregon Country
(4) the Gadsden Purchase
(5) Florida

30. The Louisiana Purchase was made during the presidency of which of the following men?

(1) George Washington (1789–1797)
(2) Millard Fillmore (1850–1853)
(3) Thomas Jefferson (1801–1809)
(4) James Polk (1845–1849)
(5) Franklin Pierce (1853–1857)

31. Which sentence is the best summary of the map's content?

(1) Texas was annexed before the Gadsden Purchase was made.
(2) The Louisiana Purchase extended from the Gulf of Mexico to the Canadian border.
(3) At the time of the Constitutional Convention, the territory of the United States was all east of the Mississippi River.
(4) The Oregon Country is north and west of the Louisiana Purchase.
(5) The expansion of the continental United States was made up of adjoining pieces of land that were added during the nineteenth century.

Items 32 to 33 refer to the following information.

When the United States entered World War I in 1917, President Woodrow Wilson said, "The world must be made safe for democracy. Its peace must be planted upon the tested foundations of political liberty." Later he said, "The Americans who went to Europe . . . in World War I . . . to die are a unique breed. Never before have men crossed seas to a foreign land to fight for a cause which they did not pretend was particularly their own, which they knew was the cause of humanity and mankind."

32. Of the following statements regarding potential U.S. courses of action in the early 1990s, which might Wilson have most strongly supported?

(1) The United States should intervene militarily in the former Yugoslavia to stop the bloodshed there.
(2) The United States should prevent the nations of Eastern Europe from joining NATO because such a situation could cause alarm in Russia.
(3) The United States should launch surprise attacks against North Korea and Iraq to eliminate their dictatorial governments.
(4) The United States should encourage the growth of economic groups like the European Common Market and the North American Free Trade Association.
(5) The United States should ignore foreign affairs as much as possible and spend more of its funds and time on domestic affairs.

33. Which of the following beliefs or actions of Woodrow Wilson was consistent with his speeches about making the world safe for democracy?

   (1) his belief in white supremacy

   (2) his belief that God had foreordained him to be president of the United States

   (3) his eight-year tenure as president of Princeton University

   (4) his appointment of Louis D. Brandeis to be the first Jewish justice of the Supreme Court

   (5) his strong support for the League of Nations and U.S. participation in it

34. Which list below places the events of twentieth-century America in the correct chronological order?

   (1) the Roaring 20s, the Great Depression, World War II, the assassination of John F. Kennedy, the Watergate scandal

   (2) the Great Depression, the assassination of John F. Kennedy, World War II, the Watergate scandal, the Roaring 20s

   (3) World War II, the Watergate scandal, the Great Depression, the assassination of John F. Kennedy, the Roaring 20s

   (4) the Watergate scandal, the assassination of John F. Kennedy, World War II, the Roaring 20s, the Great Depression

   (5) the assassination of John F. Kennedy, World War II, the Great Depression, the Roaring 20s, the Watergate scandal

35. Which of the following situations was not an outcome of World War I?

   (1) a drop in immigration from Italy, Austria-Hungary, and Russia to the United States between 1910 and 1920

   (2) the influenza epidemic of 1918

   (3) the creation of the American Expeditionary Force to Europe

   (4) the Treaty of Versailles

   (5) the League of Nations

Items 36 and 37 refer to the following information.

Clinical depression is a treatable, medical illness. Many Americans get the treatment they need. However, elderly people often fail to seek treatment even though statistically the elderly are more likely to suffer from clinical depression than any other age group in America.

36. Which choice would not be a reasonable cause of this low level of treatment among the elderly?

   (1) They are of a generation that views depression not as an illness but as a symptom of weakness or laziness.

   (2) They are already suffering from other illnesses, such as diabetes, heart disease, and kidney and liver disease, that sometimes alter the brain chemistry and set off depression.

   (3) They are often taking numerous medications that may precipitate depression.

   (4) They are in the age group most likely to develop other diseases, such as Alzheimer's, that may cause symptoms similar to depression and thus lead to misdiagnosis.

   (5) They often lead such busy lives that it is difficult for them to find time to get a thorough diagnosis.

37. Someone who suspects that he or she may be suffering from clinical depression would do best to seek advice from

   (1) a friend who may also have the disease

   (2) an X-ray technician

   (3) a doctor

   (4) a close relative

   (5) a psychologist

Item 38 refers to the following cartoon.

A WIDELY HELD VIEW OF AMERICAN TROOPS IN FOREIGN LANDS

38. Which statement is the best summary of the meaning of this 1993 cartoon?

   (1) American troops are often not as well trained as their foreign enemies.

   (2) American troops are often too lightly armed when they go into combat.

   (3) Saddam Hussein failed to defeat America and its allies in the Gulf War.

   (4) American troops often become targets themselves when they try to settle conflicts between two foreign adversaries.

   (5) American troops are better at fighting wars at home than they are at fighting wars abroad.

Items 39 to 43 refer to the following information.

    Below are some highlights of former President Herbert Hoover's career:

- He created the Wickersham Commission (in 1929), which concluded that Prohibition was a failure but nevertheless opposed its repeal.

- He signed into law the Smoot-Hawley Tariff, which set off a global trade war.

- He headed, at the end of World War I, the American Relief Administration, which distributed $5.2 billion in aid to Europe.

- He established the Hoover Institution on War, Revolution, and Peace at Stanford University.

- He ordered the clearing by force in 1932 of the Washington, D.C., camp of the Bonus Army, which consisted of needy World War I veterans who came to the capital to seek early payment of a bonus Congress had promised them.

39. Which event in Hoover's career contributed to his sometimes being called the Great Humanitarian?

   (1) the Wickersham Commission
   (2) the Smoot-Hawley Tariff
   (3) the American Relief Administration
   (4) the Hoover Institution
   (5) the Bonus Army

40. Which situation showed Hoover's lack of understanding of the suffering of individuals during the Great Depression?

   (1) the Wickersham Commission
   (2) the Smoot-Hawley Tariff
   (3) the American Relief Administration
   (4) the Hoover Institution
   (5) the Bonus Army

41. At the end of World War II, President Harry S. Truman appointed Hoover as coordinator of Food Supply for World Famine. Which of Hoover's earlier experiences gave him the qualifications to head this group to alleviate world suffering?

   (1) the Wickersham Commission
   (2) the Smoot-Hawley Tariff
   (3) the American Relief Administration
   (4) the Hoover Institution
   (5) the Bonus Army

42. In 1917, Hoover said, "War is a losing business. . . . Its greatest compensation lies in the possibility that we may instill into our people unselfishness." Which part of Hoover's own career might he have pointed to as an example of this unselfishness?

   (1) the Wickersham Commission
   (2) the Smoot-Hawley Tariff
   (3) the American Relief Administration
   (4) the Hoover Institution
   (5) the Bonus Army

43. In 1920, Franklin Roosevelt said of Hoover, "He is certainly a wonder and I wish we could make him president of the United States. There could not be a better one." However, in 1932 Roosevelt said, "I accuse the present [Hoover] administration [of having failed] to anticipate the dire needs of and the reduced earning power of the people." What may so drastically have changed Franklin Roosevelt's opinion of Hoover?

(1) the fact that Roosevelt had contracted polio and had permanent paralysis in his legs by 1932

(2) the fact that Roosevelt was running for president in 1932 against Hoover, the incumbent

(3) the fact that both Hoover and Roosevelt had served in the administrations of previous presidents

(4) the fact that Hoover was often associated with California whereas Roosevelt was associated with New York

(5) the fact that Hoover opposed U.S. entry into World War II until after the Japanese attack on Pearl Harbor

Items 44 to 47 refer to the following information.

The World's Columbian Exposition was held in Chicago from May through October, 1893. It was held to celebrate (one year late) the 400th anniversary of Columbus's crossing of the Atlantic Ocean and to honor the progress of American civilization. Some facts concerning the fair are listed below.

- Some 28 million people visited the fair.

- Adults paid an entry fee of $0.50, a high price for the time.

- Nicknamed the White City, the fair's buildings were sheathed in a lightweight mixture of plaster, cement, and white paint.

- The fair had some 3,500 flush toilets, a new invention that, at the time, most fairgoers had never seen before.

- The world's first Ferris wheel (named for its inventor, George Washington Gale Ferris), which had thirty-six cars that could carry forty people each, was a highlight of the amusements.

- Countries that had their own official "government" buildings at the fair included Brazil, Canada, Ceylon, Colombia, France, Germany, Great Britain, Haiti, Japan, Norway, Siam, Spain, Sweden, Turkey, and Venezuela.

- The fair was illuminated by electric lights, which were first turned on by U.S. President Grover Cleveland when he tapped a gold-plated telegraph key.

- Speakers at the fair included feminist Susan B. Anthony, social reformer Ida B. Wells, politicians Theodore Roosevelt and Woodrow Wilson, historian Frederick Jackson Turner, scientist Booker T. Washington, African-American leader Frederick Douglass, and poet Paul Laurence Dunbar.

- The amusements included a toboggan ride, an exotic dancer known as Little Egypt, and ethnic villages from India, Java, Ireland, Lapland, Austria, and Turkey.

44. According to the passage, the greatest number of countries having official government buildings were from

(1) Asia

(2) South America

(3) Europe

(4) North America

(5) the Caribbean

45. On the opening day of the fair, social reformer Jane Addams had her purse snatched, and on American Cities Day, October 28, Chicago mayor Carter Harrison, the day's triumphant host, was shot and killed by a deranged job seeker. What do these two events say about America of the late nineteenth century when compared to America of the late twentieth century?

(1) American officials and notables have long received poor protection from their security forces.

(2) Criminals often prey on unsuspecting women.

(3) America has long been a violent society.

(4) America is more violent in the late twentieth century than it was in the late nineteenth century.

(5) America was more violent in the late nineteenth century than it is now.

46. One way the Columbian Exposition honored American civilization was by

    (1) the erection of ethnic villages

    (2) the fair's being nicknamed the White City

    (3) the great number of official "government" buildings

    (4) having the President of the United States open the fair

    (5) the inclusion of technological wonders of the times, such as the Ferris wheel, electric lights, and flush toilets

47. One of the following statements is a conclusion about the Columbian Exposition. All of the others are supporting statements. Which one is the conclusion?

    (1) The Columbian Exposition brought together a wide spectrum of nineteenth-century peoples, cultures, and technology to be seen by millions of Americans and others.

    (2) Some 28 million people visited the fair over its six-month run in 1893, during which the fair took in almost $32 million in entrance and other fees.

    (3) The 60 nations represented at the fair included Austria, Brazil, Ceylon, Germany, Haiti, Norway, Siam, and Venezuela.

    (4) Many dignitaries visited the fair, and some—like Roosevelt, Wilson, Douglass, and Wells—spoke there also.

    (5) Technology highlighted the fair with such novelties of the times as a Ferris wheel, flush toilets, and electric lights.

Items 48 and 49 refer to the following cartoon.

The NORTH ATLANTIC TEA & ORIGAMI Society

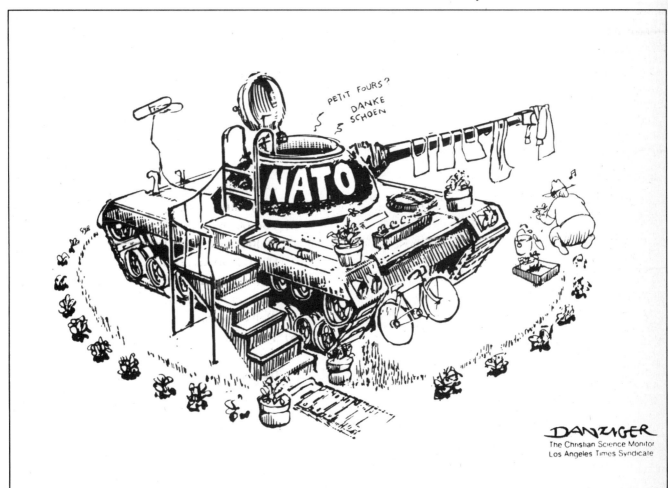

48. Which statement is the best summary of this 1990 cartoon's meaning?

    (1) NATO has become too involved in Japanese affairs.
    (2) NATO is not a well-managed organization.
    (3) NATO has become ineffectual since the fall of communism.
    (4) NATO needs to undertake joint training exercises with the former communist countries of Eastern Europe.
    (5) NATO was a better organization when it had a strong adversary.

49. With which of the following statements would the cartoonist probably most agree?

    (1) NATO needs a powerful enemy to be strong itself.
    (2) France needs to rejoin NATO before the organization can become strong again.
    (3) NATO has never been a useful organization for the United States to be a part of and it never will be.
    (4) NATO should become a worldwide security group.
    (5) NATO's benefit to the West has ended and it should be disbanded.

Items 50 and 51 refer to the following cartoon.

50. Which choice best summarizes the cartoonist's point?

    (1) Poverty, drugs, and ignorance are root causes of gangs.
    (2) Gangs are the root cause of poverty, drugs, and ignorance.
    (3) Experts agree that poverty, drugs, and gangs are the major causes of ignorance.
    (4) Drugs are the major cause of gang violence.
    (5) Few people believe that poverty, drugs, and ignorance are root causes of gangs.

51. With which point of view would the cartoonist most clearly agree?

    (1) The only way to end gang violence is to eliminate poverty.
    (2) Gang violence can be ended only by implementing a law that puts repeat offenders in jail permanently.
    (3) Drugs are the major cause of gangs.
    (4) Only by eliminating poverty, drugs, and ignorance will we be able to end gangs and their violence.
    (5) The government has spent too much money trying to eliminate poverty and drugs.

Items 52 to 55 refer to the following table.

IMPORTANT JOB FACTORS

Job Factor	Percentage Who Rated It "Very Important"
Open communication in company	65%
Effect of job on personal/family life	60%
Supervisor's management style	58%
Job security	54%
Job location	50%
Family-supportive policies	46%
Fringe benefits	43%
Salary/wages	35%
Management/promotion opportunities	26%
Size of company	18%

52. According to the table, which aspect of their jobs do workers consider most important?

    (1) job security
    (2) fringe benefits
    (3) open communication
    (4) management opportunity
    (5) salary/wages

53. According to the table, which job factor is least important to employees?

    (1) family-supportive policies
    (2) the supervisor's style of management
    (3) the size of the company
    (4) the effect on personal/family life
    (5) fringe benefits, such as health insurance

54. Which of the following combinations might be most likely to make employees unhappy enough to consider leaving their jobs?

    (1) few management opportunities and few fringe benefits
    (2) an uncommunicative supervisor and a company atmosphere of secrecy
    (3) a small number of total employees and an out-of-the-way office location
    (4) policies that are not family supportive and few fringe benefits
    (5) lack of management opportunities and a large number of staff members

55. If you are the owner of a small business and you are trying to hire a potentially valuable employee away from a large multinational competitor, what should you stress in interviews?

    (1) that you expect the size of your business to grow rapidly
    (2) that the lines of communication will always be open between the two of you, both formally and informally
    (3) that the prospective employee will never be fired or terminated
    (4) that you cannot offer many fringe benefits now, but you have great plans for such things in the future
    (5) that you plan to move the business to a newer building

---

Items 56 and 57 refer to the following cartoon.

56. Which statement best describes the cartoon's meaning?

    (1) Repeat offenders are a problem in American society.
    (2) Parole boards should carry malpractice insurance as doctors do.
    (3) Only high wage earners such as doctors can afford to carry malpractice insurance.
    (4) Parole boards should be held more accountable for those they release from prison.
    (5) Parole boards should have more minority members.

57. If this cartoonist could speak to the parole board, what would he probably ask them to do?

    (1) be less lenient with probable repeat offenders
    (2) spend more time reviewing each case
    (3) grant paroles to first-time offenders only
    (4) work with state legislators to increase the funds available for building more prisons
    (5) grant more paroles to drug dealers

Items 58 to 61 refer to the following passage.

Although people sometimes think of the earth as unchanging and solid, this is not really true. In fact, the earth is changing constantly, both on and beneath the surface. Evidence of this activity can be seen in the United States today. Active volcanoes are found in both Oregon and Hawaii. Earthquakes are common in California, especially along the San Andreas Fault. The New Madrid Fault, a less active but well-known fault, runs from southern Illinois through Missouri, Tennessee, and Arkansas.

Weather has a big effect on the shape and form of the earth's surface. Tornadoes are common during some seasons in Iowa, Nebraska, Kansas, Illinois, Wisconsin, and other states in the Midwest. Heavy rains sometimes cause flash floods in Texas, Arizona, New Mexico, and California. Hurricanes are annual events and sometimes strike Florida, the Carolinas, and other states along the eastern seaboard.

58. Someone who lives near the San Andreas Fault probably worries most about the danger from

(1) hurricanes
(2) tornadoes
(3) earthquakes
(4) volcanoes
(5) flash floods

59. In 1811 and 1812, the Mississippi River changed its course through Tennessee, Missouri, and Arkansas. What most likely forced this change?

(1) hurricanes
(2) tornadoes
(3) earthquakes
(4) volcanoes
(5) flash floods

60. Ancient peoples believed that earthquakes and volcanic eruptions were caused by the gods. Why did they believe this?

(1) The explanation fit the level of knowledge at the time.
(2) The ancient people rejected the actual scientific explanations.
(3) Earthquakes and volcanic eruptions were more common in ancient times than they are today.
(4) Most of the earth's population in ancient times lived in the Eastern Hemisphere, where earthquakes and volcanic eruptions are more common than in the Western Hemisphere.
(5) Ancient peoples wanted to believe that their gods had great powers.

61. An expert in volcanic activity would be able to combine business with pleasure if she or he took a vacation in

(1) Florida
(2) Illinois
(3) Hawaii
(4) California
(5) Texas

Items 62 to 64 refer to the information below.

The following materials and help for small businesses are available from the federal government.

- a directory of 320 firms that make equity investments in small, qualified companies

- brochures on how a small company can do business with the federal government

- training and individual counseling from the Service Corps of Retired Executives (SCORE)

- quarterly publications on how a small business can qualify for federal research and development funds

- seminars on management skills

- a booklet on available loans, counseling, and special programs for businesses in rural areas

490

62. A small business owner who wanted to get some government contracts would probably do best to start by

   (1) finding a firm that would make an equity investment in the business
   (2) getting individual counseling from a SCORE volunteer
   (3) reading materials about services available for rural businesses
   (4) studying brochures on how to do business with the federal government
   (5) attending seminars on management skills

63. Four of the following sentences are opinions. Which one is a statement of fact?

   (1) The federal government holds specialized management seminars too infrequently.
   (2) Retired business executives do not provide enough help with accounting procedures.
   (3) More than 300 firms make equity investments in small U.S. businesses.
   (4) Many federal government publications are high-quality materials that are very helpful to small businesses.
   (5) Federal government publications on small businesses in rural areas are hard to get because too few are printed.

64. A recent immigrant from the former Soviet Union might question the worthiness of federal government publications because

   (1) similar publications in the Soviet Union were not very well written
   (2) immigrants generally do not like to ask the government for help
   (3) other recent immigrants have already been disappointed in the quality of the materials and have said so
   (4) immigrants from the former Soviet Union usually did not trust anything their government said and may have carried this negative feeling about government with them
   (5) many immigrants from the former Soviet Union and elsewhere do not know enough English to be able to take full advantage of the publications and might misinterpret the materials

To check your answers, turn to page 532.

SCIENCE

95 Minutes ❖ 66 Questions

Directions

The Science Test consists of multiple-choice questions intended to measure the general concepts in science. The questions are based on short readings that often include a graph, chart, or figure. Study the information given and then answer the question(s) that follow. Refer to the information as often as necessary in answering the questions.

You should spend no more than 95 minutes answering the questions in this booklet. Work carefully, but do not spend too much time on any one question. Be sure you answer every question. You will not be penalized for incorrect answers.

Do not mark in this test booklet. Record your answers to the questions on the separate answer sheet provided. Be sure all requested information is properly recorded on the answer sheet.

To record your answers, mark the numbered space on the answer sheet beside the number that corresponds to the question in the test booklet.

Do not rest the point of your pencil on the answer sheet while you are considering your answer. Make no stray or unnecessary marks. If you change an answer, erase your first mark completely. Mark only one answer space for each question; multiple answers will be scored as incorrect. Do not fold or crease your answer sheet.

FOR EXAMPLE

Which of the following is the smallest unit in a living thing?

(1) tissue
(2) organ
(3) cell
(4) muscle
(5) capillary

① ② ● ④ ⑤

The correct answer is "cell"; therefore, answer space 3 would be marked on the answer sheet.

GED Test _____

Name _____

Date _____

- Use a No. 2 pencil.
- Mark one numbered space beside the number that corresponds to each question you are answering.
- Erase errors cleanly and completely

1. ① ② ③ ④ ⑤
2. ① ② ③ ④ ⑤
3. ① ② ③ ④ ⑤
4. ① ② ③ ④ ⑤
5. ① ② ③ ④ ⑤
6. ① ② ③ ④ ⑤
7. ① ② ③ ④ ⑤
8. ① ② ③ ④ ⑤
9. ① ② ③ ④ ⑤
10. ① ② ③ ④ ⑤
11. ① ② ③ ④ ⑤
12. ① ② ③ ④ ⑤
13. ① ② ③ ④ ⑤
14. ① ② ③ ④ ⑤
15. ① ② ③ ④ ⑤
16. ① ② ③ ④ ⑤
17. ① ② ③ ④ ⑤
18. ① ② ③ ④ ⑤
19. ① ② ③ ④ ⑤
20. ① ② ③ ④ ⑤
21. ① ② ③ ④ ⑤
22. ① ② ③ ④ ⑤

23. ① ② ③ ④ ⑤
24. ① ② ③ ④ ⑤
25. ① ② ③ ④ ⑤
26. ① ② ③ ④ ⑤
27. ① ② ③ ④ ⑤
28. ① ② ③ ④ ⑤
29. ① ② ③ ④ ⑤
30. ① ② ③ ④ ⑤
31. ① ② ③ ④ ⑤
32. ① ② ③ ④ ⑤
33. ① ② ③ ④ ⑤
34. ① ② ③ ④ ⑤
35. ① ② ③ ④ ⑤
36. ① ② ③ ④ ⑤
37. ① ② ③ ④ ⑤
38. ① ② ③ ④ ⑤
39. ① ② ③ ④ ⑤
40. ① ② ③ ④ ⑤
41. ① ② ③ ④ ⑤
42. ① ② ③ ④ ⑤
43. ① ② ③ ④ ⑤
44. ① ② ③ ④ ⑤

45. ① ② ③ ④ ⑤
46. ① ② ③ ④ ⑤
47. ① ② ③ ④ ⑤
48. ① ② ③ ④ ⑤
49. ① ② ③ ④ ⑤
50. ① ② ③ ④ ⑤
51. ① ② ③ ④ ⑤
52. ① ② ③ ④ ⑤
53. ① ② ③ ④ ⑤
54. ① ② ③ ④ ⑤
55. ① ② ③ ④ ⑤
56. ① ② ③ ④ ⑤
57. ① ② ③ ④ ⑤
58. ① ② ③ ④ ⑤
59. ① ② ③ ④ ⑤
60. ① ② ③ ④ ⑤
61. ① ② ③ ④ ⑤
62. ① ② ③ ④ ⑤
63. ① ② ③ ④ ⑤
64. ① ② ③ ④ ⑤
65. ① ② ③ ④ ⑤
66. ① ② ③ ④ ⑤

Directions

Choose the one best answer to each item.

Items 1 to 3 refer to the following information.

All ordinary materials offer some resistance to the flow of electrons, or electricity. Metals such as copper and silver are good conductors; that is, their resistance to the flow of electricity is low. A metal's resistance to the flow of electricity becomes even lower as the temperature decreases. The resistance of most metals does not decrease below a certain value, even at extremely cold temperatures.

Other materials, called superconductors, show an extraordinary drop in resistance at extremely cold temperatures. Lead, for example, gradually decreases in resistance until it reaches a certain temperature. At that point, the resistance of lead drops to zero.

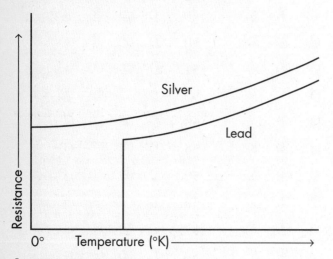

1. What is resistance?

   (1) the flow of electrons
   (2) a metal that conducts electricity
   (3) a substance that is a superconductor
   (4) the slowing down of the flow of electrons
   (5) a substance such as copper or silver

2. A material with extremely high resistance would most likely be used as

   (1) electrical wiring
   (2) the filament in a light bulb
   (3) a battery
   (4) a covering for electrical wiring
   (5) a lightning rod

3. Which of the following statements is supported by the information given?

   (1) As the temperature decreases, the resistance of any material decreases until both values are zero.
   (2) As the temperature increases, the resistance of any material decreases.
   (3) The resistance of lead falls to zero at extremely low temperatures.
   (4) The resistance of conductors falls to zero at extremely low temperatures.
   (5) Resistance is measured in ohms.

4. The amount of carbon dioxide in the atmosphere is increasing, partly as a result of many human activities. For example, carbon dioxide levels are increased by burning fuels and by reducing the amount of plant life on Earth.

   Which of the following activities would not tend to increase carbon dioxide levels in the atmosphere?

   (1) increasing the use of automobiles
   (2) increasing the amount of electricity generated from solar energy
   (3) cutting and burning large areas of rain forest
   (4) replacing forests and fields with cities and parking lots
   (5) incinerating garbage instead of taking it to a landfill

5. Bread mold grows in fruits as well as in bread and other baked goods. The mold reproduces by forming dry spores that grow best in a warm, moist environment. The spores travel through the air from one object to another. Using this information, how can you keep bread from getting moldy?

   A. Store bread in a cool place.
   B. Keep bread wrapped tightly.
   C. Throw away other moldy foods as soon as you see them.

   (1) A only
   (2) B only
   (3) C only
   (4) A and B
   (5) A, B, and C

494

Items 6 to 9 refer to the following information.

The basic unit of all living things is the cell. A thin membrane holds the contents of the cell together. Most of the cell is made up of a jellylike material called cytoplasm.

Each cell has one nucleus, which controls the activities of the cell. In addition, each cell has mitochondria, sometimes called the powerhouses of the cell because they release energy from food. Cells also have storage areas called vacuoles. Ribosomes are cell parts that make proteins for the cell. A typical animal cell is shown here.

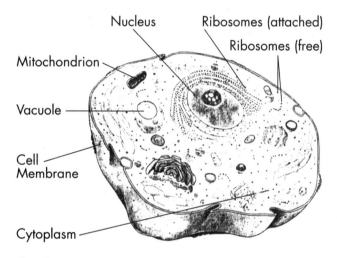

6. The control center of a cell is the

(1) nucleus
(2) cytoplasm
(3) ribosome
(4) vacuole
(5) membrane

7. Some cells, such as muscle cells, are very active. Which of the following parts are active cells most likely to have?

(1) a very thick cell membrane
(2) many ribosomes
(3) a very large vacuole
(4) many mitochondria
(5) very little cytoplasm

8. A ribosome could best be compared to

(1) a warehouse
(2) a factory
(3) a power plant
(4) a furnace
(5) an office

9. The first structure of living cells to be seen through the microscope was the nucleus. Which of the following statements is the most likely reason for this?

(1) The nucleus is the most important part of the cell.
(2) The nucleus is found in the center of the cell.
(3) The nucleus is the densest structure in the cell.
(4) The nucleus controls the activities of other cell structures.
(5) The nucleus is the source of energy for the cell.

Items 10 and 11 refer to the following information.

Light consists of electromagnetic waves that are visible to the human eye. The color we see depends on the wavelength of the waves. Of the visible electromagnetic waves, red has the longest wavelength and violet the shortest.

Most of the light we see consists of a mixture of wavelengths and, therefore, a mixture of colors.

10. What is light?

(1) electromagnetic waves visible to the human eye
(2) the color red, with a long wavelength
(3) the color violet, with a short wavelength
(4) electromagnetic waves of the same wavelength
(5) laser beams

11. Which of the following is a use of visible electromagnetic waves?

(1) heating
(2) AM radio
(3) FM radio
(4) radar
(5) photography

Items 12 to 14 refer to the following information.

A lever is a bar or rod that tilts on a fulcrum, or pivot. When you apply a force at one point on a lever, the lever tilts on the fulcrum to provide a force at another point. The force you apply is the effort, and the weight moved or resistance overcome is called the load. The effort times its distance from the fulcrum equals the load times its distance from the fulcrum.

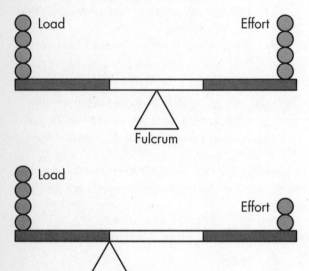

12. What would be the effect of moving the fulcrum from the center toward the effort?

    (1) The effort required to raise the load would decrease.
    (2) The effort required to raise the load would increase.
    (3) The weight of the load would increase.
    (4) The weight of the load would decrease.
    (5) The load and the effort would be equal.

13. The levers illustrated are first-class levers, in which the fulcrum is positioned between the load and the effort. In a second-class lever, the fulcrum is at one end, the effort is at the other, and the load is in the middle. Which of the following is a second-class lever?

    (1) a balance scale
    (2) a crowbar
    (3) the claw end of a hammer
    (4) a seesaw
    (5) a nutcracker

14. Which of the following statements is supported by the information given?

    (1) A fishing rod is a type of third-class lever in which one hand functions as the fulcrum and the other as the effort.
    (2) In a first-class lever, the farther the distance between the effort and the fulcrum, the less effort is needed to move a load.
    (3) The load and the effort are always equal in a first-class lever.
    (4) The greater the load, the less effort is required to move it.
    (5) All first-class levers have fulcrums equally distant from the load and the effort.

Items 15 to 20 refer to the following information.

A solute dissolves in a solvent to form a solution, a homogeneous mixture. Water is called the universal solvent because so many substances dissolve in it. However, solutes and solvents may be gases, liquids, or solids. Solutions may be characterized by the amount of solute that is dissolved:

Diluted: a solution in which a small amount of solute is dissolved in a solvent

Concentrated: a solution in which a large amount of solute is dissolved in a solvent

Saturated: a solution in which all the solute that can be dissolved in the solvent at a given temperature is dissolved

Unsaturated: a solution in which more solute can be dissolved in the solvent at a given temperature

Supersaturated: a solution that holds more solute than it normally can in the solvent at a given temperature.

15. Which of the following substances can act as solvents?

    A. Gases
    B. Liquids
    C. Solids

    (1) A only
    (2) B only
    (3) C only
    (4) A and B
    (5) A, B, and C

16. A woman was mixing sugar with water in preparation for making candy. She added a cup of sugar to some cold water and stirred. No matter how long she stirred, some of the sugar would not dissolve. The solution of sugar and water was

    (1) diluted
    (2) concentrated
    (3) saturated
    (4) unsaturated
    (5) supersaturated

17. The woman heated the solution of water and sugar until it was boiling. All the remaining sugar quickly dissolved. She added another spoon of sugar and it too dissolved quickly. The solution of sugar and water was now

    (1) diluted
    (2) concentrated
    (3) saturated
    (4) unsaturated
    (5) supersaturated

18. Vinegar is a solution of acetic acid and water. When making a sauce, a man added two tablespoons of vinegar to a cup of water before adding it to the other ingredients. The vinegar solution was

    (1) diluted
    (2) concentrated
    (3) saturated
    (4) unsaturated
    (5) supersaturated

19. At room temperature, ammonia is a gas. However, the ammonia used as a household cleaner is a liquid. Which of the following is the most likely reason for this?

    (1) Household ammonia contains a cleaning agent other than ammonia.
    (2) Household ammonia consists of water with ammonia gas dissolved in it.
    (3) Household ammonia is made in temperatures low enough for ammonia gas to become a liquid.
    (4) When ammonia gas is placed in containers, it becomes a liquid.
    (5) Household ammonia, when mixed with bleach, produces a toxic gas.

20. Which of the following statements is supported by the information provided?

    (1) Solids can act as solutes but they cannot act as solvents.
    (2) Gases can act as solvents but they cannot act as solutes.
    (3) A concentrated solution may be saturated or unsaturated.
    (4) The solubility of gas decreases when the temperature is increased.
    (5) To make a diluted solution concentrated, more solvent must be added.

> Items 21 and 22 refer to the following information.

When a large piece of raw beef is sliced, it is a purple color because of the presence of a chemical called myoglobin. As myoglobin is exposed to the air, it combines with oxygen to form oxymyoglobin, and the meat turns bright red. If the meat is sealed in airtight wrapping at this point, bacteria consume some of the oxygen in the oxymyoglobin, yielding metmyoglobin, which is brown. The meat is still fresh, but it no longer has the bright red color consumers associate with freshness.

21. What would be the result if the meat were wrapped in a substance that allows oxygen to pass through?

    (1) The meat would still turn brown, because bacteria are consuming all the oxygen, yielding metmyoglobin.
    (2) The meat would remain red, because even though bacteria are consuming some oxygen, more oxygen is available to combine with myoglobin to form oxymyoglobin.
    (3) The meat would remain purple, because the myoglobin would not combine with oxygen from the air.
    (4) The meat would turn red, then purple, because the oxygen in the air was drawing out the oxygen from the oxymyoglobin.
    (5) The meat would no longer be fresh even though it had just been cut.

22. If you slice a piece of raw beef that's brown on the outside, the newly cut surface will turn bright red. Which of the following is the cause of this color change?

(1) Oxygen from the air combines with myoglobin.

(2) Bacteria consumes oxygen in oxymyoglobin.

(3) Oxygen from the air combines with metmyoglobin.

(4) Blood flows from the meat.

(5) Oxygen from the air combines with oxymyoglobin.

Items 23 to 27 refer to the following map.

TODAY'S HIGH TEMPERATURES AND PRECIPITATION

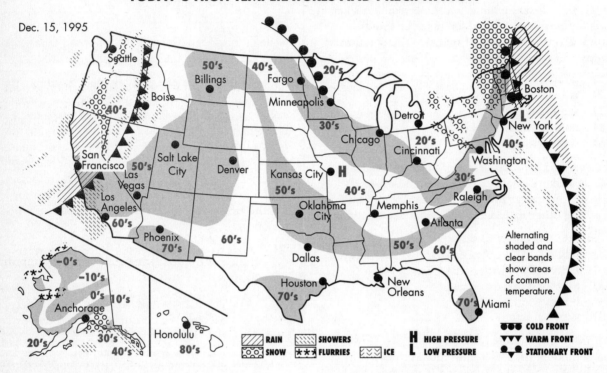

Dec. 15, 1995

23. In which of the following cities is it raining?

(1) Miami, Florida
(2) Dallas, Texas
(3) Minneapolis, Minnesota
(4) Las Vegas, Nevada
(5) San Francisco, California

24. The movement of fronts across the United States is generally from west to east. The local weather forecast in one city is for clearing skies and colder temperatures in the 20s. Which of the following cities is the forecast for?

(1) Washington, D.C.
(2) Atlanta, Georgia
(3) Denver, Colorado
(4) Los Angeles, California
(5) Houston, Texas

25. The local weather forecast in another city is for sunny weather with temperatures in the 40s or 50s. Which of the following cities is the forecast for?

(1) Detroit, Michigan
(2) New Orleans, Louisiana
(3) Los Angeles, California
(4) Memphis, Tennessee
(5) New York, New York

26. Which of the following statements is supported by the information in the map?

    (1) Salt Lake City and Kansas City have temperatures in the 40's.
    (2) It is usually colder in Billings than it is in Atlanta.
    (3) Areas of low pressure are associated with precipitation.
    (4) Cold polar air masses originate over the Arctic.
    (5) Winds generally blow from areas of high pressure to areas of low pressure.

27. A stationary front is one that is not moving or is moving very slowly. In which of the following cities is the weather likely to remain the same for a few days?

    (1) Seattle, Washington
    (2) Las Vegas, Nevada
    (3) Minneapolis, Minnesota
    (4) Boise, Idaho
    (5) Boston, Massachusetts

Items 28 to 32 refer to the following information.

There are thousands of different kinds of proteins in the human body. The enzymes that digest food, the hormones that control many body functions, and the clotting factors in blood are examples of proteins. Furthermore, much of the body itself is made of proteins.

All proteins are made up of sequences of simpler materials called amino acids. Although there are thousands of proteins in the human body, they are made from only 20 different amino acids. By forming different combinations and arrangements of these amino acids, the body makes the wide range of proteins that it needs. A small protein contains about 40 amino acids, while larger proteins contain as many as 500.

The formation of proteins from amino acids is controlled by deoxyribonucleic acid (DNA). DNA contains the code that tells the cells of the body how to assemble each kind of protein.

28. How many different amino acids make up the proteins in the human body?

    (1) 20
    (2) 40
    (3) 500
    (4) 1,000
    (5) 3,000

29. The way amino acids are put together to make different proteins is most like the way

    (1) bricks are put together to make a building
    (2) vegetables are put together to make soup
    (3) pages are put together to make a book
    (4) letters are put together to make words
    (5) pearls are put together to make a necklace

30. The human body does not make its own amino acids. Instead, it must get them from food. Foods that supply amino acids are

    (1) sugars
    (2) starches
    (3) fats
    (4) oils
    (5) proteins

31. A change in DNA is called a mutation. A mutation in the part of DNA that has instructions for the production of the protein insulin could cause all of the following except

    (1) one amino acid to be substituted for another
    (2) one amino acid to be left out
    (3) the production of insulin to stop
    (4) a different protein to be made
    (5) one amino acid to change into another amino acid

32. Which of the following statements is supported by the information provided?

    (1) Amino acids are the building blocks of proteins.
    (2) The body manufactures the amino acids it needs.
    (3) Proteins contain nitrogen, carbon, hydrogen, and oxygen.
    (4) Proteins help carry out chemical reactions.
    (5) All amino acids contain nitrogen and hydrogen.

33. Biomass, any plant or animal material, is a renewable resource that can be used to produce energy. Which of the following is an example of the use of biomass?

    (1) using flowing water to generate electricity
    (2) using gasoline to power an automobile
    (3) harnessing wind to generate electricity
    (4) burning sugar cane to generate electricity
    (5) using solar collectors to heat a house

Item 34 refers to the following information.

The second law of thermodynamics states that every time energy is transformed, it becomes less useful. For example, when electric energy runs a motor, no more than 80 percent of the energy is actually used. The rest becomes heat, which is given off by the machine. Waste heat is always generated by any use of energy. Even machines that use heat energy, such as a steam engine, take in very hot steam but discharge wastewater that is still warm.

34. Which of the following statements from the passage is a conclusion supported by the details given?

(1) Every time energy is transformed, it becomes less useful.
(2) When electric energy runs a motor, no more than 80 percent of the energy is actually used.
(3) The rest becomes heat, which is given off by the machine.
(4) Steam engines take in very hot steam.
(5) Steam engines discharge wastewater that is still warm.

Items 35 to 37 refer to the following information.

All living things are made from elements, simple materials found in nature. Although there are about 100 elements found in nature, about 99 percent of the weight of living organisms consists of just 10 elements, as shown.

THE TEN MOST COMMON ELEMENTS FOUND IN LIVING THINGS

Element	Percent by Weight
oxygen	65.0
carbon	18.0
hydrogen	10.0
nitrogen	3.0
calcium	1.5
phosphorous	1.0
potassium	0.1
sulfur	0.2
sodium	0.1
chlorine	0.1

35. What is the percent by weight of calcium in living organisms?

(1) 18.0
(2) 3.0
(3) 1.5
(4) 1.0
(5) 0.1

36. Iron is another element, not listed, found in living things. The percent by weight of iron cannot be more than

(1) 0.1 percent
(2) 0.5 percent
(3) 5 percent
(4) 10 percent
(5) 15 percent

37. The elements listed in the table are not evenly distributed throughout the human body. Which of the following statements supports this idea?

A. Water, which is made of hydrogen and oxygen, makes up over 70 percent of body weight.
B. There are large deposits of calcium and phosphorous in bones.
C. All cells contain about the same amount of sodium.

(1) A only
(2) B only
(3) C only
(4) A and B
(5) A and C

38. Mosses are small plants that grow in shady, damp places. Mosses lack true roots, and do not have veins as larger plants do. When mosses reproduce sexually, sperm produced on one plant swim to eggs produced on another plant. Why don't mosses grow in dry, sunny places?

(1) They need water to put down roots.
(2) They need water for sexual reproduction.
(3) They need sunlight to make their own food.
(4) They need minerals found in soil.
(5) They only grow underwater.

39. Navel oranges are naturally seedless oranges. The first seedless oranges were found on an orange tree in South America. All navel oranges can be traced to that one tree. Taking cuttings from a navel orange tree is the only way to increase the number of navel orange trees. Why must cuttings be used to propagate the navel orange?

(1) Cross-breeding of orange trees may reduce the number of valuable traits in the next generation.

(2) Cross-breeding of orange trees may cause the next generation of navel oranges to have seeds.

(3) Planting navel orange seeds takes too long to produce mature trees that are ready to bear fruit.

(4) The seeds of a navel orange are not able to sprout.

(5) There are no navel orange seeds to plant.

Items 40 and 41 refer to the following illustration.

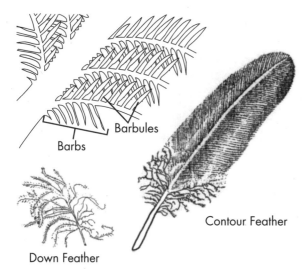

Barbules

Barbs

Contour Feather

Down Feather

40. The function of contour feathers on the wing is to make a large surface that provides lift and balance for flight. What characteristic of contour feathers is helpful for flying?

(1) The barbules on adjacent feathers hook together to form a strong surface.

(2) The fluffy barbs near the base of the feather are soft.

(3) Oil on the feathers makes a waterproof surface.

(4) The contour feathers give the bird its color.

(5) The contour feathers are located on the bird's breast.

41. The down feathers are fluffy and small, and are found beneath the other feathers. What is their function?

(1) They help the bird flap its wings.

(2) They make a large wing surface for flight.

(3) They trap air in the spaces and keep the bird warm.

(4) They make the bird a bright color to attract a mate.

(5) They enable the bird to dive beneath the water.

42. Pheromones are chemical substances that insects use to attract a mate. The female silkworm moth gives off a pheromone that attracts males. The male can smell this pheromone even if it is diluted to only one molecule in one trillion. Which of the following is the most likely explanation for this?

(1) The pheromone smells sweet.

(2) The male has a very sensitive sense of smell.

(3) The female has a very sensitive sense of smell.

(4) The female makes a large amount of pheromone.

(5) The male makes a large amount of pheromone.

43. The black soot that settles on the windowsills and furniture of city dwellers is visible air pollution. The soot consists primarily of tiny carbon and sulfur particles released by cars, trucks, and buses as a result of incomplete combustion of fuel. What would the effect be if vehicles used purer fuel that is low in sulfurs?

(1) Air pollution levels would decrease.

(2) Air pollution levels would increase.

(3) Traffic levels would increase.

(4) Traffic levels would decrease.

(5) Water pollution would increase.

Items 44 to 46 refer to the following information.

A beehive contains three kinds of bees:

- one queen, who produces eggs

- many males, called drones, whose only function is that one drone mates with the queen; she stores the sperm to use for the rest of her life

- workers (the most numerous type), sterile females who make honey and take care of the queen and the hive

44. Sometimes, when food is scarce, the workers drive the drones out of the hive. Why does this not harm the hive?

    (1) Males can be replaced as the queen lays more fertilized eggs.
    (2) Workers can breed more males.
    (3) The workers can take over the jobs the drones do.
    (4) The queen can take over the jobs the drones do.
    (5) Drones have no function in the hive.

45. Which of the following bees would a beekeeper need to start a new hive?

    A. a queen who has mated
    B. a drone
    C. a worker

    (1) A only
    (2) B only
    (3) C only
    (4) A and B
    (5) A, B, and C

46. Which of the following conclusions is supported by the information provided?

    (1) The taste of honey depends on the type of pollen the bees use.
    (2) Only the drone bees can sting when disturbed.
    (3) When bees swarm, they are always driving out the drones.
    (4) Bees are animals that cooperate in order to survive.
    (5) The worker bees live longer than the queen bee.

47. The adult frog has a shorter digestive system than the tadpole has. This change is most likely related to

    (1) the change from breathing water to breathing air
    (2) the change from eating plants to eating insects
    (3) the change from swimming to hopping
    (4) the growth to larger body size
    (5) the loss of the tail

48. A solar eclipse occurs when the moon blocks the sun's light from reaching parts or all of Earth. A solar eclipse can best be compared to

    (1) a guard blocking a forward's attempt to get a basketball into the basket
    (2) a security guard preventing people from entering a store before it opens
    (3) a person blocking the light of a slide projector and casting a shadow on the screen
    (4) a runner alternately jogging and walking on a track
    (5) a person using a flashlight to find something lost in the dark

49. Leaves contain many pigments, or types of coloring matter. The main pigment is chlorophyll, which is green. It masks the other pigments, which may be red, orange, and yellow. Although all pigments are sensitive to temperature changes, chlorophyll is especially so. Even a mild frost can destroy chlorophyll. Why do leaves change color in the fall?

    (1) The orange pigment destroys the chlorophyll.
    (2) The leaves make extra red pigment.
    (3) The chlorophyll combines with red pigment.
    (4) The tree destroys its own chlorophyll.
    (5) The chlorophyll breaks down and the other pigments become visible.

The Shoemaker-Levy comet was on a collision course with the largest planet in the solar system, Jupiter. At one time, the comet passed so close to Jupiter that it was broken into many fragments by the planet's gravity. The scattered fragments were expected to collide with Jupiter over a six-day period in 1994.

Scientists were not sure what would happen when the comet pieces descended into Jupiter's atmosphere. Some thought that the fragments would explode soon after entering the atmosphere. Others thought that the comet fragments would penetrate much deeper into Jupiter.

50. Which of the following sentences best summarizes the passage?

(1) Jupiter is the largest planet of the solar system.

(2) A comet was broken into fragments by Jupiter's gravity.

(3) Scientists were studying the effect of comets on the atmosphere of Jupiter.

(4) Scientists were not sure what would happen when a comet collided with Jupiter.

(5) A comet was expected to collide with the planet Jupiter over a six-day period.

51. Which of the following statements represents an opinion held by scientists who predicted the collision?

(1) Jupiter is the largest planet in the solar system.

(2) A comet is on a collision course with the planet Jupiter.

(3) Jupiter's gravity broke the comet into many pieces.

(4) The collision will occur over a six-day period.

(5) The fragments will explode soon after entering Jupiter's atmosphere.

52. Many seeds go through dormancy, an inactive period, before sprouting. Seeds produced in the fall lie dormant in winter. Then spring rains cause them to swell and sprout. What is the advantage to a species of having its seed go through a dormant period?

(1) It keeps the seeds from sprouting when there are leaves on the trees.

(2) It keeps the seed from sprouting when it is too cold.

(3) It keeps the seed from sprouting when there is too much water.

(4) It keeps the seed from sprouting when there is too much light.

(5) It keeps the seed from sprouting when there is no food available.

Substances pass through the food chain as one organism feeds on another. For example, an oil called omega-3, produced by fish, is found in polar bears. Seals eat fish year-round, and polar bears feed heavily on the seals' skin and blubber during the winter. Polar bears eat nothing during the summer months, when seals are not available.

Omega-3 has been found to lower blood cholesterol in humans. During the winter, polar bears have lower blood cholesterol levels than in summer.

53. Which of the following is the food chain described in the passage?

(1) fish, seal, polar bear

(2) fish, polar bear, seal

(3) seal, polar bear, fish

(4) omega-3, cholesterol

(5) omega-3, cholesterol, humans

54. How can eating seal blubber lower a polar bear's cholesterol?

(1) Seals make omega-3 in their bodies.

(2) Polar bears make omega-3 in their bodies.

(3) Polar bears eat mostly fish, and the omega-3 builds up in their bodies.

(4) Seals eat fish, and the omega-3 builds up in their bodies.

(5) Polar bears' fat cells change seal blubber into omega-3.

Items 55 and 56 refer to the following information.

A chemical reaction is one in which there are changes in the composition and structure of one or more substances, called reactants, to produce new products. Activation energy is needed to start a reaction. One type of chemical reaction, an exothermic reaction, is shown in this graph.

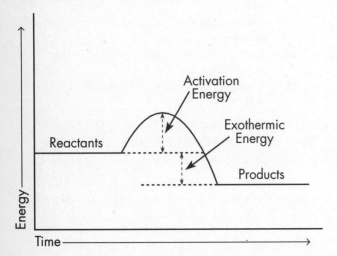

55. According to the graph, which of the following has the least energy?

(1) products
(2) activation energy
(3) reactants
(4) exothermic reaction
(5) reaction time

56. In a chemical reaction, energy can be neither created nor destroyed. Which of the following is most likely to happen to the energy that results from an exothermic reaction?

(1) It is released in the form of heat or light.
(2) It is absorbed by the products of the reaction, which have more energy than the reactants.
(3) It is absorbed by the reactants, which have more energy than the products.
(4) It turns into activation energy.
(5) It turns into a chemical substance.

57. As fruits ripen, they give off ethylene gas. This gas can speed up the ripening process in nearby fruits, especially when the fruits are in a container. Which of the following sayings reflects this information?

(1) An apple a day keeps the doctor away.
(2) One rotten apple spoils the whole barrel.
(3) The apple doesn't fall very far from the tree.
(4) She is the apple of her father's eye.
(5) Comfort me with apples for I am sick of love.

Items 58 to 60 refer to the following information.

Isostasy means that the top layer of Earth, the crust, floats on the next layer of Earth, the mantle, in a state of balance. For example, if the crust presses down in one area, it is pushed up in another. The crust floats on the mantle because it is less dense than the mantle. Heavy parts of the crust sink deeper into the mantle than light parts. For example, thick, dense mountain crust sinks deeper into the mantle than thinner, lighter crust.

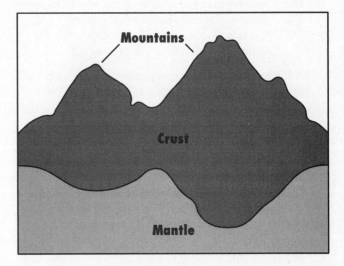

58. Dense mountain crust sinking deeper into the mantle than lighter crust is most similar to

(1) a loaf of bread rising higher in a warm place than in a cold place
(2) a pothole forming on a street during the winter rather than during the summer
(3) a loaded freighter floating deeper in the water than an empty freighter
(4) a swimmer being more buoyant in the ocean than in a lake or pool
(5) an athlete training by lifting weights rather than doing aerobic exercise

504

59. Which of the following is most likely to result if the mountain is worn away by erosion?

(1) Because the mountain weighs more, it sinks deeper into the mantle.

(2) Because the mountain weighs more, it rises higher in the mantle.

(3) Because the mountain is worn away on the surface, its position in the mantle remains the same.

(4) Because the mountain weighs less, it sinks deeper into the mantle.

(5) Because the mountain weighs less, it rises higher in the mantle.

60. Which of the following statements is supported by the information given?

(1) The rising or falling of crust cannot be observed because it happens so slowly.

(2) Fault-block mountains result from the uplift of large sections of crust along faults.

(3) Folded mountains sometimes develop where large sections of crust meet.

(4) Since the mantle and crust are in a state of balance, if the crust rises somewhere it sinks somewhere else.

(5) The crust is between 5 and 65 kilometers thick.

Items 61 to 64 refer to the following information.

Cholesterol, a fatlike substance, is one of several factors that increase a person's risk of heart disease. Although some cholesterol is normally found in the body, many people have too much. Excess cholesterol builds up along the walls of blood vessels. As cholesterol buildup increases, less blood is able to carry oxygen to the heart muscle.

Cholesterol buildup in the arteries of the heart can cause a heart attack, a blockage of blood flow to part of the heart. Sometimes the blockage is caused entirely by cholesterol buildup. At other times the blockage occurs when a blood clot becomes trapped in a blood vessel already narrowed by cholesterol. Cells in the part of the heart that is not getting enough oxygen may die, permanently damaging the heart.

Several other factors increase a person's risk of heart attack. Smoking and being overweight are two such risk factors. So is an inactive lifestyle. Diet is a well-documented risk factor. A diet high in cholesterol or saturated fats, such as found in meats and dairy products, increases the risk of heart attack. High blood pressure increases the risk of heart attack because it increases the rate at which cholesterol builds up in

blood vessels. The risk of heart attack increases as you get older, or if you are male, or if you have a family history of heart disease.

61. Which of the following <u>increases</u> the risk of heart attack?

(1) shortness of breath

(2) smoking

(3) damaged cells in the heart

(4) exercising

(5) low-fat diet

62. Which of the following is a <u>direct</u> cause of a heart attack?

(1) dizziness

(2) high blood pressure

(3) diet rich in fat

(4) cholesterol buildup in blood vessels

(5) diet rich in grains and vegetables

63. Which of the following risk factors is a person able to control?

(1) family history of heart disease

(2) sex

(3) exercise

(4) age

(5) body type

64. A person who wanted to reduce the risk of coronary heart disease could do all of the following except

(1) go to a stop-smoking program

(2) increase the grains, fruits, and vegetables in her diet

(3) go to an exercise class three times a week

(4) go on a diet if she is overweight

(5) eat more meat and dairy products

65. Life scientists divide all living things into five kingdoms as shown here:

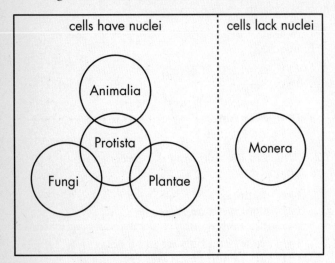

Which of the following statements is supported by the information in the diagram?

(1) Human beings are the only species in their kingdom.

(2) The cells of plants and animals have nuclei.

(3) Plants and animals are more closely related to organisms in the kingdom Monera than they are to each other.

(4) Bacteria are examples of organisms in the kingdom Monera.

(5) Plants are one-celled organisms.

66. Nuclear fission is the process in which the nuclei of atoms are split by an additional neutron, resulting in a large release of energy. As a nucleus is split, it releases several neutrons, which in turn split other nuclei. The first neutron sets off a chain of fissions, called a chain reaction. Unless the chain reaction is controlled, enormous amounts of heat energy are produced in a fraction of a second, as in an atomic bomb.

What would be the result of slowing and controlling the chain reaction?

(1) The amount of heat energy produced would increase sharply.

(2) A more powerful bomb could be manufactured.

(3) Additional neutrons would be released.

(4) Heat production would take place at a decreased, steady pace.

(5) The chain reaction would not begin.

To check your answers, turn to page 534.

INTERPRETING LITERATURE AND THE ARTS

65 Minutes ❖ 45 Questions

Read each excerpt first and then answer the questions that follow. Refer back to the reading material as often as necessary in answering the questions.

Each excerpt is preceded by a "purpose question." The purpose question gives a reason for reading the material. Use these purpose questions to help focus your reading. You are not required to answer these purpose questions. They are given only to help you concentrate on the ideas presented in the reading materials.

You should spend no more than 65 minutes answering the questions. Work carefully, but do not spend too much time on any one question. Be sure you answer every question. You will not be penalized for incorrect answers.

Do not mark in this test booklet. Record your answers on the separate answer sheet provided. Be sure all requested information is properly recorded on the answer sheet. To record your answers, mark the numbered space on the answer sheet beside the number that corresponds to the question in the test booklet.

Do not rest the point of your pencil on the answer sheet while you are considering your answer. Make no stray or unnecessary marks. If you change an answer, erase your first mark completely. Mark only one answer space for each question; multiple answers will be scored as incorrect. Do not fold or crease your answer sheet.

FOR EXAMPLE

It was Susan's dream machine. The metallic blue paint gleamed, and the sporty wheels were highly polished. Under the hood, the engine was no less carefully cleaned. Inside, flashy lights illuminated the instruments on the dashboard, and the seats were covered by rich leather upholstery. The subject ("It") of this excerpt is most likely

(1) an airplane
(2) a stereo system
(3) an automobile
(4) a boat
(5) a motorcycle

① ② ● ④ ⑤

The correct answer is "an automobile"; therefore, answer space 3 would be marked on the answer sheet.

GED Test _____

Name _____

Date _____

- Use a No. 2 pencil.
- Mark one numbered space beside the number that corresponds to each question you are answering.
- Erase errors cleanly and completely

1. ① ② ③ ④ ⑤	16. ① ② ③ ④ ⑤	31. ① ② ③ ④ ⑤
2. ① ② ③ ④ ⑤	17. ① ② ③ ④ ⑤	32. ① ② ③ ④ ⑤
3. ① ② ③ ④ ⑤	18. ① ② ③ ④ ⑤	33. ① ② ③ ④ ⑤
4. ① ② ③ ④ ⑤	19. ① ② ③ ④ ⑤	34. ① ② ③ ④ ⑤
5. ① ② ③ ④ ⑤	20. ① ② ③ ④ ⑤	35. ① ② ③ ④ ⑤
6. ① ② ③ ④ ⑤	21. ① ② ③ ④ ⑤	36. ① ② ③ ④ ⑤
7. ① ② ③ ④ ⑤	22. ① ② ③ ④ ⑤	37. ① ② ③ ④ ⑤
8. ① ② ③ ④ ⑤	23. ① ② ③ ④ ⑤	38. ① ② ③ ④ ⑤
9. ① ② ③ ④ ⑤	24. ① ② ③ ④ ⑤	39. ① ② ③ ④ ⑤
10. ① ② ③ ④ ⑤	25. ① ② ③ ④ ⑤	40. ① ② ③ ④ ⑤
11. ① ② ③ ④ ⑤	26. ① ② ③ ④ ⑤	41. ① ② ③ ④ ⑤
12. ① ② ③ ④ ⑤	27. ① ② ③ ④ ⑤	42. ① ② ③ ④ ⑤
13. ① ② ③ ④ ⑤	28. ① ② ③ ④ ⑤	43. ① ② ③ ④ ⑤
14. ① ② ③ ④ ⑤	29. ① ② ③ ④ ⑤	44. ① ② ③ ④ ⑤
15. ① ② ③ ④ ⑤	30. ① ② ③ ④ ⑤	45. ① ② ③ ④ ⑤

Directions

Read each passage; then answer the questions that follow. Choose the <u>one best answer</u> to each item.

Items 1 to 4 refer to the following excerpt from a nonfiction book.

WHAT HAPPENED AT THIS NUCLEAR PLANT?

Line   At 1:23 [a.m.] the emergency regulating valves to the turbogenerator were turned off so that if necessary the test could be repeated. Metlenko switched on the oscillograph; and Kirschenbaum
5   shut off the steam from the turbine. As he did so, Toptunov noticed that the reactor's power had begun to rise. He alerted Akimov who, glancing at the computer printout, shouted to Dyatlov that he was going to shut down the reactor and pushed
10   the emergency AZ button to lower the control rods into the core.

There was a thud followed by further thuds from deep inside the building. . . . Akimov looked up at the instruments and saw that the descending
15   control rods had stopped. He immediately disconnected the servo to let them fall under their own weight. They did not move. Then simultaneously there came a terrible tremor together with a sound like a clap of thunder. The walls shook;
20   the lights went out; and a drizzle of plaster-dust rained down from great cracks in the ceiling. . . .

At 23 minutes past one, Leonid Shavrey was woken by the explosion which shook the glass in the windows of the fire station. He leapt off the
25   bunk and ran out into the road. He saw that the roof of the fourth unit was on fire, and that a strange cloud was rising from the reactor. . . .

With no special clothing to protect them from radiation, firemen climbed up the [reactor's]
30   exterior staircases and turned their hoses on the patches of burning bitumen which had been ignited by a shower of hot black rock.

The temperature was so high that the roof melted beneath their feet; and as soon as one fire
35   was put out, another would start. After only half an hour or so, the first teams on the roof . . . began to feel giddy. Ivan Shavrey, standing on the external staircase 72 meters above the ground, felt his feet grow weak and a sweet taste came into
40   his mouth, as if he had eaten some chocolate. He staggered down the stairs. His brother, Leonid, too, began to feel weak and sick.

—From *Ablaze: The Story of Chernobyl*
by Piers Paul Read

1. Which of the following problems is most similar to that in the passage?

(1)   an auto accident caused by driving under the influence of alcohol
(2)   the contamination of fresh water from a chemical spill
(3)   a fire that results from a lightning bolt
(4)   the collapse of a coal mine caused by too many workers
(5)   an emergency landing due to an airplane's faulty brake gear

2. Which word best describes the tone of this passage?

(1)   suspenseful
(2)   inspirational
(3)   sarcastic
(4)   humorous
(5)   emotional

3. Why do Leonid and Ivan Shavrey and other firefighters go to the plant?

(1)   The entire town is on fire.
(2)   They feel an explosion and see a fire.
(3)   They need the special radiation suits that are stored there.
(4)   They are the only ones qualified to fight this kind of fire.
(5)   Metlenko asks them to come.

4. ". . . the first teams on the roof began to feel giddy. Ivan Shavrey . . . felt his feet grow weak and a sweet taste came into his mouth . . ." (lines 36–40)

These physical effects are all the result of

(1)   eating too much sugar
(2)   water pollution
(3)   air pollution
(4)   exposure to radiation
(5)   a flu epidemic

Items 5 to 7 refer to the following excerpt from a play.

HOW DO THESE MEN FEEL ABOUT ANN WHITEFIELD?

Line | |
--- | --- | ---
 | Tanner: | Ramsden, do you know what this is?
 | Ramsden: | (*loftily*) No, sir.
 | Tanner: | It's a copy of Whitefield's will. Ann got it this morning.
5 | Ramsden: | When you say Ann, you mean, I presume, Miss Whitefield.
 | Tanner: | I mean our Ann, your Ann, Tavy's Ann, and now, Heaven help me, my Ann!
10 | Octavius: | (*rising, very pale*) What do you mean?
 | Tanner: | Mean! (*He holds up the will.*) Do you know who is appointed Ann's guardian by this will?
15 | Ramsden: | (*coolly*) I believe I am.
 | Tanner: | You! You and I, man. I! I!! I!!! Both of us! (*He flings the will down on the writing table.*)
 | Ramsden: | You! Impossible.
20 | Tanner: | It's only too hideously true. (*He throws himself into Octavius's chair.*)
 | Ramsden: | Get me out of it somehow. You don't know Ann as well as I do. She'll commit every crime a respectable
25 | | woman can; and she'll justify every one of them by saying that it was the wish of her guardians. She'll put everything on us; and we shall have no more control over her than a
30 | | couple of mice over a cat.
 | Octavius: | Jack, I wish you wouldn't talk like that about Ann.
 | Tanner: | This chap's in love with her: that's another complication. Well, she'll
35 | | either jilt him and say I didn't approve of him, or marry him and say you ordered her to. I tell you, this is the most staggering blow that has ever fallen on a man of my age and
40 | | temperament.

      —From *Man and Superman*
      by George Bernard Shaw

5. From this discussion, you can assume that Ann's father

  (1) never liked Tanner
  (2) disinherited Ann before he died
  (3) wanted Tanner to look after Ann
  (4) loved Ann more than his other children
  (5) was Tanner's best friend

6. Based on this passage, Tanner probably would describe Ann as

  (1) beautiful
  (2) honest
  (3) compassionate
  (4) calculating
  (5) boring

7. Which of the following situations is most similar to Tanner's?

  (1) A couple decides to start a family.
  (2) A godparent receives custody of a godchild.
  (3) A young man gets married.
  (4) A woman suddenly loses custody of her children.
  (5) A man is jilted by his sweetheart.

Items 8 to 10 refer to the following excerpt from a short story.

WHO ARE NORMAN AND WILLIE?

Line Norman was not the kind of kid who would cause you to break out in a grin if you saw him ride your way on a bike.

5   1. He couldn't ride a bike.
  2. He rarely emerged from his house.
  3. He was considered . . . well . . . weird.

This last opinion was based on the fact that Norman would only be seen heading toward or leaving the library, and always hugging an armful
10 of books. To the townfolk it seemed unhealthy for a young boy to read so much. They predicted a total loss of eyesight by the time he reached nineteen.

    Willie, however, was a kid who, had there
15 been a Normal Kid Pageant, would have won first and tied for second and third. A dynamic baseball player, daring bike rider, crackerjack newspaper delivery boy—he was the town's delight. Never mind that he was flunking all school subjects and
20 had a reputation as a bully, he was, after all, "a real boy."

    The differences did not escape the boys themselves. Though neighbors, separated only by

splintery bushes, they never as much as shared a
25 "Hi."

To Willie, Norman was simply the kid with
the yellow eyes. Not that they were actually
yellow—more of a brown-hazel—but often, the
way the sunlight bounced off the thick eyeglasses,
30 it seemed to create a yellow haze. . . .

To Norman, Willie was exhausting. He talked
fast, ran fast, walked fast, and, he suspected, even
slept fast. (If such a thing could be measured.) It
was tiring just to sit behind him in class and listen
35 to his endless chatter.

If Norman was slow motion, Willie was
definitely fast forward.

—From "The Boy With Yellow Eyes"
by Gloria Gonzalez

8. The central message of lines 4–6 is that Norman

(1) has a unique sense of humor
(2) is an unusual child
(3) is a popular boy
(4) enjoys sports except for bike-riding
(5) is an all-American boy

9. Based on the information in this passage, the
relationship between Willie and Norman could
best be described as

(1) close
(2) dependent
(3) practically nonexistent
(4) forced
(5) uncomfortable

10. The structure of this passage could best be
described as

(1) a study of a young boy named Norman
(2) a study of the friendship between two boys
(3) a comparison of two young boys
(4) a contrast between two very different boys
(5) a list of activities that a boy named Willie
enjoys

Items 11 to 14 refer to the following excerpt from a
novel.

HOW DOES MACON FEEL ABOUT BEING ALONE?

Line   After his wife left him, Macon had thought the
house would seem larger. Instead, he felt more
crowded. The windows shrank. The ceilings
lowered. There was something insistent about the
5   furniture, as if it were pressing in on him.

Of course Sarah's personal belongings were
gone, the little things like clothes and jewelry. But
it emerged that some of the big things were more
personal than he'd imagined. There was the
10   drop-leaf desk in the living room, its pigeonholes
stuffed with her clutter of torn envelopes and
unanswered letters. There was the radio in the
kitchen, set to play 98 Rock. (She liked to keep in
touch with her students, she used to say in the old
15   days, as she hummed and jittered her way around
the breakfast table.) There was the chaise out back
where she had sunbathed, planted in the only spot
that got any sun at all.

He looked at the flowered cushions and
20   marveled at how an empty space could be so full
of a person—her faint scent of coconut oil that
always made him wish for a piña colada; her wide,
gleaming face inscrutable behind dark glasses; her
compact body in the skirted swimsuit she had
25   tearfully insisted on buying after her fortieth
birthday. Threads of her exuberant hair showed
up at the bottom of the sink. Her shelf in the
medicine cabinet, stripped, was splashed with
drops of liquid rouge in a particular plummy shade
30   that brought her instantly to Macon's mind. He
had always disapproved of her messiness but now
those spills seemed touching, like colorful toys left
on the floor after a child has gone to bed.

—From *The Accidental Tourist*
by Anne Tyler

11. What event is Macon adjusting to in this passage?

(1) a death
(2) a divorce
(3) a career change
(4) a new baby
(5) a new house

12. Based on the information in this passage, you can infer that Macon

(1) is glad that Sarah's personal belongings are finally gone
(2) fought with Sarah when she lived there
(3) did not expect to notice Sarah's absence so much
(4) is a teacher, as Sarah was
(5) enjoys being alone in a big house

13. The structure of this passage could best be described as

(1) a list of a character's belongings
(2) a series of causes and their effects
(3) an interview with Macon
(4) a series of letters to Sarah
(5) a biography of Macon

14. According to the passage, why did Sarah listen to 98 Rock?

(1) to win radio contests
(2) to practice her singing
(3) to learn how to dance
(4) to give herself music to cook by
(5) to understand her students

Items 15 to 17 refer to the following excerpt from a book review.

WHAT IS THE SUBJECT OF THIS BOOK?

Line There is a lot to recommend in Cathy Luchetti and Carol Olwell's beautiful book, *Women of the West* (The Library of the American West, Orion Books; $22). There are the vintage photographs of the
5 pioneers who were part of the great migration into the western territories during the latter half of the nineteenth century and photographs of the Native Americans who preceded them. And there are the stories—in the form of diaries, books, and
10 letters written by 11 remarkable women, 10 who were immigrants and one, a Paiute, who tried to help her tribe adjust to the inevitability of that immigration. . . .
    But the diaries tell the real story here. These
15 are women who, predictably, endured great hardship. They delivered children alone on the prairie and often buried them there. They suffered terrible loneliness, cold, and hunger. Yet the overwhelming impression is of hardheaded
20 independence. Clearly, these women were an exceptional lot—dogged in their efforts to have a voice in their own lives, even if it was a private one, recorded in their journals and letters. A

surprising number were determined to stand equal
25 to their husbands in the decisions that would shape their future. One actually took the extraordinary step of divorcing hers when he failed to live up to her expectations. . . .
    . . . some of the entries are simply too brief.
30 We don't learn enough about Pauline Lyons Williamson to understand or care much about her, and we struggle to keep the characters in Helen Wiser Stewart's life straight. But this is a quibble. On the whole, the language of these women
35 literally rings with the hope and surety of people who have no doubts about the fragility of life and its rare moments of contentment.
    —From "At Home on the Range: Portraits of Women Who Tamed the West" by Nancy F. Smith

15. Based on the information in this passage, who are Pauline Lyons Williamson and Helen Wiser Stewart?

(1) friends who lived in the early 1900s
(2) the first American divorcees
(3) pioneer women from the late 1800s
(4) coauthors of *Women of the West*
(5) American history researchers

16. Smith's one negative comment about this book is that

(1) the women who wrote the diaries never meant for their words to be published
(2) no diaries from African-American pioneers have been included
(3) the authenticity of some of the diaries is questionable
(4) its characters are strong-minded and optimistic
(5) there is not enough information about some characters

17. A movie based on *Women of the West* probably would most appeal to an audience that

(1) liked to see strong leading men
(2) appreciated a character's determination and individualism
(3) enjoyed stories about the struggles between Native Americans and white settlers
(4) appreciated suspenseful and complicated plots with surprising twists
(5) enjoyed special effects

Items 18 to 22 refer to the following excerpt from a play.

HOW ARE THE MOTHERS AT GRAND ISLE DEPICTED?

Line It would have been a difficult matter for Mr. Pontellier to define to his own satisfaction or any one else's wherein his wife failed in her duty toward their children. It was something which he
5 felt rather than perceived, and he never voiced the feeling without subsequent regret and ample atonement.

If one of the little Pontellier boys took a tumble whilst at play, he was not apt to rush
10 crying to his mother's arms for comfort; he would more likely pick himself up, wipe the water out of his eyes and the sand out of his mouth, and go on playing. Tots as they were, they pulled together and stood their ground in childish battles with
15 doubled fists and uplifted voices, which usually prevailed against the other mother-tots. The quadroon nurse was looked upon as a huge encumbrance, only good to button up waists and panties and to brush and part hair; since it seemed
20 to be a law of society that hair must be parted and brushed.

In short, Mrs. Pontellier was not a mother-woman. The mother-women seemed to prevail that summer at Grand Isle. It was easy to know
25 them, fluttering about with extended, protecting wings when any harm, real or imaginary, threatened their precious brood. They were women who idolized their children, worshiped their husbands, and esteemed it a holy privilege to
30 efface themselves as individuals and grow wings as ministering angels.

Many of them were delicious in the role; one of them was the embodiment of every womanly grace and charm. If her husband did not adore
35 her, he was a brute, deserving of death by slow torture. Her name was Adele Ratignolle. There are no words to describe her save the old ones that have served so often to picture the bygone heroine of romance and the fair lady of our
40 dreams.

—From *The Awakening* by Kate Chopin

18. Based on lines 8-13 and 22-24, the setting of this passage is most likely a

(1) steamy, hot city
(2) relaxed vacation site
(3) bustling, overcrowded train
(4) grand old mansion
(5) formal hotel

19. Based on lines 8-13, which of the following best characterizes Mrs. Pontellier as a mother?

(1) warm and loving
(2) strict yet comforting
(3) cruel and abusive
(4) somewhat distant
(5) overprotective

20. ". . . since it seemed to be a law of society that hair must be parted and brushed." (lines 19-21)

Which of the following best decribes the tone of this statement?

(1) serious
(2) respectful
(3) social
(4) studious
(5) exaggerated

21. Based on lines 27-31, what is the meaning of *efface?*

(1) erase
(2) strengthen
(3) condemn
(4) praise
(5) support

22. What do lines 32-36 suggest about Adele Ratignolle?

(1) She exemplified the "mother-women" that summer.
(2) She was frequently spoiled by her family and friends.
(3) She was envied by the other women.
(4) She cooked delicious meals for her family.
(5) Her husband never treated her well.

Items 23 to 25 refer to the following poem.

WHAT ABOUT NATURE DOES THIS POET PRAISE?

Line Glory be to God for dappled things—
For skies of couple-colour as a brindled cow;
For rose-moles all in stipple upon trout that swim;
Fresh-firecoal chestnut-falls; finches' wings;
5   Landscape plotted and pieced—fold, fallow, and
           plough;
And all trades, their gear and tackle and trim.
All things counter, original, spare, strange;
Whatever is fickle, freckled (who knows how?)
10   With swift, slow; sweet, sour; adazzle, dim;
He fathers-forth whose beauty is past change:
Praise Him.

—From *Pied Beauty*
by Gerard Manley Hopkins

23. Based on the images in this poem, the best
meaning of dappled (line 1) is

(1) exciting
(2) confident
(3) unattractive
(4) covered with patches
(5) living

24. To what purpose does the speaker include images
of trout, finches, and fields?

(1) to reveal the speaker's dislike of the outdoors
(2) to show that he is afraid of animals
(3) to honor the beauty and variety of nature
(4) to prove his talent as a painter
(5) to contrast nature and technology

25. Which of the following titles would be most likely
for a poem with a theme similar to that of "Pied
Beauty"?

(1) "Peoples of the World"
(2) "The Sameness of the Desert"
(3) "Lake Whitefish"
(4) "A One-Color Sunset"
(5) "Singing Bluebird"

Items 26 to 28 refer to the following excerpt from a
journal.

WHAT DOES THE SPEAKER REMEMBER?

Line When I look back over the years I see myself, a
little child of scarcely four years of age, walking in
front of my nurse, in a green English lane, and
listening to her tell another of her kind that my
5   mother is Chinese. "Oh, Lord!" exclaims the
informed. She turns me around and scans me
curiously from head to foot. Then the two women
whisper together. Tho the word *Chinese* conveys
very little meaning to my mind, I feel that they are
10   talking about my father and mother and my heart
swells with indignation. When we reach home I
rush to my mother and try to tell her what I have
heard. I am a young child. I fail to make myself
intelligible. My mother does not understand, and
15   when the nurse declares to her, "Little Miss Sui is
a storyteller," my mother slaps me.

Many a long year has passed over my head
since that day—the day on which I first learned
that I was something different and apart from
20   other children, but tho my mother has forgotten
it, I have not.

I see myself again, a few years older. I am
playing with another child in a garden. A girl
passes by outside the gate. "Mamie," she cries to
25   my companion, "I wouldn't speak to Sui if I were
you. Her mamma is Chinese."

"I don't care," answers the little one beside
me. And then to me, "Even if your mamma is
Chinese, I like you better than I like Annie."

30   "But I don't like you," I answer, turning my
back on her. It is my first conscious lie.

—From "Leaves from the Mental Portfolio of
an Eurasian" by Sui Sin Far

26. The fact that the speaker is punished for lying
(lines 11–16) is ironic because she

(1) betrayed her parents
(2) was actually lying
(3) was telling the truth
(4) has been adopted
(5) actually enjoys storytelling

27. The series of remembrances in this passage
documents the speaker's

(1) passage into adulthood
(2) experiences with prejudice
(3) denial of her family history
(4) relationship with her mother
(5) inability to form friendships

28. From the events in lines 27-30, you can conclude that the speaker

- **(1)** accidentally insults her friend's family
- **(2)** truthfully admits that she does not like a friend
- **(3)** convinces a friend that her mother is not Chinese
- **(4)** confidently defends her ethnic heritage
- **(5)** intentionally tries to hurt her friend's feelings

Items 29 to 32 refer to the following excerpt from a novel.

HOW DOES NELLY RESPOND TO CATHERINE?

Line I was superstitious about dreams then, and am still: and when Miss Cathy, who had listened to the hubbub from her room, put her head in, and whispered:

5   "Are you alone, Nelly?"

"Yes, miss," I replied.

She entered and approached the hearth. I, supposing she was going to say something, looked up. The expression of her face seemed disturbed
10 and anxious. Her lips were half asunder, as if she meant to speak, and she drew a breath; but it escaped in a sigh instead of a sentence. I resumed my song; not having forgotten her recent behavior.

15   "Where's Heathcliff?" she said, interrupting me.

"About his work in the stable," was my answer.

He did not contradict me; perhaps he had
20 fallen into a doze. There followed another long pause, during which I perceived a drop or two trickle from Catherine's cheek to the flags. Is she sorry for her shameful conduct? I asked myself. That will be a novelty: but she may come to the
25 point as she will—I shan't help her! No, she felt small trouble regarding any subject, save her own concerns.

"Oh, dear!" she cried at last, "I'm very unhappy!"

30   "A pity," observed I. "You're hard to please: so many friends and so few cares, and can't make yourself content!"

"Nelly, will you keep a secret for me?" she pursued, kneeling down by me, and lifting her
35 winsome eyes to my face with that sort of look which turns off bad temper, even when one has all the right in the world to indulge it.

"Is it worth keeping?" I inquired, less sulkily.

"Yes, and it worries me, and I must let it
40 out! I want to know what I should do. Today, Edgar Linton has asked me to marry him, and I've given him an answer. Now, before I tell you whether it was a consent or denial, you tell me which it ought to have been."

—From *Wuthering Heights* by Emily Bronte

29. The narrator of this passage is

- **(1)** Catherine
- **(2)** an unnamed woman
- **(3)** Heathcliff
- **(4)** Nelly
- **(5)** Catherine's sister

30. Based on lines 25-27, Nelly would be most likely to describe Catherine as

- **(1)** self-centered
- **(2)** doubting
- **(3)** intellectual
- **(4)** beautiful
- **(5)** generous

31. In this passage, the narrator's attitude could best be described as

- **(1)** loving and admiring
- **(2)** wary yet forgiving
- **(3)** relieved and grateful
- **(4)** sad yet hopeful
- **(5)** selfish and undependable

32. Based on descriptions in this passage, what would Catherine be most likely to do if her best friend were upset?

- **(1)** ask Nelly to go and visit the friend
- **(2)** listen sympathetically to her friend's problems
- **(3)** remain focused on her own problems
- **(4)** gossip about her friend's problems with other people
- **(5)** ask the friend for advice about Edgar Linton

Items 33 to 36 refer to the following poem.

HOW DOES THIS SPEAKER FEEL ABOUT WORK?

Line Work
    I don't have to work.
    I don't have to do nothing
    but eat, drink, stay black, and die.
5   This little old furnished room's
    so small I can't whip a cat
    without getting fur in my mouth
    and my landlady's so old
    her features is all run together

10 and God knows she sure can overcharge—
Which is why I reckon I does
have to work after all.
—From *Necessity* by Langston Hughes

33. From this poem, what can be concluded about the speaker?

 (1) He owns a house.
 (2) He resents the freedom of animals.
 (3) He admires his landlady.
 (4) He rents an apartment.
 (5) He has two jobs.

34. If the poem ended at line 3, the speaker might have had to

 (1) leave this apartment
 (2) rent a larger apartment
 (3) eat more food
 (4) sue his landlady
 (5) buy a house

35. "This little old furnished room's/so small I can't whip a cat/without getting fur in my mouth" (lines 5–7)

 The tone of this figurative statement could best be described as

 (1) exaggerated
 (2) cruel
 (3) angry
 (4) proud
 (5) embarrassed

36. ". . . my landlady's so old/her features is all run together" (lines 8–9)

 This figurative description reveals that the landlady's skin is

 (1) smooth and firm
 (2) damaged from the sun
 (3) a soft tan color
 (4) wrinkled and sagging
 (5) covered with freckles

Items 37 to 42 refer to the following excerpt from a drama review.

WHAT IS THIS PLAY ABOUT?

Line It would be nice if revolutions could happen the
way Ladysmith Black Mambazo sings—as easily
and inexorably as a force of nature. But the
overthrow of apartheid in South Africa is taking
5 place amid blood and pain, and the presence of
the great a cappella choral group in *The Song of
Jacob Zulu* adds an ironic beauty to its tragic
story. The nine-man group, which became world
famous for its work on Paul Simon's album
10 "Graceland," becomes the ultimate Greek chorus,
reflecting the acting in eloquent, elegiac songs.
They mourn "those for whom the good news of
the end of apartheid comes too late." One of
these is Jacob Zulu, the central figure of Tug
15 Yourgrau's play.
 Zulu is based on Andrew Zondo, a 19-year-
old black man who in 1985 set off a bomb at a
shopping mall, killing five and wounding more
than 50, both black and white. Yourgrau, a white,
20 Johannesburg-born writer who immigrated to
America at the age of 10, has shaped his play
around the records of Zondo's trial and execution
by hanging. Jacob (K. Todd Freeman) is a minis-
ter's son, a mild, scholarly boy who shied away
25 from the political activism of his fellow students.
Trying to explain how such a youth came to
commit an act of terrorism, the play shows Jacob
being radicalized by the violence of a society
fractured by racism. He flees to Mozambique, joins
30 a militant group, and eventually returns to South
Africa, where he plants his bomb, is arrested, and
brought to trial. . . .
 Freeman movingly captures the trapped
anguish of this character. Eric Simonson has
35 transferred the play sensitively to Broadway for
Chicago's noted Steppenwolf Theatre Company.
But it's Ladysmith Black Mambazo that lifts the
play to another level. Their name, meaning the
black ax of the township of Ladysmith, belies the
40 gentle power of their singing. . . . Their angelic
harmonies and hypnotic rhythms are the sound of
sunrise, the inevitable sunrise of a new society.
—From "Sunrise in South Africa"
by Jack Kroll

37. In describing this play, the reviewer focuses primarily on

 (1) how the plot and the music work together
 (2) the pain and anguish of Andrew Zondo
 (3) the political forces that rule South Africa
 (4) how gifted the lead singer of Ladysmith Black Mambazo is
 (5) the talent of Tug Yourgrau, the playwright

38. According to this review, the event that provides the background for the play's action is the

 (1) introduction by Tug Yourgrau
 (2) hanging of Jacob Zulu
 (3) first song by Ladysmith Black Mambazo
 (4) end of South African apartheid
 (5) Broadway debut of *The Song of Jacob Zulu*

39. The reviewer compares Ladysmith Black Mambazo to "a force of nature" and an "inevitable sunrise" (lines 3 and 42) to show how the group's songs

    (1) provide sound effects of wind and rain
    (2) help create a sad atmosphere
    (3) lend hope and strength to the play
    (4) overshadow the action of the play
    (5) focus only on natural images

40. Lines 10–13 suggest that the "Greek chorus" in old Greek dramas

    (1) took attention away from the actors
    (2) provided an onstage audience for the actors
    (3) was not as effective as Ladysmith Black Mambazo is today
    (4) sang to complement the action of the play
    (5) was beloved by Greek audiences

41. The reviewer illustrates the irony of Jacob Zulu's life by contrasting

    (1) the lives of playwright Tug Yourgrau and subject Jacob Zulu
    (2) Zulu's quiet childhood with the later violence he committed
    (3) the evils of apartheid with the peacefulness in the township of Ladysmith
    (4) Zulu's public reputation with his family life
    (5) Ladysmith Black Mambazo's beautiful music with the barren stage

42. Which of the historic events below is most similar to the end of South African apartheid?

    (1) the end of World War II, following the first use of atomic weapons
    (2) the start of the twentieth century
    (3) the first manned moon landing
    (4) the collapse of the Soviet Union
    (5) the end of school segregation in the United States

Items 43 to 45 refer to the following poem.

WHAT THOUGHTS CONCERN THIS SPEAKER?

Line They speak to you the words of death,
"forget, forget."
Riding alone your ears make voices
out of the wind, *"forget, forget you are."*
5   This car can't be a horse,
but it's night and speed
that matters, as you knife through the
canyon.
You know everything watches this flight,
10 a tire grazes the rim.
You will not feel it,
"forget, forget you are Indian!"
On the next curve you will break into stars.
— From *Riding Song of One* by Jo Cochran

43. The speaker in this poem is

    (1) driving along the edge of a Native American reservation
    (2) riding a horse along the edge of a highway
    (3) running away from her home
    (4) driving near the edge of a canyon
    (5) traveling alone on a hot day

44. In lines 2, 4, and 12, what do the words in italics symbolize?

    (1) the voices of friends who are no longer living but who loved the speaker
    (2) the voices of people who want the speaker to dismiss her heritage
    (3) the whisper of wind through the canyon
    (4) the spirit of Native American civilizations throughout the centuries
    (5) the sounds made by passing cars

45. Based on line 13, which of the following events is most strongly foreshadowed?

    (1) The speaker will study the stars.
    (2) The speaker will wish for peace in the world.
    (3) The speaker will drive her car off the edge.
    (4) The speaker will turn around and go home.
    (5) The speaker will wish out loud that she were not Native American.

To check your answers, turn to page 537.

MATHEMATICS

90 Minutes ❖ 56 Questions

You should spend no more than 90 minutes answering the questions in this test. Work carefully, but do not spend too much time on any one question. Be sure you answer every question. You will not be penalized for incorrect answers.

Formulas you may need are given on page 544. Only some questions will require you to use a formula. Not all the formulas given will be used.

Some questions contain more information than you will need to solve the problem. Other questions do not give enough information to solve the problem. If the question does not give enough information to solve the problem, the correct answer choice is "Not enough information is given."

Do not mark in this test booklet. Use blank paper for your calculations. Record your answers on the separate answer sheet provided. Be sure all requested information is properly recorded on the answer sheet.

To record your answers, mark the numbered space on the answer sheet beside the number that corresponds to the question in the test booklet.

Do not rest the point of your pencil on the answer sheet while you are considering your answer. Make no stray or unnecessary marks. If you change an answer, erase your first mark completely. Mark only one answer space for each question; multiple answers will be scored as incorrect. Do not fold or crease your answer sheet.

FOR EXAMPLE

If a grocery bill totaling $15.75 is paid with a $20.00 bill, how much change should be returned?

(1) $5.26
(2) $4.75
(3) $4.25
(4) $3.75
(5) $3.25

① ② ● ④ ⑤

The correct answer is "$4.25"; therefore, answer space 3 would be marked on the answer sheet.

GED Test _____

Name _____

Date _____

- Use a No. 2 pencil.
- Mark one numbered space beside the number that corresponds to each question you are answering.
- Erase errors cleanly and completely

1. ① ② ③ ④ ⑤
2. ① ② ③ ④ ⑤
3. ① ② ③ ④ ⑤
4. ① ② ③ ④ ⑤
5. ① ② ③ ④ ⑤
6. ① ② ③ ④ ⑤
7. ① ② ③ ④ ⑤
8. ① ② ③ ④ ⑤
9. ① ② ③ ④ ⑤
10. ① ② ③ ④ ⑤
11. ① ② ③ ④ ⑤
12. ① ② ③ ④ ⑤
13. ① ② ③ ④ ⑤
14. ① ② ③ ④ ⑤
15. ① ② ③ ④ ⑤
16. ① ② ③ ④ ⑤
17. ① ② ③ ④ ⑤
18. ① ② ③ ④ ⑤
19. ① ② ③ ④ ⑤

20. ① ② ③ ④ ⑤
21. ① ② ③ ④ ⑤
22. ① ② ③ ④ ⑤
23. ① ② ③ ④ ⑤
24. ① ② ③ ④ ⑤
25. ① ② ③ ④ ⑤
26. ① ② ③ ④ ⑤
27. ① ② ③ ④ ⑤
28. ① ② ③ ④ ⑤
29. ① ② ③ ④ ⑤
30. ① ② ③ ④ ⑤
31. ① ② ③ ④ ⑤
32. ① ② ③ ④ ⑤
33. ① ② ③ ④ ⑤
34. ① ② ③ ④ ⑤
35. ① ② ③ ④ ⑤
36. ① ② ③ ④ ⑤
37. ① ② ③ ④ ⑤
38. ① ② ③ ④ ⑤

39. ① ② ③ ④ ⑤
40. ① ② ③ ④ ⑤
41. ① ② ③ ④ ⑤
42. ① ② ③ ④ ⑤
43. ① ② ③ ④ ⑤
44. ① ② ③ ④ ⑤
45. ① ② ③ ④ ⑤
46. ① ② ③ ④ ⑤
47. ① ② ③ ④ ⑤
48. ① ② ③ ④ ⑤
49. ① ② ③ ④ ⑤
50. ① ② ③ ④ ⑤
51. ① ② ③ ④ ⑤
52. ① ② ③ ④ ⑤
53. ① ② ③ ④ ⑤
54. ① ② ③ ④ ⑤
55. ① ② ③ ④ ⑤
56. ① ② ③ ④ ⑤

Directions

Choose the one best answer to each of the following items. (You may use the formulas on the inside back cover of this book if you need to.)

1. Betty uses 6 ounces of adhesive for every 8 square meters of geometric patterns she irons onto T-shirts. If she ironed 168 square meters of patterns on last month's order, how many ounces of adhesive did she use?

   (1) 21
   (2) 28
   (3) 126
   (4) 224
   (5) 1,008

2. How many meters long is one side of the square dance floor shown below?

   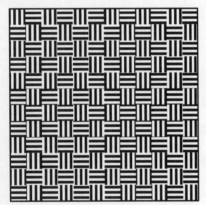

   144 square meters

   (1) 12
   (2) 24
   (3) 36
   (4) 72
   (5) Not enough information is given.

3. Johnathan made 14 sales calls during the first three days of the week. He hoped to make an additional 26 calls to complete his customer list. Which of the following equations could be used to find c, the number of calls on his customer list?

   (1) $26 - 14 = c$
   (2) $c + 14 = 26$
   (3) $\dfrac{c}{14} = 26$
   (4) $c - (14 \times 3) = 26$
   (5) $c - 14 = 26$

4. Maryanna paid for 10 cans of soup with a $20 bill. Each can of soup was priced at $0.79. How much should Maryanna receive in change?

   (1) $19.21
   (2) $12.10
   (3) $10.00
   (4) $7.90
   (5) $2.10

Item 5 refers to the following information.

REGIONAL ELECTION RESULTS
Total Votes Cast: 20,000

Candidate	Percent of Votes Received
Porter	28%
Ricks	19%
Holliday	21%
Young	15%

5. Which of the candidates received more than 4,000 votes?

   (1) Only Porter and Holliday
   (2) Only Porter
   (3) Only Ricks
   (4) Only Porter, Holliday, and Ricks
   (5) Only Holliday

6. If Ed's salary s is more than 3 times Ellen's salary g, which of the following statements is true?

   (1) $g < 3$
   (2) $g < 3s$
   (3) $g > 3s$
   (4) $g < \dfrac{s}{3}$
   (5) $g > \dfrac{s}{3}$

7. At The Candy Grab, a child pays $0.05 for 2 pieces of gum. How many pieces of gum can Justin buy with $0.75?

   (1) 187
   (2) 150
   (3) 30
   (4) 25
   (5) 7

8. Mara took 50 minutes to complete a test, and George took an hour and 20 minutes. What was the *average* number of minutes it took to complete the test?

(1) 65
(2) 70
(3) 120
(4) 130
(5) Not enough information is given.

Item 9 refers to the following graph.

1993 UNEMPLOYMENT IN EUROPE

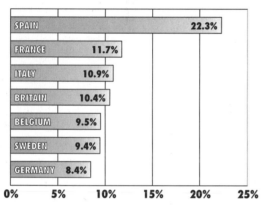

SPAIN	22.3%
FRANCE	11.7%
ITALY	10.9%
BRITAIN	10.4%
BELGIUM	9.5%
SWEDEN	9.4%
GERMANY	8.4%

0%   5%   10%   15%   20%   25%

9. In 1993, the number of people able to work in Italy was about 36 million. *Approximately* how many people were unemployed?

(1) 39,000
(2) 4,000,000
(3) 10,900,000
(4) 33,000,000
(5) 40,000,000

10. A lab worker recorded a controlled room temperature of −17 degrees at 9:00 a.m. At 10:00 a.m. the temperature was recorded as 5 degrees. What happened to the room temperature between 9 and 10 a.m.?

(1) It fell 12 degrees.
(2) It rose 12 degrees.
(3) It rose 5 degrees.
(4) It rose 22 degrees.
(5) It fell 22 degrees.

---

11. Of every 120 toy trains that come from assembly station 3, 18 of them are damaged and cannot be shipped. What percent *can* be shipped?

(1) 15%
(2) 18%
(3) 82%
(4) 85%
(5) 102%

Items 12 and 13 refer to the following chart.

TAX AND SHIPPING COSTS

Amount of Order	Add
Under $50.00	$ 3.50
$50.00–$99.99	$ 7.00
$100.00–$149.99	$ 9.50
$150.00–$199.99	$12.50

12. From a discount catalog, Juanita bought 4 toddler outfits for $12.99 each and a boy's winter coat for $45. She had to pay shipping according to the rates above. What did Juanita pay in all for this order?

(1) $55.46
(2) $96.96
(3) $103.96
(4) $106.46
(5) Not enough information is given.

13. Which of the following expressions shows the amount a customer would pay for the purchase and shipment of 2 pairs of pants at $27.50 each and 2 hats at $5.99 each?

(1) $(2 \times \$27.50) + \$3.50$
(2) $2(\$27.50 + \$5.99) + \$3.50$
(3) $2(\$27.50 + \$5.99) + \$7.00$
(4) $\dfrac{\$27.50}{2} + \dfrac{\$5.99}{2} + \$3.50$
(5) $(\$27.50 + \$5.99) + \$3.50$

14. An automated sorter discards all wingnuts that are not within 0.1 centimeter of the regulation diameter of 1.5 centimeters. Which of the following measurements would *not* be discarded?

(1) 2.60 centimeters
(2) 2.40 centimeters
(3) 1.81 centimeters
(4) 1.51 centimeters
(5) 1.30 centimeters

15. Ted got a 78% score on a job-entrance exam. What fraction is closest to this percent?

(1) $\dfrac{7}{8}$

(2) $\dfrac{6}{7}$

(3) $\dfrac{5}{6}$

(4) $\dfrac{3}{4}$

(5) $\dfrac{1}{2}$

16. A survey reports that 2 out of 3 people prefer Brand X toothpaste. According to the survey, how many people in a bus holding 210 people would prefer Brand X?

(1) 630
(2) 420
(3) 208
(4) 140
(5) 70

17. A pair of shoes is priced at $29.99. Tino bought the shoes with a 10% employee discount. Which expression shows the amount Tino paid?

(1) 0.10 × $29.99
(2) $29.99 + (0.10 × $29.99)
(3) $29.99 − (0.10 × $29.99)
(4) $29.99 − 0.10
(5) $29.99 − 10

18. If BC = 12 meters, how many meters is DE?

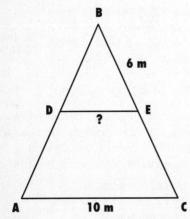

(1) 2.5
(2) 4
(3) 5
(4) 60
(5) Not enough information is given.

Items 19 and 20 refer to the figure below.

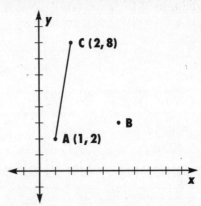

19. What is the slope of line AC?

(1) 6
(2) 5
(3) 4
(4) 3
(5) Not enough information is given.

20. What are the coordinates of point B?

(1) (3, 5)
(2) (5, 3)
(3) (2, 4)
(4) (4, 2)
(5) Not enough information is given.

21. A trash-collection company services 300 residences in an 8-hour day with 4 trucks. At this rate, how many residences could it serve in a 40-hour week?

(1) 375
(2) 1,200
(3) 1,500
(4) 6,000
(5) 9,600

22. A computer disk already holds 1.4 megabytes of formatted data. If Wayne has 30% of the total disk space free for use, what fraction of the disk space has been filled with data?

(1) $\dfrac{21}{52}$

(2) $\dfrac{3}{10}$

(3) $\dfrac{2}{3}$

(4) $\dfrac{7}{10}$

(5) Not enough information is given.

Items 23 to 25 refer to the following graph.

CORN, SOYBEANS, AND WHEAT
U.S. Production and Exports: 1991

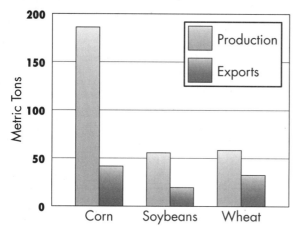

23. *Approximately* how many times as many metric tons of corn were produced as were exported in 1991?

(1) $\frac{1}{4}$

(2) 2

(3) 4

(4) 8

(5) 4,000,000

24. Which of the categories on the graph did not surpass the 25-Million-Metric-Ton mark?

(1) Corn exports

(2) Soybean exports

(3) Soybean production

(4) Wheat production

(5) Wheat exports

25. Which of the following statements is true based on the graph?

(1) Soybean and wheat production is leveling off.

(2) In 1991, more corn was exported than produced.

(3) In 1991, a metric ton of wheat cost less than a metric ton of corn.

(4) In 1991, less than 25 metric tons of corn were exported.

(5) In 1991, the amount of soybeans and wheat produced was about equal.

26. A limousine service charges a fee of $15 for each passenger picked up, then $0.75 per mile for distances less than 10 miles, or $50 per hour for distances greater than 10 miles. What more do you need to know to find out the total cost of a trip from Arlington Station to Downtown Crossing, a distance of 12 miles?

(1) The time it took to get from Arlington Station to Downtown Crossing

(2) The miles per hour driven by the limousine

(3) The time of the ride

(4) The number of passengers picked up

(5) The rate per minute for the limo

27. Custom Catering says that a customer should order about 2½ bottles of water for every 9 guests expected. Mr. and Mrs. Yun expect 200 guests at their daughter's wedding reception. Which of the following expressions represents the number of bottles of water the Yuns should order?

(1) $\dfrac{9 \times 200}{2.5}$

(2) $(9 \times 200) \times 2.5$

(3) $\dfrac{9 \times 2.5}{200}$

(4) $\dfrac{200}{9 \times 2.5}$

(5) $\dfrac{2.5 \times 200}{9}$

28. A traffic-control officer recorded the following numbers of children crossing at the intersection of First Street and Dudley Avenue over a 4-hour period. What was the mean number of crossings *per hour* over the five-day period?

Day	Number of Children
Monday	140
Tuesday	144
Wednesday	100
Thursday	86
Friday	90

(1) 7

(2) 28

(3) 112

(4) 140

(5) Not enough information is given.

Items 29 to 31 refer to the following drawing.

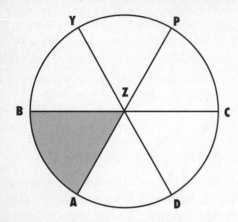

29. If ∠AZB = 60 degrees, what percent of the circle is shaded, expressed to the nearest hundredth?

   (1) 16%
   (2) 17%
   (3) 33%
   (4) 67%
   (5) Not enough information is given.

30. If ∠BZC is a straight angle and ∠CZD = ∠AZB, how many degrees is ∠YZP?

   (1) 30°
   (2) 45°
   (3) 60°
   (4) 90°
   (5) Not enough information is given.

31. If AZ = 7 cm, which of the following expressions represents the circumference of the circle?

   (1) $2 \times 7 \times \dfrac{22}{7}$

   (2) $7 \times \dfrac{22}{7}$

   (3) $2 \times 3.14 \times (7)^2$
   (4) $3.14 \times (7)^2$
   (5) Not enough information is given.

32. What is the greatest number of $12.99 picture frames Manuel can buy with $100?

   (1) 6
   (2) 7
   (3) 7.7
   (4) 13
   (5) 15

Items 33 and 34 refer to the following information.

The company where Barry works is holding a raffle. Each ticket costs $15, and only 250 tickets will be sold. The winner will receive $325 per month for a year.

33. If Barry buys 10 tickets, what are the odds that he will win the raffle?

   (1) 1 in 250
   (2) 1 in 125
   (3) 1 in 25
   (4) 2 in 25
   (5) Not enough information is given.

34. One hundred of the tickets are purchased by nonemployees. What are the chances that an employee will win the raffle?

   (1) 1 in 5
   (2) 2 in 5
   (3) 3 in 5
   (4) 4 in 5
   (5) Not enough information is given.

35. What is the value of $-12 - (3 - 4)$?

   (1) −19
   (2) −13
   (3) −11
   (4) −5
   (5) 5

36. Nan's truck odometer read 45,987.5 at the start of her trip and 46,011.2 at the end. If her truck gets about 20 miles per gallon, which of the following expressions can be used to determine how many gallons of gas she used on this trip?

   (1) $(45{,}987.5 + 46{,}011.2) \times 20$

   (2) $\dfrac{45{,}987.5 + 46{,}011.2}{20}$

   (3) $(46{,}011.2 - 45{,}987.5) \times 20$

   (4) $\dfrac{46{,}011.2 - 45{,}987.5}{20}$

   (5) Not enough information is given.

37. Dara bought 4 pounds of cheddar cheese and a $4.89 roast. She paid for her purchases with a $50 bill. How much change should she receive?

   (1) $30.44
   (2) $38.89
   (3) $45.11
   (4) $49.56
   (5) Not enough information is given.

38. Marge's exercise class walks 3.2 miles to the gym every weekday for three weeks. How many miles did the class walk in all?

   (1) 9.6
   (2) 16
   (3) 48
   (4) 96
   (5) 160

> Items 39 and 40 refer to the following graph.

U.S. PRISON POPULATION
1980–1992

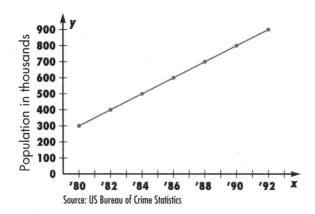

Source: US Bureau of Crime Statistics

39. In what year did the U.S. prison population first reach 400,000?

   (1) 1980
   (2) 1982
   (3) 1984
   (4) 1986
   (5) Not enough information is given.

40. By about how much did the U.S. prison population increase between 1980 and 1992?

   (1) 600
   (2) 900
   (3) 1,000
   (4) 600,000
   (5) 900,000

41. According to the chart below, how many more people attended the 9:00 a.m. workshop than the 10:00 a.m. workshop?

ATTENDANCE RESULTS

Workshop	Percent of Attendance
9:00 a.m. Session	47%
10:00 a.m. Session	32%
11:00 a.m. Session	21%

   (1) 11
   (2) 15
   (3) 47
   (4) 53
   (5) Not enough information is given.

42. The best picking crew at Door's Apple Orchard yields 450 bushels of fruit in 9 days. At this rate, how many days would it take this crew to pick 2,000 bushels?

   (1) 400
   (2) 222
   (3) 50
   (4) 40
   (5) 20

> Items 43 and 44 refer to the following diagram.

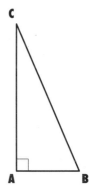

43. If $\angle ABC = 62°$, which expression represents the number of degrees in $\angle BCA$?

   (1) $360 - (90 + 62)$
   (2) $360 - 62$
   (3) $180 - 62$
   (4) $180 + 62$
   (5) $180 - (90 + 62)$

44. If AB = 8 meters and BC = 20 meters, *approximately* how many meters long is AC?

(1) between 6 and 7
(2) between 11 and 12
(3) between 18 and 19
(4) between 27 and 28
(5) Not enough information is given.

45. The automated machinery at Cray Industries can seal 4.8 large cartons per second at full speed. The manual laborers seal an average of 0.5 carton per second. About how many times as fast is the automated sealer?

(1) $\dfrac{1}{10}$
(2) 1
(3) 10
(4) 20
(5) 100

46. Mustapha paid $320 for a bicycle at a 20%-off sale. What was the original price of the bike?

(1) $1,600
(2) $1,200
(3) $400
(4) $256
(5) $64

47. What is the value of the expression $x^3 + x$ if $x = 4$?

(1) 16
(2) 24
(3) 64
(4) 68
(5) 256

48. A community center charges $5 per 45 minutes of computer time. How many 2-hour time slots can be filled in a 7-hour day?

(1) 4
(2) 5
(3) 9
(4) 10
(5) 47

49. Which of the following expressions shows the amount of interest paid on a $2,000 loan at an 8.5% annual interest rate over 6 months?

(1) $2,000 × 0.85 × 6
(2) $2,000 × 0.085 × 0.5
(3) $2,000 × 0.085 × 0.6
(4) $\dfrac{\$2,000}{0.085 \times 0.5}$
(5) $\dfrac{\$2,000}{8.5 \times 6}$

Items 50 to 52 refer to the following diagram.

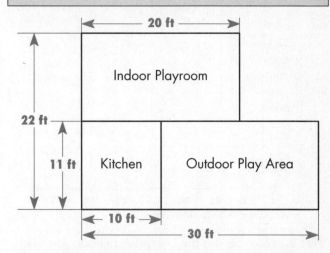

50. The director of the preschool plans to cover the outdoor play area with a rubber surface. If the surface costs $30 per square foot installed, what will it cost to cover the outdoor play area?

(1) $19,800
(2) $16,500
(3) $6,600
(4) $2,460
(5) Not enough information is given.

51. Which of the following expressions represents the number of feet in the perimeter of the indoor playroom?

(1) 20 × 22
(2) 20 + 22
(3) 20 × 11
(4) 2(20) + 2(11)
(5) 2(22) + 2(20)

52. One-third of the kitchen floor is covered with 2-ft-by-2-ft linoleum tiles. Which of the following expressions represents the number of tiles used?

(1) $\dfrac{\frac{1}{3} \times 110}{4}$

(2) $\dfrac{1}{3} \times 10 \times 4$

(3) $\dfrac{\frac{1}{3} \times 4}{110}$

(4) $110 \times 3 \times 2$

(5) $\dfrac{11 + 11 + 10 + 10}{4}$

53. The point $(1, 5)$ is on the graph of which equation below?

A. $y = 3x + 2$
B. $y = x + 4$
C. $y = x - 5$

(1) A and B only
(2) A only
(3) B only
(4) C only
(5) A, B, and C

54. Sandy worked h hours at the health club and earned \$7.85 per hour. She also worked 10 hours overtime at twice that rate. Which of the following expressions represents the total amount Sandy earned?

(1) $(h + 10)\ \$7.85$
(2) $(h + 10) \times (\$7.85 \times 2)$
(3) $(\$7.85h) + (10 \times 2 \times \$7.85)$
(4) $(\$7.85h) + (2 \times \$7.85)$
(5) $(h + \$7.85) \times 10$

Item 55 refers to the following diagram.

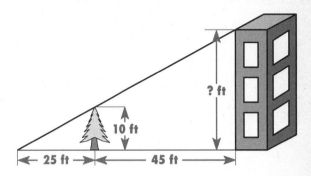

55. According to the diagram above, how tall is the building?

(1) 35 feet
(2) 28 feet
(3) 18 feet
(4) 15 feet
(5) Not enough information is given.

Item 56 refers to the following figure.

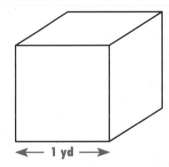

56. How many cubic *feet* is the cube above?

(1) 1
(2) 3
(3) 9
(4) 27
(5) Not enough information is given.

To check your answers, turn to page 540.

ANSWERS TO THE PRACTICE TEST

WRITING SKILLS		SOCIAL STUDIES		SCIENCE		LITERATURE AND THE ARTS		MATHEMATICS	
Part I		1. 3	33. 5	1. 4	34. 1	1. 2	24. 3	1. 3	29. 2
1. 1	40. 2	2. 4	34. 1	2. 4	35. 3	2. 1	25. 1	2. 1	30. 3
2. 3	41. 5	3. 2	35. 2	3. 3	36. 1	3. 2	26. 3	3. 5	31. 1
3. 2	42. 2	4. 1	36. 5	4. 2	37. 2	4. 4	27. 2	4. 2	32. 2
4. 3	43. 2	5. 4	37. 3	5. 5	38. 2	5. 3	28. 5	5. 1	33. 3
5. 5	44. 1	6. 2	38. 4	6. 1	39. 5	6. 4	29. 4	6. 4	34. 3
6. 4	45. 5	7. 5	39. 3	7. 4	40. 1	7. 2	30. 1	7. 3	35. 3
7. 3	46. 1	8. 5	40. 5	8. 2	41. 3	8. 2	31. 2	8. 1	36. 4
8. 4	47. 4	9. 1	41. 3	9. 3	42. 2	9. 3	32. 3	9. 2	37. 5
9. 4	48. 3	10. 2	42. 3	10. 1	43. 1	10. 4	33. 4	10. 4	38. 3
10. 3	49. 5	11. 3	43. 2	11. 5	44. 1	11. 2	34. 1	11. 4	39. 2
11. 1	50. 3	12. 5	44. 3	12. 2	45. 1	12. 3	35. 1	12. 3	40. 4
12. 4	51. 3	13. 2	45. 3	13. 5	46. 4	13. 1	36. 4	13. 3	41. 5
13. 5	52. 3	14. 3	46. 4	14. 2	47. 2	14. 5	37. 1	14. 4	42. 4
14. 2	53. 5	15. 1	47. 1	15. 5	48. 3	15. 3	38. 4	15. 4	43. 5
15. 3	54. 5	16. 2	48. 3	16. 3	49. 5	16. 5	39. 3	16. 4	44. 3
16. 4	55. 2	17. 3	49. 1	17. 4	50. 4	17. 2	40. 4	17. 3	45. 3
17. 5		18. 1	50. 1	18. 1	51. 5	18. 2	41. 2	18. 3	46. 3
18. 2	**Part II**	19. 4	51. 4	19. 2	52. 2	19. 4	42. 5	19. 1	47. 4
19. 4	Turn to	20. 3	52. 3	20. 3	53. 1	20. 5	43. 4	20. 2	48. 3
20. 5	pages 453	21. 3	53. 3	21. 2	54. 4	21. 1	44. 2	21. 3	49. 2
21. 2	and 532.	22. 2	54. 2	22. 1	55. 1	22. 1	45. 3	22. 4	50. 3
22. 3		23. 3	55. 2	23. 5	56. 1	23. 4		23. 3	51. 4
23. 3		24. 1	56. 4	24. 1	57. 2			24. 2	52. 1
24. 3		25. 1	57. 1	25. 4	58. 3			25. 5	53. 1
25. 4		26. 3	58. 3	26. 3	59. 5			26. 4	54. 3
26. 2		27. 3	59. 3	27. 5	60. 4			27. 5	55. 2
27. 2		28. 4	60. 1	28. 1	61. 2			28. 2	56. 4
28. 3		29. 2	61. 3	29. 4	62. 4				
29. 4		30. 3	62. 4	30. 5	63. 3				
30. 1		31. 5	63. 3	31. 5	64. 5				
31. 4		32. 1	64. 4	32. 1	65. 2				
32. 3				33. 4	66. 4				
33. 2									
34. 5									
35. 2									
36. 1									
37. 4									
38. 4									
39. 2									

Answers and Explanations
PRACTICE TESTS

Practice Test 1: Writing Skills
PART I

1. **The correct answer is (1)** The original sentence is a fragment. Choice (1) corrects this error by providing a verb *(is)* for the subject *(Cryonics)*. Choices (2) and (3) do not correct the fragment, and they insert unnecessary commas. Choice (4) does not correct the fragment.

2. **The correct answer is (3)** The original sentence needs a comma to separate an introductory sentence from the main clause of the sentence. Choice (3) corrects this error by inserting the needed comma. Choices (2) and (4) add a word that confuses the sentence. Choice (5) removes a needed word.

3. **The correct answer is (2)** The original sentence uses a verb tense that does not fit with the sentences leading to it. Choice (2) corrects this error by using the present tense *(could result)*. The other choices use the wrong tense.

4. **The correct answer is (3)** The original sentence incorrectly capitalizes a common noun. Choice (3) corrects this error by removing the capital letter from the common noun *physicist*. Choices (1) and (2) use the wrong verb tense. Choice (4) inserts an unnecessary comma.

5. **The correct answer is (5)** The original sentence uses the wrong word to connect it with the preceding sentence. Choice (5) corrects this error, replacing *for example* with *however* to express the right relationship between the two sentences. The other choices do not express the right relationship between the two sentences.

6. **The correct answer is (4)** The original sentences are best combined in choice (4). Choice (1) creates a comma splice. Choices (2) and (5) suggest that one thing caused the other. Choice (3) suggests that one thing happened after the other.

7. **The correct answer is (3)** The original sentence uses a word that expresses the wrong relationship between this sentence and the previous sentence. Choice (3) corrects this error by changing the word *therefore* to *however*. *Therefore* incorrectly suggests that the second sentence follows from the first. *However* correctly suggests that the sentences present contrasting information. Choices (2) and (4) do not correct the original error. Choice (5) uses the correct word, but a comma after *However* is missing.

8. **The correct answer is (4)** The original sentence uses a verb tense that neither matches the rest of the paragraph nor logically expresses the meaning of the sentence. Choice (4) corrects this error by using the future tense *(will not work)*. The other choices do not use the right verb tense.

9. **The correct answer is (4)** The original sentence uses a pronoun that does not agree with the word it refers to. Choice (4) uses *he or she* (singular) to refer to *person* (also singular). Choice (3) also uses this combination of words, but it assigns a plural verb *(are)* to the singular *he or she*. Choice (2) incorrectly uses *he or she* (singular) to refer to *people* (plural). Choice (5) uses *they* (plural) to refer to *people* (plural), but it assigns a singular verb *(is)* to the plural *they*.

10. **The correct answer is (3)** The original sentence has a comma splice. Choice (3) corrects this error. It uses the word *which* to refer to *cryonics* and to add information about this word not strictly essential to the meaning of the sentence. Choices (2) and (5) each create a comma splice. Choice (4) inserts the word *and*, which does not express the right relationship between the two parts of the sentence.

11. **The correct answer is (1)** In the original sentence a comma is needed to set off a phrase that interrupts the main clause of the sentence. Choice (1) inserts a comma to set off the phrase *unsure of what the future holds*. Choice (2) incorrectly capitalizes a common noun. Choice (3) removes a needed comma. Choices (4) and (5) insert unneeded commas.

12. **The correct answer is (4)** The original sentences are best combined in choice (4), which uses the word *because* to show that one statement (the second) causes the other (the first). Choice (1) creates a comma splice. The other choices do not express the right relationship between the two statements.

13. **The correct answer is (5)** Choice (5) removes the unnecessary comma after the word *muggings*. Commas are not needed to separate items in a series of only two. Choices (1) and (2) create verb-tense errors; (3) and (4) introduce additional comma errors.

14. **The correct answer is (2)** The original sentence is a fragment. Choice (2) corrects this error by inserting a verb *(will be)* for the subject *(crimes)*. Choice (4) also inserts a verb *(will be committed)*, but changes the meaning of the sentence. Choice (3) inserts both verbs *(will be* and *will be committed)*, leaving the subject of the sentence unclear. Choice (5) creates a command, which changes the point of view of the paragraph.

15. **The correct answer is (3)** The original sentence is a run-on sentence. Choice (3) separates the two complete sentences and uses a connecting word *(Therefore)* to express the right relationship between them. Choice (2) creates a comma splice. Choices (4) and (5) use connecting words that express the wrong relationship between the two parts of the sentence.

16. **The correct answer is (4)** The original sentence contains an error in word usage. Choice (4) correctly uses *their* instead of *there* to show possession. Choice (1) creates a verb-tense error. Choices (2) and (3) insert unneeded commas.

WRITING SKILLS PRACTICE TEST ANALYSIS CHART

Use this table to determine your areas of strength and areas in which more work is needed. The numbers in the boxes refer to the multiple-choice questions in the practice test.

Content Area	Sentence Correction	Sentence Revision	Construction Shift	Score
Unit 1 **Sentence Structure** (pp. 74–87)				
Fragment	1, 33	14	31	
Run-on	36	15		
Comma splice	28	10		
Coordination	19, 39	5, 7	44	
Subordination			6, 12	
Clarity, modification, parallelism	32, 48	34	46	_____ of 19
Unit 2 **Usage and Grammar** (pp. 88–105)				
Subject-verb agreement	18	40, 41	26	
Verbs	17, 20, 24, 30, 50	3, 8, 27, 37	35	
Pronouns	21, 43	9	45	_____ of 18
Unit 3 **Mechanics** (pp. 106–124)				
Capitalization	4, 29, 47, 52, 54			
Punctuation	11, 13, 22	2, 25, 42, 49		
Spelling, possessives, contractions, homonyms	16, 23, 53, 55	38, 51		_____ of 18
Score	_____ of 28	_____ of 19	_____ of 8	_____ of 55
Unit 4 **Essay Writing** (pp. 125–130)	Strengths: Weaknesses:			

17. **The correct answer is (5)** The original sentence uses a verb tense that does not match the main verb tense of the rest of the paragraph. Choice (5) corrects this error, using the future tense *(will also appear)* to match the future tense used in similar statements throughout the paragraph. Choices (3) and (4) change the verb tense but do not use the correct tense. Choices (1) and (2) remove needed commas.

18. **The correct answer is (2)** The original sentence uses a verb that does not agree with its subject. Choice (2) uses *exists*, not *exist*, to agree with the subject *(technology)*. Choices (3) and (5) create verb-tense errors. Choice (4) creates a subject-verb agreement error in addition to an error in verb tense. Choice (1) inserts an unnecessary comma.

19. **The correct answer is (4)** The original sentence connects two similar verbs using an incorrect form: *either . . . and*. Choice (4) uses *either . . . or* to connect the two verbs: either *have not foreseen* or *have been slow*. Choices (1) and (2) create spelling errors. Choice (3) creates a verb-form error. Choice (5) creates a tense error.

20. **The correct answer is (5)** The original sentence uses an incorrect verb form. Choice (5) correctly uses *has begun*. Choices (1), (2), and (3) create errors in word usage. Choice (4) inserts an unnecessary comma.

21. **The correct answer is (2)** The original sentence uses a pronoun *(they)* with an unclear reference. Choice (2) corrects this error by replacing *they* with a clearer reference *(companies and governments)*. Choice (1) also replaces *they* but with the wrong reference. Choices (3) and (4) create verb-tense errors. Choice (5) creates a spelling error.

22. **The correct answer is (3)** The original sentence needs a comma to separate an introductory sentence from the main clause of the sentence. Choice (3) corrects this error by inserting a comma after *criminal*. Choices (1), (2), and (4) insert unnecessary commas.

23. **The correct answer is (3)** The original sentence has a spelling error. Choice (3) spells *guarantees* correctly. Choices (1) and (2) incorrectly remove capital letters from proper nouns. Choice (4) inserts an unnecessary comma.

24. **The correct answer is (3)** The original sentence has a verb-tense error. Choice (3) replaces *live* (present tense) with *had lived* (past tense), which clarifies the meaning of the sentence. Choice (1) creates another verb-tense error. Choice (2) creates a subject-verb agreement error. Choice (4) inserts an unnecessary comma. Choice (5) creates a spelling error.

25. **The correct answer is (4)** The original sentence needs a comma to connect two independent clauses joined by *and*. Choice (4) inserts the needed comma. Choice (2) inserts the comma in the wrong place. Choice (3) inserts both the needed comma and an unnecessary one. Choice (5) creates a comma splice.

26. **The correct answer is (2)** The original sentence uses a verb *(is)* that does not agree with its subject *(restrictions)*. Choice (2) uses the correct verb *(are)*. Choices (3) and (4) use verbs that agree with *restrictions* but are in the wrong tense. Choice (5) creates an unclear sentence.

27. **The correct answer is (2)** The original sentence uses a verb tense that does not match the rest of the paragraph. Choice (2) corrects this error by replacing *will fail* with the present tense *(may fail)*. Choice (4) makes sense, but the tense does not match that of the rest of the paragraph. The other choices use the wrong verb tense.

28. **The correct answer is (3)** The original sentence has a comma splice. Choice (3) corrects this error by inserting the connecting word *or* to join what would otherwise be two full sentences. Choices (1) and (4) create sentences with unclear pronoun reference. Choice (2) creates a spelling error. Choice (5) uses the wrong verb tense.

29. **The correct answer is (4)** The original sentence has a capitalization error. Choice (4) removes the capital letter from the common noun *courts*. Choices (1) and (2) insert unnecessary commas. Choice (3) creates an error in word usage.

30. **The correct answer is (1)** The original sentence uses a verb tense that does not match the rest of the paragraph. Choice (1) uses *have been sued* instead of *will be sued*. Choices (2) and (3) create comma errors. Choice (4) creates another verb-tense error.

31. **The correct answer is (4)** The original sentence is a fragment. Choice (4) supplies the correct verb tense for the revised sentence. Choice (1) does not correct the original error. Choice (2) creates a subject-verb agreement error. Choices (3) and (5) create new verb-tense errors.

32. **The correct answer is (3)** The original sentence lacks parallel structure. Choice (3) replaces *to do* with *doing*, thereby making *doing* and *publishing* parallel. Choice (1) incorrectly replaces *that* with another word. Choice (2) inserts an unnecessary comma. Choices (4) and (5) create awkward sentences.

33. **The correct answer is (2)** The original sentence is a fragment. Choice (2) removes the word *who*, making both *disagree* and *claim* verbs for the subject *(people)*. Choice (1) removes the subject, which is essential for clear meaning. Choices (3), (4), and (5) insert unnecessary commas.

34. **The correct answer is (5)** The original sentence has a misplaced modifier. Choice (5) places the modifier *only* as close as possible to the phrase it modifies *(a strong press)*. The other choices place *only* in places that suggest that it modifies other words or phrases.

35. **The correct answer is (2)** The original sentence uses the wrong verb form. Choice (2) replaces *have saw* with the correct form *(have seen)*. Choice (1) does not correct this error in form. The other choices use the wrong verb for the subject *(viewers)*.

36. **The correct answer is (1)** The original sentence is a run-on sentence. Choice (1) corrects this error by separating the run-on in the right place to make two sentences. Choice (2) creates a comma splice. Choice (3) separates the original run-on sentence in the wrong place. Choices (4) and (5) are not punctuated correctly.

37. **The correct answer is (4)** The original sentence uses a verb tense that does not match the main tense of the rest of the paragraph. Choice (4) replaces *reflected* (past tense) with *reflects* (present tense). Choices (2) and (5) do not correct the original tense error, and they insert unnecessary commas. Choice (3) inserts an unnecessary comma.

38. **The correct answer is (4)** The original sentence contains an error in word usage. Choice (4) corrects this error by replacing *to* with *too*. Choices (2) and (3) do not correct this error. Choice (5) inserts an unnecessary comma. Choices (2), (3), and (5) remove a needed comma.

39. **The correct answer is (2)** The original sentence incorrectly uses two words to connect the two clauses of the sentence. Choice (2) removes the word *so*, leaving *if* to connect the clauses. Choice (1) expresses the wrong relationship between this sentence and the one before it. Choices (3) and (4) do not correct the original error.

40. **The correct answer is (2)** The original sentence has a subject-verb agreement error. Choice (2) correctly uses the plural verb *hire* to agree with the compound (plural) subject *(producer and director)*. Choices (3), (4), and (5) use the wrong verb tense.

41. **The correct answer is (5)** The original sentence has a subject-verb agreement error. Choice (5) correctly uses *tells* to agree with the nearer of the two subjects *(announcer)*. Choice (2) creates a fragment by changing the form of the verb. Choices (3) and (4) use the wrong verb tense.

42. **The correct answer is (2)** The original sentence has an unnecessary comma. Choice (2) corrects this error by removing the comma. Choice (4) simply moves the comma. Choices (3) and (5) create fragments by dividing the original sentence.

43. **The correct answer is (2)** The original sentence has a pronoun whose reference is not clear. Choice (2) corrects this error. It replaces the pronoun *this* with the noun to which it refers *(the reenactment)*. Choices (1) and (4) insert unnecessary commas. Choice (3) creates a spelling error.

44. **The correct answer is (1)** The rewritten sentence uses the phrase *not only . . . but also* to connect its two parts (clauses). Choice (1) correctly completes the sentence. The other choices do not follow the *not only . . . but also* pattern.

45. **The correct answer is (5)** The original sentence changes the point of view of the paragraph. Choice (5) replaces the pronoun *you* with *viewers*, which is consistent with the point of view of the paragraph: *According to critics, television shows should not be promoted as news when they do not provide viewers with clear, factual news.* Choice (1) creates an unclear reference for the pronoun *them*, thereby leaving it to refer to *shows*. Choices (2) and (3) use a point of view that does not match the rest of the passage. Choice (4) creates an unclear sentence.

46. **The correct answer is (1)** The original sentence has a misplaced phrase. Choice (1) places the phrase *in the early part of the next century* nearer to the word it modifies *(work)*. The rewritten sentence is *Experts who study society and job trends can tell you a lot about your work in the early part of the next century.* Choice (2) uses a word that is not needed when the sentence is rewritten. The other choices create sentences in which a modifying phrase is misplaced.

47. **The correct answer is (4)** The original sentence has a capitalization error. Choice (4) removes the capital letter from *summer*. Choice (1) removes a needed comma. Choice (2) creates a spelling error. Choice (3) creates a verb-tense error.

48. **The correct answer is (3)** The original sentence lacks parallel structure. Choice (3) changes *to emphasize* to *will emphasize* to be parallel with *will run* and *will teach*. Choices (1) and (2) create verb-tense errors. Choice (4) creates a spelling error.

49. **The correct answer is (5)** The original sentence uses commas incorrectly to mark a series of three items. Choice (5) inserts a comma between *collect* and *transmit* and removes the comma after *retrieve*. The other choices use commas incorrectly to punctuate the series.

531

50. The correct answer is (3) The original sentence uses the wrong verb tense. Choice (3) replaces *declined* (past tense) with *will decline* (future tense) to match the future tense of the paragraph. Choice (1) inserts an unnecessary comma. Choices (2) and (4) change the tense of the sentence but do not correct it. Choice (5) creates an illogical series of tenses.

51. The correct answer is (3) The original sentence contains an error in word usage. Choice (3) replaces *your* (possessive form) with *you're* (contraction of *you are*). Choices (2) and (4) change the wrong *your*. Choices (2) and (5) misspell *likely*.

52. The correct answer is (3) The original sentence has capitalization errors. Choice (3) removes capital letters from *streets* and *boulevards,* which are common nouns when not used in a specific address. Choices (1) and (4) insert an unnecessary comma. Choice (2) creates another capitalization error.

53. The correct answer is (5) The original sentence is correct. Choices (1) and (3) create spelling errors. Choice (2) creates two sentences, one of which is a fragment. Choice (4) makes no sense.

54. The correct answer is (5) The original sentence is correct. Choices (1) and (4) create capitalization errors. Choice (2) creates two sentences, one of which is a fragment. Choice (3) inserts an unnecessary comma.

55. The correct answer is (2) The original sentence has a spelling error. Choice (2) spells *intelligence* correctly. Choice (1) uses a contraction *(it's)* when the possessive *its* is required. Choice (3) removes a needed comma. Choice (4) creates a comma splice. Choice (5) creates another spelling error.

PART II

Essays will vary. A sample follows.

To the Editor:

I would like to state my support for canceling the highway building project and for avoiding any more damage to the insects in that area. We can bring the highway's benefits to this area in other ways, but we don't know the possible effects of killing or moving the insects.

People who support the highway have said that it will bring customers to the businesses nearby. This may be true, but this business is not badly needed. The area along this route has grown a lot within the past few years. The number of businesses moving there suggests that the highway is not needed for businesses to do well. They are doing very well already. To increase business even more, we could adjust city bus routes to carry more people to the area. In fact, this option is much cheaper for taxpayers than paying for a new highway.

Furthermore, adding bus routes will not harm our environment as a new highway would. Killing a few thousand bugs seems harmless enough, but we really don't know the damage we could be doing. Plants, insects, and other animals (including people) are linked to each other in many ways we don't see or even fully understand. By changing or removing one link, we could be putting other links in danger.

Let's try to keep the city from taking over the surrounding environment. We can do this by canceling the highway project and, if necessary, adapting bus routes to meet our needs.

Practice Test 2: Social Studies

1. The correct answer is (3): (Application) Profit is the amount of money remaining after a company's bills have been paid. Frequently, a part of the profit is distributed to the company's shareholders on a quarterly basis.

2. The correct answer is (4): (Application) When more Japanese goods are sold in the United States than U.S. goods are sold in Japan, America has an unfavorable balance of trade with Japan. In recent years, this unfavorable balance of trade has become one of the major points of contention between the United States and Japan.

3. The correct answer is (2): (Analysis) Memories of the difficulties caused by galloping inflation led the German government to refuse to lower its interest rates.

4. The correct answer is (1): (Analysis) Monopolies are allowed to operate (under government supervision) so as to benefit the customers of the monopolies, so choice (1) is correct. Choice (4) is only a partial answer.

5. The correct answer is (4): (Application) If the cost of production rises but the selling price remains the same, the result is lower profitability.

6. The correct answer is (2): (Comprehension) One of the major beliefs of communism is that no enterprise should earn a profit. According to this view, profits are ill-gotten gains. Thus, choice (2) is the correct answer.

7. The correct answer is (5): (Analysis) Choice (5) is the only one that describes the situation regarding immigration from Japan and China to America.

8. The correct answer is (5): (Comprehension) More than 90 percent of the immigrants were from Europe.

9. The correct answer is (1): (Evaluation) The large number of immigrants from Europe, who, it must be assumed, were processed through Ellis Island, would indicate that choice (1) is the correct answer.

10. The correct answer is (2): (Analysis) The great racial tensions between African Americans and whites of European descent probably caused immigration from Africa to be almost nonexistent.

11. The correct answer is (3): (Comprehension) New York City is three time zones to the east of San Francisco, so it is three hours later in New York.

12. The correct answer is (5): (Application) Because Washington, D.C., is in the Eastern time zone and Portland, Oregon, is in the Pacific time zone, the time difference is three hours, so when it is 9 a.m. in Portland, it is noon in Washington.

13. The correct answer is (2): (Analysis) Originally, each town across the country set its own time by the position of the sun, so it was impossible to figure the arrival and departure times of trains. The creation of time zones solved this problem.

14. The correct answer is (3): (Comprehension) According to the graph, the year of highest profits was 1989.

15. The correct answer is (1): (Evaluation) Reducing costs (i.e., salaries) would have helped increase profits. The other four choices would not have increased the profitability of the store; in fact, choices (2) and (3) would have actually added to the problem.

16. The correct answer is (2): (Analysis) The year the business opened, 1984, would have been the one during which the most employees would have been hired, because it can be assumed that a full staff would have been put in place that year.

17. The correct answer is (3): (Comprehension) This answer can be derived by looking only at the latitudes of the various options. Only choices (3) and (5), points C and E, are in the south latitudes, so the other three choices can be eliminated immediately. Choice (5) is at 60 degrees south latitude, so choice (3), point C, can be determined to be the correct answer by the process of elimination.

SOCIAL STUDIES PRACTICE TEST ANALYSIS CHART

Use this table to determine your areas of strength and areas in which more work is needed. The numbers in the boxes refer to the multiple-choice questions in the practice test.

Content Area	Comprehension	Application	Analysis	Evaluation	Score
Unit 1 **History** (pp. 144–155)	8, 34, 46, 48	39, 40, 41, 42, 44	7, 10, 47	9, 43, 45, 49	_____ of 16
Unit 2 **Geography** (pp. 156–162)	11, 17	12, 18, 58, 59	13, 61	60	_____ of 9
Unit 3 **Political Science** (pp. 163–171)	19, 48	21, 22, 28, 29, 31	20, 30, 35	23, 24, 32, 33	_____ of 14
Unit 4 **Economics** (pp. 172–177)	6, 14	1, 2, 5	3, 4, 16, 62, 63	15, 64	_____ of 12
Unit 5 **Behavioral Science** (pp. 178–186)	50, 52, 53, 56	55, 57	25, 26, 27, 36, 54	37, 51	_____ of 13
Score	_____ of 14	_____ of 19	_____ of 18	_____ of 13	_____ of 64

18. **The correct answer is (1): (Application)** By locating points B and D on the globe, it should become apparent that point B is both west and north of point D, so choice (1) is correct.

19. **The correct answer is (4): (Comprehension)** Between 1965 and 1971, spending declined for only one category—training of federal personnel—so choice (4) is correct.

20. **The correct answer is (3): (Analysis)** Choices (1), (2), (4), and (5) may or may not be true statements; they cannot be verified by the information in the bar graph. Only choice (3) contains information that can be verified by the bar graph.

21. **The correct answer is (3): (Application)** The Iraqi government under Saddam Hussein is a dictatorship.

22. **The correct answer is (2): (Application)** Great Britain and Northern Ireland are considered to be a model example of a constitutional monarchy. The current ruler is Queen Elizabeth II.

23. **The correct answer is (3): (Evaluation)** Because the Irish Republican Army strongly opposes British rule of Northern Ireland, the group would probably call the British government a dictatorship.

24. **The correct answer is (1): (Evaluation)** A belief in the right of people to have a say in their government is a traditional, strongly held American belief.

25. **The correct answer is (1): (Analysis)** Child abuse would probably be the major concern of someone involved in child welfare, so choice (1) is correct. The growth in the number of children who are involved in random shootings might also be a concern, particularly in terms of preventing such behavior, but this would still come under the overall heading of preventing child abuse.

26. **The correct answer is (3): (Analysis)** Of the types of violence listed, the AARP would probably be most interested in crimes directly targeted at its members, the elderly.

27. **The correct answer is (3): (Analysis)** Street gangs are most often associated with drive-by and random shootings of members of other such gangs, either in retribution for past incidents or as a way to gain territory.

28. **The correct answer is (4): (Application)** The Gadsden Purchase was added in 1853, making it the final acquisition to the continental United States.

29. **The correct answer is (2): (Application)** The Mexican Cession was added to the United States in 1848 as a result of the Mexican War, which ended that year.

30. **The correct answer is (3): (Analysis)** The Louisiana Purchase was made in 1803, during the presidency of Thomas Jefferson.

31. **The correct answer is (5): (Analysis)** Choice (5) summarizes the entire map; each of the other choices describes only one part of it.

32. **The correct answer is (1): (Evaluation)** Wilson's belief in the need for America to make the world safe for democracy would probably lead him to support military intervention in the former Yugoslavia, because that area's problems beginning in the early 1990s were heavily involved in the persecution of minority groups and the implementation of authoritarian rule.

33. **The correct answer is (5): (Evaluation)** Wilson's support for the League of Nations was directly tied to his belief that nations should, and could, talk together to settle differences in an open, fair, and democratic way.

34. **The correct answer is (1): (Comprehension)** The correct order of events is: the Roaring 20s (1920-1929), the Great Depression (1929-1941), World War II (1939-1945), the assassination of John F. Kennedy (1963), and the Watergate scandal (1971-1974).

35. **The correct answer is (2): (Analysis)** The influenza epidemic was not tied to World War I; all the other choices were.

36. **The correct answer is (5): (Analysis)** Choices (1) through (4) describe situations that face many elderly Americans and may prevent them from receiving proper treatment for clinical depression. Choice (5) describes a situation that is not true for a large percentage of older people.

37. **The correct answer is (3): (Evaluation)** The most appropriate person to seek advice from would be a medical doctor. Only a person with medical training could determine if other illnesses are involved. Choice (5), a psychologist, might also be useful after diagnosis, but would not have the training to rule out other medical problems such as Alzheimer's disease.

38. **The correct answer is (4): (Comprehension)** The cartoon's view of American soldiers in the sights of a gun indicates that the cartoonist believes U.S. troops often become targets when they go abroad to solve conflicts between other groups.

39. **The correct answer is (3): (Application)** The American Relief Administration, a humanitarian effort, led to Hoover's being called the Great Humanitarian.

40. **The correct answer is (5): (Application)** The Bonus Army was made up of needy veterans, and Hoover's handling of the affair indicated that he didn't understand the extent of their problems.

41. **The correct answer is (3): (Application)** Hoover's qualifications for leadership of world famine relief would be based mostly on his work with the American Relief Administration.

42. **The correct answer is (3): (Application)** The major career experience that showed Hoover's unselfishness among the choices was his leadership of the American Relief Administration.

43. **The correct answer is (2): (Evaluation)** The fact that Roosevelt was then running against Hoover for the presidency may be viewed as the major reason for the change in Roosevelt's opinion of Hoover.

44. **The correct answer is (3): (Application)** The greatest number of nations listed in the passage as having government buildings at the fair were European countries, so choice (3) is correct.

45. **The correct answer is (3): (Evaluation)** The passage shows that there was already much violence in America in the 1800s, as there is today.

46. **The correct answer is (4): (Comprehension)** Having the President of the United States open the fair was a way of honoring American civilization.

47. **The correct answer is (1): (Analysis)** Choice (1) is the only one that makes a broad statement about the fair.

48. **The correct answer is (3): (Comprehension)** The key word is *ineffectual*, because the drawing shows that the tank and its occupants have little to do except decorate a garden.

49. **The correct answer is (1): (Evaluation)** The cartoon implies that NATO's reason for existence (the Soviet Union) has disappeared. Therefore, the cartoonist would probably agree that a powerful enemy once again would lead to a stronger NATO.

50. **The correct answer is (1): (Comprehension)** The drawing shows gangs growing out of poverty, drugs, and ignorance.

51. **The correct answer is (4): (Evaluation)** The correct answer is choice (4), because the cartoonist, who sees poverty, drugs, and ignorance as the causes of gangs, would probably agree that the only way to end gang violence is to eliminate these causes.

52. **The correct answer is (3): (Comprehension)** According to the table, open communication is the most highly valued job factor, with 65 percent of respondents saying they rate it "very important."

53. **The correct answer is (3): (Comprehension)** The table indicates that the size of the company is the least important factor.

54. **The correct answer is (2): (Analysis)** The flow of communication within the company and the management style of the supervisor are two of the three most highly rated qualities in their importance to workers.

55. **The correct answer is (2): (Application)** Because open communication is highly desired by most employees, the interviewer would be wise to talk about the company's ability to fulfill this desire.

56. **The correct answer is (4): (Comprehension)** The problem of repeat offenders who had been released early by parole boards is shown in the cartoon as the responsibility of the boards themselves.

57. **The correct answer is (1): (Application)** The cartoonist would probably tell the parole board to be less lenient and more cautious about whom they release, because such leniency is the issue of the cartoon.

58. **The correct answer is (3): (Application)** Because the San Andreas Fault is a major source of earthquakes, choice (3) is the correct answer.

59. **The correct answer is (3): (Application)** The passage describes the New Madrid Fault as running through the area, so choice (3) is the correct one.

60. **The correct answer is (1): (Evaluation)** Lack of scientific knowledge led ancient peoples to attribute to supernatural beings those natural occurrences that they could not easily explain. "The gods" were often believed to be in charge of such events, because people commonly believed that only supernatural powers could have such huge effects.

61. **The correct answer is (3): (Analysis)** The passage states that active volcanoes are found in Oregon and Hawaii. Of these, only Hawaii is listed as an answer, so choice (3) is correct.

62. **The correct answer is (4): (Analysis)** The first thing the business owner should do is get a general overview of the possibilities for landing government contracts, and the brochures described in choice (4) would probably be the best source for this overview.

63. **The correct answer is (3): (Analysis)** Choice (3) is a simple statement of fact, so it is the correct answer. Choices (1), (2), (4), and (5) contain value judgments ("too infrequently," "don't provide enough help," "high-quality materials," "too few are printed") and therefore are opinions, not facts.

64. **The correct answer is (4): (Evaluation)** A background in the former Soviet Union would probably have colored an immigrant's views of life in the West and what types of people and institutions are to be trusted. In the Soviet Union, the government was widely suspected of dishonesty.

Practice Test 3: Science

1. **The correct answer is (4): (Comprehension)** According to the passage, resistance is the degree to which the flow of electricity is slowed.

2. **The correct answer is (4): (Application)** A material with extremely high resistance to electricity would be needed to cover electrical wires and protect people from shock. All the other choices have very low resistance and conduct electricity well.

3. **The correct answer is (3): (Evaluation)** According to the passage and graph, lead reaches zero resistance at extremely low temperatures. Choices (1), (2), and (4) are contradicted by the graph. Choice (5) is true, but it is not supported by the information given.

SCIENCE PRACTICE TEST ANALYSIS CHART

Use this table to determine your areas of strength and areas in which more work is needed. The numbers in the boxes refer to the multiple-choice questions in the practice test.

Content Area	Comprehension	Application	Analysis	Evaluation	Score
Unit 1 Life Science (pp. 194–208)	6, 28, 35, 49, 53, 61, 62	5, 7, 8, 29, 30, 41, 45, 57, 64	31, 36, 38, 39, 40, 44, 47, 52, 54, 63	9, 32, 37, 42, 46, 65	_____ of 32
Unit 2 Earth Science (pp. 209–214)	23, 27, 50	24, 25, 33, 48, 58	4, 43, 51, 59	26, 60	_____ of 14
Unit 3 Chemistry (pp. 215–223)	15, 55	16, 17, 18	21, 22, 56	19, 20	_____ of 10
Unit 4 Physics (pp. 224–229)	1, 10	2, 11, 13	12, 34, 66	3, 14	_____ of 10
Score	_____ of 14	_____ of 20	_____ of 20	_____ of 12	_____ of 66

4. **The correct answer is (2): (Analysis)** Carbon dioxide levels are increased by the burning of fuels, choices (1) and (5). Carbon dioxide levels are also increased by the reduction of plant life, choices (3) and (4). The correct choice, generating electricity from solar energy, does not involve burning fuels or destroying plants.

5. **The correct answer is (5): (Application)** Storing bread in a cool place will slow the growth of any mold spores that might get on the bread. Keeping bread wrapped and throwing away sources of spores are ways of keeping spores away from fresh bread.

6. **The correct answer is (1): (Comprehension)** The passage states that the nucleus controls the activities of the cell.

7. **The correct answer is (4): (Application)** The passage states that mitochondria release energy from food. A very active cell uses a large amount of energy, and would have many mitochondria. The ability of a cell to provide enough energy to be very active would not be affected by the thickness of the membrane, the number of ribosomes, the size of the vacuole, or the amount of cytoplasm.

8. **The correct answer is (2): (Application)** The passage states that the ribosomes make protein. Because they make a product, the ribosomes are like a factory. Ribosomes do not store materials, as the vacuoles do. Mitochondria, not ribosomes, are like power plants or furnaces.

9. **The correct answer is (3): (Evaluation)** The densest structure in the cell is the most likely to be visible, which explains why the nucleus was the first structure to be seen through the microscope. Choices (1) and (4) are true statements, but they do not explain why the nucleus is visible. Choice (2) is not necessarily true. Choice (5) is not true.

10. **The correct answer is (1): (Comprehension)** In the passage, light is defined as electromagnetic waves that are visible to the human eye.

11. **The correct answer is (5): (Application)** Of the choices listed, only photography makes use of visible electromagnetic waves, or light, to create images on paper. The other choices all involve invisible electromagnetic waves.

12. **The correct answer is (2): (Analysis)** As the distance to the fulcrum decreases, the effort required to lift the load increases. When the fulcrum is in the center, effort and load are equal. When the fulcrum is moved toward the load, as shown in the second diagram, the effort required decreases. Choices (3) and (4) are incorrect because the load does not change.

13. **The correct answer is (5): (Application)** In a second-class lever the load is between the fulcrum and the effort. Of the choices listed, only the nutcracker fits this description. The fulcrum is the hinged end, the effort is your hand at the other end, and the load is the nut in the middle. All the other choices are first-class levers.

14. **The correct answer is (2): (Evaluation)** The diagrams show that as the distance between the fulcrum and the effort increases, the effort decreases. Choice (1) happens to be true, but the information provided does not support it. Choices (3), (4), and (5) are contradicted by the information given.

15. **The correct answer is (5): (Comprehension)** According to the passage, gases, liquids, and solids can all act as either solvents or solutes.

16. **The correct answer is (3): (Application)** A solution in which all the solute that can dissolve has dissolved is saturated; no more can be dissolved.

17. **The correct answer is (4): (Application)** Heating a solution of water and sugar increases the amount of sugar that will dissolve. Because the sugar was still dissolving rapidly, the solution was unsaturated.

18. **The correct answer is (1): (Application)** Vinegar is a solution of acetic acid and water; by adding more water, the solvent, the man diluted the solution.

19. **The correct answer is (2): (Evaluation)** As the passage explains, a gas can be a solute. Since household ammonia is used at room temperature, the ammonia in it is still in gas form. Choice (1) may or may not be true, but it does not explain why household ammonia is a liquid. Even if choice (3) were true, the ammonia would become a gas again once it heated up to room temperature. Choice (4) does not make sense. Choice (5) is true, but it does not explain why household ammonia is a liquid.

20. The correct answer is (3): (Evaluation) A concentrated solution is one with a lot of solute; it may have reached saturation capacity or it may not. Choices (1) and (2) are contradicted by the passage. Choice (4) is true, but it is not supported by the information given. Choice (5) does not make sense; more solute must be added to make a solution more concentrated.

21. The correct answer is (2): (Analysis) The breathable wrapper would allow oxygen to continue to combine with myoglobin, even though bacteria would use some of the oxygen. Therefore, the meat would remain red. Choice (1) is incorrect because there would be a constant supply of oxygen available from the air. Choice (3) is incorrect because myoglobin would combine with oxygen from the air. Choice (4) does not make sense. Choice (5) is incorrect because color changes do not necessarily indicate freshness.

22. The correct answer is (1): (Analysis) The newly exposed surface would contain myoglobin, which would react with oxygen to form oxymyoglobin, giving the new surface a red color. The red color of beef is not caused by blood.

23. The correct answer is (5): (Comprehension) According to the map's key, slanted lines indicate rain. Of the answer choices, the only city in an area of slanted lines is San Francisco.

24. The correct answer is (1): (Application) As the cold front continues to move out into the Atlantic, Washington's weather will clear. The air will get colder as the area of temperatures in the 20s moves eastward. None of the other choices is experiencing such cold temperatures or is near an area of such cold temperatures.

25. The correct answer is (4): (Application) Memphis is in an area clear of precipitation, with temperatures now in the 40s and likely to rise into the 50s as the high pressure area moves east. Choices (1) and (5) are incorrect because they are too cold. Choice (2) is incorrect because it is too warm. Choice (3) is incorrect because it is likely to continue to rain there.

26. The correct answer is (3): (Evaluation) The two areas of precipitation, along the west and east coasts, are low pressure areas, as indicated by the letter L on the map. Choice (1) is incorrect because it is in the 50s in Salt Lake City. Choice (2) may be true, but on the day shown by the map, it is colder in Atlanta than in Billings. Choices (4) and (5) are true, but are not supported by the information given.

27. The correct answer is (5): (Comprehension) According to the map, Boston is experiencing a stationary front, a front that does not move or moves only slightly for several days. All the other cities listed are near moving cold or warm fronts, so their weather is likely to change.

28. The correct answer is (1): (Comprehension) According to the passage, the thousands of proteins in the human body are made of only 20 amino acids.

29. The correct answer is (4): (Application) A limited number (26) of different letters in our alphabet can be put together to form thousands of different words. Similarly, 20 different amino acids are combined into thousands of different proteins. Choices (1) and (5) are incorrect because the bricks and pearls would all be the same. Choice (2) is incorrect because soup has no organization or structure. Choice (3) is incorrect because each page in a book is different, and none is repeated.

30. The correct answer is (5): (Application) The passage states that proteins are made up of amino acids. Thus, protein foods can provide the body with a supply of amino acids.

31. The correct answer is (5): (Analysis) The passage states that DNA contains the code that tells the body how to assemble proteins. It does not control the nature of amino acids. If the DNA is changed, choices (1) to (4) are all possible results. A change in the identity of an amino acid cannot result.

32. The correct answer is (1): (Evaluation) Choice (2) is incorrect because it is contradicted by the passage. Choices (3), (4), and (5) may or may not be true, but you cannot tell from the information provided.

33. The correct answer is (4): (Application) Only sugar cane is an example of biomass. Choices (1), (3), and (5) are other types of renewable resources. Choice (2) is a fossil fuel.

34. The correct answer is (1): (Analysis) Choice (1) is a conclusion, a general law. Choices (2) to (5) are all statements of facts that support this conclusion.

35. The correct answer is (3): (Comprehension) According to the table, calcium makes up 1.5 percent by weight of living organisms.

36. The correct answer is (1): (Analysis) Iron is not listed in the table, so it is not one of the ten most common elements. The tenth element in the table makes up 0.1 percent of a living thing. If iron were the eleventh element, it could not be more common than the tenth element, so iron could not make up more than 0.1 percent of a living thing.

37. The correct answer is (2): (Evaluation) According to statement B, bones contain large deposits of calcium and phosphorous. This statement indicates that other structures contain less calcium and phosphorous than bones do. Statement A says nothing about the distribution of oxygen and hydrogen. Statement C indicates that sodium is evenly distributed throughout living things.

38. The correct answer is (2): (Analysis) Mosses reproduce sexually by forming sperm that swim to eggs. Water is needed for this transfer, so mosses could not reproduce sexually in dry places. Choice (1) is incorrect because mosses do not have roots. Choice (3) is incorrect because a sunny place would provide plenty of sunlight. Choice (4) is incorrect because moisture and sunlight do not determine the amounts of minerals found in soil. Choice (5) is not true.

39. The correct answer is (5): (Analysis) Because the navel orange is a seedless fruit, there are no seeds to plant. Cross-breeding is pointless if there will be no seeds, so the only method left is taking cuttings, a vegetative method of producing more trees.

40. The correct answer is (1): (Analysis) The barbules of the feathers hook together to produce the large surface that keeps the bird in the air. Choice (2) is incorrect because the fluffy base of the feather has nothing to do with flying. Choices (3) and (4) are not related to flight either. Choice (5) is not true.

41. The correct answer is (3): (Application) The down feathers keep a bird warm. Any fluffy substance that can trap air makes good insulation. The other choices are incorrect because down feathers cannot help the bird fly or dive, and since they are not visible, they do not attract a mate.

42. The correct answer is (2): (Evaluation) The male can recognize the pheromone even when it is greatly diluted. The most likely explanation for this is that the male has a keen sense of smell. The nature or amount of the smell does not explain why the male can detect the chemical in minute amounts.

43. The correct answer is (1): (Analysis) If vehicles burn purer fuel, there will be less production of carbons and sulfates because of incomplete combustion, so air pollution levels will drop.

44. The correct answer is (1): (Analysis) The queen is able to store sperm, so once she has mated, the drones are not needed. As she continues to lay eggs, some of them will develop into males, and the drones will be replaced. Choice (2) is incorrect because workers are sterile and cannot breed. Choices (3) and (4) are incorrect because the queen and workers are female, and cannot do the reproductive job of the males. Choice (5) is not true.

45. The correct answer is (1): (Application) Only the mated queen would be needed, because she would produce the workers and drones from sperm already stored in her body.

46. The correct answer is (4): (Evaluation) Since the different types of bees have different functions that enable the hive to survive, bees are animals that cooperate. The truth of the other choices cannot be verified by the information in the passage.

47. **The correct answer is (2): (Analysis)** A change in the digestive system is most likely related to a change in diet. Plant matter takes longer to digest than animal matter, and plant eaters generally have a longer digestive system than do animals that eat other animals.

48. **The correct answer is (3): (Application)** The key elements in the comparison are a source of light and something blocking it. Only choice (3) has both elements. Choice (5) is incorrect because nothing is blocking the beam of the flashlight.

49. **The correct answer is (5): (Comprehension)** The passage states that chlorophyll is more sensitive to temperature changes than the other pigments. Frosts occur in the fall as nights become cooler, so the chlorophyll is destroyed before the other pigments, revealing the colors once hidden by the chlorophyll.

50. **The correct answer is (4): (Comprehension)** This choice best summarizes the two main ideas of the passage: first, that a comet was expected to collide with Jupiter, and second, that scientists were not sure exactly what would happen when it did. Choices (1), (2), and (5) are details from the passage. Choice (3) is not what the passage is about.

51. **The correct answer is (5): (Analysis)** No one knew what the fragments would do, so choice (5) represents an opinion. Choices (1) to (4) are all facts stated in the passage.

52. **The correct answer is (2): (Analysis)** Dormancy keeps the seed from sprouting under unfavorable conditions. Spring brings warmer temperatures and abundant water, which the young plant will need to grow. Choice (1) is incorrect because in spring the trees are getting new leaves. Choices (3) and (4) are incorrect because spring is the season when available water and light are increasing. Choice (5) is incorrect because a seed contains stored food, and the new plant will make its own food.

53. **The correct answer is (1): (Comprehension)** According to the passage, fish are eaten by seals, which are eaten by polar bears.

54. **The correct answer is (4): (Analysis)** Since polar bears cannot make omega-3, they must get it from the food they eat. Their main food is seal, so the omega-3 must come from that. Choices (1) and (2) are incorrect because fish make omega-3. Choice (3) is incorrect because polar bears eat mostly seal. Choice (5) is incorrect because the original source of the omega-3 is fish.

55. **The correct answer is (1): (Comprehension)** The graph shows that the energy level of the products is the lowest energy level in an exothermic reaction.

56. **The correct answer is (1): (Analysis)** Since there is less energy in the products than in the reactants in a exothermic reaction, the excess energy must be released. Choice (2) is contradicted by the graph. Choice (3) is incorrect because the reactants do not absorb the energy that is produced by the reaction. Choice (4) is incorrect because activation energy is the energy needed to start the reaction, not a result of the reaction. Choice (5) is not true.

57. **The correct answer is (2): (Application)** In a container (like a barrel), the ethylene gas given off by a ripening apple can cause the others to ripen and then become overripe, or spoiled. No other choice reflects the information in the passage.

58. **The correct answer is (3): (Application)** The heavier the freighter, the deeper it will sink in the water. This is similar to the crust sinking deeper where it is heavier. The key element in the comparison is the contrast between dense and light material floating in something. Choice (4) is incorrect because the density of the swimmer does not change. He or she floats more easily in the ocean because salt water is denser.

59. **The correct answer is (5): (Analysis)** When a mountain wears away, it weighs less because it contains less material. Crust that weighs less rises in the mantle.

60. **The correct answer is (4): (Evaluation)** To maintain a state of balance, rising crust in one area must be offset by sinking crust in another. All the other choices may or may not be true, but they are not supported by the information given.

61. **The correct answer is (2): (Comprehension)** According to the passage, smoking is a risk factor for heart attack. Shortness of breath, choice (1), is a symptom of a heart attack. Damaged cells, choice (3), result from a heart attack. Exercising, choice (4), and a low-fat diet, choice (5), are lifestyle choices that can reduce the risk of heart attack.

62. **The correct answer is (4): (Comprehension)** Heart attacks are the result of cholesterol buildup in arteries. Although high blood pressure, choice (2), and a fatty diet, choice (3), increase cholesterol buildup, they are not the direct cause of heart attacks.

63. **The correct answer is (3): (Analysis)** A person cannot change his or her family history, sex, or age—choices (1), (2), and (4). However, a person does determine the amount of exercise that he or she gets. Choice (5) is incorrect because body type is not indicated as a risk factor, although body *weight* is a factor and can be controlled.

64. **The correct answer is (5): (Application)** Choices (1) to (4) will reduce the risk of heart attack. If smoking, eating a high-fat diet, and being overweight increase the risk of heart attack, reversing these conditions should reduce the risk.

65. **The correct answer is (2): (Evaluation)** According to the diagram, fungi, plants, animals, and protista all have cells that contain nuclei. Choice (1) is not true; there are many species in the kingdom Animalia. Choice (3) is contradicted by the diagram. Choice (4) is true, but it is not supported by the information given. Choice (5) is not true.

66. **The correct answer is (4): (Analysis)** By slowing and controlling the fission chain reaction, the heat production can be decreased to a steady pace. In fact, this is what is done in nuclear reactors. Choices (1), (2), and (3) would be the result of speeding up the chain reaction. Choice (5) is incorrect because the reaction would be slowed, not prevented from starting.

Practice Test 4: Interpreting Literature and the Arts

What Happened at This Nuclear Plant? *(page 509)*

1. **The correct answer is (2): (Application)** Just as radiation can contaminate the air, so chemicals can contaminate fresh water. Choices (1), (4), and (5) are less similar because they do not involve an environmental hazard. Choice (3) is an accident caused by natural forces, not human.

2. **The correct answer is (1): (Analysis)** The serious consequences of a meltdown make the atmosphere tense. Choices (2) and (4) suggest the opposite. Choice (5) can be eliminated because, while the passage itself may stir the reader's emotions, its story is told in an unemotional way. The passage is a straight factual account, so choice (3) is incorrect.

3. **The correct answer is (2): (Literal comprehension)** Lines 22–26 state that Leonid Shavrey "was woken by the explosion . . . and saw that the roof of the fourth unit was on fire." There is no evidence that the whole town is on fire, as choice (1) suggests; that they have seen a meltdown before, as choice (4) states; or that Metlenko has contacted them, as choice (5) indicates. They do not look for or find special radiation suits at the plant, so choice (3) can be eliminated.

4. **The correct answer is (4): (Inferential comprehension)** Details such as "With no special clothing to protect them from radiation" make it clear that the sickness is the result of radiation poisoning. Although water and air pollution are long-term effects of radiation contamination, these are not the direct causes of the firemen's symptoms, so choices (2) and (3) can be eliminated. There is no evidence for choices (1) and (5).

INTERPRETING LITERATURE AND THE ARTS
PRACTICE TEST ANALYSIS CHART

Use this table to determine your areas of strength and areas in which more work is needed. The numbers in the boxes refer to the multiple-choice questions in the practice test.

Content Area	Literal Comprehension	Inferential Comprehension	Application	Analysis	Score
Unit 1 Nonfiction (pp. 238-243)	3, 8, 9	4, 5, 6	1, 7	2, 10	_____ of 10
Unit 2 Fiction (pp. 244-249)	11, 14	12, 15, 18, 19, 21, 22		13, 20	_____ of 9
Unit 3 Poetry (pp. 250-253)	26, 43	23, 27, 28, 33, 45	25, 34	24, 35, 36, 44	_____ of 13
Unit 4 Drama (pp. 254-258)	29, 30	31, 40	32, 42		_____ of 6
Unit 5 Commentary on the Arts (pp. 259-266)	16, 38		17	15, 37, 39, 41	_____ of 7
Score	_____ of 11	_____ of 15	_____ of 7	_____ of 12	_____ of 45

How Do These Men Feel About Ann Whitefield? (page 510)

5. **The correct answer is (3): (Inferential comprehension)** Because Mr. Whitefield made Tanner one of Ann's guardians, you can conclude that he wanted Tanner to look after her. Choice (1) is not logical because, since Mr. Whitefield selected Tanner as a guardian, he must have liked him. The other choices are not supported by the passage.

6. **The correct answer is (4): (Inferential comprehension)** In lines 23-28, Tanner implies that Ann is calculating when he says Ann will do anything she wants and then "put everything on us." Choice (1) is incorrect because he does not mention her looks. Choices (2), (3), and (5) each suggest a person who would not behave as these men expect Ann to do.

7. **The correct answer is (2): (Application)** In this passage, Tanner suddenly receives guardianship, just as a godparent might suddenly receive custody of a child. Choices (4) and (5) describe a situation in which a child or sweetheart is lost, not suddenly gained. Choices (1) and (3) can be eliminated because they describe situations in which the person makes a choice.

Who Are Norman and Willie? (page 510)

8. **The correct answer is (2): (Literal comprehension)** Lines 4-6 state that, since Norman doesn't ride a bike and rarely plays outside, he is seen as different or unusual. This characterization makes Norman sound serious, not humorous, so choice (1) can be eliminated. Since he is considered "weird" (line 6), he wouldn't be described as popular or all-American, so choices (3) and (5) are unlikely. Choice (4) is incorrect since nothing is said in these lines about Norman's interest in other sports besides bicycling.

9. **The correct answer is (3): (Literal comprehension)** According to lines 24-25, ". . . they never as much as shared a 'Hi.'" Choices (1) and (2) are incorrect because they imply a strong relationship. Since Willie and Norman ignore each other, their relationship could not be forced or uncomfortable, so choices (4) and (5) can be eliminated.

10. **The correct answer is (4): (Analysis)** The passage describes great differences in the behavior and appearance of the two boys. Choice (3) is incorrect because the passage does not describe any ways that they are alike. Choices (1) and (5) are incomplete answers; the passage also studies Willie and describes activities that Norman enjoys. The boys are not friends, so choice (2) is incorrect.

How Does Macon Feel About Being Alone?
(page 511)

11. **The correct answer is (2): (Literal comprehension)** This passage describes a separation or divorce rather than a death, as choice (1) indicates; the passage begins, "After his wife left him . . ." Choice (5) is incorrect because Macon has clearly stayed in the house that he and Sarah shared. There is no evidence for choices (3) and (4).

12. **The correct answer is (3): (Inferential comprehension)** Macon's focus on Sarah's belongings, and the fact that the house seems smaller when he expected it to feel larger, show that he is surprised to be feeling her absence so keenly. Choices (1) and (5) suggest the opposite, and there is no evidence to support choice (4). It is possible that Macon and Sarah fought, but the passage does not mention this; therefore, choice (2) can be eliminated.

13. **The correct answer is (1): (Analysis)** The second and third paragraphs list Sarah's personal belongings. Macon is thinking, not being interviewed or writing to Sarah, as choices (3) and (4) suggest. The passage does not discuss events in Macon's life, so choice (5) is incorrect. Although Sarah's belongings influence Macon's emotions, this cause-and-effect relationship is not the main focus of the passage, so choice (2) can be eliminated.

14. **The correct answer is (5): (Literal comprehension)** Lines 13-14 state directly that "She liked to keep in touch with her students . . ." There is no evidence for choices (1), (2), or (4). Choice (3) is incorrect because, though the passage suggests that she is dancing, it does not indicate that she is learning to dance.

What Is the Subject of This Book? (page 512)

15. **The correct answer is (3): (Inferential comprehension)** Lines 30-33 describe the entries about Pauline Lyons Williamson and Helen Wiser Stewart, two of the pioneer women profiled in the book. The review does not state that these women knew each other or that they divorced their husbands, as choices (1) and (2) state. The authors of *Women of the West* are named in lines 1-2, so choice (4) can be eliminated. It can be assumed that the authors are also researchers, so choice (5) can be eliminated.

16. **The correct answer is (5): (Literal comprehension)** The reviewer voices this complaint in lines 29-33. Choices (2) and (3) are incorrect, respectively, because the reviewer mentions neither African Americans nor the reliability of the sources. The fact that the characters are strong-minded and optimistic, as described in choice (4), is what the reviewer praises about *Women of the West*. Choice (1) may be true, but it is not mentioned in the review.

17. **The correct answer is (2): (Application)** The reviewer praises the fact that *Women of the West* presents a picture of pioneer women's determined, individualistic spirit. A movie that was true to the book would present a similar picture. It would focus little on men, so choice (1) can be eliminated. Choice (3) can be eliminated because only one Native American woman is mentioned (lines 10-13), and that is not in a warlike setting. Choices (4) and (5) are incorrect because *Women of the West* is a straightforward presentation of basic, real-life hardships and joys.

How Are the Mothers at Grand Isle Depicted?
(page 513)

18. **The correct answer is (2): (Inferential comprehension)** Lines 8-13 and 22-24 mention sand, water, and summer, so the setting is probably a vacation site—a seashore or an island. Choices (1) and (3) can be eliminated because they describe crowded, stressful situations. Although the families may be staying in large old homes or even hotels, there is no evidence to support these ideas; therefore, choices (4) and (5) can be eliminated.

19. **The correct answer is (4): (Inferential comprehension)** Since Mrs. Pontellier's child is "not apt to rush crying to his mother's arms for comfort" (lines 9-10), she is probably a somewhat distant mother. Choices (1) and (5) suggest the opposite, whereas choice (3) is too strongly negative a description based on the passage. There is no evidence that Mrs. Pontellier is

or is not strict, but the speaker does indicate that she is not comforting, so choice (2) is incorrect.

20. **The correct answer is (5): (Analysis)** Since hair parting cannot be an actual law, the speaker is humorously exaggerating its importance to the characters in this passage. Choices (1), (2), and (4) all suggest that the speaker is serious. Although the speaker is describing a social custom or standard, her tone could not be characterized as social; therefore, choice (3) can be eliminated.

21. **The correct answer is (1): (Inferential comprehension)** The point of this statement is that the women direct so much of their energy toward their husbands and children that their own personalities are nearly erased, or *effaced*. Choices (2), (4), and (5) are incorrect because they suggest that the women are building up, not erasing, their own personalities. Choice (3) is not the best choice because the women are not criticizing, or condemning, themselves—they simply aren't paying any attention to their own needs.

22. **The correct answer is (1): (Inferential comprehension)** As the "embodiment of every womanly grace and charm" (lines 33-34), Adele is the model, or perfect example, of the "mother-woman." Choices (2), (3), and (4) may be true, but they are not supported by the passage. Adele's husband is not described, so choice (5) is incorrect.

What About Nature Does This Poet Praise?
(page 514)

23. **The correct answer is (4): (Literal comprehension)** The natural things that the speaker praises—for example, stippled trout (line 3), a landscape that looks like patchwork (line 6), and anything that is freckled (line 10)—have irregular patterns and colors. The speaker praises their beauty, so choice (3) is incorrect. Choice (1) suggests how these images make the speaker feel, not what they look like. Choices (2) and (5) do not make sense in this context.

24. **The correct answer is (3): (Analysis)** These images illustrate the speaker's admiration of the variety and beauty of nature. Choices (1) and (2) are incorrect because it is clear that the speaker loves the outdoors and is not afraid of animals. The poem does not mention painting or technology, so choices (4) and (5) can be eliminated.

25. **The correct answer is (1): (Application)** A poem called "Peoples of the World" might celebrate the variety of people, much as this poem praises the variety of nature. Choices (2) and (4) imply descriptions of things that have only one color or that are the same. There is not enough information in the other titles to suggest a similarity of theme.

What Does the Speaker Remember? (page 514)

26. **The correct answer is (3): (Literal comprehension)** The speaker tells her mother the truth but has trouble explaining what happened. Choice (2) is incorrect since the speaker told the truth. The speaker defends her mother, so choice (1) is incorrect. "Telling stories" in this context means *lying*, so choice (5) is incorrect. There is no evidence for choice (4).

27. **The correct answer is (2): (Inferential comprehension)** The speaker describes two childhood experiences involving prejudice—shown on one occasion by an adult and on another occasion by a girl her own age. Though the speaker is now an adult, the passage focuses on her childhood, so choice (1) is incorrect. The speaker does not deny her mother's Chinese heritage, so choice (3) can be eliminated. Though her mother is the subject of the remembrances, as choice (4) suggests, the focus of the passage is the speaker's response to prejudice. A friendship is mentioned, so choice (5) can be eliminated.

28. The correct answer is (5): (Inferential comprehension) When the speaker says, "But I don't like you" (line 30), she is lying and is saying something hurtful. Since she is lying intentionally ("It is my first conscious lie," line 31), choices (1) and (2) are incorrect. The speaker never refutes the fact that her mother is Chinese, so choice (3) can be eliminated. Choice (4) is incorrect because although the speaker is not ashamed of her heritage, she does not defend it in this passage, either.

How Does Nelly Respond to Catherine? *(page 515)*

29. The correct answer is (4): (Literal comprehension) Nelly is narrating this passage—events are told from her point of view and she is the "I" referred to throughout. Catherine's actions and words are being described by Nelly, so choice (1) is incorrect. Heathcliff is mentioned but does not appear, so choice (3) is incorrect. There is no mention of any other woman or of Catherine's sister, so choices (2) and (5) can be eliminated.

30. The correct answer is (1): (Literal comprehension) In these lines, Nelly says clearly that Catherine does not worry about anyone but herself. There is no evidence for the other choices.

31. The correct answer is (2): (Inferential comprehension) Nelly is wary, or suspicious, of Catherine's selfishness; still, as suggested in lines 34-37, she is willing to forgive her. It is Catherine who could be described as selfish and undependable, so choice (5) is incorrect. The other choices are not supported by the passage.

32. The correct answer is (3): (Application) Nelly's comments highlight Catherine's extreme self-interest. With such an attitude, Catherine probably would remain focused on herself in the situation given. There is no reason to believe Catherine asks Nelly to take care of personal business, so choice (1) is unlikely. Choice (2) would be the action of a selfless person. Though Catherine's current dilemma regards Edgar Linton, she would not necessarily mention this, so choice (5) can be eliminated. There is no evidence for choice (4).

How Does This Speaker Feel About Work? *(page 515)*

33. The correct answer is (4): (Inferential comprehension) The speaker mentions that his landlady overcharges (line 10); thus, he does not own his home, as choice (1) suggests. The speaker's feelings about animals in general cannot be inferred from his mention of one cat, so choice (2) can be eliminated. Since he resents his landlady, choice (3) is incorrect. Choice (5) can be eliminated because the specifics of the speaker's work situation are not given.

34. The correct answer is (1): (Application) At the end of line 3, the speaker has not yet decided that work is essential. Without working, he could not afford the rent and might have to move. Without working, he probably could not rent a larger apartment, eat more, or buy a house, so choices (2), (3), and (5) are incorrect. By the end of line 3, the speaker has not yet mentioned a grievance against his landlady, as choice (4) suggests.

35. The correct answer is (1): (Analysis) The speaker does not actually "whip a cat" to prove how small his apartment is, so this figurative statement is humorous and choice (2) is incorrect. Though the apartment is very small, the speaker does not seem especially angry, proud, or embarrassed by that fact; thus, choices (3), (4), and (5) can be eliminated.

36. The correct answer is (4): (Analysis) If the landlady's features look as though they run together, her skin must be wrinkled and sagging. Choice (1) suggests the opposite. The color of the landlady's skin and freckles are not mentioned, so choices (3) and (5) can be eliminated. Her skin may be damaged from the sun, but this is not stated in the passage; thus, choice (2) is incorrect.

What Is This Play About? *(page 516)*

37. The correct answer is (1): (Analysis) Throughout, the reviewer praises how well the actors and singers work together. Choices (2)

and (3) are incorrect because he does not focus much on Andrew Zondo (the real-life Jacob Zulu) or on political forces in South Africa. Choices (4) and (5) are incorrect because the reviewer does not mention the lead singer or directly praise the playwright.

38. The correct answer is (4): (Literal comprehension) Lines 3-5 state that "the overthrow of apartheid in South Africa is taking place. . . ." The reviewer does not mention an introduction by the playwright or the first song by Ladysmith Black Mambazo, so choices (1) and (3) can be eliminated. While the play does describe the trial and hanging of Jacob Zulu, as choice (2) states, these events are not the background for the action—they are results. Choice (5) can be eliminated because although the review describes the play's Broadway debut, that information is not related to the play's action.

39. The correct answer is (3): (Analysis) These images convey strength and hope—a new era dawning for South Africa. The reviewer does not suggest that the songs sound like nature or describe only natural images, so choices (1) and (5) are incorrect. Choice (2) suggests the opposite of strength and hope, and choice (4) contradicts the balance between action and song suggested by the reviewer.

40. The correct answer is (4): (Inferential comprehension) These lines state that Ladysmith Black Mambazo is the "ultimate Greek chorus, reflecting the action in eloquent . . . songs." The implication is that Greek choruses complement the action of a play by commenting on it, not that they take attention away from the actors or are observers, as choices (1) and (2) suggest. Choice (3) is incorrect because the reviewer does not contrast the effectiveness of Ladysmith Black Mambazo with that of a Greek chorus. The response of Greek audiences is not mentioned, so choice (5) can be eliminated.

41. The correct answer is (2): (Analysis) The reviewer shows irony by describing how calm Zulu's early years are and how surprising it is that he committed a violent act later. Choices (1) and (5) are incorrect since the life of Tug Yourgrau is not described and because there is no comment on the stage or setting. The town of Ladysmith is mentioned only in connection with the singers, so choice (3) is incorrect. Zulu's family life is not mentioned, so choice (4) can be eliminated.

42. The correct answer is (5): (Application) With the end of apartheid came the end of segregation in public places, including public schools. The end of World War II, the start of the twentieth century, the first moon landing, and the collapse of the Soviet Union did not arise from racial issues, so the other choices can be eliminated.

What Thoughts Concern This Speaker? *(page 517)*

43. The correct answer is (4): (Literal comprehension) Line 5 refers to the speaker's car, and lines 7-8 mention the canyon alongside the road. Although the speaker is Native American, and although she seems to be fleeing from something, there is no evidence that she is near a reservation or running away from home, so choices (1) and (3) are incorrect. Since she is driving, choice (2) is incorrect. Line 6 mentions the night, so choice (5) is incorrect.

44. The correct answer is (2): (Analysis) In actuality the speaker hears only the wind, but the sounds symbolize "voices" (line 3) that tell her to forget that she is Indian (line 12). There is no reason to believe these mysterious voices are those of loved ones no longer living, or that they specifically represent the spirit of past Native American civilizations, so (1) and (4) are not the most likely choices. Choices (3) and (5) can be eliminated because they ignore the symbolism in the sound of the wind.

45. The correct answer is (3): (Inferential comprehension) The speaker is driving fast along a steep canyon. Line 13, "On the next curve you will break into stars," suggests that the speaker may drive off the road. Choice (1) is incorrect because the speaker is not referring literally to the stars. There is no mention of world peace, so choice (2) is incorrect. She is driving quickly and does not turn around, so choice (4) can be eliminated. The speaker seems to be upset by the symbolic voices that tell her to forget her heritage, so choice (5) is incorrect.

Practice Test 5: Mathematics

1. **The correct answer is (3): 126**

$$\frac{6 \text{ ounces}}{8 \text{ sq meters}} = \frac{z \text{ ounces}}{168 \text{ sq meters}}$$

$$6 \times 168 = 8 \times z$$
$$1{,}008 = 8 \times z$$
$$1{,}008 \div 8 = z$$
$$126 = z$$

2. **The correct answer is (1): 12** Use the formula for area of a square.

$$A = s^2$$
$$144 = s^2$$
$$12 = s$$

3. **The correct answer is (5):** $c - 14 = 26$

4. **The correct answer is (2): $12.10**

$20 - (\$0.79 \times 10)$
$20 - \$7.90 = \$12.10$

5. **The correct answer is (1): Only Porter and Holliday**

Porter: $0.28 \times 20{,}000 = 5{,}600$
Ricks: $0.19 \times 20{,}000 = 3{,}800$
Holliday: $0.21 \times 20{,}000 = 4{,}200$
Young: $0.15 \times 20{,}000 = 3{,}000$

6. **The correct answer is (4):** $g < \dfrac{s}{3}$

7. **The correct answer is (3): 30**

$$\frac{\$0.05}{2} = \frac{\$0.75}{g}$$
$$\$0.75 \times 2 = \$0.05 \times g$$
$$\$1.50 = \$0.05 \times g$$
$$30 = g$$

8. **The correct answer is (1): 65**
50 min + 1 hr 20 min
$50 + 60 + 20 = 130$ min

9. **The correct answer is (2): 4,000,000**

Use estimation.
Italy's unemployment rate:
$10.9 \approx 10\%$

People able to work:
36 million $\approx$ 40 million
0.10×40 million = 4 million
or 4,000,000

10. **The correct answer is (4): It rose 22 degrees.**

$$17 + x - 5$$
$$x = 5 + 17$$
$$x = 22$$

11. **The correct answer is (4): 85%**

$120 - 18 = 102$
$102 \div 120 = 0.85 = 85\%$

12. **The correct answer is (3): $103.96**

$(\$12.99 \times 4) + 45 = 96.96$
$\$96.96 + \$7.00 = \$103.96$

13. **The correct answer is (3):** $2(\$27.50 + \$5.99) + \$7.00$

14. **The correct answer is (4): 1.51 centimeters**

15. **The correct answer is (4):** $\dfrac{3}{4}$

$$78\% = \frac{78}{100} \approx \frac{75}{100} = \frac{3}{4}$$

16. **The correct answer is (4): 140**

$$\frac{2}{3} = \frac{x}{210}$$
$$3x = 210 \times 2$$
$$3x = 420$$
$$x = 140$$

17. **The correct answer is (3):** $29.99 - (0.10 \times \$29.99)$

18. **The correct answer is (3): 5**

Use similar triangles and a proportion.
$$\frac{BE}{BC} = \frac{DE}{AC} \quad \frac{6}{12} = \frac{x}{10}$$
$$60 = 12x$$
$$5 = x$$

19. **The correct answer is (1): 6**

$$m = \frac{y_2 - y_1}{x_2 - x_1}$$
$$= \frac{8 - 2}{2 - 1}$$
$$= 6$$

20. **The correct answer is (2): (5, 3)**

21. **The correct answer is (3): 1,500**

The number of trucks is unnecessary information.
$$\frac{8}{40} = \frac{300}{x}$$
$$8x = 12{,}000$$
$$x = 1{,}500$$

22. **The correct answer is (4):** $\dfrac{7}{10}$

$$\frac{1.4}{x} = \frac{70\%}{100\%}$$
$$70\% \, x = 1.4(100\%)$$
$$x = \frac{1.4}{0.70}$$
$$x = 2 \text{ megabytes}$$
$$\frac{1.4}{2.0} = \frac{7}{10}$$

23. **The correct answer is (3): 4**

Corn produced:
about 200 million metric tons

Corn exported:
about 50 million metric tons
$200 \div 50 = 4$

24. **The correct answer is (2): Soybean exports**

Soybean exports did not come to halfway between 0 and 50 metric tons.

25. **The correct answer is (5): In 1991, the amount of soybeans and wheat produced was about equal.**

The bars for these two categories are approximately the same height.

26. **The correct answer is (4): The number of passengers picked up**

27. **The correct answer is (5):** $\dfrac{2.5 \times 200}{9}$

$$\frac{2.5}{9} = \frac{x}{200}$$
$$9x = 2.5 \times 200$$
$$x = \frac{2.5 \times 200}{9}$$

MATHEMATICS PRACTICE TEST ANALYSIS CHART

Use this table to determine your areas of strength and areas in which more work is needed. The numbers in the boxes refer to the multiple-choice questions in the practice test.

Content	Item Number	Page Reference	Score
Unit 1 **Arithmetic** (pp. 275–280)	32, 37	524	_____ of 2
Unit 2 **Understanding Word** **Problems** (pp. 281–286)	26, 48, 50	523, 526	_____ of 3
Unit 3 **Decimals** (pp. 287–291)	4, 14, 38, 45	520, 521, 525, 526	_____ of 4
Unit 4 **Fractions** (pp. 292–301)	15, 22	522	_____ of 2
Unit 5 **Ratio and Proportion** (pp. 302–307)	1, 7, 16, 21, 42	520, 521, 526	_____ of 5
Unit 6 **Percent** (pp. 308–313)	5, 11, 46	520, 521, 526	_____ of 3
Unit 7 **Data Analysis** (pp. 314–326)	9, 12, 23, 24, 25, 39, 40, 41	521, 525	_____ of 2
Unit 8 **Measurement** (pp. 327–339)	2, 8, 28, 33, 34, 51, 52, 56	520, 521, 523, 524, 526, 527	_____ of 8
Arithmetic Score			_____ of 35
Unit 9 **Algebra** (pp. 340–358) Signed Numbers Expressions Equations Inequalities	 10, 35 13, 17, 27, 36, 47, 49, 54 3 6	 521, 524 521, 522, 523, 524, 526 520 520	 _____ of 2 _____ of 7 _____ of 1 _____ of 1
Algebra Score			_____ of 11
Unit 10 **Geometry** (pp. 359–378) Angles and Triangles Circles and Cylinders Coordinate Geometry	 18, 43, 44, 55 29, 30, 31 19, 20, 53	 522, 525, 526, 527 524 522, 527	 _____ of 4 _____ of 3 _____ of 3
Geometry Score			_____ of 10
Total Score			_____ of 56

28. **The correct answer is (2): 28**

    (140 + 144 + 100 + 86 + 90) = 560
    560 ÷ 5 = 112 (daily average)
    112 ÷ 4 = 28 (average per hour)

29. **The correct answer is (2): 17%**

    circle = 360°

    $\dfrac{60}{360} = \dfrac{1}{6} = 0.166\ rounds\ to\ 0.17$

30. **The correct answer is (3): 60°**

    $\angle AZD = 60°$ because
    $\angle AZB + \angle CZD = 120°$.
    $\angle YZP$ and $\angle AZD$ are vertical angles and therefore equal.

31. **The correct answer is (1):** $2 \times 7 \times \dfrac{22}{7}$

    Use the formula for the circumference of a circle.
    $C = \pi d$
    $C = \dfrac{22}{7} (2 \times 7)$

32. **The correct answer is (2): 7**

    Estimate: $12.99 is about $13.

33. **The correct answer is (3): 1 in 25**

    $\dfrac{10\ tickets}{250\ tickets} = \dfrac{1}{25}$

34. **The correct answer is (3): 3 in 5**

    250 − 100 = 150
    Tickets bought by employees:
    $\dfrac{150}{250} = \dfrac{3}{5}$

35. **The correct answer is (3): −11**

    $-12 - (3 - 4) = x$
    $-12 - (-1) = x$
    $-12 + 1 = -11$

36. **The correct answer is (4):**

    $\dfrac{46{,}011.2 - 45{,}987.5}{20}$

37. **The correct answer is (5): Not enough information is given.**

    You do not know how much the cheese costs.

38. **The correct answer is (3): 48**

    3.2 × 5 = 16 mi per week
    16 × 3 = 48 mi in three weeks

39. **The correct answer is (2): 1982**

    The data line reaches the 400,000 mark in 1982.

40. **The correct answer is (4): 600,000**

    900,000 − 300,000 = 600,000

41. **The correct answer is (5): Not enough information is given.**

    You do not know how many people attended in all.

42. **The correct answer is (4): 40**

    $\dfrac{450}{9} = \dfrac{2{,}000}{b}$
    $450b = 2{,}000 \times 9$
    $450b = 18{,}000$
    $b = 40$

43. **The correct answer is (5): 180 − (90 + 62)**

    A triangle is 180° total. $\angle CAB$ is a right angle, 90°.

44. **The correct answer is (3): between 18 and 19**

    Use the Pythagorean formula.
    $$c^2 = a^2 + b^2$$
    $$(20)^2 = 8^2 + b^2$$
    $$400 - 64 = b^2$$
    $$336 = b^2$$
    b is between 18 and 19

45. **The correct answer is (3): 10**

    4.8 rounds to 5

    $\dfrac{5}{0.5} = 10$

46. **The correct answer is (3): $400**

    $\dfrac{\$320}{0.80} = \$400$

47. **The correct answer is (4): 68**

    $4^3 = 64$
    64 + 4 = 68

48. **The correct answer is (3): 9**

    $7 \div \dfrac{3}{4} = 7 \times \dfrac{4}{3} = \dfrac{28}{3} = 9\dfrac{1}{3}$

    Only 9 of the $\dfrac{3}{4}$-hour time slots can be completed in 7 hours.

49. **The correct answer is (2): $2,000 × 0.085 × 0.5**

    $I = prt$
    $p = \$2{,}000$
    $r = 8.5\%$ or 0.085
    $t = 6$ months, or ½ year, or 0.5

50. **The correct answer is (3): $6,600**

    Area of outdoor play space: $A = l \times w$
    $A = 20 \times 11 = 220\ ft^2$
    $220 \times \$30 = \$6{,}600$

51. **The correct answer is (4): 2(20) + 2(11)**

    $P = 2l + 2w$

52. **The correct answer is (1):** $\dfrac{\frac{1}{3} \times 110}{4}$

    Area of floor: 11 × 10 = 110
    ⅓ of area: ⅓ × 110
    Area of each tile: 2 × 2 = 4

53. **The correct answer is (1): A and B only**

    A. $5 = (3 \times 1) + 2$
    B. $5 = 1 + 4$
    C. $5 \neq 1 - 5$

54. **The correct answer is (3): ($7.85b) + (10 × 2 × $7.85)**

55. **The correct answer is (2): 28 feet**

    Use similar triangles and a proportion.

    $\dfrac{10}{25} = \dfrac{b}{25 + 45}$
    $10 \times 70 = 25b$
    $700 = 25b$
    $b = 28$

56. **The correct answer is (4): 27**

    $V = s^3$
    $V = 1\ yd \times 1\ yd \times 1\ yd$
    $V = 3\ ft \times 3\ ft \times 3\ ft$
    $V = 27\ ft^3$

Description	Formula
Area (A) of a:	
square	$A = s^2$; where s = side
rectangle	$A = lw$; where l = length, w = width
parallelogram	$A = bh$; where b = base, h = height
triangle	$A = \dfrac{1}{2}\,bh$; where b = base, h = height
circle	$A = \pi r^2$; where $\pi = 3.14$, r = radius
Perimeter (P) of a:	
square	$P = 4s$; where s = side
rectangle	$P = 2l + 2w$; where l = length; w = width
triangle	$P = a + b + c$; where a, b, and c are the sides
circumference (C) of a circle	$C = \pi d$; where $\pi = 3.14$, d = diameter
Volume (V) of a:	
cube	$V = s^3$; where s = side
rectangular container	$V = lwh$; where l = length, w = width, h = height
cylinder	$V = \pi r^2 h$; where $\pi = 3.14$, r = radius, h = height
Pythagorean relationship	$c^2 = a^2 + b^2$; where c = hypotenuse, a and b are the legs of a right triangle
distance (d) between two points in a plane	$d = \sqrt{(x_2 - x_1)^2 + (y_2 - y_1)^2}$; where (x_2, y_1) and (x_2, y_2) are two points in a plane
slope of a line	$m = \dfrac{y_2 - y_1}{x_2 - x_1}$; where (x_1, y_1) and (x_2, y_2) are two points in a plane
mean	$\text{mean} = \dfrac{x_1 + x_2 + \ldots + x_n}{n}$; where the x's are the values for which a mean is desired, and n = number of values in the series
median	median = the point in an ordered set of numbers at which half of the numbers are above and half of the numbers are below
simple interest (i)	$i = prt$; where p = principal, r = rate, t = time
distance (d) as a function of rate and time	$d = rt$; where r = rate, t = time
total cost (c)	$c = nr$; where n = number of units, r = cost per unit

INDEX

NOTES